6,000 YEARS

OF HOUSING

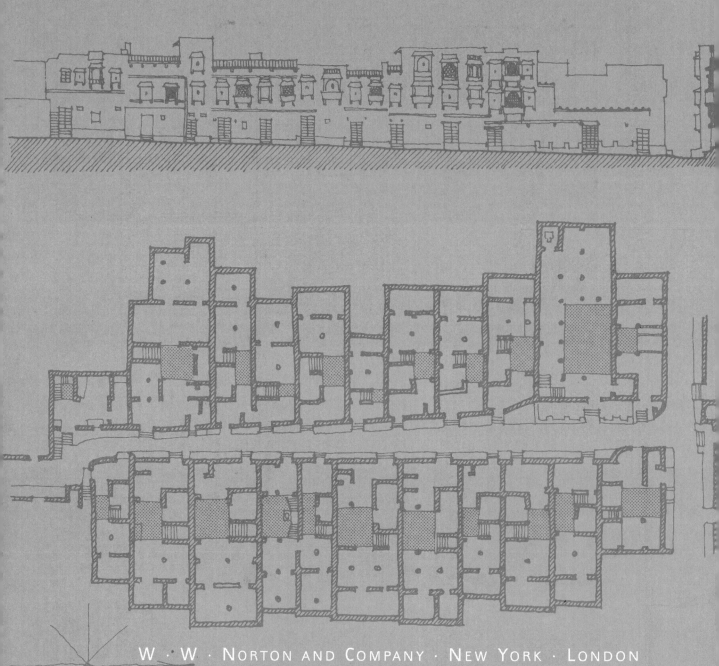

W · W · NORTON AND COMPANY · NEW YORK · LONDON

0 10 20 30 40 50 ft

0   5   10   15 m

6,000 YEARS

OF HOUSING

REVISED AND EXPANDED EDITION

NORBERT SCHOENAUER

The text of this book is composed in Filosofia with the
display set in Filosofia Grand and Jeunesse Sans
Composition and production by Ken Gross
Manufacturing by Edwards Brothers Incorporated
Book design by Antonina Krass

**Library of Congress
Cataloging-in-Publication data**

Schoenauer, Norbert, 1923–
    6,000 years of housing/Norbert Schoenauer.—Rev. &
expanded ed.
        p.   cm.
    Rev. ed. of: 6,000 years of housing. Vol. 1. 1981.
    Includes bibliographical references and index.
    ISBN 0-393-73052-2
    1. Dwellings—History. 2. Architecture, Domestic—
    History. 3. Vernacular architecture—History. I. Title:
    6,000 years of housing. II. Schoenauer, Norbert, 1923–
    6,000 years of housing. III. Title.
NA7125.S383   2000
728'.09—dc21   00-024458
    ISBN 0-393-73120-0 (paperback)

W. W. Norton & Company, Inc., 500 Fifth Avenue, New York, N. Y. 10110
www.wwnorton.com
W. W. Norton & Company Ltd., 10 Coptic Street, London WC1A 1PU

To my students,
for whom I wrote this book

Contents

PREFACE 9

PART I
The Pre-Urban House

INTRODUCTION 11

1. EPHEMERAL OR TRANSIENT DWELLINGS 14
African Bushmen Skerm 16
BaMbuti Pygmy Hut 18
Arunta Hut 19
Prehistoric and Historic Ephemeral Dwellings 20

2. EPISODIC OR IRREGULAR TEMPORARY
DWELLINGS 22
Inuit Igloo 23
Plains Indian, Tungus, and Lapp Tents 28
Communal Episodic Dwellings 32
Wai-Wai and Yanomamö Communal Dwellings 34
Erigbaagtsa and Cubeo Maloca 36
Prehistoric and Historic Episodic Dwellings 38

3. PERIODIC OR REGULAR TEMPORARY
DWELLINGS 41
The Mongolian and Kirgizian Yurt 42
Äir-Tuareg Tent 44
Bedouin Black-Tent 45
Prehistoric and Historic Periodic Dwellings 47

4. SEASONAL DWELLINGS 48
Navaho Hogan and Ramada 49
Nuer Kraal 51
Masai Boma 52
Barabaig Gheid 54
Pokot Dwelling 55
Prehistoric and Historic Seasonal Dwellings 56

5. SEMIPERMANENT DWELLINGS 57
Luyia and Luo Dwelling 58
Mesakin Quisar Cluster Dwelling 60
Awuna Cluster Dwelling 62
Gurunsi Compound Dwelling 63
Dogon Cluster Dwelling 64
Mayan Oval House and Mexican Jacal 66
Pueblo 68
Prehistoric and Historic Semipermanent Dwellings 70

6. PERMANENT DWELLINGS 73
Chinese Cave Dwellings 75
Italian Trullo 77
Slovakian Village Farmhouse 79
The Hungarian Farmstead 81
The Low German Farmhouse 83
Bernese Farmhouse 85
New England Homesteads 87
The Traditional Quebec Farmhouse 89

SUMMARY 91

PART II
The Oriental Urban House

INTRODUCTION 95

1. ANCIENT CIVILIZATIONS 100
Mesopotamia 100
Egypt 108
Indus Civilization 112
China 119

2. THE GREEKS AND THE ROMANS 123
Hellenic, Hellenistic, and Roman Cities 123
The Greek Peristyle House 129
The Roman Atrium House 136

3. THE TRADITIONAL ISLAMIC CITY AND ITS URBAN HOUSE 145
The al-Fustat House and the North African Dar 151
The Urban House of Cairo 161
The Baghdad House 168

4. THE TRADITIONAL URBAN HOUSE IN INDIA 179
Jaisalmer 181
Jaipur 184
Udaipur 188
Ahmadabad 189

5. THE TRADITIONAL URBAN HOUSE IN CHINA 193
The City of Beijing 193
The Beijing House 196

6. THE JAPANESE URBAN HOUSE IN KYOTO 204
The City of Kyoto 204
The Kyoto Merchant's House 205

SUMMARY 209

PART III
The Occidental Urban House

INTRODUCTION 213

1. THE DARK AGES 217
The Eclipse of Roman Cities 217
The Emergence of Medieval Cities 223
The Early Medieval Urban Dwelling 229

2. THE MIDDLE AGES 234
Medieval Fortress Cities 234
Dubrovnik 240
Rothenburg ob der Tauber 248
Salisbury 254
The Late Medieval Urban House 258

3. THE AGE OF THE RENAISSANCE 267
The Impressive City 267
Residential Squares and Crescents 270
The Town House 282

4. THE NINETEENTH CENTURY 289
Industrialism and Urbanism 289
Back-to-Backs, Tenements, and Bylaw Housing 293
From Villadom to Suburbs 302
Nineteenth-Century Suburban Development 306
Riverside, Illinois 307
Bedford Park, London 309
Parisian Apartment Buildings 311
Apartment Buildings in Great Britain 323
New York City Apartment Houses 332
Studio Apartment Houses 339
Apartment Hotels 341

5. TWENTIETH-CENTURY HOUSING (1900–1950) 344
Domestic Revival in Great Britain 344
Arts and Crafts in North America 356
Avant-Garde Movements of Europe: Art Nouveau, Jugendstil, Secession, National Romanticism, and Nieuwe Kunst 369
Housing Between the Two World Wars 382

6. TWENTIETH-CENTURY HOUSING (1950–2000) 413
Decline of American Cities 413
Court-Garden Homes 422
Attached Town House Dwellings 426
High-Rise Luxury Apartments 432
High-Rise Tenements 437
Point Blocks 442
Mixed-Use Buildings 445
Mid-Rise Housing 452
Collective Habitation and Communal Dwellings 460
Residential Conversions 466
Neotraditional Dwelling Design and New Urbanism 468

CONCLUSION 472
BIBLIOGRAPHY 475
ACKNOWLEDGMENTS 487
INDEX 489

PREFACE

6,000 Years of Housing is a brief history of the evolution of dwellings from the dawn of urban civilizations to the end of the twentieth century. In order to keep the book manageable, the domestic architecture of many countries was omitted. The manuscript is profusely illustrated with the author's freehand drawings, in the belief that, indeed, a drawing is worth a thousand words.

The book is divided into three parts. Part I, The Pre-Urban House, describes the sequence of six dwelling prototypes ranging from the simplest transient huts of nomadic food-gathering/hunting societies, to the permanent homesteads of sedentary societies with a surplus agricultural economy—the stage at which the basic prerequisites are reached for the birth of urban settlements. This part of the manuscript—in a more condensed form—was originally published in 1973 under the title *Introduction to Contemporary Indigenous Housing* (Montreal: Reporter Books). It was republished in expanded forms, in 1981, as Volume 1 of *6,000 Years of Housing* (New York: Garland STPM Press), and, in 1992, as Part I of *History of Housing* (Montreal: McGill University School of Architecture), a limited edition textbook complementing a course offered by the author.

Part II, The Oriental Urban House, reviews ancient inward-looking house forms of the four urban civilizations of antiquity (Mesopotamia, Egypt, the Indus Valley and China). Included are descriptions of dwellings with one or more private courtyards, both classical Greek and Roman urban dwellings, and traditional urban houses of North Africa, the Middle East, India, China, Japan, and Latin America. This part of the book was published as Volume 2 of *6,000 Years of Housing* and later as Part II of *History of Housing*.

Part III, The Occidental Urban House, outlines the development of the occidental urban house form from the Dark Ages to the end of the twentieth century. Since the occidental urban dwelling is outward-looking, it is in some ways the antithesis of the oriental urban dwelling. This part of the book was published as Volume 3 of *6,000 Years of Housing* and later, with additions to the nineteenth-century section, as Part III of *History of Housing*. The present edition is further expanded with a new section on the twentieth century with liberal use of material from both *Arts & Crafts and Art Nouveau Dwellings* (1996) and *Cities, Suburbs, Dwellings in the Postwar Era* (1994), two textbooks published by the author in an in-house limited edition (Montreal: McGill School of Architecture).

Until fairly recently, traditional domestic architecture was not a topic of great interest to architectural historians. Even today, by rejecting the notion that architecture has its roots in the humble beginnings of indigenous dwellings, some contemporary scholars insist that housing is not architecture. Yet it stands to reason that architecture had humble beginnings; indeed, there is documented evidence that in the distant past, houses of worship were modeled on human dwellings.

The author is under no illusion that the basic subject matter of this book is novel, and acknowledges that its content is far from comprehensive. Nevertheless, it is hoped that it will help dispel a persistent myth that the first dwellings were invariably caves, when they were far more frequently huts; similarly, the poetic rendition by ex-Jesuit Abbé Laugier that a man invented the primitive rectangular hut has no credence, since the earliest huts were round and most likely built by women.

PART I

The Pre-Urban House

INTRODUCTION

In this study pre-urban indigenous housing is viewed as an architectural response to a set of cultural and physical forces intrinsic to a particular socioeconomic and physical environment. This view has not always been espoused. Similarities in building forms of two widely separated simple societies are often attributed to some common prehistoric heritage, cross influences, or even chance or coincidence. In most instances, however, these notions are not based on fact. A more realistic and plausible explanation is found in the theory that similar determinative forces cause similarities in building form. Naturally, this environmental determinism includes not only the forces of physical and human geography, but also those determinants that derive from the relationships between man and his culture; the latter is the product of social, economic, religious, political, and physical forces.

The phenomenon of similarity resulting from environmental determinism is demonstrated most easily by the dwelling forms found in the simplest social organizations, such as those of the African Bushmen and Australian Aborigines. Both groups inhabit beehive-type huts practically indistinguishable from each other, both forms being simple architectural responses to a few identical causal forces. It must be realized that the likelihood of identical dwelling forms decreases proportionately with increased complexity and variation in the determinant forces. (Similarities in building form, however, reappear in advanced and literate societies where the exchange of ideas brings about a certain conformity in the transplanted architecture, which is often quite incongruous with its new setting.)

Acceptance of this emphasis on anthropogeographic and socioeconomic factors calls for the adoption of a primary classification similar to that used by Gabriele Schwarz in her *Allgemeine Siedlungsgeographie* to study the hierarchy of pre-urban indigenous dwelling types. Six categories emerge for such a system, each with its distinct social, economic, and political structure complemented by its respective settlement pattern and dwelling prototypes:

1.   Ephemeral or transient dwellings—the dwellings of nomadic band–type societies whose existence depends on a simple hunting/food-gathering economy.

2.   Episodic or irregular temporary dwellings—the dwellings of nomadic band–type societies whose existence depends on either advanced hunting or advanced food-gathering practices; the former is a stepping-stone to pastoralism and the latter to rudimentary agriculture.

3.   Periodic or regular temporary dwellings—the dwellings of nomadic tribal societies with a pastoral economy.

4.   Seasonal dwellings—the dwellings of tribal societies with a seminomadic way of life based on both pastoral and marginal agricultural pursuits.

5.   Semipermanent dwellings—the dwellings of sedentary folk societies or hoe peasants practicing subsistence agriculture.

6.   Permanent dwellings—the dwellings of sedentary agricultural societies that have a political social organization as a nation and a surplus agricultural economy.

Only at the sixth stage of socioeconomic development are the basic prerequisites provided to foster urban settlement.

The geographic distribution of these six dwelling forms reveals a general pattern congruous with the particular stage of socioeconomic development of their respective societies. Predictably, simple societies are found in the least desirable regions, and more complex societies claim the more favorable regions. Ephemeral and episodic dwellings, for example, are indigenous to arid tropical deserts, humid equatorial jungles, or arctic and subarctic barrens. Periodic and seasonal dwellings are predominantly found in arid marginal areas of the subtropical and temperate zones. Subtropical and temperate regions that have adequate water for cultivation contain semipermanent or permanent dwellings.

It must be emphasized that the evolution of these six categories of dwelling prototypes rarely follows our model sequence. Intermediate stages are frequently bypassed. This is particularly true of stages three and four, of which both have a pastoral economy at their base; accordingly, a purely agricultural sequence model is simply stages 1-2-5-6, namely, food gathering and hunting, followed by slash-and-burn primitive cultivation, followed by hoe-peasant cultivation, and ending with surplus agriculture. Of course, there are other conceivable combinations as well, with perhaps only the common denominator that all models start at the first, or ephemeral, stage.

Of course, one invariably encounters exceptions as some societies are in a transitional stage of development between two adjacent categories. These societies have either primitive or advanced dwelling forms that are not representative of their respective stages of social development. Notwithstanding these exceptions, the classification suggested does provide an overview of the patterns of development in pre-urban indigenous housing.

A study of the hierarchy of pre-urban dwelling types based on anthropogeographic and socioeconomic criteria reveals many new insights into architectural form. For example, the study indicates that circular dwellings are primordial, and predate the rectangular shape of indigenous shelters. Moreover, gradual increase in dwelling size or even complexity does not necessarily signify socioeconomic development; indeed, several very large collective dwellings are built by members of simple social organizations. These are but two unexpected observations that emerged from the research.

The present study deals predominantly with contemporary dwelling forms rather than with historic or prehistoric shelters. The objective—to illustrate the developmental stages of pre-urban housing by means of dwellings currently inhabited—is still possible but probably not for very long. Simple social organizations are disappearing through acculturation at an ever-increasing rate, and with this phenomenon will vanish the opportunity to present a "history" of housing prototypes based on examples of contemporary indigenous dwellings.

CHAPTER ONE

EPHEMERAL OR TRANSIENT DWELLINGS

The simplest dwelling types are ephemeral or transient dwellings. As their name indicates, these dwellings generally are not used for more than a few days since their inhabitants are primitive food gatherers and lowly hunters, constantly on the move in an endless pursuit of food.

Man is primarily a social animal. "He is understandable only in terms of his social relationships. Man, as a solitary individual, is basically helpless, despite his vaunted intelligence" (Bates 1961, 7). If one tries to visualize the life of human beings in the Old Stone Age, one can see that only by cooperating as a unit could people ensure that they obtained the food they needed. Moreover, cooperation was vital to ward off enemies. Thus social organization was as necessary in the past as it is today.

The social structure of primitive peoples is characterized by small groups called *bands*—that is, members of associated families living together and maintaining face-to-face relations under nomadic conditions. The bands self-regulate in a completely informal manner. As occasion demands, leadership is assumed by a skilled hunter or by an older man; these headmen have no special powers and are considered only first among equals. The band is of necessity a cooperative, identifiable, self-contained social entity.

The economic success of primitive hunters and food gatherers depends upon the cooperation of every individual and family within the group. The economic unit is the band, and the needs of the band take precedence over all other considerations. At an elemental level man feels a sense of ownership over the wild plants and animals on his territory, but his degree of control over them is small. Hence, actual ownership of property or resources by groups or individuals is either nonexistent or limited to a few material possessions, such as clothing and hunting gear. As a result, at the elemental level of a hunting and food-gathering economy there is considerable harmony among individuals, families, and groups.

Since primitive nomads do not cultivate food but subsist on game and plants, they must leave their campsite as soon as food resources within walking distance are exhausted. Primitive nomads do not roam aimlessly, however, but migrate within recognized band territories. Their movements often follow a seasonal pattern related to the availability of food. Their mode of life is precarious, depending greatly on an intimate knowledge of their respective territories: they must know the location of water holes, where certain edible plants grow, and where game can best be stalked. In some instances hunters and food gatherers increase their supply of food by burning the bush at certain seasons to inhibit the growth of undesired vegetation, by protecting seedlings, or by channeling watercourses to provide better irrigation to a particular area to encourage an abundance of wild edible plants.

Food gathering and hunting as the sole means of subsistence represents the most primitive phase in the hierarchical system of social evolution, preceding the pastoral and agricultural stages of human societies. In primordial times all human beings lived entirely on wild plants and game. Of necessity, in a purely food-gathering and hunting society, population densities had to be low. People lived in ecological balance with the environment, affecting it in ways and to degrees no different than large animals did; their numbers were rigidly controlled by a food supply determined by forces over which they had little, if any, control. It is estimated that, depending on prevailing climatic conditions, each person required an area of 4,500 to 320,000 acres (1,800 to 130,000 hectares) for subsistence in this mode of life.

The generic form of the dwellings of primitive nomads has several basic characteristics in addition to its ephemeral nature. Primitive dwellings are simple shelters, small in size, constructed solely of building materials collected in the immediate vicinity of the campsite, and are erected in a very short time, usually a few hours. The workmanship is so unskilled that only the most elementary form of interior climate control is provided. The circular shelters are covered by a beehive-type, or domed, roof structure. There are no vertical walls, windows, or smoke holes but only an entranceway without a door. The low interior space of the ephemeral dwelling is not divided into areas of specific use.

African Bushmen and Pygmies, several food gathering peoples of southern India, and Australian Aborigines still live in dome-shaped beehive-type huts. As recently as the fifties, the Alakaluk Indians of southern Chile built wigwams, a dwelling form akin to the beehive hut. The size and shape of these simple dwellings are basically similar in most respects except for the covering which may be leaves, bark, mats, or skins. Carleton S. Coon asserts that dome-shaped or beehive dwellings once had a worldwide distribution. Judging by archaeological evidence, this dwelling type may be over a quarter of a million years old. "One might almost say that the domed hut is as

specific to man, in a cultural sense, as the oriole's special kind of nest is instinctively specific to orioles" (Coon 1971, 28–29).

Ephemeral dwellings are indigenous primarily in two climatic regions—the desert and the tropical rain forest. Neither has a substantial seasonal variation; therefore, the building materials used are characterized by low heat capacity offering maximum shade and good ventilation. An open fire outside the shelter provides the necessary comfort on cool nights.

One exception to the prototypical ephemeral dwelling is the home of the cave-dwelling Tasaday. These recently discovered bands inhabit the almost impenetrable rain forest of the southern Philippines and live in three limestone and conglomerate caves about 500 ft (150 m) up a mountain slope. Their sedentary way of life is made possible by the abundance of food in the jungle territory over which the Tasaday range, a territory that is relatively small, extending not further than 5 miles (8 km) from their caves.

As described by Kenneth MacLeish, a Tasaday cave dwelling has an arched entrance, roughly 15 ft (4.5 m) high by 35 ft (10.6 m) wide, and the cave's depth is about 50 ft (15.2 m). A narrow, shoulder-high buttress divides the cave into two sections. A nestlike space of no more than 8 by 8 ft (2.4 by 2.4 m) located on one side of the buttress shelters a family, the parents with their few young children, and the rest of the group clusters in a large bay on the other side of the dividing wall.

The walls of the cave dwelling have not been changed or in any way decorated. The natural niches and ledges in the cave are used for storage of tools and implements. The stone axes are very similar to those used in Europe during the Old Stone Age; they are merely split pebbles polished along the cutting edge and bound into cleft sticks.

The Tasaday use a fire drill, another device from prehistory, to kindle their fire. "A slender rod that, set in a wooden socket and whirled back and forth between a man's palms, produced a spark to be nursed into flame with dried threads of vegetable fibre" (MacLeish 1972, 242). Such implements represent all Tasaday material culture. Leaves and bamboo sections are their containers, and leaves are their clothing. The Tasaday do not hunt but occasionally trap animals. The food gatherer often eats his fill while collecting for his family—a job that takes only a few hours a day. "Deft hands grab tadpoles, frogs, and freshwater crabs from swift-flowing streams. These are wrapped in orchid leaves and put next to hot coals for cooking. The staple of the Tasaday diet, biking, . . . is a wild yam, a root dug with a sharpened stick. Rotted logs provide fat grubs . . . a favorite of the tribe (actually the band)" (MacLeish 1972, 238–39). A variety of palm fruit, wild bananas, and edible leaves complete their diet.

There is no division of labor, nor is there a special sense of property. Everything is shared, and if food is scarce, children eat first. The Tasaday have no leader and make all decisions jointly. Each person does what he or she can do best.

It is tempting to conclude from the discovery of the Tasaday band (as well as from evidence found in certain caves indicating their use as shelters by prehistoric man) that man began his existence as a cave dweller. Of course, caves could have been used as shelters only by sedentary food gatherers and primitive hunters, who, like the Tasaday, inhabited an abundant paradise. In prehistoric times and less abundant areas, most food gatherers must have led a nomadic existence in constant search of food, therefore the man-made ephemeral shelter was the simplest and most common dwelling form.

Bushmen skerm

lead to quarreling. Their peaceful approach to communal life is dictated by the tenuous conditions under which they must live, and is manifested in the way they share food and all material goods. It is unthinkable that a Bushman would refuse to share food or water with his other band members. Without this rigid cooperation, they could not survive the famines and droughts that frequently occur in the Kalahari desert. Their few material possessions are freely shared among the members of this nomadic group in order to prevent jealousies and hostility (Thomas 1963, 32–33).

AFRICAN BUSHMEN SKERM

The grass *skerm* of the African Kung Bushmen who live in the arid Kalahari Desert may serve as a prototype for ephemeral dwellings.

Kung Bushmen call themselves *zhu twa si* ("the harmless people") while a stranger is always referred to as *zhu dole* ("dangerous person"). Bushmen rarely fight and almost never use their only real weapon, the arrow poison for which there is no antidote, against each other. They go to any length to avoid potential disagreements that might

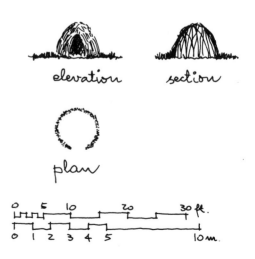

elevation   section

plan

0 5 10   20   30 ft.

0 1 2 3 4 5   10 m.

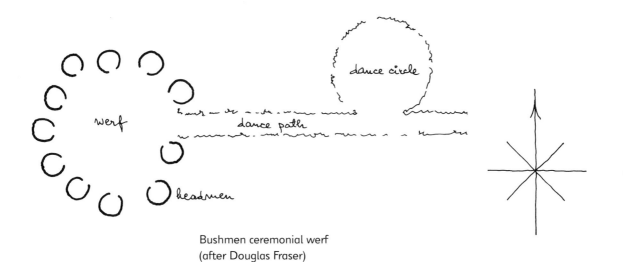

Bushmen ceremonial werf
(after Douglas Fraser)

In *The Harmless People*, by Elizabeth Marshall Thomas, an old Bushman describes the genesis of his people in a story of the grass fiber and the reim (a narrow, very long leather rope made from the hide of a cow that is useful for harnessing oxen or building a hut):

"In the earliest days," the old man said, "the Bushmen and the non-Bushmen were all one nation, and the great god came to earth and gave them a rope. Half the rope was made of reim and half was made of grass fiber. The great god told all the people to pull on the rope, and the non-Bushmen came away with the reim, but the Bushmen got only the grass fiber. After that, the non-Bushmen had cattle and reims and all those things, but the Bushmen had only the things that are in the veld. If this ever happened again," the old man said, "I would tell the Bushmen to make sure they got the reim half." (Thomas 1963, 34)

Kung Bushmen follow the aboriginal pattern of nomads by relying on collective hunting and gathering, and their bands usually consist of about twenty-five to thirty persons. In their territory food is scarce during most of the year, and they constantly migrate in search of a new supply. The bow and poisoned arrows and the club are their chief hunting weapons. Women use digging sticks to pull up roots. Men hunt, make weapons, and prepare skins for loincloths; women gather food

and wood, build the huts, kindle the fire, cook, and keep the campsite clean.

The small grass shelters of the Bushmen are erected by the women in one or two hours and are abandoned after a few days when the band moves on. The building procedure begins with the gathering of grass until a large pile is collected. The women then break a few branches from a nearby tree and drive them upright into the ground. The branches are arched together to form a rudimentary skeleton structure that then supports the grass covering. Each shelter is then tied around once with a sinew string.

Elders and unmarried members of the band are sometimes left without a hut; to give themselves a place of their own, they thrust an upright branch into the ground and place a few belongings beside it. Bushmen prefer to sleep in the open beside the fire and frequently store their few possessions in the skerms.

The various grass shelters of the band are usually arranged under the branches of a single large tree. This encampment is called a *werf*. Kung campsites are always built within easy reach of food, but a mile or so away from a water hole in order not to interfere with animals. The huts are usually clustered together without a fixed pattern, and entrances may point in any direction. During initiation rites the werf layout is circular and more formal, with an entrance facing east and leading to a dance path.

BAMBUTI PYGMY HUT

Another example of an ephemeral dwelling type is the BaMbuti Pygmy beehive hut. The BaMbuti are forest people who inhabit Africa's Ituri Forest, a vast expanse of dense, dark, damp, and inhospitable jungle. They call the forest *Ndura*, a word that also means the entire world.

The BaMbuti are small people, averaging less than 4 1/2 ft (1.3 m) in height; they are powerful and tough and have the ability to run swiftly and silently, essential characteristics for survival in a primitive hunting existence. The BaMbuti hunt the animals of their region and gather wild fruit, roots, and mushrooms. They roam the forest in hunting bands of at least six to seven individual families, each with its own hunting net; only in this way can they have an efficient net hunt. The women and children drive the animals into the long circle of nets, joined end to end. In addition to nets, they use spears and bows and poisoned arrows to hunt animals and birds. BaMbuti clothing is minimal, consisting of a simple loincloth made of bark.

Once again the women construct the shelter. In a squatting position, they drive young saplings into the ground with sharp thrusts, each time in exactly the same place, until the saplings are firm in the ground. When a circle of straight saplings surrounds them, the women stand up and skillfully bend the saplings over their heads, twisting and

BaMbuti hut

twining smaller saplings across until a lattice framework is formed.

After the framework is completed, the women gather the large, heart-shaped mongongo leaves collected by the men and slit the stalks toward the end (like clothespins), then hook two or three of them together and hang them on the framework like roof tiles, overlapping each other to form a waterproof covering. Sometimes as many as four women work on thatching a hut. Some hang leaves from the outside, working upward; others work from the inside, pushing the leaves through the lattice frame and fastening leaves from the top down. At first this covering leaks when it rains, but once the leaves have settled down, not even the hardest rain can penetrate it, and it remains watertight until the leaves dry out and begin to curl. The entrance is simply a gap in the framework of the shelter.

The BaMbuti are clean people and do not like to sit on the bare ground. Most often they sit on logs, even on the end of a log that is sticking out of a fire. Sometimes they pull a mongongo leaf from the roof of the nearest hut and sit daintily on that. They also make simple chairs by cutting four sticks, each about 3 1/2 ft (1.1 m) long, and twisting a vine thong around the middle of the bundle. The bundle of sticks is stood on the ground and then, with a turn of the hand, the ends of the bundle are splayed out and a seat is formed.

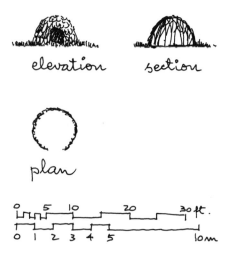

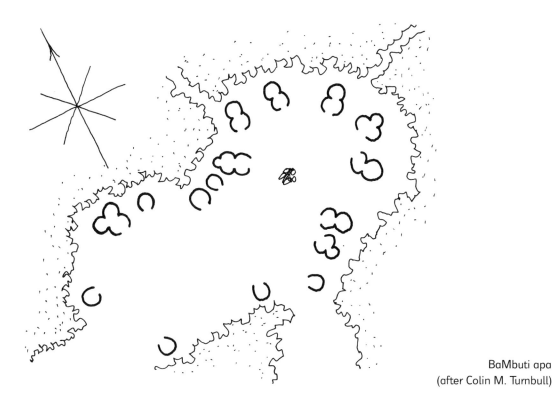

BaMbuti apa
(after Colin M. Turnbull)

The BaMbuti may sleep on a layer of dry leaves or sticks placed directly on the ground. Sometimes they make an elevated bed of sticks lashed together and bound by vine thongs to a frame.

Normally, the fire is made outside the entrance of the beehive hut. During a spell of rain, it is moved inside the hut, but as soon as the rain stops, it is rekindled in its usual position outside.

Usually the campsite (apa) of the BaMbuti is erected in a forest clearing near a stream. The huts are placed near the edge of the clearing, and depending on the number of huts required to house the hunting band, one or two circular communal open spaces are defined by their position. The entrances of the huts point in different directions, usually toward friends or relatives but never toward the forest; if a woman has a grudge against a neighbor or a dislike for someone who has built a hut opposite hers, she will rearrange her hut's entrance to face another direction or move her hut altogether. Little jealousies are inevitable in small communities, and since most of the women continually add to their huts, the layout of the apa is in a continuous state of change during the BaMbuti's stay of about one month in the same camp.

ARUNTA HUT

The hut of the Arunta, Australian Aborigines, is also an ephemeral dwelling type. The Arunta live in the desert environment of central Australia and subsist by food gathering and hunting. Small bands, of one to three families, forage the desert in constant quest for food. The men's sole hunting weapons are spears and boomerangs; the women use a digging stick with a crude point to dig for roots and tubers. Although it is often bitter cold at night, the Arunta have no clothing or even wraps to cover themselves while asleep; on cold nights the family huddles with its dogs for warmth. Indeed, the Arunta note the temperature by the number of dogs per person required to feel comfortable; a three-dog night is unusually cold.

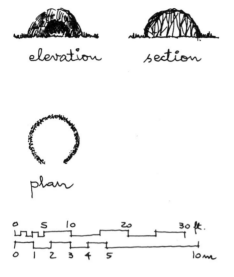

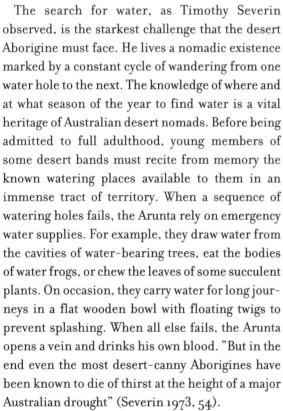

Arunta hut

The search for water, as Timothy Severin observed, is the starkest challenge that the desert Aborigine must face. He lives a nomadic existence marked by a constant cycle of wandering from one water hole to the next. The knowledge of where and at what season of the year to find water is a vital heritage of Australian desert nomads. Before being admitted to full adulthood, young members of some desert bands must recite from memory the known watering places available to them in an immense tract of territory. When a sequence of watering holes fails, the Arunta rely on emergency water supplies. For example, they draw water from the cavities of water-bearing trees, eat the bodies of water frogs, or chew the leaves of some succulent plants. On occasion, they carry water for long journeys in a flat wooden bowl with floating twigs to prevent splashing. When all else fails, the Arunta opens a vein and drinks his own blood. "But in the end even the most desert-canny Aborigines have been known to die of thirst at the height of a major Australian drought" (Severin 1973, 54).

The Arunta live in crude shelters made by lacing branches into a low dome-shaped framework and thatching this latticed structure with grass, leaves, reeds, or whatever is available. They use no furniture. A small fire is kept in front of or inside the shelter; people huddle close around it for warmth. The typical Arunta encampment consists of a few huts in close proximity. If the camp is very temporary, the families shelter themselves from the wind with a rough lean-to or windscreen of shrubs.

When a band member dies, his hut is burned, and his few personal belongings are destroyed. The other members move to a new campsite, fearful of the spirit that is believed to stay near the grave until a purification ceremony is later performed.

PREHISTORIC AND HISTORIC EPHEMERAL DWELLINGS

The precise form of prehistoric ephemeral dwellings is not known, and may never be, but it is unlikely that these dwellings were very different from those used at present by the few primitive hunters and food-gathering bands still roaming in isolated parts of our globe. Their lifestyle represents an Old Stone Age culture that has survived into our time.

wigwam-type

dome-shaped

Yaguan huts

Brian M. Fagan (1977) estimates that in 15,000 B.C. all humans were still hunters and food gatherers, and that only several thousand years later (ca. 8000 B.C.) some people began to cultivate wild cereals or root crops. George Murdock (1968) suggests that by the late fifteenth century, when Columbus sailed to America, only 15 percent of the world's land mass was inhabited by primitive hunters and food gatherers.

Hunting and food-gathering societies no longer exist on the American continent, but at the time of its discovery the American continent was peopled by several hunting-gathering societies. The Karankawa Indians and the Ute Indians, among others, were the hunter-gatherers of North America, while the Pelche, Tehuelche, Querandi, Ona, and Yaguans were their counterparts in South America. Not many decades ago the Ona and Yaguans still roamed the barrens of the Tierra del Fuego archipelago at the foot of South America. The shelters of American hunter-gatherers were similar to the skerms of the present-day African Bushmen and were invariably ephemeral dome-shaped or wigwam-type circular brush huts.

CHAPTER TWO

EPISODIC OR IRREGULAR TEMPORARY DWELLINGS

Like the ephemeral dwellings, simple episodic or irregular temporary dwellings are shelters inhabited by food gatherers and hunters living in a band type of social organization. These nomadic bands, however, are skilled hunters or fishermen living in a richer environment than that of the hunters described in Chapter 1. They are primarily hunters (or fishermen) and only secondarily food gatherers. Although their shelter is erected within an hour or two, the period of use generally extends to several weeks rather than to several days.

Advanced hunters and gatherers live for the most part in ecological balance with the natural environment. Although they do not have direct control of this natural environment, they do have a greater effect on it than the primitive hunters since they frequently prey on selected animals and gather large quantities of certain plants for food. Often they are so successful that they alter the ecological balance of their environment, and they become the dominant animals in their ecological communities.

The social structure of these more advanced societies does not differ greatly from that of the lowly hunters and food gatherers. Both societies are characterized by small groups in which all interpersonal relations are face-to-face. This interaction of the members of closed groups is of necessity based on involuntary associations, and their interrelationship is often many-stranded. In other words, members of primitive bands seldom have the choice of associating with preferred persons and their relationship to each other can take many forms; a father-son relationship, for example, can also be teacher-pupil, chieftain-subordinate, healer-patient, high priest–worshipper, and so forth.

Differences in cultural inheritance and mode of life rather than in social structure set the skilled hunters apart from the primitive hunters. The skilled hunters have more personal belongings in the form of clothing, tools, and weapons. They also have vehicles, such as sleds or *travois*, to transport their belongings and domesticated working animals, such as dogs, to pull the vehicles. Advanced hunters and gatherers possess a technology in which they use constructive methods of combining various materials to make their artifacts. They are aware of the basic properties of various materials and combine them efficiently to make complex tools. Their shelters, clothes, and vehicles are put together from various materials and demonstrate both ingenuity and creativity. As Richard A. and Patty Jo Watson (1969) rightly postulate, craftsmen who are skilled in the production of complex tools are capable of conceiving and executing the construction of such complex art forms as sculpture and painting. In fact, skilled hunters such as the Inuit are known to have considerable skills in both drawing and sculpting.

While the differences between lowly and advanced hunters may appear to be slight, they are substantial enough to bring about considerable changes in dwelling forms. The foremost characteristic of a dwelling of a more advanced society of hunters or fishermen is the adjustment to adverse climatic conditions. The function of climate control is more sophisticated and is complemented by the degree of skill manifested by these people in their clothing design. Indeed, these band societies often have two distinguishable dwelling types—one for the winter and the other for the summer. A second difference in the episodic dwellings is their relative size; both the surface area as well as the height of the interior are considerably greater than in the ephemeral shelter. The interior is divided into sleeping and cooking areas with a designated place for the fire or hearth. Sleeping inside the shelter and making a fire indoors are both characteristic of skilled hunters. Moreover, at least some of the building materials of the dwelling are transported and reused when the band moves to a new encampment. Finally, an obvious characteristic that sets episodic dwellings apart from ephemeral dwellings is the greater variety of form.

The generic plan of an episodic dwelling is similar to the ephemeral dwelling in that it also has a circular plan, but this simple form has either a dome or conical enclosure above. The supporting structure in the dome-shaped episodic shelter can be a wooden frame (Chippewa Indian hut) or a vaulted dome of snow blocks (Inuit igloo). The conical shelters have a primary tripod or tetrapod frame that supports a set of secondary poles; a cover made of hides (Plains Indian tepee) or of strips of birch bark (Tungus tepee) is stretched over this supporting structure.

Episodic dwellings are found in arctic, subarctic, and the Great Plains steppe regions. The thermal characteristics of these regions vary from intense cold with high winds in winter to moderate to warm daytime temperatures in summer. Because of these weather conditions, episodic shelters are invariably built so that there is a minimum exposed surface to the elements relative to volume and maximum stability of the structure. Building elements have a low heat capacity; consequently the interior of the episodic dwelling responds quickly to the warmth generated by the interior hearth.

INUIT IGLOO

Perhaps the most fascinating prototype of an episodic dwelling is the *igloo* built by the Inuit living in the treeless tundra of the Canadian north. (*Inuit* is the Eskimos' name for themselves, meaning in their own language "men" or "people.")

Since the inhospitable arctic country does not produce enough vegetation to sustain life for its inhabitants, the Inuit depend primarily upon animal food. The seal, which is abundant in their habitat, is by far the most important prey. The

Inuit Igloo

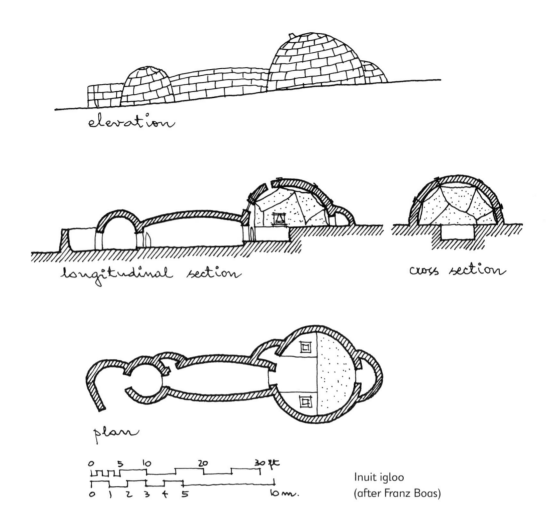

elevation

longitudinal section

cross section

plan

Inuit igloo
(after Franz Boas)

Inuit depend on this aquatic mammal for the basic necessities of their life. The seal is used in the following ways: seal meat is almost the sole staple food during the winter months; seal skins furnish materials for clothing as well as for lining the inside of the igloo or covering the summer tent; seal blubber affords the indispensable fuel for cooking, and for heating and lighting the igloo during the long dark winter; the Inuit feed the intestines and scrap flesh to the dogs that pull their sleds; finally, some bones of the seal are used for various utensils. Nothing is wasted in the harsh world of the Inuit.

The Inuit have two—and sometimes even more—distinct settlements, determined primarily by the economic activity of the season. The longest period of residence is at the winter site, which is normally located on a sheltered bay or on the lee side of an eminence. Here an Inuit builds his igloo, a dome-shaped snow house that serves as the winter home. The igloo builder has to locate snow for his building materials and not just any snow will do. He must find snow wind-packed to the right consistency, neither too hard and icy, nor too soft and powdery. Then, with a long knife (made of bone, ivory, or metal) he cuts rectangular blocks measuring about 3 ft (90 cm) long, 20 in (50 cm) wide, and from 6 to 10 in (15 to 25 cm) thick, and slightly beveled so as to corbel when laid in a continuous spiral, thus forming a dome. The first step in the building process is to lay a number of blocks on edge until the circular base of the wall is complete;

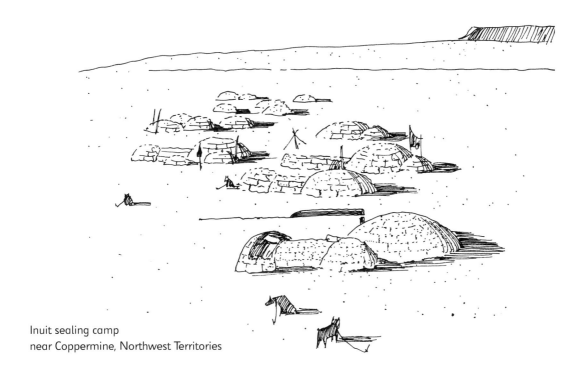

Inuit sealing camp
near Coppermine, Northwest Territories

thereafter, the Inuit trims the top of the base to form an even slope starting from the ground to the height of a full block to enable the placing of consecutive snow blocks in a spiral pattern.

Working from the inside, the builder lays one snow block next to another in upward spiraling rows, each block tipped inward slightly to narrow the circle. Thus, a dome structure results, ingenious in its method of construction, since scaffolding to support the dome during construction is made unnecessary by the spiraling rows, which prevent the walls from caving in.

When the dome is almost complete and only the so-called key block is missing, the builder lowers it into place. (The Inuit can cut blocks very rapidly and, with his eye, can measure their size to such accuracy that the key blocks almost invariably fit their intended places.) To complete the igloo, the builder cuts an exit passage near the bottom of the hut and constructs several additions to the igloo. A low vaulted tunnel or passageway called *igdluling* links the igloo with a domed antechamber called *uadling*. Often the low entrance tunnel has to be negotiated on hands and knees; moreover, its floor is set about one ft (30 cm) lower than that of the main igloo, to further minimize any draft of cold air. A windscreen usually protects the entrance-way, and a large snow block, which stands in the passage during the day, is placed in front of the opening at night.

Additional small vaults are invariably attached to the igloo and its entrance tunnel. A semicircular vault called *audlitiving* is often built at the rear of the main dome; this vault serves to store meat for future use. One smaller storage vault, called *igdlu-arn*, is usually constructed on the left side of the entrance to the igloo and is used, not unlike a pantry, for keeping the daily supply of meat and blubber. Additional igdluarns sometimes are constructed on the opposite side of the entrance and along the entrance tunnel. Finally, a vault for the storage of clothing and harnesses, a *sirdloang*, is placed at the junction of the antechamber and the entrance passage (Boas 1964, 133).

A window located above the entrance is made of a sheet of ice or the translucent membrane of a seal's

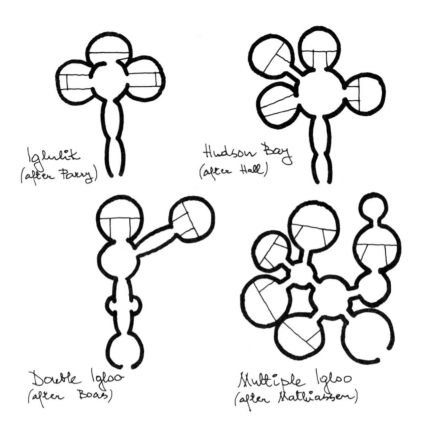

Iglulik
(after Parry)

Hudson Bay
(after Hall)

Double Igloo
(after Boas)

Multiple Igloo
(after Mathiassen)

Typology of igloo clusters

intestine and lights the igloo. Above the window and near the top of the dome there is a small hole for ventilation.

Once the building is finished, blubber lamps are lit in the interior. The igloo is vacated, and all openings are sealed, including the entranceway. In this way the lamps heat up the interior space, and the inside wall surfaces begin to melt. Because of the inherent characteristics of the dome shape, excess water from the sweating walls does not drop to the floor but slowly trickles downward on the inside surface until it is totally absorbed by less saturated wall sections in the lower parts of the walls.

In a short while the entire inside surface is permeated with moisture. As soon as this stage of moisture saturation is reached, the main doorway and the ventilation hole near the top of the dome are opened, and cold air rushes into the dwelling while the warm air escapes through the vent. The

inside surface is suddenly chilled, and the water-permeated walls freeze solid into a monolithic structure. Similarly, prolonged occupancy invariably makes an igloo more substantial since the occasional slight melting inside inevitably freezes again. Igloos are known for their rigidity, and they can easily support the massive body of a wandering polar bear.

Drifting snow invariably piles over and around the igloo, protecting it from the below-freezing temperatures of the outdoors. Moreover, insulation of the interior is often enhanced by lining walls and ceilings with hides and sealskins; these are held in place by cords passing through the snow blocks and secured by toggles. Not only do the hides improve the comfort of the igloo, but the air space created between the exterior walls and the hides augments the insulation of the snow house. The door leading to the igloo is also usually made of

Inuit tupiq

suspended hides, and frequently a double-door effect is obtained through the use of several hides. Even when extreme low temperatures prevail outdoors, the inside of the igloo presents a comfortable environment, and the Inuit may remain in their snow huts for several days in a row.

A sleeping platform raised well above the floor occupies the rear half of the main chamber. This large platform is made of snow and is covered with moss or willow twigs overlaid with caribou furs. On both sides of the igloo's entrance are smaller platforms. The Inuit places cooking utensils as well as shallow saucer-shaped stone lamps on top of these side benches. By burning animal fat (such as seal blubber) in these lamps, the igloo dweller solves the problem of heat and light throughout the long, cold, and dark winter season.

Igloos may be built as large as 15 ft (4.6 m) in diameter and more than 10 ft (3 m) high at the center. Given the proper snow, a man can erect within an hour's time one large enough to shelter his entire family. As a rule, the snow houses are built for one family only, but in certain territories communal snow houses may be found. These compound structures consist of a number of round igloos linked to each other with short vaulted tunnels. Most of the linked dome structures are

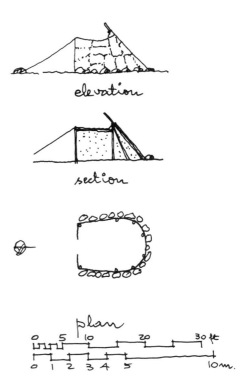

Inuit tupiq
(after Franz Boas)

dwelling units similar to the main chamber of the igloo described above; others serve as storerooms and/or assembly rooms where all the inhabitants of the communal house gather.

Although snow may seem to be the least likely building material in the intense and extremely cold arctic region, it is the substance that best meets the criterion of a low-heat-capacity wall enclosure. The analysis of the igloo made by James Marston Fitch and Daniel P. Branch supports the contention that on a purely theoretical basis it would be difficult to conceive of a better shelter against the arctic winter. The igloo's admirable performance is attributed to both form and the material used in its construction. A hemispherical dome exposes the least surface and offers the maximum resistance to chilling winter winds. The dome encloses a large volume within a relatively small structure, and an oil lamp effectively heats its interior space. Warm air rises and, since the volume of the igloo decreases towards the top, it is forced to occupy a broader zone and provide a considerable degree of comfort for its occupants.

The igloo is abandoned when the sun begins to melt the dwelling. In any case, the Inuit is now ready to leave his winter settlement to move to the spring and summer hunting grounds where he will live in seal tents suitable to this period of his nomadic life. The abandoned igloo melts away, leaving no trace.

The seal tent of the Inuit is called *tupiq*. The framework consists of poles, made of many pieces of wood ingeniously lashed together. The interior layout is similar to that of the igloo. At the entrance and at the edge of the bed two pairs of converging poles are erected. A little below the intersection two cross poles are firmly attached, forming a ridge; at the bed end additional poles are placed to form a tepeelike frame. Combined with the poles at the entrance, this frame forms the skeleton on which the sealskin cover is placed. It is tightly fitted and secured at the periphery with heavy stones. Overlapping sealskin doors prevent the wind from blowing into the tupiq.

PLAINS INDIAN, TUNGUS, AND LAPP TENTS

THE PLAINS INDIANS

There is little doubt that the best known examples of episodic dwellings are the tepees of the North American Plains Indians. These tribes followed

Plains Indian tepees

the trek of the immense bison (buffalo) herd roaming the plains or prairies of the continent. Two prototype tepees can be distinguished by whether their relative basic skeletal structure consists of either three or four poles. Of the two types, the three-pole tepee was inherently more stable. This was used by the Cheyenne, Sioux, and Cree nations, while the Crow, Shoshone, Blackfoot, and Comanche used the four-pole tepee.

The skeletal structure of the Plains Indian tepee was made by tying the top ends of the supporting poles (either three or four poles) together and standing them up; then additional poles, up to about twenty, were placed against the tripod or tetrapod. A tailored buffalo-hide cover was placed on the pole skeleton and was staked or weighted down with stones all around the bottom edge. A hole was left at the crossing of the poles to allow smoke from the interior fire to escape. All tepees were slightly tilted so that the smoke hole was off center toward the front side, thereby facilitating the closing of the hole in wet weather. The two flaps, or "ears," of the smoke hole were each fastened to a separate pole enabling the adjustment of the aperture in accordance with the prevailing wind or to close it so that the tepee could be weathertight. The fire was built directly below the smoke hole, and the bedsteads were placed on the ground around the circumference except at the doorway, which habitually faced the rising sun.

Camp on the Blackfoot reserve, Alberta
(after William Notman 1887)

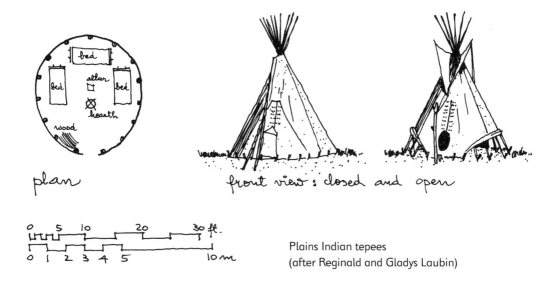

plan

front view: closed and open

Plains Indian tepees
(after Reginald and Gladys Laubin)

The average tepee was 10 to 12 ft (3.0 to 3.6 m) high and had a diameter of 12 to 15 ft (3.6 to 4.5 m). To cover it required as many as twenty buffalo hides. Sometimes an additional hide lining covered the ground and ran up the tepee's sides for 4 to 5 ft (1.2 to 1.5 m). This second layer of skin formed a closed bowl shape and prevented drafts from creeping in under the edges of the outer covering. The buffalo hides were more windproof than canvas. The air space between the outer and inner skin covers provided additional insulation in winter. In contrast, during the summer the bottom edge of the outer cover was raised to permit ventilation without draft.

The poles of the tepee were carefully prepared by the men of the tribes. The poles were chosen for length and straightness and stripped of bark and branches before being seasoned. They were considerably longer than required and projected beyond the tepee cover in accordance with the Indian aesthetic ideal.

The tanning, cutting, and sewing of the buffalo-hide covers of the tepees was the work of the women. Often elaborately painted decorations adorned the covers. There were many traditions associated with the sewing of the tent cover. For example, the Blackfoot's tepee had to consist of an even number of skins and only those from the buffalo cow. Moreover, they believed that if the cover was sewn by a jealous or quarrelsome woman, the tepee would invariably be smoky regardless of wind conditions. Consequently, a good-natured woman was always chosen for this task.

The erection and dismantling of the tepee was also the women's task. The tepee could be pitched within an hour's time and dismantled in less than that. The poles were used to form travois for transporting their owners' belongings. Initially, as the Plains Indians followed the buffalo herds, they used dogs to drag the travois, but later they used horses.

THE TUNGUS

The northern Tungus who inhabit the great expanse of eastern Siberia also use a tepeelike "tent." The nomadic Tungus move about within a defined clan territory with a sparse population density of about one person for every 100 square miles (259 km²). They are both reindeer herders and hunters. In winter they roam the taiga (northern forested areas) rich in mosses, lichens, shrubs, and dwarf willows, all of which are food for reindeer. Snowfall is relatively light, but temperatures can reach as low as -80°F (-62°C). The herds are constantly on the move since the snow becomes packed from the trampling of the herd and then animals cannot dig through it to find food. In summer the herd moves to the tundra for pasture where it must fatten on grass, willow shoots, lichens, and reeds to withstand the harsh eight to nine months of the long winter season. The herd is not shepherded; it is left to itself to find pasture and water.

The Tungus milk their reindeer for food, but even under the best conditions the animals do not give more than 1 pint (0.5 l) of milk a day after suckling their fawn. Reindeer are also used as mounts and pack animals.

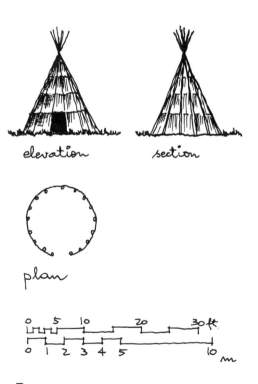

elevation   section

plan

Tungus tent

The basic economic and social unit of the Tungus is the nuclear family, augmented perhaps by an older surviving relative of the husband; it is a small household. There is a precise division of labor between Tungus males and females. The principal daily activity of the male is hunting and trapping. In addition, he performs other outdoor tasks, such as loading of pack animals, slaughtering and skinning animals, and cutting firewood. The women care for the children, cook, milk reindeer, dress the skins of animals, and make clothing and tent covers.

Of necessity, the Tungus dwelling is easily transportable (in contrast to the ephemeral structure, which was simply abandoned). It resembles a tepee in form and structure. The conical framework consists of a number of poles leaning against each other. In the winter, the framework is covered with skins and in the summer with birch bark. Except for smoke holes, the tent is kept tightly closed and a fire is kept burning to keep out the intense cold in winter and to inhibit insects in summer. Consequently, the interior is always smoky.

The right-hand place from the entrance is reserved for the husband and his wife's place is adjacent; the left side is occupied by the oldest son, followed by other members of the family; the area opposite the entrance is reserved for the spirits or for an eminent male visitor.

THE LAPPS

Like the Tungus, the Lapps of northern Europe are nomads who live off great herds of reindeer augmented by hunting and fishing. But most of all, they live by the whim of the herd. Whenever the urge to move is upon the reindeer herd, the Lapps follow the animals, because any attempt to halt them is doomed to failure. Only when the urge has spent itself, and the reindeer are tired and hungry, does the herd settle down to feed and rest, and the Lapp herders follow suit.

The Lapps call themselves *Samelats*. They live in portable tepeelike tents called *kota*. The base structure of the kota is a tripod of 12-ft (3.6-m) long forked poles. Other tall poles are placed against the tripod to form a wide circle. A tent cover made of reindeer skins is pulled over this skeletal structure leaving a vent at the top. A layer of birch branches is spread on the snow-covered

Lapp tents

ground to keep an insulating airspace between the reindeer-skin floor cover and the snow. Sacks containing the family's possessions are placed all around the tent walls. A fire is lit in the center of the tent, and a cauldron hangs above the fire suspended from a chain attached to the framework.

In contrast to the unadorned kota in a monochromatic landscape of snow, the clothes of the Lapps are "beautifully ornamented with multicolored ribbons and braidwork in vivid red and yellow on a deep-blue background" (Bruemmer 1974, 168).

The transition from skilled hunting of the wild bison herds by the Plains Indians to the graduated domestication of the reindeer herds by the Tungus and the Lapps illustrates the evolutionary steps leading to a pastoral economy.

COMMUNAL EPISODIC DWELLINGS

An aberrant and more complex form of episodic dwelling is the large communal dwelling developed by slash-and-burn cultivators living in tropical forest regions. In contrast to semiarid steppes or arctic regions, the lush tropical forests allow simple societies with few and simple wants to support themselves without the need for frequent migrations in pursuit of food. These living conditions encourage the formation of larger social communities, namely subtribes, as well as the development of a rudimentary and collective agricultural technology. Usually these subtribes form autonomous communities and live in communal types of episodic dwellings. Coupled with hunting, fishing, and food collecting, the subtribes practice shifting or slash-and-burn cultivation, a form of migratory agriculture predominantly associated with a tropical rain forest region; it represents the simplest, most ancient, and least productive use of cropland. Only a few implements such as the axe, the machete, and a digging-planting stick are

employed; moreover, in the absence of domesticated draft animals, labor energy is provided solely by human effort.

On the whole, the tropics offer uniquely favorable conditions for plant life. The luxuriance and variety of plant growth in the humid tropical forest is unparalleled anywhere; in addition, animal life as well as microorganisms flourish in humid tropical climates. Frequent precipitation ensures a year-round growing season, but the rain also reduces the soil's nutrient value by leaching minerals from it. Thus, there is a limit to the economic exploitation of this luxuriance because shallow root crops do not reach minerals from the unbleached lower layers of the soil. Under these conditions cultivators must regularly shift their fields from deteriorated land to new sites.

Shifting or slash-and-burn cultivation entails several steps. First, a patch of forest is cleared by burning off the existing vegetation cover. Then, crops are planted in the clearing, without manuring other than the mineral nutrients provided by the ashes of the burned vegetation. The plot is cultivated for a few years until the soil ceases to be productive. Then it is abandoned and a new plot is cleared for cultivation, usually in a distant location offering better hunting opportunities. This short-term use of forest plots is called *milpa* in Latin America and *ladang* in Indonesia.

The "fields" of the slash-and-burn cultivators seldom exceed 1 acre (0.40 hectares). They invariably remain full of stumps and logs during their cultivation. Crops are often grown mixed. This rudimentary form of agriculture primarily involves the cultivation of root crops. "In 1952, Carl O. Sauer published a remarkable essay on agricultural origins, an ecological analysis of food production. He saw the origins of food production as a change in adaptation, a change in the way culture and environment interacted" (Fagan 1977, 179). Sauer proposed that rain forests were major centers of plant domestication, where root crops were grown by semisedentary societies. "Root crops such as the African yam are relatively easy to cultivate by simply planting the chopped-off top of the

Makiritare communal dwelling,
Venezuela

yam and watching it regerminate. The transition from intensive gathering to deliberately conserving and cultivating root crops probably was almost unconscious, brought on by the sorts of adaptive pressures that were found in more arid areas like the Near East" (Fagan 1977, 183). Although few scholars at the time accepted Sauer's theory, he has proved remarkably astute on the importance of root crops and the antiquity of food production especially in Southeast Asia; today, however, root cultivation is predominantly a South American Indian phenomenon, with the staple crops being manioc and potatoes.

Several factors are inherent to slash-and-burn cultivation: a large collective labor force in the absence of plow and draft animals, a large amount of reserve land to allow for the customary fallows of eight years or longer, and adequate hunting territory. Consequently, population densities are frequently less than 10 persons per square mile (3.9 persons per square kilometer), or 1 person per 64

acres (1 person per 26 hectares), for equilibrium between man and nature to be maintained.

The day-to-day routine of these rudimentary cultivators involves considerable hunting, food gathering, fishing, and tilling the soil. Men hunt in short treks through the rain forest and are often accompanied by women gathering wild fruits and berries. Fishing is done with traps and weirs, dragnets, spears, and poison. The men also use the bow and arrow to shoot fish, which is a remarkable feat because the marksman has to allow for the refraction of the target in the water.

Although the interpersonal relationships of slash-and-burn cultivators are similar to those of the skilled hunters, other characteristics, such as the greater stability of their settlements, bring about some changes in the form of their housing as well as in the number and kind of their personal possessions. In keeping with their collective economy, their dwellings are large detached communal structures of a circular, doughnut, oval, or rectangular plan. An increase in the number of occupants in a communal dwelling eventually necessitates a departure from the primordial circular plan. Structural considerations limit the span of circular buildings; thus, beyond a certain limit floor area can only be increased by means of either a doughnut plan or an oval plan that ultimately becomes rectangular in form. The dwellings of slash-and-burn cultivators often resemble large haystacks situated in the middle of an oval forest clearing. A tropical rain forest setting with intense sunlight means extreme heat during the day and warm nights throughout the year. A building with low-heat-capacity walls and a roof providing maximum shade and good ventilation is the proper design response to this environment, and the inhabitants of tropical forests in South America have evolved such house forms.

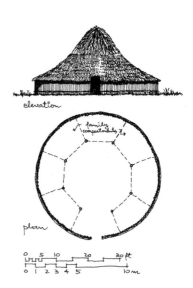

Wai-Wai communal dwelling

WAI-WAI AND YANOMAMÖ COMMUNAL DWELLINGS

The Wai-Wai of British Guiana practice shifting cultivation and live in large circular communal dwellings in small isolated groups. Their simple, rugged pattern of communal agriculture is augmented by hunting, fishing, and food gathering. Land is cleared in the jungle by felling trees and the repeated burning of the dense tree-strewn field. Crops include cassava, sugar cane, bananas, pineapples, and tubers, all planted indiscriminately among the unburned stumps and tree trunks cluttering the field. The fields are seldom used for more than two or three years because the soil wears out. Consequently, the Wai-Wai abandon their settlements and move on to new territory; they seldom return to a previously used site.

The indigenous communal dwelling of the Wai-Wai is a single, circular hut with walls built of vertical poles supporting a large, cone-shaped, thatched roof. The hut is not divided by partitions, but each family has a designated area between two roof posts. Each compartment has its own hearth for cooking and generating the warmth required at night. Sleeping hammocks are draped between the hut's posts, with the woman's hammock slung beneath her husband's. Dogs, the only domesticated animals, are tethered on platforms along the walls and are walked with leashes. Cassava cakes and smoked meat are piled on racks; feather ornaments, gourds of palm oil, baskets, and arrows hang from the ceiling. Since there is no chimney, smoke escapes through apertures in the thatched roof.

The Wai-Wai seldom penetrate the jungle and then only to hunt. They fish by poisoning the water or shooting larger fish with arrows. Their highway is the river and their transportation mode a dugout canoe. Distances are measured in paddling time or by the number of river bends.

Labor is usually divided between the sexes. Men build the communal house, hunt, fish, clear land, plant, and sometimes help women harvest the crops; they also weave hammocks, baskets and cloth. Women tend children, cook, fetch water, chop firewood and keep the fire going all night, weave bead aprons, spin cotton, and make cassava graters.

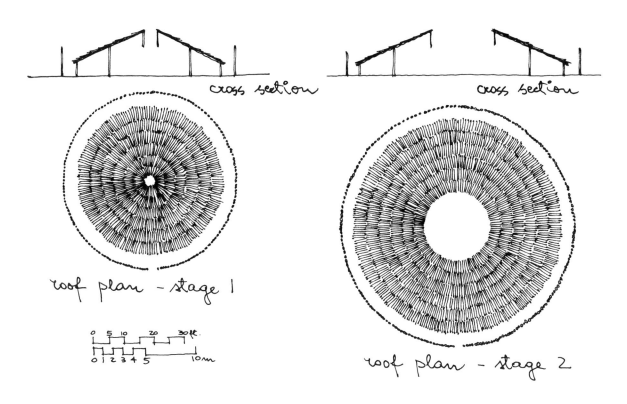

Yanomamö communal dwellings
(after Napoleon A. Chagnon)

Although their clothing consists only of a loin-cloth, the Wai-Wai are very fastidious about their appearance. Their bodies are invariably decorated with plant juice to ward off harmful spirits; they wear earrings, necklaces of red beads, armbands of white and legbands of blue and white beads. Their hair is combed and dressed with palm-nut oil, then fashioned into a tight pigtail adorned with feathers.

The Yanomamö Indians, who inhabit the Orinoco River basin in southern Venezuela, also practice shifting cultivation and live in circular communal dwellings.

When the subtribal community of the Yanomamö is still relatively small, it builds a circular haystacklike communal dwelling known as a *shabono* with a smoke hole at its apex. As soon as the subtribe population increases and exhausts the

potential of its fields, it abandons the old building and clears a new and bigger site for cultivation. The tribe then builds a new and larger circular dwelling to accommodate all its members.

The span capacity of the available timber is limited: the resulting buildings eventually become doughnut-shaped and the original smoke hole a courtyard. This pattern of expansion presents an interesting example of the evolutionary process in which one of the origins of the courtyard dwelling is illustrated. (The additive growth pattern is the other evolutionary process leading to the courtyard house form.)

All building materials for the shabono come from the jungle: poles, vines, and leaves. Each family builds its own section of the shabono. The man usually does all the heavy work of locating and fetching poles for the frame, placing them into the ground or tying them overhead, and weaving the numerous leaves into the roof thatch. The wife helps by gathering the leaves and vines used in the construction.

> The first step in building a new shabono is the selection of the site. . . . The four main posts of the individual house are then sunk into the ground, two short ones about 5 ft (15 m) high at the back, and two longer ones about 10 ft (3 m) high at the front. The rear posts are placed about 8 or 9 ft (2.4 or 2.7 m) away from the front posts, and both pairs are approximately the same distance from each other as well. After these have been tamped securely into the holes, cross poles are lashed to the tops of them, and then long, slender saplings some 20 to 30 ft (6 to 9 m) long are laid about a foot (30 cm) apart from each other on top of the cross poles and secured with vine lashings. Since the two rear posts are only half as high as those at the front, the long roof poles protrude upward at an angle of 25 to 30 degrees toward the village clearing. A vine is then strung along the bottom of the long, protruding saplings, looped around each pole, and run the entire length of the house. The leaves used in the thatch have a long stem; the individual leaves are bent over the vine where the stem joints the leaf, and the first row of thatching goes on. When this row is completed, another vine, about 8 in (20 cm) above the first one, is again strung along the entire length of the house and secured to each of the long saplings where it crosses them. The next row of thatch is then put in place; the leaf is inserted into the thatch of the first row of leaves when it is bent down. The leaves are placed about an inch (2.5 cm) apart, resulting in a thoroughly impermeable roof (Chagnon 1968, 25–26).

The completed communal building resembles a series of open-faced dwellings encircling a large communal courtyard; a fringe of palm leaves decorates the edge of the roof around the plaza. A narrow passageway surrounds the shabono at the rear and is defined by a 10-ft (3-m) high palisade of logs. A new shabono is very attractive, clean, and tidy and smells of freshly cut leaves. However, the dwelling only lasts one or two years because the leaf-made roof begins to leak and often becomes infested by cockroaches, scorpions, spiders, and other vermin.

ERIGBAAGTSA AND CUBEO MALOCA

The *maloca* of the Erigbaagtsa Indians, who live in the northwestern part of the Amazon basin, is a good illustration of the oval-shaped communal shelter inhabited by slash-and-burn cultivators.

In building a maloca, a large open space is carefully leveled in the center of the forest clearing. The main supporting structure is then erected—three pairs of large trunks with connecting beams, one pair located at each end of the designated space, and a third pair in the middle of the long side. Between these, smaller posts braced with horizontal members, secured entirely by liana thongs, are introduced to stabilize the structure. The roof and sides are thatched with thick layers of babussu palm fronds.

Depending on the number of families inhabiting the maloca, the dimensions vary, but it is not unusual for the length to exceed 100 ft (30 m), its width 60 ft (18 m), and its height 30 ft (9 m). Essentially, the maloca is a large, dark one-room shelter with the central part reserved for public receptions and dances. Small fires flicker on the ground, and the hammocks of each family are slung from the rafters and posts adjacent to each individual fire. There are no separating partitions or windows; several entrances tightly closed with thick palm-frond door panels protect the inhabitants from gnat-size blood-sucking flies called *piums*. To escape these pests, the near-naked dwellers of the maloca spend much of their lives indoors, venturing into daylight only to hunt and fish, bathe, and fetch wood and water. They work their fields of corn, manioc, and cotton before dawn.

Life within the maloca is communal; all participate in building the house and tilling the plot. Only weapons are personal property. Harmony usually prevails in the community, where all men are blood relations. Everybody is friendly and soft-spoken. Women spin cotton into cord for hammocks, cook monkey meat or wild pork, roast corn, and lie in hammocks tending their babies. Men and boys squat on tree trunks that are placed to

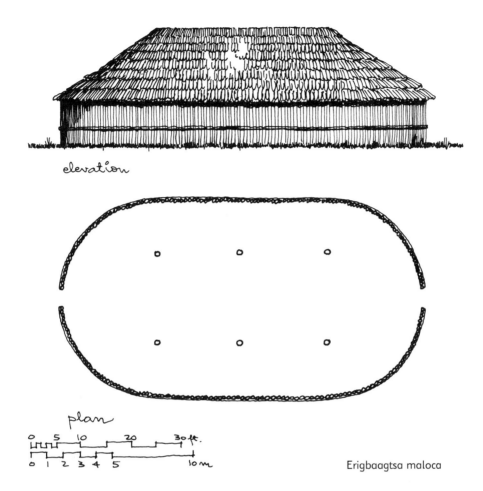

elevation

plan

0 5 10   20   30 ft.

0 1 2 3 4 5   10 m

Erigbaagtsa maloca

form a rectangle and chat while making bows and arrows and feather decorations. This log rectangle is reserved for menfolk; here they eat their meal together and tend a fire at its center. The nights are cool, but everyone sleeps naked. Small children sleep with their mothers, older ones in their own hammocks, and young boys sleep apart with the unmarried men.

The Cubeo Indians also live in the northwestern part of the Amazon basin. Like the Erigbaagtsa, they practice shifting or slash-and-burn cultivation and live in communal dwellings or malocas. Lounging in hammocks, the Cubeo spend most of their leisure time indoors. The Cubeo maloca, as Irving Goldman observes, "is no mere shelter or sleeping barracks," it is also a vital social and religious center. In addition to the normal daily household activities, all other social and religious

functions take place within the large maloca, including the burial of the dead. Hosts greet guests at the doorway and invite them inside to a reception area near the entrance, equipped with low benches that face the interior of the large communal structure (Goldman 1963, 39).

Since all inhabitants of the maloca accept the authority of the headman, he is known as the owner of the communal dwelling. However, the allocation of space in the maloca does not follow a precise order of status, although the headman prefers to occupy a central bay on one side of the dwelling.

Building the maloca is a major technical and social undertaking. Its mere size—75 ft by 55 ft by 21 ft (23 m by 17 m by 6.4 m)—demands a solid structure built with the greatest care. The headman together with his closest relatives erect the central framework, consisting of three pairs of heavy

Caraya maloca, Brazil

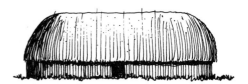

Paressi maloca, Brazil

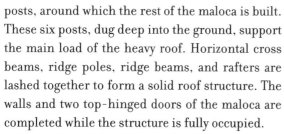

Waura maloca, Brazil

Yecuana communal dwelling, French Guiana

posts, around which the rest of the maloca is built. These six posts, dug deep into the ground, support the main load of the heavy roof. Horizontal cross beams, ridge poles, ridge beams, and rafters are lashed together to form a solid roof structure. The walls and two top-hinged doors of the maloca are completed while the structure is fully occupied.

The maloca of the Cubeo is divided into specific use areas. Along the side walls are the living quarters; for example, a twelve-household maloca has two parallel rows of seven posts along the side walls of the building, and each bay, defined by two posts, is designated as a living area for a family. The family hearth of three pottery cylinders is located in the center of each bay; at night a fire is kept burning in each family space. Several hammocks are hung from the posts of each bay at night, but during the day most are stored neatly away. A shelf built under the roof as well as several baskets and calabash bowls suspended from the roof structure serve as storage places. Although there are no partitions separating the family quarters, the privacy of each family space is respected by everyone.

The central corridor area of the maloca is used for dancing, and most evening meals are eaten communally in this area. Evening meals are prepared in the communal kitchen, which has a large ceramic oven for baking manioc. Both the kitchen and the women's quarters are located in the rear of

the maloca. The formal reception area as well as the burial ground is at the front of the dwelling.

Other examples of communal dwellings in South America include the Caraya, Waura, and Paressi oval malocas in Brazil, the Yecuana circular dwelling in French Guiana, and the Makiritare circular dwelling in Venezuela.

An additional example of communal shelters is the *bohio* of the Motilone Indians who live in the Catatumbo River area of Venezuela. The bohios resemble giant haystacks. There are twelve entrances with paths radiating like spider legs from them. The bohio interior is smoky and crowded since it is not uncommon for more than seventy people to occupy one dwelling. The Piaroa Indians of the Orinoco River jungle are another of the numerous Indian tribes who inhabit bohio-type palm-thatched communal dwellings.

PREHISTORIC AND HISTORIC EPISODIC DWELLINGS

In prehistoric times numerous skilled hunters roamed the Eurasian, African, and American continents. For example, advanced hunters inhabited

Dwelling of mammoth hunters
(after Brian M. Fagan)

the banks of the Don River and hunted the mammoth. These giant elephants supplied them with meat, skins for their tent covers, and bones for building materials and utensils as well as a substitute for firewood.

These "hunters sometimes lived in large, irregular dwellings partially scooped out of the earth, probably roofed with bone and huge mammoth skins. Movable bone poles probably supported the hides; the edges of the tents were weighted with huge bones and tusks, which were found lining the hollows at Kostenki and Gagarino in Russia, at Dolni Vestonice in Czechoslovakia and in other localities" (Fagan 1977, 117–18). The prehistoric episodic dwellings of these skilled hunters were remarkably like the Inuit summer tents in appearance if not in size.

Among the leading tribes of North American Indians the agrarian Onondaga, Oneida, Seneca, Cayuga, Mohawk, and Iroquois all lived in communal

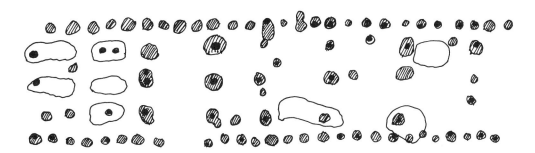

Danubian long house from Olszanica, Poland
(after Brian M. Fagan)

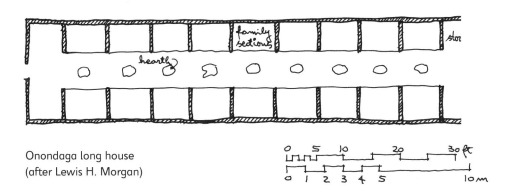

Onondaga long house
(after Lewis H. Morgan)

longhouses at the time of America's discovery. Their dwellings sometimes reached 125 ft (38 m) in length.

Within living memory communal dwellings built of cedar planks were inhabited by the coastal Indians of the Northwest, namely the Haida, Kwakiutl, and Salish. Living in a rich environment, they had an economy of plenty. They gathered shellfish, harpooned seals, porpoises, sea lions, and whales, and caught the teeming runs of salmon, using weirs, traps, nets, and hooks; they rounded out their diet with wild fruits, roots, nuts, and green shoots.

The prehistoric communal dwellings of primitive agrarian people such as the Danubians were similar to communal dwellings of the North American Indians. The Danubians lived in north-western Europe during the fifth millennium B.C. and introduced a rudimentary agriculture technology to this region. They lived in villages containing several large rectangular houses from 54 to 138 ft (20 to 50 m) long, built of timber, and with thatched roofs. These large houses were each occupied by several families and presumably also sheltered their livestock.

Brian M. Fagan suggests that originally the Danubians probably came from the Starcevo culture group, and they developed their wasteful agricultural practices on the rich loess lands of eastern Europe. As their population increased, some groups were forced to move to less fertile lands in northwestern Europe and to supplement the crops derived from cultivation with hunting and food gathering (Fagan 1977, 199).

CHAPTER THREE

PERIODIC OR REGULAR TEMPORARY DWELLINGS

The portable tents of the pastoral nomads represent the third evolutionary stage of dwelling forms: temporary dwellings that are inhabited on a periodic or regular basis. Pastoral nomads have a hierarchical social organization consisting of migrating bands or other subgroups united by a tribal chiefdom. Tribal societies represent a category of cultural development intermediate in complexity between hunting/food-gathering bands and agrarian folk societies.

A tribe is a body of people of common derivation and custom in possession and control of its own extensive territory. It is characterized by widespread cohesion and some centralization of authority at higher levels. This hierarchy is needed to blunt the frequent collisions between neighboring camps, to coordinate the use of pasture, and to maintain an equitable use of resources.

The characteristics of tribal societies that set them apart from hunters and food gatherers are primarily their pastoral economy, their homogenous culture, and the possession of some form of political organization. In the more advanced stages of pastoral nomadism, there appears to be an increasing dependence on settled agriculture. However, this dependence is facultative only; in other words, it may, but need not, occur. Such a relationship is in great contrast to their obligate relation to the livestock upon which their survival depends.

Although some pastoral tribes depend to a certain extent on hunting and food gathering, most nomads rely solely on domesticated livestock for subsistence. Their cyclical or seasonal migration pattern depends on the topography and climate prevalent in their established territory. Some groups, along with their livestock, migrate hundreds of miles between their winter quarters in the south and their summer pastures in the north; others move only a few miles from their winter settlements at the foot of a mountain range and the summer grazing areas on the higher slopes of the mountain. Population densities range mainly between one and five persons per square mile (two persons per square kilometer) or the equivalent of one person per 125 to 640 acres (50 to 244 hectares).

Nomads spend most of their time outdoors. Hence proper clothing is often of greater importance for survival than the effectiveness of their shelter. In fact, among some desert dwellers, young boys are initiated to adulthood by being sent off with the herd and forced to live for a considerable length of time in the open with no other protection against the elements but their clothing. Thorvald Faegre's implication that the nomad lives not so much in his tent as outdoors in the desert or steppe is no exaggeration.

Portable tents do not accentuate the boundaries between outdoors and indoors as more permanent structures do. Although in colder regions tents are built quite weathertight, in the deserts they are often mere sunshades without vertical walls to define where the dwelling begins and ends. Weather permitting, women do many chores under the open sky, and looms, churns, and querns are more often seen outside the tent than in it (Faegre 1979, 7).

In fact, many nomads are so accustomed to the temporary nature of their dwellings that they feel uncomfortable in solid buildings and often suffer claustrophobia; moreover, they dread to enter multistoried buildings. This fear, in the past, was exploited in the building forms developed by sedentary peoples subjected to frequent incursions by tent-living nomads. For example, tower-like stone dwellings were adopted by sedentary farmers in the Caucasian mountain valleys and they were habitually subjected to harassment by raiding nomads.

The usual household in pastoral tribes includes two or more married couples and their children—an extended family. If the polygynous family is the rule, a man's sons ordinarily break away upon marriage and establish a new or neolocal residence.

The pastoral nomad's dwelling is generically a portable tent consisting of a tensile felt or skin membrane stretched over a wooden framework. The materials are lightweight so that they are easily transported from one periodic settlement to another. Periodic dwellings are indigenous to continental steppes and deserts. Climatic forces and the nomadic life of tribal societies are the predominant forces determining the shape, structure, and construction method of the dwellings. In some instances the intense cold in winter influences the shape of the dwelling, dictating that it have a minimum of exposed surface and maximum stability in order to withstand high winds. Naturally, a dome-shaped structure consisting of a skeleton and membrane cover lends additional strength to the shelter. Lightweight building materials possess a low heat-storage capacity, which is advantageous in winter when a quick heat response to the fire is required and in summer when shade and ventilation are easily afforded during the long warm days.

The steppes are intensely and continuously cold in winter; there are high winds and negligible solar heat. In summer there are long warm days and cool night. The deserts have little or no seasonal variations, little precipitation, very low humidity, and intense solar radiation, resulting in very hot days and cold nights. Nevertheless, the architectural response to both the continental steppe and desert climate is similar because it is dictated by the need for portability of the dwelling. This imposes a restriction upon the size of the structure. Hence, most periodic or temporary shelters are relatively small in area, and their spaces are carefully organized in conformity with the basic needs of their inhabitants.

THE MONGOLIAN AND KIRGIZIAN YURT

An excellent example of a portable dwelling used by nomadic tribes living in the rich steppe lands of Asia is the *yurt*. "The steppe tribes that dwell in yurts may be divided into two groups according to the type of yurt they use . . . The Mongol or Kalmuck yurt has straight roof poles making the roof a cone. The Kirgiz or Turkic yurt has a curve in the roof poles which makes the roof into a dome" (Faegre 1979, 81).

The yurt is an ingenious and weatherproof dwelling that affords its occupants a remarkable degree of protection against inclement weather and, in particular, the strong steppe winds. The yurt has a circular plan with a diameter of 10 to 20 ft (3 to 6 m). Its walls are about 4 ft (1.2 m) high and consist of lightweight willow latticework sections, called *khana*, that can easily be folded up like a children's safety gate. In their expanded form, four to eight khanas and a door frame are lashed together to serve as a circular supporting wall of the roof. To the top of this wall are fastened the curved (if Kirgiz) or straight (if Mongol) roof poles radiating

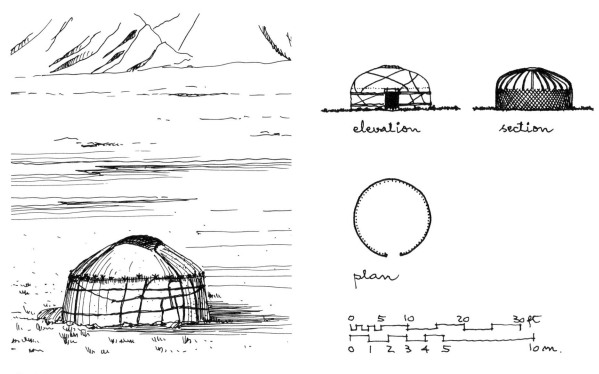

Kirgizian yurt

toward the center and fitted into a wooden ring about 4 ft (1.2 m) in diameter. This compression ring at the top of the yurt also functions as the smoke hole. The forces that push outward are neutralized by a tension band tied around the top of the wall. Because of the yurt's shape, wind pressure acting upon the structure results in anchoring it more firmly to the ground. At times, to increase the structure's stability, a heavy stone is suspended on a rope from the central wooden ring.

Over the entire framework of the yurt, large pieces of heavy felt (*mundahs*) are fastened, sometimes in two or even three layers, with air space in between in order to increase the comfort of the interior. A felt curtain, often ornamented, is hung over the door, which invariably faces south or southeast away from the direction of the prevailing wind. The door curtain as well as the wall panels can be rolled up to give good cross-ventilation if so desired. Curtains are also hung in the interior and can be let down to form separate compartments. Women always set up and dismantle the yurt.

The eastern half of the yurt's interior is the women's side; the western half, the men's and visitors' side. Storage boxes and bags as well as rolled-up bedding and carpets are placed along the walls.

A fire of *argol* (dried yak or camel dung cakes) is made in the center of the yurt and is surrounded by dry stunted brush. The smoke escapes through the

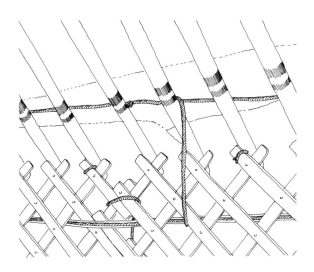

Yurt wall and roof assembly

central hole in the roof; when necessary, the smoke hole can be closed by a piece of felt drawn across by a string so that even in severe weather the yurt offers its occupants adequate warmth. The overhead smoke hole acts as a time clock for the yurt's occupants; since the yurt always faces more or less the same direction, sunrays reaching through the hole into the yurt show the time of the day.

Although the framework is lightweight, the covering material is cumbersome and relatively heavy. However, the nomads' pack animals (camels, horses, and yaks) provide the means to transport not only the portable dwellings but also rugs and other household and personal belongings.

Unquestionably, the horse is the steppe nomad's prized possession, but his survival depends on breeding sheep and goats that provide milk, meat, and wool. Only a few families camp together for most of the year to prevent overgrazing and to extend the duration of their stay in one location. In winter a large tribal group assembles in a sheltered area, and they await the arrival of spring in their circular campsite called *aul*.

spiral to make an oval mat. Several mats are thrown over the tent framework and tied down securely. The wall mats are made of straw or grass and are woven in decorative patterns.

The typical tent consists of three wooden arches of slender poles lashed together.

These three arches are placed in the middle of the tent at right angles to its longitudinal direction. The two curved wooden pieces which together constitute an arch are not of equal length. The arch piece which is fixed in the soil at the frontal end is very long, while the other curved piece attached to it and buried in the ground at the back is shorter. . . . Parallel to the

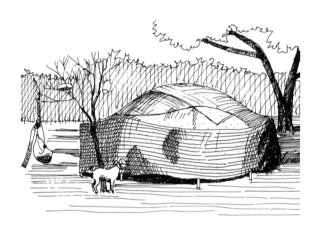

ÄIR-TUAREG TENT

The hutlike tent developed by the Äir-Tuaregs is another periodic shelter. These pastoral nomads live in the arid plains of the Sakelian Zone on the fringes of the Sahara Desert. Although nomads, the Äir-Tuaregs are related to the sedentary Berbers. They are usually very poor, subsisting on a meager staple of goat's milk with wheat and millet added. Owen Lattimore's definition of a pure nomad being a poor nomad aptly describes their condition. Interestingly, Äir-Tuareg men, not women, wear veils.

The Äir-Tuareg tent consists of a dozen or so slim poles and laths made from acacia or palm leaf stems bent and laced to form a framework not unlike the skeleton of a dome-shaped hut. The mat roof cover, the *arsala*, is woven of doum palm leaf fibers. Narrow plaited bands are sewn into a large

elevation   section

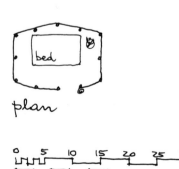

plan

Äir-Tuareg tent

three arches there are two pairs of cross-bars supported by vertical sticks, a pair being placed at both sides of the arches to form the narrow sides of the dwelling. . . . Over this skeleton of arches and cross-bars supported by vertical sticks are placed a number of slender curved rods. . . . These rods form semi-arches in the longitudinal direction of the tent. Each of these semi-arches consists of two identical rods fastened to the horizontal cross-bars at their thick end, while at their thin ends they are lashed together and fastened to the true arches (Nicolaisen 1963, 350–51).

This latticework of arched rods is lashed together with cords to form a stable framework to receive the mat covers.

The sole furnishing in the tent is a couch supported by carved poles and built 15 in (38 cm) off the ground. The couch (which is actually set up before the tent is pitched) occupies nearly the whole floor area of the dwelling. Here the family sits and sleeps. Äir-Tuaregs have few personal possessions and few cooking utensils, in keeping with their nomadic existence.

Women pitch and strike the tent. "Pitching the tent should not be too time-consuming, since it is nice to have a roof over your head soon after arriving at a new spot. The tent must provide shade, protection from the sun and from the cold at the nights. The tents of the Tuaregs have met these requirements most excellently" (Gardi 1973, 13).

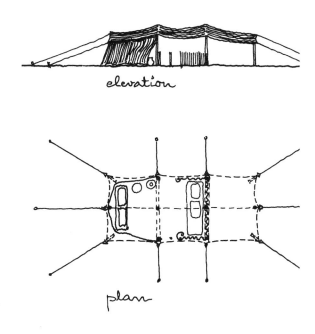

elevation

plan

Bedouin black-tent

BEDOUIN BLACK-TENT

The Bedouin, the hardy desert herdsmen of western Asia and North Africa, live in a periodic portable dwelling—the Bedouin black-tent. In fact, the word *Bedouin* means "man of the tent."

These herdsmen raise camels, sheep, and goats, and roam with their livestock through the severe environments of the endless deserts of Arabia and the Sahara. During the height of summer, when the grazing is poor, the Bedouin are forced to camp near towns or farm settlements that provide access to stubble of harvested fields. They also depend to a large degree on towns for vital products, such as metal utensils, weapons, clothing, and footwear.

The typical Bedouin black-tent has a supporting structure of vertical poles, and its coarse black clover is made of woven goat's hair fabric reinforced by tension bands. The Bedouin call their tent *beit sha'r*, or "house of hair."

The tent is always pitched by women. The first step entails the clearing of the site on level ground. Next the tent cover is spread on the ground. Then the ropes are pulled out and staked. Starting from one corner, poles are pushed up one by one. When the tent roof is aloft, the rear wall (*ruag*) as well as the dividing curtain (*qata*) are pinned in place. This whole operation is usually completed within an hour.

Being a tensile structure, the typical black-tent uses very little wood for its supporting frame. In contrast to the skeleton of the yurt, which is stable

Bedouin black-tent
(after Gyula Hajnoczi)

Ouled Naïl tent (Central Algeria)
(after C. G. Feilberg)

Moor tent (Mauretania)
(after Torvald Faegre)

Pushtun tent (Afghanistan)
(after Torvald Faegre)

without its cover, the black-tent's frame is unstable without the stayed tensile cover. Its poles are mere compression members supporting the weight of the tent cover, and all tensile stresses and lateral wind forces are borne by the cover and its stays. (The tent's long rope stays are only allowed to cross another tent's stays if their respective households are related in some way.)

The roof line of the black-tent is very flat to minimize resistance to winds and sandstorms. The front of the tent is oriented either toward Mecca or toward the south if protection from the northern winds is desirable. The women's side of the tent, often bigger in area than the men's side, is the living and working area of the whole family; the men's side, covered with carpets, is the reception area. The contents of the tent are scanty, consisting mainly of cooking utensils, pack saddles, water skins, wheat bags, halters, bowls, and various weapons. A stranger must always approach a Bedouin tent from the front.

The average length of the Bedouin tent ranges from 20 to 30 ft (6 to 9 m); the depth is rarely more than 10 ft (3 m); and the height goes from 5 to 7 ft (1.5 to 2.1 m). A sheikh's tent, however, may attain a length of 70 ft (21 m).

The black-tent is indigenous to the area between the 30° and 35° north parallels. Basically, it provides shade in an area marked by clear skies and intense solar radiation. Using very little wood for its structure, the black-tent is an admirable adaptation to regions where wood is a scarce commodity. But this dwelling is less than ideal in areas with considerable precipitation because its cover is not completely waterproof. Indeed, when waterlogged, it is both heavy and cumbersome to move.

With the exception of Tibet and Afghanistan, the distribution of the black-tent coincides with that of the camel. In addition to the Bedouin, the black-tent serves as a portable dwelling for the Berbers, the Algerian nomads of North Africa, the Kurds, Baluchi, Afghans, and the Tibetan nomads of Asia. Although the basic design of the tent is the same, there is a variation in detail from tribe to tribe. For example, various methods are used for stay fastening by different Bedouin tribes. These various black-tents present a rich typology of tensile structures adhering to a single design principle, but each has its intrinsic departures in detail.

Lady Wen-chi's canopied yurt (second century) (after Frank Trippett)

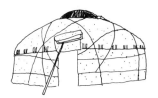

Kazakh yurt (nineteenth century)

PREHISTORIC AND HISTORIC PERIODIC DWELLINGS

By their very nature, portable shelters such as tents do not leave lasting imprints for archaeologists to study. Nevertheless, portable dwellings were probably used in prehistoric times. Certainly during biblical times the black-tent was a common dwelling form, particularly for nomadic herdsmen tending their flocks of sheep. Abraham, born in Ur of the Chaldees, adopted and lived the pure life of the nomad and "pitched his tent having Bethel on the west, and Ha'i on the east" (Genesis 12:8).

The housing and the way of life of mounted nomads roaming the Eurasian steppes have not changed substantially over the years from those of their ancestors, the first horsemen of antiquity. The remains of rugs and other fabrics that have been found in the tombs of the Scythians are evidence that the interiors of their felt tents "were floored with richly patterned carpets, the walls brightened with tapestries or felt hangings with elaborate appliqué designs depicting men, beasts and birds" (Trippett 1974, 15–18).

In the fifth century B.C. the Greek historian Herodotus described the Scythians and their nomadic existence. His account was similar to a later description of the Huns by Lady Wen-chi, an educated Chinese woman from Shensi who in A.D. 196 was abducted by a raiding band of Mongolian horsemen, the Hsiung-nu (Huns). The illustrations of her story made on a silk scroll show several yurts.

In the late nineteenth century, a Ukrainian photographer, Samuel M. Dudin, recorded the lifestyle of the Kazakhs, a tribe whose name in Turkish means "riders of the steppes." The kazakh yurt was portrayed with a Spartan simplicity on the outside, but behind its felt curtain door, called *ish kir mas* (the dog shall not enter), "there was hardly an inch of space that was not covered by woven carpets, and rugs, hangings and mats of felt. The felts were lavishly embroidered or appliquéd with floral designs, animal motifs, and arabesques" (Trippett 1974, 146).

CHAPTER FOUR

SEASONAL DWELLINGS

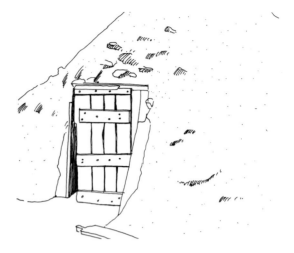

In this chapter the dwellings of the seminomads—the fourth category in our classification system—are considered. These dwellings are occupied seasonally or for several months at a time.

Seminomads practice some form of cultivation (that is, they plant and harvest crops) between seasonal migrations in their quest for survival as hunters and stock breeders. Their social organization is that of a tribal community, composed generally of a number of clans bound by strong social ties. This type of social structure is found predominantly in the continental steppe and the subtropical savannah regions.

Since the seminomadic society represents a transitional phase in the evolutionary process, it could also be described as semisedentary, especially since many tribes have abodes in a fixed locality to which they return from time to time. As is to be expected, common traits exist between nomadic and seminomadic housing forms. Members of both communities use temporary shelters during the migratory period of the year. The similarities in dwellings are especially evident in the summer shelters of the seminomads.

People who are dependent primarily on cultivated plants and domesticated animals for food are, of course, bound to more limited areas than nomadic hunters and food gatherers. The dependency upon adequate land for subsistence, coupled with direct control over cultivated plants and domesticated animals, develops an explicit notion of property

that is absent in the previously mentioned social organizations. However, this notion of property ownership of land still has the simple characteristic of communal property in contrast to one of personal or individual ownership. Depending on the degree to which a group of semisedentary people relies upon the collective labor of its members, property becomes either community or family oriented, and the extent of necessary group participation is inversely proportionate to the effectiveness of productivity. Thus, the greater the level of productivity in farming and herding, the fewer the members who are required to contribute. The prerequisite of family holdings instead of group holdings is the development of means by which each family can, through its own labor, produce enough food for its own needs.

The diversity of environmental factors and the prevailing level of productivity among the seminomadic or semisedentary people bring about a great variety of building types. Nevertheless, the dwellings share certain characteristics. To begin with, these people often utilize distinct types of dwellings: a substantial one for their sedentary period of life and a temporary structure for the duration of their migratory life. The first type, the more substantial of the two, naturally varies in size and complexity according to the size of the conjugal family, the extended family or "clan" that occupies the single or compound dwelling. Such dwellings are often clustered in a villagelike setting. In contrast, the shelters used during the migratory period are scattered and are designed to accommodate only small social units.

If a part of their economy is based upon cultivation, seminomads must have some form of granary or storage buildings adjacent to their dwellings. When there is very strong social cohesion, it is not unusual for them to have communal storehouses as well.

Not all seminomads, however, cultivate crops in addition to their animal husbandry. Some tribes in the arid savannah regions of Africa are exclusively cattle herders. The dependence on cattle is so complex and so complete that virtually all facets of life are either influenced or governed by the needs of, and yields from, the herd.

Their staple food is cow's milk, which is prepared in numerous ways including a mixture with cow's blood. This mixture is either imbibed raw or cooked to form a paste. When cattle are diseased or too old to breed, they are slaughtered; their meat is eaten, their hides are made into garments and bed covers, and their horns become containers or cups. Even the urine and the dung are put to use. The urine is used for rinsing milk gourds and as an antiseptic on cuts and scratches. The dung, mixed with mud, is applied as a plaster in building construction.

These "cattle complex" people have only one type of housing, a semisubstantial structure that is not transportable. When new pasture is sought for the cattle in a distant location, the dwelling is abandoned.

As expected, the generic form of seasonal dwelling varies with the prevailing climate of the environment. The steppe climate requires high-heat-capacity walls and roofs for the substantial winter residence to keep out intense cold and high winds, and low-heat-capacity walls and roofs for the temporary summer shelter. The winter residence is frequently a semisubterranean dwelling covered with earth that offers the maximum protection from cold and wind; the summer shelter, on the other hand, is often a mere sunshade and windscreen.

The subtropical savannah climate—characterized by little or no seasonal change, hot days and cool nights, low humidity, and little precipitation—demands one generic dwelling type: a structure with high-heat-capacity walls and roofs so that the thermal mass of the building will release at night the heat absorbed during the day; conversely, the night-cooled walls cool the interior of the dwelling during at least part of the day.

NAVAHO HOGAN AND RAMADA

The two seasonal living quarters of the Navaho Indians—the *hogan* and the *ramada*—serve as good prototypical examples of substantial and temporary family-sized dwellings.

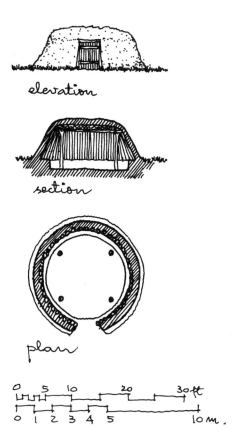

Navaho hogan

The Navaho live in the arid regions of the south-western United States, an area characterized by high mesas, large sand and gravel plains, deep canyons, and rugged mountains. In spite of considerable rainfall, this region stays arid because most of the precipitation falls in torrents that erode the land rather than make it fertile. In summer the Navaho move to the highlands, which are more favorable for farming, to cultivate their crops, whereas during fall, winter, and spring they live in the lowlands with their livestock.

The basic social unit of the Navaho is the extended family; this group consists mainly of the parents and the married daughters and their families. Two or more extended families have an established right over a territory that is cultivated collectively. This larger new division or subgroup of the tribe is the clan of the mother.

The traditional, and more substantial, dwelling of the Navaho—the hogan—is a low, one-room, mud-covered log hut with a doorway facing the east, the direction from which all good spirits come (a belief that probably has its roots in sun worship). Only one family occupies a dwelling; several hogans are grouped together to house the individual units of the extended family.

Hogans are rarely built in isolation; they usually occur in clusters. These small settlements are formed by a matrilinearly related group that may be composed of three generations. Each nuclear family occupies at least one hogan, while other hogans are used for storage. A ceremonial hogan without a smoke hole is often constructed to serve as the sweathouse for a small settlement.

There are several types of hogans. The older, circular type consists of three forked poles locked together at the top with other poles leaning on them; the whole structure is then covered with earth. The later and more usual type has a circular plan with four upright forked poles supporting a log deck and sloping walls, all covered with tamped earth. These dome-shaped huts do not have windows; the smoke of the open fire escapes through the smoke hole in the roof. A blanket is often used for a door.

Navaho hogan

The construction of the conventional four-post hogan commences with the digging of a 2-ft (60-cm) deep circular pit. The forked posts are then erected near the edge of the pit, roughly 10 ft (3 m) from each other; these posts are usually very crooked since only scrubby short trees are found in this arid region. Two long poles are laid parallel across two sets of forks to act as supporting beams for a number of lighter poles and branches spanning the two beams; still lighter branches may be laid at right angles on top of these to make the roof deck stronger, not dissimilar in principle to the reinforcing rods of a two-way reinforced concrete slab. To construct the wall of the hogan, branches from nearby bushes are collected and stuck into the ground along the periphery of the circular pit. They are bent so that they will touch the roof's edge. The upright branches are tied at the top to the roof structure and other branches interwoven horizontally around the frame. A door opening is left (facing the east) just high enough for a man to enter in a stooped position.

Finally, the whole brush framework is covered with moist desert earth that has been scraped up in baskets after a rain. After a while the desert earth gets very hard and dry in the sun, making the walls and the roof cover almost like plaster. Indeed, the hogan is very comfortable both during the day and at night, since the diurnal extremes of temperature

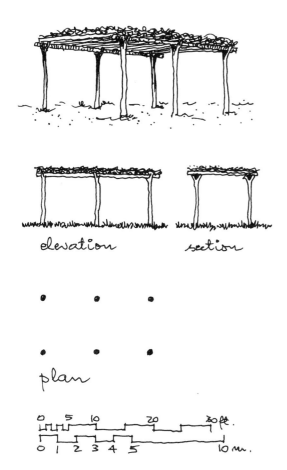

elevation   section

plan

Navaho ramada

NUER KRAAL

The Nuer, a Nilotic tribe living in the Sudan, provide another example of a cluster of seasonal dwellings, called the *kraal*, which is a fence-enclosed homestead.

The Nuer are essentially a pastoral people. They do grow a few crops to augment their food supply, but cultivation of the soil is a secondary activity and is considered degrading. Stock breeding, on the other hand, is viewed with great pride. Milk, the tribe's staple food, is drunk fresh, eaten mixed with millet as a porridge, eaten sour, or churned into cheese. During the dry season, when cows run dry, the Nuer bleed their cattle from a small cut in the neck vein; they boil the blood until it is thick or let it coagulate, after which it is roasted and eaten. Cattle are only slaughtered and eaten when they are injured or too old for breeding.

During the rainy season the Nuer live on the upper plateaus of the southern Sudan in villagelike settlements of fifty to several hundred persons. Here they breed cattle and cultivate small plots. At the end of the rainy season, after the ground becomes arid, they set fire to the grass to prepare new pastures for the following season and set off to camp near streams or rivers for the next six months. Frequent migrations during the dry season are necessary to ensure adequate pasture for their livestock.

of the region are evened out by the lag in heat gain and heat loss of the thick layer of mud covering. Thus, a hogan is cooler than the outdoors in daytime, and warmer at night.

The Navaho summer home—the ramada, little more than a sunshade—is essentially an open structure of four or six upright forked posts supporting a flat roof of poles and brush. Its sides are open and only seldom do the inhabitants erect a pole-and-brush wall on the windward side. The ramada is also used in many parts of Latin America.

House building, well digging, fence making, and other major endeavors are usually communal activities for the Navaho. Men do most of the field work; women keep the dwellings and tend the young children; and the older children and the aged are expected to look after the livestock.

Nuer kraal

The village community of the Nuer is known as the *cieng*, which may be translated as "home," and the cattle camp used in the drought season as *wec*, meaning "camp." Grazing land and all vegetation in a given area are the common property of all members of a community.

The Nuer kraal is a substantial homestead containing a cluster of round mud huts and stables constructed of wattle and daub (a framework of interwoven rods and twigs between upright posts, then plastered with mud). Each kraal is inhabited by the minimum socioeconomic unit: one conjugal family or an extended family composed of a patriarch and several sons and their families. A single round hut is occupied by a wife and her children and at times by her husband. If there is a polygamous family group, the homestead consists of several round huts plus the cow barn. A family grouping is called the *gol*, a word synonymous with "hearth." Each gol herds its own cattle and performs its domestic tasks independently.

Building and repairs generally take place early in the dry season when there is plenty of straw for thatching. Fences are erected between the stables along the sides of the kraal and around huts to control the movement of cattle in the rainy season. During the rainy season economic activities of the homesteads are individualized (done communally by each gol), but during the period of camp living the economic activities of the Nuer are performed communally by all families. All cattle are herded together and milked at the same time.

E. E. Evans-Pritchard in his study of the Nuer provides an apt description of their living arrangements:

> Nuer are forced into villages for protection against floods and mosquitoes and to engage in horticulture, and are forced out of villages into camps by drought and barrenness of vegetation and to engage in fishing. . . . In dry-season camps men sleep in windscreens and women in beehive-huts, or both sexes in beehive-huts. These flimsy shelters are erected a few yards from water, generally in a semi-circle or in lines with their backs to the prevailing wind, and are simply constructed, the roots of grasses, or occasionally stems of millet, being tightly packed in a narrow trench to make windscreens, and the tops of the grasses being bound together and plastered with dung on the outside to make huts. . . . The whole space within a windscreen is occupied by a hearth of ashes on which the men sleep around the fire, and the openings face the kraal. If people do not intend to spend more than a few days at a site they often sleep in the open and do not trouble to erect windscreens and huts. These light dwellings can be erected in a few hours (Evans-Pritchard 1940, 63, 65–66).

MASAI BOMA

The shelters of the Masai tribes living on the rolling plains of Kenya and Tanzania are also seasonal dwellings.

Small groups of Masai families travel with the seasons and herd cattle in a cyclical fashion by following the rain and the availability of pasture. Skill in cattle breeding has made the Masai tribes among the wealthiest of Africa's pastoralists. By 6 years of age, boys have already begun to learn how to handle cattle, and at 10 or 12 they take care of the family herd. As young men, they become herders and warriors to protect the large tribal herds from wild animals. A *moran*, a warrior, is not allowed to do any other work, drink alcohol, smoke, or eat vegetable food. He must live on milk and blood alone, the staple food of the Masai. The cattle are bled from the jugular vein, the bull about a gallon (3.78 l) a month, and the cow about a pint (0.47 l). The Masai eat only the meat of their own cattle, sheep, and goats; consequently, they do not hunt the wild herds of zebra, wildebeest, and other animals grazing peacefully side by side with the domesticated cattle. They live in harmony with the wildlife in the natural haven of the Serengeti Park.

The Masai homestead, called *boma*, is a circular kraal ringed with high thorn fences. Several huts are erected just inside and adjacent to the protective fence. On the right side of the gate, at the entrance to the boma, stands the first or main wife's hut; the second wife builds hers on the left side, and the third to the right of the first, and so on.

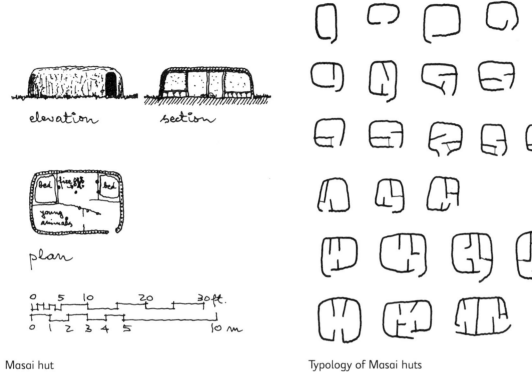

Masai hut
(after Kaj Blegvad Andersen)

Typology of Masai huts
(after Kaj Blegvad Andersen)

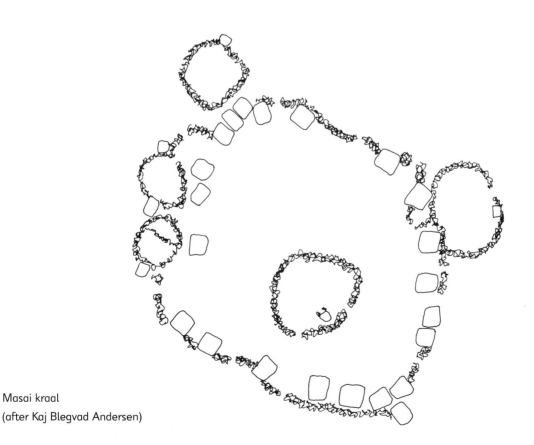

Masai kraal
(after Kaj Blegvad Andersen)

The Masai hut is built by the woman, and she alone decides who enters it. The construction of the low and oblong hut takes about a week. It begins with the gathering of building material and involves a search for posts from small forests or wood stands which may be at great distances from each other in the savannah. The posts are usually short and rarely exceed 5 ft (1.5 m) in length. Several posts are pounded into the ground along the perimeter of the dwelling and then are tied together horizontally with saplings. Additional saplings are lodged between the top horizontal ties and bent over to reach the opposite sides to be fastened there. This type of roof construction results in the typical humped roofline of the Masai hut. Intermittent posts in the interior of the hut lend support to the flimsy latticework of the roof and reinforce the screens or partitions dividing the hut into designated use areas.

Twigs, leaves, and grass are interwoven between the posts and the roof latticework to complete the structure. The entire structure is then plastered from the outside with a mixture of cow dung and mud. The first areas to be plastered are the round corners forming the transition between the walls and the roof. In exceptional cases, the inside of the hut is also finished with cow-dung plaster (Andersen 1977, 176).

The huts resemble rectangular earth mounds measuring from 7 to 10 ft (2.1 to 3 m) in width and 10 to 13 ft (3 to 3.9 m) in length. They are so low that one cannot stand upright inside them. The interior, lit only through a narrow door opening, is divided into two specific use areas. Immediately inside the hut is usually a privacy wall and an enclosure for young animals, which occupies about a third of the total area. Beyond this enclosure is the living quarter with its central hearth. Flanking the hearth are two beds, one for the older children and a second one for the mother. The children's bed is used for sitting during the daytime; the woman's bed is considered private and therefore screened off and not used during the day.

The doorway of the Masai hut is so low that one must stoop when entering. "The door itself is made of reeds held together by strips of leather. This framework is also used as a pack-saddle on a donkey when the family moves camp" (Andersen 1977, 184).

At night the cattle are driven into the central space of the kraal for protection against wild animals. When the dry season forces the Masai to move in search of new waterholes and better grazing grounds (or if someone dies inside a boma), the kraal is abandoned. The Masai load their goods onto donkeys to be transported to the new site, and their former homes are set afire before they leave.

BARABAIG GHEID

The Barabaig of Tanzania are another of the few surviving "cattle complex" people. These seminomads also inhabit seasonal dwellings. They must

Barabaig gheid

migrate with their herds in response to climate and vegetational changes. Although they do cultivate small plots of maize, the Barabaig are primarily cattle breeders.

A Barabaig kraal or homestead is called *gheid* and consists of a thorn-bush enclosure built in the shape of a figure eight. The fence is about 8 to 10 ft (2.6 to 3 m) in height and is usually uninterrupted except by an opening at the tangential point of the two circles of the figure eight. One circular enclosure is called *samod* and contains the dwellings of the Barabaig, while the other, the *muhaled* is a cattle corral. Both people and cattle enter and leave the kraal through a joint gateway that provides access to both enclosures.

The typical dwelling of a nuclear family is small in size and has only two rooms: the *huland* for the husband and the *ged* for the wife. Each room has its own hearth, but only the woman's firestead is used for cooking. Sometimes a dwelling may contain a third room called *dododa muhog* where sheep, goats, and young calves are sheltered overnight (Klima 1970, 34–36).

The walls of the huts are built of upright poles that are interlaced with saplings before they are plastered with mud and cow dung. The roof beams are supported on forked posts and are covered with twigs, thatch, and a finishing layer of mud mixed with cow dung.

POKOT DWELLING

The pastoral Pokot inhabit the highlands that form the northern extreme of the Cherangany Hills of Kenya. They live in large circular buildings topped by a dome that is only slightly arched. A cluster of dwellings is built in a kraal-like setting surrounded by a thorn brush fence; a second, smaller corral within the larger enclosure harbors the cattle at night.

The typical Pokot dwelling has a diameter of from 10 to 32 ft (3 to 10 m). Its walls consist of sets of paired posts at about 12-inch (30-cm) intervals

around the perimeter of the building; the gap between the paired posts is packed with horizontally laid saplings. The main roof beams are gently sloped and rest on this wall. They are additionally supported by freestanding forked posts within the building. Secondary roof beams span the space between the main beams. An additional layer of thin branches and twigs completes the domelike supporting structure that is topped by a layer of grass superimposed by a thick layer of earth. A continuous gap at the eaves ensures cross-ventilation in the dwelling.

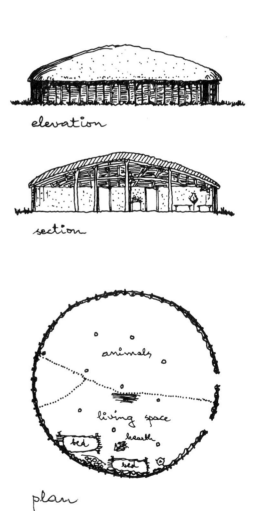

Pokot dwelling
(after Kaj Blegvad Andersen)

Larger houses are divided into two main sections, one serving as the living quarters and the other as a stable for goats and young calves. The shoulder-high dividing partition, as well as the inner surface of the outside wall, is usually plastered with a mixture of cow dung and mud. Separate doorways give access to the two sections of the building.

The furnishing of the living quarters is sparse. Bed platforms constructed of wood sticks are placed adjacent to the exterior walls and near the family hearth.

Round Pan-p'o dwelling
(after Jonathan N. Leonard)

PREHISTORIC AND HISTORIC SEASONAL DWELLINGS

The remains of hoganlike seasonal dwellings dating from 4,000 B.C. were identified in the village of Pan-p'o in China. In each dwelling a dirt ramp descended from the door to the interior of the circular semisubterranean dwelling of 17 ft (5.1 m) in diameter. The roof structure, covered with mud and sod, was supported by six posts surrounding a central hearth. Beside the round houses archaeologists also found several square dwellings measuring 18 by 18 ft (5.5 by 5.5 m). These buildings resembled the round ones in construction. The floors were also semisubterranean, but the roof and covered entrance passage were thatched.

The hoganlike structure, in fact, was a widespread dwelling type used in many regions of the world. Prehistoric examples were discovered in Japan as well as in the Near East. In North America several Indian tribes lived in semisubterranean dwellings resembling the Navaho hogan. The Mandan, for example, an Indian farming tribe

Square Pan-p'o dwelling
(after Jonathan N. Leonard)

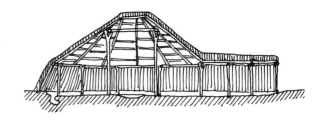

Mandan dwelling
(after Albert F. Bemis)

encountered in 1738 by the explorer La Vérendry, built earth lodges that were admirably suited to the severe winters of the Northern Plains. Additional historic examples are the earth lodges in California of the High Sierra Maidu and the tribes of the Sacramento Valley, and the lodges of the Mogollon from New Mexico.

CHAPTER FIVE

SEMIPERMANENT DWELLINGS

The fifth stage of the evolutionary hierarchy of dwelling types includes the semipermanent huts and houses of a sedentary society. This type of society, which has a predominant social organization known as a folk community, subsists mainly by the cultivation of staple crops. Its members are commonly referred to as hoe peasants, for although they may use a rudimentary plow, they have not yet reached the advanced stage of agriculture in which more sophisticated plows and other farm implements are used. These primitive cultivators have to leave their lands fallow for a few years after their crop yield decreases, except where they have irrigated the land. This, of course, has a direct effect on their housing patterns. In accordance with their cultivation system, the use period of the hoe peasants' semipermanent dwellings varies from a few to about fifteen years.

The development of agriculture and the domestication of animals was a gradual, pervasive revolution in the history of the world. The effect of this revolution upon man's history was as profound as that of the Industrial Revolution despite the fact that most agrarian societies remained at the subsistence level of food production. Agricultural people who had direct control over domesticated plants and animals developed an explicit notion of property and its ownership. In comparison with the vast territories of hunters and food gatherers, their land holdings were very small, often not more than a few acres. Moreover, the ecological conse-

quences from the small size of their property coupled with the nature of its exploitation resulted in considerable modification of their physical environment. Land holdings that were passed down along hereditary lines brought about class distinctions between large and small property owners, but these distinctions had little impact on the basic, social structure of the hoe peasant "...since the imperatives of land labor will not allow greatly diverse property holdings" (Watson and Watson 1969, 101).

There is no single pattern of culture or form of socioeconomic organization that is truly characteristic of hoe peasant society. A wide range of physical environments, along with a great diversity of crops, techniques of cultivation, organization of manual labor, and cultural inheritance bring about many types of settlement patterns. Yet, in spite of these complex variables, some general traits pertaining to this social group and to the dwellings they build can be discerned.

In contrast to the social groups already considered—the hunters, food gatherers, fishermen, and pastoral nomads who do occasionally cultivate naturally productive areas—the hoe peasant deliberately cultivates through regular planting of selected seeds, tubers, or cuttings in fields that are prepared to yield staple crops. Over and above an empirical knowledge of plant life, the cultivator has to have foresight and an established routine in order to ensure a continuing supply of food. For example, he has to store supplies not only for that period of the year when there is no produce, but also for the sowing or planting of the following year's crops. The most elementary ways of tilling the land involve one or more of the following steps: clearing and burning over the plots in the dry season, using digging sticks as planting implements for ridge-and-mound cultivation, or planting irrigated plots enclosed by embankments. The storage of cultivated food supplies allows greater numbers of people to live in a given area which, in turn, leads to a greater concentration of dwellings, sometimes clustered in the form of villages.

The anticipated use of a dwelling for a period of years rather than for several days or months naturally imposes greater care in its construction. The resulting building thus is more durable than most nomadic or seasonal dwellings.

The basic dwelling forms of a sedentary society are the cylindrical hut with a conical thatched roof, the oval house, and the rectangular dwelling with rounded corners and a saddle-type roof. In its simplest form the semipermanent dwelling has only one room, which the human occupants often share with small domestic animals. The most complex form is a dwelling compound of interrelated clusters of huts. These are usually occupied by an extended polygamous or composite family. Indeed, some hoe peasants have adopted a large collective dwelling form; these additive structures are either single-storied or multistoried buildings whose flat roofs are used to reach the interior dwellings as well as to communicate from one unit to another.

Since storage facilities are required by the hoe peasants, structures serving this purpose are constructed. Other ancillary buildings may also be built, such as pens and stables for domestic animals, and kitchen huts. It is of interest to note that public buildings such as places of worship make their appearance as well at this level of social organization.

The most widespread generic form of subtropical semipermanent dwellings is the adobe round hut with a thatched roof. The thermal mass of the cylindrical walls balances the fluctuating diurnal temperature changes between hot days and cool nights, and the low-heat-capacity thatched roof provides excellent protection from the rays of the sun as well as from precipitation while allowing warm air to escape between its fibers. In arid regions flat roofs plastered with adobe are predominant, especially in multistoried collective dwellings such as the pueblo and the Moroccan ksar.

In tropical regions the generic house form is cylindrical, oval, or rectangular with low-heat-capacity walls and roof. Walls are frequently constructed of vertical stalks with narrow gaps between them to ensure good cross-ventilation; roofs are invariably thatched.

LUYIA AND LUO DWELLING

The detached cylindrical huts of the agricultural Luyia and Luo are good examples of simple semipermanent dwellings. The Luyia are settled in Kenya's fertile rolling hills and the Luo in the low-lying areas around Lake Victoria. Their main crop is maize, but a variety of other grains and vegetables as well as bananas are also cultivated.

The circular plan of the Luyia dwelling is delineated with the help of a string attached to a central peg. An outer circle marks the position of the verandah posts; an inner circle designates the position of the dwelling's exterior wall. A number of posts are dug into the ground in a row along the two circles; the outer row of posts are spaced farther apart than the inner posts because only the inner wall is laced with horizontal saplings to form a supporting lattice for the adobe wall. Beams span the distance from post to post and support the rafters of the conical roof structure. Auxiliary posts are positioned inside the building to lend additional support to the roof structure. A continuous gap of 6 in (15 cm) at the eave level and between the rafters ensures good air circulation. The roof thatching is either layered, which results in a stepping effect, or flush; an extra layer of thatch usually

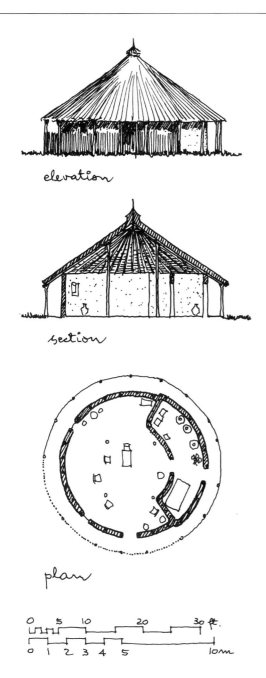

elevation

section

plan

Luyia dwelling
(after Kaj Blegvad Andersen)

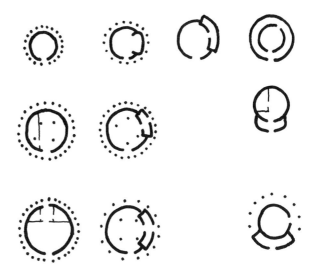

Typology of Luyia and Luo dwellings
(after Kaj Blegvad Andersen)

crowns the apex of the roof. Papyrus reeds are used extensively for thatching.

The traditional dwelling of the Luyia is divided into two sections—a large reception area where social activities are held and a smaller section, often paralleling the exterior wall that serves as the living quarters where the occupants sleep, cook, and eat. Separate entryways give access to the two sections from the outside, but an inside doorway links the two spaces. The dwellings are furnished with bedsteads and three- or four-legged stools as well as sophisticated armchairs made of green saplings with a finely woven rattan seat.

To store their grains, the Luyia construct thatch-roofed granaries of wickerwork or papyrus stems on raised platforms. Wide eaves protect the grains both from the sun and rain.

The Luo, neighbors of the Luyia, also inhabit cylindrical mud huts with a thatched conical roof. The Luo dwellings are constructed the same way as those of the Luyia, but often have two concentric walls of vertical posts covered with adobe. In contrast to the Luyia house (where the outer wall defines a verandah), the outer wall of the Luo house is often enclosed and the corridorlike space thus formed is divided into kitchen, storage, and pen sections. The central room is reserved for sleeping and social activities.

MESAKIN QUISAR CLUSTER DWELLING

The Mesakin Quisar, a Nuba people of the Sudan, live in round-hut clusters that typify the multiunit semipermanent dwelling pattern.

The chief activity of the Mesakin is the cultivation of fields for their staple food, *durra*, a variety of millet resembling maize. Sowing commences in April, when the rainy season begins, and is completed by the end of May. The fields are tended during the long growing season until November when the harvest starts. The harvest is a community endeavor. Neighbors and relatives join in reaping a man's crop and then move on to another's. Men wield knives or iron spearheads to cut the grainbearing ears from the stalks and flail the ears of millet with flat clubs to thresh out the grain. Women clean the grain by lifting filled calabashes in the air and trickling their contents into baskets while the wind carries off the chaff. The women then transport the baskets to the granaries of their homes.

Cattle are driven to the fields after the harvest to graze on the stubble; however, cattle raising is only of secondary importance in this region of scanty grazing. Before the next sowing season the fields are burned over in preparation for spring planting.

A typical Mesakin dwelling consists of five or six windowless round huts constructed on stone foundations around a courtyard. The base is carefully prepared to allow rain water from the inner courtyard to drain off easily. The huts, as well as the walls closing off the spaces between them, are built of adobe, 12 in (30 cm) at the base and thinner above. The walls of the huts are from 7 to 10 ft (2.1 to 3.0 m) high and are mud-plastered smoothly inside and out; wooden pegs are set into the wall for hanging calabashes and working tools. The huts, which may be from 11 to 13 ft (3.3 to 3.9 m) in diameter, enclose a private courtyard. The center of it is the family cooking area. A conical grass roof covers each round hut, giving it a turret effect. A roof of loosely woven grass and boughs shades the inner courtyard.

elevation

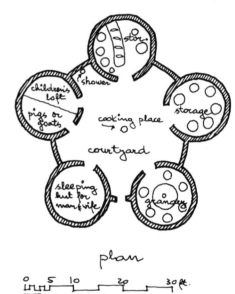

plan

Mesakin Quisar cluster dwellings

If the dwelling cluster consists of five huts, the entrance door is in one of the connecting walls and leads directly into the inner courtyard; if there are six huts, the entrance leads into one of the larger huts, usually the guest house, and only from there can one reach the courtyard. The main portal to the compound has the shape of a keyhole to admit a person bearing a bulky load. A hut is illuminated by the light coming through the entryway, a small round or oval opening with a high mud threshold.

Each hut is reserved for a particular household activity. For example, one hut is the main sleeping hut, one is an animal pen for chickens, goats, or pigs, and several are storehouses. The animal shelter often contains a loft that is reached by a

Mesakin Quisar cluster dwelling
(after Oskar Luz)

separate entrance on a higher level and is used as a sleeping platform for the young boys of the family; older girls sleep in the hut where the corn is ground. Between two turrets of a cluster dwelling an elementary shower is constructed from a calabash cradled on a pair of antelope horns; the bather has to reach up to tilt the water-filled container forward so water can trickle from a hole near the rim of the vessel.

The courtyard of the round-hut cluster is the principal space of the Mesakin dwelling. It is where most social activities, eating, and cooking take place. A hearth consisting of three rounded stones to support cooking vessels is found in the center of the courtyard, and other stones to sit on as well as simple chairs made from branches are scattered around the hearth. The exterior walls of the cylindrical huts defining the courtyard are equipped with pegs on which weapons, tools, calabashes, and a variety of pots hang.

The courtyard also functions as a hallway since all huts are entered from the court. The entrances are usually oval and have a high threshold. A few huts that are used as bedrooms and on occasion as granaries have very small entrance holes measuring between 12 and 14 in (30 to 35 cm) in diameter and placed as high as 5 ft (1.5 m) above ground level. The grace and agility with which the Mesakin use these narrow entrance holes is astonishing. The smallness of the apertures ensures a more desirable indoor climate, which is cool in the middle of a warm day and warm on a cool night. Moreover, it is difficult for snakes and scorpions to enter the hut over the high threshold wall. Finally, when huts are used as granaries, it is easy to seal off the entrance (Riefenstahl 1973, 15–16).

Externally, the Mesakin hut cluster is plain, but the inside walls of the dwellings, including the connecting walls, are often covered with shiny blue glazing, mainly done to be ornamental but also to harden the surface and make it smooth. The glazed effect is achieved by smearing the walls with earth containing graphite and then hand-rubbing it until the blue sheen appears. The mud walls are also painted with a wide ornamental border. The shower section in particular is richly adorned with painted decorations, no doubt to protect the adobe walls from water erosion.

When first married, husband and wife live with their respective families until the wife becomes pregnant. At this time the husband starts building the dwelling complex. It takes a man two years to build a cluster, since during the five-month rainy season building activity ceases and during the dry season the fields are tended.

The family life of the polygamous Mesakin is harmonious. If the husband has several wives, he provides separate dwellings for each and must have additional fields and livestock to support each family.

Awuna cluster dwelling

AWUNA CLUSTER DWELLING

Indigenous to Ghana and to the Upper-Volta region is the residence of the Awuna (or Fra-Fra), a typical African round-hut compound dwelling. Each dwelling unit consists of a cluster of round huts facing an enclosed central courtyard. The Awuna, like the Mesakin Quisar, practice polygamy. Since each wife and her children occupy one cluster dwelling, several clusters surround the perimeter of the greater extended-family compound, which is also enclosed by a circular or elliptical wall centering on a cattle corral.

Each cluster dwelling of these settled, agricultural people is designed to accommodate animals, such as goats, domestic hens, and guinea fowl, in addition to its human inhabitants. The various round huts of the cluster have assigned functions: one is a sleeping room, one a kitchen, one a storehouse. Others may be used as a children's sleeping room, a fowl house, or a goat pen, according to particular needs.

The round huts and enclosing walls are constructed of mud, and most huts are roofed with thick thatches of straw on a framework of cut branches. The storehouse roof is made of mud laid

elevation

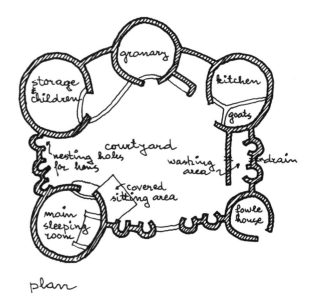

plan

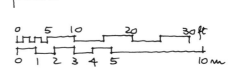

Awuna dwelling
(after Charles Cockburn)

on wooden rafters and is usually flat for use in drying corn and other farm produce. After the roof is completed, a wood fire is kindled inside the hut to blacken the rafters, the wood frame, and the thatch in order to discourage termites.

The mud walls and flattened floors of the dwelling are plastered with mud mixed with cow dung and a juice extracted from the locust bean pod. This mixture hardens into a waterproof and smooth finish. The huts have no windows. Light enters through low doorways that are only 4 ft (1.2 m) high. Mud thresholds, 9 in (23 cm) high, are placed just inside the door openings to keep out the rain. In the main sleeping hut the bed is molded out from the wall. In the kitchen a low mud wall separates a section for the goats, which are tethered to posts.

The courtyard has a gentle fall and is drained through a channel under the outer wall and adjacent to a screened-off bathing area. Conical nesting boxes for domestic fowl are built into the enclosing yard walls, and shallow seats are molded out of the high wall surrounding the outdoor cooking area. The section of the yard used for drying produce is enclosed by a 1-ft (30-cm) high mud wall that also serves as seating. The thatched roof of the main sleeping hut is extended outward to provide a sheltered outdoor sitting area near the main entrance to the dwelling cluster.

Gurunsi compound and baobab tree

GURUNSI COMPOUND DWELLING

The Gurunsi also inhabit the Upper-Volta region, but, in contrast to the neighboring Awuna, they live in large and integrated extended-family compounds. The Gurunsi are also polygamous, and since several brothers with their families may live together in a compound, their circular building site may exceed 200 ft (60 m) in diameter. A typical large compound, as described by René Gardi for example, may be occupied by several brothers who have among them sixteen wives and thirty-five children. The oldest brother is the head of the extended family and wields considerable authority. The individual dwellings of the sixteen households occupy the periphery of the compound and enclose a large courtyard. Within this courtyard are the family head's dwelling, numerous storehouses, granaries and stables.

From the outside the compound resembles a regular fortress, since the dwellings on its periphery are windowless. The main entrance to this large complex is located near a great baobab tree and, like the two secondary entrances, is barred at night. The individual dwellings along the periphery of the compound are attached to other dwellings and are "boxed up in each other with [such] irregular floor plans that the only way to more or less sort out the confusion is from the rooftops" (Gardi 1973, 138). The private outdoor extensions of an individual dwelling are defined by walls of various heights; laundering and bathing, for example, are done behind a high wall.

The adobe dwellings on the periphery of the compound vary in size from three to five rooms. Although most dwellings are attached to neighboring units, they have no direct access between them. A typical home consists of a large elongated living space, a circular kitchen, and bedrooms. The living space usually has a small altar in one corner, and a

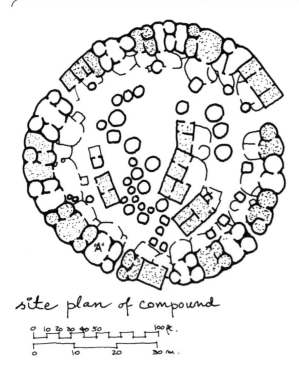

site plan of compound

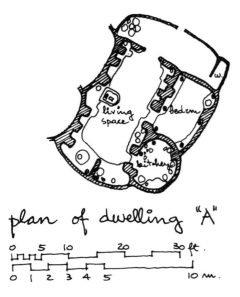

plan of dwelling "A"

Gurunsi dwelling
(after René Gardi)

like the kitchen, have no bedsteads; mats are spread out on the floor at night for sleeping.

The small screened-off yard fronting each dwelling and the roof terrace are important spaces as most living is done outdoors. A corner of the front yard is used as a beer kitchen, another as a laundry. A notched tree trunk in the yard gives access to the mud-plastered flat roof, which becomes a sleeping platform on hot nights. At other times the roof may serve as a drying platform for produce or, on occasion, as a chicken yard.

It is interesting to note that several structures within the compound are rectangular in shape, including the main building occupied by the head of the extended family. There is little doubt that the rectangular structures are foreign to the area and represent a deliberate departure from the traditional pattern.

DOGON CLUSTER DWELLING

The Dogon people of Mali also live in a cluster-type dwelling, but in contrast to those of their neighbors of the Upper-Volta, Dogon huts are mostly rectangular or square in plan.

The Dogon are agriculturalists who cultivate their meager arable land collectively. Each man has the right to farm certain parcels of land, but he may never own them. However, he cannot be deprived of access to these fields as long as he has descendants who will till the soil.

The Dogon live in compact village communities near the cliffs of the Bandiagara Plateau. There are two basic village types—the "plateau" type situated on elevated tablelike rock outcroppings between arable fields and the "cliff-debris" type situated on the steep slopes of fallen rock along the Bandiagara escarpment. The cluster dwellings of the village are built collectively and adjacent to each other. This collective facet of the Dogon's life explains the compact nature of their communities.

Dwellings are placed around a family courtyard defined by dry stone walls linking the main house, granaries, and secondary huts. The huts and

wide earthen ledge extends along the rear and two side walls on which drinking water and beer jars as well as containers of millet, corn, and beans are placed. This ledge may also serve as a bench. Buttresslike piers and freestanding posts support the flat roof structure.

The circular kitchen is used mainly during the rainy season; a stove, pots, jars, and calabashes are placed along its wall. The bedrooms, windowless

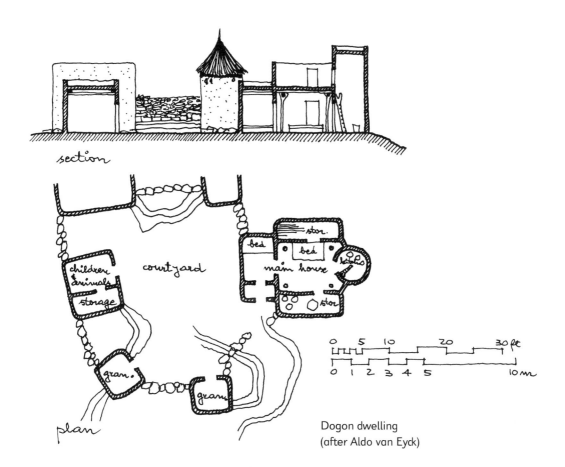

section

plan

children & animals

storage

courtyard

gram.

gram.

stor.

bed

bed

main house

patio

stor.

0 5 10   20   30 ft

0 1 2 3 4 5   10 m

Dogon dwelling
(after Aldo van Eyck)

granaries rest on foundations of stones and tree trunks. Their walls are constructed of sun-dried mud bricks reinforced with bits of straw and then plastered with mud.

The courtyard is the principal living space of the family: it is the kitchen and workshop during the dry season and a pen for the family's domestic animals. The main house, a multiroom complex, has an anteroom, the family room, storage rooms, and a kitchen used in the rainy season. The kitchen section has the primordial circular plan, but instead of the conical roof of cylindrical huts, like the rest of the house it is covered with a flat roof. The mud-plastered roofs are supported by wooden rafters, beams, and freestanding columns where needed. From the anteroom or kitchen a notched tree-trunk ladder gives access to the roof, where the family sleeps during the hot, dry months. Beams and rafters protrude beyond the outside face of the walls in order to act as scaffolding when the mud walls need repair.

Each family has several granaries, some for storing a portion of the harvest to feed the family during the dry season, others for storing grains for sowing during the following season, and yet others for storing grains as insurance against crop failure. The latter granaries have wooden doors that are sealed with mud plaster; the grain inside is first sprinkled with ashes as protection against insect damage. The flat roofs of the granaries are often covered with an additional conical straw roof. These straw roofs are assembled on the ground like straw hats and placed on the square-based towerlike granaries. Since the conical straw roofs do not fit the square shape of the granaries, the eaves are always irregular.

The Dogon dwelling is a good example of an advanced stage of the evolutionary process from the circular to the rectangular building plan; moreover, it illustrates the mixed use of the single-room and multiroom structure.

Finally, in contrast to the Mesakin dwellings, which are scattered in the landscape, Dogon clus-

Plateau-type Dogon village

Cliff-debris type Dogon village

ter dwellings are built close together to form close-knit settlements. The plateau-type villages are small in comparison to the larger cliff-debris type villages. All Dogon settlements have a network of irregular and narrow pathways with an organic rather than a geometrically rectilinear pattern. The large villages are divided into districts, each with its own religious center. A public square and a meeting house for men, called *toguna*, are the focal points of large villages. The toguna is, in effect, a council house where the men meet, presided over by the village elder.

The Dogon village, inhabited by a multitude of nonrelated families, is a well-organized community and typifies an early stage in the developmental sequence of human settlements (Van Eyck 1961, 186).

MAYAN OVAL HOUSE AND MEXICAN JACAL

Another prototypical semipermanent dwelling is the Mayan oval house found in the village communities of the Yucatán peninsula in Mexico.

The Mayan people are agriculturalists living in almost self-sufficient villages. They are predominantly tillers and all specialized occupations, such as carpentry and storekeeping, are subordinate to farming. When a family's arable land becomes depleted, they must leave the village and move to another site in order to cut and burn new fields out of an overgrown wilderness. The new site may have been cultivated years ago. At first the family retains its ties with the home village, but these ties eventually vanish when a new village community is established.

In autumn, at the beginning of the dry season, a new field is cleared with a small axe. After a few months the field is burned over, and just before the rainy season in late spring maize, beans, and squash are planted in small holes made with a digging stick. Following the planting, the fields are hardly cared for until harvest time in the late fall.

A Mayan settlement is grouped around a square with a common well and a place of worship and consists of simple one-room homes with corn stalks or wattle-and-daub walls and thatched roofs. The house is oval in shape with entrances placed in the center of its broad sides. Although it has no door, neighbors respect the privacy of the occupants. The interiors of these homes are simply furnished with hammocks for sleeping and little

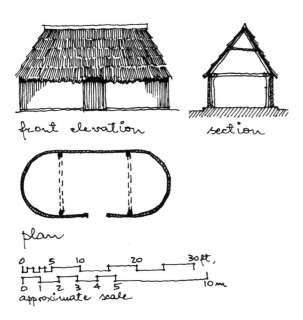

Mayan oval house
(after P. M. Bardi)

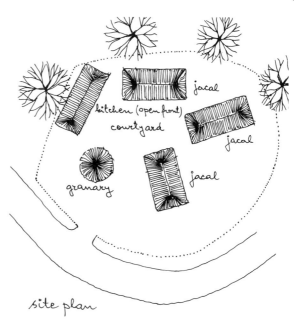

Mexican jacal compound
(after Eleanor Smith Morris)

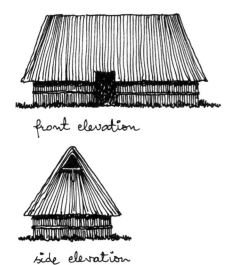

Mexican jacal
(after Eleanor Smith Morris)

wooden benches for seating. Cooking is done in one section of the room on a small stone hearth. The food is either boiled in a clay pot or baked on a clay griddle.

The *jacal* is similar to the Mayan oval house and found in the villages of southern Mexico. Their inhabitants also are primarily agriculturalists and descendants of the indigenous Indian tribes. The jacal is rectangular and constructed of corn stalks tied together with vines. The roof is also made of knotted twine and forms a gabled thatched roof. There are no windows in the jacal, but the apertures between the vertical stalks allow cooling breezes to blow through the hut. The jacal has a tamped dirt floor and a single doorway to the interior.

Usually the jacal is part of a compound of huts surrounded by a cornstalk fence. The sleeping quarters for the parents and their young children is the largest hut in the compound. Often a second or even a third jacal is built as sleeping quarters for older children. The kitchen hut is similar to a sleeping hut, but has one or more sides open toward the courtyard; molded low adobe platforms serve as cooking hearths, and stone metates are used to grind the corn. A circular granary called *cuescomatl* is erected near the center of the compound. Its floor is elevated above the ground to protect the corn from rodents. Its supporting structure is plastered inside and out with clay to keep it dry, and its conical roof is thatched to shed the rain.

Taos pueblo

PUEBLO

An interesting and very picturesque example of a collective semipermanent dwelling form is the American *pueblo* inhabited by the Hopi, Zuni, Acoma, and other Pueblo Indian tribes living in the semidesert plateaus of Arizona and New Mexico. Pueblos are multistoried buildings of many dwelling units arranged in tiers. Usually several of these building masses enclose one or more plazas.

The Pueblo Indians, a sedentary and peaceful people, cultivate staple crops on lands that are marginal because of limited rainfall and growing seasons curtailed by frost. To secure adequate harvests of maize, beans, squash, gourds, tobacco, and cotton, they must take advantage of the runoff and seepage from the higher plateaus and mesas that receive more rain. They have to use drought-resistant and quick-growing plant varieties suitable for deep and widely spaced planting. The fields are perpetually suited for cultivation since soil fertility is constantly restored by wind-blown and alluvial deposition of new soil. Even today few Pueblo Indians own plows, preferring the simple wooden digging sticks, weed cutters, and hoes of pre-Columbian times. Men perform the great bulk of

the agricultural work, assisted by women only during planting and harvesting.

Prior to the arrival of the white colonists the turkey and the dog were the only domesticated animals. Sheep and other livestock were introduced by the colonists. In addition to farming, the Pueblo Indians at one time did some hunting of buffalo, deer, and, above all, rabbits; women collected fruits of the yucca and cacti as well as berries and piñon nuts, especially during times of famine. However, the framework of Pueblo life centered then, as it still does today, around agriculture.

The Pueblo Indian view of nature and human society is governed by balance and harmony and men's and women's tasks complement each other. In their communalistic society, the notion of "my room" is unknown and impossible to express in their language. Social organization is based on a matrilineal and matrilocal clan system and tribal society. The clan owns the springs, gardens, and farmland. Women own the home furnishings and the stored crops, while men own the livestock, tools, personal effects, and religious ceremonial objects.

The collective pueblo is composed of numerous rooms—sometimes hundreds. It forms a homogeneous tiered structure. This closely built building mass is usually three to five stories high. Each flat-roofed and terraced upper story on the plaza side is set back from the one beneath it, but it ends with a multistoried perpendicular wall in the rear. In other words, the plaza side of the pueblo is usually tiered, while the outside multistoried wall resembles a fortification wall. The pueblo is an additive and cumulative building structure that accommodates the spatial needs of either a diminishing or increasing number of its inhabitants; in fact, the pueblo periodically changes its mass and shape as the result of the construction of additional units as well as the demolition of dilapidated sections.

Today the thick walls are made of adobe brick or stone laid in adobe mortar; in the past they were often made of tamped mud laid in formwork. Both externally and internally the walls are plastered with clay mud; in addition, the interior is either whitewashed with a fine white clay or colorfully decorated.

Peeled cedar beams about 1 ft (30 cm) in diameter are laid across the walls with small poles placed transversely and close together. Cedar bark, brushwood, and grass are then placed on the poles to form a support for a 3- to 4-in (7.5- to 10-cm) coat of adobe. Since the main floor beams of cedar are precious building materials rarely found in an arid region, they are constantly reused and are not trimmed to the specific length required to span the bearing walls. The excess length of beam penetrates beyond the face of the exterior wall and thereby creates a characteristic visual feature of the pueblo. Some of the floor or roof beams of the pueblos that one finds in the southwest United States have been used for centuries.

Traditionally, the external walls had no door openings and only a few small windows. Access to the rooms was gained through an opening in the roof through which rude ladders permitted passage. Today, however, side doors and larger glazed windows are common. Ladders still give access—as in the past—to the first and each successive recessed roof terrace. These ladders and the projecting ends of ladders through the roof holes are another unmistakable visual characteristic of the pueblo.

Taos pueblo

Each dwelling unit consists of a number of rooms, each measuring from 6 to 8 ft (1.8 to 2.4 m) in width and 8 to 12 ft (2.4 to 3.6 m) in depth. These are usually arranged two or three deep and connected to each other by small doors. The innermost room is used for storage. A fireplace is usually built in a corner of the main room, and a hood over it carries the smoke to the chimney. In another corner, parallel with the wall, are the slab-lined mealing bins with stone metates for grinding corn.

The extensive roof terraces are used for sitting, sleeping, winnowing grain, drying crops, and—just as important—as viewing platforms to observe public religious ceremonies and dance performances held in the plaza below.

Religion pervades the Pueblo Indian life to such an extent that it is estimated that Pueblo men

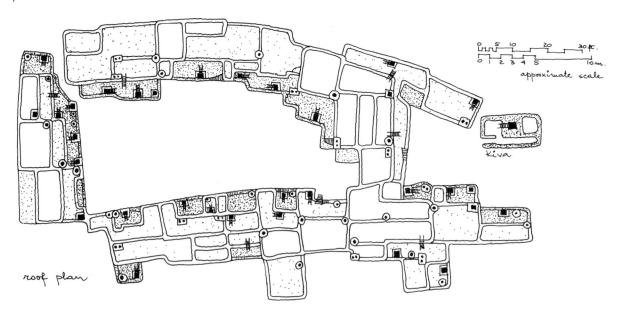

Shipaulovi Pueblo (nineteenth century)
(after Cosmos Mindeleff)

spend at least half their time engaged in religious rites that are performed to bring rain and abundant crops. The secret part of the religious rituals is performed in the *kiva*, "sacred room." Kivas are located in the plaza area near the base of the pueblos. Traditionally, they are large circular subterranean chambers and resemble an earlier form of the Pueblo pithouse. In addition to serving as places of worship, kivas are used as council chambers, meeting rooms, and workshops by initiated men only. A kiva is entered by a ladder through an opening in the roof. It is carefully oriented with a raised platform for observers in the southern section of the chamber and a fire pit and the *sipapu*, or "place of emergence," situated in the northern part. To the poetic Pueblo Indian the kiva represents the universe; the roof and walls are the firmament; the floor is the earth. Along the walls are benches for the initiated members of the Pueblo society, and above and beyond these are the imaginary "cloud seats" where the gods watch ceremonies in their honor.

Pueblos are frequently built on high steep-sided mesas, sites that are unsuitable for cultivation. The use of these elevated sites for settlements prevents the wasteful deployment of agricultural land. In addition such sites were advantageous in former times for purposes of defense. As a result of increasing outside influences during the last century, the Pueblo Indians' way of life has undergone some significant changes. These changes are reflected in the tendency in several contemporary pueblos to scatter the dwellings. This is in marked contrast to the compactness of former pueblos, as exemplified by the plan of Shipaulovi Pueblo as it appeared during the nineteenth century. To a far greater extent than today, the collective building forms and large mass of the historic pueblo, as well as the adobe color itself, blended with the natural surroundings to such a degree that the pueblo was almost indistinguishable from the dramatic mesa formations of its setting.

PREHISTORIC AND HISTORIC SEMIPERMANENT DWELLINGS

Traces of protoneolithic circular dwellings from about 7000 B.C. and 6000 B.C. have been found in Cyprus, Jordan, and Israel. The stone dwellings of Khirokitia in Cyprus measured from 10 to 26 ft (3 to 8.7 m) in diameter, while those at Wadi Fallah on

Round dwelling, Beidha, Jordan (7000 B.C.)
(after Jonathan N. Leonard)

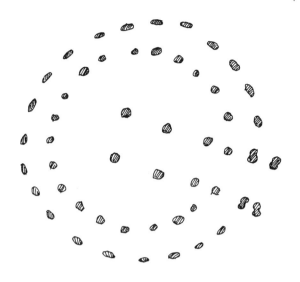

Iron Age farmstead, Little Woodbury, Wilts
(after Derek Roe)

Mount Carmel varied from 6 to 17 ft (2 to 5.6 m). In the village of Beidha, in Jordan, circular cluster dwellings that precede the rectangular dwellings used a half-millennium later have been excavated.

During the pre-Roman Iron Age, circular semipermanent dwellings and farmsteads were common in Yorkshire, Wiltshire, Sussex, and the highland areas of the British Isles. They were defended by simple timber palisades and in structure strongly resembled the Middle Bronze Age farming settlements.

A typical farmstead from the Iron Age was excavated at Little Woodbury in Wiltshire. The main structure of this farmstead had a circular plan with the entrance facing east. Two concentric rows of posts and four central columns supported the rafters of the roof structure. Additional structures which served as barns and granaries formed part of the homestead. The compound was encircled by palisades (Roe 1970, 202–6).

Smaller circular dwellings and farmhouses, clearly appropriate to a harsher terrain, were found over wide areas of the northern and western Scottish highlands and islands. These "wheelhouses," which take their name from the radial, buttresslike piers inside the circular stone walls, probably supported a wooden roof structure. The Little Woodbury farmstead closely resembles a contemporary Luyia dwelling just as the piers of a wheelhouse are similar to those found in the compound dwelling of the Gurunsi.

A collective habitation with several shrines, similar to the pueblo sites of the southwestern United States, was unearthed at Catal Hüyük in Anatolia. The agrarian occupants of Catal Hüyük built their collective dwelling of adobe bricks, and their contiguous dwelling units were entered from the roof by means of wooden ladders placed against the

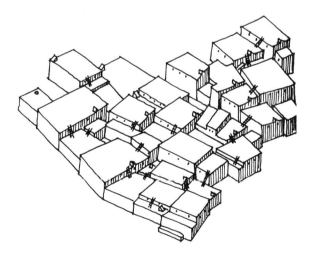

Catal Hüyük (level VI), Anatolia (6000 B.C.).
Schematic reconstruction of houses and shrines
(after Brian M. Fagan)

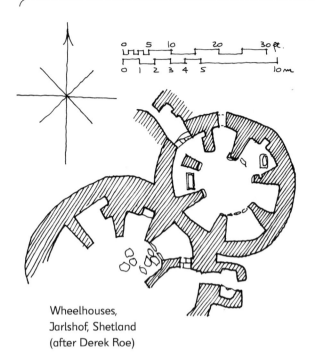

Wheelhouses,
Jarlshof, Shetland
(after Derek Roe)

south wall. The roof entrance also served as a smoke hole. Since access to the various dwellings of this tiered agglomeration of dwellings was from the roof, the peripheral windowless walls were solid and functioned as veritable defense ramparts. Ladders connected the various terraces to each other, and a great part of the villagers' lives was probably spent on these roof terraces, as is still the custom in many Anatolian villages today.

The principal rooms of the dwellings had at least two platforms, of which the main platform was framed by wooden posts. These platforms served as sitting, working, and sleeping areas, and the dead were buried below them (Mellaart 1965, 81–82).

CHAPTER SIX

PERMANENT DWELLINGS

The dwellings in our sixth group—permanent homesteads—are those of advanced agricultural societies. Members of these rural societies depend upon the land that they till and are usually an ultrasedentary people. The effective use period of their homes—both the isolated farmhouse and the village house—is that of a lifetime or, indeed, of several generations.

The basic unit of social organization is the family. Depending upon the state of agricultural technology and the number of people required to produce food, the type of family unit varies; with less advanced technology the extended or composite family is the basic social unit, while with advanced technology it is the conjugal or nuclear family. In any case, the social hierarchy is well established and is complemented by a political hierarchy that commences with the village, township, or county and ends in nationhood.

Advanced and stabilized food production is accompanied by fulltime division of labor, and people not needed for food production can specialize in other endeavors. This complex way of life rcprcscnts the most advanced stage in social development discussed thus far.

At this level surplus food is produced with the aid of compound tools with a power source other than man. Moreover, there are storage and distribution facilities for the surplus as well as a fairly well-developed transportation system to carry the produce to distant markets. Farming at this stage of social development is still the basic occupation of a large segment of society, for it is the farmers who provide essential food supplies.

The primary social consequence of the proliferation of food production, accompanied by specialized manufacture of goods and their distribution through commerce, leads to a weakening of the social structure based on lines of kinship and a strengthening of ties along occupational lines as well as a differentiation of wealth. Furthermore, in an advanced agricultural society, when there is increased control over crops and domesticated animals, the notion of property evolves and land becomes property, explicitly and privately owned.

At the sixth evolutionary level agriculturalists permanently clear the land. They rotate crops, and fallow and fertilize the fields. Their attention is directed to the care of the field rather than to the care of individual plants. Oriental agriculturalists who concentrate on rice growing use such horticultural techniques as terracing, irrigation systems, diked fields, transplantation of seedlings, intercropping of several kinds of plants, and organic fertilizers, which ensures the permanent use of fields without rotation or fallowing. Occidental agriculturalists, on the other hand, use farming techniques such as plowing dry fields, adding organic and mineral fertilizers, broadcasting seed, cultivating a single crop in each field, and rotating crops and allowing fields to lie fallow.

The impact of agriculture on the natural landscape is immense since it implies a permanent clearing of the indigenous vegetation of large expanses of land and replacing them with cultivated fields. Soil impoverishment and accelerated erosion often follow, but they are neither omnipresent nor inevitable. Indeed, agriculture can be in balance with nature.

Due to local variations in natural endowment, land-use practices, and the various degrees of market economy developments, the population densities of sedentary agricultural societies vary from a few hundred to several thousand persons per square mile.

Since the number of variables—building materials, climate, topography, crop cultivation, and cultural heritage—are numerous at this level of agricultural development, there naturally are a multitude of permanent dwelling prototypes ranging from cave dwellings to complex communal farmsteads. A complete description of the many manifestations of these forms presents a formida-

Regional English dwellings

ble task. Hence, it is necessary to generalize when describing the common or shared characteristics of the many types of indigenous permanent dwellings and also to describe only a few examples in detail.

The permanent dwelling is invariably constructed from durable building materials; its walls are either of wood or masonry construction. The permanent character of the dwelling and locally available occupational specialization ensure better workmanship and detailing; thus, doors, windows, roofs, floors, and chimneys are more elaborate. Interior climate control is no longer designed to the criterion of survival but to that of comfort. The dwelling is generally more spacious than previous types described, and it is usually a multiroom building (although the one-room dwelling is still found). The various rooms are designed for specific functions: single-purpose rooms as bedrooms, parlors, and kitchens, and multipurpose rooms as kitchen/living rooms.

Traditionally, materials indigenous to a given region were used for building, resulting in various regional characteristics congruous and in harmony with that region (and incidentally providing variety from one region to another). These characteristics, imposed by the intrinsic quality and texture of the materials, combine with the needs imposed by climate to produce a specific design, such as the inclination of a roof, the projection of its eaves, and the size and shape of windows as well as other building features. Thus, for example, the cob (straw and clay mixture) cottages of Suffolk made of thick rounded walls and thatched roofs are markedly different from the slate (both walls and roof) cottages of Cornwall, the limestone Cotswold cottages of Gloucestershire, the brick and tiled cottages of Kent, the timber-framed cottages of Berkshire, or the pargetted (plastered with a relief decoration) cottages of Norfolk. These idyllic regional prototypes represent only a small sample of the many indigenous permanent dwelling types in England. Many other countries have an equally rich typology of regional permanent dwellings, each possessing a particular charm quite in keeping with its environmental setting.

CHINESE CAVE DWELLINGS

About forty million Chinese rural people, descendents of a very ancient agricultural civilization, live in earth-sheltered permanent dwellings—caves that are protected from the high winds and low temperatures of the steppe winter and are pleasantly cool during summer months. Since timber is scarce in this region, subterranean dwellings offer a reasonable solution to the problem of shelter, and exploit the unique self-supporting quality of the local soil. These multiroom caves are quite sophisticated dwellings with standards of comfort and hygiene equal to most other permanent dwellings inhabited sequentially by two or three generations. Invariably these cave dwellings are clean and free of vermin, and are designed to take advantage of favorable orientation, avoiding, for example, having main rooms face the north (Knapp 1990, 17).

We can distinguish two basic types of caves: the cliffside caves dug into escarpments and the subterranean dwellings of the plateaus hollowed out from the level ground. Both are indigenous dwelling prototypes of the rich and fertile loess or "yellow earth" regions of north and northwest China. Loess is a deep and unstratified loamy soil deposited by the wind; it is usually a calcareous mixture of silt, and because of its high porosity it is easily carved with simple tools.

Usually the cliffside cave dwellings consist of several vaulted chambers, which are on average 10 ft (3 m) wide, 20 ft (6 m) deep, and 10 ft (3 m) high, and tunneled into a south-facing hillside of loess. Excavation of a chamber may take about forty days, but up to three months are required for the walls to dry completely. The vaulted ceiling commences about 6 ft 6 in (2 m) from the floor level and all interior surfaces are coated with a plaster of loess or a mixture of loess and lime to prevent scaling; at times a brick or stone revetment is built to provide a more permanent inner surface. The front of the chamber is sealed by a masonry wall that contains a doorway and windows, apertures that are the sole sources of light for the cave's occupants. A *kang*, or raised masonry platform heated from below, is

Underground village in northern China
(after Bernard Rudofsky)

built near the entrance, while some alcoves along the longitudinal walls are used for storage and display of religious images. The bedrooms are partitioned off in the rear of the chambers (Boyd 1962, 109).

Cliffside caves often open onto walled courtyards with masonry surface buildings along one side and a privy in a corner. Two-storied caves have an external stairway leading to a balustrade-protected terrace, where access is gained to the upper chambers. For structural reasons second-story chambers are located above the walls separating the lower chambers.

The typical plateau-type cave dwelling consists of a large 30-ft (9-m) deep excavated pit, usually square in shape, with vertical sidewalls oriented towards the cardinal points. Access to the pit is gained through an L-shaped descending ramp or stairway that emerges from the north-facing sidewall into the sunken courtyard. The subterranean main chambers of this dwelling are dug into the south-, east-, and west-facing sidewalls of the courtyard. The south-facing side, warmed by the winter sun, is occupied by the head of the family.

The chambers are constructed and appointed in a similar way to those of the cliffside caves. While the sunken courtyard also serves as the main circulation space, its more important function is that of an outdoor living room when weather permits. A privy is often found adjacent to the descending stairway.

There is an uncanny similarity between the Chinese courtyard cave dwellings and the Troglodyte dwellings in the Matmatas of southern Tunisia. The Troglodytes also live underground in caves scooped out from the ground. The hub of the dwelling, the court, is a round, rather than square, crater open to the sky, and has sloping walls and a flat bottom. In the walls of the crater, caves are dug for the different rooms comprising the dwelling, and below the courtyard another cavern is dug for a rainwater cistern. Access to this dwelling is through a descending open trench that turns into a tunnel before it reaches the court; in some cases a stable is scooped out from the side of this passageway. Like the Chinese plateau-type cave dwellings, the Tunisian Troglodyte caves are found in large village formations and, with fields above them,

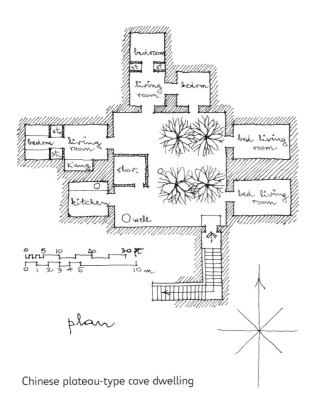

Chinese plateau-type cave dwelling

these cave-dwelling agglomerations optimize agrarian land-use efficiency. However, cave dwellings are not easily defendable against hostile incursions; on the other hand, a certain defense feature derives from the fact that underground dwellings are not easily detectable.

The cave dwellings of rural China, although numerous, are by no means typical permanent dwelling forms. More common are the rectangular, masonry, above-ground buildings that evolve through an increase in family size into compound dwellings. The core of the compound is a south-facing main building with a large central room, the ancestral hall, flanked by bedrooms. With the addition of detached side wings a courtyard is formed, defined on the south side by a masonry wall with a gate. Additional expansion often results in a large compound dwelling, but the axially central ancestral hall forever remains the most venerable place of the extended family's dwelling.

The typology of Chinese permanent dwellings is very rich and includes, apart from caves and traditional compound dwellings, the large communal houses of the Hakka people (Boyd 1962, 103).

These indigenous multistoried fortresslike structures house many families practicing collective agriculture. The plan of the communal building can be circular, horseshoe-shaped, or rectangular, with the south-facing ancestral hall central in the building complex.

ITALIAN TRULLO

The *trullo* is the traditional permanent building form of the inhabitants of the Murgia in the region of Apulia in southeastern Italy. Adaptations of this form of dwelling are found in both villages and towns of this region of Italy.

Farming is still the main occupation in the rural districts of Apulia. Grapes and olives are the primary crops, and wheat, beans, tomatoes, and other small crops are planted among the olive trees. The fields are usually small and enclosed with thick, dry stone walls. The land is tillable only through great expenditure of labor. The limestone bedrock was originally covered with but a few inches of organic soil. The preparation of a field entailed,

Trullo farmstead

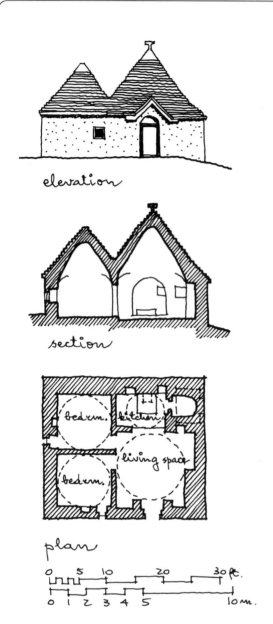

elevation

section

plan

Trullo
(after Edward Allen)

limestone. Finally, the stored topsoil was carefully spread over the bolo.

Very rocky areas in the district serve as pasture land, most often for sheep. Rabbits and chickens are raised in the yards, and small game is hunted in the countryside.

The trulli are mostly constructed with stones from the fields. Another source is the stone quarried in the process of providing large rainwater cisterns or wine tanks beneath the dwelling being built. Bare bedrock serves as the foundation for the trullo. The rectangular rooms are enclosed by thick stone walls that are hollowed in places to make alcoves and niches. The walls support a conical stone dome covered with overlapping flat stones. Similar flat stones are used for finishing the floor of the house. The tiny windows are spanned with stone lintels, and door openings are arched. The walls are invariably whitewashed and so is the capstone of the dome. Rainwater is collected from the roofs in a cistern.

In a typical multiroom farmhouse the largest dome spans the main living space; the kitchen has a large open hearth whose dome ends in a chimney; bread-baking ovens are either built outside the house or adjacent to the kitchen; other rooms serve as bedrooms.

During the warm season the stone trulli are comfortably cool. In winter they are cold and damp; therefore, the doors are kept open during the day to keep the interior dry. Women sit just outside the doorway to do such tasks as mending and knitting; as modesty demands, they face the house as they work.

Entire farmsteads are built as trulli clusters, sometimes numbering up to two dozen. Hay barns have a truncated roof cone, capped with a large and flat removable stone, with steps built into the roof to allow the farmer access to this hatch to fill the barn. Animal barns and storehouses also have the shape of domed trulli, and even the chicken house is a low but crude trullo. One structural unit is attached to the next so that the roof plan of a cluster is characterized by a graceful transition from one building to the next.

first, the removal of the thin topsoil and its temporary storage. Then the exposed limestone bedrock was broken up to a depth of 2 ft (60 cm); the best stones were saved for building construction and the rest replaced, the coarse pieces on the bottom and the finest on top. Red soil, called *bolo*, was brought from a nearby depression and tamped into a layer of 15 to 20 in (38 to 50 cm) on the loose

Slovakian Village Farmhouse

The Slovakian farmstead represents a generic type of permanent homestead where diverse structures define the farmyard. It is still much in evidence in the agricultural regions of Kysuce and Orava in Czechoslovakia.

Slovakia is a mountainous region, and its inhabitants engage in the typical occupations of such a region. Those of the lower altitudes farm while those living at higher altitudes harvest timber from

Slovakian farmhouse

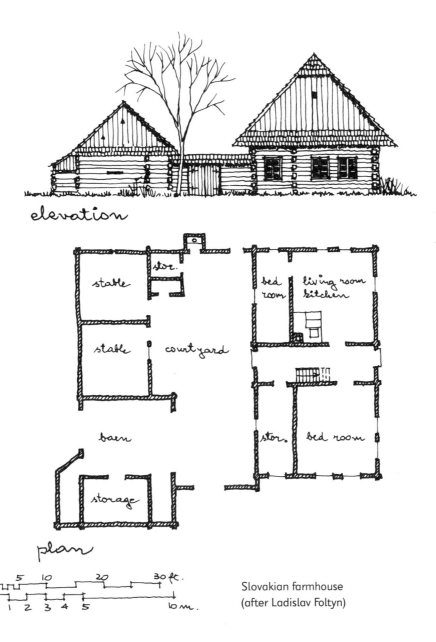

elevation

plan

Slovakian farmhouse
(after Ladislav Foltyn)

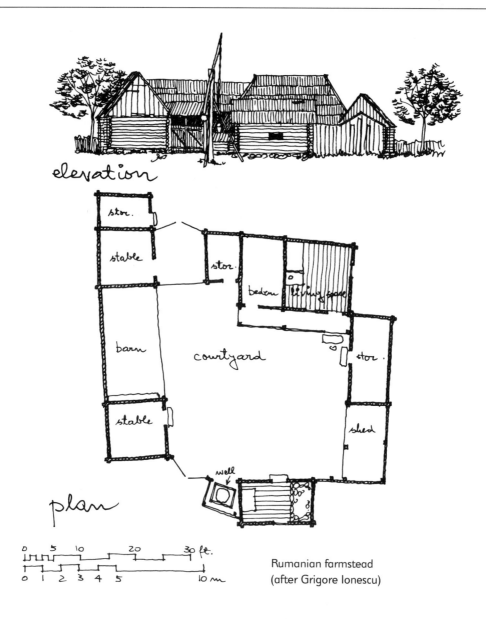

elevation

plan

Rumanian farmstead
(after Grigore Ionescu)

the forest. Wind shelter, the slope of the field, and soil conditions of the mountains coupled with frequent temperature inversions produce sharp local climatic differences that determine whether wheat, rye, barley, or oats will be cultivated or whether root crops such as sugar beets and potatoes should be grown. Although there is some collectivization of agriculture in Slovakia, there is still agricultural land cultivated by independent farmers practicing small-scale mixed farming. The livestock raised are chiefly cattle and pigs.

The typical farmhouse of the Kysuce and Orava regions is constructed of logs cut from the abundant pine wood in the mountains. It is a single-story structure except where slope conditions require a partially exposed cellar. This lower story is then used as a storage space, workshop, or pen. The foundation is constructed of fieldstone and supports the horizontally laid log walls with interlocking corners; all joints are pointed with mortar. Walls, interior posts, and beams form the base of a large roof, which is usually shingled. The gable ends are hipped near the ridge and at eave level in order to protect the end walls. Weather boarding covers the vertical gable section between the ridge hip and the eaves. The windows are framed by a plaster architrave, and simple carvings and decorations adorn the exterior of the house.

The floor plan is an elongated rectangle with a transverse central vestibule dividing the house into two equal parts. From the vestibule one gains access to most rooms as well as to the loft and cellar. The principal room is the multipurpose family room; it is used for family activities. The family cooks, eats, socializes, and even sleeps there. Its dominant feature is a large built-in hearth located in the innermost corner. The hearth, originally made of clay, used to serve as stove and oven; it now has been replaced by a rectangular tile stove. Wooden benches, a table, large armoires, and one or two beds are the traditional furnishings. A small bedroom frequently opens onto the family room. On the opposite side of the vestibule from the family room is a second set of two rooms—usually unheated—that are used as a bedroom and a storage area.

Wherever possible, the entrance side of the farmhouse faces the south and encloses the north side of the farmyard. A parallel building, elongated and less substantial, serves as barn, stable, and storage rooms and forms the southern boundary of the yard; a roofed fence and large portal on the village street side and sheds, privy, and fences on the rear complete the yard enclosure.

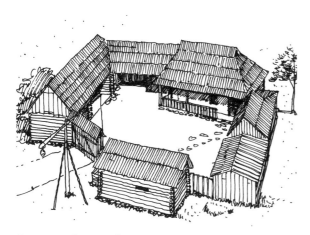

Rumanian farmstead
(after Grigore Ionescu)

The farmyard formed by a dwelling, stables, and other ancillary buildings is also characteristic of other regions of southeastern Europe. The Rumanian farmstead illustrated here has many affinities with the Slovakian farmhouse; both are indigenous to the Carpathian Mountain region where wood is abundant and therefore the prevalent building material.

THE HUNGARIAN FARMSTEAD

The most typical Hungarian village farmstead is composed of house, storage, stable, and barn attached to each other in a linear arrangement, but without indoor connections between them. An open porch, often arcaded and oriented towards the south, serves as a sheltered link between the various functions, including communication between the kitchen (the "little house") and the living room (the "big house").

Since the axis of the stable and barn is at right angles to that of the house and storage, the building assembly becomes L-shaped, a form that in conjunction with the neighboring house results in a clear definition of the farmyard on three sides; the fourth and open side of the yard, facing the roadway, is enclosed by a wooden fence with a gate next to the house and an often elaborate arched portal high enough to clear a loaded hay wagon. Because the narrow front of the plot faces the road, this planning arrangement is land-use efficient and therefore widespread.

Invariably, the gable end of the farmhouse with the living room's two small windows, often shuttered, faces the road or common and a small fenced-in flower garden frequently separates the front of the house from the public domain. In the absence of a front garden, portals with some fencing links one house to the next, thereby providing a continuous building façade towards the road.

The living room is multifunctional, in spite of its small size, serving as a living/dining/sleeping room as well as for reception. It is a smoke-free space with an oven and its fuel door built against the kitchen wall; stoking the oven from the kitchen made it possible to keep the living area not only

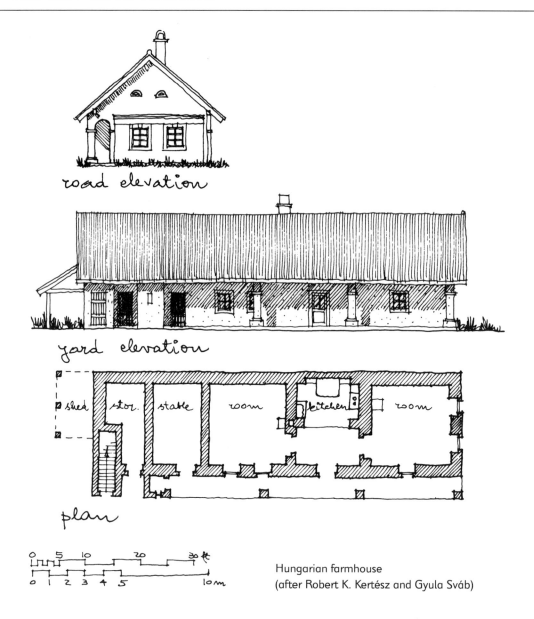

road elevation

yard elevation

plan

0 5 10   20   30 ft

0 1 2 3 4 5   10 m

Hungarian farmhouse
(after Robert K. Kertész and Gyula Sváb)

clean from smoke, but also from the dirt and ashes generated by tending the fire. The kitchen itself is dominated by a large firestead.

The various stages in the evolution of the fireplace can still be studied in various regions of the country. In the Upper-Tisza River region the kitchen is a walk-in chimney called *pitvar*, a transitional stage between the open-hearth kitchen (where smoke dissipates through the loft and exits through smoke holes in the roof) and the smoke-free kitchen with a fireplace-with-chimney or stove. As its name implies, the walk-in chimney is a room-size fireplace used for cooking and baking, as well as drying and smoking food; in addition, stokeholes to fire chambers in adjacent rooms

allow the heating of the house from a central space. Masonry-constructed walk-in chimneys, at times called "black kitchens," are not indigenous to Hungary only, but were used in the past in Denmark, Poland, and the Baltic countries, among other regions.

In the three-room farmhouse, the kitchen is a central heating space and functions as an entrance hall as well. With two windows facing the road and one window facing the yard, the front room serves as a reception room, while the rear room is used as a family room and a bed/sitting room. A porch, along the yard side of the house, provides additional workspace and allows sheltered access to the stable and the privy.

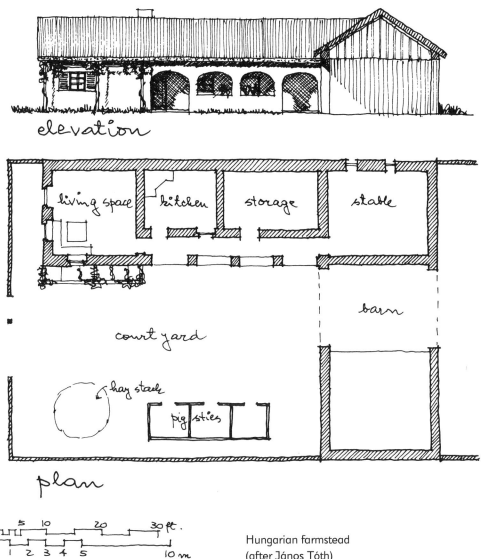

elevation

living space kitchen storage stable

court yard

barn

hay stack

pig sties

plan

0 5 10   20   30 ft.

0 1 2 3 4 5   10 m

Hungarian farmstead
(after János Tóth)

In the plains of Hungary, where wood is scarce, the use of wood in construction is limited to floors; roofs, fences, and the walls of the farmstead are built of adobe or brick masonry.

THE LOW GERMAN FARMHOUSE

In contrast to permanent homesteads composed of diverse buildings, such as the dwelling, the barn, and the stable, the Low German farmhouse combines all these elements in a single large rectangular structure, a dwelling/stable/storage building.

In keeping with ancient north European traditions, in this generic building type, people, farm animals, and crops are sheltered under one roof, with domestic and husbandry activities spatially interlinked through a central space called a *diele*, or hall. In northwestern Germany, the use of these dwelling prototypes was widespread throughout the Middle Ages and subsequent periods until the end of the nineteenth century. Because of advances in agricultural technology and mechanization, not to mention rural lifestyle changes, these large farmsteads are no longer built. Since their average life span extends to three-hundred years or more, there are still many hall-type farm buildings dotting the rural landscape of this region.

The Low German farmstead is a large, impressive three-aisled structure, usually 40 ft (12 m) in width and in excess of 80 ft (24 m) in length. Originally, it was sheltered by a huge hipped roof, but was gradually replaced by a saddleback roof. The building is entered through a large barn door, located at one gable end, which leads to the central aisle, or hall. This wide central space is flanked by narrower side aisles divided into stalls for cows and horses that face inward; the floor level of the stalls is slightly below that of the hall. In contrast to the 6 ft 6 in- (2-m) ceiling height of the stables, the clearance in the hall is about 12 ft (3.6 m), in order to allow the passage of a fully loaded hay wagon.

Conceptually, the hall is the central space, the heart of the house, and it is multifunctional. It serves as an entrance hall, a corridor and distribution space, a feeding aisle for the stabled animals, a threshing floor, a work space to prepare flax and do other chores, a *festsaal*, or feast hall (Schäfer 1906, 54), where dances are held on happy occasions, and also where the bier of a deceased member of the household is placed during mourning. Above the diele is a cavernous loft for hay and grain storage.

Beyond the stables, the hall space expands into side aisles, and with the addition of these two alcoves, the hall becomes T-shaped. This widened section, or cross hall, usually two bays deep, is called the *flett*, and constitutes the kitchen/dining/living space of the dwelling. Dominated by a large fireplace (originally an open hearth), the flett is essentially an open continuation of the hall with cooking activities at the intersection of the two axes of the T-shaped hall. This central position allows the housewife to keep an eye on all activities within the hall. From two sides, large windows in the alcoves light this three-aisled domestic space with its stone paved floor slightly raised above the hall floor. A long dining table with benches along the walls, a space often occupied by the men both during and after meals, occupies one alcove, while the other alcove is designated as the washing area. From it a so-called Dutch door (with two separate leaves, one above the other operated independently or together) gives access to the side yard and

elevation

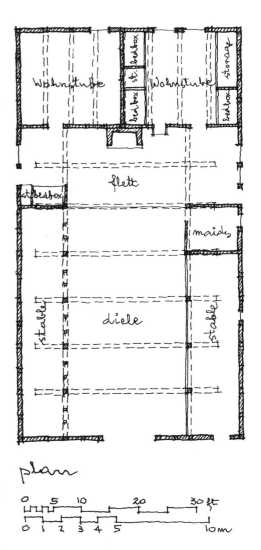

plan

Low German farmhouse
(after Dietrich Schäfer)

water well; the upper leaf of this door is often kept open for better ventilation (Klöckner 1991, 51).

After the sixteenth century, it was common to extend the hall by adding two bays beyond the flett to provide additional habitable rooms. This so-called *Kammerfach*, or chamber bay, usually contains two or three rooms with fenestration in the rear gable wall. One of the rooms serves as a *Wohnstube* or *Donse*, a smoke-free living and reception space heated by a cast-iron oven stoked from the flett. This room is well appointed and furnished with a table, chairs, benches, an armoire, and one or two bed boxes with sliding doors. Occupied by the head of the family with his wife and small children, the bed box adjacent to the flett frequently has a little window in the wall to afford a view into the hall. The other smaller rooms of the Kammerfach could be used for sleeping, storage, or working places. A small cellar was often excavated below this section of the house and an attic floor built above, both accessible from the flett.

The support structure of these farmsteads consists of a sophisticated heavy timber framework, with oak posts along the hall defining bays ranging in width from 6 ft 6 in (2 m) to 8 ft (2.5 m). External walls were of half-timber construction, with wattle-and-daub infilling; later, brick, a more permanent material, was used for the same purpose, and the pattern of the brick infill panels are often very decorative.

As mentioned above, the Low German farmstead is rooted in an old building form, and it is there-fore not surprising that it is remarkably similar in concept to a farmhouse found at Feddersen Wierde, an Iron Age hamlet excavated in 1955 near Bremerhaven. This first century A.D. farmstead was also a rectangular three-aisled building with a T-shaped hall. Four ranges of round oak posts, the two inner ones taller than the outer ones, supported the thatched roof of this 19 ft 6 in- (6.5-m) wide and 98-ft (29.5-m) long structure. The external wall was built along the inner face of the outer posts and constructed of wattle-and-daub.

As in the Low German farmstead, the main entrance was at one gable end and led into a hall flanked by stables; two additional doors, one in each alcove of the T-shaped hall, were also identified. At the far end of the structure, entered from the hall, was a large room with a central open hearth, presumably a multifunctional room.

BERNESE FARMHOUSE

Another example of a permanent dwelling is the Bernese farmhouse, the indigenous dwelling of lower-lying midland Switzerland. The economy of the rural Bernese is mixed agricultural-pastoral. The chief crops are wheat, barley, rye, oats, and potatoes, and the pastoral economy is predominantly based on dairy produce.

A typical Bernese farmstead consists of a cluster of detached buildings. The main farmhouse, how-

Bernese farmhouse with granary

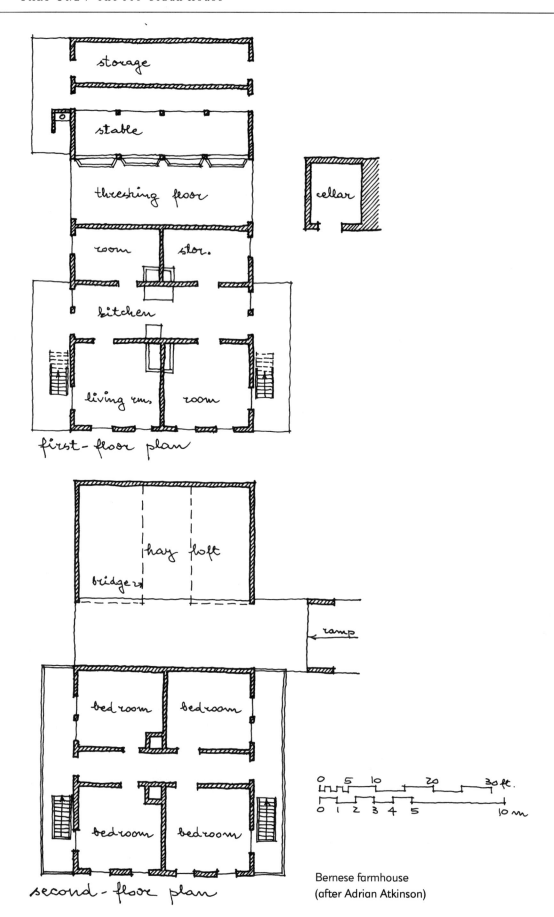

storage

stable

threshing floor

cellar

room   stor.

kitchen

living rm,   room

first-floor plan

hay loft

bridge

ramp

bedroom   bedroom

bedroom   bedroom

second-floor plan

0   5   10   20   30 ft.

0 1 2 3 4 5   10 m

Bernese farmhouse
(after Adrian Atkinson)

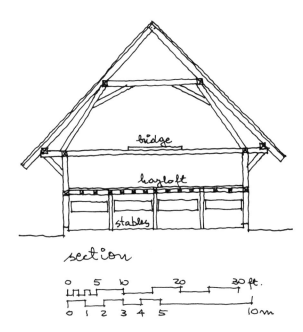

Bernese farmhouse
(after Adrian Atkinson)

ever, is the dominant structure and is surrounded by smaller secondary buildings such as the *stöckli* (the home reserved by parents for their use when they give the farm to their heirs), the *speicher* (the lavishly decorated granary), wood sheds, pigsty, barn, and bake house.

The main farmhouse contains the family quarters, the stable, the hayloft (reached by a ramp), storerooms, and the threshing floor. The threshing floor separates the family quarters from the stable and hayloft. On the ground floor of the dwelling are the living room and bedroom (or less formal living room), both lit from the gable end. Behind, a large kitchen stretches the full width of the building, followed by two other rooms used as bedrooms and storage space. Identical rooms on the upper floor are used as a bedroom or a storage room. Access to the upper level is by a steep exterior staircase to a balcony.

The main entrance to the dwelling leads into the large kitchen; from here one gains access to the two pairs of rooms situated on either side of the kitchen. Each set of rooms shares a *kachelofen*, an elaborate ceramic tile oven stoked from the kitchen.

The living room is a quiet area where the family has its meals, the farmer reads, and the women spin. One corner is reserved for the dining table with built-in benches against the wall. At meals the father occupies the head of the table, flanked on his right by his sons and on his left by his wife and daughters; the children take their places according to their age. Workhands and servant girls sit at the end of the table. The corner nearest the head of the table is called *Herrgottswinkel*, or "altar corner," for a cross or painting of the Holy Family is placed there.

The farmhouse has stone foundations topped with a huge ring-beam. The walls, of post-and-beam construction, support the large roof structure with its ridgepoles and close-centered rafters. Overhanging eaves protect the balconies and walls. The craftsmanship displayed in the Bernese farmhouse is very advanced and reflects a great concern for aesthetic considerations.

While the dwelling section of the Bernese farmstead is covered by the same roof that shelters the stable and the threshing floor, farmstead dwellings in most other regions of Europe are distinctly identifiable buildings, as illustrated by previous examples.

NEW ENGLAND HOMESTEADS

The early settlers of North America built their homesteads in the way they were accustomed to do in the old country. Hence, the typology of permanent dwellings in rural areas of the United States and Canada is varied, and reflects the influences of French, Dutch, Spanish, German, Scandinavian, and, above all, English vernacular dwellings.

One of the most familiar American rural dwelling prototypes is the Cape Cod–style farmhouse in New England. Its use can be dated back to the colonial period and its origins to vernacular homes in lowland England, especially those in the eastern counties. The main feature of the rectangular two-room Cape Cod house is a massive central chimney with back-to-back fireplaces at its base. The central entrance leads to a vestibule,

elevation

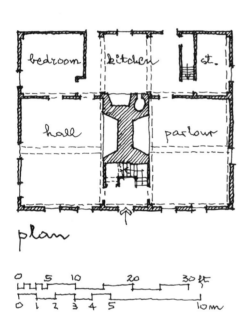

plan

New England farmhouse
(after N. M. Isham and A. F. Brown)

usually with a staircase leading to the attic or upper-story bedrooms. One of the ground floor rooms was a parlor, used as a formal reception room, and the other, called a "hall" or *keeping room*, functioned as an all-purpose family room. Traditionally, each of these rooms had a set of two windows facing the street and either a single or double set of two windows in the gable end wall.

While the earliest dwellings were only one room deep, measuring on the average 40 ft (12 m) in length and 20 ft (6 m) in width, later, with the addition of a lean-to, these houses acquired a 30-ft (9-m) depth. In homes with a lean-to, the kitchen was in the rear with another fireplace built into the

central chimney, and on occasion, even had a built-in bake oven. A pantry and another similarly sized room, the latter often used as a bedroom, flanked the central kitchen at the rear; a trap door or steep staircase gave access to the cellar below the kitchen. The hall remained a family room, but cooking and baking were now relegated to the kitchen.

The early Cape Cod–style house was built of heavy post-and-beam frames filled in with wattle and daub, which proved to be inadequate in regions with a harsher climate than that of England. Invariably, these structures had to be covered with wooden clapboard for additional protection, and this led to the abandonment of wattle and daub in newer building construction in favor of wood plank, balloon frame, or masonry. The joists supporting the attic floor rested on the front and rear walls with additional support given in the center by a beam called the *summer*, which spanned each room from the chimney to the gable end wall. The joist and beams were often exposed and the ceiling height was relatively low, with a clearance of about 6 ft 3 in (1.9 m) below the central beam.

A two-story Cape Cod–type dwelling with a one-story lean-to at the rear is commonly known as a *saltbox*. These buildings were often oriented with the high front elevation to the south, and the low rear elevation to the north; during the winter months, snow or bales of hay were banked against the north side for greater protection from the cold northerly winds.

The ancillary farm buildings of these early New England homesteads were usually detached structures placed around the farmyard. A scattered arrangement of farm buildings proved to be inconvenient in the severe winters of the northern parts of New England. To facilitate access between buildings during the cold winter months, a linear form of farmstead was developed that connected the main house to all ancillary structures. This arrangement is known as "big house, little house, back house, barn." The "big house" in this linear sequence was the Cape Cod–type or saltbox described above, but it was connected to a "little house" with a large winter kitchen, a smaller summer kitchen, and a woodshed; the little house, in turn, was attached to a "back house" containing a large workshop and a privy; the last building in the sequence was a barn with a hayloft, threshing floor, and a stable; the large barn door opened upon the yard. By using setbacks for the little house and back house, two yards were defined, namely, the front yard next to the big house and the dooryard fronting on the other three buildings; a third yard, the barnyard, was at the rear of the barn (Hubka 1984, 70).

The L-shaped plan of the connected farm buildings of New England resembles in concept the layout of central European village farmsteads. In the European setting, the arrangement of the L-shaped farmsteads is more compact and consists of rows of narrow front lots abutting each other and strung along the roadway. Typically, the village front of a lot consists of a gable-ended farmhouse linked to its neighbors by a large portal that gives access to the farmyard. Such villages are prevalent, for example, in the Burgenland of Austria, the Saxon settlements of Transylvania, and several regions of Hungary.

THE TRADITIONAL QUEBEC FARMHOUSE

The building tradition of rural Quebec had its origins in France, particularly in the countryside of northwestern France. One prototype, the central hearth farmhouse, is indigenous to Normandy and the other, the gable hearth farmhouse, to Brittany. However, the North American climate and harsher living conditions gradually forced upon the builders of New France the adoption of several modifications that led to the emergence of a Québecois rural architecture.

With their roots in Normandy, the oldest farmhouses had a low, broad appearance with high pitched roof and gable verges. The low walls were constructed of wooden planks laid horizontally

upon each other, and covered on the exterior face with vertical boarding, often whitewashed; the roof was framed together with heavy timbers and covered with cedar shingles, which weathered over time to a slate gray color. The only building elements constructed of masonry were the stone foundations and chimney, the latter rose from the cross wall of a two-room house and penetrated the roof in a slightly off-central location if the two rooms were of unequal size. The Brittany-type two-room farmhouse underwent similar changes, but was always distinguished by its two chimneys, one at either gable end.

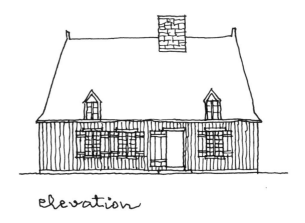

elevation

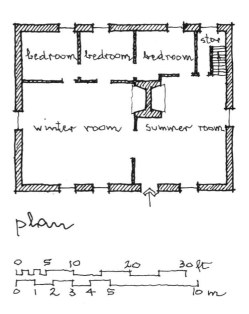

plan

Quebec farmhouse
(after Ramsay Traquair)

The front door opened directly into the work room or "summer room" with a large fireplace and a steep ladderlike stair leading to the attic. From the first room one entered the "winter room," used by the family as a multipurpose space during the cold winter months; during the summer, this elaborately furnished room, with its yellow wooden floor covered with homemade rugs, served as a parlor in which distinguished visitors were received. The windows had lace curtains, but during summer months the window panes were shaded with blue paper to keep it dark and cool. According to tradition the blue shade also kept the room free of flies, a belief shared by many rural people in many parts of the world. Frequently, two small bedrooms were partitioned off from the winter room; each room contained only a large bed and chest.

At a later period, thick masonry walls built of fieldstone gathered from the clearings replaced timber construction. Concurrently, other changes were also introduced. The floor level was raised above the ground level, metal sheeting replaced roof shingles, eaves widened, and the gable verges steepened until they became gables.

A further evolution derived from raising the floor above the snow level and expanding the width of the eave to protect the walls from snow and rain and shade them during the hot summer months, while allowing sun penetration in winter. These changes led to the emergence of the popular "gallery house" with the typical curving extended eave (bellcast) at the bottom of the roof.

Stables, barns, dairies, and other auxiliary farm buildings were detached structures grouped around a farmyard. Although a planning approach common in northwest France, it was used in Canada mainly to safeguard against fire spreading from one wooden building to another. Another reason for the scattered arrangement of farm buildings was probably the abundance of land in the early days of colonization.

Summary

Many insights into the development of architectural form can be gained from this study of indigenous pre-urban dwellings. Indeed, even the history of architecture appears in a different light, for as one studies these dwellings it is evident that time is not the only or even the most important criterion for judging architectural development. Certainly time is a factor, but it is only one among many others. Anthropogeographic and socioeconomic factors have at least an equal bearing. Thus, time is a relative factor. Therefore, although this study has dealt primarily with contemporary housing, most of the architecture described nevertheless predates, in terms of cultural criteria, the urban architecture of antiquity.

Today it is still possible to see at first hand Stone Age cultures that, chronologically speaking, should have predated Sumerian culture by thousands of years. Though, admittedly, it will not be long before all existing Stone Age societies disappear as the result of acculturation, it seems unreasonable that most historians of architecture deal with the Stone Age as a mythicized period of the distant past.

If one applies knowledge acquired from the study of contemporary Stone Age cultures to view prehistoric ones, it is difficult to accept the notion that man was originally a cave dweller. For example, although the Kalahari Desert has many caves suited for shelter, the Bushmen seldom use them for that purpose. With the exception of the Tasaday, there is no evidence of any existing band-type societies living in caves. Food-gathering nomads are constantly on the move, and the notion of sedentary cave living is inconsistent with this activity. A sedentary lifestyle belongs to a more advanced society. Indeed, caves are inhabited by contemporary peoples, but in most instances these people are pastoralists, agriculturalists, or even urban dwellers (for example, Guadix, in Andalusia, Spain), and thus several stages removed from a primitive hunting and food-gathering society.

The evidence found in many caves points to the fact that they were used as shelters by prehistoric man, but it is likely that caves were merely one alternative, when available, to the more prevalent beehive huts and windbreaks. The inherently permanent nature of caves ensured the survival of middens and paintings left behind by their early occupants, whereas the fragility of ephemeral dwellings for the most part prevented, over the span of several millennia, the survival of any traces of their occupancy. Hence, evidence favors the assumption that caves rather than other forms of shelter were mankind's original dwelling. Despite the popular acceptance that caves were the primordial dwellings of paleolithic people, this belief seems also untenable because it implies that human evolution was at the outset restricted to those geographic areas where caves existed.

Another interesting inference derived from the study of indigenous housing relates to the notion that the circular plan predates the rectangular plan

Cappadocian cave dwellings

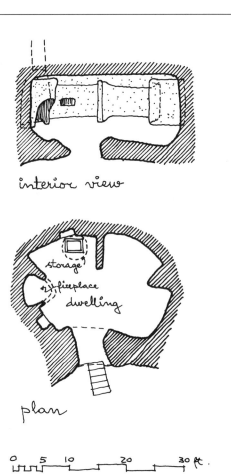

interior view

plan

Italian cave dwelling, Massafra, Apulia
(after Edward Allen)

of indigenous shelters. The circular or horseshoe-like plan represents the simplest form of shelter. The concave shape is womblike and maternal: it invites, harbors, and shelters, and the concave circular plan is an "intuitive" form, in sharp contrast to the square and rectangular forms, both of which are rationally or intellectually devised.

The circular plan also appears frequently in the indigenous architecture of societies that developed the more sophisticated rectangular form. Invariably, however, the presence of such circular plans can be linked to primordial dwelling forms that have survived, for example, as places of worship, such as the traditional kiva of the Pueblo Indians or the kitchen round hut of the Dogon dwelling.

The circular plan has two intrinsic characteristics restricting its maximal development. First, structural considerations limit its being enlarged or expanded: with the increase of area the diameter increases proportionately, and spanning the structure becomes a difficult task, especially in societies in which only simple tools and building materials are used. In contrast, while expansion is limited in width, the rectangle is unlimited in length. The second restriction of the circular plan is the difficulty in adapting it to cumulative or additive

growth. The adaptability of the rectangle or square to expansion, on the other hand, is much more feasible and more economical in terms of both building materials and efficient space utilization. The development of dwelling prototypes, thus, is manifested by a sequence of plan shapes commencing with the circle, developing into the oval, then the elongated rectangle with rounded corners, and finally the angular rectangle or square.

Obviously, a progression may also be distinguished in terms of the complexity of building construction. The simplest shelter, such as the beehive hut, has a space enclosure that is both roof and wall; there is no differentiation between the two. The next stage is the separation of wall and roof. At first the same building material, such as wood and thatch, is used for both, but then different materials are applied, such as adobe for the wall and thatch for the roof. Similarly, the door in the simplest dwelling functions as window and chimney as well. Gradually the various functions are delegated to single-purpose building elements; then it is the door that provides access, the window that lets in light, and the chimney that lets out smoke. The word "window," in fact, is derived from "wind eye," which meant an opening in the roof, a combination of smoke hole and open skylight.

Another interesting conclusion derived from this study concerns building size. Socioeconomic development is not necessarily complemented by an increase in the size of dwelling structures. The malocas and bohios of the Amazon Valley Indians are much larger than most dwellings of more advanced societies. Similarly, the pueblos are both larger and more complex in spatial organization than homesteads of agriculturalists using more sophisticated farming methods. This seemingly inconsistent development is attributable primarily to the socioeconomic structure of the societies involved. The size of a viable economic and social unit, in terms of the number of people required for subsistence cultivation, is inversely proportionate to its degree of technical advancement. In other words, the more primitive the method of cultivation, the greater the number of workers required to till the land in order to ensure a sufficient harvest for subsistence. Collectivism and communalism at this level are the essential lifestyles for survival, and the construction of large communal dwellings is the response to the particular lifestyle.

As agricultural methods improve, the viable economic unit decreases from that of the tribe to a composite or extended family, followed by the conjugal family, first with many children and later with few. Naturally, the dwelling size complements these changes in the number of inhabitants, and gradually spatial needs become smaller until the stage is reached where additional improvements to agricultural methods replace the "survival criterion" with a "comfort criterion." At this point the

Guadix cave dwellings

size and complexity of the dwelling becomes a function of increased affluence.

The pre-urban dwellings described in the six previous chapters represent a very long evolutionary period of human development. For by far the longest period of his existence, which is estimated to be more than a million years, man was a food gatherer and hunter. It took many hundreds of thousands of years for him to break through the Old Stone Age or paleolithic stage of economic life. With the domestication of plants and animals that marks the beginning of the New Stone Age or neolithic revolution, the process of development gradually gained momentum, but as late as 4,000 B.C. only a few societies had surpassed the subsistence level of agricultural production. In these latter societies, fewer people were required for food production, and members not engaged in cultivation could specialize in such endeavors as the manufacture of goods and their distribution through commerce. Only at this stage of socioeconomic development were the basic prerequisites provided to foster urban development and, with the surplus agricultural economy, urban civilizations were born. Thus began the evolution of a new house form, and the beginning of 6,000 years of urban housing.

PART II

The Oriental Urban House

INTRODUCTION

The earliest civilizations evolved from agrarian societies inhabiting the fertile alluvial valleys of great rivers. Fertile river banks enabled indigenous agriculturalists to go beyond subsistence farming, and the rivers themselves became arteries of communication and transport with a unifying influence upon their users. Also required for the development of civilizations along these river valleys was physical protection from incursions by neighboring nomadic tribes. Such protection was provided in some cases by the inhospitable deserts or mountain ranges flanking the river valleys. In fact, this was the setting of four early cradles of civilization that gave rise to urban development and with it to the emergence of the ancient urban dwelling. The alluvial regions in which these four urban civilizations evolved were:

1. The Tigris-Euphrates valleys in Mesopotamia
2. The valley of the Indus River and its tributaries in Pakistan and India
3. The valley of the Nile River in Egypt

4. The networks of the Hwang Ho and Yangtze rivers in China

A very long evolutionary period of human development preceded the beginning of urban life. Since man's existence on earth is estimated to be more

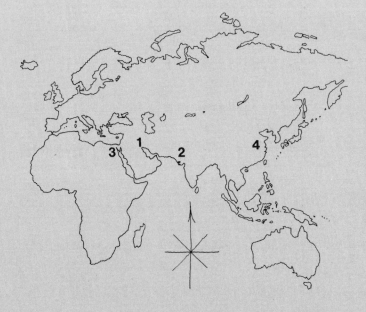

than one million years and since towns probably did not antedate 4000 B.C. by very much, urban living environments are relatively recent phenomena.

All ancient cities were built by civilizations deriving their wealth from agricultural pursuits. Initially these urban dwellers represented only a very small fraction of their respective total population. It is estimated by Philip M. Hauser (1957) that, as late as the 1800s, only 3 percent of the world's population lived in urban settlements of 5,000 or more inhabitants. After 1800, however, the proportion of urban residents increased steadily and rapidly. By 1850 the urban population had risen to 6.4 percent; by 1900 it became 13.6 percent; and in 1950 it had reached 29.8 percent.

Since 1950 the overall urban population of the world has grown annually at an average rate of about 3 percent. The urban growth rate has been even more rapid in several less developed regions and has exceeded 4 percent, with the result that urban populations in developing regions have almost doubled from 15 to close to 30 percent. This increase has occurred despite a high rural growth rate of about 1.5 percent.

In more developed and industrialized regions, the rural population declined during the postwar decades. Although urban growth has decelerated since 1950, it has nevertheless exceeded an annual growth rate of 2 percent. As a result, the proportion of urban population has grown over the past 25 years from 55 percent to 70 percent (*The World Population Situation in 1977* 1979, 63).

By 1975 the urban population of the world had risen to 37.8 percent, and by 1997 to 46.1 percent; corresponding figures for industrialized countries were 74.9 and 77.8 percent. It is estimated by the United Nations that by the year 2015 the overall urban population will be 54.4 percent, while in the more industrialized countries it will amount to 81.6 percent (UNDP 1999, 200).

It must be borne in mind that in the ancient Orient, when the population was very small and urban development was indeed a very slow

process, the adaptation of indigenous rural dwellings to new urban conditions was gradual, measured, and complementary to both basic psychosocial needs and economic forces. Since technology was still rudimentary, the urban dweller had to work in harmony with physical, social, and economic forces. This necessary harmony eventually culminated in an urban dwelling concept shared by all four ancient civilizations mentioned above—the court-garden dwelling, the inward-looking oriental urban house.

The rural courtyard house antedates its urban prototype. The simplest expression of an open-space enclosure was that of food-gathering and primitive hunting people. The BaMbuti, who inhabit Africa's vast Ituri forest, still erect their campsite in a forest clearing close to a stream with the ephemeral dwellings or huts placed near the edge so that a communal open space, or large courtyard, is defined by their position. The North American Plains Indians, the Cheyenne, who were skilled hunters, also formed circular episodical encampments through the positioning of their tepees, not dissimilar in shape to that of the North African pastoral nomads, the Bedouin. The Bedouin encampment, called *douar*, is formed by a circular arrangement of tents with all entrances facing a central open space; the rear of the tents is protected by a thorn bush fence.

Some contemporary seminomadic pastoral tribes also site their huts at the periphery of a circular or near circular plot. The Masai kraal is a good example of such a space enclosure. It is ringed by a high thorn fence, and in the central part of this enclosure, a corral for their cattle is frequently built as additional protection against wild animals.

Examples of dwellings clustered around a courtyard are very common in societies dependent upon a subsistence agricultural economy. The Mesakin Quisar semipermanent dwelling, already mentioned, is one representative prototype, and numerous other cluster dwellings abound on the African continent.

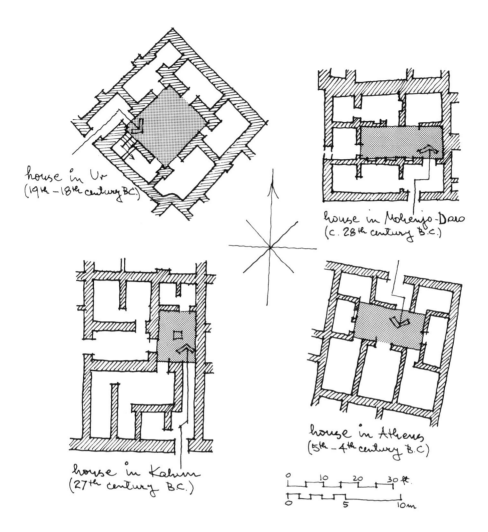

house in Ur
(19th – 18th century BC.)

house in Mohenjo-Daro
(c. 28th century B.C.)

house in Kahun
(27th century B.C.)

house in Athens
(5th – 4th century B.C.)

Finally, the courtyard is also an intrinsic feature of most dwellings of agriculturalists practicing a surplus agricultural economy. The enclosed farmyard is an essential feature of homesteads on all continents.

The sequence of dwelling forms just described, each representing a society with a particular socio-economic background, illustrates the genesis of the courtyard house as well as the innateness of a "central open space." But this sequence only illustrates the evolution of the courtyard dwelling from one point of departure, namely, the additive evolutionary process in which the juxtaposition of a number of building elements around a central open space brings about the courtyard house.

The additive evolutionary process was not the origin of the courtyard concept in the case of the single, large communal dwelling. For example, the Yanomamö, inhabiting the jungle forests of the Orinoco River basin and subsisting on slash-and-burn cultivation, present an evolutionary process of the courtyard dwelling that is nonadditive. When the tribe is still relatively small, it inhabits a circular haystacklike communal dwelling with a smoke hole at its apex. As soon as the tribe increases in numbers and exhausts the potential of its fields, it abandons the old building and fields and clears a new and bigger site for cultivation. The tribe builds a new and larger circular dwelling, but since the span capacity of the available timber is limited, the resulting building becomes doughnut shaped and the original smoke hole a courtyard.

The Greek peristyle house with its large court garden is the classical prototype of the additive evolutionary process. The expansionary process is well

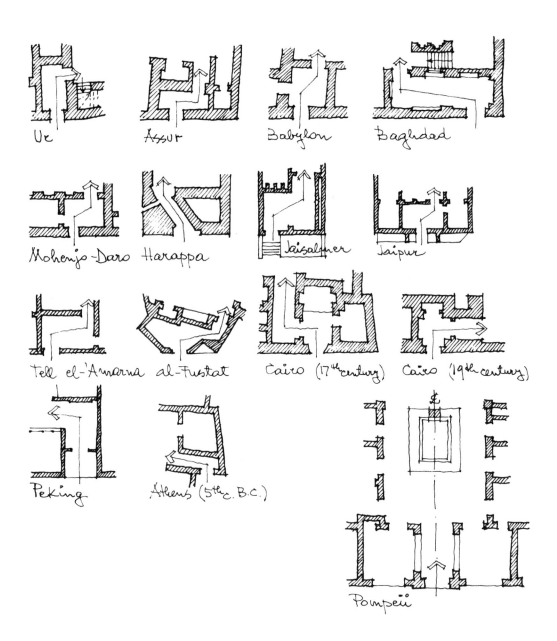

illustrated by the Etruscan house with its character-istic small atrium.

Four factors contributed to the uniform acceptance of the oriental court-garden house. First, there was a psychosocial consideration: the inward-oriented dwelling provided privacy from neighbors in respect to both household activities and material posses-sions. Second, there was an economic factor: the fortifications surrounding ancient cities greatly restricted the amount of land available for housing, and the court-garden house permitted the greatest density, barring multistoried development, which, at that time, was technologically inconceivable. Third, climatic conditions favored the court-garden house: in contrast to the detached dwelling exposed on four sides to the sun and weather, the court-garden house was attached to other dwellings and was pro-tected by them on all but the narrow, shaded, and wind-protected alley side giving access to the house. Moreover, the court could readily, through the use of water and planting, provide a favorable micro-climate. The fourth factor had a religious connotation: the open interior court garden had an affinity with man's image of paradise or oasis in the wilderness; its two lateral dimensions were defined but its third dimension, its height, was limitless.

An intrinsic feature of many court-garden houses is the design of the entryway with a wall positioned to ensure visual privacy of the interior. Increased density coupled with the desire to retain some sense of privacy resulted in the evolution of the spirit wall, a screen that blocks the view from the outside into the house and the court. The Balinese call this screen wall *aling aling* and believe that it prevents the entry of evil spirits, which are reportedly unable to travel around corners. Chinese houses and numerous other contemporary indigenous dwellings make use of the spirit wall and thereby block the view of many evil eyes to their family domain. This traditional entranceway does indeed enhance the inherent privacy of the court-garden house. It is hardly surprising, therefore, that the attributes of the privacy screen were well known to ancient urban dwellers; indeed, most ancient street entrances of urban houses were designed with a privacy wall. This ancient tradition came to an end with the advent of "classical" architecture, perhaps because the exigency of axial planning prevented the privacy screen. Thus, the Roman *domus* never had a spirit wall.

CHAPTER ONE

ANCIENT CIVILIZATIONS

MESOPOTAMIA

THE EMERGENCE OF CITY-STATES

Mesopotamia, "the land between the rivers," the Euphrates and Tigris, forms part of the eastern section of the "fertile crescent" stretching from Egypt through Palestine and Syria to Mesopotamia. In this region barley and wheat still grow wild and the pursuit of agriculture can be traced back to 8000 B.C. In fact, remnants of the earliest known agricultural community were unearthed in the 1950s by Robert J. Braidwood at Jarmo in the foothills of the Zagros Mountains, only 150 miles from Baghdad. This prehistoric farming community was close to the cultural borderline between hunting-gathering and rudimentary agriculture.

More than 4,000 years passed before the inhabitants of Mesopotamia reached the surplus agricultural economy that enabled the establishment of the first extensive civilization known to man—the city-states of Sumer.

The valleys of the Euphrates and Tigris provided ideal conditions for the development of urban civilization. First, the fertility of the land was assured by their seasonal flooding. Second, both navigable rivers acted as ready-made highways, fostering communication as well as trade and commerce beyond the river delta and across the Persian Gulf. Third, sheltered by the Zagros Mountains to the

northeast and the inhospitable Arabian Desert to the southwest, Mesopotamia was protected from barbarian incursions at least until the nomadic tribes domesticated the horse. After that, mounted nomads increased the range and speed of their mobility and, from the eighth century B.C. onward, nomadic invaders became a new and powerful force that threatened the very survival of the sedentary urban civilizations of Mesopotamia. Less than a thousand years later, mounted nomads precipitated the collapse of the Roman Empire.

The Sumerian civilization developed around 3500 B.C. It consisted of several city-states with an inventive and highly organized population who practiced a division of labor. Sumerian citizens

developed the earliest forms of writing and mathematics; they drew up the first code of written law, which predated the Ten Commandments by almost a thousand years. They developed a political system deeply rooted in religion, a system of local government controlled by an assembly of elders that delegated executive powers to a *lugal*, or "big man," who was regarded as the secular representative of the city's guardian deity. The abuse of this power led eventually to the replacement of city-states by "kingdoms."

The Sumerians were the first to use gold and silver as standards of value. In addition they made business contracts and introduced the credit system. Their pottery was simple earthenware, but their gold and silver jewelry was exquisite. They also worked in copper and used ornamental metals.

The absence of local stone and the scarcity of timber gave rise to a sophisticated building technology based on brick masonry construction with an architectural vocabulary of columns, piers, arches, and vaults. The Sumerians built great cities with monumental buildings for places of worship and large palaces for their kings. Their cities were fortified with ramparts and defensive walls.

These fortification walls were more than a mere defense demarcation line between city and countryside. In fact, in conjunction with their gateways they were dominant features of urban architecture that displayed the wealth of the city's inhabitants. In addition to warding off enemies, the monumentality of the fortification walls and gateways was also intended to impress visitors to the city. Sections of the walls were placed under the protection of various deities, and the space just within the gateways functioned as a civic center of the quarter to which the gate led. In this space the statues of victorious conquerors were erected and the assembly of city elders also met to administer the affairs of the quarter's inhabitants (Oppenheim 1977, 128).

Within the ramparts was a maze of streets, alleys, and dead-end streets, filled with the "busy hum of man, with street vendors but without beggars, domestic animals could be encountered, cripples, and prostitutes. Indeed, the noise and bustle of a city day, the eternal coming and going, was effectively contrasted by the poets with the quiet nights when the city slept under the starry sky, behind locked gates. Only the night watchmen made their rounds" (Oppenheim 1977, 141–42).

The houses of the citizens were built around a central court with most rooms opening upon it; there were no windows facing the street or the outer world. The inner walls were plastered and painted. There was little furniture, but both beds and armchairs were often decorated.

Without wanting to imply that there is a link between the Sumerian language and the Sumerian house, it should, nevertheless, be noted that both are additive. The Sumerian language was an agglutinative language: it preserved the root of the word and expressed the various morphemic changes by linking prefixes and suffixes to the root. The Sumerian house is also agglutinative because the court garden is the unaltered root and all other living and work spaces are linked to it.

The village, no doubt, preceded the city and may in some instances have formed the original nucleus of a future city. However, it can be readily understood that with the growing importance of trade and commerce and the consequent development of a means of transportation (the use of the wheel), the efficiency of transportation increased manyfold—since an ox hitched to a cart could pull three times the load it had borne on its back. Such technological devices coupled with better methods of cultivation increased agricultural output while diminishing the numbers of workers required in the field and in transportation.

The Sumerian cities depended upon neighboring agricultural communities for their supply of food. Their principal staples were barley, wheat, and dates. Many small mud-brick villages with a family-clan social pattern dotted the rural land around cities. The villagers tilled the rich alluvial fields watered by irrigation channels. Uruk, one of the biggest and richest Sumerian cities (known in biblical times as Erech and in Arabic as Warka) was surrounded in 3000 B.C. by at least one hundred and forty-six outlying villages. It is interesting that even in ancient times the attraction of city life was irresistible to rural dwellers. In the period between 3000 and 2700 B.C. villagers drifted toward the growing cities, and the number of villages gradually decreased from one hundred and forty-six to seventy-six. A further reduction to twenty-four villages had occurred near Uruk by 2400 B.C.

A passage in a Sumerian poetic text written in praise of Ur asserts that even a native of Markasi—a mountain region of Elam—becomes civilized when living in Ur, so proudly certain were its inhabitants of achieving the acculturation of any paganus (peasant or villager) (Oppenheim 1977, 111).

Eridu, Uruk, Ur, Larsa, Lagash, and Nippur were all major Sumerian cities, but Ur, being until now the most explored city, offers the best insight into the physical form of the Sumerian urban house and its residential urban environment.

THE URBAN HOUSE IN MESOPOTAMIA

Reputedly the home of Abraham, Ur was located close to the confluence of the Euphrates and Tigris rivers, close to the low hills near the edge of the Arabian Desert, and relatively close to the sea. It commanded the trade routes of both rivers and drew upon the agricultural wealth of their fertile valleys.

The Golden Age of Ur lasted from 2474 to 2398 B.C.; as the capital of the neo-Sumerian Empire under Ur-Nammu, it experienced a second period of prosperity between 2112 and 2095 B.C. The city area covered about 220 acres (89 hectares) and had at its peak about 34,000 inhabitants; its gross urban density at the period was 150 persons per acre (370 persons per hectare). After 1700 B.C. until 1854, when the first excavations identified it, Ur was a forgotten city. It was only in the twentieth century that the serious excavations made by Hall and Woolley revealed with some certainty the extent of its physical environment and its residential districts.

The typical urban house in Ur consisted of several rooms around a central court. A staircase, usually near the entrance, led either to the roof or to the

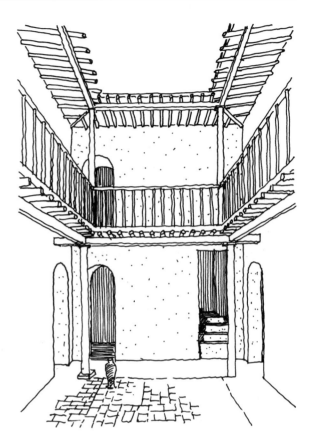

Ur: Reconstruction of a private house (No. 3 Gay Street) (after C. Leonard Woolley)

upper floor. A reception room, kitchen, and other ancillary household rooms faced the courtyard at ground level. In two-story structures bedrooms and private family rooms were located on the upper floor, also facing the courtyard. The roof of single-story houses was often used as a sleeping platform, but in humbler dwellings the reception room had to serve also as a bedroom.

The essential features of the Ur house survived a life span of over 6,000 years; the traditional Baghdad house in Iraq today retains all the intrinsic elements of the Ur house. This similarity prompted Cantacuzino to state: "The plan [of the Ur house] is a lasting solution to urban life. The house is insulated against the bustle of the street, defended against marauders, and protected against the fierce climate" (1969, 17).

In the west section of the city of Ur, Sir Charles Leonard Woolley (1880–1960) excavated a small residential area consisting of about a dozen houses

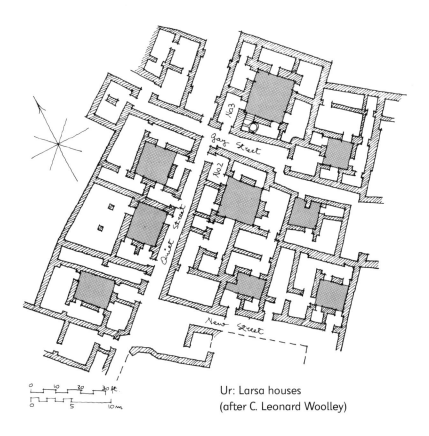

Ur: Larsa houses
(after C. Leonard Woolley)

dating from the Larsa period (nineteenth to eighteenth century B.C.) A narrow and angular street system and near-square buildings characterize this enclave. The most publicized Ur house is located in this area and is identified as No. 3 Gay Street. It is entered from Gay Street through an oblong vestibule with a privacy wall at its end facing the front door that blocks any direct view from the street into the house. At the far end of the vestibule, adjacent to the privacy wall, an entry leads to the paved court, the nucleus and main distributor space of the house. Immediately next to this entry point was a staircase, probably leading to an upper-level gallery surrounding the court that served as a verandah and circulation space for the bedrooms on the upper floor. The reception room was probably the central space on the ground floor located on the northeast side of the court.

The other houses of this cluster of homes are variants of the design just described with the exception of No. 2 Quiet Street, a double house with one entry on Quiet Street and a second one on New Street. A well-to-do family may have lived in one house and may have acquired the neighboring dwelling to enlarge its residence, a practice that is still widespread in Islamic cities. Whether one house was subsequently used as the formal and public dwelling and the second one as the informal and private dwelling (a contemporary custom in the Orient) is not known.

A larger residential district, also excavated by Woolley and dating from the Larsa period, is located in the eastern part of Ur. The layout of the primary streets was irregular, but the narrow residential lanes and blind alleys were more or less rectilinear. To the western eye this pattern appears chaotic, haphazard, or at best disorderly. In reality, the pattern reflects a natural or organic growth rather than an artificial growth, and as such it possesses a hierarchical order that distinguishes between main commercial streets and local residential streets in contrast to the rigid "orderly" grid pattern of more recent cities. The precise grid inhibits this natural hierarchy.

Although it was so called, the excavated eastern section of Ur was not a purely residential area in

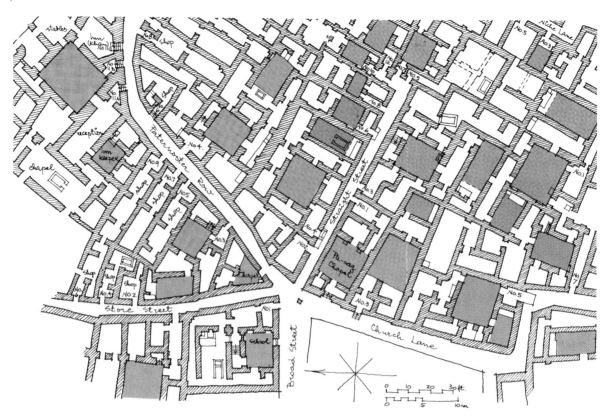

Ur: Eastern residential quarter
(after C. Leonard Woolley)

our terms. Along the main streets—Broad Street and Paternoster Row—there were, as identified by Woolley, several chapels, a two-classroom school, a large inn, several shops, an eating house, and a cooperage. The inn had three separate street entrances and consisted of a large building complex, including at the ground-floor level the innkeeper's dwelling. (It is important to remember that in ancient cities urban houses frequently combined family accommodations with the workshops of their owners. The separation of "home" and "work," perfectly natural to us, would have seemed absurd to the city dwellers of antiquity.)

Most residences in the district had their entrances from narrow lanes, even where corner properties could have had an entrance from a main street. Small and large homes, presumably occupied by poor and rich families, were intermingled in this district, but their two basic design features—the central court and the shielded entryway—were common to all. Such intermingling is not surprising when the dwelling is inward-look-

ing. In fact, the practice of poor and rich living next to each other is still commonplace in traditional oriental cities whose inhabitants have adhered to the inward-looking urban house concept and, of course, to the old oriental custom of avoiding public ostentation.

In Sumeria this apparently natural intermingling of the wealthy and the poor may not be attributable solely to the inward-looking nature of the urban house, but perhaps also to social policy. An inscription from the twenty-sixth century B.C. suggests that Gudea, an enlightened monarch of Lagash, gave evidence of the tempering of strength with mercy in his statement that "the maidservant was the equal of her mistress, the slave walked beside his master, and in my town the weak rested by the side of the strong" (Durant 1954, 122).

"Civilization, like life, is a perpetual struggle with death. And as life maintains itself only by abandoning old, and recasting itself in younger and fresher forms, so civilization achieves a precarious survival by changing its habitat or its blood.

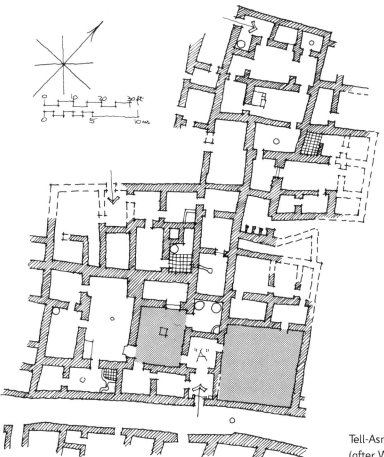

Tell-Asmar c. 2250 B.C.
(after Winifred Orthmann)

It moved from Ur to Babylon and Judea, from Babylon to Nineveh" (Durant 1954, 218) and from these eventually to other centers of Egypt, Greece, and Rome. In this way Will Durant expressed the profound and inevitable changes that accompany urban development.

Ur declined in importance and was replaced by the cities of Babylonia and Assyria. Babylon, Borsippa, Assur, Nimrud, and Nineveh (as indeed all cities) had their intrinsic and unique character principally in their natural setting, their fortifications, their monumental buildings for deity, and their great palaces for royalty, but their residential quarters did not vary substantially from those of the Sumerian cities. This can be seen from the following descriptions of urban houses and their immediate environment in both Assyria and Babylonia.

Late Akkadian urban house forms dating from about 2250 B.C. were found at Tell-Asmar. Although it is asserted that most dwellings had a central hall rather than a court, it is, nevertheless, conceded that house "A" did have a court garden. Since no trace was left of their roof structures, the existence of roofed-over central halls is only conjectural. Many similarities in layout shared with later Mesopotamian court-garden houses suggest that the likelihood of open central courts in the Tell-Asmar houses cannot be so easily discounted.

A neo-Assurian residential quarter consisting of about twenty-five dwelling units was unearthed by Preusser (1954) and is attributed to the period between 687 and 637 B.C. The largest dwelling unit of this precinct is the "red house," which had two courts. An entrance court surrounded by housekeeping rooms formed the public, or *babanu* section of the house, while a larger central court garden with the family quarters was the private, or *bitanu*, section. The street entrance door led into a vestibule with a privacy wall, and through a short

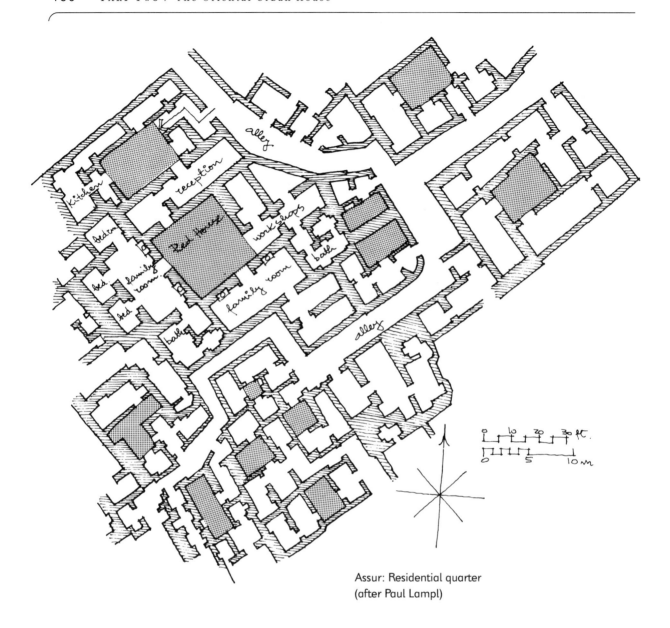

Assur: Residential quarter
(after Paul Lampl)

passage the front court. On the south side of this court was the reception room, which was linked through an anteroom to the larger family court garden.

On the west side of the family court was the main family room with small bedrooms opening from it. The bathrooms were in the southernmost corner. The south side of this court gave access to other living accommodations, while the east side probably contained the workrooms of the master. The two main living rooms each had two wall recesses with alabaster shelves to support water-filled, porous earthern vessels to cool and humidify the interior. The smaller homes feature only one court, but they

retain the essential characteristics of the oriental urban house, namely a central open court, privacy wall at the entrance, and family accommodations at the furthest distance from the entry point.

The street layout in this neo-Assurian residential sector is typically oriental in character, consisting of curving streets and narrow blind alleyways; moreover, it also characteristically has a very dense land-use pattern, in which the area of building coverage exceeds the combined areas used for courtyards and public access lanes. Finally, the large homes of the well-to-do and the small homes of the workers are intermixed. There is no homogeneous residential district for the wealthy or for

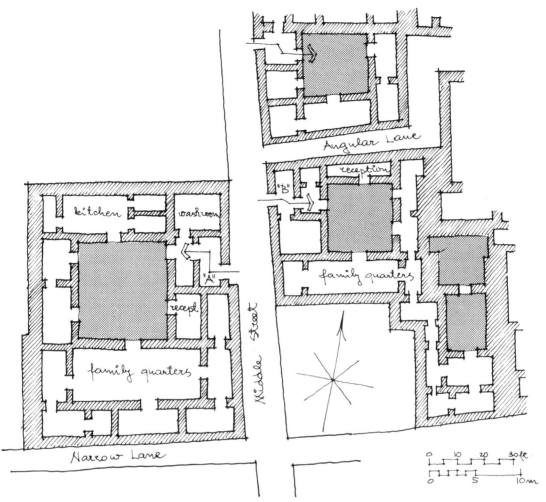

Babylon: Merkes quarter
(after E. Unger)

the poor; segregation according to income groups was absent in the older city of Assur.

Late Babylonian urban houses in the period 700 to 600 B.C. are well illustrated by Reuther's (1926) plan of the Merkes Quarter of Babylon. The street layout here has all the appearances of a planned city.

A typical medium-sized dwelling was house "A" situated at the corner of Middle Street and Narrow Lane. The street entrance was near the northeast corner of the property and led through a passage into a large courtyard; on the north side of this passage was a washroom. The kitchen and other ancillary facilities occupied the north side of the court, while the west side was a two-room interconnected apartment. The multiroom family suite was located in the southern and shadowy part of the house and was thus protected from the heat of the midday sun. There was a reception room, facing the court garden, just south of the entry passage.

House "B," at the intersection of Angular Lane and Middle Street, had an entrance with a double vestibule rather than a privacy wall. It had three small courts, a central one and two additional secluded ones, the latter no doubt for family use only.

Some of the houses of the Merkes Quarter of Babylon were inhabited continuously from 700 B.C. until the Seleucid era. Only in 275 B.C., when the inhabitants of this great city were moved to the new city of Seleucia, does the history of Babylon as a living city end.

EGYPT

FROM MENES TO CLEOPATRA

To Herodotus, Egypt was "the gift of the Nile," and, indeed, as the river inundated the land with its silt-laden flood, the fertile soil was yearly renewed to make Egypt a land of plenty. The domestication of plants and animals in this great alluvial valley dates back to about 5000 B.C. and as early as 3600 B.C. crop storage was practiced. Thus, with the existence of surplus agriculture and the protection provided against frequent incursions by deserts on both sides, this fertile river valley possessed the essential conditions to become a most significant cradle of civilization.

The people of ancient Egypt developed a territorial government along the Nile consisting of a number of *nomes* (provinces), each inhabited by people of one stock, obeying the same chief, and worshipping the same gods. They primarily cultivated wheat and barley but gradually increased the range of their crops to include figs, dates, grapes, beans, and other vegetables. Extensive cattle raising supplied dairy products and meat, the latter preserved with salt. Agriculture assisted by controlled irrigation created Egypt's wealth and enabled the division of labor that led to the establishment of urban centers where metal was worked, pottery manufactured, and writing developed.

After uniting the "two lands," Upper and Lower Egypt, around 3100 B.C., Menes became the first pharaoh. He built a new city—Memphis—on the Nile near the border between the former two lands. Located about 14 miles (22.5 km) south of Cairo, Memphis served as the Old Kingdom's capital until the seat of power was moved to Thebes, about 300 miles (500 km) south, during the Middle Kingdom (c.2160–c.1580 B.C.).

The Golden Age of Egypt was reached during the reign of the Eighteenth Dynasty, when Thutmose III invaded southwestern Palestine. Gradually the borders of the early New Empire were extended until they embraced Nubia and Cush in the south and the lands of the Euphrates in the north. Thebes remained the capital of the empire from the Middle Kingdom onward, with the exception of a few decades when Amenhotep IV devoted himself to the cult of the sun god Aton, no doubt after realizing that the sun was the most visible source of life. Amenhotep changed his name to Ikhnaton (Akhnaton), or "It Pleases Aton," and established a new capital city called Akhetaton, meaning "the Horizon of Aton." After his death, however, the new city declined and Thebes once again became the capital.

We know very little, in general, about the physical form of ancient Egyptian cities compared to those of Sumeria. The Egyptians produced great and monumental architecture, and certainly they would also have had the technology to build great cities. However, evidence points to the fact that they devoted their skills primarily to the construction of permanent shelters for the dead instead of for the living. Perhaps this emphasis upon death and its permanence resulted from the major upheavals and changes that they experienced. For millennia Egypt's indigenous people lived as nomads, and with the development of agriculture some became sedentary in a world where

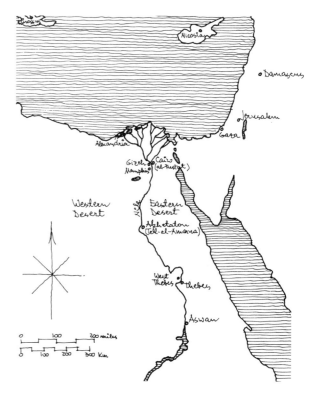

nomadism, certainly in the initial stages, prevailed. Symbols of permanence were perhaps needed to express the new condition of sedentary life paralleled with a set of new values. Pyramids were ideal reminders of permanence because they were heaps of stones that could neither collapse nor become ruins because of their inclined planes. An Arab proverb expresses their permanence best: "All the world fears Time, but Time fears the Pyramids" (Durant 1954, 150).

In contrast to the stone-built pyramid and the rock-hewn necropolis, the Egyptian homes were probably constructed of frail building materials, such as sun-dried bricks that did not withstand the ravages of time. Another theory expressed by some Egyptologists is that the cities in Egypt, a relatively peaceful country, did not have to be fortified. Therefore, they had an open form; this meant that the city structure was looser and its component parts were not fixed within the constraint of a circumvallation.

The most reliable examples of Egyptian housing were unearthed on former town sites built for workers engaged in the construction of a pyramid or a necropolis. These towns were in fact enclosed by a wall, but the enclosure may have been designed as much to retain the foreign workers within the settlement as to protect the inhabitants against incursions.

The Egyptian empire came to an end in 526 B.C. when the Persians invaded Egypt, and for centuries thereafter the country was under foreign dominance. The Persians were ousted by the Macedonians in 332 B.C., when Alexander the Great occupied Egypt. He founded the Hellenistic city of Alexandria, which subsequently became the capital of Egypt and remained so for over a thousand years. Its plan was drawn by Deinocrates of Rhodes and embraced within its boundaries the old pharaonic city of Rhacotis. Many Greek immigrants came to Egypt and influenced its future development.

After the death of Alexander his empire was partitioned and Egypt fell to Ptolemy, the son of Lagus and founder of the Ptolemaic dynasty. With the death of the last Ptolemaic ruler, Cleopatra, in 30 B.C., Egypt became a Roman province and until A.D. 640 a major supplier of grain to Rome.

HOUSING IN KAHUN, DEIR EL MEDINA, AND TELL EL-'AMARNA

Sesostris II (Usertesen), of the Twelfth Dynasty, around 2670 B.C. built the Illahun pyramid as his tomb. He established a 20-acre town site—Kahun—for people engaged in its construction. The town was divided into two parts. The eastern part was nearly square and the western part was a narrow oblong, consisting primarily of small workmen's houses (Badawy 1968, 5).

In the northwest corner of the eastern sector of Kahun was the acropolis with a public square and a guard house to its south. An east-west main street radiated from this square and formed the processional spine of the community. Along this artery were nine palatial residences, six on the north side and three on the south side. Each of these palatial homes had more than fifty rooms as well as several courtyards and atria. The balance of the western sector had a geometric street layout with workmen's houses lining the streets.

The principal building of the western section was the temple; it was located at the southwest corner of the town site and had an open square with a

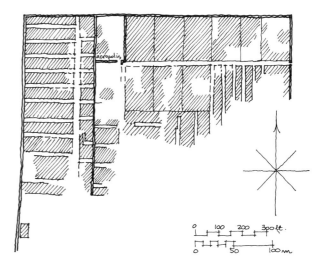

Kahun
(after W. M. Flinders Petrie)

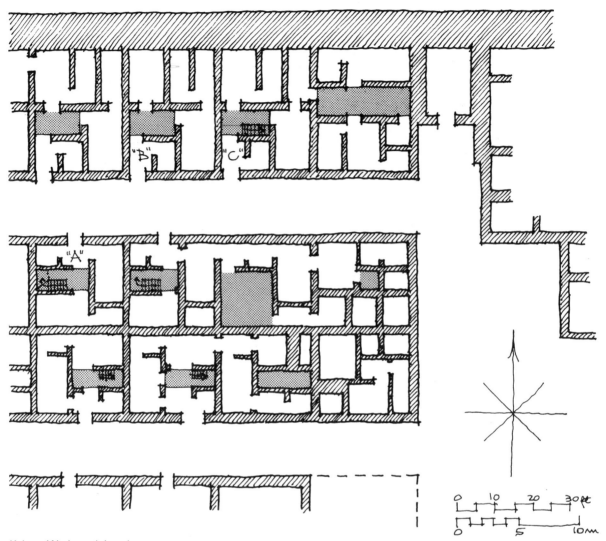

Kahun: Workmen's housing
(after W. M. Flinders Petrie)

guard house in front of it. Here, too, a geometric street pattern formed the base of the western community, but with a north-south main street and intersecting east-west narrow blind alleys lined on both sides with workers' houses. Although most houses had a similar plan, their entrances were invariably staggered so that they never faced each other across the street. All streets had a stone gutter down the center to drain off waste water and occasional rainwater.

The workmen's houses of the western section of Kahun were modular in plan, but close examination of the site reveals that they were certainly not uniform, a contention that is often made in the description of these homes. In some cases two or three modules were joined together to form a single residence. Dwelling sizes varied considerably. The houses along the north wall, for example, were deeper than those opposite them. Several city blocks varied in depth with one being, in fact, twice as deep as the narrowest block.

The smallest houses, such as house "A," had at least five separate spaces, namely an open courtyard and four rooms. No doubt the flat rooftop, reached through a staircase from the court, provided additional living space. Larger dwellings, like house "B," had five rooms in addition to the courtyard. Compound dwellings, like "C," for example, had eleven rooms and two courtyards. The largest residence of the western sector, located

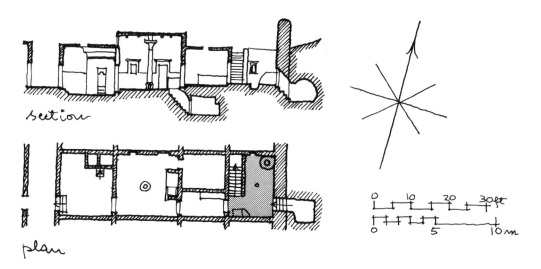

Deir el Medina: Typical house
(after Alexander Badawy)

in the northeast corner, had over twenty rooms and a large north-facing *mandarh*, or reception room, adjacent to a large courtyard.

Under Thutmose I (Thothmes) (1540–1501 B.C.), Deir el Medina, another community, was built near Thebes for workmen engaged in constructing the royal necropolis. This community was enlarged three times. Its street plan was less regular and more organic in comparison with the plan of Kahun.

The typical house of Deir el Medina was a one-story structure placed on a deep rectangular plot. The rooms were arranged in a single row, starting with an entrance hall or courtyard, followed by the main hall, a bedroom paralleled by a corridor, and ending in a rear open courtyard. The floor of the entrance space was three steps below street level. In one corner a shrine dedicated to a god or goddess was usually placed. Opposite the street entrance was the entry to the main hall, whose level was two steps above that of the entrance space. A central wooden column in this hall gave additional support to the ceiling, and a low dais was placed between the doors leading to the bedroom and the corridor. Below the dais a staircase, reached through a trap door, led to a cellar. The bedroom and the corridor were raised slightly above the main room, and the rear courtyard was elevated still higher. The rear court served primarily as a kitchen space, and its typical built-in facilities were a clay oven, a stone basin, a kneading vessel, and a silo. From this courtyard a staircase led to the flat rooftop of the house and a second stairway reached into another cellar.

These houses were built of sun-dried brick, with ceilings of palm trunks and stalks covered with earth; the floors were of rammed earth, probably whitewashed. The interior walls, especially where the shrine was placed, were covered with paintings representing the images of popular deities. These wall adornments reveal an art-loving people who were very skilled craftsmen. The dais in the main room was also built of brick, but with limestone edges and elbow rests at the sides. Windows were placed high, just under the ceiling, and had wooden or stone gratings (Badawy 1968, 67).

Another workmen's town site, east of the capital of Akhetaton, was developed during the reign of Ikhnaton, the effeminate pharaoh married to the lovely Nefertiti. Leonard Woolley excavated this site, which is commonly known as Tell el-'Amarna.

Tell el-'Amarna was less than 2½ acres (1 hectare) in area and enclosed on its four sides by 230-ft (70-m) long walls. It was divided into two sections, an eastern sector that, as in Kahun, comprised four-fifths of the total area and a western sector. The street pattern was geometric with streets running in a north-south direction; single rows of uniform houses lined the streets in the eastern division. In the western section there was

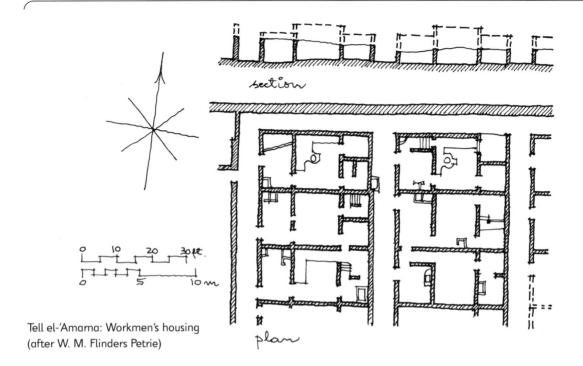

Tell el-'Amarna: Workmen's housing
(after W. M. Flinders Petrie)

only a single street, and two rows of houses facing each other lined it.

An elongated square was located just within the southern wall enclosure; the only gateway to the town was in this square and there was a shrine adjacent to the gateway. The southeast corner of the town site was occupied by a large house. It is assumed that this belonged to the overseer of the artisans engaged in the construction of the rock-cut tombs of the pharaoh.

The typical houses of Tell el-'Amarna measured about 16½ ft (5 m) in width and about 33 ft (10 m) in depth. Uniform in style, they were divided into three areas: a front hall or courtyard, a central hall, and a bedroom and a kitchen at the rear. Within this general layout there were slight variations, especially the location of the staircase to the roof platform. The front courtyards were used for various purposes. Some housed animals, others workshops or household activities such as food preparation. The main living space, however, was usually the central hall. The roof of this hall was supported by a central column. It is not unlikely that in some instances this central space was an open courtyard and that the entrance space was roofed over.

Certainly the large house of the overseer in Tell el-'Amarna had a central courtyard with a staircase leading to the upper stories and the roof space at its west side. The principal living spaces all opened from the court.

The Nuba living in Sudan today often cover their courts with mats or brushwood to give some semblance of shade while allowing unhindered air circulation in their central open living space; this contemporary practice suggests that a similar arrangement may have occurred in Tell el-'Amarna houses. A base for the column was not found in the central space of every home, and even where it was found it can be conjectured that it supported a beam for a shade canopy that may have been erected only at certain seasons.

INDUS CIVILIZATION

THE GARDEN OF SIND AND PUNJAB

Watered by the Indus River and its many tributaries, the Garden of Sind and Punjab became the setting of the ancient Indus civilization. (The Garden of Sind is the alluvial plain created and watered by the Indus, while the Punjab is the land of the five tributaries of the Indus.) Archaeological

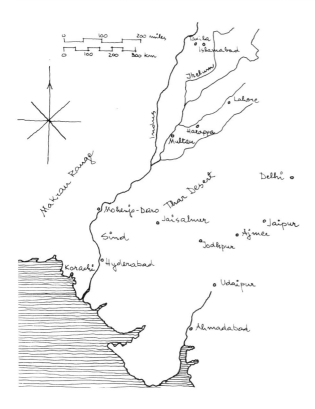

excavations by John Marshall and others at Mohenjo-Daro and Harappa brought to light conclusive evidence of an urban civilization that reached the height of its prosperity at the close of the fourth millennium B.C. It was also ascertained that this early urban society's wealth derived from a surplus agricultural economy coupled with trade and commerce. Trade appears to have extended far from the homeland, since seals bearing the characteristic "Indus" pattern from the pre-Sargonic period have been found at Ur and Kish of Mesopotamia, implying that commerce between these two ancient civilizations certainly existed by 2800 B.C.

Wheat, barley, and the date palm were cultivated by the people of this ancient society. They domesticated the zebu, buffalo, shorthorn bull, camel, and elephant, as well as the chicken, pig, and dog, but the cat and the horse were unknown to them. Spinning and weaving were widely practiced; it is known that at this period the use of cotton for textiles was exclusive to India. Domestic vessels were commonly of earthenware turned on the wheel and were frequently decorated.

The Indus culture had arisen in a "chalcolithic" age, that is, in a period in transition from the use of stone to bronze as the material for tools. Consequently, metal was frequently used for weapons as well as for many farm implements and household utensils; even copper, bronze, and silver were occasionally used for household vessels. In addition to these metals, gold was also fashioned into elaborate and skillfully wrought jewelry. Transport was provided by wheeled vehicles to which either oxen or buffalos were probably yoked.

The Indus civilization possessed a very advanced building technology. The builders of Mohenjo-Daro used burnt brick for their massive battered walls, with the inner face invariably vertical and finished in clay plaster. The exterior surface of the walls appears to have been unfinished, and only larger buildings appear to have been battered. The foundations were carried to a considerable depth and were built with great care. Floors were usually paved with brick, laid flat in most rooms but on edge in areas of excessive wear, such as bathrooms.

The true arch was probably unknown. While the corbeled arch was used for recesses in the massive walls (and infrequently for spanning wall openings), the masonry above door and window openings was usually supported by wooden lintels. Wood construction was also used for upper floors and flat roofs. These consisted of beams and planking. In addition, the roofs were probably covered by beaten earth and a protective layer of brick.

Fireplaces were rarely built, but portable braziers may have served for cooking and heating. Since most dwellings had an upper story, stairways were common elements and were rather steep compared to today.

Most buildings had their own wells, circular in plan and built of burnt brick. All dwellings had bathrooms linked to a very elaborate drainage system; vertical drain pipes were constructed of terra cotta while horizontal ones were of the omnipresent brick. Very often rubbish chutes were built within the thickness of the exterior wall, and they emptied on the outside into a bin or pit.

It appears that the citizens of Mohenjo-Daro had developed organized means for ensuring the peaceful conduct of everyday affairs with some sort of law system, because archaeologists found that

Mohenjo-Daro had little one-room guardhouses built into the corners of intersecting thoroughfares, where "policemen" were presumably installed to help keep order. The citizens of Mohenjo-Daro appear to have been the first urban dwellers with a broadly based, comparatively high standard of living. In fact, they appear to have lived in considerable comfort. Although the size of their dwellings varied, other aspects of their residential environment—building methods, drainage systems and street façades were virtually the same. This similarity struck one archaeologist as "miles of monotony," but as Dora Jane Hamblin (1973) rightly observes, this monotony suggests, "in its uniformity, an even distribution of material goods among a large segment of the population, and thus the well-being that goes with a large, prosperous middle class" (1973, 144).

THE URBAN HOUSE OF MOHENJO-DARO AND TAXILA

John Marshall estimates that the life span of the city of Mohenjo-Daro was approximately 500 years between 3250 and 2750 B.C. The boundaries of the town site have not been determined and it cannot yet be ascertained whether the city was protected by fortifications.

A certain regularity in its street layout suggests that the early Indus civilization inclined toward geometric order in its cities. All main streets and thoroughfares of the excavated areas were oriented to the points of the compass. First Street, or the main thoroughfare, had a north-south orientation and was about 30 ft (9 m) wide, while other parallel streets were much narrower, though rarely less than 10 ft (3 m). Certain streets were lined with shops, and judging from the number of bazaar streets, the city appears to have been prosperous. In Marshall's view, there is every indication that the customs of the people of Mohenjo-Daro were similar to those observed at present in any large-sized town in India.

Narrow lanes, varying from about 3 to 6 ft (1 to 2 m) in width, linked the primary and secondary streets. These lanes did not necessarily run in straight lines from one street to another; occasionally they took right-angle turns; moreover, the levels of the lanes were considerably higher than those of the secondary streets or the main thor-

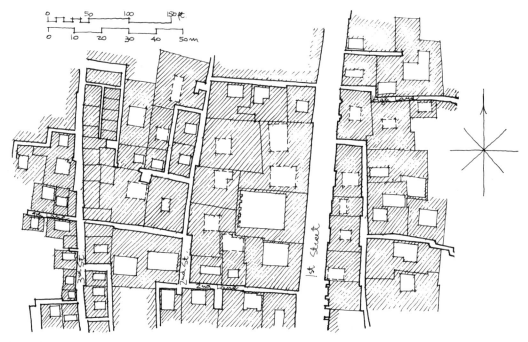

Mohenjo-Daro: Residential district
(after John Marshall)

oughfare. Probably frequent floods necessitated that residential areas be built at higher levels.

Most of the excavated areas of Mohenjo-Daro appear to have been residential. The size of buildings ranged from humble two-room dwellings to large multiroom houses that could be ranked as palaces. Invariably, however, the typical dwelling unit of Mohenjo-Daro is an inward-looking courtyard house. Naturally, the smaller homes had only one courtyard, whereas the larger ones had several courts.

A typical small but comfortable dwelling is house No. 54; it formed part of a cluster of similar-sized dwellings along Ninth Lane. A relatively wide doorway with a brick front step and threshold gave access to a vestibule. The western section of this entrance chamber was used as a bathroom and was equipped with an outlet for waste water that led to a large jar placed in a brick-lined pit against the exterior wall and buried below the surface of the lane; a second adjacent pit received rubbish from the upper floors of the house through a vertical chute contained within the thickness of the exterior wall.

The open courtyard, located along the north wall, was linked to the vestibule by a passage, and a spirit wall ensured its privacy. Two principal rooms opened toward the courtyard, and between them a steep staircase led from the court to the private family quarters on the upper floor. The finding of grindstones suggests that the northwestern room served as a kitchen.

Building No. 52 was most likely a shop with a small storage room at its north end. Most probably shops also lined the eastern side of Third Street. Here there was also a one-room structure immediately south of No. 43, which appears to have been "a piau, or public drinking place, similar to those so common in modern bazaars. One corner of the room is occupied by a finely built well with a neat brick paving laid over the rest of the floor. The shallow round pits in the floor near the well were meant to hold pottery jars which were kept filled with water, and by them sat the attendant to dole out draughts to thirsty persons" (Marshall 1973, vol. 1, 205).

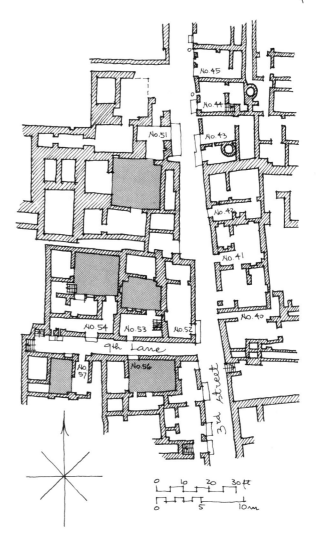

Mohenjo-Daro: Third Street area
(after John Marshall)

A slightly larger dwelling was house No. 12, a corner property with two entrances, one from Second Street and another from Second Lane. Seven chambers surrounded a central courtyard, but their individual functions were not identified by the archaeologists who uncovered this structure.

Also fronting on Second Street was house No. 23, a larger home with a central rectangular courtyard surrounded at ground level by thirteen rooms. The entrance hall was probably centrally located along Second Street, but the east wall unfortunately is so ruined that no trace of either the threshold or the door jambs has survived. A water well, constructed

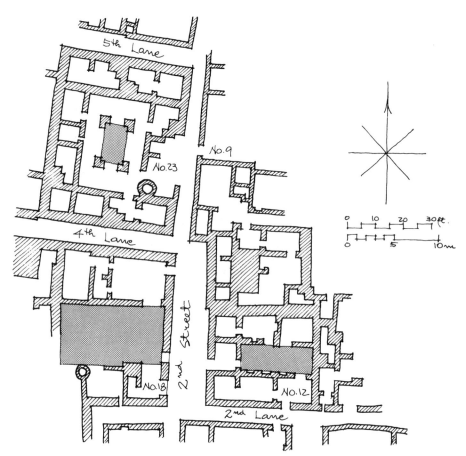

Mohenjo-Daro: Second Street area
(after John Marshall)

of brick and provided with a covered drain to carry off waste water, has survived in the south section of the entrance hall. This house had four brick piers in the four corners of the courtyard, no doubt intended to support an upper-story access gallery to the family quarters; the similarity of this classical courtyard to those of the much later Hellenistic courtyard house or the tetra-style Roman atrium is unquestionable.

The four chambers along the north wall may have been bathrooms linked through stairways directly to the upper-floor family quarters. A chamber in the southeast corner and the one in the northeast corner were stair halls giving access to the upper floors.

An even larger home was identified by Marshall as an "average upper-class house." Fronting on High Lane, house No. 8 was located close to the main thoroughfare of Mohenjo-Daro. A broad entryway—wider than the lane—led to a front courtyard with a porter's lodge. A short passage led from the entrance court to the central large courtyard. All rooms on the ground floor and upper levels were grouped around the open courtyard. The apartment immediately north of the porter's lodge was probably for guests; although the guest chamber opens onto the courtyard, its access is isolated from the rest of the house and is, of course, directly accessible from the entrance hall.

The well chamber, adjacent to the short passage leading to the courtyard, had a raised floor and was connected through an aperture wide enough to permit small vessels to be passed through it to the neighboring bathrooms. The raised floors of both these chambers were paved with brick, and the bathroom was divided with a low curb into two separate use areas. A hole through the exterior wall allowed the drainage of waste water into the lane. A

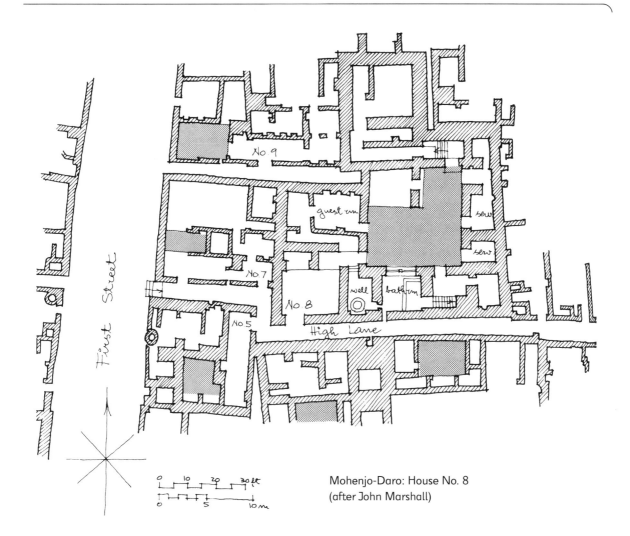

Mohenjo-Daro: House No. 8
(after John Marshall)

staircase appears to have linked the family quarters on the upper floor to the bathroom below, which was probably not accessible from the ground floor; the aperture toward the courtyard was clearly meant as a window, perhaps screened with lattice-work.

The small rooms along the east wall of the house were probably the servants' quarters, while the slightly raised south-facing alcove in the courtyard may have served as a kitchen. The family's living and sleeping rooms were all on the upper floor and were reached through the main staircase located on the north side of the courtyard.

Archaeological evidence indicates that the ancient Indus Valley civilization came to an end before the arrival of the seminomadic Aryan tribes who invaded the Punjab and the Garden of Sind

around 1500 B.C. About one thousand years lapsed before the birth of the classical period of the Indic civilization, which roughly dates from 500 B.C. to A.D. 700. During this classical period Hinduism developed, while Buddhism rose, flourished, and declined in India. This was also the period when the Hellenistic culture left its imprint upon Indian civilization following the invasion of India by the Macedonians led by Alexander the Great (356–323 B.C.).

The city of Takshasila, or Taxila, as it is known to Europeans, was established during the classical period. It was located between the Indus and Jhelum rivers and at the crossroads of three important trade routes between India, central Asia, and western Asia.

The oldest city excavated at Taxila is known as the

Taxila
(after John Marshall)

Bhir Mound City. As in the case of most ancient tells, it had several strata dating between the fifth or sixth and second centuries B.C. While the principal street, named First Street, followed a straight line in an approximately north-south direction, other streets were less regular. The average width of the principal street was 22 ft (6.7 m) and the width of the other streets varied from 9 to 17 ft (2.7 to 5.2 m). In contrast, the residential lanes were extremely narrow; in fact, so narrow that the passage of two people side by side was often made very difficult. However, this tightness was now and then relieved by the widening of a lane into a small open space (Marshall 1960, 48–49).

Most of the excavated city blocks contained dwellings and shops, the latter consisting of rows of chambers fronting the main streets. The dwellings were typically oriental in character and consisted of rooms facing one or several sides of an open court. Although all dwellings adhered to this principle, the diversity in its application was found by Marshall to be so chaotic that it was sometimes difficult to determine where one house ended and another began. Marshall surmised that these dwellings probably resembled the contemporary flat-roofed houses (yet uneven in height) of modern towns in northwest India. "That the roofs in olden days were flat and covered with earth is sufficiently demonstrated both by the complete absence of any kind of tiles on the site and by the layers of earth, sometimes half burnt and mixed with charcoal, which had evidently fallen from the roofs as they collapsed" (Marshall 1960, 51–53).

In the beginning of the second century B.C. the Bactrian Greeks transferred the city of Taxila from the Bhir Mound to a new site. This new site, called Sirkap, was located only a few hundred yards to the north of the old site and presented topographic features that must have appealed to Hellenistic city builders. It had considerable level ground, streams along its perimeter, and an isolated hill within the town site suitable for an acropolis.

Sirkap was surrounded by a fortification wall 15 to 20 ft (4.5 to 6 m) wide and 20 to 30 ft (6 to 9 m) high, equipped with bastions and gateways. Its plan was a Hellenistic chessboard pattern with the main thoroughfare running north-south and emanating from the northern gateway but offset to the east of center, so that the thoroughfare itself was masked from view as one entered the city.

On both sides of this main street were rows of shops. In John Marshall's words:

They are small, single-storey structures of one or two rooms, raised on a high plinth above the roadway and often with a shallow verandah or open platform in front. The rows of these shops are not continuous. At short intervals, their shadows are broken by streaks of sunlight from the narrow side-streets which cut from east to west across the city; and here and there, too, between the shops can be seen sacred temples and shrines [stupas] overlooking the main thoroughfare. . . .

At the back of the shops and shrines, and reached usually through entrances in the narrow side-streets, were the private dwelling-houses of the citizens. A few, adjacent to the city wall were poor, mean habitations, occupied probably

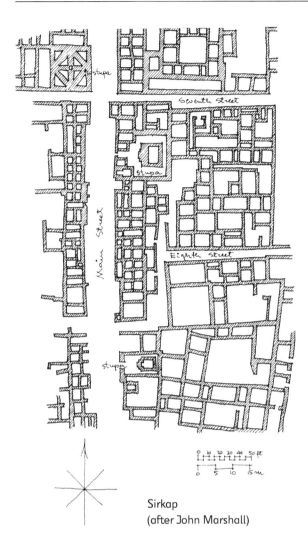

Sirkap
(after John Marshall)

when a new city was built called Sirsukh, which was located about 1 mile (1.6 km) distant from Sirkap's northern fortification wall. Sirkap continued to be occupied for a while, just as Bhir Mound City had been occupied for some time after the establishment of Sirkap.

Sirsukh had a rectangular site plan and was also a fortified city with a strong wall reinforced at 90-ft (27.4-m) intervals by semicircular bastions. Existing villages built on top of Sirsukh's ruins and the existence of several graves have limited archaeological excavations of this town site. Consequently, very little is known of the city and the dwellings of its former inhabitants.

CHINA

CHINESE CITIES AND URBAN DWELLINGS

From time immemorial, agriculture has been a sacred occupation in China and remains so today. The God of the Soil, one of the oldest Chinese deities, was greatly revered and gradually became identified with the land of the family. Much emphasis was placed upon family life, which led to ancestor worship and an ultrasedentary society. With its fertile valleys, great alluvial plains, the loess soil, and favorable climate (and usually adequate rainfall), China possessed the ideal conditions for the emergence of a surplus agricultural economy. Indeed, "Chinese literature reveals that the knowledge of agricultural methods, water regulations, etc., was already well advanced in early times, i.e., between 2357 and 1122 B.C." (Gutkind 1946, 203–4).

It is certain that during the Shang dynasty (c.1765–c.1122 B.C.) the Chinese people had discovered the art of writing and were making bronze utensils of unusual beauty. By this time they had also domesticated cattle, pigs, sheep, dogs, and chickens as well as the horse. The cowrie shell served as the monetary unit, and building technology was developed to the degree that sizable buildings could be constructed.

by the soldiers who manned the ramparts, but most houses within the city were large and probably belonged to the well-to-do (1960, 65–66).

The dwellings rarely exceeded two stories in height and were flat-roofed courtyard houses with chambers (*chatuhsala*) grouped around the open courts that provided light and air. When used in the exterior walls facing the street, windows were merely narrow slits to protect the inhabitants' privacy.

In the Greek stratum of Sirkap courtyard houses were more symmetrical in plan than those of the subsequent strata with the exception of the last, the Parthian, where irregular plans again gave way to symmetrical ones. After an existence of about three centuries, Sirkap was gradually abandoned

The formative centuries that produced the basis for the development of Chinese literature and philosophy were the centuries of the Zhou dynasty (1122–255 B.C.). *I Ching*, the Book of Changes, dates from the beginning of this period, while the works of Lao-tse, Confucius, and many other philosophers were written during the later part.

During the Zhou reign hundreds of principalities emerged out of the need to defend agricultural communities against the encroaching barbarians. The resulting feudalistic states usually consisted of a walled town and several other smaller walled communities, all of which dominated the surrounding agricultural land. Gradually the weaker feudal states were conquered by stronger ones until the strongest of them all succeeded during the third century B.C in establishing a unified empire ruled by the Qin dynasty. Qin, formerly known as Ch'in, also "gave to China the name by which it is known to nearly all the world but itself" (Durant 1954, 645).

The building of the Great Wall of China began during the Qin dynasty (255–206 B.C.), but equally significant in this period was the introduction of a land settlement policy based on a balance between the density of population and cultivable land area. Scores of towns and cities were established, and reached over one thousand in number before the

Han dynasty (206 B.C.– A.D. 220) was established and made China an empire with the capital at Changan (today's Xi'an).

A rural-urban interdependence was an important concept of the Chinese settlement policy and brought about a hierarchical organization of cities commencing with the district center called *xian*, followed by the small town, or *yi*, and ending with the large city or capital called *du*. All of these urban areas had one characteristic in common: they had a square or nearly square plan. This was based on an ancient Chinese conception that the earth was square and that the sky or heaven was round. Not only were the physical layout and the subdivision of Chinese towns and villages rectilinear, but the fields were also arranged more or less symmetrically in squares. "All occidental peoples (indeed, all other civilizations) of ancient times conceived the world and the universe as being circular and flat, and this cosmogony dominated directly or indirectly their life and their work. The question why the square plays so important a part among the Chinese, both in their cosmic conceptions and in many other respects, must remain unanswered" (Gutkind 1946, 202).

In contrast also to cities in other ancient civilizations, the Chinese city was conceived from its very outset as a coherent whole that would not grow beyond its established boundaries. Initially, it contained large open spaces within its walls; one of the few exceptions to this was Beijing. Otherwise, cities were governed by simple planning principles used by other ancient civilizations; this involved the concepts of wall enclosure, north-south orientation, rectilinear or checkerboard street pattern, and the courtyard urban dwelling. For reasons of defense, the Chinese city was surrounded by impressive walls. This feature is reflected in the Chinese language, which makes no distinction between "city" and "city wall," the word for both being *cheng*. In fact, walls dominated not only the external appearance of the city but also its interior, since all important groups of buildings with their respective courtyards formed separate small enclosures, as was the case with the humblest court-garden dwellings.

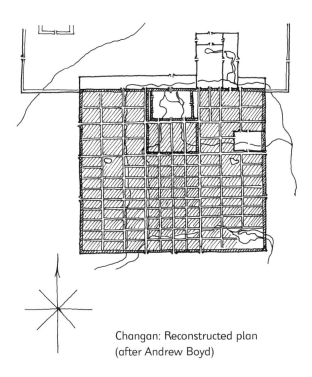

Changan: Reconstructed plan
(after Andrew Boyd)

Another intrinsic feature of Chinese cities was based on climatic considerations and manifested itself in the southern orientation of all walled enclosures. Large and small groups of buildings were organized in such a way that their outdoor spaces were sheltered from the cold northern winds and acted as sun traps. This effect was achieved by siting main buildings parallel with the north side of the courtyard, while secondary buildings protected the east and west sides of the court. Larger compounds consisted of a series of similar building clusters arranged in sequence along a north-south axis (Boyd 1962, 49–50). The sheltered court garden is known as *tianjing* or "the well of heaven," a poetic and appropriate name for this pleasant and private outdoor space.

The streets in Chinese cities ran typically north-south and east-west, thus resulting in a number of rectangular superblocks. Principal streets led to the city gates. The secondary streets within this network were less systematic because the primary elements within the city blocks were the houses. Consequently, secondary streets were often broken at right angles and narrow access streets were blind alleys. In fact, the Chinese city was composed

of individual elements that were governed by a hierarchical order, such as districts, compounds, and houses, and where the larger element encompassed the smaller one, not unlike the Chinese box. This concept, for example, also applied to the walled royal palace of Beijing, which was within the walled enclosure of the Imperial City, which, in turn, was within the enclosure of the Inner City of Beijing.

The streets served as marketplaces. While in smaller towns commercial activities were restricted to a few streets, in larger cities whole districts pulsated with intense commercial activity. Different categories of craftsmen and shopkeepers were grouped together along a particular street so that each street catered to special crafts or trades. Shopkeepers in some streets often formed guild-like associations to protect their interests.

Most manufacturing of goods was done in the home and was paid on a piecework basis if it was farmed out. Thus, dwellings were designed to fulfill the needs of family life, but also had to function as workshops for the occupants. The Chinese bourgeoisie that emerged as a result of the flourishing trade in the cities possessed almost modern comforts. Will Durant's assertion that "their standard of living was probably higher than that of their contemporaries in Solon's Greece, or Numa's Rome" (1954, 647) is probably correct. The Chinese bourgeoisie wore leather shoes and clothes of homespun silk; they lived in well-built houses furnished with beds, tables, and chairs; they ate from plates made of ornamented pottery and china; and they traveled on land by chariot and on the waterways by boat.

The entrances of houses were oriented to the south wherever possible; this partly explains the existence of a maze of many little streets within a city block. The typical urban house was a compound dwelling consisting of several buildings surrounding a central courtyard. One reached the house through the main gate and immediately faced a screen or spirit wall. The screen, according to popular belief, prevented the entry of evil spirits, whom the Chinese believed traveled only in straight lines. The belief was that, once inside, even a tiny evil spirit could expand and dislodge the occupants.

Throughout China one-story dwellings were the rule. It was considered presumptuous to live in a house that was higher than the walls that surrounded the city. A climatic consideration seems to have governed the relationship between the areas of courtyards and houses; in the north the courtyards were larger than the houses, whereas the opposite was true in the south. Moreover, in the south projecting roofs of the houses partially sheltered the courtyards from the strong heat of the sun.

The street façade of Chinese urban houses was very simple; they seldom had more than a window, pitched high up under the eaves, and a door. The residential streets were very narrow but picturesque, owing to the homogeneous appearance of the buildings, with the branches of an occasional courtyard tree waving over the rooftops. Although the plan of the courtyard was often symmetrical, the main entrance was not in its central axis. This would have been interpreted as an offense against the gods, for human things could not be perfect.

CHAPTER TWO

THE GREEKS
AND THE ROMANS

HELLENIC, HELLENISTIC, AND ROMAN CITIES

The classical period of urban development in both Greece and Ionia evolved during the period between 900 and 600 B.C. Athens, for example, became significant as a city after it succeeded in unifying Attica in the eighth century, reached its first eminence under the able administration of Pisistratus (546–527), and enjoyed its Golden Age under Pericles (443–429).

The Hellenic civilization (pre-Macedonian) is inextricably linked with the development of the Greek *polis*, an urban-rural entity, in which the city and its rural surroundings were politically and socioeconomically interdependent. The term "city-state" does not fully describe the meaning of polis; some scholars, in fact, object to this translation. Certainly there was a difference between the polis and the city-states of the ancient civilizations; for example, in the polis rural dwellers were, in a sense, equal to their city counterparts, a relationship that probably did not exist in the Sumerian city-states. But, there also was a similarity between these two urban forms of antiquity; like the Sumerian city-states the Greek *poleis* (plural of polis) were often in conflict with each other and joined forces only when a common enemy attacked. Moreover, the result of the intermittent conflicts between the poleis brought about shifts of

power from one urban center to another, as also occurred in Mesopotamia.

A unique feature of the Greek polis was its policy of growth control and expansion. When a city reached a certain size, further growth was curtailed and a new polis established. The new cities thus formed became quasi-colonies of the parent city. This policy must have been based on the concern for maintaining an ecological balance between the size of the city population and the capacity for food production in the surrounding arable land. It must be remembered that the fertility of the Greek soil was limited and could in no way be compared with the fertile alluvial valleys inhabited by the ancient civilizations. Another important by-product of the

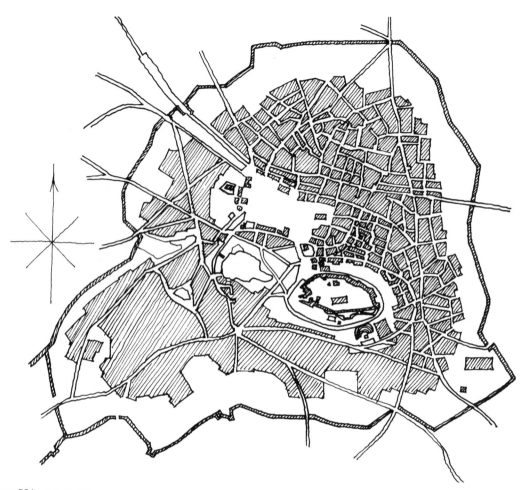

Athens: fifth century B.C.
(after Arnold Whittick)

Greek satellite growth policy was its inherent expansion of trade and commerce, one of the cornerstones of civilization.

Miletus, the richest city of the Ionian confederacy, played a major part in the widespread trading activities of Hellas and encouraged new ideas and influences that contributed greatly to the uniqueness of the Greek civilization. Many cities were founded on the mainland along the Asian shore, in Sicily, in the Italian peninsula, and in distant lands as far as ancient France (Gaul). The Persians invaded Ionia during the first decade of the fifth century and later mainland Greece, temporarily arresting the proliferation of the Greek cities, but they could not extinguish the Greek civilization despite laying to ruin many cities, including Miletus in 494 B.C. and Athens in 480 B.C. After two decades of struggle, the Greeks defeated the Persians and subsequently, during a relatively short period of prosperity, created an urban society of philosophers, scientists, and politicians whose thoughts left an indelible imprint upon most aspects of the occidental way of life—an exception being the concept of housing.

After the Persian devastation the ruined cities of Greece had to be rebuilt. Athens chose to restore its former organic urban pattern while Miletus, in keeping with its tradition of fostering new ideas, rejected the old pattern and rebuilt the city with a gridiron street pattern that became a hallmark for many centuries of occidental town planning. Hippodamus of Miletus, an architect, is credited with the design of Miletus's master plan, which governed its development throughout its subsequent history including a major expansion under the Romans during the first century A.D. The total

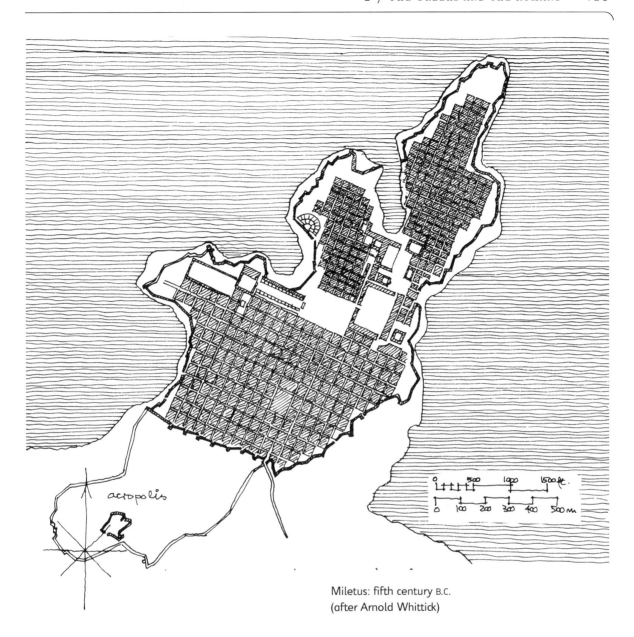

Miletus: fifth century B.C.
(after Arnold Whittick)

area of Miletus within the confines of its fortification walls was about 220 acres (89 hectares), a relatively small area affording pedestrian access to its most distant parts as well as to the adjacent countryside beyond its walls. Indeed, cities of antiquity usually occupied a small area, a characteristic that may explain why inhabitants of Greek cities and their oriental predecessors were content with small courtyards in a dense urban residential setting; the countryside with its wide open space was always close at hand. Incidentally, this compactness was also shared by the inhabitants of medieval occidental cities, but with a significant difference in housing concept—the homes looked outward rather than inward toward a courtyard.

The principal urban components of the Hellenic city were the *acropolis*, a fortified last refuge for the citizenry under siege (the religious precinct often coincided with the acropolis); the *agora*, the central public square of the city and the seat of democracy; and cultural centers such as theaters and arenas. The residential quarters obviously occupied the largest area of the city, but for some inexplicable reason the architecture and planning of residential areas rarely caught the interest of architectural historians.

Initially the residential districts of Greek cities resembled those of the oriental cities with a maze-like street pattern and a myriad of narrow lanes, the result of agglutinative organic growth. And like their oriental counterparts, the houses were unpretentious, in keeping with a democratic dislike for display; moreover, the houses were small. However, nearly every citizen owned his own courtyard house, and within this private domain much of the family's life was lived and much of its work was done. Apart from courtyards, gardens were rare in the city and at best were narrow outdoor spaces behind or next to the dwelling. The interior of the houses was simple and the decoration minimal. Furniture was scanty. It consisted of beds and couches with mattresses and pillows, chairs, a few small tables, and some chests for storage. Cooking was done over an open fire. Tables were brought into the room with the food and removed after the meal; at mealtime women and boys sat before small tables while men reclined on couches. To eat alone was considered barbarous, and fine table manners were considered an indication of culture. The family ate together when there were no visitors, but if male guests were entertained, the women retired to the private sector of the house. After the *deipnon*, or dinner, came the *symposion*, or drinking together.

After the death of Pericles (429 B.C.) Greece was afflicted by troubled times, and no new towns were established until the Macedonian era, which heralded the Hellenistic Age. Marked by the triumphs of Alexander the Great (356–323 B.C.), a new era began which saw the founding of numerous towns over the span of two centuries. The layout of these towns reveals the maturity of Greek urban planning (Hiorns 1956, 40).

During the Hellenistic Age (which followed the Hellenic Age) the Greek sphere of influence followed the routes of the conquests of Alexander the Great and reached into Egypt, Mesopotamia, Persia, and India, four vast geographic areas of which three had given birth to ancient civilizations. Scores of new cities were built during the Macedonian Empire, and each had a plan that followed the Hippodamian model used at Miletus.

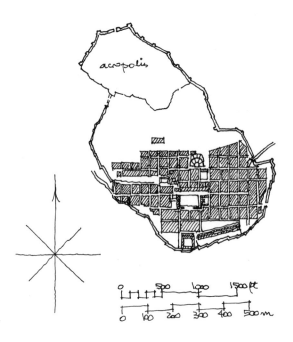

Priene: c. 300 B.C.
(after A. Von Gerban as cited in F. R. Hiorns)

Priene and Pergamon on the Ionian coast, Alexandria on the coastal formation of the Nile delta, Seleucia along the Tigris River, Sirkap along the Jhelum River of the Punjab, and Pompeii at the foot of Vesuvius are only some of the well-known Hellenistic cities. Cities so widely distributed and occupying such distinct geographic areas had, of course, unique and intrinsic features, but their residential districts all copied the time-proven model of the inward-looking courtyard house, larger in size and with more adornment but basically similar to the courtyard house of the earlier Hellenic Age.

The transition from the Hellenistic to Roman civilization was gradual and one has to agree with Frederick R. Hiorns, a scholar of Hellenic and Roman societies, who professed that "the late phase of Greek city-building merged so gradually into such influences as evolved from Roman practice that no line of division can be drawn" (Hiorns 1956, 44). Certainly at the outset of the transition that was the case because "the cultural and artistic technique of the Greeks was far superior to the Roman and accepted as such. In Greco-Roman

Macedonian Empire

Roman Empire

towns, among which Pompeii must now be regard-ed as pre-eminent, no outstanding changes of town pattern or stylistic building became apparent until the Roman Empire was firmly established" (Hiorns 1956, 45).

Indeed, the Roman civilization was built on a culture Hellenic in origin, but Rome "gave it order, prosperity, and peace for 200 years, held back the tide of barbarism for two centuries more, and transmitted the classic heritage to the West before she died" (Durant 1939, 671). Before their demise the Romans ruled a vast empire that controlled the whole of Europe with the exception of its northern part and today's Russia; moreover, they ruled over Asia Minor, the entire Fertile Crescent, including Mesopotamia, Judea, and Egypt, as well as the whole northern Mediterranean coast of Africa.

To maintain this empire, the Romans built thou-sands of fortified legionary camps. Each *castrum* was built according to a standardized plan that was axial in design with its two main roads (*decumanus* and *cardo*) at right angles to each other; many of these intersections formed the nucleus of later cities. The Romans also built scores of new cities and Romanized hundreds of existing ones. They classified the cities of their empire into three cate-gories, the *coloniae* (plural of colonia), or princi-pal cities allied to Rome and therefore enjoying full privileges, *municipia* (plural of municipium), or cities with inhabitants whose Roman citizenship was only partial, and *civitates* (plural of civitas),

which were market and administrative towns. There were also three categories of streets in Roman cities—the *via*, which was wide enough for two passing carts; the *actus*, permitting the passage of only one cart; and the *itiner*, wide enough only for pedestrians. Larger cities were equipped with a sewage system, and potable water was brought in by aqueduct.

The *forum*, an agoralike central district, was the heart of the Roman city. Here the city's mercantile, judicial, and political business was conducted. It was an ostentatious place designed to be imposing, as was certainly the case of the Forum Romanum Magnum of Rome. Other public facilities were the *thermae* (the public baths), theaters, and the *cir-cus* and *colosseum*, or arenas for entertainment.

It was the residential quarters, however, that formed the largest segment of the Roman cities. Initially in Roman cities established before the classical era, including Rome itself, these residen-tial districts were oriental in character. The areas were densely built with a network of mazelike lanes and narrow streets. The dwellings were inward-looking *atrium* (courtyard) houses with a plain street façade. Rich and poor lived side by side; the workers' homes intermingled with the patricians' residences. There was no such thing as a separate working-class district (Morris 1972).

The average Roman preferred the oriental her-itage of housing, but this sentiment was not shared by his rulers, who wanted to bring monumental order to the city. In A.D. 64 the burning of Rome obliterated three city districts and hopelessly damaged seven others out of a total of fourteen. "Premeditated or not, this fire was needed to remove the worst excesses of high density, shoddy buildings and grossly inadequate streets, in order to give an opportunity for comprehensive rebuilding, which the Romans would not otherwise have accepted" (Morris 1972, 44).

The conflagration set the scene for a policy of "urban renewal" based on the rectilinear gridiron street network of Hellenistic origin and a rectangular city block development. The city blocks, or *insulae*, were clogged with multistoried tenement houses, also known as insulae. In Rome "in the middle of the fourth century A.D., 1,797 domus were recorded: this compared with 46,662 insulae each, according to Caropino, with an average of five flats whose average occupancy was at least five or six persons" (Morris 1972, 45). Although they were sometimes six to seven stories high, many tenements were built so carelessly that several collapsed, killing hundreds of people. In spite of the fact that already during the reign of Augustus (27 B.C.–A.D. 14) the height of buildings was limited at the front of the property to 70 ft, apparently the law permitted greater heights toward the rear. Martial, a Roman epigrammatist of the first century A.D., tells of a poor servant whose attic dwelling was two hundred steps up.

Most insulae had shops or *tabernae* (plural of taberna) on the ground floor and dwelling units on mezzanine floors, some with balconies. Now and then, facing tenements were linked with each other across the street by arched structures "containing additional rooms—precarious penthouses for particular plebeians" (Durant 1944, 341). With these insulae the oriental tradition of dispersement of income groups throughout the city came to a gradual end in Rome. Insulae replaced the domus in many sections of the city, including Palatine Hill and the noisy brothel-ridden district that stretched from the Viminal to the Esquiline Hills. Here also lived longshoremen, butchers, fishmongers, vegetable vendors, and workers employed in factories, clerkships, and trades. As Durant has

aptly observed, "the slums of Rome lapped the edges of the Forum Romanum Magnum" (1944, 341).

There is conclusive evidence that insulae were also used in cities smaller than Rome—in Ostia, for example—but it is doubtful whether citizens occupying *cenacula*, or flats, in insulae in the smaller cities represented a majority of these inhabitants. Consequently, in most cities the old oriental tradition of the dispersement of rich and poor throughout the city was retained for a while longer.

Rome during its Golden Age became a very large city, a metropolis in the true sense of the word, with a population of over one million. Such a sizable population could no longer rely on a food supply from its immediate rural surroundings and had to import most of its food and other necessities. *Horrea* (warehouses) were built to store the food and goods before distribution. The 290 or so warehouses, some of which measured 218 by 169 yd (200 by 157 m), formed regular warehouse districts, occupying considerable sections of Rome's waterfront along the Tiber. The daily supplies were distributed by wholesale vendors at special markets, such as "the holitarium for vegetables, boarium for horned cattle, suarium for pigs, vinarium for wine-merchants, and piscarium for fishmongers. Other trades gradually established themselves in their own districts and streets" (Morris 1972, 47).

Inevitably, Rome experienced traffic congestion. During the reign of Julius Caesar the street network of Rome had already become clogged with traffic. To ease the congestion and the conflict between pedestrian and vehicular movement, Caesar banned most carts from the city streets during daylight hours. Exceptions were granted only in the case of builders' carts and the chariots of some officials. Later these limitations on vehicular movement were extended to other cities of the Empire and additional restrictions were also implemented by limiting the size of teams and cartloads allowed to enter the city (Morris 1972, 45).

The expanse of large cities also inhibits access to the open countryside. In Rome not only were the distances too great from the central areas to the periphery, but large segments of its immediate countryside were occupied by the summer villas and palaces of its wealthy and aristocratic inhabitants. Public parks had to be established and "by the third century A.D. there were several campi, or commons, green spaces set apart mainly for foot-races and gymnastic exercises; and twenty or more parks and gardens which, first laid out by wealthy citizens for their private use, became absorbed into the Imperial domain by right of purchase, bequest or confiscation" (Hiorns 1956, 65).

Because its size and centralized government required a series of administrative units, Rome was divided into fourteen districts or regions, and each region, in turn, into several *vici*, or wards, presided over by its own magister (the warden of the city quarter). In A.D. 73 there were 265 such vici in Rome. If we assume an even distribution of population, each *vicus* must have represented about three thousand inhabitants.

The Roman civilization was not eternal as it was thought to be. In the fifth century A.D. the empire collapsed, and the remnants of Roman civilization moved to the East, to Constantinople, the capital of the Byzantine Empire, where some aspects of Roman urban civilization continued to flourish for almost a thousand years. But in the rest of Europe the collapse of the Roman Empire resulted in the chaos of the Dark Ages, centuries lacking in urban traditions until the emergence of the medieval occidental city. In the intervening period the concept of the oriental inward-looking urban house, with its central courtyard, was almost forgotten; it survived only in the cloisters and monasteries of the Christian Church.

THE GREEK PERISTYLE HOUSE

Both archaeological and literary records provide evidence that from the fifth century B.C. onward the indigenous Greek *megaron* or hall-type house

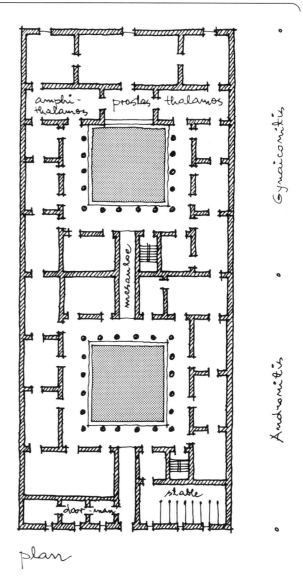

Plan of Vitruvius's Greek house
(after Vitruvius)

was gradually replaced in urban areas by the peristyle house, a Greek adaptation of the oriental urban courtyard house.

The central space of this new urban house was the *peristyle*, a courtyard surrounded on several sides by colonnades, which gave access to adjacent rooms. The number of rooms and the size of the dwelling varied according to the wealth of the family; indeed, large homes frequently had more than one courtyard. However, Greek houses generally had an unpretentious character when viewed from the street; the courtyard principle made it unnecessary to have window openings in external walls and street elevations were both modest and of simple design. While the social status of the occupants was rarely recognizable by the exterior, the interior could be lavish.

Courtyards were indispensable features of most Hellenic urban homes; they served as sources of light and air for the surrounding rooms and enabled the inhabitants, throughout the greater part of the year, to carry on many household activities in the open while remaining in comparative privacy from the outside world. Whenever the court was acentral and therefore contiguous to the street or a neighbor, it was screened by a masonry wall called the *herkos*. A common feature of the courtyard was an altar dedicated to Zeus Herkeios, the god of the courtyard.

The peristyle was usually located in the southern part of the house in order that the principal rooms might receive better insulation. Otherwise, courts varied as to size and proportion of the total area of the house within rather wide limits.

The Greek courtyard house was generally a single-storied structure, but on occasion larger houses had two stories with a two-tier colonnade in the courtyard similar to the Ur houses nearly two millennia earlier. Homes were built of mud, brick, or stone with floors of hard-packed earth or mosaic, either of pebbles or of elaborately cut stone.

Access to the Greek house was through a single or double wooden door, which was often recessed into the wall from the narrow street so as to give shelter and protection to anyone waiting to be admitted to the house. Through this recess, the *prothyron*, one entered directly or by way of a short access corridor (*thyron*) into the courtyard.

In Book Six of his work, *On Architecture*, Vitruvius described the classical Hellenic house. His version of the prototypical peristyle house had two courtyards each with its attendant set of rooms. The first part of the house, that closest to the main entrance, was called the *andronitis* and the second, more secluded section, the *gynaeconitis*; the former was predominantly designated for men and guests, the latter for women and children.

This description has not been verified by archaeological evidence, but it is possible that two

adjacent houses were joined to make one house as, in fact, appears to be the case in an excavated house at Priene (a practice still customary in the Islamic world today where a neighboring courtyard house is acquired for expansion and linked to the original home). The passageway connecting the two peristyle court areas is referred to by Vitruvius as a *mesauloe* because it was situated midway between the two courts.

According to Vitruvius (1960, 186) the typical peristyle of the family section of the house ideally had colonnades on three sides only. The fourth side, which faced south, contained the main section of the house and consisted of a portico defined by two antae or pilasters carrying an architrave. The depth of this portico was two-thirds of its width. This portico was called by some writers *prostas* and others *pastas*. Beyond the portico were large living rooms occupied by the women of the house. A chamber called *thalamos* and another called *amphithalamos* flanked the portico. Additional chambers, the dining rooms for everyday use, and rooms for the slaves were situated along the colonnades.

As cited by Hiorns, the street elevation of the city blocks of Olynthos reflected the unpretentious character of Greek house design. The court-garden principle was universally used and resulted in a rational compactness and lack of street fenestration. Although far from uniform, the internal planning of the dwellings was simple and modest. "Indeed, what some call 'class' distinctions were rare, or at least not overemphasized, in the Greek houses" (Hiorns 1956, 32).

The coupled city blocks of Olynthos consisted of two sets of five houses, each covering an area roughly 60 ft (18.2 m) square. The length of the block was about 300 ft (91.5 m) and the total width 120 ft (36.5 m). A narrow lane, probably used for drainage, separated the two rows of houses. The streets were about 16 ft (4.8 m) wide, ran in an east-west direction, and led to wider avenues with a north-south orientation.

The layout of the dwellings varied considerably, although all dwellings had a pillared portico facing south and opening onto a courtyard. The construc-

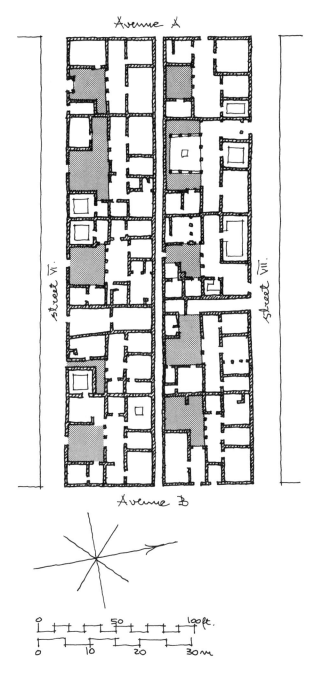

Olynthos: Coupled house block
(after D. M. Robinson as cited in F. R. Hiorns)

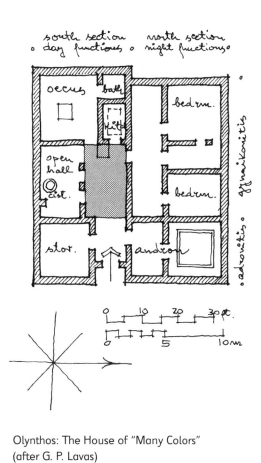

Olynthos: The House of "Many Colors"
(after G. P. Lavas)

tion of the walls was of brick, the roof covering was of tile, and the columns and roof-supporting structure were largely of wood.

The Olynthos "house of the many colors," which dated from the middle of the fifth to the early part of the fourth century B.C., reflected the internal structure of the Greek family, especially the role

and social position of the woman, who seldom went out; it was also an expression of the man's desire to guard his own private life. This peristyle house was analyzed by C. P. Lavas, and its internal organization exemplifies that of a typical Greek house. With the exception of a recessed entrance, the east-facing street façade was a blank wall that did not reveal any detail of the sophisticated interior arrangement of the house. The interior arrangement was only visible from within the dwelling and reflected the day-to-day activities as well as the structure of the family inhabiting it. It was a zoned dwelling that separated daytime activities from nighttime activities and the women's quarters from those used by the men (Lavas 1974, 334). Thus, the east section consisting of the entrance hall, a storeroom to the left, and an anteroom and the *andron* (room reserved for men) to the right constituted the domains of the men. The latter suite of two rooms was used for entertaining and banquets.

The balance of the house was reserved for the women and centered around the courtyard. The principal spaces were (1) a covered open hall facing north, used for eating and as general living quarters, and (2) the *oecus* also general living quarters, principally for the women where housework other than cooking was done; it was adjacent to the kitchen and bathroom.

The southern part of the house was used predominantly for daytime activities and the northern part, the most private section, with three bedrooms reached through a corridor, was used only at night. Essentially, there were intersecting lines dividing the house: one divided it into a men's and women's section and the other into a day and night section.

In the houses at Olynthos the floors were usually of beaten earth, except in the dining room, where pebble mosaic made it possible to wash down the surface.

An example of two attached houses in Athens dating from the fifth or fourth century B.C. demonstrates further variations on the courtyard theme. The smaller dwelling did not have a division between the andronitis and gynaeconitis, but the larger dwelling, possibly a shopkeeper's house, had a marked division between the public and private domain of the dwelling. Judging from the

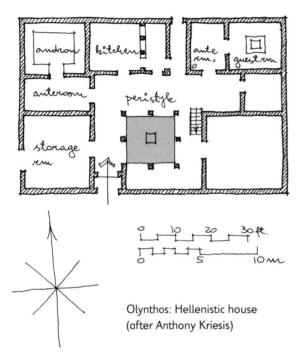

Olynthos: Hellenistic house
(after Anthony Kriesis)

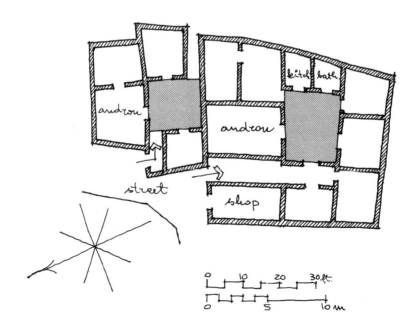

Athens: Two attached houses (fourth or fifth century B.C.)
(after Anthony Kriesis)

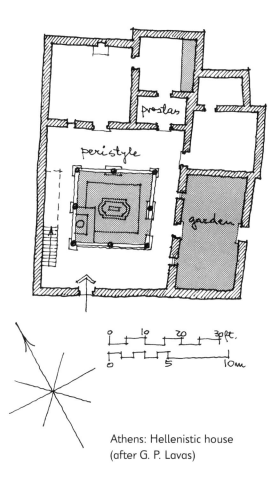

Athens: Hellenistic house
(after G. P. Lavas)

accumulated in these dark streets and the fact that sewer and water pipes had been left in disrepair indicate that the Greek urban dwellers paid little attention to public health. Despite their dedicated use of gymnasia, their disregard for minimum standards of hygiene led to frequent outbursts of pestilence.

Accordingly, when the Golden Age was reached under Pericles, the magnificence that gave glory to the Acropolis, to the agora quarter, and to the temples and gymnasia near the boundaries of Athens was not reflected in the residential provision and health services of the city. To that extent there was a conflict between Hellenic theory and practice. The way in which Athens was afflicted by pestilence and plague is graphically described by Thucydides. Though the frequent and long-continued warfare between the states made works of construction and improvement difficult, it is necessary to give emphasis to this adverse side of town development in Attica and Greece generally (Hiorns 1956, 35).

There is no doubt that Hiorns's description of residential living conditions in Athens and other mainland Greek cities is reasonably accurate. It is also reasonable to conjecture that even with a spacious grid pattern, sanitary conditions in Athens might not have been very different. The assumption that narrow, crooked, and dark streets are synonymous with unsanitary conditions is not necessarily tenable.

A Hellenistic courtyard house in Athens probably built after the Macedonian conquest indicates that irregular building plots were still the rule. The central space of this classic example was a true peristyle courtyard, and a staircase leading to the upper floors suggests that the family quarters, the private domain of the house, must have occupied the second-floor area, the whole very much resembling the Baghdad house. An unusual feature of this sophisticated house was an additional open space, a small garden, located at the southeast corner of the property.

A cluster of five homes in a residential area in Delos shows a modified gridiron street network, probably resulting from topographic considerations. The houses of this cluster were relatively

location of its entrances and from the irregular shape of its building plot, this example suggests that the street pattern was not "orderly," that is, that it resulted from agglutinative growth rather than from planned development. This example also confirms the assumption that Athens' street pattern resembled that of oriental cities and was the result of chance growth. In Hiorns's words:

A very ancient origin and gradual, unforeseen increases in building afford some explanation of this, and may be applied to the mainland cities generally. Though Platonic philosophy was to teach that things of the mind and spirit were much more important than those of the body, this could give no excuse for disregard of the health and amenity arrangements of cities, such as was apparent in Athens (Hiorns 1956, 33).

The improvements that Themistocles implemented in Athens, however, left residential streets narrow, crooked, and unpaved. The filth that had

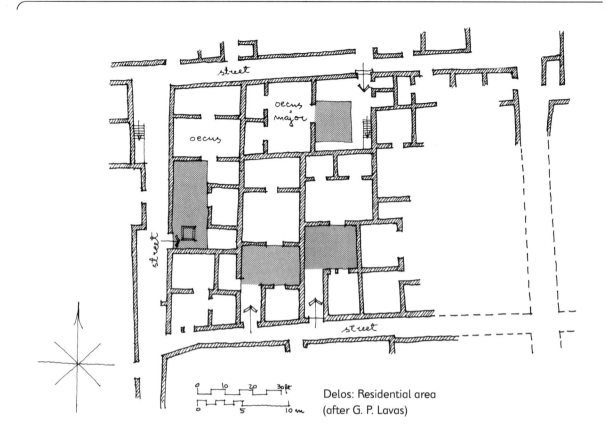

Delos: Residential area
(after G. P. Lavas)

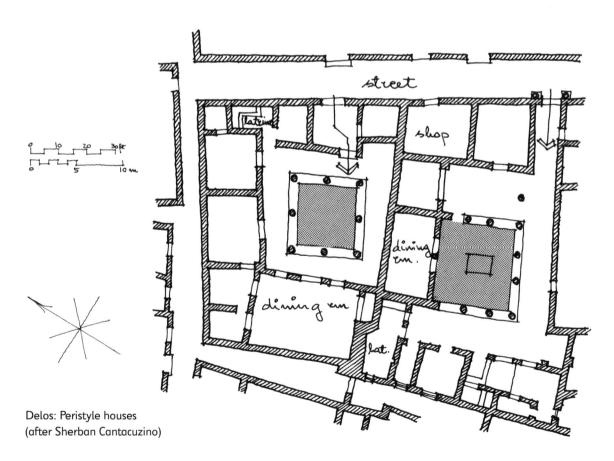

Delos: Peristyle houses
(after Sherban Cantacuzino)

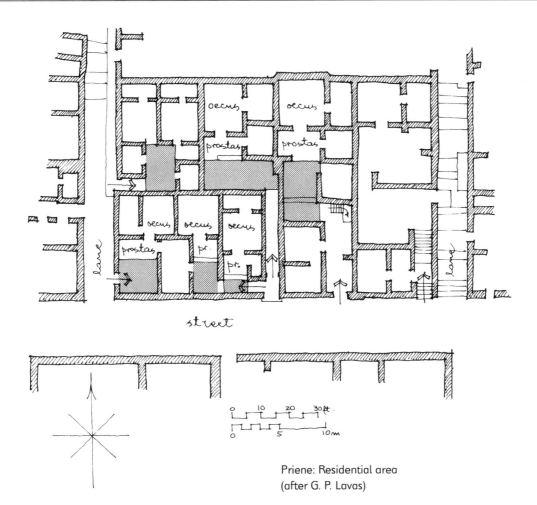

Priene: Residential area
(after G. P. Lavas)

small and simple. The house at the southwest corner had only two rooms adjacent to a court. Four of the five houses appear to have been single-story homes, while a larger home, situated at the north side of the block, had probably been a two-story structure. Here, too, the juxtaposition of very small and large houses implies that there was no separation according to income. The variety of status of the occupants is quite evident from the range of dwelling unit sizes.

Two classical examples of a medium-sized Greek peristyle court-garden house on the island of Delos illustrate the organization of dwellings at a time when the island enjoyed prosperity under Roman rule. Dating from the second or first century B.C., these dwellings were built of stone, which was abundant on the island. This durable material ensured a reasonably good preservation of building elements rarely matched in mud brick houses.

The adjoining dwellings were entered from a street on the east side of the property. The entrance passage led past a porter's lodge to a central peristyle court with inward-sloping roofs to collect rainwater, which was then stored in cisterns built in the court. Several of the rooms had mosaic floors of cut stone; in the dining rooms the pattern of the mosaic reflected the position of the couches. In each case, the dining room and most other rooms faced the court, the focal point of the house. Bathrooms were absent due to the preciousness of water, but each house had a latrine that discharged into drains under the street (Cantacuzino 1956, 20).

The street layout of Priene, which dates from the Hellenistic period, appears to have been more regular than that of Delos; however, the homes themselves were very similar. This similarity was so striking "that on seeing isolated examples [of houses] one would not be able to pinpoint their origin. In both towns the form of the house remains the same because the fundamental element, i.e., the concept of space, is common to both" (Lavas 1974, 332).

THE ROMAN ATRIUM HOUSE

The typical Roman house, the *domus*, was a composite derived from the Etruscan and Hellenistic house forms. The Etruscan dwelling prototype was characterized by an axial plan with a central hall and open skylight, which perhaps had been a smoke hole in an ancient version of the house and had eventually become a courtyard well and atrium. "The courtyard wells, exemplified at Marzabotto, would ultimately yield to the compluvium-impluvium arrangement. As cities became more populous and the pressure on building space intensified, the courtyard wells yielded to the compluvium and cistern arrangement familiar in Pompeii, Herculaneum, and Ostia at a later date" (McKay 1977, 22).

The typical Etruscan urban dwelling had the following arrangement: Facing the entrance way, or *fauces*, and across the atrium, the central courtyard, was the *tablinum*, originally perhaps the main bedroom but later a record (*tabulum*) depository and reception room. The principal space of the house was, of course, the atrium. Its far end was flanked by two *alae*, or alcoves. At the rear of the tablinum and accessible through a corridor adjacent to this reception room was an *hortulus*, an enclosed garden, no doubt affording an admirable vista along the axial sequence starting from the entrance, then through the atrium space and the tablinum, and ending in the small garden.

As a result of the Hellenistic influence, the typical Roman urban house in time became a composite of the Etruscan atrium house and the Greek peristyle house with its oriental heritage. Thus, the typical urban house that emerged during the Late Roman period had two rectangular interior court

gardens, the smaller called the atrium and the larger, the peristyle. Quite frequently it had a third outdoor space, a small rear garden. The atrium with its surrounding area formed the more public section of the house, while the peristyle section, the more secluded area, was the private or family quarters.

Viewed from the street, the Roman atrium houses seemed surprisingly small and remarkably similar. The façades were rather simple with few openings toward the narrow street and were interrupted only by recessed areas that were used for shops. Most windows opened onto the courtyards and in larger homes also onto an enclosed garden in the rear. The remains of Pompeiian houses suggest that the Roman domus was usually a one-story building.

In contrast to the exterior simplicity, the interior of the domus was sumptuous. The floors were patterned mosaic or marble, the walls were decorated with frescos, and the ceiling timbers were often gilded. In addition to the family altar in the atrium, the two courtyards were lavishly adorned by fountains, statues, vases, and other embellishments.

The main entranceway to the house had a recess, called *vestibulium*, before the fauces. The wooden front door had a particular importance. It was usually decorated, and on feast days it was carefully lit and garlanded. In fact, the doorway was a sacred object protected by four deities: Janus guarded the doorway itself; Forculus, the cornice; Limentius, the threshold; and Cordea, the hinges. The door led to the fauces, which in turn opened into the atrium. The images of the Lares, or household gods, were placed in the hallway with a lamp burning in their honor. The hallway was guarded by the porter, a slave; frequently a long chain was attached to his foot to prevent him from leaving to gossip with the neighbors.

The atrium, as mentioned earlier, served as a center for the more public functions of the home and was surrounded by small rooms and recesses. Some of these rooms, lit only from their doorways, were used as bedrooms for guests (*hospitia*), others were used by slaves (*ergastuae*). Recesses (alae)

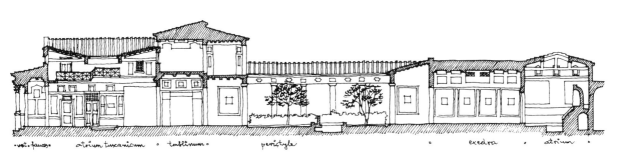

Longitudinal section

Pompeii: House of the Centenary
(after L. Chifflot as cited in H. D'Espouy)

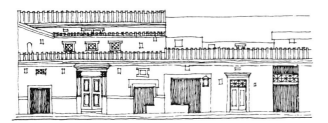

Street elevation

Pompeii: House of the Centenary
(after L. Chifflot as cited in H. D'Espouy)

were used as either reception rooms or conversation rooms. A protective roof called the *compluvium*, supported on brackets projecting from the wall, gave shelter around the periphery of the atrium and shed the rainwater toward the center into the *impluvium*, or catch basin, sunk in the pavement. In the tetrastyle atrium columns at the four corners of the courtyard supported the roof girders.

Opposite the entranceway the atrium was linked to the peristyle area by narrow passageways as well as by an open reception room (tablinum), which could be curtained off. The peristyle area was used for family activities and was usually larger than the atrium. It, too, had an impluvium for rainwater, but here the roof was supported by a colonnade. In the absence of a rear garden (and in contrast to the hard surface of the Hellenistic peristyle) the Roman peristyle often served as a garden with climbing vines and potted plants. In summer additional shade was provided by red-dyed veils called *courtinae*. The rooms surrounding the peristyle

were the bedrooms (*cubicula*), which had stone slab beds; the dining room (*triclinium*) with couches; recesses for conversation (alae); the family reception room (oecus); and the kitchen (*culina*) with its ancillary storage rooms.

Pompeii, buried in pumice stone and light ash to a depth of 10 to 23 ft (3 to 7 m) after the eruption of Vesuvius in A.D. 79, provides us with the most reliable information available on the structure of Roman residential areas as well as the form of Italic and Hellenistic-Roman urban houses. A few years before its destruction, Pompeii had suffered damage from an earthquake; hence many of the houses show traces of the renovation and enlargement made just prior to the city's demise.

Pompeii was small by modern standards like nearly all cities of antiquity. According to Hiorns (1956), the area within its walls was about 160 acres (64.6 hectares). Its population may have numbered between 25,000 and 30,000; a considerable proportion composed of leisured and cultured

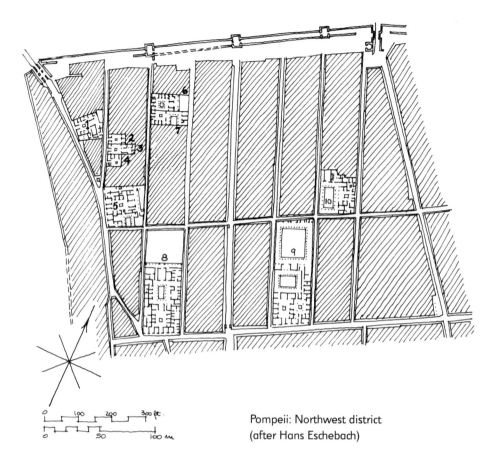

Pompeii: Northwest district
(after Hans Eschebach)

people of the patrician and middle class, including wealthy merchants.

Pompeii was a fortified city with eight gates, one of them leading to the waterfront. Its streets were well paved and were provided with raised sidewalks. Mercurio Street was the widest at 32 ft (9.7 m), and the lesser roads of the gridiron network ranged between 12 and 18 ft (3.6 and 5.5 m).

The city was a planned community with no evidence in its street layout of any improvisation. It had a copious water supply stored in tanks and water towers, and its sewage system was reasonably effective. Shops were built into the fronts of houses along the main streets and supplemented the provisions made by the residents of Pompeii in the central marketplace. Even palatial homes, such as the House of Pansa (No. 8) and the House of the Faun (No. 9), had shops and workshops built into their street façades but without communication to the interior.

The dwelling units of the sixteen-block residential area of Pompeii show a great disparity in sizes

ranging from the palatial to a tiny dwelling with a total area equal to that of the mere atrium of the largest homes. Even the smallest, unnamed dwellings appear to have atria, but have neither a peristyle court garden nor a rear hortulus. It appears that in Pompeii, too, there was a mix of income groups in a given residential quarter, especially if one takes into account that the large palatial homes had, in addition to shops, a number of cenacula built into their peripheral walls. It can also be observed that the housing plots within the city blocks were less orderly than the street layout itself, yet another characteristic of the residential quarters of oriental cities. Probably the irregular building plots evolved over time through accretion, just as in oriental cities, when a resident acquired a portion of a neighbor's property in order to enlarge his own home.

The dwellings identified on the plan of this residential quarter are, from left to right and top to bottom: No. 1, the House of the Surgeon; houses No. 2, 3, and 4; No. 5, the House of Sallust; houses No. 6

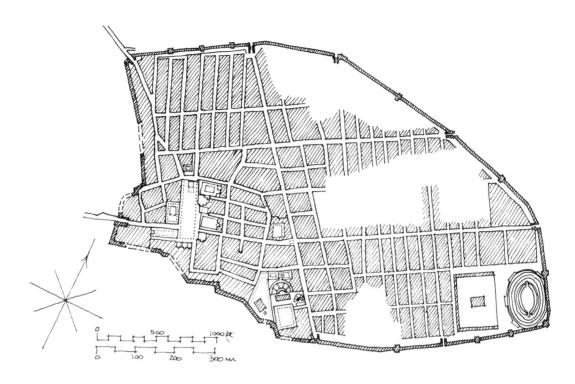

Pompeii
(after Hans Eschebach)

and 7; No. 8, the House of Pansa; No. 9, the House of the Faun; and No. 10, the House of the Vettii.

An excellent early example of an urban dwelling with an atrium but without a peristyle court is the House of the Surgeon, named for the surgical instruments found in its ruins. This dwelling dates from the fourth or third century B.C., a period when Hellenistic influences such as peristyle courtyards had not yet enriched the plan of the Roman domus. The massive walls were built of sandstone blocks and the successive courses of blocks were laid with mud. Two shops flanked the entrance along the street façade.

The House of the Surgeon was basically a cavernous and austere dwelling meagerly lit through the wood-beamed square atrium. Arranged in a traditional and axial fashion around the atrium with its catch basin were the cubicula, the alae, the triclinia, and the tablinum; the latter also opened upon a portico and a small garden beyond, a feature that no doubt made this important reception room also the brightest room of the house.

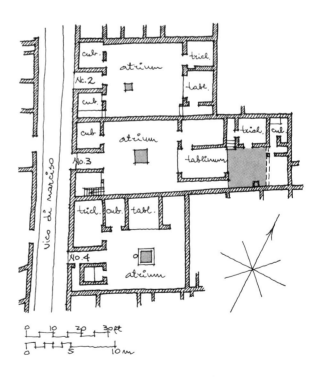

Pompeii: Houses no. 2, 3, and 4
(after Hans Eschebach)

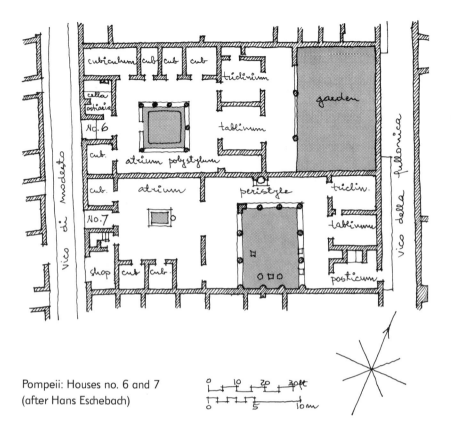

Pompeii: Houses no. 6 and 7
(after Hans Eschebach)

"Between the tablinum and impluvium in the atrium court, the architect located the traditional dining table (cartibulum), which a more prosperous age transformed into an elegant marble table with elegantly carved legs. Behind the tablinum was the walled garden and, in a corner, the shrine of the Lares (lararium), the household's protective gods" (McKay 1977, 37).

The House of Sallust is a good example of the tufa (the oldest) period, to which the Roman luxuries of a peristyle with summer triclinium and separate kitchen were later added. Several shops occupied the main street front of this house. The largest commercial establishment was a bakery (pistrinum) complete with mills, oven, and storage space as well as living accommodations on the upper story. A cook shop (thermopolium) was located adjacent to the main entrance and may have been operated by the slaves of Sallust's household.

The principal space of this dwelling was the atrium, a Tuscan hall with an impluvium in its center. Along the main axis of the atrium was a large tablinum or drawing room, which opened upon a rear portico and a *viridarium* (pleasure garden) beyond. The narrow garden contained potted plants and the rear wall was painted with trees and shrubs to give the illusion of space. A rear entrance (*posticum*) led to a secondary street.

A passage linked the atrium of the old house to the peristyle addition of the house. In this addition, a flower garden was enclosed on three sides by colonnades. Two richly ornamented bedrooms and a large summer dining room faced the garden; a staircase led to a balcony and additional rooms on the upper floor. The mural paintings in this part of the house belong to a later and less severe Roman style than those of the older part of the house (Longfellow 1895, 316).

The House of the Vettii also exemplifies a luxurious middle-class dwelling with a large peristyle courtyard addition. The house was entered through a fauces from the east and was protected by a servant whose *cella ostiaria* (doorman's room) was nearby. The atrium ensemble was unusual in this dwelling because of the absence of a tablinum. Another departure from typical dwelling layouts

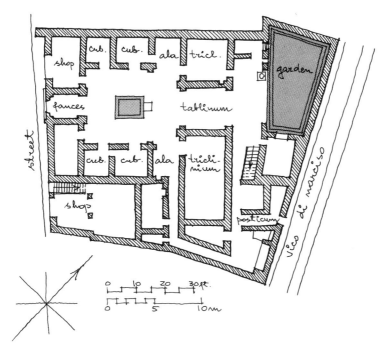

Pompeii: House of the Surgeon
(after A. G. McKay)

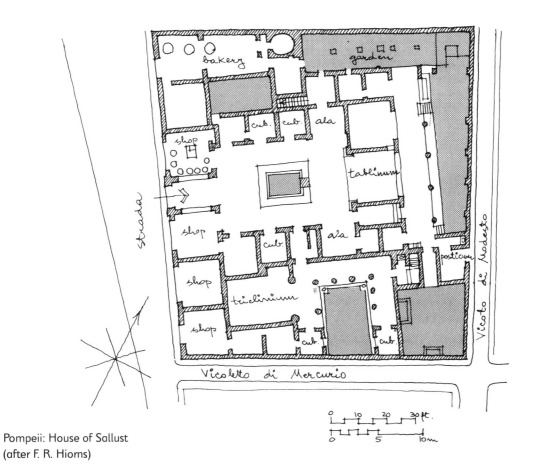

Pompeii: House of Sallust
(after F. R. Hiorns)

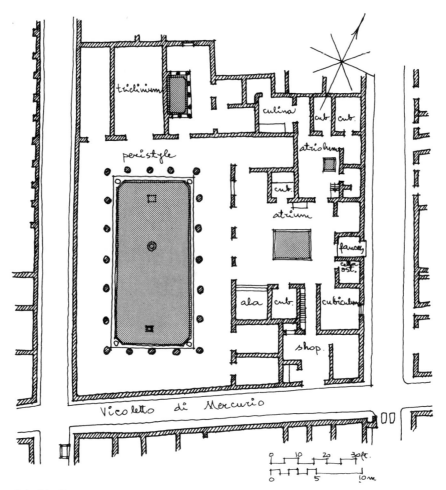

Pompeii: House of the Vettii
(after Hans Eschebach)

was the provision of a second, smaller atrium, called an *atriolum*, which was the focal point of the kitchen and servants' quarters located north of the main atrium. A beautiful lararium, or shrine, adorned one of the walls of the atriolum. A large peristyle court garden occupied the southwest corner of the property. It was directly linked with the atrium, and several large rooms opened upon it. A second smaller and more secluded peristyle court with an elegant dining room was located in the north section of the house (McKay 1977, 56–58).

Also of the tufa period is the large and stately palatial dwelling with a classical plan known as the House of Pansa. This dwelling shows additions and modifications to the original house. For example, numerous shops or tabernae were added along the front of the house, including a large bakery. Several of the shops had living accommodations

above, and therefore formed small houses in themselves. The main doorway of the house was in a small recess or vestibule and led through a corridor to a large Tuscan-type atrium with a central *piscina* (pool). Traditional rooms surrounded the atrium, and the axial tablinum together with an adjacent fauces linked the formal section of the house to the private part, which was dominated by a spacious peristyle court garden. The central piscina was surrounded by sixteen columns that supported a gallery on the second story. Bedrooms, dining rooms, and a large living room, or *exedra*, opened upon the peristyle court. Beyond the exedra was a covered walk, or *xystus*, which overlooked a garden arranged in parallel beds, probably used to grow vegetables. Several of the second-story bedrooms have survived, and many ornaments and toilet accessories used by the

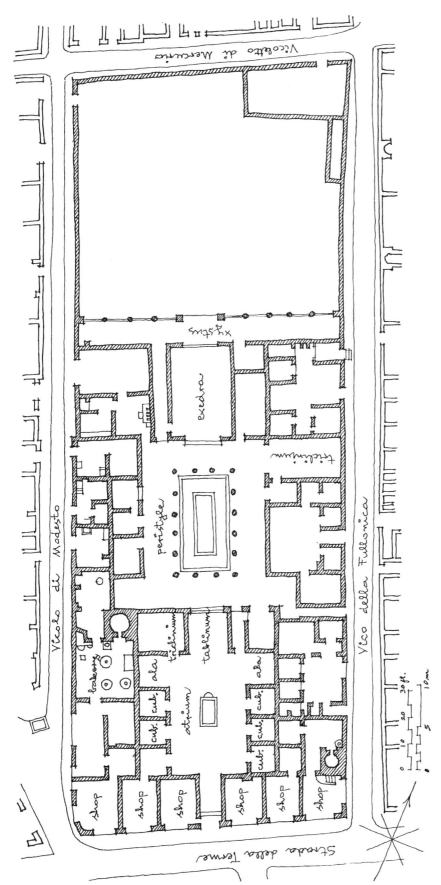

Pompeii: House of Pansa
(after A. G. McKay)

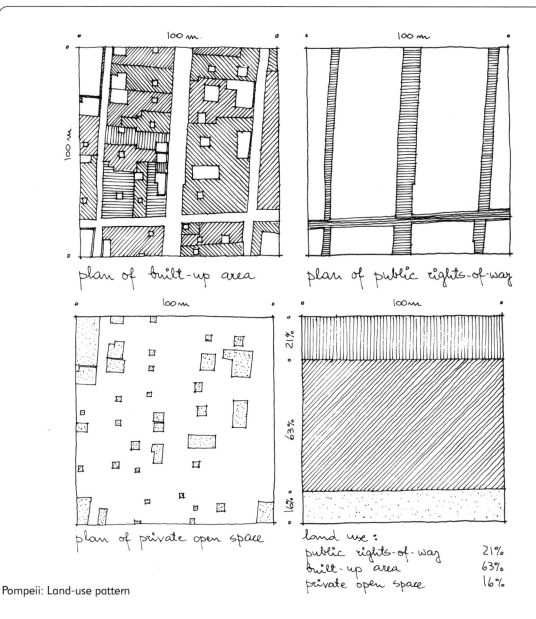

plan of built-up area

plan of public rights-of-way

plan of private open space

land use:
public rights-of-way   21%
built-up area   63%
private open space   16%

Pompeii: Land-use pattern

women of the household were found in them (Longfellow 1895, 315).

Urban houses excavated in Herculaneum and Ostia are very similar in principle to the Pompeiian dwellings, and it seems reasonable to assume that they also represent the typical Roman house in most cities of the empire including its capital, Rome. Of course, the domus, as mentioned earlier, represented only a small fraction of Rome's housing stock, since by far the most numerous dwellings were tenement flats.

An analysis of the land-use efficiency of a typical residential area in Pompeii shows that the area devoted to public rights-of-way is 21 percent. The percentage of the area occupied by buildings is 63 percent. Private court gardens represent a mere 16 percent.

It is clear from the foregoing that the Roman house is closely related to the oriental urban house in both character and design. The central courtyard, the recessed alcoves off the atrium, the centrally located large reception room, the kitchen, in some cases with its own courtyard, and the separation of the family quarters from the public area of the house are also indigenous elements of the urban house in the Orient.

THE TRADITIONAL ISLAMIC CITY AND ITS URBAN HOUSE

Alexander the Great (356–323 B.C.) invaded Asia Minor in 334, crossed the Tigris River in 331, and brought the entire twin-river valley under the sphere of Macedonian political and cultural influence. After Alexander's death and the partition of the Macedonian Empire, Seleucus, who accompanied Alexander in the Indian campaign, became first the head of the Babylonian province and later of what came to be known as the Seleucid Empire. The Hellenistic culture entered the Near East and flourished for several centuries.

Alexander founded twenty-six cities in the captured lands, and Seleucus added sixty to them. Greek urban planning principles characterized these new cities with their gridiron road pattern, agora, public baths, gymnasium, and theater. The population of these cities was predominantly Greek and enjoyed the privileges of Greek citizenship. The Hellenistic influence lasted for almost a thousand years and came to a gradual end with the rise of Islam.

The medieval Islamic concept of the city was unlike the Hellenistic concept; in fact, it was more closely related to the concept underlying the ancient cities of Mesopotamia. The Muslim conquerors gradually imposed their way of life on the Hellenistic cities, and although they retained the fortification walls of the city for defensive reasons (as exemplified by the plans of Aleppo), they changed the urban fabric within. The agora gave way to the *jami'* mosque (the religious and political center of the city), the colonnaded avenues became the *suq*, or bazaar streets; the basilica, the *qaysariyyah* (market hall) or *khan* (inn or lodging for travelers as well as a storehouse). The baths naturally remained as public baths, or *hammams*, but the gymnasium and theater had no useful purpose for the conquerors since the social and educational aspects of their societies were centered in the mosque. These adaptive changes were relatively minor compared to changes that took place in the street network; in time, the gridiron street pattern was gradually eradicated as new buildings replaced the old in a more oriental and less rigid urban pattern. An unquestionably central part of

Arab Empire, A.D. 750 (A.D. 632–1258)

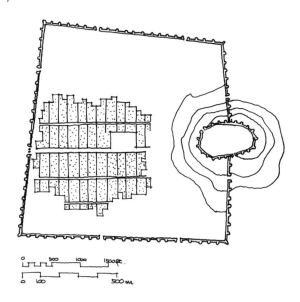

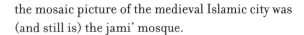

Aleppo, 333 B.C.– A.D. 286
(after Jean Sauvaget)

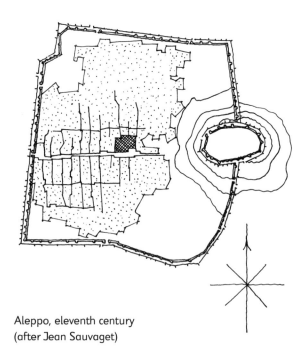

Aleppo, eleventh century
(after Jean Sauvaget)

the mosaic picture of the medieval Islamic city was (and still is) the jami' mosque.

In medieval Islam, religion, law, education, and government were so integrated that an orthodox Muslim would hardly try to distinguish them as separate entities. Therefore, the classic jami' mosque was to function as a religious entity, a court of justice, and an intellectual and educational center. It was also a place of secular activity, such as eating and drinking, as well as providing recreation for many people (Ismail 1972, 117).

As it was the hub of the city, the jami' mosque usually was located at the intersection of two major traffic arteries. However, this strategic location was not exploited in a monumental treatment of the mosque's street façades except for the entrance portal. In fact, the jami' mosque was hidden by many buildings and narrow streets, and its rich internal architectural form was only betrayed from the outside by distant views of its dome and minarets. "The minaret was the tallest structure in the city. It marked the skyline of the early urban scene. As the cities expanded and the need for public services multiplied accordingly, most of the jami' mosque's functions were transferred to other departmentalized buildings converted to such

usages, but always in close proximity to the mosque" (Ismail 1972, 117).

Such functions were assigned to the *madrasah* and the hammam. The madrasah was a school of legal and moral teachings based on the Koran and the sayings of the Prophet of Islam; it also served as a dwelling for the resident teachers and their outstanding students. The hammam was primarily a public bath, for the rich and the poor, and was also important in the ritual of ablution; it was a social institution for informal business conversation and social contact between members of different residential precincts.

The commercial hub of the city and surrounding rural area was the suq (bazaar) and the *maydan* (open market). Because of their importance in the economic integration of the city with the surrounding countryside, they were supervised by a public official called a *hisbah*. The main duties of this market supervisor were to ensure fair dealings in business transactions, the maintenance of proper physical facilities, and the implementation of building control regulations. "He helped to settle commercial or business disputes and supervised the standardization of weights and measures. Along with the judiciary and the city police, it was one of the most important administrative offices.

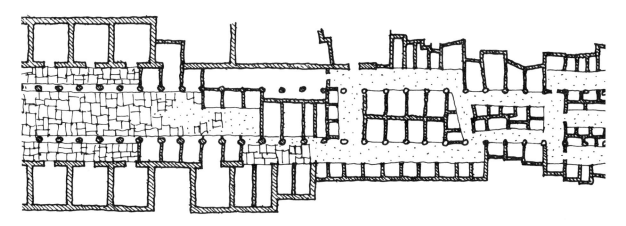

Transformation of a classical colonnaded avenue to an Islamic bazaar street
(after Jean Sauvaget)

These all helped to regulate the economic and social life of the inner city" (Hassan 1972, 111).

The traditional suq was a maze of narrow shopping lanes often covered and usually in the vicinity of the jami' mosque. It contained not only stores but also a number of workshops. In a typical guild-like fashion, related activities were grouped together and the location of these various activities relative to the mosque followed a certain predetermined pattern. Accordingly, closest to the mosque were the vendors of clean and valuable goods as well as those selling candles, incense, oils and essences; booksellers and bookbinders were also in this area. Usually at a right angle to a main street, in close proximity (but not abutting the mosque proper), was the qaysariyyah, a large hall where jewelry, gold, and precious stones as well as fine textiles and expensive imported goods were sold. Adjacent to the qaysariyyah were the coffee shops and food vendors, followed by the tailors and cobblers and, beyond them, the metal workers. At the greatest distance from the mosque were located the potters, tanners, and dyers.

Also part of the suq precinct were the khans, the caravansarai-like storehouses with lodgings in the upper levels for merchants. Khans were also located near the city gates, and access to them was controlled by gatekeepers.

In contrast to the suq, the maydan, the open market, was also a formal square. It was frequently

Hellenistic street network in Old Damascus
(after Jean Sauvaget)

used for public events. Other public institutions were the *maristans*, or hospitals; these public health centers amazed the crusaders, who had not seen their like before.

With the exception of the suq, all public institutions followed a design concept based on the utilization of central open courts. Thus the mosques,

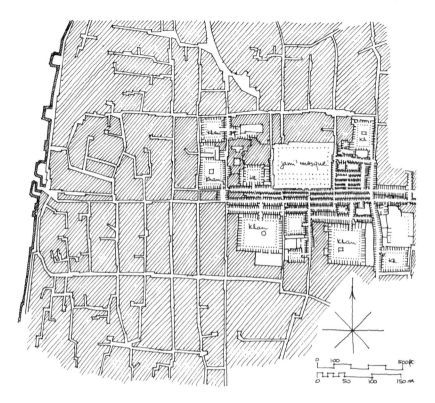

Aleppo: Nineteenth-century town center
(after Jean Sauvaget)

madrasahs, hammams, maristans, khans, and qaysariyyahs were all inward-looking buildings facing at least one courtyard. In this they were akin to the oriental urban house.

Islamic cities were well ordered, and their urban spaces and facilities followed a hierarchical pattern that in its sophistication surpassed that of their counterparts, the occidental medieval cities. Islamic citizens also possessed a broader view than the burghers of occidental cities. An Islamic city dweller did not see himself primarily as a citizen of a particular city nor as a citizen of a nation in the occidental sense; rather he felt himself to be a member of the 'ummah, or "great-community," established by the Prophet, which knew no geographic bounds. This broader viewpoint is also reflected in the Islamic trade guilds. The guilds played a role in the organization of occupational activities similar to that of the occidental guilds in that they provided training and capital for their members as well as regulating and protecting their craft, but unlike their occidental counterparts,

which were closed institutions, the Islamic trade guild did not exclude non-Muslims.

The occupants of Islamic cities adhered to the ancient concept of closed precinct neighborhoods, which was probably rooted in the tribal tradition of solidarity and proximity. The checkerboard city blocks and the open-ended urban system left by the Greek conquerors could not be adapted to this basic residential requirement, for it was antithetical to the traditional cluster concept.

In time, the cities' residential sectors were altered into precincts called *mahalahs*, each composed of a closely knit and homogeneous community with its own intrinsic physical character. The *assabiyyats*, or "solidarities," such as ethnic groups, sectarian religious affiliations, occupational groups, and multiracial groups unified by association with a particular sheikh or madrasah, inhabited specific mahalahs. In fact, non-Muslim citizens, namely Christians, Jews, and Maronites, also had their own mahalahs.

Although not quite analogous, a similarity does

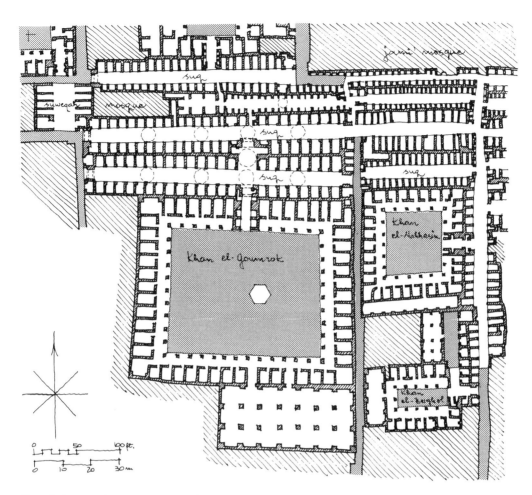

Aleppo: Part of nineteenth-century town center
(after Jean Sauvaget)

exist between the "natural areas" of North American cities, as defined by sociologists, and the mahalahs; both performed similar important functions in the areas of social control, socialization, and mutual assistance when required by their residents. Hence, mahalahs were secure shelters for newcomers to the city who shared affinities with the respective residents. However, in one important respect mahalahs differed from their American counterparts: they were communities for both rich and poor. Important administrative responsibilities devolved upon the residents of the mahalah, including that of policing. The natural formation of the community, accessible only by means of one or two gates, provided the populace security during revolts, civil wars, and enemy invasions as well as during the dreaded onslaught of pestilence. A continued isolation was possible when necessary in the case of larger mahalahs, which were self-sufficient neighborhoods and quasi-cities. They had their own mosque, madrasah, hammam, *suweqah* (small suq), and many workshops—all local community facilities serving the mahalah residents only. While all mahalahs were supervised, under normal circumstances they were not restricted to their own residents only. In their totality they formed a mosaic-like city.

As the jami' mosque was the focal point of the Islamic urban community, so the *sakan* or *maskan*, the Arab words for house, was the center of the basic social unit, the family. The word sakan is "related to the word *sakinah* meaning peaceful and tranquillity. The inward-looking sakan, open to

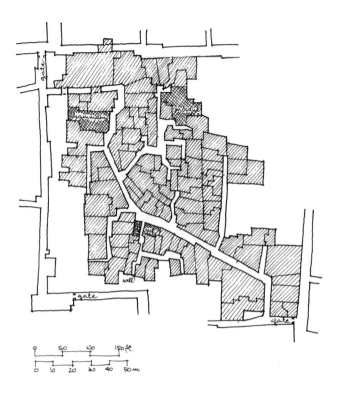

Mahalah in Damascus
(after Jean Sauvaget)

the calm of the sky, made cool by the element of water, self-contained and peaceful, the deliberate antithesis of the harsh public world of work, warfare and commerce, is the place where the early Arab family found its *sakinah*" (Ismail 1972, 115).

The medieval Islamic urban house had its roots in the ancient urban dwellings of Mesopotamia. There was indeed an affinity between the ancient and Islamic concepts of the urban house. Both cultures believed in maximum privacy, in protection from strangers, and in the humble appearance of the exterior of the home; moreover, climatic conditions being virtually the same throughout the world of Islam, they elicited similar physical responses in dwellings. These conditions were best met by the courtyard concept. Of course, in many respects the Islamic house is more sophisticated than its precursor.

To enhance the privacy and security of the family, the Islamic urban house (as indeed was the case with most large rural homes) was frequently divided into two sections: the *salamlik* and the *haramlik*. The former served as the public part of the house, where male visitors and friends were received, while the latter was a private and secluded sanctuary reserved for the family. In larger homes these two parts were separate and their respective rooms grouped around their own separate courtyards. In smaller houses the separation was vertical, the salamlik occupying the ground floor and the haramlik the upper level of the house around a single courtyard. Here, too, considerations of privacy governed the design of the entrance, which was protected by a privacy wall to inhibit a direct view from the street. In addition, the whole disposition of the house was designed to preclude the possible visual intrusion by neighbors or strangers. When window openings were placed in the haramlik either facing the street or central open space, trellised bay windows, or *mashrabiyyahs*, protected them. These trellised apertures enabled the occupants of the haramlik to satisfy their curiosity about the outside world without being seen.

The Islamic ideology initially encouraged the use of insubstantial building materials to accentuate

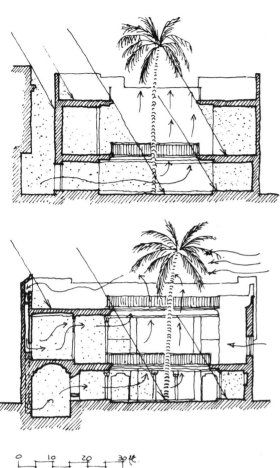

Climate control in Islamic dwellings

court), verandahs, and galleries, were oriented to take advantage of climatic realities. *Malqafs*, or wind traps, equipped with cooling jars and linked to a vertical air duct, brought fresh and humidified air into the dwelling and helped in general to create better air circulation in the house. A disproportionately high ceiling in the living rooms enhanced air circulation. By sitting at floor level the occupants enjoyed the coolest indoor environment. The trellised mashrabiyyahs eliminated glare and provided a pleasant level of illumination to the interior. Finally, the Islamic urban houses were grouped closely together; thus a minimum surface was exposed to the merciless hot sun.

THE AL-FUSTAT HOUSE AND THE NORTH AFRICAN DAR

The Muslims began their conquest of Egypt in A.D. 639 when an army, under the command of Amr ibn-al-As, was sent by the second caliph, Omar I, against Egypt. Only two years later, and after his return from the siege of Alexandria, Amr founded the first Islamic city of Egypt, which he called al-Fustat. Named after the camp (fossatum) occupied by Amr while besieging Babylon (a Roman-Byzantine city that was located near the site of today's Old Cairo), al-Fustat soon became an important trade center. It flourished until the great famine and the epidemic that followed it in A.D. 1054. Subsequently, the city was abandoned and its ruins served for many years as a convenient quarry of building materials for the construction of Cairo.

The typical al-Fustat house had one or two central courtyards, each with a basin in its center. Symmetrically and axially planned, triple-arched *iwanat* (porticos) surrounded the court on one or several sides; the central arch of these iwanat was twice as wide as the two side arches. In keeping with Islamic custom, larger homes were divided into two quarters, namely, a salamlik, or public sector, and a *harem*, the private or family sector of the house, each surrounding a court garden.

the humbleness of the dwelling. Houses preferably were not to exceed two stories, for luxurious and multistoried buildings were symbols of pride and arrogance and represented homage to material things. Although in later periods these values were not strictly adhered to, the exterior façade of the dwellings remained relatively simple and plain in contrast to the richness of the interior.

The medieval urban house of Islamic cities was designed to create favorable microclimatic conditions in its interior. Water fountains, basins, and *salsabils* (fountains in which water tumbled over a ridged surface into a pool and through evaporation cooled and humidified the air) as well as planted or potted trees created a cool ambience in the courtyard in sharp contrast to the aridity and heat of the street outside. Semiopen spaces, such as *iwanat* (recessed porticos with open arches facing the

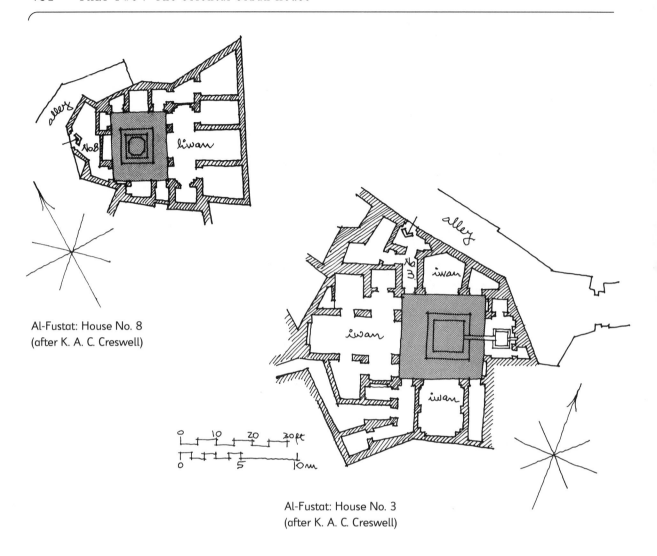

Al-Fustat: House No. 8
(after K. A. C. Creswell)

Al-Fustat: House No. 3
(after K. A. C. Creswell)

House No. 8 was a relatively small dwelling and thus had only one court garden. A privacy wall blocked the view from the street into the interior, and a bent corridor linked the entrance hall to the court. The principal suite of living spaces, namely, the T-shaped and triple-arched iwan group with a transverse portico, opened toward the court. In the middle of the courtyard was a water basin, square above and octagonal below, with water supplied from a cistern. Although the plot of this house was very irregular, the interior, which had an axial layout, appeared symmetrical and rectangular.

House No. 3 was a larger single court-garden dwelling. The street entrance door faced a spirit wall and a short corridor linked the vestibule with the court. The west side contained the typical T-shaped iwan group, and just south of this suite was a bent corridor, which most likely led to a side

entrance. Simple iwanat were located on the north as well as on the south side of the court garden, while an alcove with a basin and a salsabil occupied the east side. Once again, an irregular building site was occupied by a building whose design was rather formal and symmetrical.

House No. 2 was still larger and virtually consisted of two separate houses joined by a narrow passageway. The south and main entrance to the formal section of the house had no privacy wall; the elongated vestibule gave access directly to the transverse portico of the main iwan group, facing the court garden with its typical basin. On the east and west side of the square court were two large reception rooms, each triple arched.

A narrow passageway on the far west side of the court led to the harem, which was raised three steps above the level of the formal house; through a

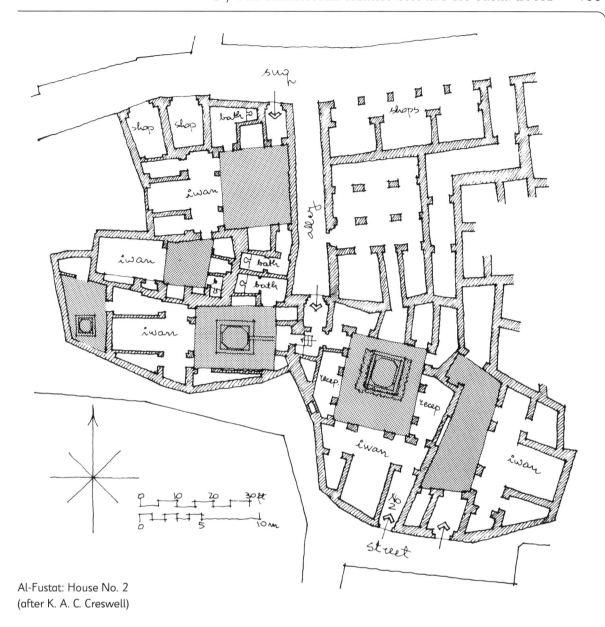

Al-Fustat: House No. 2
(after K. A. C. Creswell)

vestibule this passageway also led to a second street entrance off a narrow blind alley that was connected to a bazaar street. This second and hidden entrance (*bab assir*) was probably used by the women and children of the household.

The harem section had a smaller court garden with the triple-arched iwan group at its west side; an additional small court or pleasure garden was hidden behind the iwan. A bathroom was located on the north side of the court garden.

The neighboring house, immediately north of house No. 2, was a medium-sized home with its entrance from the bazaar street. Perhaps it was a shopkeeper's dwelling. Although more modest than its neighbor, this home also had two court gardens and had both formal and family living areas, in accord with the tenets of Islam.

The dating of these al-Fustat houses is uncertain, but most likely they were built around the tenth or eleventh century. The tripartite façades of the iwan group are "similar to the Abbasid *bayts* at Ukhaidir and Samarra and were probably introduced into Egypt under the Tulunids" (Hoag 1977, 150).

In 640, under the command of Abdallah ben Said, the successor to Amr, the founder of al-Fustat, the Arab conquerors of Egypt continued the expansion of the realm of Islam beyond Egypt. By

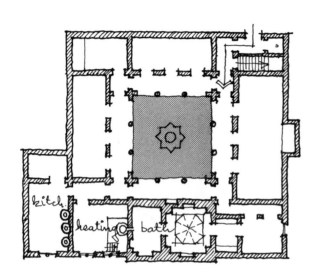

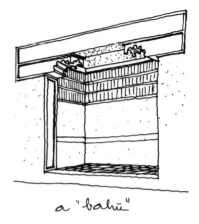

a "bahū"

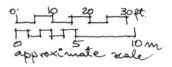

Moorish dar
(after Jean Galotti)

670 they controlled the north coast of Africa, including Tunisia, Algeria, and Morocco. The Arabs called this conquered territory Maghreb, the West. Aided by the Berbers, they launched their invasion of Spain from Maghreb in 671.

The oriental courtyard concept of urban housing followed the path of the conquerors and has survived to the present day as the prototypical urban dwelling of this region. Of course, the Romans, who had occupied the territory prior to the Arabs, also lived in courtyard houses, but, as we saw in chapter 2, the domus too was a concept influenced by the Orient.

It is likely that the *dar*, the North African urban house of the medieval period, did not look very different from today's traditional urban dwelling of the region. The dar in its simplest form is a rectangular or square dwelling with an open court, called *wast-eddar*, in its center. Facing three or four sides of the open court are the main rooms, each with a central doorway, which also allows light to penetrate. These rooms are long and narrow, and their width seldom exceeds 10 ft (3 m); this narrow dimension is dictated by the length of the beams available in a region where wood is a scarce com-

modity. The disproportionate narrowness of the room is usually offset by the provision of a wide bay called a *bahū* in the wall opposite the entrance, as well as by the fact that built-in cabinets occupy both ends of the room; in this way, the room plan takes on a T-shape.

One of the corners of the property contains the entrance hall, which is invariably shaped in such a way as to impede a view of the interior of the dar from the street even when the door is open. Secondary spaces, such as the staircase leading to the upper floor or roof, a kitchen, bathrooms, and toilets, may occupy the other corners of the dar.

The dar frequently has some living accommodation on a second story, but in the more elaborate dwellings it has two complete stories with a gallery built along all four sides of the courtyard. The upstairs rooms are lit by windows or doors opening onto the gallery. External windows are only provided where they cannot overlook a neighboring court or terrace.

The plan of the dar may vary in detail, but its basic characteristics are always the same. Thus, for example, one would never encounter a polygonal, circular, or triangular courtyard. Nor would one

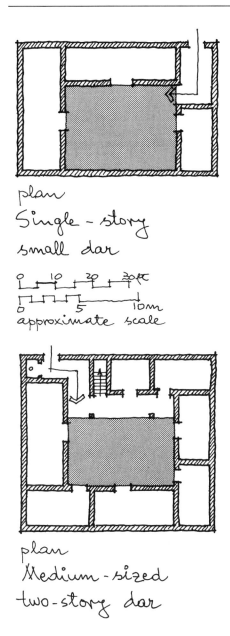

Moorish dars
(after Jean Galotti)

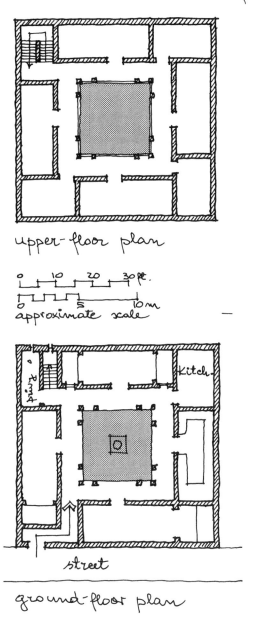

Two-story dar
(after Jean Galotti)

find a doorway which did not (in the best Muslim tradition) completely guard the privacy of the family from the prying eyes of strangers. The dar isolates its inhabitants from the outside world. Not only are they sheltered from the public, but also from extreme climatic conditions—the pitiless sun and the grinding sandstorms.

There is marked contrast between the blinding whiteness, nakedness, and heat of the outside and the intimate narrowness, deep shade, and coolness of the dar's interior.

Two adjacent dars are occasionally joined to form a single dwelling when a well-to-do Moroccan family purchases a neighboring property and connects them with a passageway. In such an instance, one of the dars becomes the private and informal domain of the family and the other becomes the reception or formal area of the household (Schoenauer and Seeman 1962, 25–29).

The similarity of the two-story dar and the typical Sumerian urban house is almost uncanny; moreover, the dar is also very similar to the Judean

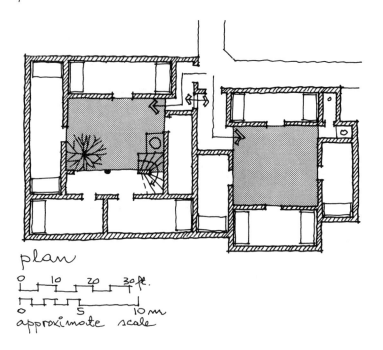

plan

Moorish connected dars
(after Jean Galotti)

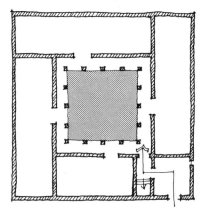

A typical dar
(after Thomas Shaw)

urban house of biblical times. It is very likely that the dar retained its basic form throughout the centuries and thus gives us a glimpse of the nature and form of the medieval Islamic house of the African continent. If we read its description by an English scholar who traveled two and a half centuries ago in North Africa, the dar does not appear to have changed very much since then.

In the early seventeen hundreds, Thomas Shaw, a fellow of Queen's College in Oxford, traveled extensively in the Islamic countries on the north coast of Africa as well as in the Levant, and he recorded his observations in a book published in 1738. Shaw was surprised to discover that Muslim dwellings had many similarities to descriptions of dwellings familiar to him from the Bible. He devoted several paragraphs to a vivid description of the typical contemporary Muslim house; it warrants extensive quotation.

But the Art, wherein the Moors (especially) are the most conversant, is Architecture: though, as Room and Convenience are the only Points regarded in their Plans, the Mallums (as they call those persons who are skilled in the designing and executing of them) are to be considered rather as Masters of a Craft or Trade, than of a Science or Liberal Profession. However, as there is a near Relation betwixt the Buildings of this Country and those that are occasionally mentioned in the H. Scriptures, it may be presumed, that a particular Account of the Structure and Contrivance of the one, will not little contribute to the clearing up such Doubts and Difficulties as have arisen, from not rightly comprehending the Fashion of the other.

Now the Method of building, both in Barbary and the Levant, seems to have continued the same, from the earliest Ages, without the least Alteration or Improvement. Large Doors, spacious Chambers, Marble Pavements, cloystered Courts, with Fountains sometimes playing in the Midst, are certainly Conveniences very well adapted to the Circumstances of these Climates, where the Summer Heats are generally so intense. Add to this, that the Jealousie, which is commonly to be met with in Masters of Families, is hereby less apt to be alarmed, whilst all the Windows open into private Courts, if we except sometimes a latticed Window or Balcony towards the Street. It is during the Celebration only of some Zeenah or publick Festival, that these Houses and their latticed Windows and Balconies are left open. For this being a Time of great Liberty, Revelling and Extravagance, each

Courtyard elevation of a dar
(after Thomas Shaw)

Tunis: Residential street
(after Jacques Revault)

Family is ambitious of adorning both the inside and the outside of their Houses with the richest Part of their Furniture: whilst Crowds of both Sexes, dressed out in their best Apparel and laying aside all Modesty, Ceremony and Restraint, go in and out where they please. . . .

If we quit then the Streets of these Cities (which are usually narrow, with sometimes a Range of Shops on each Side), and enter into any of the principal Houses, we shall first pass through a Porch or Gate-Way, with Benches on each Side, where the Master of the Family receiveth Visits and dispatcheth His Business; few Persons, not even the nearest Relations, having Admission any further, except upon extraordinary Occasions. From hence we are received into the Court, which lying open to the Weather, is, according to the Ability of the Owner, paved with Marble or such proper Materials, as will immediately cary off the Water. There is something very analagous betwixt This open Space in the Moorish Buildings, and the Impluvium or Cava Aedium of the Roman Architecture; both of Them being alike exposed to the Weather and giving Light to the House. When much People are to be admitted, as upon the Celebration of a Marriage, the Circumcising of a Child or Occasions of the like Nature, the

Company is rarely or never received into one of the Chambers, but into the Court, which is strewed accordingly with Mats and Carpets for their more commodious Entertainment. Now as this Part of the House is always allotted for the Reception of large Companies, being also called (El Woost) The Middle of the House, and so far litterally answering to the tò mesou of St. Luke, it is probable that the Place, where our Savior and the Apostles were frequently accustomed to give their Instructions, might have been in the like Situation.

It is usual in the Summer Season, and upon all Occasions, when a large Company is to be received, to have the Court sheltered from the Heat or Inclemency of the Weather, by a Velum, Umbrella or Veil, as I shall call It, which being expanded upon Ropes from one Side of the Parapet Wall to the other, may be folded or unfolded at Pleasure. The Psalmist seems to allude to some Covering of this Kind in that beautiful Expression, of spreading out the Heavens like a Curtain.

The court is for the most Part surrounded with a Cloyster; as the Cava Aedium of the Romans was with a Peristylium or Colonnade; over which, when the House hath one or more Stories, (and I have seen Them with two or three) there is a Gallery erected, of the same Dimensions with the Cloyster, having a Ballustrade, or else a Piece of carved or latticed Work going round about It. From the Cloyster or Gallery, we are conducted into a large spacious Chambers, of the same Length with the Court, but seldom or never communicating with one another. One of them frequently serveth a whole Family, particularly when a Father indulgeth his married Children to live with him; or when several Persons joyn in the Rent of one House. From whence it is, that the Cities of these Countries are so exceedingly populous, and that such Numbers of People are always swept away by the Plague. . . .

In House of better Fashion, these Chambers are hung with Velvet or Damask from the Middle of the Wall downwards: the rest is adorned with the most ingenious Wreathings and Devices in Stucco and Fret-Work. The Cieling is generally of Wainscott, either very artfully painted, or else thrown into a Variety of Pannels, with gilded Mouldings and Scrolls of their Coran intermixed. The Prophet Jeremiah 22.14. exclaimeth against some of the Eastern Houses that were cieled with Cedar, and painted with Vermilion. The floors are laid with painted Tiles or Plaister of Terrace; but the Eastern Nations making no use of Chairs (either sitting cross-legged. or lying at length upon these Floors), they have them constantly spread over with Carpets, which sometimes are most beautifully designed, and of the richest Materials. For their further Ease likewise and Convenience, there is a Row of Damask or Velvet Bolsters, ranged along each Side of the Floor; an Indulgence that seems to be alluded to by the sowing of Pillows to Armholes, as we have It expressed by the Prophet Ezekiel (13.18. and 20). At one End of each Chamber, there is a little Gallery, raised four or five Foot above the Floor, with a Ballustrade in the Front of It. Here They place their Beds; a Situation frequently alluded to in the H. Scriptures.

The Stairs are sometimes placed in the Porch, sometimes at the Entrance into the Court. When there is one or more Stories, they are afterwards continued, through one Corner or other of the Gallery to the Top of the House, whither they conduct us through a Door, that is constantly kept shut to prevent the domestick Animals from spoiling the Terrace, and thereby the Water which falls from thence into the Cisterns below the Court. This Door, like most others we meet with in these Countries, is hung, not with Hinges, but by having the Jamb formed at each End into a Axle Tree or Pivot; whereof the uppermost, which is the longest, is to be received into a correspondent Socket in the Lintel, whilst the other falls into a Cavity of the like Fashion in the Threshold. . . .

I do not remember ever to have observed the Stair-Case conducted along the outside of the House; neither indeed will the Contiguity and Relation, which the Houses bear to the Street, and to each other (exclusive of the supposed Privacy of Them), admit of any such Contrivance. However we may go up or come down them, by the Stair-Case I have described, without entering into any of the Offices or Apartments, and consequently without interfering with the Business of the House. . . .

The Top of the House, which is always flat, is covered with a strong Plaister of Terrace; from whence, in the Frank Language, It hath attained the Name of The Terrace; a Word made use of likewise in several Parts of these Countries. It is surrounded by two Walls; the outermost whereof is partly built over the Street, partly maketh the Partition with the contiguous Terraces, being frequently so low that one may easily climb over It. The other, or the Parapet Wall, as we may call It, hangeth immediately over the Court, being always Breast high. . . . Instead of this Parapet Wall, some Terraces are guarded. in the same manner the Galleries are, with Ballustrades only or Latticed-Work. . . . Upon these Terraces, several Offices of the Family are performed; such as the drying of Linnen; preparing of Figs and Raisins; where likewise they enjoy the cool refreshing Breezes of the Evening; converse with one another and offer up their Devotions. When one of these Cities is built upon a Plat of level Ground, we can pass from one End of It to another, along the Tops of the Houses, without coming down into the Street (Shaw 1738, 273–77).

Many dars dating from the eighteenth century, and perhaps from the time when Thomas Shaw traveled in North Africa, have survived in the Medina section of Tunis. A typical example of a "bourgeois" residence of this period was Dar Sfar, a commodious house bearing not only similarities to houses described by Shaw, but also many char-

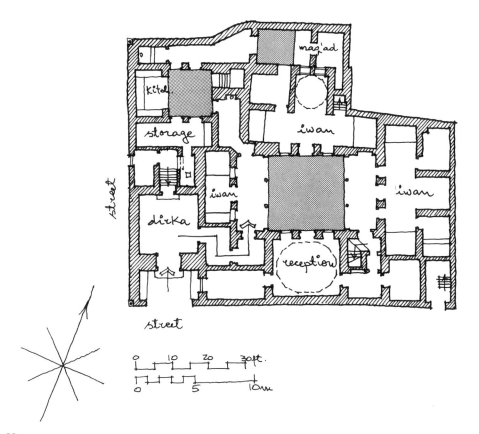

Tunis: Dar Sfar
(after Jacques Revault)

acteristics of Islamic domestic architecture that are almost identical with al-Fustat residences. Certainly, three of the four iwanat surrounding the central courtyard had a remarkable similarity to the iwanat of the large al-Fustat house. The fourth iwan had been modernized and its form is attributed to European influences. As well as the central court, Dar Sfar had two additional small courts, one a service court adjacent to the kitchen and the other a pleasure court garden facing the *maq'ad* (open loggia) of the main traditional iwan. This iwan was used most frequently by the master and the mistress of the house as their day-to-day living quarters, while the large modernized iwan was used exclusively for receptions. The small iwan adjacent to the entrance hall was only used by the mistress of the house to receive her parents and close relatives.

An analysis of the land-use pattern of the residential areas of the Medina in Tunis reveals that the homes and the courtyards are larger than those of Pompeii. Since larger homes require inherently less area for streets, the land-use diagram shows less area devoted for public rights-of-way, i.e., 9 percent; the built-up area represents 74 percent and private open spaces 17 percent.

In 1923, the French colonial authorities of Casablanca built a new medina, El-Habous, to provide decent dwellings for families living in squatter settlements or *bidonvilles*. Typically, these makeshift settlement dwellings were constructed primarily of discarded waste materials. Since bidonvilles lacked basic municipal infrastructures, they represented a health threat for the whole community.

Designed by the distinguished Ecole des Beaux Arts–trained French architect-planner Albert Laprade, the new medina reflected the time-honored local traditions of the country in the design of residential buildings as well as of public baths, mosques, and schools. Similarly, in 1948, a housing development for the rapidly increasing

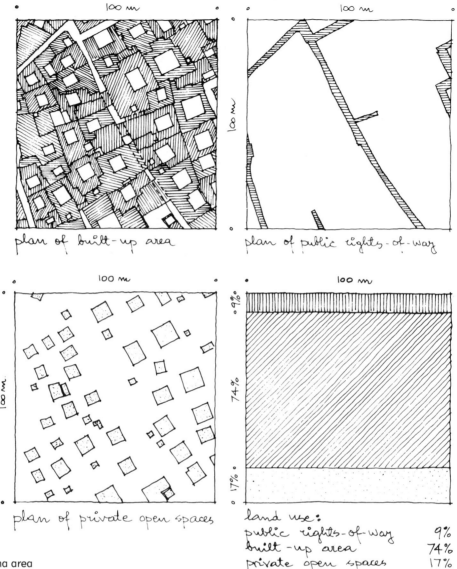

plan of built-up area

plan of public rights-of-way

plan of private open spaces

land use:
public rights-of-way   9%
built-up area   74%
private open spaces   17%

Tunis: Medina area

Tunisian population was designed by B. H. Zehr-fuss, J. Drieu, and J. Kyriakopoulos, where all elements of traditional North African court dwellings were retained. The same year, G. Glorieux and L. Glorieux-Monfred built the Cité Musulmane el Omrane, which comprised about one hundred single-story courtyard houses sited on a slope facing the Gulf of Tunis. Both these developments used attached, whitewashed vaulted houses without fenestration towards the street and with a spirit wall blocking a view to the courtyard when the front door was opened.

Of course, housing built for Europeans in Morocco and Tunisia conformed to European stan-dards. This resulted in a contrasting juxtaposition of two distinct urban environments in close proximity: the Old Medina with its mazelike narrow alleys, and the European district of Tunis with its commercial Avenues de France and Habib Bourguiba, both wide thoroughfares with a central promenade.

The population growth of North African cities exceeded the supply of adequate housing by colonial authorities. By the fifties, traditional design was compromised in new construction to speed up access to wholesome housing for bidonville residents. When Le Corbusier's former followers Georges Candilis, Shadrach Woods, and Vladimir

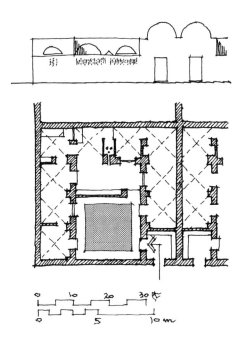

Court house development (1948), Tunis,
B. H. Zehrfuss, et. al.

older members of the extended family to climb, but also because the shared space was not easy to clean. Other criticisms concerned the upkeep of common corridors, the limited storage area allocated to each family, and the prohibition on keeping domestic animals. Cooking and heating with charcoal was also forbidden. Finally, the possibility of expanding the dwelling was curtailed with the sole exception of converting the balcony into an additional living space.

THE URBAN HOUSE OF CAIRO

Bodiansky began working (1951–55) for the African office of ATBAT (Atelier des Bâtisseurs) in Casablanca, a new rational design for three- to five-story apartment buildings was introduced. Each dwelling now had access to a two-story balcony, called a "suspended courtyard," a design concession not only to local domestic lifestyles, but also reminiscent of Le Corbusier's 1922 project, where each dwelling of Immeubles-Villas had access to a *terrasse-jardin*.

After the establishment of the French Moroccan Building Association (FMBA), multiple buildings that denied cultural design concessions were built. This approach was compared to the design of machines that are both international and universal. FMBA erected several five- to seven-story tenements for Casablanca's bidonville residents at several locations including Carrières Centrales, the site of the first squatter settlement. Although these buildings were economical and well-constructed, they were nevertheless disliked by their tenants, who were used to having a private street entrance to their dwelling. They also disliked the large windows which deprived them of privacy, and the staircase because it was not only difficult for

When the Fatimids, the Shiite Muslims, conquered Egypt during the reign of the Caliph al-Muizz, the foundations were laid in 969 for a new Islamic city called al-Qahira, or The Triumphant. Al-Qahira occupied a site northeast of the old town site of a Roman-Byzantine city called Babylon, which was captured and destroyed by Amr ibn-al-As, the founder of al-Fustat, during the seventh century.

The new city of al-Qahira, now known as Cairo, became a typical fortified medieval Islamic city adhering to the principles of Muslim urban planning. A major north-south street formed its spine and linked two important city gates, the Bab al-Futuh and Bab Zuwayla; part of this street still exists and is now called Sharia al-Muizz. On both sides of this main artery a palace was built with a large square separating the eastern and western buildings comprising the palace compound. Just south of the eastern palace stood the Mosque of al-Azhar. In contrast to the formality of the spine, the residential quarters, the major part of any city, had an informal and oriental character in keeping with the traditions of Islam, and so their houses, the dars, were inward-looking dwellings with a central courtyard. Small and large dwellings were intermingled, forming cohesive mahalahs (neighborhoods).

After 1250 the Mamluk sultans ruled Egypt until they in turn were ousted by their own countrymen,

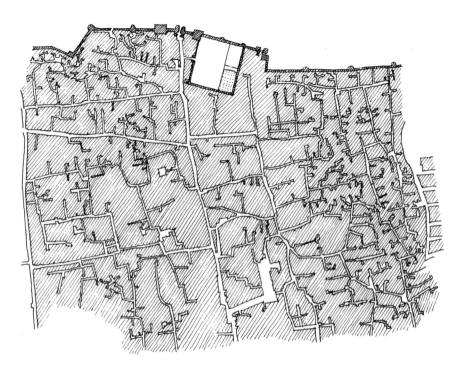

Old Cairo: Street plan of northern section

the Ottomans, in 1517. The Ottoman influence lasted until the end of the nineteenth century, when Egypt was occupied by the British.

Initially, the Turkish influence upon Cairo's residential quarters was negligible. Being Muslims also, but less orthodox than the Shiites, the Ottomans also built their houses in the Islamic tradition. Each residence had two distinct parts—a formal (or public) and an informal (or private) section. Moreover, the mahalah, the neighborhood block of oriental cities, was a familiar concept to the Ottomans since it was a common feature of their own cities.

Eventually some unique Turkish characteristics were adopted in the urban houses of Cairo. The most significant was the diminishing of restraint in the display of both wealth and social status in the exterior as well as the interior. Opulence in architectural details became a characteristic of most larger residences. The most modest homes, for obvious reasons, remained simple in detail. Even as late as 1637, when Gamal al-Din-al-Zahabi built a house for himself, the dwelling was in the Islamic style. Although Egypt had already been under Ottoman rule for over a century, this residence did

not betray any Turkish influence in its style or construction. In John D. Hoag's opinion, "Gamal al-Din's house provides a model of all the features of a luxurious Mamluk residence unchanged since at least the fourteenth century if not before" (1977, 181–82). It appears that Turkish influences shaped domestic architecture in Cairo only during the nineteenth century, and even then this influence was modified by European attitudes.

The residence of Gamal al-Din occupied an irregular building site that accommodated, in addition to the dwelling itself, four shops (*dukkans*) near the intersection of two streets. There were two street entrances, each with an offset passageway, called *dirka*; one entrance led to the mandarh, or public reception hall, the epicenter of the salamlik; the other entrance led into the *hosh*, or central court garden, of the harem.

Invariably located on the ground-floor level, the mandarh was in essence a suite of rooms. Its central and cross-vaulted space, called the *durqā'ah*, very often had an inlaid marble mosaic floor, and a basin or fountain (*fisqiyyah*) was generally placed in its center. Opposite the entrance door was a decorated wall recess, often adorned with small

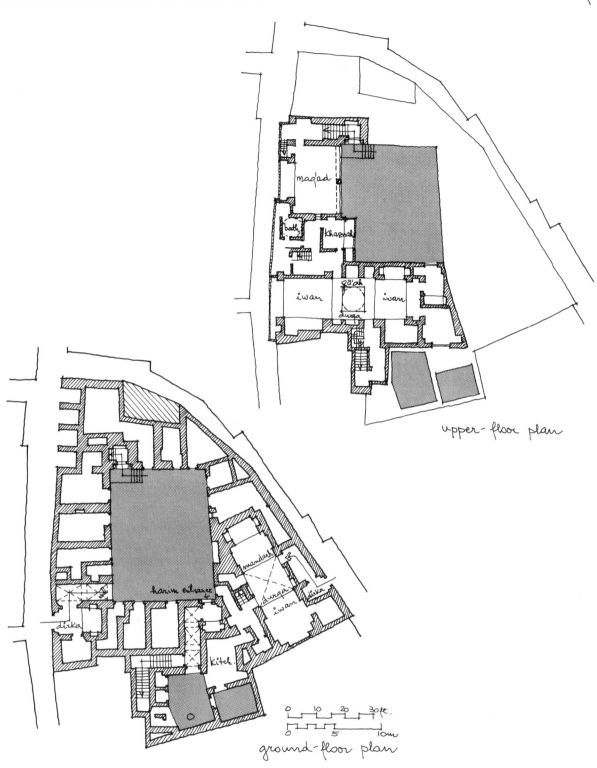

upper-floor plan

ground-floor plan

Cairo: House of Gamal al-Din-al-Zahabi
(after Franz-Pascha)

columns (*zufa*). The durqā'ah functioned as a hall-way, and during receptions servants were stationed there. Flanking both sides of the durqā'ah were the main iwanat, the reception alcoves with symmetrical wall recesses (*sidillahs*) in the traditional Islamic fashion. A narrow, winding passageway

House of Gamal al-Din-al-Zahabi: The Qā'ah
(after Martin S. Briggs)

House of Gamal al-Din-al-Zahabi: The courtyard and maq'ad
(after Martin S. Briggs)

linked the mandarh to the hosh and to the household utility rooms.

As was customary, the ground-floor level of the harem section of Gamal al-Din's home mainly contained secondary and utility rooms. The principal living quarters were on the upper level, reached from the hosh through adorned portals giving access to two main staircases. One staircase led to an open porch, the maq'ad. On to the maq'ad opened the *khazneh*, or private reception hall, equipped with a projecting balcony with a mashrabiyyah over the court. Through the intricate wooden screen of this bay window the women of the residence could observe, without being seen, the activities of a reception in the hosh or the maq'ad. Beyond the khazneh were the private living quarters of the harem's occupants, the qā'ah. In the style of the mandarh, the qā'ah's central space was a sunken durqā'ah, lit from above through a windowed wooden dome. Two iwanat, their lower walls in marble and their ceilings of exposed and painted wooden beams, faced each other across the durqā'ah. The second set of stairs off the hosh, restricted to private use, linked the qā'ah to the ground-floor service rooms.

The Egyptians adopted very little of the architectural style of the Turks, as already noted. It is not until the nineteenth century that one finds a strong impact by Turkish and European design elements in the dwellings of Cairo and changes in the traditional Islamic layout. A large and luxurious Cairo house probably dating from the nineteenth century reveals both Turkish and European influences in its design. The court garden is no longer central to the house, and in one of its corners one finds a Turkish *kiosk* (open pavilion). Several rooms have windows toward the street, and although the division between the public and private sector of the house does exist, it is certainly less explicit.

In contrast to Gamal al-Din's home, this house has only one street entrance, also a dirka impeding (but, here, not completely obscuring) a direct view from the street into the courtyard. The kiosk is placed in a garden setting, close to the side wing of

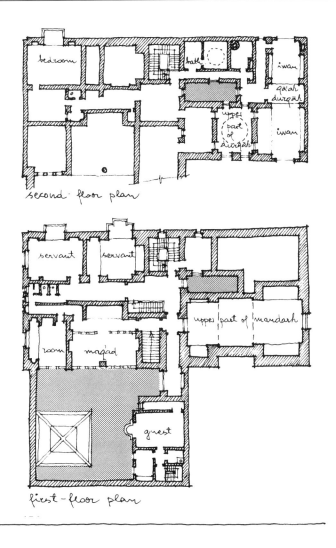

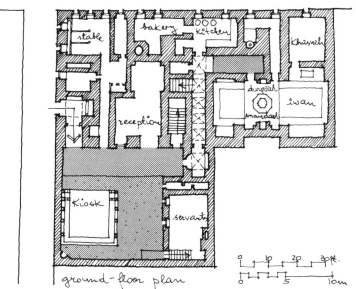

Cairo: Urban house (c. nineteenth century)
(after Franz-Pascha)

Cairo: Residential alley
(after Franz-Pascha)

Cairo: Residential street
(after Martin S. Briggs)

the house, which contains at ground level servants' quarters and on the upper levels guest apartments reached through a separate staircase. The main reception rooms, the mandarh, are located on the ground level of the main house; a long vaulted corridor leads to a small open court, and hence to the durqā'ah of the mandarh. The durqā'ah has a central fountain and is an impressive three-story domed space lit from above. In addition to the two iwan alcoves of the mandarh, there is a third secluded space, a cabinet or *khizaneh*, a private space of the master of the house. The balance of the ground-floor area is occupied by a less formal reception room facing the court, a kitchen and bakery opening on the mandarh corridor, and a small stable near the entrance reached through a separate passageway.

The second level contains a two-story, twin-arched maq'ad, an open reception porch facing the courtyard, reached through a separate staircase. With the exception of a few servants' rooms, guest suite, and the main staircase leading to the qā'ah, the rest of this floor is occupied by the upper spaces of the ground-floor mandarh.

On the third floor of the house are the family's private quarters, the qā'ah; its durqā'ah is smaller than the mandarh's. Two iwanat open from the central space of the durqā'ah, both lit by windows; two small additional windows open into the durqā'ah of the mandarh. A bathroom suite is located along the corridor linking the main staircase to the qā'ah.

In the twentieth century, western design approaches became dominant in Cairo, and foreign housing standards were introduced. The traditional oriental urban house, however, has not entirely disappeared, especially from the older sections of Cairo. A new consciousness of indigenous and traditional values in architecture initiated by Hassan Fathy, a traditionalist architect, and his followers may ensure that the courtyard house does survive.

Cairo: Courtyard of a Mamluk house

The old section of Cairo retains the ingredients of an oriental city. Its wider streets are lined with shops and workshops, but its twisting narrow alleys give access to traditional courtyard dwellings. Intersections open into small squares accommodating street vendors and small temporary commercial stands.

The pattern and hierarchy of Cairo's streets have an environmental rationale. North-south streets are wide and their sidewalks are shaded by canopied buildings; east-west streets, running parallel to the path of the sun, are narrow and bending and often contain overhangs to prevent overexposure to the sun of the south-facing buildings. The northern prevailing winds follow the commercial streets, and at intersections a drop in pressure results; thus, air is drawn down the narrow side streets by suction (Development Workshop 1976, 20).

Pressure-differential-induced air movement is also used in the design of larger homes that have two court gardens. Air moves from cooler, small, shaded courts to warmer, sunny, open court gardens with lighter, lower-pressure air.

The oriental city pattern is the result of harmony between environmental, social, and economic forces and is still evident in the old section of Cairo, but unfortunately its survival is not assured.

In spite of early ties to the modern movement, Hassan Fathy, a noted Egyptian architect and former head of the School of Fine Arts in Cairo, sought design inspiration in indigenous rural buildings for moderate- to low-income housing. In 1945, the Ministry of Antiquities granted Fathy a commission to relocate a village built on ancient tombs near Luxor. In his design of New Gourna village, Fathy employed a simple architectural vocabulary entailing the square-domed and rectangular vaulted structures which were indigenous to the region. All buildings were constructed of traditional sun-dried bricks. Unfortunately, Fathy's chef-d'oeuvre was never completed for two

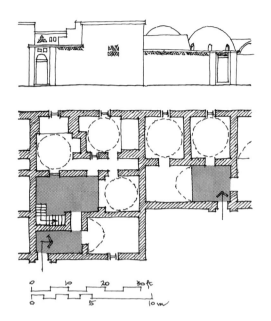

New Gourna (1945–47), Hassan Fathy

reasons: First, the villagers sabotaged the project by refusing to move to the new location, and second, Fathy received little official support. Nevertheless, enough of New Gourna was built to demonstrate the economic viability of Fathy's application of both local construction technology and building materials. He also succeeded in giving an example of the aesthetic prowess of indigenous architecture.

Although Fathy had the support of a large number of architects, most major commissions by both Egyptian government and private companies are awarded either to foreign architectural firms or to Egyptian architects who follow international design trends. Egypt is not unique in this tendency to ignore local talent.

THE BAGHDAD HOUSE

The city of Baghdad, founded in A.D. 762 by the Abbasid ruler Abu Jafar al-Mansur, was planned as a circular city with three concentric fortification walls, four city gates, and a large central area set aside for a mosque and a palace. The residential areas were contained between the second wall, or main fortification wall, and the third wall, which encircled the palace area.

The residential zone was divided into four quadrants by the vaulted commercial galleries which linked the four city gates to the central palace area. These residential quadrants were bounded on both their outer and inner perimeters by concentric ring roads which at certain intervals were linked to each other by spokelike connecting streets; the latter were the spines of the residential quarters and were protected at either end by strong gates (Creswell 1940, 15–16).

Baghdad, or Dar-es-Salaam (Abode of Peace), became the nodal point in east-west caravan routes; it also commanded the two waterways, the Tigris and Euphrates, and through them had easy access to the sea. Baghdad's commercial position was unrivaled and, under the rule of Harun-al-Rashid, it became a center of culture and one of the most magnificent cities in the whole Muslim Empire.

A great flood in 942 severely damaged large segments of the city, and in 1258, when the Mongolian hordes overran Mesopotamia, the City of the Arabian Nights was destroyed. Although Baghdad was rebuilt, it did not regain its former eminence during the subsequent centuries of foreign domination. Only during the twentieth century did it once again become a capital city, but there is no trace left of its former circular plan.

Urban houses that were built before the beginning of the twentieth century in Baghdad and in other Iraqi cities, such as Karbala, Najaf, Mosul, and Basra, retained the essential features of the medieval Islamic house. They were indigenous courtyard houses, and they were divided into a public and a secluded family section, although this separation was less rigidly observed. As can be expected, the long Ottoman occupation of "the land between the rivers" left an imprint upon the Baghdad house; also detectable is a strong Persian influence in the design of the house, especially in the religious centers of Karbala and Najaf.

If one compares the various spatial elements of the Baghdad house with those of the occidental

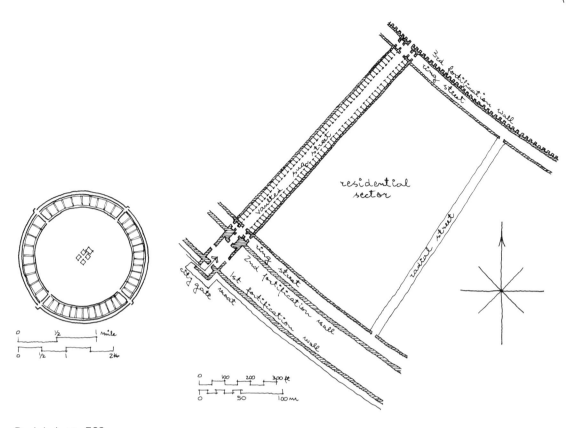

Baghdad, A.D. 762
(after K. A. C. Creswell)

house, one realizes a great difference in their spatial organization. This difference is primarily attributable to the different perception of a home's function. The Baghdad urban dweller, for example, did not perceive the various spaces of his house as living rooms, dining rooms, bedrooms, and so on but viewed each space in the light of its optimum usefulness in winter or summer, in the morning, at noon, or in the evening. Hence, depending on the season of the year and the time of the day, the resident used the particular area of the house, including the basement and roof space (*sath*), that offered maximum comfort at a given time. The Baghdad house did not have a bedroom or dining room, per se, but most principal spaces had a multifunctional use; for example, a room that was used in winter as a bed-sitting room became in summer only a living room since roof terraces were cooler and more desirable for sleeping.

Family meals were not taken in the occidental manner. The master of the house ate with his sons and male relatives and was served by the women of the household; when unrelated and important male guests were entertained, the master served the meals himself and did not partake in the meal until his guests had finished eating. Food was served on large metal trays placed on a low stool and was consumed while the diners sat on carpets, an arrangement that afforded greater flexibility than the use of a dining table and chairs.

The most common living space in the traditional Baghdad house was the *oda*, frequently without windows and lit by a transom above the door. In larger homes there would be more than one oda. A larger space was the *'ursi*; it invariably had a vertical sliding window wall and was well lit compared to the oda. Both these spaces were used predominantly during the cool seasons of the year.

An important living space, always located on the upper level of the house, was the *shenashil*. An inherent feature of this room was the large bay window, occupying the full width of the room and

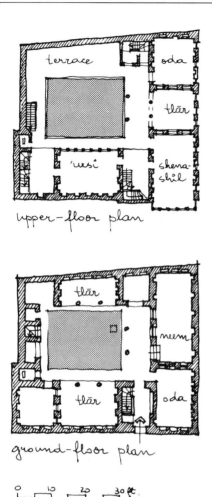

Typical house in Baghdad
(after Oscar Reuther)

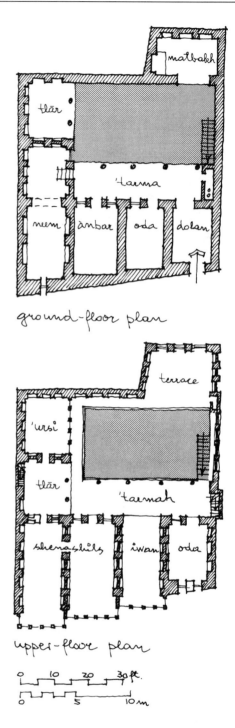

Baghdad: House of Ustad Abdallah Kadimeïn
(after Oscar Reuther)

cantilevered over the street. The folk ethnological meaning of shenashil derives from *shah-neshin* or "the seat of the king" and refers more accurately to the bay window itself. In this room the women of the household gathered socially, and through the bay window they observed the activity of the street below.

A *tlār* was also an important living space and was enclosed on three sides with the fourth open to the ῾tarmah, a porchlike anteroom, which in turn opened onto the hosh, the courtyard. (Generally it was a square court called the *hosh murabba'*.) The tlār was an elongated rectangular space with its long axis parallel to the court and its roof supported on a set of columns. Often its floor was raised a

few steps above the level of the court or gallery. It was usually entered through side doors rather than from the front.

Similar to the tlār was the iwan (shaded portico), but in contrast to the former this space had its long axis at a right angle to the court and, consequently, did not require column support at its open end. North-oriented tlārs and iwanat were in perpetual shade and were used during the summer months. Those facing south, being protected from the cold winter winds but exposed to the warm radiation of the winter sun, were favorable outdoor spaces during sunny winter days.

During the hot summer months, when the midday temperature was extremely warm, Baghdad residents retreated to the *neem*, a semibasement room, or to the *serdab*, a cellar living room. The neem's floor was between 1 ft 8 in to 3 ft 4 in (0.5 to 3 m) below grade with apertures opening through a ˙tarmah at grade into the courtyard; this arrangement was also called "tlār Baghdadi." An elevated platform at one or both narrow sides of the neem, the *taktabosh* offered the advantage of a dry floor in contrast to the damp floor of the neem; the space below this platform was excavated slightly deeper than the floor of the neem and was used as a storage space. The word taktabosh derived from a Persian and Turkish word with the combined meaning "a platform with a hollow space below."

The serdab was a subterranean and domed living space below the courtyard and was lit through skylights. This space had, on one or several sides, iwanlike recesses with benches and in the middle of the space a fountain, a *faskije*, placed in an octagonal basin. Access to the serdab was commonly through the neem.

The entrance to the traditional Baghdad house at the beginning of this century was either a *majaz* or a *dolan*. The former was an angular entrance hall with a privacy wall facing the door, or *bab*, while the latter was usually a square or octagonal domed vestibule equipped with a second set of doors preventing a direct view from the street into the courtyard. Both types of entryway were provided with benches.

The *matbakh* (kitchen) and most other ancillary rooms such as the *ànbar* (storage room) were situated at ground-floor level; in larger homes the matbakh faced a secondary small courtyard or was lit and ventilated through a light shaft. The servants'

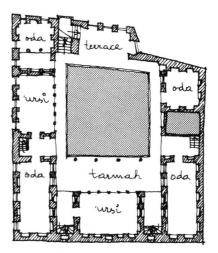

upper-floor plan

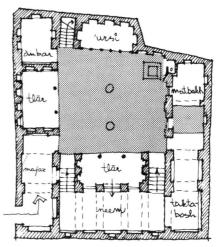

ground-floor plan

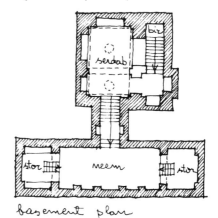

basement plan

Baghdad: House of Shashur
(after Oscar Reuther)

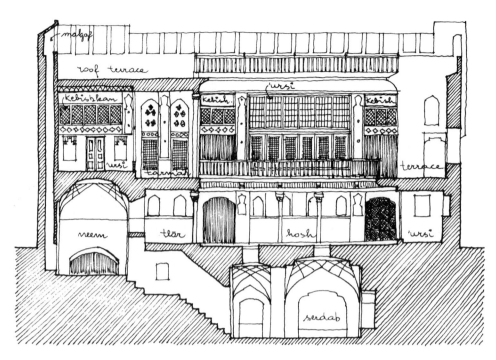

Baghdad: Section through the Shashur House
(after Oscar Reuther)

rooms were invariably located next to their place of work; for example, the cook was next to the kitchen, the doorman (or *bawab*) next to the entrance. Also at grade level were the hammams (baths) and the *mirhad* (toilet).

Staircases (*daraj*) linked the various levels of the house. Next to the stairs were located additional mirhads at the upper level. Corridors giving access to the main high-ceilinged rooms supported mezzanines at mid-level, thereby avoiding a disproportionate scale between the narrow width of the corridor and its otherwise excessive height. The corridors were called *iwentshes* and the mezzanines above them *kebishkans*. The kebishkans had trellised windows overlooking the principal rooms and were frequently used by the occupants of the haramlik, who could thus participate unseen in the activities of a formal reception held in the adjacent reception space.

Although the division of the house into the salamlik and haramlik (or *diwan* and *haram* in Baghdad) was traditional in Iraqi cities, the separation was less rigid than in the medieval Islamic cities, except, of course, for very religious homes.

In large homes where a horizontal separation between the two sections was economically feasible, there were virtually two homes, a public and a private one, each with its own court garden functioning as the nucleus of their respective living spaces. However, the vertical separation of the single courtyard house so strictly enforced in the medieval period lost its rigidity in the Baghdad house during the nineteenth century. Unrelated male guests were often received in upper-level living spaces; the existence of several staircases enabled the women in the family to move about the house without undue exposure to guests.

The traditional Baghdad house still exists and is most common in al-Kazimiyah, a former Shiite city that now constitutes a section of Baghdad, and in other deeply religious centers like Karbala and Najaf. Unfortunately, today most old homes in the central districts of Baghdad are abandoned and serve as storage warehouses for the nearby bazaars.

Al-Kazimiyah is an excellent example of a traditional Islamic city. It owes its survival to its religious importance as a Shiite holy place. In its center is the great mosque with two gilded domes, each

Baghdad: Southeast corner of courtyard (upper level)

erected above the tomb of an imam from the ninth century. This mosque also has four gilded minarets and a tiled gate tower that leads to an enclosed courtyard. This large courtyard accommodates the crowds of Shiite pilgrims that frequently visit the venerable place. In fact, al-Kazimiyah's economy is centered upon the service it provides to pilgrims.

Shiite Muslims are very conservative and adhere tenaciously to old traditions; consequently, their communities reflect perhaps more than others the character of medieval Islamic cities. Unfortunately, some parts of al-Kazimiyah were modified during the twentieth century; for example two wide avenues for motorized vehicular traffic were cut through its tight urban texture, and, in the name of progress and urban renewal hundreds of residential and community buildings crowding the holy mosque were demolished to be replaced by large and mercilessly sun-drenched open spaces and parking lots.

Nevertheless, the medieval urban pattern of a myriad of narrow twisted and shaded alleyways and cul-de-sacs still predominates in most of al-

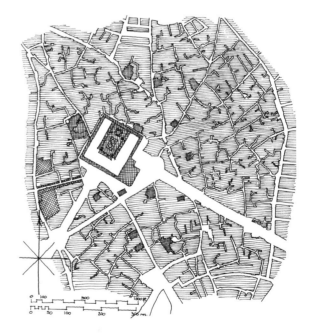

Al-Kazimiyah
(after Andrzej Basista)

Kazimiyah. The covered suq is still near the main entrance of the great mosque, and smaller mosques and madrasahs as well as hammams and khans are distributed in the tight-knit urban mass

Al-Kazimiyah alley

Al-Kazimiyah street

formed by residential buildings. This can be witnessed from the survey plan made several years ago by the Polish architects of Miastroprojekt, Cracow (Basista 1976a, 1976b).

The residential sectors of al-Kazimiyah no longer consist of clearly defined mahalahs, and their gates, or babs, are now absent. However, the hierarchical street network or primary streets, secondary alleys, and tertiary or intimate blind alleys are still very much in evidence. The building sites are very irregular both in shape and in size. Moreover, with the exception of small courtyards, a building site is usually occupied entirely by building structures. In fact, the upper levels of buildings often project beyond the street line and thereby cast shadow on the narrow public right-of-way.

It must be remembered that Islam does not have a common law parallel to its religious laws. Furthermore, since religious laws are primarily oriented toward the behavior of the individual, no provision is made for restrictive regulations, such as bylaws, that govern building development. For example, according to religious laws of conduct, an individual must not overlook a neighbor's property nor is he allowed to interfere willfully with a neighbor's right of access to his property, although

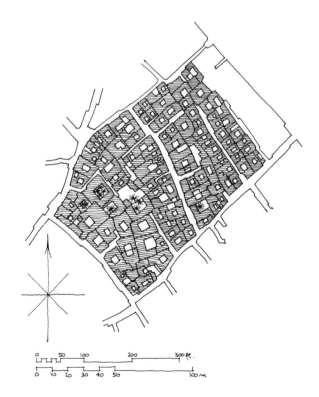

Residential sector in al-Kazimiyah
(after Andrzej Basista)

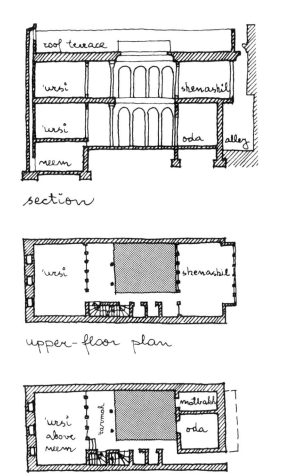

Al-Kazimiyah small house
(after Andrzej Basista)

immediate neighbors, but traditionally he is not required to make allowances for through traffic to ease accessibility from one neighborhood to another.

Although no religious restrictions apply to the interior arrangement of a dwelling, a certain uniformity prevails. The typical al-Kazimiyah house is in the traditional court-garden form, and the size of its central open space is more or less in proportion to the size of the building plot and dwelling unit. Today it is rare to find a courtyard shaded by its own palm tree, but as Andrzej Basista (1976a) rightly observed, the unevenness created by roots still buried below many courtyard pavings gives evidence that trees must have been very common elements of courtyards long ago. The layout of the dwellings in al-Kazimiyah is very similar to that of the traditional Baghdad urban house already described with the exception of the unusually beautiful wooden tracery on the stained glass windows that invariably face the private court garden. These window walls have a similar motive of overlapping circles familiar in Persian architecture, but their scale is minute and complementary to the domestic environment.

From a city plan of an old residential district of Baghdad, a sequence of land-use plans, 2.47 acres (1 hectare) in area, was made by the author to compare the land-use efficiency of the oriental mahalah with that of a residential section of a typical North American suburb. In Baghdad the building coverage appears to be about 72 percent versus 17 percent in the North American example. If we assume an average building height of two stories for the oriental dwelling and one story for the suburban home, their respective floor space indices, or floor area ratios, are 1.5 and 0.12. In other words, the oriental mahalah's building mass is more than tenfold that of the occidental suburb. Moreover, court gardens cover 12 percent of the oriental building plot, while lawns, side yards, and backyards surrounding the typical bungalow amount to 54 percent of the suburban lot size.

As is the case throughout the Near East, the majority of Iraq's population has adopted occidental customs and occidental house forms—slightly

the street fronting each house is rightfully private up to the center line of the alley or street. In addition, he cannot deny the use of an external wall by his neighbors and must even allow them to place load-bearing beams into it, as long as the builder does not physically damage the property in question. Moreover, religious laws clearly favor neighborhood interests rather than the interest of the community at large. In other words, a citizen must ensure free passage in front of his house to his

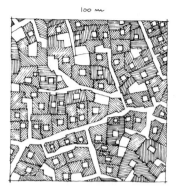

plan of built-up area

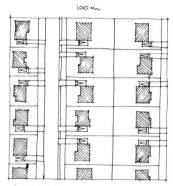

plan of built-up area

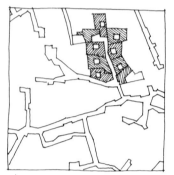

plan of street-related neighborhood

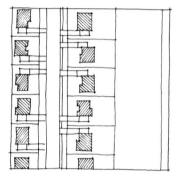

plan of street-related neighborhood

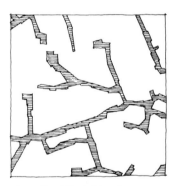

plan of public rights-of-way

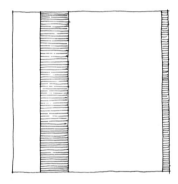

plan of public rights-of-way

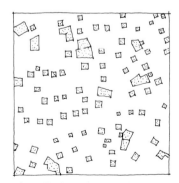

plan of private open spaces

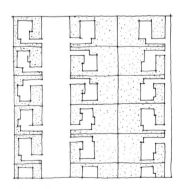

plan of private open spaces

Baghdad   North American suburb

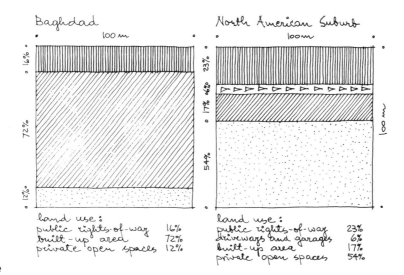

Land use

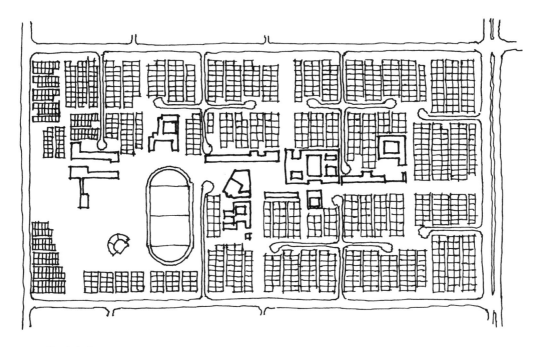

Human sector, Baghdad
(after Constantinos A. Doxiadis)

modified, of course, to make them bearable in an arid and very hot climate. Since affluent people are generally the first to adopt foreign customs, many mahalahs have lost their wealthier residents, who have moved to "better" sections of the city. Furthermore, government policy favors the open-ended street pattern of occidental cities for new residential areas, in spite of the fact that land-use efficiency of the old pattern innate to mahalahs is superior.

Freestanding villas of the upper-income residential districts are made more comfortable by adding air conditioners and landscaping, both of which make the extreme climatic conditions bearable. Lower-income residential areas, however, which accommodate the large influx of rural immigrants seeking their fortunes in the big city, lack both air conditioning and shade trees. Baghdad's Al-Thawra low-cost housing district, planned by Constantinos Apostolou Doxiadis and Associates (1963), is divided by an orthogonal grid of very wide treeless avenues into large residential megablocks—called "human sectors" by the designers. To form a self-sufficient neighborhood entity, each megablock has its mosque, school, commercial center, and recreational areas. The low-rise courtyard houses of this development are small, and the use of the courtyard for many domestic activities is indispensable although its privacy is unprotected by a spirit wall. The roof of the house is terraced to serve as a sleeping space on warm nights; a pierced parapet wall ensures privacy and catches the breeze. The wide streets and plazas of this development do not provide relief from the intense, searing summer heat, and because of the water shortage it is questionable whether trees and landscaping could ever be lush enough to ameliorate its microclimate.

The open-ended street pattern and occidental urban spatial standards, along with the segregation of income groups, is contrary to oriental principles of environmental harmony, and is incongruous with the climatic realities of Iraq and many other regions of the Near East and North Africa.

CHAPTER FOUR

THE TRADITIONAL URBAN HOUSE IN INDIA

The courtyard or court-garden house is the indigenous urban dwelling of the Indian subcontinent. If stone is unavailable or economically out of reach, urban dwellings are built of brick and the upper stories of timber frame with adobe or brick infill panels. The roof is either flat and covered with mud or sloping and tiled, depending on the region. In humble dwellings floors are beaten earth at ground level and paved only in the open court, passages, and washrooms. The toilet is frequently located next to the entrance and consists of no more than a hole in the paved floor with a basket below, which is emptied at night by the official sweeper, an arrangement that resembles the ancient sanitation practices of the Mohenjo-Daro dwellers.

In Hindu homes, where the preparation of food is a religious ritual, the kitchen is placed next to the family shrine. It is a chimneyless room with one or more earthen fireplaces raised above the floor. Otherwise, most Indian homes have multifunctional interior spaces with little furniture: mats are used for sitting, quilts for sleeping, and chests for storage. Unlike those of the historical examples discussed earlier, the façades of many urban dwellings are frequently austere and anonymous; they rarely reflect the class distinction of the occupants. Color is reserved for religious buildings.

Dwellings bordering on major streets, or bazaars, traditionally have shops on the ground floor that open out into the street during the day, but the privacy of the home behind or above the shops is inviolate. The house itself is a private shelter for home life, but it represents only one aspect of city life. Another aspect, namely the street life within the community, is an important corollary to home life in India.

To the superficial occidental eye, the residential districts of oriental cities appear chaotic, but in fact they have an inherent order much more sophisticated than the simpler order of contemporary western residential suburbs. Equally superficial is the view that economic ghettoism existed in oriental residential areas. In fact, traditionally, areas of homogeneous income levels did not exist; such differentiation in oriental cities is a recent phenomenon.

In general, the traditional cities of the Indian subcontinent have a cellular structure composed of residential neighborhoods or precincts. In Old Delhi they are called *mohallas*, in Ahmadabad *puras*. A mohalla or pura is an identifiable residential entity with a homogeneous population related through occupation, religion, geographical origin, or caste membership. In recent years increasing social mobility has reduced to some extent the homogeneity of the respective inhabitants of the mohalla or pura. Nevertheless, these districts still have a well-defined social hierarchy. A local council enforces rules governing public and private behavior. "A Mohalla may contain its own

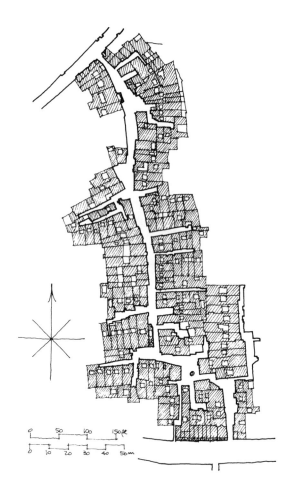

Ahmadabad: Mamunaik Pol
(after Mahendra Shah and Vikram Bhatt)

Bazaar, mosque or temple, school, and through its council cares for orphaned children. The isolated aspect of these social units is broken by the need for community cooperation (with the rest of the city) during religious festivals and the Bazaar, which retails the artifacts produced within the unit" (Fonseca 1969, 109).

As in ancient cities, a spine street links the mohalla to main thoroughfares or bazaar streets and its exits are often protected by gates, whose watchmen are called *chowkidars*. Many of these gates are not in use today, especially in larger cities, but some are still maintained and are closed after certain hours. Gateways are usually unadorned to avoid displaying the wealth of their respective mohalla inhabitants. The gateways or

control points at every exit of a mohalla are defensive elements that in bygone days made the mohallas individual fortresses within a large fortified city; but they also unified their inhabitants into a social unit, a cohesive whole.

Not unlike the street pattern of the ancient cities, the traditional Indian city has narrow blind alleys or lanes (*khanchos*) that branch off the spine street and reach into the mohalla to link all its dwellings to each other with an intricate network of public rights-of-way. *Kucha* and *gali* mean street in Delhi; *chatta* is the name used for a street or lane that has a residential structure built over it.

The *chowk* or small square is an important outdoor space in a mohalla and is used sequentially throughout the day by various groups—for example, by women washing clothes in the morning, by children playing during the day, and by adults meeting informally in the evening. In essence, the mohalla is to the community what the home is to the family.

The home, the lane, spinal street, and main thoroughfare represent a gradual hierarchical order, a continuum of an expanding living environment that complements admirably the gradual and safe exploration of their world by growing children. This order shuns a sudden confrontation of incompatible land use and subscribes instead to gradual transition. The sequence of private, semiprivate, semipublic, and public spaces cannot fully convey the intrinsic spatial qualities of oriental residential districts.

In India traditional values as well as the timeless way of building compact residential environments are now threatened by new and foreign influences from the Occident. These influences are incompatible with the climate of the country and traditional culture of its people. They have a dispersing effect upon the compact urban environment, loosening the once close social ties that gave a sense of community to a group of people.

The oriental concept of the urban house with its central and private courtyard still determines today the physical form of the indigenous house of Indian cities such as Jaisalmer, Jaipur, Udaipur, Ahmadabad, and several others.

Jaisalmer: The walled town
(after Arnold Whittick)

JAISALMER

Jaisalmer is a fortress city founded in A.D. 1156 by Rao Jaisalji as a military fort and trading post for the east-west caravan route crossing the Thar Desert. It owed its wealth to the fact that it was the capital of a princely state as well as a trade center for wool, camels, cattle, and sheep. The Jaisalmer region is arid with only sparse vegetation and saline ground water. Spring crops of wheat or barley are very rare, and only the poorer rain crops can be relied upon. Herds of camels, horned cattle, sheep, and goats augmented the food supply. The main source of potable water is still Garisar Lake, fed by a rivulet just outside the fortification walls.

The city's site has an irregular polygon shape within which is a hill surrounded by a second fortification wall. This city within a city is triangular in shape and contains the royal palace in addition to numerous common dwellings. A winding path leads from the lower city to the only gateway of the upper city.

Both the upper and lower cities of Jaisalmer are compact in urban form. The streets are narrow; the buildings are on a deep lot, have a narrow front, and are multistoried. They possess the generic urban form that desert towns develop for climatic and defensive reasons.

The street network of the upper city is irregular, whereas that of the lower city has a predominant grid pattern. However, the grid is not a rigid one since the width of the streets changes frequently; moreover, at junctions the streets and lanes often widen, thereby creating a series of interesting and picturesque street views.

The typical urban house of Jaisalmer is attached on its sides and at the back, leaving only a narrow façade with screened openings exposed to the street. To guard the privacy of the house, the ground floor rarely has any apertures toward the street other than the necessary entrance door. On the

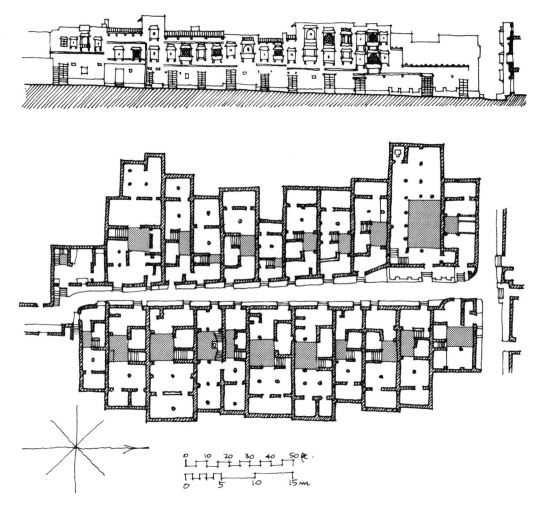

Jaisalmer: Typical residential street
(after Kulbhushan Jain)

outside, adjacent to the entrance, there is an elevated platform or porch and just within the doorway a privacy wall usually blocks a direct view of the dwelling's interior. The entrance hall itself is a spacious room called *moda* and serves as both a transitional area leading to the courtyard and as a sitting room. From the courtyard, the central space of the house, there are generally one or two steps leading up to a *chaupala* or *pattasala* around which are grouped several rooms, one of which is used as a kitchen and the other as a storage room called *ovra*.

Women's activities are centered in the chaupala, traditionally, a living room,

> where spinning and weaving too were done, and where the family ate their meals or enjoyed their midday rest. Here too in one of the front niches

the family deities, usually a Devi [Indian deity] or an impression of Sati's [a deity] palm were enshrined to guard the material goods of the house or safeguard the destiny of the members of the family. In some cases the plan of the ground floor was repeated on the upper storey which was connected by a staircase by the side of the chaupala. The arrangement of the upper storey varied slightly. There was an open terrace for sleeping in summer and a chitrasali, with balcony and arched niches over the ovra, which served the purpose of a bed and drawing-room. As the name signifies, it was usually decorated with paintings of various types and kept scented with burning of perfumed oil lamps. The adjoining room called medi was meant for keeping valuables, money-chest and private records or documents. If there was a third storey, it was an open

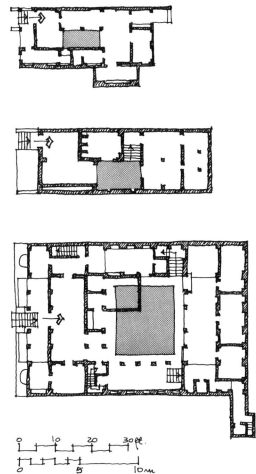

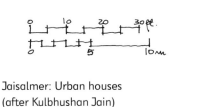

Jaisalmer: Urban houses
(after Kulbhushan Jain)

Jaisalmer: Street façade of an urban house
(after Kulbhushan Jain)

terrace all over the building. Only on one side there was a small room for use as a bedroom in rainy season or summer nights, furnished with paintings, beds and other toilet equipment (Sharma 1968, 65).

With the exception of a few service areas, the various rooms of the Jaisalmer house are rarely designated for a single activity. The use of most spaces changes both diurnally and seasonally. This is especially true of the interior open spaces, namely, the courtyards, terraces, galleries, and balconies. Thus, for example, in the late morning the kitchen activities spill into the courtyard, whereas in the afternoon other household chores are done below the open sky. In winter, however, it is not uncommon for cooking to be done on the upper terrace, the space that during the summer serves as a sleeping platform below the cool evening sky.

The urban homes of Jaisalmer vary considerably in size according to the wealth of their occupants, but there is no segregation according to income groups; the rich and poor live side by side, but various castes formed distinct residential districts. The smallest typical dwelling is two bays wide, one bay the width of the courtyard. With increased width and depth the houses become more luxurious, and beyond a certain depth two courtyards supply light and air to their surrounding rooms. The two-courtyard house is divided into a formal, semiprivate front section and an informal, private rear section reserved for the family.

A cross section through a typical street reveals the unique relationship between the entrance to the home and the public right-of-way. The street level is about 3 ft (90 cm) below the threshold of the main door. Raised platforms, usually flanking the staircase leading to the entrance, are used by male residents as outdoor extensions of the home, enabling them to participate in the activities of the narrow and busy street. Projecting screened oriels called *zarookhas* allow women to view street life from above without being observed. These zarookhas are more efficient than mere windows since they afford side views down the length of the narrow street; moreover, zarookhas together with shade canopies (*chajjas*) and balconies crowd the façades of most buildings and provide welcome shade to the street.

Most houses in Jaisalmer are built of local yellow sandstone and utilize prefabricated standard building elements acquired from stone carvers. Thus, columns, brackets, balconies, zarookhas, and chajjas are similar throughout the city. The diversity of building width and height is unified by the use of similar building materials and building elements, resulting in a pleasing balance between unity and diversity.

JAIPUR

Maharaja Sawai Jai Singh (1699–1743) was the founder of the walled city of Jaipur built during the second quarter of the eighteenth century as the new capital of his Rajput state. The former fortress capital, Amber, nestled in the Aravalli Hills, was relatively inaccessible, and this handicapped its commercial development at a time when the new political realities no longer justified such isolation for the purpose of defense.

Construction of the new town commenced in 1727 and its main sections were completed within the following six years. The physical form of the walled city was conceived as an orderly orthogonal cluster of nine roughly equal-sized square wards, or "superblocks."

Jaipur: Bazaar street scene

Jai Singh's plan for Jaipur conformed to the traditional agrarian society's view that a city consisted of a collection of villages, but one cannot exclude the possibility of a certain influence of eighteenth-century European planning practices. As was characteristic of Europe during that period, strict design control of buildings was exercised by Jaipur's founder along the principal thoroughfares and bazaar streets.

No doubt the cardinal points of the compass also imposed an important discipline on Jaipur's plan. The practice of a north-south and east-west orientation of street networks had a precedent in the ancient Indus Valley civilization, as exemplified by the excavations both in Mohenjo-Daro and Harappa, as well as later, in the Hellenistic city of Taxila, built after the conquest of the Punjab by Alexander the Great.

The principal axis of the city was formed by an east-west bazaar street which linked the Surajpol (Gates of the Sun) to the Chandpol (Gates of the Moon) and thereby divided the city into two unequal halves; the eastern extension of this axis led to the Temple of the Sun. The southern half of the city had four superblocks, while the northern part had five, two of which, the central ones, were merged into one to form the palace precinct with its extensive gardens. The entire town site was surrounded by crenelated fortification walls 25 ft (7.6 m) high and

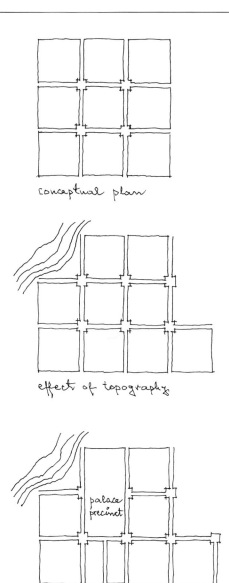

conceptual plan

effect of topography

palace precinct

final plan

Jaipur: Evolution of city plan
(after Kulbhushan Jain)

9 ft (2.75 m) thick. Access to the city was provided by eight main gates, each equipped with heavy bronze doors and preceded by a barbican. The city gates were closed every night at eleven o'clock and opened at daybreak. Nobody could enter or leave the city during the night, a custom also practiced in medieval cities in Europe. This custom lasted in Jaipur until 1923, when Chandpol first was left open during the night for the convenience of train travelers using the nearby station.

The palace precinct was also surrounded by fortification walls similar to those surrounding the city and its corresponding gates, some of which still retain the original bronze doors, and must have represented a second line of defense within the city proper. The rectangular wards, or superblocks, called *chowkris*, were identified individually with a particular name. Typically each chowkri was further subdivided into a number of mohallas, or residential precincts, inhabited by a particular caste, religious group, or members of a trade guild. The square chowkri located immediately south of the palace precinct was divided into two wards by a new bazaar street developed during the nineteenth century; this bazaar street extended the north-south axis of the palace precinct and eventually received its own gate, which is still known as the New Gate. It, of course, had no barbican.

Unquestionably, the founder of Jaipur envisaged a hierarchical order of street networks. The main bazaar streets, about 108 ft (33 m) in width, were the primary arteries delimiting the various chowkris and the palace precinct. A secondary grid of streets, about half the width of the bazaar streets, subdivided the chowkris into city blocks, each of which was then penetrated by a tertiary network of shaded narrow lanes, alleys, and cul-de-sacs. The primary roads or bazaar streets were not only wide and straight, but were also subject to regulations that prescribed the spatial organization and aesthetic treatment of the buildings lining them in order to ensure an effect of beauty. Accordingly, the main bazaar streets had on both sides a wide sidewalk that ran parallel to a modular arcade fronting a row of shops; the arcades and shops were in some cases built by the state, but the *havelis*, or large townhouses, two to three stories in height surmounting the shops behind the arcade were most often built by individuals. The façades of these havelis were also subject to some regulations and were generally adorned in the Hindu tradition with bay windows and *chatris*, to enhance the visual appeal of the street façade and the façade's silhouette. In most instances, the havelis had their main entrance from the rear street, but infrequently they could be reached from the front

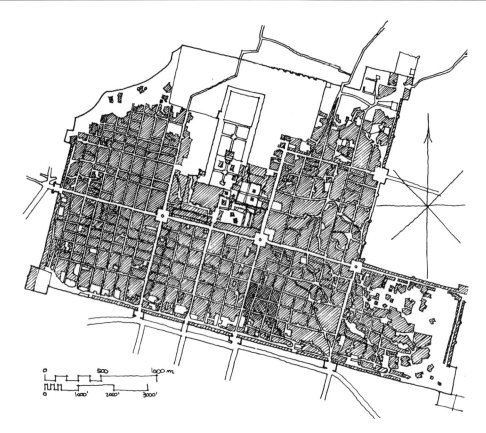

Jaipur
(after Kulbhushan Jain)

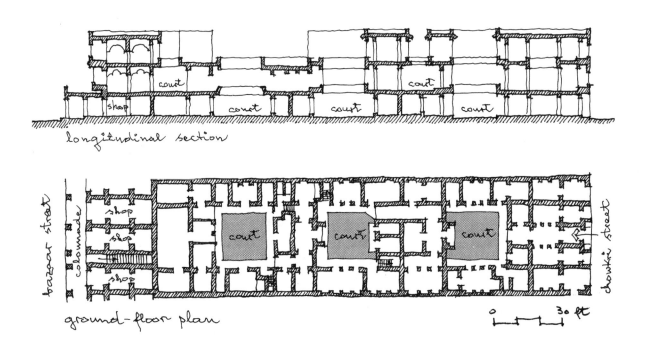

Large haveli along Bazaar street in Jaipur
(after Kulbhushan Jain)

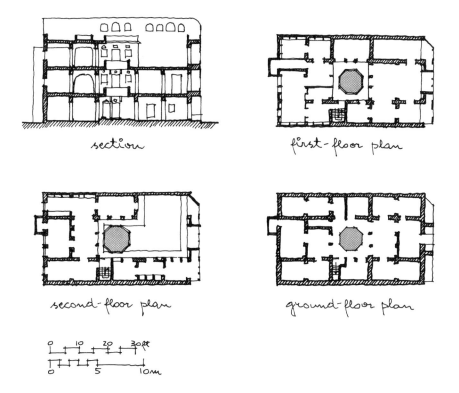

section   first-floor plan

second-floor plan   ground-floor plan

Jaipur: Urban house
(after Kulbhushan Jain)

through a staircase wedged between two shops leading to the continuous roof terrace of the arcades. At the intersection of the major north-south and east-west bazaar streets, the building lines recessed to form large squares which became important nodal points, or *chaupars*, of the city. We can identify three chaupars along the main axis of Jaipur, namely, Ramgay ki chaupar, Sangener ki chaupar, and Amber ki chaupar. At these nodes are the important buildings and temples, the latter built on elevated platforms and reached by a wide and formal stairway ascending from the pavement to the platform, lending an additional aura of importance to the religious shrines.

Of course, the palace precinct occupied a central and strategic position in the city, and its buildings were the dominant elements of Jaipur. In front of the eastern gate of the palace precinct was a large square called Jaleb Chowk that in the past served as the assembly area for state processions with their various conveyances, including elephants. The surrounding chambers of this square accommodated the retinue of the Maharaja. To the south of

Jaleb Chowk was the Jantar Mantar, the astronomical observatory built by Jai Singh.

Although most palatial buildings were secluded from public view to ensure the privacy of the Maharaja's household, one palatial building, Hawa Mahal, or the Palace of the Winds, did front on a bazaar street in order to provide members of the Maharaja's court and harem windows to the city. Hawa Mahal, built in 1799 by Jai Singh's grandson, Pratap Singh, was not a residential structure, but merely an ornate multistoried façade with a multitude of screened oriels and balconies to provide viewing platforms for members of the royal court who had to respect the *purdah* and were forbidden to mingle with ordinary people, but were nevertheless curious about them; their privacy was assured by the screened apertures, and the members of the harem could gaze on the activities of people in the streets below.

The courtyards of the havelis in Jaipur were unusual in that they most often had an octagonal plan and were relatively small. The size of the courtyard was justified by the extreme heat that prevails for many months of the year. Courtyards that were narrow and deep prevented sunlight from radiating into the dwelling. Moreover, the well-like courtyards retained the cool air accumulated during the night and, later in the day during the heat build-up, acted as chimneys by inducing a constant air movement in the surrounding habitable rooms. Climatic realities not only influenced the design of houses in Jaipur but also shaped the pattern of its streets and alleys in order to moderate effects of climate upon the urban environment. The pressure differential created between the wide sunny streets and narrow shaded alleys induces air movement even on calm days and a favorable microclimate thus results.

The typical dwelling unit is similar in principle to that of Jaisalmer and is basically an attached multistoried townhouse built of stone with one or several interior courtyards. Whatever the size of the dwelling, the courts never exceed a certain optimum size in order to afford protection from the sun. "The privacy-oriented house is totally closed to the street at ground floor level in order to block any view from the street. Only the entry door opens on the street. This door is also blocked by a baffle wall within a few feet of the entry; this space is called modh, the turn" (Jain 1978, 119).

Originally Jaipur was a white city and only after some experimentation in the colorings of buildings along the various streets—green, yellow, and pink, among others—did Ram Singh adopt pink as the trademark of Jaipur. He had all buildings along the main thoroughfares painted pink on the occasion of a royal visit. From that time Jaipur became known as the Pink City.

UDAIPUR

Udaipur is an equally picturesque city. Like Jaisalmer and Jaipur it has retained its architectural heritage because so-called progress was slow in the state of Rajasthan, the geographic and political setting of these three cities.

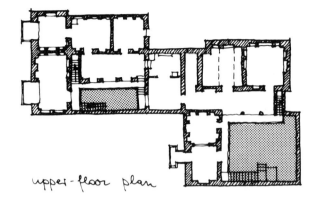

upper-floor plan

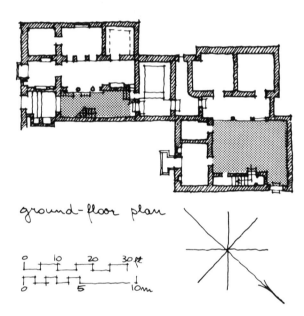

ground-floor plan

Udaipur: Urban house
(after Mahendra Shah)

The streetscape and urban form of Udaipur are also similar to those of Jaisalmer and Jaipur, and, indeed, so are its typical urban houses. Here, too, the courtyard is the center of the house, its pivotal point. Verandahs, terraces, and balconies overlook this open space and form the transitional areas leading to the more secluded chambers, thus guarding the privacy of the family when guests are present.

The buildings are constructed mainly of sandstone and adorned by precarved building elements similar to those at Jaisalmer. The stone walls are often whitewashed, which enhances the shadow effect of a building's sculptural façades and at the same time reduces the heat absorption of its walls.

AHMADABAD

Founded in A.D. 1411 by the Muslim ruler of Gujarat, Sultan Ahmed Shah, Ahmadabad was also a fortified city and an important trade center. In contrast to the desert cities described above, Ahmadabad is located in a fertile agricultural region along the Sabarmati River.

The residential quarters of the city were located on both sides of a main thoroughfare (now called Gandhi Road) that linked the city's administrative center, the royal palace, with its religious and commercial center comprising the jami' mosque and the adjacent marketplace.

The subsequent occupation of Ahmadabad by the Mogul emperor Akbar also left its imprint upon the city. The Mogul practice of settling the generals and troops with their respective families near the gateways of the city brought about a cellular urban structure of quasi-autonomous subcities, each forming an entity in itself. These subcities were further divided into puras inhabited by a specific guild, caste, or religious group. Each pura in turn had a spinal street, or *pol*, with small blind alleys or lanes branching from it; gates at both ends of the pol barred entry into the pura to strangers at night. Each pura usually had a small chowk, or square (often not more than a widening of the street), where public activities of these close-knit communities took place. Puras often had their own water wells and *vadies*, or community open spaces for communal feasts, caste meetings, or religious hearings. Public notices and news bulletins were placed on notice boards next to the gateways.

The city was divided into homogeneous community cells, but these cells or residential precincts were not based on income levels of their inhabitants; rich and poor lived side by side with their guild or caste fellows.

A typical house, described by Mahendra Shah and Vikram Bhatt (1974), is located in the central section of Mamunaik Pol on Sarkarno Khancho, a side street. The building site is 20 ft (6 m) wide and about 46 ft (14 m) deep. The house is attached on two sides and at the back to other houses. The building materials are brick for load-bearing walls

Ahmadabad street scene

and wood for the floor and roof structures. Wood columns, brackets, railings, doors, and windows are adorned with beautifully carved ornaments.

The heart of the Ahmadabad house is its central courtyard, which is smaller than that of its Udaipur counterpart in response to climatic forces. Thus, the narrow and deep courtyards (also called chowks) of Ahmadabad seldom receive sunshine at the ground-floor level; a favorable microclimate is created in these outdoor spaces where most household activities occur. The ground-floor level has an open plan with the entrance hall (the *khadaki*), the courtyard, the shaded open verandah (*parsal*), and the staircase leading to the upper floors. Adjacent to the parsal is the kitchen area and a large storage room for food supply and household utilities.

The upper-floor level contains a front sitting room with a screened oriel overlooking the street, a rear sitting room lit from the courtyard, and a storage room. The top floor consists of a family bed-sitting room, a bedroom, and a storage room. A small balcony, above the first-floor oriel, overlooks the street below.

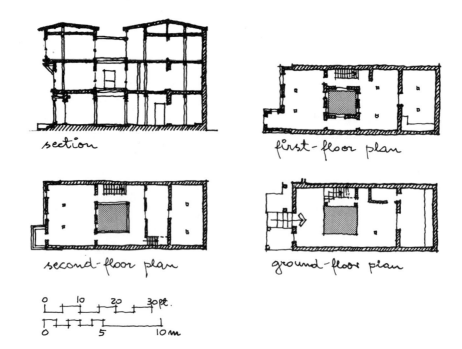

section

first-floor plan

second-floor plan

ground-floor plan

Ahmadabad: Urban house
(after Mahendra Shah and Vikram Bhatt)

An important element of the Ahmadabad house is a front porch (also called parsal) or a platform (an *otta*), a semiprivate space that links the public street with the private domain of the family.

The land-use efficiency of a typical and traditional residential district in Ahmadabad today is very similar to that in Baghdad. However, the population density is probably higher in Ahmadabad since the dwelling unit count per hectare (2.47 acres) is about 33 percent higher than that of Baghdad.

India's liberation from colonial rule in 1947 was followed by submission to a cultural domination by masters of the International Style, first through the influence exerted by Le Corbusier and his European associates, and later through American design by Louis Kahn. It must be acknowledged to the credit of these masters that the implementation of their work was accomplished by employing both local building technology and materials which, at least in the realm of domestic architecture, blunted the sharp edges of occidental architectural influences.

The plan for the new capital of the state of Punjab, Chandigarh, as well as the design of the new capital's government buildings, was entrusted to Le Corbusier, while the design of residential and commercial quarters was allocated to Pierre Jeanneret, Maxwell Fry, and Jane Drew. Nevertheless, Le Corbusier's influence on domestic design in India was still considerable through the design commission he received from a wealthy industrialist to design the Sarabhai House (1955–56) in Ahmadabad. In fact, a noted Indian architect, Balkrishna Doshi, who apprenticed earlier with Le Corbusier in his Paris atelier (1950), supervised the Ahmadabad works. Le Corbusier's sensitive design of this house, with its brise-soleil and Catalanian vaulted ceilings supporting a sod-covered roof, as well as the siting of the building to enhance natural cross-ventilation of the interior, were appropriate design responses to the prevailing climate in Gujarat. The Sarabhai House was much admired.

After completion of his supervisory work for Le Corbusier, Doshi opened his own office and committed himself to the advancement of low-cost housing. One of his first commissions was the construction of the staff housing for the Ahmadabad Textile Industries Research Association (ATIRA).

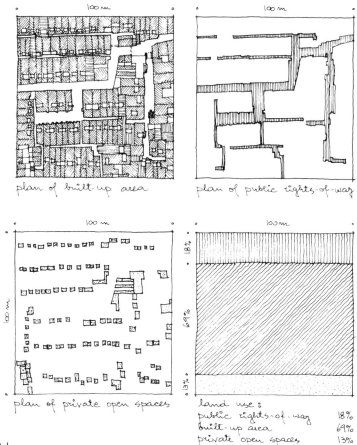

plan of built-up area

plan of public rights-of-way

plan of private open spaces

land use:
public rights-of-way   18%
built-up area   69%
private open spaces   13%

Ahmadabad: Kadwa Pol

As cited by Bhatt and Scriver in their book *Contemporary Indian Architecture*, Doshi's domestic architecture in this project was affordable even for the lowest-paid wage earner.

Since the early seventies, Indian authorities promote the cost-effective site-and-services planning concept to be used for human settlements of lower-income groups. This design approach entails the provision by the authorities of essential services, such as roads, water supply, storm and sanitary sewers, and, occasionally, a small structure with a toilet, while the owner of the site builds his home.

With user participation, architect Kirtee Shah designed the Vasna site-and-services housing development consisting of 2,248 low-cost dwelling units in Ahmadabad. Endorsed by the Amadabad Municipal Corporation, with additional financial support from OXFAM, the Housing and Urban Development Corporation, and the Gujarat state government, the project was completed in 1975. With exposed-brick walls and roofs of corrugated asbestos cement, the size of a typical two-room dwelling was 260 sq ft (24 m²). A verandah—a semiprivate zone—provided the transition space between the street and the house, while a service courtyard with two toilets and four wash spaces in the rear was shared by four families.

By the late eighties, Doshi directed the Aranya housing project to accommodate about 60,000 people in Indore for the Vastu-Shilpa Foundation in collaboration with a multidisciplinary team of planners, engineers, and architects. In keeping with traditions, the Aranya township was planned as a collection of low-rise, high-density self-contained villages. Each village was to have a mixed cross-section of income groups and all residents are ensured direct access to streets and public open spaces. Essentially, the design of this housing development is based on sites-and-services

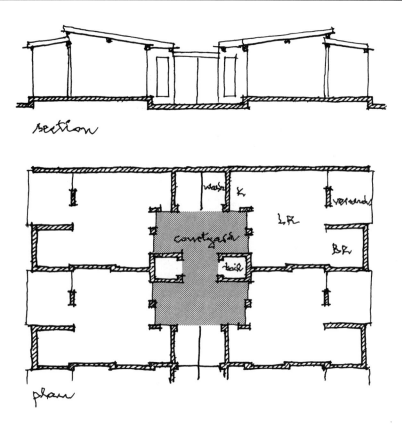

Vasna Housing Development, 1975, Kirtee Shah
(after V. Bhatt and P. Scriver)

provided by the Indore Development Authority, while the construction of dwellings is left to the users. The project is still under construction.

Bombay's landmark, the nearly thirty-story Kanchenjunga luxury elevator-serviced apartment tower (1983), is an anachronism. Designed by Charles Correa, with associate architect Pravina Mehta, this high-rise building with split-level apartment suites, each with access to a two-story corner terrace, contravenes the "site responsive" residential work done in India during the sixties and seventies by architects like Doshi and Correa himself too.

CHAPTER FIVE

THE TRADITIONAL URBAN HOUSE IN CHINA

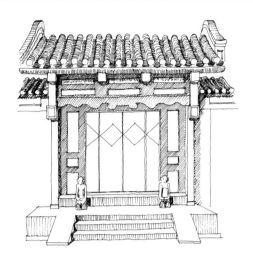

THE CITY OF BEIJING

The first known city on the site of the present city of Beijing was Ch'i, built in 1121 B.C. as the capital of Yen, the most northerly of the feudal states within the authority of the Zhou dynasty. It was located at the convergence of several important trade routes, namely, from Manchuria through Shanhai-kuan, the gate between the mountains and the sea, from the Mongolian plateau through the valley of the Yungting Ho and the Nankow Pass, and from the southern provinces of China toward the north.

Destroyed by the first emperor and founder of the Quin dynasty during the third century B.C., the city of Ch'i was rebuilt as You Chou in A.D. 70 during the subsequent rule of the Han dynasty. At the end of this dynasty, the city came under Tartar control. Under the Liao dynasty in A.D. 986 it was again rebuilt, this time on a larger scale with two gates on each of its four enclosing walls. "The towers above the gates were 99 Chinese feet high, not one foot higher, for at a height of 100 feet demons were believed to fly" (Gutkind 1946, 324–25). The palace of the emperor stood in the southwest corner of the city.

During the twelfth century the city was enlarged to almost twice its former size. Built east of the original city, the extension was a monumental undertaking, involving the labor of 800,000 coolies and 400,000 soldiers. The extended city was named *Chung Du* or "middle capital" until Genghis Khan conquered it and made it the capital of his new Mongolian province. It was then called *Khanbaliq*, or "city of the Khan," later to be Beijing. After the extension of the Grand Canal during the thirteenth century, Beijing was connected to a waterway transport system that reached far into the country.

Marco Polo described the Khanbaliq of this period as a city divided in squares, like a chessboard. Its streets were lined with booths and shops, and everything that was precious and rare on earth was brought to the capital, resulting in the exchange of

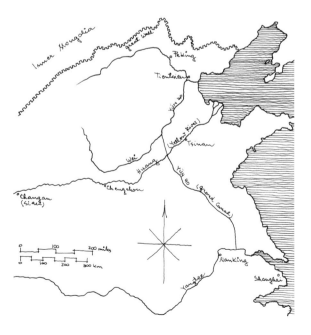

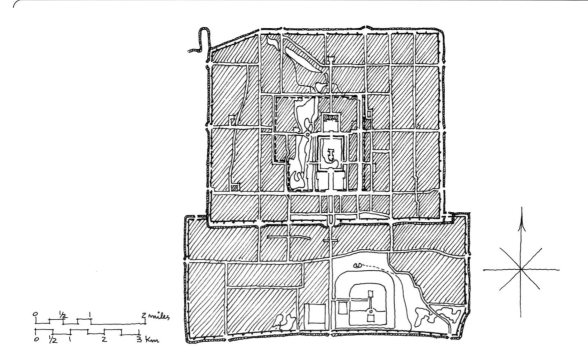

Beijing: Simplified plan of inner and outer cities

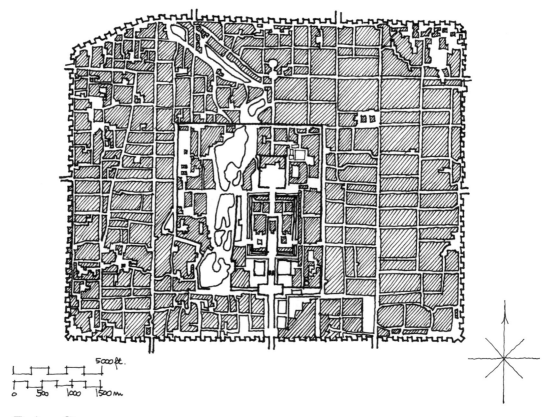

Beijing: The Inner City
(after E. A. Gutkind)

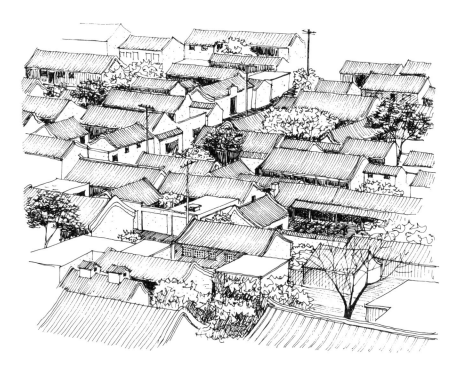

Beijing: Residential area

goods surpassing the trade of all other Chinese cities. Along the roads leading to the various provinces, and at a distance of 25 to 31 miles (40 to 50 km) apart, large villages arose. The peasant residents were settled there by the emperor. Between these rural communities and at a distance of 3 miles (2.5 km), small villages with forty houses on the average were established.

After the ousting of the Mongolian rulers, the Ming emperors moved their capital to Nanking, or "southern capital." Khanbaliq, now known as Peiping, was a border garrison town, but the third Ming emperor transferred his court to the north and Peiping was renamed Beijing, or "northern capital." It has remained the capital of China ever since, save for two decades prior to 1949.

The Manchu conquest in 1644 brought China once again under Tartar domination, but the Qing, or Manchu, dynasty

made no basic changes in the shape of the city, merely reconstructing many of the buildings and adding a number more, especially around the lakes. The Manchus monopolized the Inner City, which became known as the Tartar City, and the Outer City was called the Chinese City.

There are many other ways in which Beijing is typical of Chinese cities. It is in its comparatively modern date, being essentially of the Ming and Qing dynasties; also it is a creation rather than an accretion, a creation deliberately based on and closely resembling many previous cities going back to remote antiquity.

The plan of the city is thus clear and easy to grasp. It has four main walled enclosures: the Outer City to the south, the Inner City to the north, the Imperial City within the Inner City and within that again the Palace or "Forbidden" City. The Outer City, Inner City, and Palace City walls were moated as well (Boyd 1962, 62–64).

The different "cities" of Beijing each had their own character. The Forbidden City, with the palace of the emperor, was both monumental and formal in its buildings and courtyards, in accordance with axial planning principles. Surrounded by a red wall (hence also called the Purple City), it covered an area of 0.64 square miles (1.65 km^2). The Imperial City, with its parklike setting dominated by natural-looking artificial lakes, had a less formal character. Built between 1406 and 1437, its wall enclosure had four gates and its area covered 1.93 square miles (5 km^2). A similar difference in character also existed between the more formal Tartar City, or Inner City, and the informal Chinese City, or Outer City.

During the rule of the Manchu dynasty, the Inner City was settled by the Tartars, and the indigenous Chinese population had to move to the Outer City. Since in the Tartar City the population was not permitted to engage in any business activity, the Chinese City evolved as the business section of Beijing.

The Tartar City had nine gates in its wall enclosure, three in the south, linking it with the Chinese City, and two in each of the other walls; its area covered 11.68 square miles (30.25 km²). The Chinese City was walled in during the sixteenth century and had ten gates, five in the north, three in the south, and one each in the west and east; it covered an area of 10.55 square miles (27.32 km²). The main streets in both cities were 100 ft (30 m) wide, and although three districts of the Chinese City were almost wholly agricultural, the population density of Beijing was very high—in some districts it reached 83,000 persons per square mile (32,000 per km²). Small shops were the rule, having 15 sq ft (1.39 m²) or less in area. There were also seventy-five markets for food and other goods. In the late 1920s 110 guilds operated in Beijing—about sixty commercial, forty craft, and ten professional ones. There were no public parks in Beijing; all large open spaces were either palace gardens or private properties of nobility or wealthy citizens.

According to Gutkind, the lowest density and the greatest poverty existed side by side in the same district. Poverty was most pronounced in the northeastern and northwestern corners of the Chinese City and in the north of the Tartar City.

A fascinating insight into the social and economic structure of a typical district is gained from a detailed account by Gutkind of a characteristic area of Beijing. This area covered about one-eighth of a square mile (0.32 km²) and was surrounded by four main streets. Most shops were located along the 100-ft (30-m) wide peripheral thoroughfares as well as along two secondary streets within the district. Naturally, the shops for general use were along the primary streets, while those serving the daily needs of the district's local inhabitants were along the secondary streets. Within the district, specialized shops and craftsmen were clustered in particular areas with dwellings interspersed everywhere. The residential streets were very narrow and were characterized by long blank walls interrupted here and there by gateways. This district contained about 1,500 buildings, of which about 500 were shops, 925 were residences, and the balance consisted of temples, schools, and other official buildings.

Mostly very small, the shops and workshops represented ninety-three different trades. Altogether the inhabitants of this typical district numbered 7,900 persons, including sixty-nine officials, one hundred soldiers, and the rest engaged in 163 different professions. Perhaps the most significant observation was that the houses and shops of rich and poor alike formed a rich mosaic (Gutkind 1946, 328).

THE BEIJING HOUSE

Dating from the early twenties, Oscar Sirén's writings illustrate the traditional characteristics of Chinese dwellings in the residential districts of Beijing. Before western influences modified planning and housing design, residential streets were lined by blank and empty walls, a monotonous streetscape relieved only infrequently by an entrance gate, a portion of a curved roof, and between them, treetops. Trees inside the cities were rigorously protected, a privilege not shared by those in the open countryside.

Along residential streets there was little indication of the life and the beauty that was hidden behind the plain gray brick or plastered reddish walls protecting the dwellings. The typical home of Beijing was an extremely well-guarded place, with the only link to the outside world a simple doorway or small porch with the characteristic small saddle roof. Essentially, every family formed a

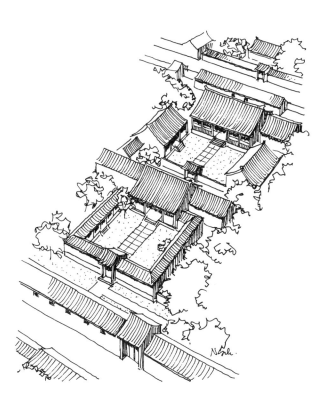

Beijing: Court-garden house
(after Steen Eiler Rasmussen)

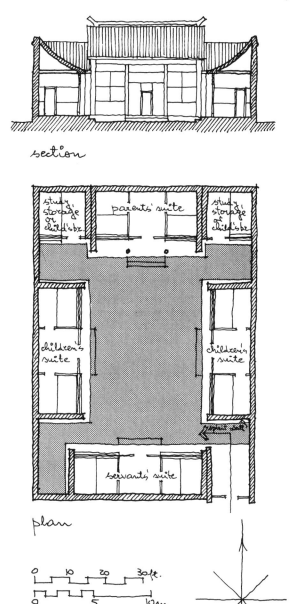

Beijing: Siheyuan house
(after Sie-Khiang Wong)

little community in itself, often quite a numerous one, since married sons shared the parental house. It is interesting to note that the walls of a family compound were often just as effective in confining the inhabitants of the compound as in protecting them against intruders; the women especially were confined within the walls. The silence of the street was now and then interrupted by the tinkling of a bell or the chiming of a bronze gong announcing an itinerant vendor.

While the street façades of the dwellings were usually monochromatic, the interior of the compounds did not lack in ornamentation. Strong colors were quite common. The brickwork and pantiles were usually gray, and all the woodwork was painted a deep red. Carved door panels were sometimes heightened with gold, and in well-to-do dwellings brackets and pillars were adorned with green and blue ornaments as well. In a setting of green foliage or blossoming trees, the courtyard views of many Beijing dwellings must have been charming.

In contrast to the quiet lanes of the residential districts, the commercial streets were much more animated. Buildings opened onto the street, and doors and windows were latticed. Shopkeepers' buildings were shaded by projecting roofs or canopies and much of the business transaction was done in the street. The inner shop in many instances was more like a living room than a place

Beijing: Courtyard views

of business. Both the proprietor and his assistants ate, slept, smoked, and sipped tea in the inner shop.

The typical Beijing house is a walled compound consisting of several buildings surrounding one or more court gardens. In dwellings where there is more than one court, the courts are laid in sequence, in a longitudinally symmetrical plan along the north-south axis. The organization of the compound could be said to resemble the traditional Chinese family structure, which was an extended family based on Confucian principles, both patriarchal and patrilocal. The father was the head of the family, but since older generations had precedence over younger ones, the older women had authority over men of a younger generation. Unmarried children and married sons with their families lived with their parents and occupied the compound in a hierarchical order, with the innermost and very private section inhabited by the family head.

The typical urban dwelling of the fairly well-to-do family was the *siheyuan*, a walled enclosure consisting basically of four buildings around a quadrangle with a north-south axis. The entrance to the compound was usually at the southeast corner of the property. This pattern was only modified if the access street's juxtaposition to the house demanded it. The front door was often painted red and was studded with bolts. The entrance hall was slightly raised above the level of the street and was often paved. Facing the door was a spirit wall, which inhibited a direct view from the street into the court garden, the central space of the siheyuan house.

Four buildings surrounded the central court garden. The south building, adjacent to the street side and facing north, was the least important in the hierarchical arrangement and usually accommodated the servant's quarters and ancillary household functions. The two side buildings, opening to east and west, respectively, were for the unmarried children and married sons with their families. The main building at the rear of the property and facing south was occupied by the head of the family and enjoyed the highest status in the hierarchical sequence.

The compound walls were usually constructed of masonry 10 to 11 ft (3 to 4 m) high, stuccoed, and with a tiled roof. Traditionally, the Beijing house had a post-and-beam structure with masonry infill

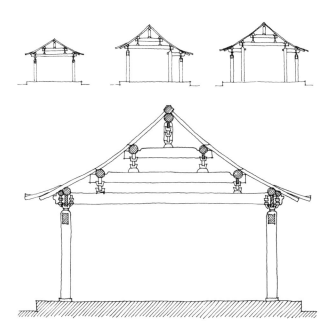

Traditional Chinese beam frame system
(after Andrew Boyd)

panels. A bay of this structure was called *jian* and was usually a rectangle with a proportion of two to three, the latter its depth. The size of the house was expressed in terms of the numbers of bays or modules it contained.

Each building was built on a rammed earth platform raised slightly above grade level; in well-to-do homes it had a brick or stone veneer. On this platform timber columns were placed on carved stone bases or dome-shaped bronze disks to protect the wood columns from the dampness of the ground. The columns supported a lintel beam parallel with the front of the house and a tiered beam frame system to span the building. This unique Chinese beam frame system made use of queen posts to support a set of secondary transverse beams and purlins; the depth of the span determined the number of queen posts and secondary beams as well as the height and the curvature of the roof structure. The purlins usually supported bamboo rafters. The roof was tiled, and projecting eaves supported on composite brackets (*san du*) protected walls. Roof tiles were glazed in various colors reflecting the rank of the occupant or the taste of the period in which it was built.

Initially, throughout the early dynasties, buildings expressed the social status of their occupants, and their size was governed by law or custom rather than the wealth of their inhabitants. Thus, for example, a person above the rank of fifth officer was entitled to build a house of five jian, whereas a commoner was only allowed a three-jian house and one without elaborate decoration. During the Han dynasty a strict etiquette determined who was allowed to be a visitor and how he was to enter the various "depths" of a house.

The Beijing house had graduated zones of privacy. A stranger or peddler was allowed to come into the entrance hall only, guests could be invited into the court garden and reception rooms, but only relatives and the most intimate friends were allowed to enter the private quarters of the home. In multicourtyard houses the sequential entry of each courtyard marked a penetration into a more secluded and intimate domain of the house. Thus, the two small corner courts adjacent to the northernmost building were the most private outdoor areas; one was reserved for the exclusive use of the head of the family and the other for his wife and daughters.

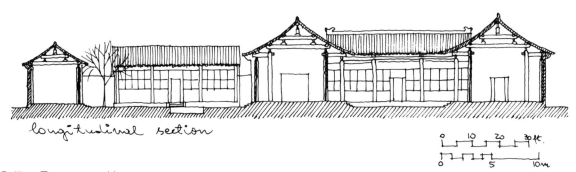

Beijing: Two-courtyard house
(after Katherine Chan and Sie-Khiang Wong)

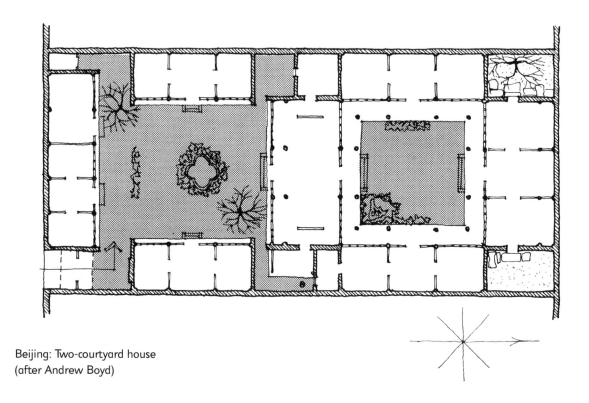

Beijing: Two-courtyard house
(after Andrew Boyd)

Broad steps led to the centrally located main door of each building of a dwelling compound: the door itself often had carved panels as well as a transom with latticework and transparent paper. Windows also had, to varying degrees, elaborate latticework covered with thick translucent paper. In spring the papers were rolled up, and throughout the warm season rooms were open toward the courtyard. Portable charcoal braziers supplied the necessary heat for most rooms during the cold season. Another method of heating was the *kang* or raised heated dais extending over part of the room; it was heated from below and served as a sitting area during the day and a sleeping platform at night.

The kitchen space was either a part of a verandah or completely in the open. There were no bathrooms as such; washing and bathing were done in the private rooms and residents used portable basins and bathtubs. The privy was most frequently a small outhouse tucked away in a corner near the street wall; it was emptied during the night, and the contents carried to rural areas to be composted.

The traditional Beijing house evolved over centuries and was shaped by collectively held conventions and traditions that changed very slowly.

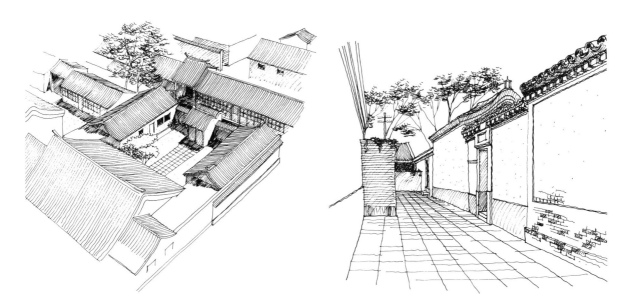

Beijing: Court-garden house

Beijing: Residential lane

Moreover, since Chinese urban dwellers did not stress individuality in the design of their homes and craftsmen adhered to traditional structural forms, the Beijing house changed little until the middle of the twentieth century. Since 1949, however, housing standards have changed radically in Beijing. The present government's policy is to preserve the harmony and integrity of Old Beijing and, indeed, to control both the height and location of new construction. However, radical socioeconomic changes made this task very difficult. Many courtyard houses have been converted into schools, workshops, and multiple dwellings. New dwelling accommodation is usually provided in three- to six-story apartment buildings; these do not reflect any aspects of the traditional oriental urban house.

Attracted by new industries located in urban areas, waves of rural people flocked to cities in search of employment—a quest naturally accompanied by an ever-increasing demand for urban housing. At the outset, housing scarcity necessitated the conversion of most single-family courtyard houses into crowded multiple dwellings, each sheltering several families. Other courtyard houses were converted into nonresidential buildings,

such as schools and workshops. The latter conversion preserved the appearance of the original family homes more accurately than those converted into multifamily dwellings with numerous lean-tos and alterations.

Since conversions alone could not satisfy the housing requirements of a rapidly growing urban population, additional dwellings built at a higher density had to be provided. A multistory walk-up residential building proved to be the most promising prototype for mass housing, in spite of the fact that this so-called *danyuanlo* did not share any features with traditional oriental urban house forms. Initially, walk-ups were built three to four stories high and had little space (37 square feet or 3.5 square meters per person), but over time spatial living standards improved to 85 square feet or 8 square meters per person. Recently, building heights increased to up to seven stories with two-story maisonette units on the top floor. Walk-up residential buildings were often built in regimented monotonous rows with predominantly south-facing façades. At present, most Chinese urban dwellings are in multistory walk-ups.

Newer and wealthier cities, such as Shenzen (established in 1980 near the border of Hong

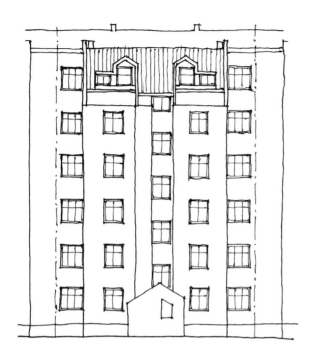

Walk-up apartments, north elevation.

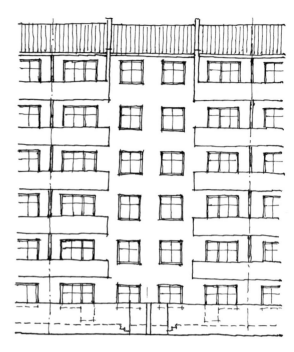

Walk-up apartments, south elevation.

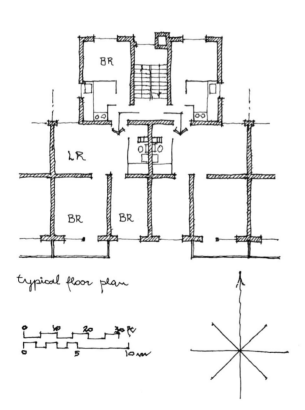

typical floor plan

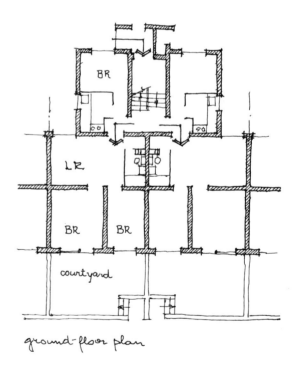

ground-floor plan

Walk-up apartments
(after Beijing Architectural Research Institute, 1991)

Kong), have high-rise elevator-serviced apartment buildings and, just as in Hong Kong, the outward appearance of these buildings resembles that of their North American counterparts. Although the spatial standards in these new high-rise buildings are more than double that of the Chinese norm (they provide up to 220 square feet or 20 square meters per person), they are still less than a third of the North American average. Admittedly, the latter is an exclusive standard unsustainable in the long run anywhere else in the world.

In contrast to the prevalent walk-ups and high-rise residential developments, Beijing's recent Ju'er Hutong experimental housing project augurs a change for the better in housing design. This low-rise housing project was ranked by Beijing residents as one of the best buildings in the capital (ahead of the Great Hall of the People), which must indicate that the Chinese public prefers low- to mid-rise housing with a human scale rather than a monumental one. Without repeating any stereotypes, the Ju'er Hutong project is described by Omar Khattab as socially, culturally, and climatically appropriate and compatible with its inner city environment (1994, 42). The Ju'er Hutong project provides a carefully designed domestic environment for its residents and Professor Wu Liangyong, the initiator of this development, received the World Habitat Award of 1993 for its design.

CHAPTER SIX

THE JAPANESE URBAN HOUSE IN KYOTO

THE CITY OF KYOTO

Modeled on the ancient Chinese capital Changan, Heiankyo ("the capital of peace and tranquility")—what is known today as Kyoto—served as Japan's capital and residence of the imperial family for more than a millennium (794–1868). Towards the end of the so-called Golden Age of Japan (1192), the population of Kyoto may have been over half a million, with more citizens than any European city of that period, with the possible exception of Constantinople and Cordova. Although smaller in area than Changan, Heiankyo (Kyoto) still measured about 4 miles (6.4 km) north to south and 3 miles (4.8 km) east to west. The emperors' palace occupied a south-facing site (0.87 by 0.68 miles or 1.4 by 1.1 km) in the middle of the northern section of the city, and a willow-lined axial wide avenue called *Suzaku* ran from the palace entrance to a gate that was built into a symbolic short fortification wall at the southern border of the city. As Japan was an island nation, like Britain, the circumvallation of cities was neither as consistent nor as important as it was on the mainland, where incursions of hostile foreign armies were a greater threat.

Divided into two halves by Suzaku Avenue, each half of the city with its own market area, Kyoto was further divided by a grid of streets into several hundred square city blocks, each about 394 by 394 ft (120 by 120 m). A single palatial residence of a Heian aristocratic family, a compound of several buildings with a south-facing ceremonial courtyard, and beyond, a pond with a central island, could cover several city blocks, while other mansions of aristocratic families occupied only a single one. Most city blocks were divided into thirty-two building lots (about 4,840 sq ft or 450 m²).

During the feudal epoch Japanese society was divided into four classes: *Samurai* (sword-bearing men), artisans, peasants, and merchants. Building

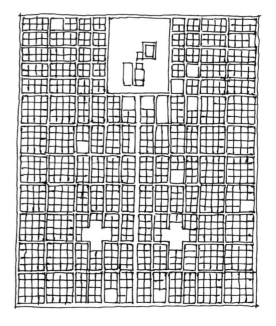

Kyoto: Palace city, eighth century
(after Kazuo Nishi and Kazuo Hozumi)

plots for merchant and artisan dwellings were located in less exclusive parts of town. Traditionally built along the periphery of the block, these dwellings had a narrow street frontage, with the center of the block serving originally as a communal open space, at times used for cultivation.

Surrounded on three sides by low mountains, Kyoto is located in the Yamashiro fault basin, and during its long history it has been rebuilt several times after being ravaged by earthquakes, firestorms, and war. In the late sixteenth century the city was rebuilt by *Taiko* (great sovereign) Toyotomi Hideyoshi, who was responsible for the many beautiful Shinto shrines, Buddhist temples, palaces, and gardens.

Kyoto, like most large Japanese cities, appears as a crowded urban agglomeration from the air, a sea of shingled or tiled roofs without chimneys, a monotony broken only by the occasional temple and its garden. And, as in other oriental cities, "you will find the houses of the wealthy in the immediate vicinity of the habitations of the poorest"(Morse 1961, 5). Moreover, the unpainted wooden façades of urban houses are more commonplace in appearance towards the street, than the picturesque shoji-screened walls facing their secluded gardens. Here, as in other oriental cultures, ostentation reflects bad manners.

The Kyoto Merchant's House

Japanese wood-constructed homes were pretty. Although they may have appeared to Americans to be fragile, in reality, they withstood earthquakes better than masonry-built dwellings, and because of frequent seismic activity they rarely exceeded two stories in height.

The traditional merchant or artisan urban house in Kyoto was the *machiya*. Like the Chinese shophouse, these elongated dwellings were built on deep lots with narrow street frontages popularly known as "eel nests."

The front room was the shop, or *mise*, where goods were displayed and sold. In linear sequence it was followed by the *nakanoma*, or middle room, with a staircase leading to the upper floor, which had a similar layout to that of the ground floor. Next to the nakanoma was the back room, or *zashiki*, which was the formal reception room as well as the master's room. With virtually no furniture, most rooms were multipurpose spaces, but they usually had ample cupboards and closet space. Bedsteads were absent in the Japanese house; mats called *futons* were used to sleep on, with a pillow and blanket as a cover. During the day the mattress

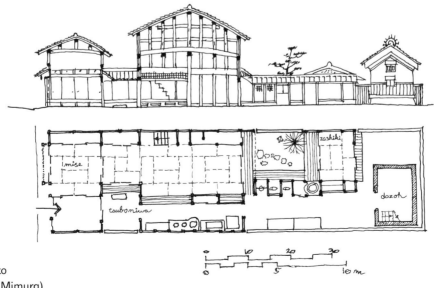

Machiya, Kyoto
(after Hiroshi Mimura)

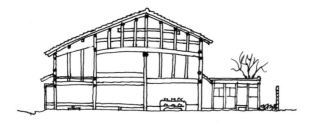

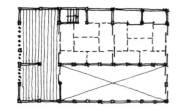

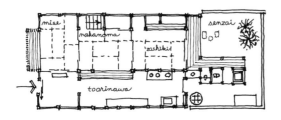

Machiya, Kyoto
(after Hiroshi Mimura)

was rolled up and stowed away in a closet with the blanket and pillows. A sliding screen made of a light frame of wood covered with paper, called *fusuma*, was used between rooms. These screens were removed to make one room out of two. Since floors were covered with standard-sized *tatami* mats, room sizes were described by the number of floor mats used.

The spine of the Kyoto shop house was a side corridor called *tooriniwa*, which ran from the street "entrance hall" to the backyard garden. This multipurpose space was open to the rafters, and in addition to serving as a passageway to most of the rooms, it also accommodated kitchen facilities and a well. The floor of the tooriniwa was of tamped earth about 20 inches below the tatami-covered floors of the various rooms accessible from it. The toilet and bathroom were located in the rear narrow wing projecting into the backyard, and were accessible both from the verandah and the spine corridor.

Being the most formal reception room, the zashiki contained the altar box of the family's ancestors as well as the recess called the *tokonoma*, the latter invariably adorned with a picture and a single flower in a vase. A wooden terrace or verandah acted as a transition space between the zashiki and the backyard garden, called the *senzai*. The exterior paneled sliding wall of this formal room varied with the seasons. In winter a wooden lattice covered on one side with translucent white rice paper, called *shoji*, was used, whereas in summer reed screens or bamboo blinds provided shade as well as privacy. At night, more solid outside sliding rain-doors were used to close the house.

Larger and more elaborate urban houses often had an interior courtyard called a *tsuboniwa* indicating the boundary between the commercial front section of the house and the dwelling. Well-to-do merchants usually built a detached fireproof masonry storehouse called *dozoh* in the rear of the property as a precaution against fire in a vulnerable timber-built urban area.

A detached zashiki was sometimes built in the back garden, where the master of the house could hold the tea ceremony for his guests. The back garden was designed to be enjoyed from the indoors when the shoji was opened to permit a garden view. Along the borders of the garden, fencing or hedge planting ensured complete privacy from the neighbors. The elements of the garden may have included stepping-stones, a water basin, and plants graduating in height as they approached the property line, but equally important vistas were the rooftops of the neighbors, the distant mountains and, above all, the sky.

During the last decades of the nineteenth century and throughout the twentieth century, Japanese art and architecture had a profound influence upon the western world. As early as the World's Fair exhibition in London (1867), Japanese colored woodcuts delighted not only artists, but lay people as well. Similarly, the Japanese pavilion at the Worlds Columbian Exposition held in Chicago (1893) enthralled many North American architects like Frank Lloyd Wright and the Greene brothers. The superb craftsmanship, and the structural and

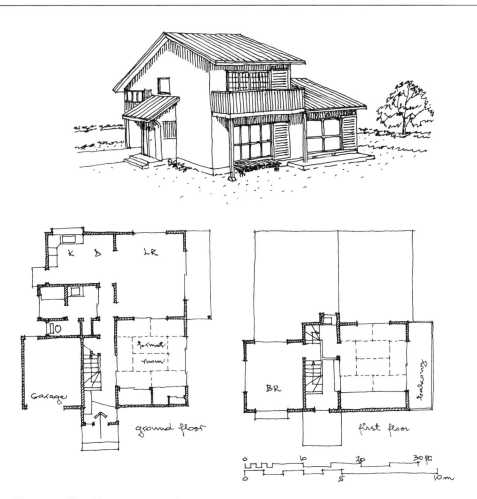

Example of Japanese "2 x 4" contemporary house
(after Home Planning, 1976)

aesthetic integrity of this pavilion embodied the very principles of the Arts and Crafts movement.

At the turn of the century, Japanese-inspired airy, bright, simple interiors greatly contrasted with the conventional somber and cluttered interiors of Victorian homes, and they became very popular with the avant garde. The simplicity and the modular nature of Japanese architecture continued to have an influence upon architecture in the west throughout the twentieth century, but the International Style of the Modern Movement also found resonance in pre-war Japan. Frank Lloyd Wright's Imperial Hotel (1915–22) and his residences were much admired, but an even greater impact was exerted by Bruno Taut, an ardent modernist architect committed to the improvement of domestic design. He spent three years in Japan studying and writing on Japanese art and culture. Antonin Raymond, who came to Tokyo with Wright, built himself a "modern" reinforced concrete house (1923) and stayed in Japan until his death.

An unprecented shortage of housing after World War II in a country where people were accustomed to shortages caused by earthquakes and fire devastation necessitated the promotion of multistory apartment buildings—a radical change from single-family traditional wood-constructed houses to multifamily structures built of fire-resistant masonry or concrete. The living spaces of apartments were consistently small, usually less than half the size of a North American dwelling intended for the same number of people.

The acceptance of multiple house forms is a slow progess since it contravenes tradition, nevertheless progress has been made. Kunio Mayekawa, who apprenticed with Le Corbusier, designed the ten-story Harumi Apartments. They are similar to the Unité d'Habitation because they have a central-access corridor on every third floor resulting in efficient elevator service and cross-ventilation in apartments on every two out of three floors. Architect Kiyonori Kikutake also built a Unité-type apartment building for a large firm at Yokohama.

In Japan, where people traditionally own and inhabit their own homes with an attached garden, experiments were initiated from the early fifties to build mass-produced single-family houses. Among others, Kenji Hiroshe has designed more than thirty types of detached houses, each with a steel frame and building components suitable for mass production. A popular prototype of a single-family detached home used during the second half of the twentieth century is the "2 x 4 House," a name derived from its wood frame construction with walls made of 2- by 4-in studs, a significant departure from the post-and-beam construction method inherent to Japan.

As in North America, the choice of housing in Japan is polarized between low-rise single-family detached houses and multistory, usually high-rise, apartment dwellings—the latter often built by a firm to house its employees.

SUMMARY

The oriental urban house has its roots in ancient civilizations and is an enduring dwelling form that has sheltered more than two hundred consecutive generations of city dwellers in the Near East, on the Indian subcontinent, in North Africa, and the Far East. The intrinsic characteristics and attributes of this inward-looking dwelling form are many, but surely the most important feature is its central and private open space, the court garden. The court is the heart of the oriental urban house and no single word in another language can equal the poetry of its Chinese name, which, translated, is "the well of heaven"; this well provides the house with light, air, and rainwater.

An intrinsic attribute of the court-garden house concept is that it offers favorable microclimatic conditions to its inhabitants; the climate in an enclosed court can be easily modified in terms of both air temperature and humidity through the use of plants, shading devices, or water fountains. Moreover, the walls of the square courtyard inherently offer exposure in four different directions; thus, the orientation of various rooms in the house is not restricted by external constraints (such as an undesirable view, for example, which all too frequently governs the layout of the occidental house). The central open space becomes what the inhabitants make of it, and since most habitable rooms face upon it, the court resembles a patio or small garden rather than the backyard of its counterpart, the occidental urban house.

Another characteristic inherent to the court-garden house is that its inward-looking form results in both acoustical and visual privacy not only from the street but also from its neighbors. Almost invariably in the oriental urban house a screen wall, or spirit wall, faces the main entrance, inhibiting a direct view from the street into the court garden; the intrusion of the curious is prevented and the privacy of the family home is thus safeguarded.

To enhance the privacy of the family, the oriental urban house is divided into public and private sections; the former is the area where guests are received, while the latter is the secluded domain of the family. In contrast to occidental custom, the family section of the oriental house is invariably the most spacious part of the dwelling, and only in very large homes does the public section approach the spaciousness and luxury of the family quarters.

Another characteristic of the oriental urban house is the flexibility of its interior spaces. Most rooms are multipurpose and are not habitually used for a specific activity such as sleeping or dining. Instead, the oriental dwelling allows rooms for specific members of the household who use their room for a number of functions: eating, sleeping, and entertaining close friends.

The typical oriental urban house has a simple and unpretentious street façade that derives from the social values of its inhabitants. Ostentation is shunned to the extent that even the building height is limited; in China, for example, traditional urban houses rarely exceeded one story and in other oriental countries, two or three stories.

It becomes evident from the foregoing observations upon privacy that the oriental urban house differs greatly in this aspect from the occidental urban home. The latter rarely has an outdoor extension, such as a patio or garden, that is not overlooked by its neighbors. Moreover, with the absence of a privacy screen, the entrance to the occidental house affords a direct view from the street into its interior, and what is not visible through the entrance is displayed through its picture windows. In contrast to the mashrabiyyah, the trellised bay window of the Islamic house, the picture window not only affords a view of the street from the interior of the house, but also a view of family life in the home from the outside. Finally, the occidental house also represents social values in its external appearance, but of a very different order, by attempting consciously to reflect the status of its inhabitants. The occidental custom in no way imposes restrictions to building size or height, both of which are in fact employed to denote status, and which result in pretentious detached estates in suburbs or ostentatious penthouse apartments on top of high-rise towers in the city, both symbols of success.

In the Orient the sensitivity expressed in house design is carried beyond the boundaries of the home into the urban residential environment and manifests itself in a spatial disposition that has a gradual hierarchical order.

Just as the oriental urban house has private and public areas, the oriental neighborhood itself has a similar order that is at least as sophisticated. Accordingly, the blind alleys or narrow local streets giving access to a cluster of private homes are semiprivate areas, while the collector or spine street with the local community facilities of its residential precinct represents the semipublic realms; beyond the gates of the spine street is the public urban domain with thoroughfares, suqs, and public institutions.

In the Orient residential precincts represent commonalities or solidarities based on ethnicity, sectarian religious affiliations, or multiracial groups unified by occupation or some other form of association, but they do not represent homogeneous income groups. Residential precincts are communities of both rich and poor and in this respect differ from the economically stratified residential urban neighborhoods of the Occident.

It is interesting to note that precincts were once fairly common in occidental cities, especially in Great Britain, although they have since become almost extinct. Precincts were basically private enclosures not penetrated by public rights-of-way. These precincts, which were adjuncts of a religious order or cathedral, were also considered to be outside the jurisdiction of the local government of the city in which they were located. The reason for enclosing religious precincts were twofold: first, to ensure discipline among the members within, and second, to provide protection against assailants from outside. In later years, when walls were no longer required for defense, they still were useful as precinct boundaries when disputes arose over jurisdiction with lay authorities, especially when fugitives sought shelter within a precinct. Probably the inherent attributes of privacy and serenity were also cherished as a relief from the crowded and noisy city (*Improvements* 1951, 132–33).

After the dissolution of monasteries in the sixteenth century, only a very few precincts remained within the walled City of London, and of these the most important were the Tower and St. Paul's. Another survived, but outside the city walls; the Inns of Court, that is, the Inner and Middle Temples, which have a great affinity to the residential precincts of the oriental city and provide a living example of a form of urban development that demonstrates the many advantages of quiet and seclusion. The very qualities that make it so desirable also tend to obscure it from the public. It is unfortunate that it was not emulated in other areas of London. In fact, quite the opposite took place in subsequent centuries, namely, the adoption of "residential squares," such as Bedford Square, where town houses faced public streets and the central fenced-in park was used exclusively by residents of the square; each family had a key to the gates of the park and preferred its use for recreation in full public view instead of its own private yard, which was relegated to household service activities and for use as a stable yard.

Oriental influences undeniably shaped both the classical Greek and Roman urban house, but after the collapse of the Roman Empire, and the Dark Ages, which lasted several centuries, the oriental heritage was forgotten or ignored in the occidental world. While it is true that the inward-looking court-garden concept continued to be used in the monasteries and convents of the Christian Church, lay buildings in cities became outward-looking. Although many medieval houses did, in fact, have courtyards, their function was different from that of the oriental urban house; they were merely backyards or service yards, and the principal orientation of the house was toward the street. The outward-looking urban house became the norm in the occidental world, the only exception being in countries where Moorish influences shaped urban residential design. From Hispania the Moorish influence was transplanted to Latin America and, thus, the oriental heritage in indigenous house design has survived in the occident only in Spanish, Portuguese, and Latin American patio houses.

Early Hispanic settlers brought with them to the Americas an architectural heritage of inward-looking rural *haciendas* and urban patio houses houses. One- or two-story patio houses, which closely imitate the urban dwellings of Spain or Portugal, still prevail in many old quarters of Latin American cities. Open to the sky, the patio is an outdoor space, yet it is neither a garden nor a courtyard, and often it is used as an indoor room. The patio is at the center of family life, the space around which the home is built.

Typically, the patio house is entered through a portal, which leads to a passageway known as the *zaguan*. At some distance from the wooden street portals there is a secondary gate, a grilled *portón* usually made of wrought iron, which gives a measure of protection from intruders when the main portal is left open during the day; this grille also

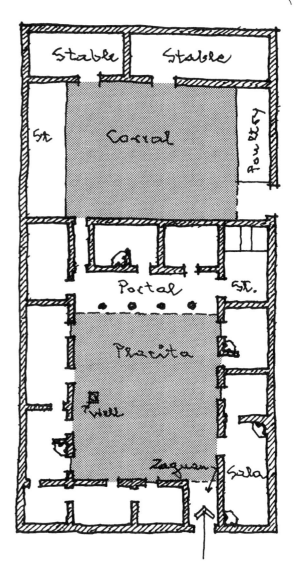

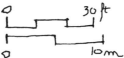

Hacienda, New Mexico

gives the passers-by a fleeting glimpse of the flower-filled patio beyond. Larger homes often have, in addition to their main patio, a second smaller patio which is surrounded by the kitchen and other service and utility rooms, an arrangement which resembles that of the atrium and atriolum of the Roman domus.

Since the fifties, the courtyard house has gained a wide acceptance in a number of European countries, and not only in those regions with a warm

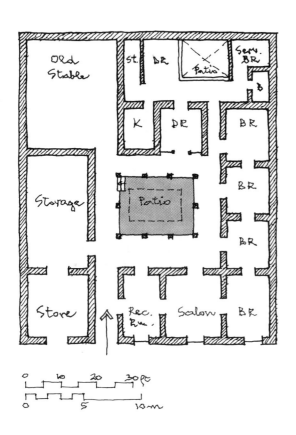

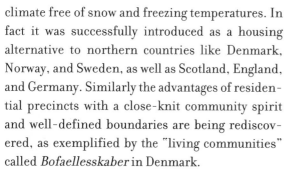

Town house, Riosucio, Colombia

Courtyard

climate free of snow and freezing temperatures. In fact it was successfully introduced as a housing alternative to northern countries like Denmark, Norway, and Sweden, as well as Scotland, England, and Germany. Similarly the advantages of residential precincts with a close-knit community spirit and well-defined boundaries are being rediscovered, as exemplified by the "living communities" called *Bofaellesskaber* in Denmark.

In a world where no nation is wealthy enough to afford waste, the land-use efficiency of the oriental urban residential pattern is worthy of emulation in terms of both land use and energy conservation. This is not to say that the oriental urban environment should be duplicated, but merely that some of its urban design principles should be adopted,

such as, for example, the hierarchical order in street networks that bring about a safer residential environment.

Moreover, planning small precincts for residential neighborhoods without through traffic would afford a more intimate identity with the residential community. In addition, a compact urban development pattern with no waste space would result in reasonable walking distances to many community facilities and would create the population density required for efficient mass transportation systems. Finally, the courtyard concept could be applied successfully in the design of both single-family dwellings as well as multiple housing in which each dwelling would have some semblance of privacy and indeed also "a well of heaven."

PART III

The Occidental Urban House

INTRODUCTION

The occidental urban civilization was influenced by the ancient oriental urban civilizations that preceded it by about 5,000 years. One of the important formative forces in its evolution was Christianity, a religion born in the Near East, a cradle of ancient civilizations. Another was the oriental influence that reached the occidental world indirectly through the Hellenic and Roman civilizations. The Romans occupied a large segment of the European continent and left an indelible imprint upon the occupied territory, especially in the cities. After the collapse of the Roman Empire a new occidental civilization arose that, in spite of its Roman roots (and despite its growth in many cases from Roman ruins), acquired a character that is manifestly different from both the Roman and oriental civilizations.

The distinct occidental character of the new urban civilization was partly attributable to the fact that the continuum of urban development on the European continent came to a sudden halt after the collapse of the Roman Empire. Centuries of chaotic conditions followed in western Europe, and during these Dark Ages urban life virtually ceased. A maelstrom of migration uprooted sedentary urban life; the inhabitants of former cities fled to isolated rural areas to escape the barbaric hordes. Cities, more than isolated rural areas, were most prone to barbaric assault, not only because of their high visibility and strategic geographic location, but also because of their riches. Not all cities were annihilated; small fragments of urban communities survived here and there, and they provided the nucleus for the relatively speedy redevelopment of the new urban society.

One of the most significant breaks with the oriental urban heritage occurred in the domain of housing. The Hellenic, Hellenistic, and Roman traditions in housing, characterized by an inward orientation, were either forgotten or disregarded. Most of the intrinsic features of oriental urban housing were absent in occidental urban housing—such as the central court garden (the focal point of domestic

Dwelling towers
(after Roland Anheisser)

life), the main entrance with a privacy screen, the division of the dwelling into two distinct segments for males and females, the unpretentious street façade, scarce or screened fenestration, and the close-knit residential precincts inhabited by mixed income groups.

It could be argued that many of the oriental characteristics in urban dwellings were abandoned in the Occident for climatic reasons. Certainly in northern climes a central open space, such as an atrium or a peristyle court garden, would have been practically useless for outdoor living during the winter season. Moreover, climatic considerations may also have led to the use of larger, more open fenestration in order to capture more sunlight. However

reasonable this argument based on climatic forces may be, it still remains inadequate as the only explanation for the radical departure from an urban dwelling tradition over 5,000 years old.

In religious architecture, however, the tradition prevailed. The cloister, basically a peristyle court-yard, has survived throughout the ages in its basic concept, whether it was built in northern or south-ern climes. The only adjustment made was the loca-tion of the cloister with respect to the main body of the church with its east-west axis. As can be expect-ed in northern climates, the cloister was invariably located along the south side of the church nave. Thus, in monastic architecture climatic forces were moderating factors only.

Austrian gabled urban dwellings
(after Roland Anheisser)

In an age marked by ongoing hostilities, defense was of primary concern. This concern is reflected in a unique early medieval house form—the dwelling tower—which was a regular fortress. It had narrow windows resembling loopholes, a crenellated parapet, and sometimes even machiculation. The entrance to dwelling towers was usually one story above ground level and reached via a ladder; by withdrawing the ladder, access to the main doorway was made nearly impossible. This early medieval dwelling form derived its intrinsic features not from climatic considerations, but from defensive ones. In effect, the tower dwelling is the complete opposite in physical design to the Roman *domus*. The former is a tall, multistoried detached structure with fenestration on all of its four exterior sides, while the latter is a rambling low building attached to its neighbors, with fenestration opening primarily toward the interior outdoor space, namely, the atrium and the peristyle court gardens. In a sense, both are defensive in nature, but their respective approaches to safety were diametrically opposed.

Dwelling towers were only one prototype of early medieval occidental urban dwellings; another was the gabled house built on a narrow but deep building plot. This second prototype had its roots in the indigenous rural dwellings of the sedentary agricultural population. Rural dwellings evolved over centuries, and of necessity their form was derived, to a considerable extent, from the climatic realities of their particular region.

This claim for a rural heritage for early occidental urban dwellings is well founded. In fact, all ancient civilizations developed their urban house forms from rural dwellings adapted and altered gradually over the course of many years to urban conditions.

This adaptation, however, altered neither the basic design principles nor the spatial relationship within the dwelling. An even more convincing proof of the gabled urban dwelling's rural heritage is the similarity between urban dwellings in medieval cities and their neighboring village or rural dwellings. Even today small-town dwellings in most isolated parts of Europe are practically indistinguishable from village or rural dwellings.

Although an interior courtyard is quite common, especially in late medieval urban houses, the function of these outdoor spaces was different from their oriental counterpart. They were service yards rather than court gardens. The medieval courtyards in merchant houses were used for loading and unloading of goods. In those of craftsmen they were spillover areas of the workshop, and in those of burghers, who cultivated land outside the city gates, they were regular farmyards. Medieval burghers who practiced agriculture as a sideline to their main profession were quite numerous, which is understandable if one remembers that horses were extensively used in that era for transportation; the upkeep of horses was greatly facilitated when their owners had access to land holdings near the city.

The use of stables, haylofts, and service quarters at the rear of urban dwellings lasted well into the nineteenth century. For example, London's fashionable terraced houses frequently had a mews with coach houses in the rear. This was especially true of the upper-income residences.

A significant change affected the urban dwelling in the eighteenth century. The home separated from the owner's workplace and the two were no longer synonymous. This separation of domestic and business activities had far-reaching consequences not only within the home, but also in the immediate neighborhood. The city eventually became compartmentalized into residential, commercial, recreational, and industrial areas. Single-use zones replaced efficient and balanced mixed land use.

Other changes affected the occidental urban house as a result of the social and physical degradation brought about by the Industrial Revolution. Cities grew too fast to provide the basic municipal services to their inhabitants, especially to those who arrived in droves from rural districts to seek their fortunes in the expanding cities. Toward the end of the nineteenth century the living standards of the great majority of urban dwellers reached the lowest point in the history of occidental urban development to that date. The city, which had been equated with freedom during the Middle Ages, became a yoke of desperation for large numbers of city inhabitants during the Victorian era. The task of improving living conditions in cities was so awesome that many city and housing reformers advocated starting anew instead of trying to solve existing problems. Thus, Ebenezer Howard's Garden City concept promised a new lease on urban life by building "New Towns" in virgin green fields, protected by a "Green Belt." This concept inadvertently avoided the problems of the existing cities and allowed the well-to-do segment of the population to escape into "suburbs" and to isolate their families from the harsh realities of city living.

The problem of providing adequate housing for the poor was not resolved during the nineteenth century when it reached desperate proportions, nor has it been adequately resolved by subsequent generations who still grope with its solution.

CHAPTER ONE

THE DARK AGES

THE ECLIPSE OF ROMAN CITIES

With the gradual decline of the Roman Empire a new epoch, later to be known as the Dark Ages, began in western Europe, and the Roman urban heritage, rooted in the Orient, gradually came to an end.

The disintegration of the Roman world lasted about three centuries. During this period of decay urban life and civilization—at least in western Europe—declined and, in many parts, virtually ceased for many centuries. The reasons for the decline were many. Paramount was the diminishing of the Roman population at a time when non-Romans experienced unprecedented growth. The educated Roman citizenry was affected by the population decline first: "The ablest men married latest, bred least, and died soonest" (Durant 1944, 666). By A.D. 100 this decline had reached the common citizens and farmers; so many farms had been abandoned in Italy that "Pertinax offered them gratis to anyone who would till them" (Durant 1944, 665).

Wars, revolutions, and pestilence also reduced the Roman population. The plague of A.D. 250–265 afflicted every family of the empire; in Rome during the height of the epidemic 5,000 deaths were recorded daily. In addition, malaria also plagued the Romans of the Campagna, especially in Latium and Tuscany.

Moral decay was another factor that contributed to the dissolution of the empire. Although it was a punishable crime, the poor resorted to infanticide as poverty grew, while the rich leaders of society practiced immoral and cruel excesses. For example, "Platianus, praetorian Prefect, had one hundred boys emasculated, and then gave them to his daughter as a wedding gift" (Durant 1944, 666).

Political decay commenced with despotism and was followed by the practice of indolence, venality, and self-indulgence on the part of the Roman Senators. Because ability was disparaged, the ablest men no longer aspired to public office. Inevitably, political ineptitude was accompanied by economic decline, confiscatory taxation to support a nonproductive and expanding bureaucracy, the depreciation of the currency, and the rising cost of armies. These manifestations of decline were common between the second and fifth centuries in Rome.

This state of affairs provided fertile ground for Christianity to root and flourish. With an ethic of nonresistance, nonviolence, peace, and charity, Christianity paradoxically possessed the most effective weapon against brutality. Moreover, its teaching encouraged humility and poverty; hence, as poverty grew, so did the numbers of Christ's followers.

The final blow to the decaying Roman Empire came in the fifth century with the invasion of Italy by the Vandals under Genseric and the subsequent sacking of Rome. By this time other barbarian chieftains had already established themselves as heads of state in Gaul, Spain, and North Africa, and with the installation of a barbarian king in Italy, the Roman Empire came to an end.

The barbarian conquests set back European civilization for centuries. "Economically it meant reruralization. The Barbarians lived by tillage, herding, hunting and war, and had not learned the commercial complexities on which cities thrived; with their victory the municipal character of Western civilization ceased for seven centuries" (Durant 1950, 43). A demographic maelstrom of migrations and invasions eventually brought about the disappearance of some ethnic groups, but it also resulted in the formation of new nations through the amalgamation of several tribes. During this period of upheaval considerable areas of Italy were denuded of population and most towns contracted their areas "as a means of economically walling them for defense; and in many cases the walls were improvised from the debris of theatres, basilicas, and temples that had once adorned the municipal splendor of Italy. . . . Rome itself shrunk from 1,500,000 souls to some 300,000 in one century" (Durant 1950, 42), and by the middle of the fifth century its population did not exceed 50,000.

Established cities were prime targets for the barbarian invaders, and practically all occidental Roman cities fell victim to their destruction. An indication of the numbers of city dwellers can also be derived from the diminution of the Judean population of western Europe during this period. Judeans who were taken from their homeland to Europe by the Roman legions during the first two centuries A.D. adapted themselves successfully and multiplied as city dwellers. It is estimated that their number in the year A.D. 300 reached almost a million. "Less than ten thousand survived as Jews by the year 800 C.E. [A.D.]" (Agus 1965, vol. 1, 15). There is little doubt that some Jews, especially the simple and uneducated ones, were converted to Christianity in the prolonged effort of the Catholic Church to crush all dissident sects, but the majority fell victim to the erosive force of the barbarians, who did not distinguish between faith and creeds. Since the barbarians exerted most of their destructive power against towns and cities and since the Jews were mainly town dwellers, they suffered much greater destruction proportionately than the native population (Agus 1965, vol. 1, 14).

Not all Roman cities, however, were destroyed. The cities of Byzantium in the eastern Roman Empire escaped destruction, at least for a while. Thus, Constantinople (Byzantium) flourished during the Dark Ages and became a center of learning and trade, and the Roman heritage, modified by Christian orthodoxy, survived for some time.

Other notable Roman cities were also saved from destruction or experienced an early revival after a brief decline. Toletum (Toledo) after the invasion by the Visigoths became their capital city; its location in the heart of the Iberian Peninsula, its strategic setting on a rugged promontory washed on three sides by the Tagus River, as well as its well-established church organization, which converted the invaders early to Christianity, ensured the survival of the city. Even after the Moorish conquest in 712, Tolaitola (as it was now called) became a capital of an Arab principality, although it lost its preeminent position to Cordova.

Toledo flourished during the Moorish occupation as a center of learning and art. Silk and wool industries founded by members of Toledo's Jewish community added great wealth to the city. The Moors gradually changed the city's Roman character and replaced it with an Islamic one. The street network, for example, became a maze of narrow lanes and squares, oriental features that were retained even after its reconquest in 1085.

Corduba (Cordova), a *colonia patricia* under the Romans, underwent similar changes. Captured in 571 by the Visigoths, it became the see of a bishop. In 711 the Moors sacked and partially destroyed the city, but during the subsequent decades rebuilt it to be worthy of a caliphate, the seat of the Omayyad dynasty. Corthobah, as it was now called, reached the summit of its splendor during the Dark Ages under 'abd al-Rahman III (912–961). The walled city covered an area of 385 acres (156 hectares) and beyond this medina, the *Alcazabah* were extensive

Arles: Medieval city within the amphitheater

suburbs that housed its large number of inhabitants. Cordova's population approached one million, and Arab accounts of the period mention
213,077 dwellings for "ordinary" persons, 60,300
residences for the upper classes, 80,000 shops,
300 mosques, 900 baths, 80 schools, and 50 hospitals. Even if these figures prove to be exaggerated, it is unquestionable that Cordova was a formidable city by the end of the tenth century; its
importance in Europe at the time was surpassed
only by Constantinople. The Berber invasion in
1010 marked the beginning of Cordova's decline,
and during the subsequent century it lost many of
its inhabitants, who fled to Granada.

Cities such as Toledo, Cordova, Granada, and
many others on the Iberian Peninsula, as well as
Palermo and other southern Italian cities that were
also under Arab occupation, continued the oriental
heritage of urban life until the Arabs were
expelled. The physical imprint of the oriental
influence upon these cities, particularly the adher-
ence to the inward-looking urban house, lived on
even after the departure of the Moors. It is still evident today. Physically, these cities are markedly
different from the medieval cities that emerged

during the Dark Ages and subsequent periods in
other parts of Europe.

In those parts of Europe that were not occupied
by the Moors or Saracens, frequent barbarian
incursions diminished and disrupted city life.
Large cities lay in ruins, and their few surviving citizens sometimes became mere squatters in a single
Roman building. Arles, in southern France, for
instance, served as the prefecture of the Gauls and
was known as Arelate during the Roman Empire.
Although pillaged in 270, it was restored and
embellished once again by the Romans to its former
beauty. After the collapse of the Roman Empire, the
city was occupied by the Visigoths and in 730 plun-
dered and destroyed by the Saracens. The few surviving inhabitants took refuge within the protective
walls of their amphitheater. The confines of this
large Roman edifice—seating capacity was 25,000—
became the setting of an emerging medieval
fortress town. With the exception of two gateways,
the two lower stories, consisting of sixty arcades,
were walled in and adapted to dwellings. The third-
floor arcade was demolished, and the building
materials so gained were used to complete the fortification installations and to build on the level site

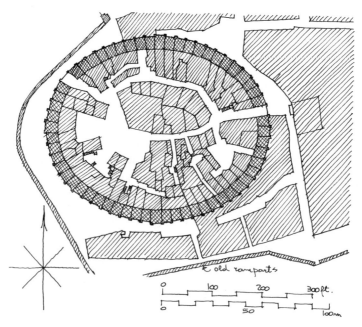

Nîmes: Medieval city within the amphitheater (1809)
(after Enrico Guidoni)

of the arena a church, chapels, and additional houses. This compact fortress settlement with its four defense towers survived the vicissitudes of many subsequent centuries and was still in existence as an identifiable city precinct at the beginning of the nineteenth century, when it was demolished to free the Roman ruins from their medieval appendices.

This adaptation of an amphitheater to a medieval fortress city was not unique. In similar circumstances the inhabitants of Nîmes, another city of southern France, transformed their amphitheater into a small medieval city of 2,000 inhabitants served by two churches. The arcades of the theater were filled in with masonry walls and served as the ramparts of the town.

Even in Rome the theater of Marcellus was altered to accommodate shops at its base and four stories of housing above. In this instance, the amphitheater was not a city in itself, but merely a city block. Amphitheaters in Florence, Lucca, and Paris, to cite but a few examples, were also changed into housing and are still easily spotted on their respective city maps.

Not only amphitheaters became places of refuge for harassed city dwellers during the Dark Ages. After the destruction of Salona in 615 by the Avars

refugee citizens sought protection within the ruined walls of Diocletian's great fortified palace, Aspalathos, named after a flower and built as a palace for retirement by the emperor. The remains of Aspalathos became the foundation of the city of Spalato (Split). The refugees modified the former emperor's palace to serve as a medieval city. They narrowed the wide colonnaded streets to provide more space for housing but left untouched the sacred buildings dedicated to Jupiter and the mausoleum of Diocletian. The former eventually became the Baptisterium and the latter, during the ninth century, a cathedral. The peristyle court in front of the octagonal mausoleum became a formal city square and the colonnaded peristyle was converted into urban housing. Above the original *prostasis* of the mausoleum a high Romanesque tower was erected.

Within the walled city, the *citta vecchia* (old city), several churches were built during the Age of Faith as well as the St. Claire monastery (S. Chiara). A Dominican monastery was located outside the east gate and a Benedictine monastery adjacent to the north gate; the latter eventually became a military hospital. The Jewish quarters occupied the northeast quadrant of the old city.

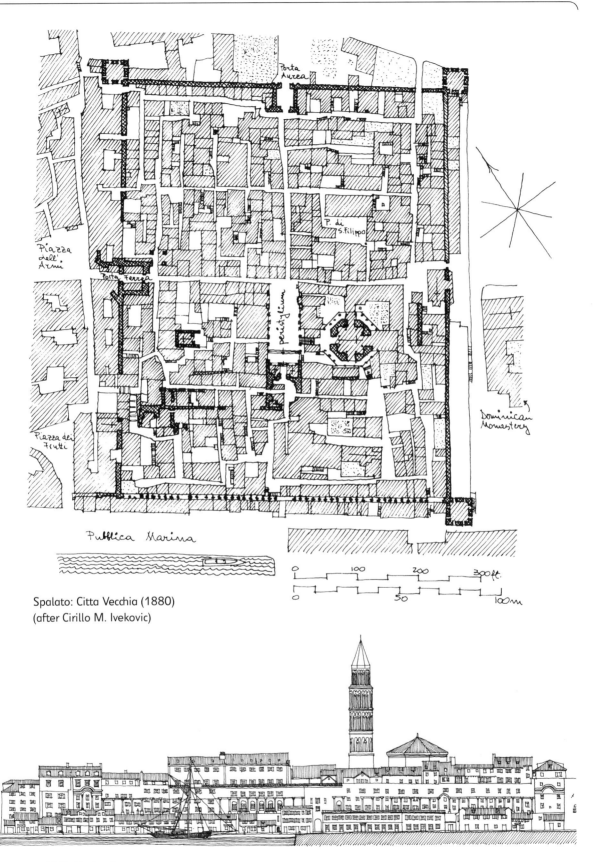

Spalato: Citta Vecchia (1880)
(after Cirillo M. Ivekovic)

Spalato (1909): Harbor front
(after Ernest Hébrard as cited in d'Espouy)

Spalato: Peristyle

Spalato: Porta Ferrea

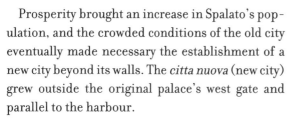

Prosperity brought an increase in Spalato's population, and the crowded conditions of the old city eventually made necessary the establishment of a new city beyond its walls. The *citta nuova* (new city) grew outside the original palace's west gate and parallel to the harbour.

Emerging cities in the Dark Ages were not always built on the ruins of Roman buildings and cities. Both Venice and Ragusa (Dubrovnik) were founded by colonists who fled their native cities after barbarian incursions and sought refuge in almost inaccessible areas that offered natural protection. Venice was founded by refugees fleeing Aquileia, Concordia, Patavium, and other mainland cities sacked and destroyed by the Huns during the middle of the fifth century and by the Lombards a century later. The survivors of these cities fled to the shallows and mud banks of the lagoons of the Adriatic Sea and established with the indigenous fishermen of the tiny islands the twelve lagoon townships, one of which, Rialto, eventually became the seat of the doge and the city of Venice.

Similarly, citizens fleeing from Epidaurum and Salona, two ancient Greco-Roman cities of Dalmatia, sought refuge during the middle of the

seventh century on the rocky island of Ragusa after the destruction of their cities by the Avars and Slavs. The island of Ragusa, situated at the foot of Mount Sergio but separated from it by a marshy sea channel, probably already sheltered a small fishing settlement. With the influx of urban colonists a small city soon emerged perched on the precipitous rocky ridge of the island.

From the outset Ragusa—today it is Dubrovnik—had several features that favored its becoming a flourishing maritime city. It was adjacent to a sheltered natural harbor, and its precipitous island setting provided protection against hostile incursions. Its geographic location ensured not only an ideally temperate climate, but also placed it in close proximity to the crossroads of major commercial land and sea routes. At Ragusa, in fact, Latins and Slavs, eastern and western churches, Christians and Muslims came in close contact with each other. From this interaction lively trade ensued, and the port emerged as a small but significant maritime city-state in the Middle Ages and rivaled mighty Venice for a thousand years.

Initially, most buildings were constructed of timber, but as early as 806 the city of Ragusa was

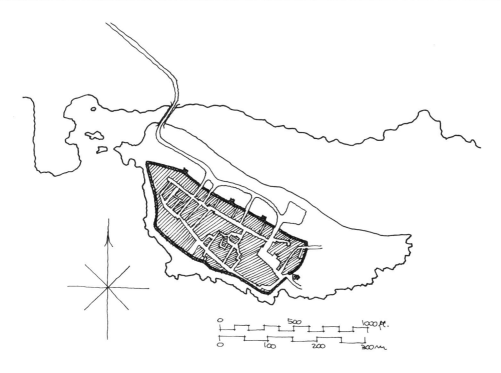

Dubrovnik: Ragusa Antiqua (ninth century)
(after Luksa Beritic)

protected by fortification walls built of stone and heavy timber. Thus, the citizens were able to hold out against a fifteen-month Saracen siege (866–867), and spurred by this success, its inhabitants maintained Ragusa as a fortress city throughout its history. Between the ninth and eleventh centuries the city fortress defended itself successfully against attacks by several foreign powers including the Venetians.

The city's peaceful prosperity and the relative absence of bigotry within its walls attracted refugees from all nations, including a colony of Slavs. The city soon had to be extended from 10 to 14 acres (4 to 5.6 hectares) in area to accommodate the population growth, and it eventually occupied the entire rocky ridge of the island. A fortification wall reinforced with six defense towers was constructed to encircle and link the extension to the old city. This extension also had a city gate, part of which still exists.

To protect the harbor, a counter fortress or "sconce," called Fort Lovrijenac, was erected on a small rocky promontory jutting out into the sea along the west side of the harbor. A defense tower was also built to protect the access to the bridge that now connected the island of Ragusa with the mainland. Finally, a shrine for the patron saint, San Biaggio or St. Vlah, was consecrated on the island side of the bridgehead.

THE EMERGENCE OF MEDIEVAL CITIES

After the collapse of the Roman Empire the economic base in western Europe again became primarily agricultural, and whatever commerce existed was local in character. The area of cultivated land was not perceptibly increased from that of the Roman era, and the peasants who tilled the land were invariably in debt to landed proprietors. In the absence of foreign trade western Europe was forced to live from its own resources. It was an age of constant predatory incursions. Sometimes, the devastation of cities or whole regions "was so complete that, in many cases indeed, the population itself disappeared" (Pirenne 1925, 21).

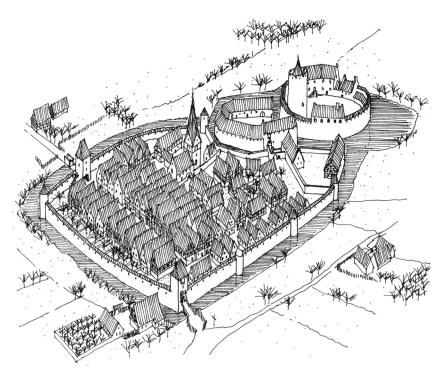

Büdingen: German medieval city
(after Karl Gruber)

In western Europe during the Dark Ages, in contrast to Spain, Italy, and Dalmatia, there was a distinct break with the civilization of antiquity.

In Britain, the break with the Roman past was perhaps unusually complete, with predictable consequences in the towns. Nowhere has convincing evidence yet been recovered of an unbroken continuity of urban life in this former Roman province. Certainly, the bones of many Roman towns survived, used by their English rulers as administrative centers and defended enceintes. But there is nothing to suggest that these towns remained in being as true "urban places," and there is good reason on the contrary to believe that the royal and ecclesiastical uses to which they were frequently put might actually have delayed their return to those primarily economic functions they were starting to resume no earlier than the late ninth and tenth centuries (Platt 1969, 18).

It was under such circumstances that feudalism arose. What had been a classless folk society based on an agricultural economy became a two-class society consisting of peasants and warriors. The latter eventually emerged as feudal lords offering protection against the attack of hostile tribes; in return for this protection and for land tenancy, peasants provided free services under oath to the lord. A highly structured society emerged. For example, Sussex was the king's land and had one royal castle. Fifteen tenants-in-chief administered this land; they were either barons or bishops and lived in manors on estates. The fifteen manorial estates were further divided into 534 subtenancies, which in turn were tilled by 5,898 villeins and serfs.

BURGHS

Throughout western Europe the Dark Ages was an era of hostilities. From the beginning of the ninth century, strongholds, or *burghs*, appeared everywhere in defense against the Saracens, Norsemen, and other incursors. Essentially, burghs were walled enclosures of somewhat restricted perimeter, customarily circular in form and surrounded by a moat (Pirenne 1925, 51). "A garrison of knights under the orders of a castellan was stationed in each burgh and a home (domus), for the

prince maintained where he stayed with his retinue in the course of the continual changes of residence which war or administrative duties forced
upon him" (Pirenne 1925, 51). A keep or fortified
tower was built near the center of the strongholds,
serving as living quarters and as last refuge in case
of attack. A chapel or church and dwellings for the
clergy and members of the periodic judicial
assemblies were also found in the burgh. A granary
and cellars for food storage with supplies adequate
to last during a long siege were invariably present.
Peasants provided for the subsistence of the garrison and supplied the necessary labor to maintain
the walls of the fortress. There were no free citizens, such as merchants and tradesmen, nor was
there any kind of communally organized local
government. Nevertheless, medieval burghs were
stepping-stones in the urban evolution of cities,
because craftmen and merchants sought the
protection provided by burghs and were often
allowed to settle outside their walls, thereby forming small communities. Thus many burghs eventually formed the nuclei of future cities.

MONASTERIES

It is indisputable that the Universal Church was a
dominant force during the Dark Ages. Not only was
it a focus for daily community life, but it also provided continuity in a fragmented world. Its spiritual center remained in Rome, the eternal city; its
language remained Latin, a universal language; and
its ecclesiastical architecture continued to be
based on Roman traditions. Thus, it is not surprising that the basilica plan furnished the design for
the places of worship in Europe, and the central
peristyle court garden became the cloister or heart
of monasteries and convents throughout the
Christian world.

Occidental monastic life, which was initiated
and formalized by St. Benedict in the early decades
of the sixth century, attracted many followers during the Dark Ages. Its *fratres* came mostly from
poor families. They sought security and peace in
the brotherhood of communal and religious life
where the three vows of obedience, chastity, and

poverty could hardly have been considered as great
sacrifices when compared with the usual life of
serfs, who were subject to military duty and high
taxation while toiling in great poverty in an eternal
struggle for survival.

The buildings of a monastery invariably enclosed
a quadrangle that was surrounded by a vaulted
colonnade. The church was usually located on the
north side of this *claustrum*, or cloister, so that its
lofty roof would not cast a shadow on the court
garden; this arrangement was particularly relevant
in northern climates. In southern climates the
reverse was often the case; the church was situated
on the south side of the cloister to shade the court
garden. But the apse of the church always faced the
east. The remaining three sides of the monastery
contained at ground level the entrance hall with the
custodian's room, the refectory or dining room,
the chapter house or meeting room, a *calefactorium* or room to warm oneself in, and the kitchen
and ancillary rooms. The bedrooms, or the *dormitoria*, were on the upper story and often were mere
cells with tiny windows and sparse furniture consisting of a bed, a table, and a chair. The dormito-
rium section was usually connected by a staircase
to the transept of the church, where rites were held
even at night. As membership in the monasteries
grew, the buildings housing them had to be
expanded accordingly. Sharing a bed with other
persons (a condition that was all too frequent at the
time in lay dwellings) was unacceptable. Thus, with
the inevitable growth many monasteries evolved
into little towns surrounded by a wall for security.

A plan of a Benedictine monastery dating from
the ninth century (and drawn on six pig skins) was
discovered in the library of St. Gallen (Switzerland). It gives new insight into the many buildings
that formed a large monastery. The principal
building was, of course, the large church with two
west towers symbolizing archangels protecting the
ecclesiastical precinct. The cloister was located on
the south side of the church. Behind the large
church was a smaller church used by novices and
aged monks. A cloister school and a hospital, each
with a colonnaded cloister, flanked the second
church. Within the walled precinct were also the

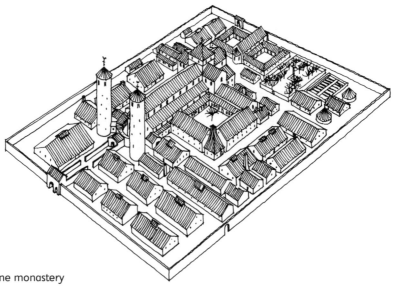

St. Gallen: Benedictine monastery
(after Karl Gruber)

large residence of the abbot, a guest house for important visitors, a hostel for pilgrims, a school for children of noblemen, several bakeries and breweries, workshops for goldsmiths, cobblers, tailors, saddlemakers, and blacksmiths, as well as a mill, many stables and chicken houses, an orchard, and herb gardens.

The monasteries that arose in this period resembled small towns. In addition to the members of the order there was a sizable population of craftsmen and workers who did not take the vows of monastic life. Moreover, since "alms and hospitality were to be given within the means of the monastery, to all who asked for it" (Durant 1950, 518), lay people often outnumbered the monks themselves. Monasteries also attracted tradesmen who, in addition to supplying the inhabitants with goods, also held markets outside the monastery gates. These markets were timed to coincide with the high mass when most people frequented the church; in fact, the German word *Messe* means both mass and fair.

Like the burghs, many monasteries also eventually became medieval cities. The strategic locations that were identified by the Romans for cities were equally desirable places for the establishment of monasteries; in addition, the ruined cities offered a reliable and easy source of building materials.

Hence, heathen buildings and cities supplied the foundations for burghs and pious monasteries, which eventually became the towns and cities of the Christian Occident.

THE RISE OF MERCANTILISM

The burghs and the monasteries were the magnets that attracted the people who collectively formed towns and cities, but neither of these two institutions yet knew of the highly complex art of living by trade and commerce, two essential preconditions for the flourishing of cities with free citizenship. As the medieval scholar Irving A. Agus writes:

> the ways of commerce are not so easily learned. To conduct business is a highly complicated art, one that requires, in addition to native ability, a long and arduous apprenticeship under the guidance of masters. How else can one explain the fact that for more than five centuries the Syrians (mostly the descendants of the ancient Phoenicians) were clearly distinguishable as "the merchants" in the Roman Empire? (1965, vol. I, 4–5).

The fact that kings of emerging European nations during the twelfth, thirteenth, and fourteenth centuries invited German burghers and western Jews to come and settle in their country, to build new towns, and to develop the commercial life of existing ones is perhaps adequate recognition of the fact that mercantilism and monetary business transaction were both highly sophisticated arts, not easily understood then, and their principles hard to reconcile with devout practice of the Christian religion.

With the exception of the *Responsa*, written in rabbinic Hebrew, reliable historic sources on mercantilism during the Dark Ages are practically nonexistent. Until its recent translation, this Hebrew source material was inaccessible even to Jewish historians because the language in which these documents are written is highly technical, involving fine points of talmudic law.

A *Responsum* is a document prepared by a talmudic scholar who analyzed a litigation, compared the problems in it to similar ones discussed in the Talmud, and expressed a decision with an explanation of the legal basis of this decision. Thus, the *Responsa* deal with the real situations and problems of everyday life, and their reliability is enhanced by the fact that litigations were scrutinized before their submission to a talmudic scholar. Jews living in western Europe during the Dark Ages had greater confidence in their own principles of justice than in those of the non-Jewish authorities; perhaps they were also careful not to expose inner quarrels that could have been used as an excuse for oppression.

Many *Responsa* dating from the tenth and eleventh centuries have survived. The content of these documents reveal that the Ashkenazic Jewry of the pre-Crusade period was a highly homogenous minority group that lived in Italy, France, and Germany. They were predominantly merchants or financial managers of large estates, even of bishoprics. Politically free, they traveled in comparative safety over long distances. They organized self-governing small communities with effective communal institutions that could render help even at a great distance from home. They dealt with princes of church and state from a position of strength that was often based on monopolistic organization, a practice that was adopted a few centuries later by the Christian burgher class in northwestern European cities.

The Jews owned property, and in the *Responsa* frequent "use of the term 'courtyard' rather than 'house' is significant, indicating that the houses were built around closed courtyards that opened into an alley" (Agus 1965, vol. I, 132). It appears from this that during the early medieval period Jews still adhered to the oriental heritage in house building. One *Responsum* dealt with two families living in one house who were in disagreement as to where the head of each family should light his Hanukkah candles. Since neither the parties involved in this litigation nor their rabbi knew of any precedent, it must have been exceptional for two families to share a house.

No doubt for reasons of security, but perhaps also in conformity with the deep-rooted oriental tradition of living in close-knit residential precincts, "the Jews preferred to live in exclusively Jewish sections of town. There they felt safe, and were free to live in accordance with their religious and social practices without offending the religious sensibilities of the non-Jews" (Agus 1965, vol. I, 132). It would be a mistake to confuse voluntary close-knit precinct living with the ghettos in which Jews were involuntarily required to live in a later period. A better comparison with precinct living would be the later medieval practice of a particular guild's members choosing to live in the same section of a city, or in the case of smaller guilds, along the same street.

A Responsum written by Rabbi Judah the Elder son of Rabbi Meir haCohen, a scholar of Mainz, contains a detailed analysis of Jewish public law as well as a discussion of the principle of 'majority rule' and community system of government which constitutes the earliest formulation of these important principles in northwestern Europe, and antedates similar discussions in non-Jewish sources by several centuries (Agus 1965, vol. I, 38).

From the evidence at hand, it is highly probable that Jews played a role in the development of self-governing communities as well as in the organization of the first merchant groups in occidental European cities. Jews may have been one of the essential forces that eventually contributed to the emergence of the occidental urban civilization.

THE EARLY MEDIEVAL CITY

The early occidental medieval city was a new creation. Although built often on the ashes and ruins of a former Roman city, it was not "an expression of continuity with the past, as scholars have often argued; what was involved was a continuity of place, and not of artistic form" (Kubach 1975, 367).

The typical city was usually a small circular urban settlement surrounded by crenellated fortification walls and a moat. A single tower above or a pair of towers flanking the few gateways guarded the entry to the city. The city's closed form had a structure that was the result of organic or natural growth; hence even when it was built on the ruins of a rectangular castrum site, the city had a tendency to be circular or amorphous in shape if the site's topographic features so demanded. The nucleus generally was either a cathedral chapter or a monastery, sometimes a burgh. Its street network consisted of picturesque, irregular, and often narrow winding lanes that broadened here and there into small odd-shaped squares.

Streets, and frequently entire neighborhoods, were reserved for particular categories of inhabitants. Merchants and craftsmen had their special districts or streets, often still reflected in their present-day names. Then as now, wealth and social position were mirrored in the size, material, and form of houses. Community buildings, churches and chapels, the town hall and mint were all situated in rows or blocks of houses or in squares. There was no rule for this, however. The main church could lie amid a tangle of narrow lanes and be accessible only through blind alleys or side streets, as is still the case in Orange, or else be on the outskirts of the town on large but vaguely defined open plots of ground, as in Pisa or Speyer or, more often, England. There was a special preference for setting the cathedral or an important abbey or collegiate church in a high commanding position—often at the center of an entire upper town, as in Laon, Langres, Lincoln, Quedlinburg, San Gimignano, and Gerona (Kubach 1975, 367).

From the above description it is evident that the classical planning of both the Hellenistic and Roman builders was either forgotten or rejected.

There was no formal or axial agora or forum in these medieval cities. In fact, they are far more akin to oriental cities, which had similarly integrated a myriad of picturesque, irregular, and narrow streets widening into small squares. In addition, the special districts or streets of particular categories of inhabitants also had their counterpart in the oriental mahalahs, although the latter were more confined. Finally, the incidental approach to some important buildings, such as the cathedral, was very similar in spirit to the siting of the all-important jami' mosque in traditional Islamic cities.

In spite of all these similarities, the occidental city differed from the oriental in one important respect—namely, in the design of the individual dwelling. In the occidental city outward-looking dwellings clearly reflected the status of their respective occupants by their size and form as well as by the materials used for their construction. In the oriental city, in contrast, dwellings were inward-looking court-garden houses with deliberately anonymous street façades; their size could not be assessed from the outside since shops and smaller dwellings were dovetailed into them, camouflaging their true extent.

The occidental city emerged with dwellings that stressed individuality. Independence was further emphasized by a gap between each house, which carried the open sewer and was intended to prevent the spread of fire. Some unity cannot be denied in medieval cities; it was the result of the use of similar building materials and the subdivision of the city into narrow and deep building parcels on which were built the individualized gable-ended dwellings that lined the streets.

This seemingly slight difference of occidental and oriental buildings is especially significant in that it mirrors the values of the respective societies. At the outset, when occidental cities were still small, this emphasis on "externality"—in contrast to "internality" of oriental cities—did not bring about negative side effects. Later, when cities grew, this "externality" manifested itself in undesirable social consequences that are not yet resolved.

THE EARLY MEDIEVAL URBAN DWELLING

While the tradition of Roman architecture persisted in churches, monasteries, and convents, after the collapse of the Roman Empire the lay people no longer followed the Roman example in their building. The domus with its atrium and peristyle court-garden ceased to be the representative urban dwelling in northwestern Europe. The few city dwellers who survived the constant or frequent onslaughts of barbarian invasions had probably neither the means nor the desire to sustain the heathen luxuries of the Roman house.

Probably most urban houses of the early medieval period were constructed of timber; therefore, they have not survived into our age. If the historic precedents of other urban civilizations have any relevance to the medieval one, it can be assumed that urban dwellings of the period differed slightly from their rural counterparts. This is understandable since city dwellers came from the countryside and brought their building traditions with them. In the Middle Ages a small minority may have been urbanites who fled to the country only to return later when things became more normal. Other exceptions were the merchants who came from other cities, but by and large city dwellers of this era had an agricultural background.

The study of early urban houses must be based on only a few surviving examples of stone buildings dating from the eleventh and twelfth centuries. These buildings survived as isolated examples rather than in rows or clusters forming a street or a city block. Apart from the great time span that separates us from the period, this scarcity of examples is due to several reasons. First, early urban houses were detached, a characteristic not only inherited from their rural origins, but also as a precaution against fire, especially when they were built of combustible building materials. Thatched roofs apparently were common and were particularly vulnerable to fire. In addition, since early cities were relatively small

settlements with a correspondingly small population, there was no pressure to crowd buildings together, especially in the absence of an advanced building technology that could help control the spread of fire from building to building. Finally, it is assumed that most buildings were built of wood, and the stone buildings still in existence today were probably interspersed among them; when the former burned or deteriorated, the latter survived in isolation.

Among the surviving examples of early medieval urban dwellings in northwestern Europe there are two distinct prototypes—the gabled house and the dwelling tower.

Although wooden buildings have not survived, it is still possible to formulate a reasonably accurate description of how the wooden gabled houses may have looked by examining later examples that have survived in small towns in Germany. Building traditions did not change as rapidly in the Middle Ages as they do today, and it usually took centuries before building practices in larger cities reached smaller towns, especially if they were somewhat isolated. It is known that while the Renaissance bloomed and flourished in Italy, other parts of Europe still adhered to the High Gothic style. It took literally centuries before the Renaissance, the Age of Enlightenment, reached hidden corners of Europe.

Dating from the 1400s, a small timber-framed gabled house in Dinkelsbühl (Koppengasse No. 4) illustrates how modest urban dwellings may have looked during the formative years of medieval cities. This building was divided by a middle wall into a front and rear section. Below the front section was a small vaulted basement reached through an external stairwell from the street. At ground level, next to the entrance hall, was a small chamber, while the rear section was probably a storage or workshop area. From the entrance hall a straight staircase led to the upper-floor hall, which, with the kitchen, shared the rear section of the house. The principal family room occupied the front section of the upper level. The attic was probably a storage space. Window openings in dwellings of the early Middle Ages were rarely

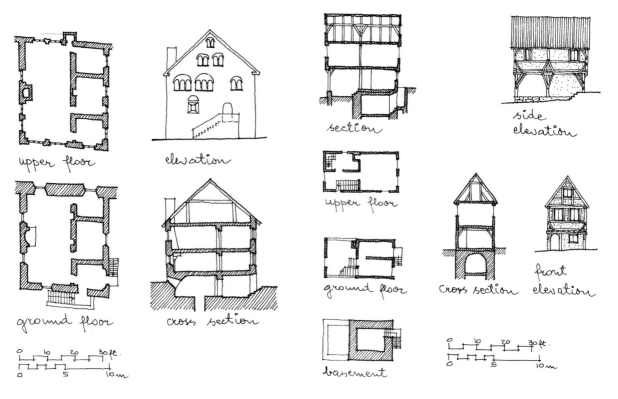

Münstereifel: Romanesque house
(after Hans Erich Kubach)

Dinkelsbühl: Koppengasse No. 4
(after Eugen Mayer)

glazed and usually equipped with wooden shutters.

As a rule, stone-built gabled dwellings also had a very simple layout with two or three rooms at each level opening directly into each other. Corridors were not yet used. The façades of these buildings were also very simple, with few adornments. The windows were very small, typically consisting of Romanesque double or multiarched narrow slits. In some parts of Europe the gables were stepped or even double-stepped, while in other parts they were simple. Thus, there were regional differences in detail in domestic architecture, but the basic principle did not vary.

The dwelling towers of the Middle Ages were a natural adaptation of dwellings as individual redoubts against frequent hostilities. In essence, these peculiar dwellings were tiny fortresses and are most evident in Italy in San Gimignano, Bologna, and Florence. However, these dwelling types were also widely used in northwestern Europe.

Dwelling towers were by no means urban inventions. Bernard Rudofsky, in his book *Architecture Without Architects* (1964), illustrates several villages that feature dwelling towers. Vatheia in the Peloponnesus, Yemen villages in Arabia Felix, and several villages in Svanetia, a high-lying valley in the western Caucasus, are just a few areas to which dwelling towers were indigenous. Some scholars contend that these building types resulted from the desire for protection during the blood feuds and vendettas that raged between families. This assertion may be true in some instances, but in others, for example those of the Caucasian villages, it can only have been a secondary consideration. The Caucasian villages were located along the path of barbarian invasions from Asia dating from the eleventh century, and their occupants must have experienced unending harassment from these

San Gimignano

Svanetian dwelling towers

invading tribes. Hence, it is more reasonable to assume that the dwelling towers in this region evolved to secure the survival of the area's sedentary and agriculturalist inhabitants. Mounted nomads who had only portable tent dwellings must have been respectful of the solidly built stone towers; not only was the scaling of these high towers an unfamiliar experience to them, but during hostilities they were probably also reluctant to descend from their mounts and venture into a narrow claustrophobic stairwell that led to the upper levels of a dwelling tower. In fact, there is evidence that during the Tartar invasion of eastern Europe high fortification towers and church steeples were not scaled by Tartars and were relatively safe places of refuge for those fleeing the barbaric hordes.

Several dwelling towers have survived in a small German town called Schwäbisch Hall. Two of these towers may serve as good illustrations of the form's organization and appearance.

The Keckenburg (Untere Herrengasse No. 8–10) dates from around 1250 and replaced an earlier tower dwelling, dating probably from the ninth or tenth century. The windows of the four-storied stone-built section of the tower reveal it to be from the late Romanesque period, while the superimposed additional story with its timber-framed three-story gable roof probably dates from around 1500. It is assumed that the vaulted basement was

originally accessible from the inside, since the existing exterior entrance to it dates only from 1627.

Perhaps the most typical example of a smaller dwelling tower is Turmhaus (Unterlimburger Strasse), also in Schwäbisch Hall. This tower is built along an escarpment and consists of two parts, a lower two-story stone building and a two-story upper dwelling, a timber-framed structure. The lower base has narrow loopholes near grade level and is accessible through an entrance at the first upper level. The entrance to the dwelling section was at the third level and probably was accessible at first only via a retractable ladder. The living room at this entrance level had a flat arched wooden ceiling.

Dwelling towers have also survived in many other German cities, including Regensburg (Ratisbon), Rothenburg, Dettwang, and Dinkelsbühl.

A dwelling tower of uncertain date in a village in Corsica, Sainte-Lucie-de-Tallano, provides a southern prototype and also illustrates the defensive character of these dwelling forms. Also built on a sloping site, the first level of this building is a mere basement space used for storage and accessible only from the outside. The entrance to the dwelling was on the first upper level, which also contained the kitchen and hearth. This fireplace was an ancient type with a sloping flue within the thickness of the wall, and it opened out onto the

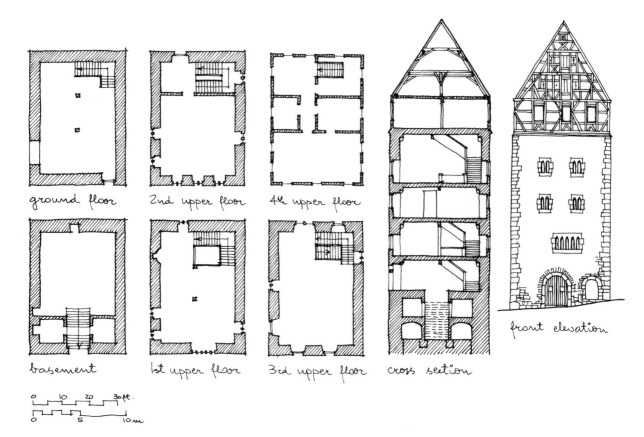

ground floor

2nd upper floor

4th upper floor

basement

1st upper floor

3rd upper floor

cross section

front elevation

Schwäbisch Hall: Keckenburg
(after Eugen Mayer)

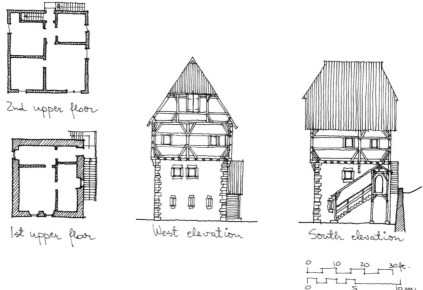

2nd upper floor

1st upper floor

West elevation

South elevation

Schwäbisch Hall: Turmhaus
(after Eugen Mayer)

Dettwang (near Rothenburg) dwelling tower
(fourteenth century)
(after Eugen Mayer)

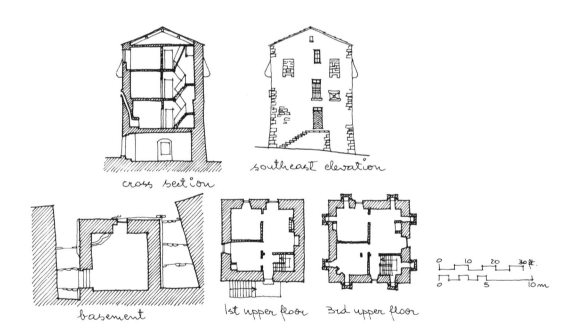

Sainte-Lucie-de-Tallano: dwelling tower
(after H. Raulin and G. Ravis-Giordani)

façade with a windowlike opening, instead of being carried through to the roof.

This tower served as a regular fortress equipped with pairs of *box-machicoulis* on each elevation and several loopholes; through the projecting machicoulis the building occupants could discharge missiles and molten pitch on any assailant attempting to scale the walls.

CHAPTER TWO

THE MIDDLE AGES

MEDIEVAL FORTRESS CITIES

With the conversion of Norsemen, Slavs, Magyars, and other heathens to Christianity, barbarian incursions subsided considerably during the tenth century, and the Dark Ages gradually gave way to a new era, the High Middle Ages. Woods, heaths, and marshes were reclaimed for cultivation, and with improved farming technology agricultural production surpassed the subsistence level. This development, coupled with an increase in population, gave rise again to a division of labor enabling trade and commerce to develop and cities to grow and flourish. "As in antiquity, the country oriented itself afresh on the city" (Pirenne 1925, 72). Trade and commerce not only revitalized several old Roman cities, but also fostered the establishment of new urban settlements "along sea coasts, on river banks, at confluences, at the junction points of natural routes of communication" (Pirenne 1925, 72). Thus, by the beginning of the tenth century towns and cities appeared in the arable rural countryside at a distance slightly less than one day's journey on foot from each other (at intervals of roughly 15 miles or 24 km), and they became marketplaces for their respective rural surroundings. A symbiotic relationship developed between the rural and urban population; each depended upon the other.

With the proliferation of medieval cities in the twelfth and thirteenth centuries, a new concept of

labor was born in Europe. Hitherto, both in the Orient and the Greco-Roman world, urbanization was invariably accompanied by slave labor, but the new medieval burghers—the merchants and craftsmen—were free and privileged men whose liberty was protected by unprecedented laws wrought from the practice of feudalism. Most of these new city dwellers were the offspring of peasants whose normal state was that of servitude in an age dominated by feudal lords and princes of the church—the only free men of the Dark Ages. It is not surprising then that the city dwellers' newly gained freedom was cherished and was of paramount importance to them. Nor is it surprising that many burghers actively sought the liberation of peasants from the yoke of serfdom. Some cities were so eager to swell the size of their population that they invited peasants to come as free men and "announced that any person living in town for 366 days without being claimed, identified, and taken as serf, became automatically free, and would enjoy the protection of the commune's laws and power" (Durant 1950, 643). *Die Stadtluft macht frei* (the city air makes you free) is a German proverb dating back to this epoch. Roland, the ideal Christian knight, became the universal symbol of free cities.

However, laws and symbols without power and strength were inadequate to ensure liberty in an age of violence. Feudal lords still wielded considerable military strength and were not averse to using it. Furthermore, the threat of incursions by a

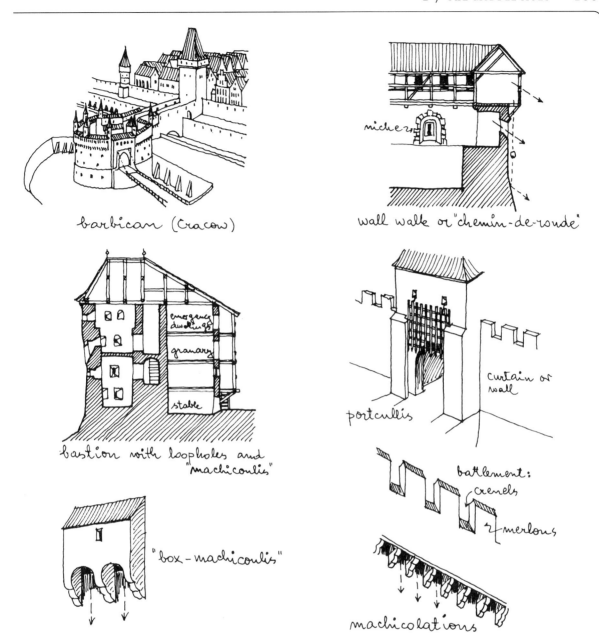

barbican (Cracow)

wall walk or "chemin-de-ronde"

bastion with loopholes and "machicoulis"

emergency dwellings
granary
stable

"box-machicoulis"

portcullis

curtain or wall

battlement:
crenels
merlons

machicolations

(after Rudolf Huber and Renate Rieth)

new wave of barbarian marauders was always present. Thus, it was obvious to all that fortification walls and other defense installations were necessary. The gate- and defense-tower-studded city walls and the deep moat surrounding the walls were hallmarks of the medieval city, as well known as the lofty Gothic church or cathedral dominating its center.

Of course, fortification walls were used in antiquity, but the medieval burghers perfected city defense and enriched the oriental and Greco-Roman vocabulary of defensive building forms and their constituent elements. Moreover, they developed an organization that delegated the responsibility of building, maintaining, and manning specific sections of the fortifications to particular guilds. The walls were usually crenellated and built with a covered walk, or *chemin-de-ronde*, behind the parapet. Numerous loopholes and embrasures enabled the defenders to shoot at attackers in relative safety. Additionally, towers and battlements were often provided with machicolation, that is, openings in the floor of projecting galleries or parapets through which missiles, hot liquid, or molten pitch could be dropped upon attackers.

Nowhere was the medieval system of city and village fortification more essential than on the eastern frontiers of central Europe, which was the traditional passageway of countless barbarian invaders. In this remote area, because Tartar and Turkish invaders retarded peaceful development, the medieval period lasted longer, and because urban expansion after the Turkish occupation was measured, fortifications have survived remarkably well; it is, therefore, appropriate to review a small chapter of the little-known medieval history of "the land beyond the forest"—Transylvania.

About the middle of the twelfth century, the Hungarian King Géza II (1141–1162) invited non-Magyar settlers from the populated regions of Franconia and Flanders to colonize the yet sparsely inhabited southern area of Transylvania. The king's objectives were twofold: first, to attract sedentary farmers, craftsmen, and merchants to populate this frontier land and, second, to delegate to the new settlers the responsibility of guarding the mountain passes adjacent to their new homeland against incursions of nomadic tribes.

King Géza's call for colonization was answered by many settlers. They came in large groups, between 1143 and 1150, to occupy the land assigned to them. The assigned land received a special status as *fundus regius*, or king's land, while its future inhabitants were granted far-reaching privileges that guaranteed near complete political and cultural autonomy, or *universitas*. This promise of freedom was a great attraction to many western European peasants who tilled a plot of land owned by a lord. Serfdom was perceived as a greater burden than the potential threat of barbarian assaults, which by then were often remembered through hearsay. In contrast to the tales of atrocities commited by barbarians, the shackles of serfdom were real. A serf had to pay to his lord (1) a land tax, (2) a small rent (cens), (3) an arbitrary charge (taille), (4) an annual share of a tenth of his crops and livestocks (tithe), (5) several days of unpaid labor (corvée), (6) a fee for the right to fish, hunt, or pasture his animals on the lord's domain, (7) military service in case of war, (8) tax on all produce sold at markets or fairs, (9) a fine if he sent his son to higher education or gave him to the church, (10) a tax when he or his children married someone not belonging to the lord's manorial land, (11) "right of the first night" with the bride (*droit du seigneur*), and several other obligations. These exactions together with the annual tithe paid to the church is estimated to have represented about two-thirds of a serf's produce in medieval Germany.

The new settlers that arrived during the twelfth century in southern Transylvania were referred to in their earliest royal charter as *hospites*, or guests; later documents refer to them as *flandrenses*. Over time, because of their Germanic origin, they acquired the designation of *Saxons* although neither their dialect nor their traditions warrant this designation. In fact, the so-called Saxons had a Mosel-Frankish dialect and their settlement pattern and property inheritance tradition resemble those of the rural people living in the Rhine and Mosel districts of Luxembourg and western Germany. At the time of their settlement, and for many centuries thereafter, the Saxon peasants practiced the open-field system of farming, a medieval tradition in which the tilled land was divided into three large fields cropped in a three-year rotation. They also followed a unique Frankish custom according to which the youngest son inherited the parents' homestead. The latter custom provided for a constant expansion of cleared land for cultivation as well as the establishment of many new villages.

The peasant colonists of the fundus regius were joined by numerous craftsmen and merchants. They settled the land in a medieval pattern, with walled city fortresses at strategic locations, often on previous settlement sites, and a number of villages each with its own church-fortress (*Kirchenburg*) distributed in the surrounding rural area of the cities. Moreover, seven peasant castles (*Bauernburgen*) were built in prominent mountain locations, and from these supposedly is derived the German name of *Siebenbürgen* for Transylvania. At the peak of the development of the region by the Saxons about a score of cities and towns had been established with a satellite network of approximately three hundred villages.

For reasons of survival, Saxon settlements were governed by an overriding concern for effective defense. This left an indelible architectural imprint upon cities and villages alike and is still discernible today more than eight hundred years after their establishment.

Unquestionably, the historic core of Saxon cities, such as Medias (Mediasch), resemble those of medieval German cities. They are invariably surrounded by ramparts, high defense walls reinforced by bastions and towers, each section originally manned by a particular guild. Gate towers, also manned by guild members, guarded the entranceways to the city's network of typically medieval narrow, crooked streets and lanes. However, a distinct feature of the Saxon city is the "church-castle" usually situated in a central location and often crowning a small hill. The church-castle, although resembling the citadels of ancient cities in their function as a second line of defense, nevertheless was different in that it was practically a miniature city in itself. Surrounded, like the city, by fortification walls studded with towers, bastions, and gate towers, it constituted an inner precinct of the city. It harbored the main church, the school, the presbytery, and nonecclesiastical buildings such as communal storage buildings, granaries, and a number of small refuge dwellings for citizens to be used in an emergency situation when attackers broke through the primary defense line and roamed through the city. The church proper, situated in the center of this inner precinct, was built as the third and last bulwark of the defense hierarchy; consequently, it was often built with a machicolated choir, nave, and tower. The tower and the loft of the church were the last retreat, and a well, which would extend the time of survival during a siege, was often found in the church nave.

The architecture of Saxon cities is characterized by simplicity with sparse use of adornment, betraying the constant struggle for survival in the wake of numerous Tartar and Ottoman assaults.

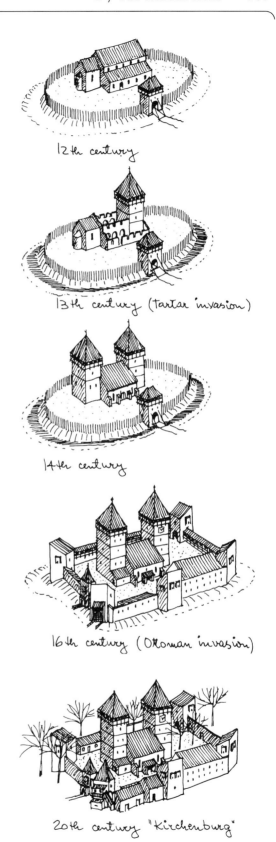

12th century

13th century (Tartar invasion)

14th century

16th century (Ottoman invasion)

20th century "Kirchenburg"

Dealu Frumos (Schönberg): Evolution of the church fortress (after H. Phelps as cited in H. Zillich)

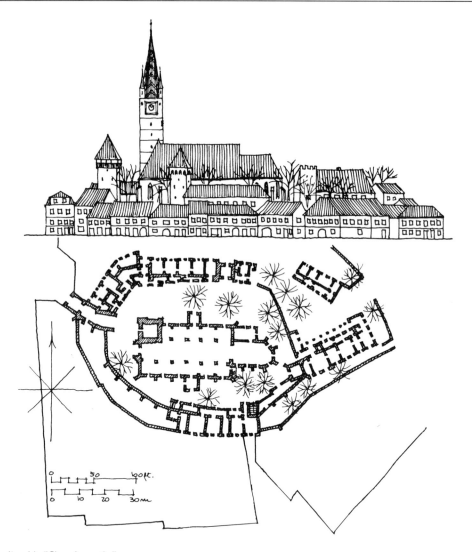

Medias (Mediasch): "Church-castle"
(after G. Curinschi et al.)

This is not to say that beauty was absent in Saxon cities, but that instead of a sophisticated Gothic aesthetic there was a robust beauty where loopholes, battlements, chemin-de-rondes, portcullises, box-machicoulis, and massive buttresses enlivened building masses. It seems reasonable to assume that the architectural vocabulary of crusaders had a great influence upon Saxon fortifications; indeed, Teutonic knights were settled for a short while (1211–1225) in the southeastern part of Transylvania until they were expelled by King Andrew II of Hungary.

Saxon cities became important trade centers and seats of local government, but they could hardly have survived without their surrounding country-side dotted with scores of fortified villages. An intrinsic symbiotic relationship flourished between the cities and their village satellites. The cities were the principal defense nodes, the spiritual, educational, and judicial seats, and the suppliers of manufactured goods, while the villages were the rear guards of the defense system and the breadbasket of the Saxon community. Generally, Saxon cities were replicas of northwestern European cities and, not unlike European cities, their population rarely surpassed 5,000 inhabitants.

Most medieval cities of northwestern Europe had a radius that seldom exceeded 800 ft (250 m), and the built-up area within the fortification walls

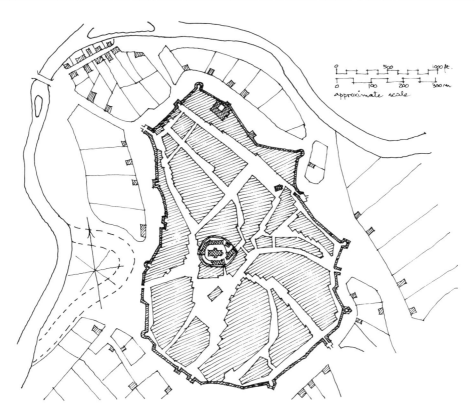

Medias (Mediasch), 1750
(after Captain Thenmern as cited in E. Greceanu)

was usually less than 50 acres (20 hectares). The overall town population density was in the neighborhood of 120 persons per acre (48 persons per hectare), although densities in residential sectors could reach 200 to 300 persons per acre (500 to 740 persons per hectare).

A typical city of the Middle Ages was Nördlingen, a city that may serve as a good illustration of the structure of the larger medieval city. The center of this community was dominated by two important buildings, the church and the city hall. Next to the church, the spiritual center of the city, was the fruit and root market, while the main marketplace was adjacent to the city hall, the lay center of Nördlingen's citizenry. From the central squares five irregular radial roads led to the five main gates of the city. Where these radial streets broadened to form additional squares other markets were established, such as the wine, produce, fish, and lumber markets. Along the ring road, which occupied the site of the fortification walls that encircled the old city before its expansion, were the granaries and the corn market. The diameter of the old city was about 1,400 ft (430 m), while that of the expanded city was about 2,950 ft (900 m). The expansion of the city occurred after 1375, when the city became an important trade center favored by its location at the crossroads of several important land routes. But even within this larger city, the distance from its periphery to the center did not exceed a quarter of a mile (1.5 km). This proximity to the open country was true for most large medieval cities. Hence, population densities in medieval cities were not oppressive, since the open countryside could easily be reached on foot in minutes, even by children.

Another characteristic of medieval cities was that they had a definite edge, an unmistakable demarcation line where the rural area ended and the city began. By entering the city through its gate tower one experienced a sudden change of environment. The solid rows of buildings defining the streets were in great contrast to the definition of the rural roads by open fields that led to the city.

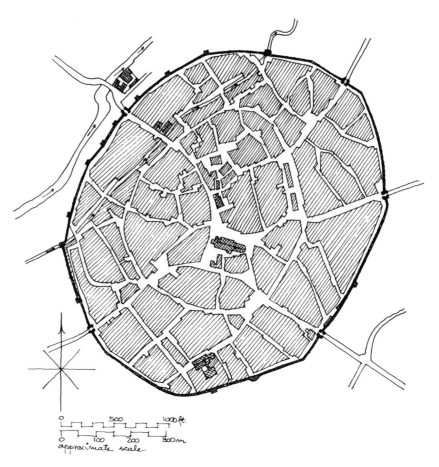

Nördlingen
(after Otto Völckers)

Behind the solid walls of the buildings were often small gardens, but these open spaces were invisible from the main streets occupied by the merchants' houses. Craftsmen's dwellings and workshops occupied the rear city blocks behind the main commercial streets; these sections of the city usually had smaller buildings and narrower streets. Some craftsmen, such as the tanners, were located at the city's edge adjacent to a small stream or canal that crossed their section of the city.

It is difficult for a contemporary city dweller who has never visited a medieval city to imagine the quality of the physical space of these cities. For example, the area of medieval Nördlingen (156 acres or 63 hectares) occupies less than a fifth of the area of Central Park (862 acres or 350 hectares) in New York City and it is smaller than Montreal's Olympic Stadium parking lots.

Even harder to imagine is the quality of life that existed within a medieval city. The descriptions of Dubrovnik, Rothenburg ob der Tauber, and Salisbury that follow may provide at least a sense of the physical surroundings of a Yugoslavian, German, and English city of the late medieval period.

DUBROVNIK

By the end of the Dark Ages Ragusa—today it is Dubrovnik—was already a significant city, and before the end of the twelfth century its citizenry had made trade agreements with many Dalmatian and Italian maritime cities; it had also received the right of free trade throughout Bosnia. Growth of

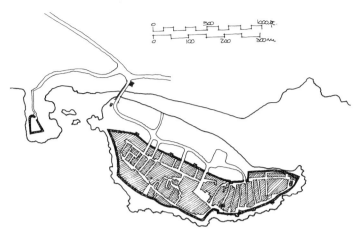

Dubrovnik: Ragusa (tenth–eleventh century)
(after Luksa Beritic)

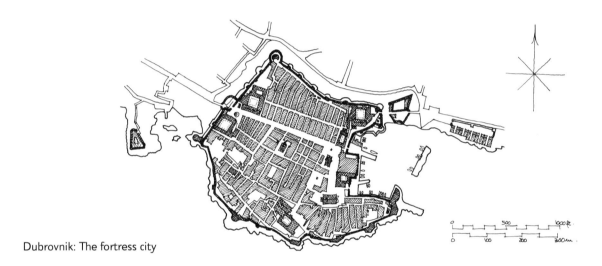

Dubrovnik: The fortress city

trade was naturally complemented by an increase in its population both within and beyond the city ramparts. A small suburb had grown outside its walls and a larger, predominantly Slavic settlement grew up over the years at the foot of Mount Sergio, along the sea channel, separating it from the island city; this Slavic suburb was named Dubrovnik after the oak forest covering the mountain slope. Over the years the sea channel had gradually turned into a marsh through alluvial deposits and was endangering the health of the inhabitants living nearby. The marshland was eventually reclaimed and the fortification walls extended to embrace the outlying settlements, including the Slavic suburb. The Placa, the main commercial street, marks the sea channel's former location in Dubrovnik today. By

the end of the thirteenth century the circumvallation was complete, and the city occupied 40 acres (16 hectares) in area.

Weakened by the Crusades, the Byzantine Empire gradually declined, and in 1205, at the time of the Fourth Crusade, Dubrovnik was forced to submit to Venice, its rival in mercantile power in the Adriatic Sea area. The Venetian sovereignty lasted about one and a half centuries; it was marked by a peaceful period and a further expansion of trade. Between 1204 and 1358 Dubrovnik was governed by Venetian rectors, and its laws, based on Roman practice, were codified into a single statute. The legislative authority was vested in the Great Council, whose members were native residents chosen by the Venetian court.

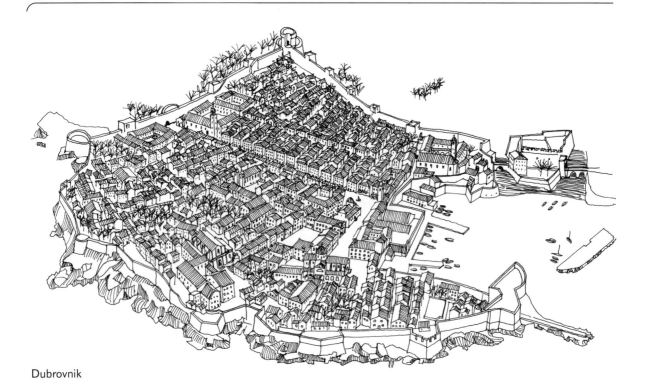

Dubrovnik

The Senate transacted most internal and external business affairs of the state, while the Small Council acted as the privy council of the rector. As Dubrovnik was an aristocratic republic, only nobility could be elected to public office. The population of Dubrovnik was divided into three classes: the nobles, the commoners or *cittadini*, and the peasants. Intermarriage of the nobility with the "inferior" classes was not permitted, and membership in the nobility was limited to descendents of families inscribed in the *Libro d'Oro* (Golden Book). The nobles of Dubrovnik were, for the most part, merchants, as were their counterparts in Venice.

In 1292 a fire destroyed most of the wooden buildings (predominantly housing). They were rebuilt shortly afterward, mostly of timber as before, in spite of a government decree against excessive use of timber because of the fire hazard. However, more effective rules were gradually drawn up to enhance the fire resistance of roofs and chimneys. Other building ordinances resulted in the widening and paving of the streets and the provision of stone steps on steep lanes to facilitate access to the upper residential quarters located on the two slopes—the rocky island slope facing north and mountain side facing south. According to city planning regulations, north-south lanes had to be 9 palmus (7.5 ft or 2.3 m) wide; the east-west streets, 14 palmus (11.75 ft or 3.6 m) wide; and the *pomoerium*, the streetlike open area running parallel with and adjacent to the interior base of the fortification walls, 6 passus (40.33 ft or 12.3 m) wide.

With the exception of Ragusa Antiqua, the physical structure of Dubrovnik, as we know it today, emerged during the Venetian period. The Placa, the 980-ft (300-m) long main commercial street, is the spine of the city and runs from the harbor to the west gate; its width gradually decreases from about 60 ft (18 m) at the harbor end to 36 ft (11 m) near the west gate. For the visitor who enters the city from the harbor the false perspective thus created makes the spine street appear much longer than it really is. Conversely, the distance to the harbor area from the west gate appears much shorter.

A number of narrow access lanes, at right angles to the Placa, give access to the various residential quarters of the city. On the north side of the spine,

Dubrovnik: Cross-section
(after Hans Hartvig Skaarup)

the lanes leading to the residential quarters of the south-facing mountain slope were inaccessible to vehicular traffic and were basically steep lanes provided with a series of steps. At roughly mid-point these lanes were linked by a level street (Prijeko) that runs parallel with the contours of the slope and was wider than the lanes in order to allow for more sunlight to reach the buildings along it. The lanes terminated at the pomoerium.

On the south side of the spine street, the lower section of the city, the street layout was roughly a grid pattern, but along the north-facing slope of the island (as on the opposite slope), the streets were actually stairways. Since their origin dates from the early medieval period, their layout is irregular. In this older section of the city the buildings are also more crowded, and the upper stories of several buildings bridge the lanes in a typical oriental city fashion.

The civic center of the city was near the harbor. Monumental public buildings such as the Sponza Palace (the customs house and mint), the clock tower, the city hall, the Rector's Palace, the cathedral, and the Bishop's Palace framed a series of interconnected squares.

In addition to the harbor gate next to the Rector's Palace, Dubrovnik had two other gates: Pile Gate (the west gate) and Ploce Gate (the east gate). Adjacent to the Pile Gate, on the north side of the spine street, was the Franciscan monastery and its church; to the south of the gate, set back to create a small square, was the St. Clair nunnery and its orphanage. The Pile Gate actually consisted of two gates linked with each other by means of a winding

ramp that overcame the difference in level between the low-lying spine street and the higher ground outside the fortification walls. A combination of a wooden drawbridge and a double-arched stone bridge spanned the moat below the ramparts. The stone bridge was equipped with stone benches along its balustrades for the convenience of visitors waiting to enter the city.

Access to the city through the east gate was more circuitous. Here, too, there was a combination of bridge and drawbridge, but entry led first to a *ravelin*, or outwork, of a fortress where a second bridge over a second moat led to another gate that opened into an ecclesiastical precinct occupied by the Dominican monastery with a church and several small chapels. Finally, a third gate led to the Placa.

The areas flanking the entry to the harbor were protected by outwork fortification, and a heavy iron chain linking these two forts barred the entry of ships during hostilities.

Neither the fortifications nor the new municipal ordinances could protect Dubrovnik's citizens from a calamity that befell many medieval cities. The plague, or Black Death, struck the city on December 15, 1348, and lasted for six months. The greatest sufferers were the artisans and workers, particularly those working with seaborne trade, but this incurable disease took its toll among all citizens. It was recorded in the archives of the city that during the height of the epidemic more than 120 persons died each day. The population was drastically reduced, and it is estimated that during the epidemic between 7,000 to 10,000 people of the

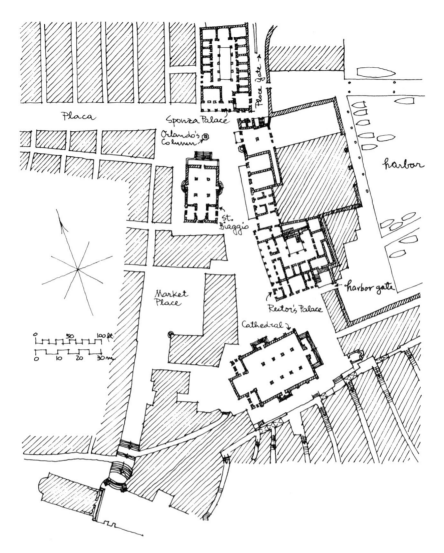

Dubrovnik: Civic center
(plan based on C. M. Ivekovic and Wayne N. T. Fujii as cited in Y. Futagawa)

republic lost their lives, including 160 nobles and 300 burghers. Because of ignorance, no sanitary precautions were taken to prevent the plague's recurrence. Instead, large sums of money were collected to build a votive church to the patron saint, St. Biaggio, and the church was quickly built in the civic square. The plague was to revisit the fortress city eleven times during the next century.

It is estimated that by 1400 the frequent recurrence of the plague had reduced the population of the city itself to about 2,500 inhabitants. The subsequent imposition of a quarantine on all foreigners who came to the republic and the prohibition of importing wheat, fruit, or cloth from places where the plague had raged brought some relief, and the population gradually increased. By 1500 the population had almost tripled, to about 7,000.

By the middle of the fourteenth century the power of the Venetian Republic was on the wane, and its rule over Dubrovnik ceased when Ludovic I, the Croato-Hungarian king, defeated Venice. Dalmatia, including Dubrovnik, surrendered in 1358. Under the protection of the Hungarian king, Dubrovnik enjoyed internal independence more fully than it had under the rule of Venice and entered a new phase of its development. "Hungarian

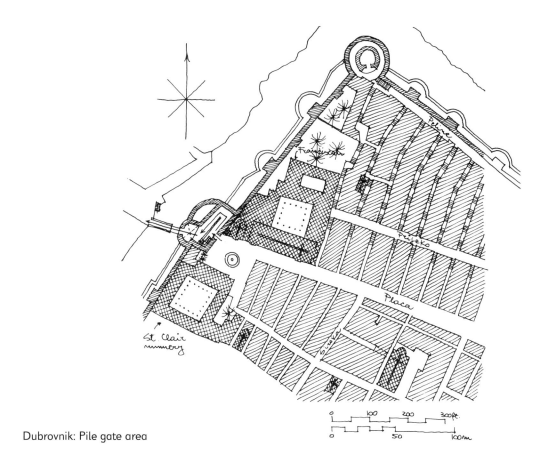

Dubrovnik: Pile gate area

authority, save for the tribute, was little more than formality" (Carter 1972, 130). Besides the nominal tribute, the city was only required to send one galley to the king's navy, and even in the case of war it was allowed to trade freely with the king's enemies; yet the king was obliged to defend Dubrovnik from all enemies. Thus, Dubrovnik became virtually a free state during the fourteenth century and prospered considerably.

With the emergence of the Ottoman Empire Hungary withdrew from the Adriatic, and Dubrovnik now became a truly independent power. The foresight of the Senate had led to the early establishment of good relations with the Ottomans. As a result, Dubrovnik merchants were allowed to penetrate the remotest part of the Ottoman Empire, where they formed permanent trading posts at a time when other Christians were either excluded altogether or limited to access to a few coastal towns. Even though a tribute was due to the sultan for these privileges, the merchants of Dubrovnik

earned handsome profits throughout this period, and their city flourished as never before.

The fortifications of the city were rebuilt with a double stone wall facing the mainland, studded with towers and bastions, and below them a deep and widened moat. The seaward walls were also reinforced with bastions and redans sheltering casemates (redans are bastions built at an acute angle to face the enemy, and casemates are shell-proof vaults protecting the men and guns) and equipped with embrasures to be used by batteries if the need arose. The ravelin near the Ploce Gate dates from this period; moreover, Fort St. John, the harbor fort, was rebuilt and reinforced as well as the Minceta Tower of the northwest corner of the city's ramparts. Dubrovnik, with its massive battered walls and bastions, became a formidable fortress city equally impressive from the coastal or inland approaches. These views can still be seen since the ramparts have survived the ravages of time.

Dubrovnik: Franciscan tower and Placa area
(after Wayne N. T. Fujii as cited in Y. Futagawa)

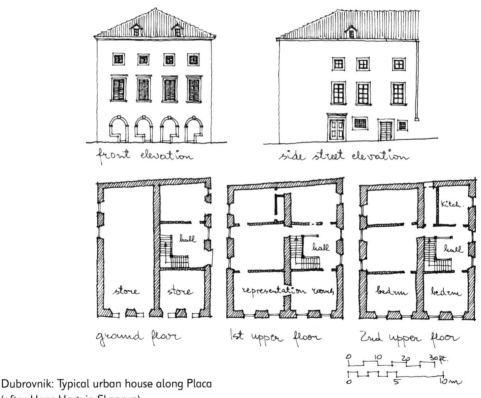

front elevation   side street elevation

ground floor   1st upper floor   2nd upper floor

Dubrovnik: Typical urban house along Placa
(after Hans Hartvig Skaarup)

The beautification of the city was also begun in the early decades of the fifteenth century. The Dominican monastery received its tower in 1424; the Rector's Palace, destroyed earlier by fire, was rebuilt by Onofrio Giardano, who also built two beautiful fountains, one near the city hall and the other in the small square near the Pile Gate. A clock tower was erected in 1444, and Roland's, or Orlando's, Column, a medieval monument that symbolized the freedom of the merchant city, was

Dubrovnik: Minceta Tower and north section of city
(after Wayne N. T. Fujii as cited in Y. Futagawa)

erected in the square in front of the Church of San Biaggio. The quadrangular column featured the carved figure of an armored knight holding sword and shield; his forearm was the standard measure of length, the Dubrovnik cubitus (1 cubitus equaled 2 palmus; 4 cubitus, 1 passus). From the column government ordinances were proclaimed and from its top the republic's standard was flown.

In 1520 a minor earthquake damaged many buildings, and on April 6, 1667, a major earthquake struck the city, followed by a fire that swept through the community. An estimated 5,000 persons were killed, and much of the city was destroyed. The greatest damage occurred in the lower city, which had been built on reclaimed land. With the exception of some large residences built of stone on the rocky ridge of the former island, most Gothic dwellings were irreparably damaged, including the arcaded buildings once fronting on the spine street. A residential quarter of small houses and narrow streets destroyed during this catastrophic earthquake became, after the reconstruction of the city, a large market square named after a local poet, Ivan Gundulic.

As the buildings were gradually rebuilt, they acquired their present appearance marked by simple but beautifully proportioned baroque façades. The typical width of an urban dwelling was 30 to 35 palmus (25 ft, or 6.8 m, to 30 ft, or 9 m) and its height between 40 to 50 palmus (33 ft, or 10 m, to 42 ft, or 12.8 m). The typical merchant's dwelling along the Placa was a three-storied building with shops at sidewalk level and a main entrance from a side street. The *piano nobile*, or first upper story, contained the formal reception rooms (known as the representation rooms), the second upper story was used for family dining rooms, living rooms, and bedrooms, while the attic contained the kitchen and storage rooms and perhaps servants' quarters.

The prosperity of Dubrovnik gradually waned from the seventeenth century onward. With the opening of the American continent trade routes changed and the decline of the Ottoman Empire eventually reduced Dubrovnik merchants' enterprises. Dubrovnik ceased to grow and retained its medieval and early Renaissance character. It is still a beautiful city, its buildings built entirely of an

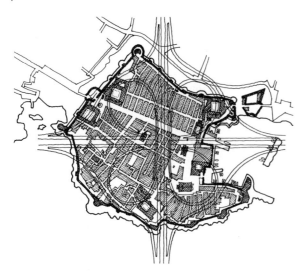

Dubrovnik: The fortress city

ivory-colored limestone as are its pavements and fortification walls. Its topographic setting and its simple plan allow even a first-time visitor to navigate every part of the town.

The fortress city of Dubrovnik today covers about 40 acres (16 hectares), an area equivalent to that of a cloverleaf intersection of a typical American interstate highway. Within this area live about 5,000 persons in about 2,000 dwelling units. This community is served by twenty-six churches or chapels, a synagogue, a mosque, two monasteries, a convent, and a college. There are scores of shops, workshops, and restaurants, one indoor and two outdoor theaters, a few museums, a palace, a city hall, a customs house and a mint, a granary, and an active harbor. The physical layout includes several squares, a wide main street (the same Placa of medieval days), and a network of pedestrian streets and lanes. It is a city where there is no wasted space, where every nook and corner is precious and cared for. Grandeur and pomposity are absent in this city; human scale and simple beauty prevail everywhere.

Like every city, Dubrovnik has its unique features, but it is also typically Mediterranean and, in its picturesque streetscapes, reveals many influences from the Orient where its medieval merchants sought their riches. In contrast, oriental influence is absent in Rothenburg ob der Tauber, a typical German medieval city.

ROTHENBURG OB DER TAUBER

Rothenburg's history began with the establishment of a burgh in Bavaria by Count Konrad der Rote, a governor of a royal demesne. With the death in battle of the last member of the count's dynasty in 1108, the lease of the demesne was transferred by the king to the Duke Konrad von Schwaben, a member of the Hohenstaufen dynasty. The original burgh, enlarged by the new lord, was located on an elevated promontory bordered on three sides by the Tauber River. A small medieval settlement grew up at the foot of this burgh over the years, and in 1172 the settlement received its charter as a free city from the Holy Roman Emperor Frederick I (Barbarossa).

The old city of Rothenburg occupied a circular area of about 34 acres (13.8 hectares). It had four gates and was surrounded by fortification walls. These walls no longer stand, but some of its gate towers have been preserved and the existing street pattern reflects quite accurately the location of the fortifications. The main church and the city hall

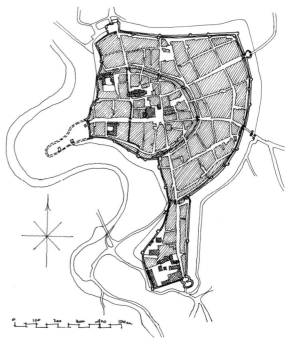

Rothenburg ob der Tauber
(after Toni Boegner)

Rothenburg ob der Tauber
(after Toni Boegner)

dominated the city center, and of course a large market fronted the city hall.

By the end of the eleventh century the city was too crowded for its physical area, and in 1204 it expanded. The new extension, in classic medieval ring fashion, more than doubled the area of the original city. New ramparts and a moat were constructed for the protection of the burghers. After the fall of the Hohenstaufen dynasty the city received permission from the king to annex a suburb to the south. An earthquake in 1356 destroyed a large section of the medieval burgh; of the lord's former residence only the *Hohe Haus*, or dwelling tower, and the principal gate tower survived.

Rothenburg reached its peak as an important trade center by 1400 and rivaled the city of Nüremberg in importance. It attained this eminent position during the mayoralty of Heinrich Toppler, a friend of the German king ruling at the time. During Toppler's tenure the city received its present character. The building of the large Gothic Church of St. Jakobs was begun, and the fortification installations completed. Five principal gates controlled access to the city and over thirty towers

and bastions protected the ramparts. Most of these defense installations are still in good repair.

The Peasants' War (Bauernkrieg) of the sixteenth century and the subsequent Thirty Years' War of the seventeenth century "weakened Germany more than any other event" (Gutkind 1964, 80). After these events the importance of Rothenburg declined. The enormous levies its citizens paid to save them from invaders prevented the city from regaining prominence. Not unlike Dubrovnik, Rothenburg stopped growing and thereby retained its medieval form and size. Thus today it is a picturesque reminder of the scale, cohesion, and beauty that were once the hallmarks of medieval cities.

Not only did the churches, fortifications. and general city plan of Rothenburg survive, but so did many medieval homes. The plan of a large house (Grüner Markt No. 2) reveals the three construction phases of its development, the earliest phase a dwelling tower dating from the thirteenth century. The tower, three stories high, was built of fieldstone, while the corners and window and door frames were of dressed stone. Each floor was a

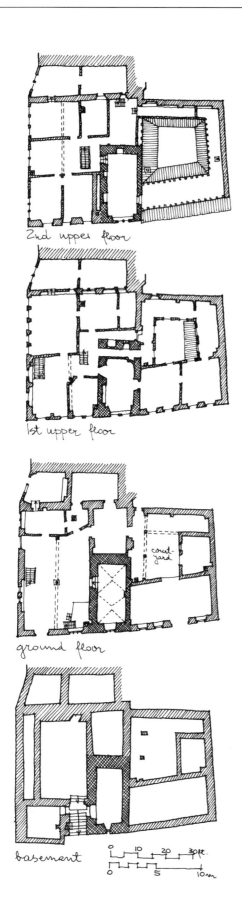

2nd upper floor

1st upper floor

ground floor

court-yard

basement

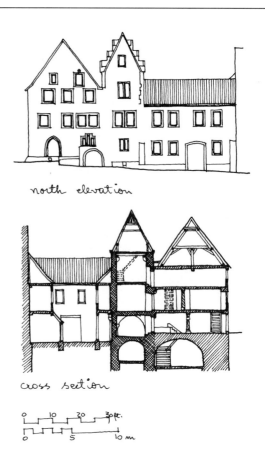

north elevation

cross section

Rothenburg ob der Tauber: Grüner Markt No. 2
(after Eugen Mayer)

single room; the basement and ground floor had vaulted ceilings while the upper floors were of timber with the two lateral supporting beams resting on stone brackets. The second phase of construction added a large hall-type dwelling to the tower structure. The middle supporting beam of the hall was itself supported in the center by a large oak column. A staircase led to the upper stories, which contained more private accommodations and presumably also storage rooms. The third stage of development consisted of a two-story household building with stables at ground level. These buildings, as well as subsequent ones, provide proof that many medieval city dwellers had agricultural landholdings outside the city and that their families complemented their city-based enterprises with cultivation.

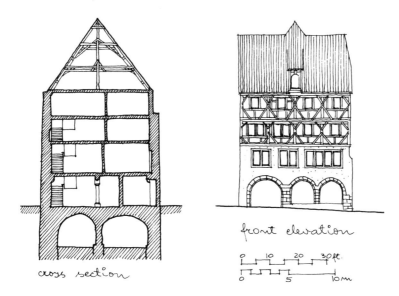

cross section

front elevation

Rothenburg ob der Tauber: Hornburghaus
(after Eugen Mayer)

Many of the patrician burghers of Rothenburg lived in so-called *Bürgerhöfe*, or dwellings with rear yards. The Hornburghaus (Herrengasse No. 46) is such an example. It is interesting to note that the width of this dwelling did not conform to the German module of 30 ft (9.75 m) employed in the subdivision of building parcels. However, in conjunction with the narrower neighboring property, both buildings have a width equal to two modules. Hence, the owner of the larger house either must have received special consideration at the outset or must have purchased additional property from his neighbor.

The Hornburghaus was originally a traditional gabled house, but during an alteration in the seventeenth century the gable was replaced by its present roof structure. The front section of the dwelling was a hall-type building. At ground level the hall was essentially a portal that allowed both vehicular and pedestrian access to the rear courtyard. Family dwelling accommodations were on the upper floor of the front section of the building, while the structures surrounding the courtyard were primarily stables and other ancillary facilities with servants' quarters above.

The cross-vaulted room adjacent to the main entrance hall originally served as a reception room for male guests (*Herrentrinkstube*). A staircase led from this hall to the upstairs halls, which throughout the building acted as distributor spaces. A gallery surrounding the courtyard was accessible from the first upper level and allowed the occupants of the house to view the activities in the courtyard.

Although physically similar to the oriental court garden, the courtyard of the medieval burgher's house was not an outdoor living space for the family; rather, it was a household yard for servants and resembled a farmyard. Since the principal rooms of the dwelling overlooked the street rather than the courtyard, the traditional oriental courtyard dwelling cannot be considered comparable to medieval buildings in northwestern Europe. Although it is tempting to draw such a parallel, it must be emphasized that the principal rooms of the medieval burgher's house overlooked the street rather than the court.

Rothenburg's Baumeisterhaus (Obere Schmidstrasse No. 343) is a classical example of a gabled burgher house with a deep frontal hall-type building and a shallow rear courtyard. The large ground-floor hall has lost its original spaciousness because of the partitioning adjacent to the street wall, but the rest of the house beautifully portrays the

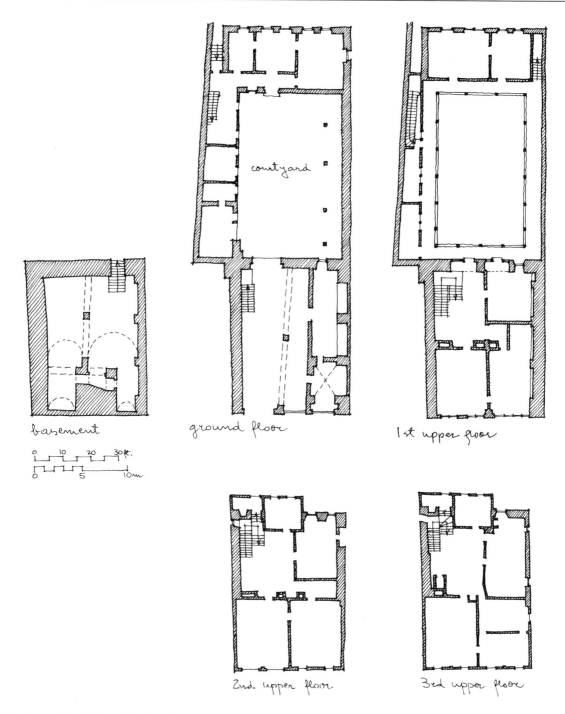

courtyard

basement

ground floor

1st upper floor

2nd upper floor

3rd upper floor

Rothenburg ob der Tauber: Hornburghaus
(after Eugen Mayer)

arrangement of a typical medieval burgher house.

Access to the large cavernous vaulted basement was through a trapdoor just within the portal, and an octagonal stair tower with winding steps led to the upper floors. The formal rooms faced the street, and a large and deep hall with a freestanding support column probably served as an all-purpose family room. The kitchen with its large fireplace opened from the hall. Also accessible from the hall was the narrow gallery that ran along three sides of the rear courtyard. The privy was located at the rear corner of the property in the

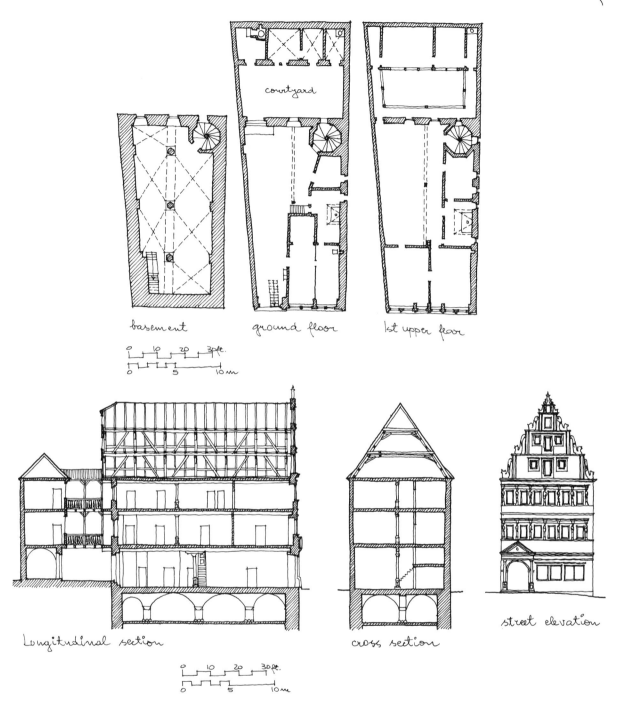

basement   ground floor   1st upper floor

Longitudinal section   cross section   street elevation

Rothenburg ob der Tauber: Baumeisterhaus
(after Eugen Mayer)

service building that had the stables and other service spaces at its ground level.

Rothenburg is but one of several well-preserved medieval cities in western Europe. Salzburg in Austria, Brugge in Belgium, Carcassonne and Mont-Saint-Michel in France are other equally picturesque cities surviving from the Middle Ages. Late medieval cities in the British Isles are less compact since defense considerations did not impose such rigid constraints upon development, and this can still be witnessed in the beautiful cathedral city of Salisbury.

Salisbury
(after Thomas Sharp)

SALISBURY

The clergy of Old Sarum—a bishopric and hilltop fortified town with a Norman castle—were granted a license in 1217 by Pope Honorius III enabling them to settle in the fertile valley at the junctions of the Avon, Nadder, Bourne, and Wylye rivers. In 1220, work began on a cathedral in this valley, located about 1.5 miles (2.4 km) from Old Sarum. Many burghers decided to follow the clergy, and shortly thereafter a new city began to grow near the ecclesiastical site. Old Sarum, which had occupied its hilltop site since the Early Iron Age, was gradually abandoned.

In 1227, Henry III granted the new city a charter, and the bishop, as lord of the manor of Milford (of which Salisbury was part), became its overlord.

The following centuries were marked by the citizens' incessant struggle to free themselves from the temporal authority of the bishop, which finally came to an end in 1612, during the reign of James I.

The graceful Early English Gothic-style cathedral with the loftiest spire in England (404 ft or 123 m) still dominates Salisbury today. The cloister along the south side of the cathedral was built shortly after the completion of the main edifice. A beautiful octagonal chapter house projects from the north wing of the cloister. The cathedral and cloister are located in the center of a large close, "the exemplar of all English cathedral closes, where cathedral, greensward, and lesser buildings seen beyond great elms, combine to produce a scene of islanded tranquility and a sense of immemorial calm" (Sharp 1949, 10). As Thomas Sharp so rightly observed, two environmental aspects con-

Salisbury: High Street gate
(after Thomas Sharp)

Salisbury: Butcher Row
(after Thomas Sharp)

tribute to the great sense of sequestration in the close: its great expanse and the contrast that is provided by the thronged streets of the busy medieval town just beyond its bounds.

The close had fortified walls and gates of its own, and with the several clusters of middle-sized and modest domestic buildings typical of cathedral precincts, it was almost a city within itself. Originally, the cathedral precinct had at least four gates, which, like the close wall, were built of stones from the demolished cathedral at Old Sarum. Two of its principal gateways still exist—one leading to High Street, Salisbury's main shopping street, and the other to St. Ann's Street. In contrast to the walled cathedral precinct, the lay city on the west side was protected only by the Avon River and, on the other sides, by an earthen rampart built in 1310, with city gates added at a later date.

Salisbury was a spacious and planned city with a pattern of five main streets running approximately north and south and six main streets running roughly east and west. Since the city occupied a low-lying marshy plain, a network of wide ditches ran along the center of each main street; one of these was a canal. This network of ditches provided the city with the necessary drainage channels and doubtless also served for sewage. Although some medieval visitors likened Salisbury to Venice, Salisbury's ditches were far from waterways and were actually a health hazard. In fact, the plague in all its virulence visited Salisbury in the spring of 1627 and claimed several hundred victims before it subsided a year later. During the following centuries, the ditches were gradually replaced by sanitary sewers and the wide canal was filled in during the nineteenth century, although the street where it once was is still named The Canal.

The planned street pattern of Salisbury defined a number of near-rectangular city blocks called chequers, one of which became the market square, the commercial hub of the medieval city renowned for its wool and cloth trades. This square was also the market place of the surrounding countryside, for villagers came weekly from far and wide with produce to sell on market days; on St. Remigius' Day (October 1st), the yearly fair was also held in this public square.

In addition to the grid of main streets, there were several narrow alleys and lanes such as the Butcher Row located just south of the market place. The designation of this lane is derived from the fact that many butchers lived there during the Middle Ages. "In general, however, the concentration of trades was by quarter rather than by street, and it could be dictated by specialist needs" (Platt 1969, 47).

It is known that in fifteenth-century Salisbury, the weavers and tuckers lived in St. Martin's Ward, the dyers in Market Ward abutting the Avon River, and the tailors, saddlers, and skinners in New Street Ward where, to minimize the bad odors of their trade, the skinners occupied the riverside locations.

Apart from the cathedral in the close, the guild hall and a few larger buildings along the market square, most buildings in Salisbury are small in scale.

> Salisbury's distinction lies in the way it has kept not merely an odd survival but many survivals of the small buildings of the early periods, taverns and cottages as well as churches and great houses. It is this that makes it seem the most "mediaeval" of all English cities, even though its genuinely mediaeval plan (which has remained almost quite unchanged) has few of the forms, the narrow crooked lanes, the irregular building lines, which are generally held to be the essential characteristics of the mediaeval city (Sharp 1949, 10).

As Sharp also remarked, Salisbury is a city wonderfully rich and varied in color— rich and yet mellow. A multitude of blackened half-timbered gables with cream and yellow plastered bays, rich red brick buildings, and blue-gray flint and gray stone structures create ever-changing picturesque streetscapes.

Apart from the cathedral, the medieval community of Salisbury was served by three parish churches, namely, St. Martin's, St. Thomas's and St. Edmund's, all still in existence. However, the friaries of the Franciscans and the Dominicans were dissolved at the Reformation.

Salisbury was an important market town throughout its medieval history, and the guilds and the well-to-do merchants played a prominent part in its life. Two guildhalls, the Joiners' Hall and the Cordwainers' Hall, as well as many medieval urban houses, especially jettied half-timbered houses,

survived not only along the main streets but also in several narrow passages and courts off the streets. Thus, for example, an alleyway near St. Thomas's Church, "with its stone flags, open gutter and tall houses almost shutting out the sky, it is for all the world like a city alley of six hundred years ago" (Whitlock 1955, 131).

Depending on the width of the burgher's plot, dwellings were typically constructed with the "hall" either parallel or at right angles to the street. Where the hall was parallel, the plan was either extended in a continuous range along the street or double-ranged with shops occupying the street front, and the hall, with its chamber block, in a second range often separated from the first by a yard. The extended house type had the simplest plan, but required a broad street frontage because the hall, chamber wing, and service wing were all arranged in a continuous row along the street. The double-ranged house plan was more economical than the extended plan in that the house was built in two parallel ranges, and required less street frontage, hence a narrower lot.

Since great value was placed on trading-street frontage, medieval plots were usually narrow and deep with a ratio of width to depth often in excess of 1:6. Given the restricted sites, the "hall at right angles" type of dwelling was the common solution. In Salisbury, this type of dwelling had two basic arrangements: narrow, with the hall occupying the entire width of the plot, or broad with the hall at one side of the plot with a narrow courtyard left beside it to let more daylight into the hall. The narrow plan generally consisted of a front part with shops at ground level and chambers above, an open hall in the middle part and service rooms with chambers above at the rear. The front part was lit from the street, and the back part from a court or garden, while the middle part (unless the house occupied a corner lot) had to be lit from windows placed above the roofs of adjoining buildings. Access from the street to the service wing at the back necessitated a passage through the body of the hall and the top of this passage then formed a gallery that linked the upper floors of the front and back parts of the house. The broad plan usually

Salisbury: Half-timbered buildings
(after Thomas Sharp)

formed part of an L-plan with shops in the cross-range parallel to the street and a courtyard flanking the hall, thereby solving the problem of light and access to the dwelling. (A wealthy medieval wool merchant, John Hall, had a house on The Canal that exemplified the broad plan; although restored, the large hall of this house now serves as a foyer to a cinema.)

While the upper floors of timber-framed houses were often jettied in the late medieval period, it is also known to have occurred in urban areas in the thirteenth century. Salisbury provides numerous examples of this type of construction, Friern Bridge is the earliest example. Probably, the jetty (overhang) was first used in towns because building space was limited. Spatial considerations may not have been the only contributing factor, however. Because of deforestation it was not only increasingly difficult to obtain long straight timbers, but the use of shorter posts superimposed one upon the other resulted in very weak joints. It was realized that joints of vertical posts in jettied construction were stronger and had the added

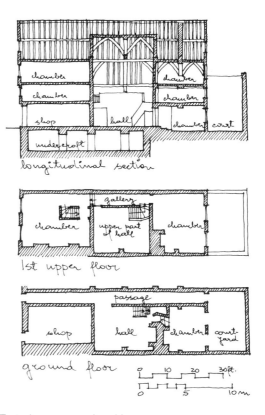

Typical narrow medieval house
(after Colin Platt)

advantage that the load-bearing capacity of the joists due to the cantilever was considerably increased. Such considerations resulted in a tendency to increase the size of the buildings at upper levels, and by the late sixteenth century many buildings were top heavy, not only in Salisbury, but also in many other cities of the British Isles.

THE LATE MEDIEVAL URBAN HOUSE

Apart from being the spiritual center, the church was also the dominant visual element of the medieval city, easily identified by its lofty roof and spire. But it was the multitude of dwellings, many of which were built in combination with shops and workshops, that gave the city its indelible character. In medieval times building ownership implied privileges that were not shared by tenants, and the number of burghers who owned their homes was considered a good index of the economic solidity of a city.

The relative width of a building's street frontage was also a clear indication of the wealth of its owner. For example, merchants, usually the wealthiest of a medieval city's inhabitants, lived in the largest buildings. Frontage along a market street was important for business, so merchants' homes were usually located along the main streets and on the market squares.

In countries where half-timber construction was prevalent, street frontage was expressed in terms of *bays*. A bay constituted the space from one vertical timber support to the next and the space between them was occupied by windows, doors, or solid masonry panels; two bays were required for a *porte cochere* or passageway leading to the rear yard. In Denmark the category of medieval urban dwellings was determined by the number of bays. For example, a merchant's house or *Købmands-gaard*, had in excess of six bays, was two-stories high, and had a porte cochere as well as a rear yard. A town house, or *Hus*, had from four to six bays and

two stories but did not have a rear yard. A simple abode, or *bode*, had fewer than four bays and a single story; tenants frequently occupied the small dwellings.

During the Middle Ages larger houses had a multifunctional nature. To a far greater extent than in any subsequent period, the medieval home provided the whole setting for the lives of its occupants. Houses were shelters from inclement weather, keeps guarding against intruders, and occasionally castles denoting the status of their owners. In addition, they were at times nurseries, schools, and hospitals and were even used on occasion as places for conducting religious services. Commercial activities were also an integral part of the home; workshops for artisans, shops for merchants, and ateliers for artists were natural extensions of the dwelling. From the beginning of medieval times a place to live was synonymous with a place to work, certainly for the self-employed, but also frequently for employees.

Thus, for a long period in our history, the city dweller's home and workshop were regarded as complementary rather than incompatible elements. Both activities evolved in harmony over many years. This concept is not very different from the notion of agrarian societies where "homestead" and "farmstead" were also synonyms. In fact, many urban dwellers also had farms and were engaged in cultivation in addition to the practice of their craft. An urban dwelling in Sesslach (Luitpoldstrasse No. 31) in Upper Franconia, Germany, illustrates this point very well. The shoemaker's workshop and dwelling is in the front section of the house, while the rear consists of ancillary buildings related to farming.

In 1958 Odd Brochmann, a well-known Norwegian architect and author, prepared a housing study for the city of Oslo that contained, among other things, a vivid description of a typical dwelling of the late 1600s. His description in *By og Bolig* is based upon authentic documents that reveal many facets of the life of a family in Oslo toward the end of the seventeenth century, at the height of the Renaissance in France but at a time when medievalism still lingered in Norway.

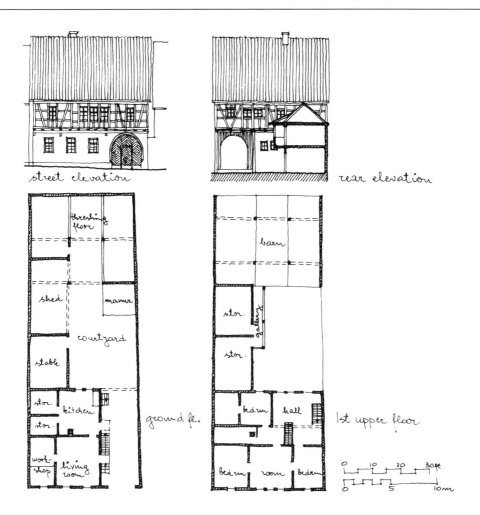

street elevation

rear elevation

threshing floor

barn

shed

manure

courtyard

stor.

stable

gallery

stor.

stor.

kitchen

ground fl.

bedrm

hall

1st upper floor

stor.

workshop

living room

bedrm

room

bedrm

Sesslach: Luitpoldstrasse No. 31
(after Wolfram von Erffa)

The head of this seventeenth-century family was a bookbinder, Frederik Jacobsen Brun. Fifteen persons worked and lived in his house on the Tollbodgaten in Oslo: some were members of his family, and others were in his trade and of his household. His property consisted of a compact two-story half-timber structure with brick-infill panels facing the street, with a porte cochere giving access to the courtyard; in addition, surrounding the interior court, were ancillary buildings constructed of wood—the workshops, stable, barn, and hayloft.

On the street side of the ground floor in the main building was the kitchen, adjacent to the porte cochere. Next to the kitchen was a large living room with a baylike projection into the street, and beyond the living room was the maid's bedroom.

The side wing contained a workshop with a store-room behind it. Abutting the rear property line were the stable and the barn, with the hayloft above.

On the upper floor of the main building were two bedrooms, flanking a spacious party room located immediately above the living room. Above the workshop there was a large storage pantry and across the courtyard a smaller storage space.

It is difficult to imagine the activities of Brun's household, separated from it as we are by three centuries. The factors that particularly obscure our understanding of their lives are those related to changes in the family structure and its physical setting. Brun's household consisted of his wife and eight children, ranging in age from a year-old baby to a twenty-one-year-old daughter. It is

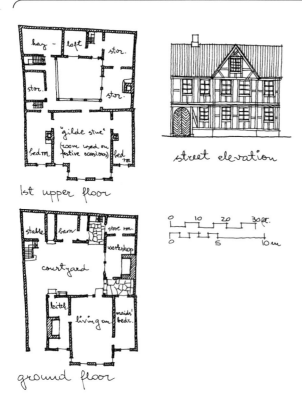

hay - loft

stor.

stor.

stor.

"gilde stue"
(room used on
festive occasions)

bedrm

bed rm

1st upper floor

street elevation

stable | barn

store rm.

workshop

courtyard

kitch.

living rm

maids'
bedr.

ground floor

Oslo, Tollbodgaten No. 14
Frederik Jacobsen Brun's house
(after Odd Brochmann)

interesting to note that a seven-year-old daughter and an eight-year-old son had not yet begun to attend school, whereas a thirteen-year-old son had completed his formal education; he was already listed as his father's apprentice. Only two girls, ages nine and eleven, were in school. An older boy of nineteen was in ill health and therefore had no training in any profession. The oldest girl was engaged to be married. Two boys in their twenties already had left the family at some earlier time; one was a goldsmith and the other served in the militia. Three boys had died in early childhood. Brun's house was also shared by three of his employees in the workshop and two maidservants in their late teens who helped with the many household chores.

The size of the Brun household, which numbered fifteen persons, is surprising in today's terms. Every day at noon the entire household gathered around the table in the living room for the principal meal; such a gathering, to us, would suggest

some festive occasion, but in Brun's time it was a commonplace occurrence. At supper time only family members ate together, but even then ten persons sat at the table.

It must also be remembered that this family was part of a society in which people were largely self-sufficient in their day-to-day needs. Food was not bought at frequent intervals in a store but was procured in season and on a large scale at the fair or market. Thus, a supply of flour was stored in sacks to last throughout the year from harvest to harvest, just as meat was carefully prepared, salted, and smoked after slaughtering to be stored for months. Storerooms had to be spacious and were important parts of the dwelling.

Other features of this family's daily routine were also radically different from the customary habits of a contemporary urban family. For example, the parents slept with their three youngest children in one bed, while the other five boys and girls in their teens shared beds in the upstairs bedroom, which could only be reached from an open gallery. The privilege of an individual bed, let alone a private bedroom, may never have occurred.

In Brun's time bathrooms did not exist, and public baths were not yet known to Oslo citizens. Small items were washed periodically in the kitchen, but the bulk of soiled clothing was laundered only twice a year, along the river bank.

The various members of the Brun household had few personal belongings and, as could be expected, there were relatively few household items and little furniture. With the exception of the living room, all other spaces in the home were sparsely furnished.

The older children usually played in the courtyard and the younger ones in the kitchen. The children who were attending school prepared their homework at the dining table in the living room; in this room everyone was well behaved and quiet.

In one respect the Brun family was well endowed—they had ample facilities for recreation. As already mentioned, above the living room there was a spacious party room used for all important family festivities. Furthermore, considerable time was spent from early spring to late fall in the open countryside, and the Brun family, with their horse and cart, often visited their fields and sometimes stayed overnight in their barn loft in the country.

The size of Brun's town property was 2,240 sq ft (208 m²); in contemporary terms this represents the equivalent of 150 sq ft (14 m²) per person or a net density of just about 300 persons per acre (721 persons per hectare). It must be remembered, however, that this apparent "high density" accommodation was limited to small urban areas that abutted either open fields or the seacoast.

The household activities and family structure just described seem to have been shared by master craftsmen in other parts of Europe. Perhaps the most significant characteristic that sets the medieval family apart from the contemporary family is its openness. Indeed the medieval family was a very open unit.

> It included, as part of the normal household, not only blood relatives but a group of industrial workers as well as domestics whose relation was that of secondary family members. This held for all classes, for young men from the upper classes got their knowledge of the world by serving as waiting men in a noble family; what they observed and overheard at mealtime was part of their education. Apprentices, and sometimes journeymen, lived as members of the master craftsman's family. If marriage was perhaps deferred longer for men than today, the advantages of home life were not entirely lacking even for the bachelor (Mumford 1961, 281).

Although everyday life in medieval homes seems to have been remarkably similar, the plan and construction of houses reflected regional characteristics, some of which were related to climatic factors, but others were derived from deep-rooted traditions that had their origin in a time that preceded the emergence of the occidental urban civilization. An example of a climate-related factor was the size and amount of fenestration used in homes; northern urban homes naturally had more and larger windows than their southern counterparts.

An example of a prototype derived from a regional tradition is the hall-type urban house; the hall or principal room open from the ground floor to the roof is a characteristic peculiar to the British Isles. An illustration of a large medieval hall-type

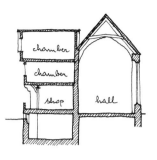

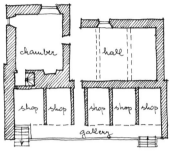

ground floor

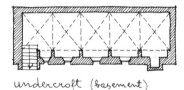

undercroft (basement)

Oxford: Tackley's Inn
(after Colin Platt)

urban house is Tackley's Inn in Oxford. Dating from the fourteenth century, this building consisted of a hall and chamber block that ran parallel with the street, but located behind an *undercroft* and row of shops. The undercroft, or basement, was reached through a staircase that descended directly from the street; this space was used as a tavern, which is known from a lease dated 1381. Above the undercroft were a gallery and five shops and the entrance to the dwelling. None of the shops had a direct connection with the domestic quarters behind them. A corridor linked the front door with the dwelling's principal room, the hall. The hall was a large space that reached from the ground floor to the rafters and had the equivalent height of

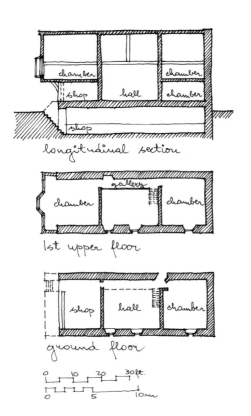

Southampton: No. 58 French Street
(after Colin Platt)

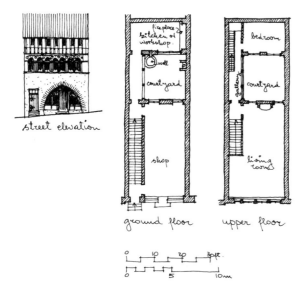

Cluny: Medieval urban dwelling
(after Otto Stiehl)

three stories. Next to the hall was a large room and additional chambers in two levels above the shops. These upper chambers were lit from the street, while the hall and its adjacent room received light from the courtyard.

In structures on narrower building lots the hall was built at right angles to the street, as described earlier. A typical example of this arrangement is a property at 36 North Street, Exeter. This building has a shop at street level and a narrow passage, the latter giving access to an open hall, three bays long. Behind the hall was a chamber block, two stories high. Above the shop were two projecting tiers of chambers that were reached through a winding staircase tucked in the corner of the hall. The kitchen occupied a rear structure on the property and was separated from the building in front by a courtyard. A service passageway led from the courtyard to a lane.

A medieval dwelling in Southampton (58 French Street) exemplifies the hall arrangement on a very narrow building site. In this example the two-bay open hall occupies the entire width of the building plot and is sandwiched between the street-front shop and the rear chamber block. The upper-level chambers were connected along the south wall of the hall by a gallery that was probably reached through an open stair from the hall. The street-fronting upper-floor chamber projected in the typical medieval fashion beyond the building line of the property. The shop and the undercroft were respectively above and below street level, and both were leased to shopkeepers.

Buildings with shops fronting the street and domestic quarters behind and above the shops were also common in other parts of Europe. A well-known example is a masonry-constructed house in Cluny in central France, which was first described by Viollet-le-Duc, the famous French architect and authority on medieval architecture. With the exception of a narrow entranceway, the entire front of this medieval building was occupied at ground-floor level by a deep shop. Behind the shop was a small yard with a well, and a narrow corridor in line with the entrance passage linked the front building with a rear structure, which, according to Viollet-le-Duc, was used as a kitchen; other medieval scholars suggest that it is more likely that this space was a workshop, since its connection with the main dwelling spaces was rather awkward. From the front door a straight staircase led to the upper-level multipurpose family room, which also had a large fireplace, probably used for cooking. The staircase landing was linked to the upper level of the rear structure, which most likely served as a bedroom. Medieval urban houses in Caen were basically similar to the Cluny house, but they were usually half-timber structures with projecting upper stories. Projecting or jettied upper stories not only increased the floor area of a dwelling, but also provided some protection from the elements for pedestrians walking beneath them. A further development of sheltered sidewalks were the picturesque arcaded houses that are found in many European regions.

Some interesting examples of arcaded medieval merchants' houses are found in Bern, Switzerland. The upper-story masonry walls of these buildings are supported on arched piers. These piers are battered toward the street and define the outside edge of the vaulted arcade. The arcades are continuous from one property to the next so that shoppers are offered shade as well as protection from rain. In a typical example in Kesslergasse (now Münstergasse), two shops face the arcade and a corridor leads to the dwelling. A corridor links the front door to a winding stair tower. It is likely that the shop to the right of the entrance door was originally part of the entrance hall and that this second shop is the result of a later addition.

At each floor level the stair tower leads to a small hall that communicates with two large rooms facing the street and to a bedroom and kitchen facing the courtyard. From the kitchen an open gallery-type corridor leads to the privy, which is placed in the rear corner of the property. Since the stair tower is designed to ensure the privacy of the inhabitants of all floors, it is probable that one or two floors may have been rented. The windows of the building were enlarged during the nineteenth century, but the oriel probably dates from the time of the building's original construction.

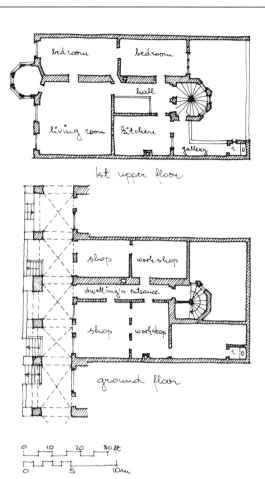

Bern: Kesslergasse, typical arcaded urban dwelling (after Otto Stiehl)

Arcaded merchants' houses were not only indigenous to Bern. They can be found in many French, German, and Eastern European cities, including some in Transylvania.

Naturally, arcades were usually part of stately buildings occupied by wealthy burghers, but in several small Silesian towns, such as Hirschberg, Schönberg, and Görlitz, there are arcaded buildings so narrow that they require only one arch to support the upper structure. It is impressive that at the time of their construction, when no municipal authority dictated a particular building plan, voluntary cooperation among burghers was so developed that there was a uniformity in the arcaded buildings surrounding the market squares.

A burgher's gabled dwelling on the market square of Hirschberg (Markt No. 44) is a charming

Hirschberg: Market place
(after Rudolf Stein)

Hirschberg: Markt No. 44
(after Rudolf Stein)

example of a narrow arcaded urban house. This building did not have a shop facing the arcade, but the owner of the building probably used his portion of the arcade to sell his goods; this is supported by the fact that next to the main entrance there is also a side entrance that gives access to a rear workshop as well as to the cellar.

The main door leads to a large entrance hall which is connected through a wide staircase to an upper-level space two stories high called a *diele*, a space akin to the hall of the traditional low German farmhouse; this central space is the heart of the dwelling and closely resembles the hall found in English medieval homes. Two galleries, each reached by an independent narrow staircase, link the bedrooms on the upper levels with the diele. The street-front rooms of the first-floor level were probably reception rooms, while the larger room facing the courtyard was the family room as well as the kitchen.

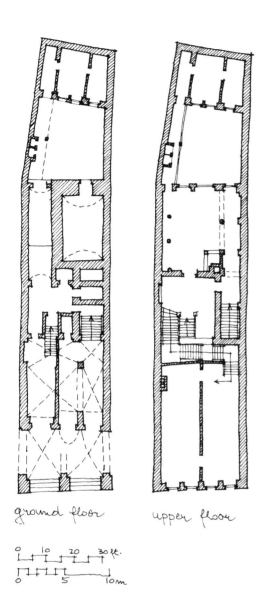

ground floor   upper floor

Görlitz: Untermarkt No. 3
(after Rudolf Stein)

A double-arched merchant's dwelling (Unter-markt No. 3) from Görlitz dates from 1535 and has a similar layout to the Hirschberg arcaded dwelling. The family room on the first upper level also faces the courtyard, but here the large hearth leaves no doubt that cooking was also done in this room. A narrow open gallery-type corridor links the family room to a small structure at the rear of the property, which presumably served as a storage building. At the beginning of the eighteenth cen-

tury the original gable of this building was altered to a saddle roof with the ridge parallel to the street line. True to their medieval character, the building plots of these Silesian cities were invariably narrow and very deep.

A unique form of English merchant dwelling similar to, yet different from, the arcaded houses of Europe is found in Chester, a medieval city built on Roman ruins. These unique merchant houses are called The Rows and share the characteristic that sidewalks, shops, and dwellings are elevated one story above the street level and are perched on top of solid, usually vaulted, cellar substructures. Shops and dwellings are linked by an elevated public walkway that runs along the entire street front and is reached intermittently by public stairways—especially at street intersections.

Leche House on Watergate Street is a typical example of such a merchant house. It is a timber-framed narrow-front building with a large and high cellar beneath it. The front part of the house contains the walkway and a shop at the elevated ground-floor level, and above them, a high and two-bay-deep bedchamber. Just beyond the shop is the hall, also two bays deep and open to the rafters; during the early sixteenth century the central hearth had been replaced by a fireplace built into the east wall of the hall. Behind the hall is a passage followed by a service room and above it a large bedchamber reached through an anteroom. A narrow side passage runs along the west wall and gives access to the dwelling and the rear yard; probably a gallery above this passage linked the front and rear bedchambers of the upper stories. The kitchen probably was along the rear property line, but this rear building was altered into a separate dwelling during the eighteenth century. The cellars of these buildings were gradually changed into shops, so that today The Rows consists of a double tier of shops. Although medieval in origin, these covered elevated sidewalks illustrate the viability of some modern planning concepts that advocate vertical separation of vehicular and pedestrian movement.

The medieval examples just described do not represent single buildings surviving here and

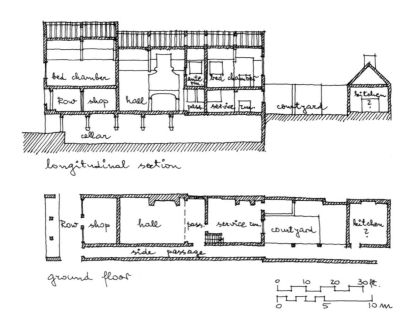

Chester: Leche House, Watergate Street
(after W. A. Pantin)

there, but form part of continuous rows of build-ings that have survived almost as they were when they were built. With the exception of interior modernizations and relatively minor changes to their exterior, the houses along Kesslergasse in Bern, the Market Square in Hirschberg, the Old Market in Görlitz, and The Rows in Chester are still as they were in the Late Middle Ages.

CHAPTER THREE

THE AGE OF
THE RENAISSANCE

THE IMPRESSIVE CITY

During the Middle Ages cities increased in number at a formidable rate; between 1220 and 1350, three hundred *bastides*, or new towns, were founded in France and it is estimated that in the course of four centuries (1000–1400) 2,500 cities were founded in Germany alone. The population of these cities also multiplied significantly, often doubling in less than a century. The population growth was especially impressive in France, England, and Italy.

The Black Death epidemic that struck Europe during the fourteenth century had a catastrophic effect. It halted city growth, killed between one-third to one-half of the total population, touching every family whether rural or urban, educated or unschooled, rich or poor. In the resulting social disorder desperate citizens repudiated the church and democratic government in favor of secular despots. Gradually many medieval institutions were demoralized, including the Universal Church, which now sold indulgences and ordained illiterates as priests.

Also, in the 1300s the medieval defense system became obsolete. Gunpowder (long known in Asia) was developed as an effective explosive, and with its widespread use the fortification walls of medieval cities became useless. A well-fortified city was no longer impregnable, as traditional defenses were no longer a match for the new form of assault. An improved and costly fortification system that consumed a lot of land was now required. With the exception of cities in England, which were relatively safe from attack because of their position on an island, most cities on the European continent had to carry the additional financial burden of erecting new lines of defense. In addition, the physical expansion of these cities became more and more difficult because the replacement cost of fortifications was prohibitive. Thus, many cities were overcrowded. Expansion could only be internal; consequently buildings grew upward. For example, during the Middle Ages (between 1200 and 1450), the area of Strasbourg was extended four times; in a later period, between 1580 and 1870, Strasbourg did not change in area although its population increased threefold.

During the fifteenth century classical influence upon the arts and literature revived, accompanied by an intellectual ferment that gave birth to the beginnings of modern science. This movement came to be known as the Renaissance. It is tempting to attribute to it the rebirth of humanism and urbanism as well, but the greater surge of urban development was in the Middle Ages, since "the real renaissance of European culture, the great age of city building and intellectual triumph, was that which began in the twelfth century and had achieved a symbolic apotheosis in the work of an Aquinas, an Albertus Magnus, a Dante, a Giotto" (Mumford 1961, 345).

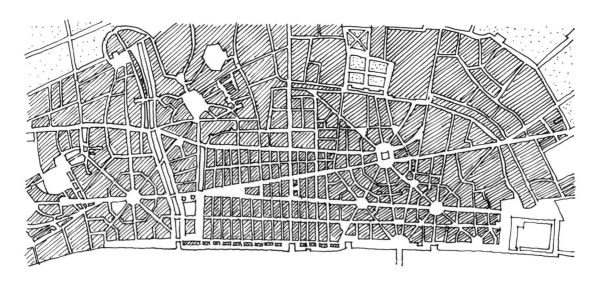

Sir Christopher Wren's plan for London (1667)

Few new towns were built during the Renaissance except as fortifications or princely residences, but considerable building activity commenced in the reconstruction and extension of existing towns. Basically, planning principles of this era advocated (1) wide avenues and straight streets with a vista, (2) the chessboard pattern of ancient city building, and (3) the extensive use of squares and groups of squares not merely as monumental, market, or traffic places, but also as domestic or residential squares.

Where a ruler had near absolute power, it was possible to apply these principles of Renaissance planning. Medieval streets, which had been narrow and crooked, were now subjected to geometric clarification, and wide avenues with a distant vanishing point were cut through the intricate and intimate maze of their medieval urban fabric. The human scale of the medieval cities gradually vanished and was too readily exchanged for a monumental and impressive scale.

Aesthetic appeal and order were not solely responsible for the transformation of the cityscape. Wheeled vehicles came into general use during the sixteenth century and demanded new standards, especially for the principal streets. Military considerations too were contributing factors to the change in street dimensions and patterns, not to mention the desire by despotic rulers to eliminate any physical reminder of the medieval urban setting that reflected the haphazard individualism enjoyed by their burghers. For example, the survival of medieval narrow streets and cul-de-sacs in Paris provided enough justification for Napoleon III to raze "whole quarters to provide wide boulevards" (Mumford 1961, 369). Avenues were envisaged as important symbols in the postmedieval city; they forced people to focus their attention upon an axis that usually ended at the palace or at a large building or monument that recalled the authority of the ruler. No other examples illustrate this contention better than the plans of Versailles and Karlsruhe.

Ambitious plans to cut avenues through medieval cities did not always succeed. For example, Sir Christopher Wren's plan for London, which was to bring order into the city after the Great Fire of 1670, was never realized; it was "foiled by tenacious mercantile habits and jealous property rights." Where Wren failed, Baron Haussmann succeeded in Paris. He built the Boulevard Saint-Michel, which "tore through the heart of ancient Latin Quarter, which had been an almost autonomous entity since the Middle Ages," an area full of life and for which there was no justification (Mumford 1961, 386, 388).

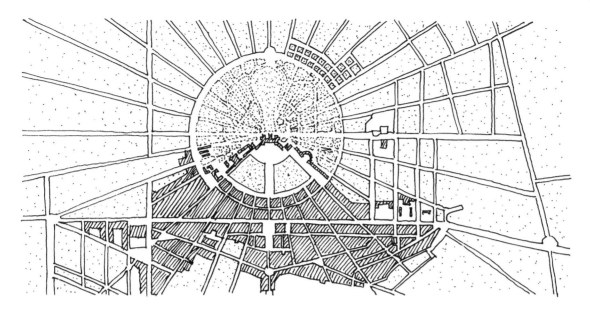

Karlsruhe (1715)

In the postmedieval period court life had an ever-increasing influence upon the city and its inhabitants, especially those of the middle class. And as Mumford insists, "one must not think of the dominance of the palace in terms of a single building with its courtly functions: the palatial style of life spread everywhere" (Mumford 1961, 378). Court etiquette influenced the manners of ordinary citizens, and the word "courtship," dating from the late sixteenth century, illustrates the extent to which courtly behavior had penetrated private and intimate affairs.

In cities the home and workplace became separate during the Renaissance, a separation that up to then had no precedent in the evolution of urban housing. From this time onward the home was a place for entertaining, eating, sleeping, and child rearing, but not where one worked to support a family. This separation first affected wealthier urban dwellers, but, as we will see, it eventually reached all city inhabitants.

The trend to separate the home from the place of business seems unimportant at first, but it had profound repercussions upon city development during subsequent centuries. Eventually, women lost touch with affairs in the outside world, and men, in turn, lost touch with domestic affairs. The basic social unit, the family, underwent a profound change. In fact, the separation of home life and business life also affected life beyond the walls of the home, and Lewis Mumford's contention that it triggered the lapse of citizenship and neighborliness is probably not exaggerated. In Mumford's words, the city became "nobody's business" (Mumford, 1961, p. 383).

The various classes of citizens began to keep to themselves. Middle-class families especially extricated themselves from daily city life and installed themselves behind the anonymous façades of town houses, which in their collectivity emulated royal palaces. If one could not afford to live in a palace, the next best thing was to live in a sector of a row of houses that looked like a palace. The medieval individualism expressed in the picturesque gabled houses of the burghers became a thing of the past. It was replaced by an enthusiasm for impersonal collectivism that employed the impressive classical order as a courtly setting for a new kind of family life.

The apparent strength and outward pomp of the absolute ruler and that of the privileged classes did not endure. The growing middle class was destined to assume power through their demand for social equality and political representation. According to Arthur Korn, the bourgeoisie and artisans numbered about half a million just before the French

Place des Vosges (Place Royale)
(after Jean-Pierre Babelon)

Revolution, while the privileged classes of the clergy and nobility numbered about 130,000. The remainder of the French people, about twenty-four million, were peasants and workers with little political power at all. Both in France and in England the bourgeoisie was an ambitious class dissatisfied with absolutism and in constant conflict with it. It was this group that brought about the victory which freed trade and ended feudalism.

RESIDENTIAL SQUARES AND CRESCENTS

At the beginning of the seventeenth century Henri IV of France planned the earliest of the residential squares in France: the Place Royale (now Place des Vosges). This enterprise was an effort to join the homes of the aristocracy with that of the king, and to recreate the great pageantry of the court in the heart of Paris. Thirty-eight three-storied buildings united at the ground level by an arcade, but articulated at the top by steeply hipped roofs, surrounded the square. Henry IV envisaged this square as providing the setting of "cosmopolitan living in the otherwise cramped city" (Rasmussen 1951, 62). The architectural treatment of the façades of these buildings was uniform; they were built of red brick masonry walls with pale stone quoins, and windows and dormers were arranged symmetrically. Two taller buildings straddled gateways in the center of the north and south side of the square. The square itself was first used for tournaments and jousting, then it became a monument square with the statue of Louis XIII in its center, and later still it was turned into a fenced landscaped park surrounded by narrow access roadways.

The concept of a residential square was a new and epoch-making idea, one that was soon adopted by other aristocrats, who thereby became the first building speculators on a grand scale. However, a government decree prohibited the construction of buildings on open land within the city. The Duke of Vendôme, an impoverished nobleman with some landholdings, circumvented the decree with a seductive proposition to create on his land a monumental place with a statue that would glorify the monarchy. Mansart was asked to draw up the plans, and in 1701, after many changes, the façades of Place Vendôme were built, before the building lots behind the façades were sold.

Residential square development was introduced to London by the fourth Earl of Bedford, whose family had received after the Reformation a confiscated convent from Henry VIII in payment of

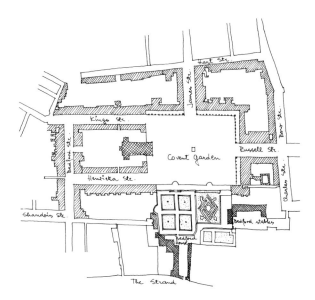

London: Covent Garden
(after map from c. 1680–85)

services rendered to the royal house. A 7-acre (2.8-hectare) area of this property was designated as a residential square, or *piazza*, and Inigo Jones was selected to draw up the plans. The large rectangular "square," now called Covent Garden, was surrounded on two sides by arcaded residential buildings with a classical façade, while a church placed along one axis and the gardens of Bedford's house along the other closed the views of its two main access streets. Behind the uniform arcades and façades of the square were individual houses of varying depth and breadth. This enterprise was an instant success. Aristocratic and wealthy families found it very fashionable to live in the stately row of houses and continued to think so even after the Duke of Bedford obtained from the crown in 1671 the right to have a daily vegetable-market in Covent Garden. This "did not in any way embellish the noble square. Early in the morning people arrived from the country with their carts and baskets and the whole morning Inigo Jones' Roman piazza rang with street cries and screams and it was overflowing with cabbage leaves and radishes" (Rasmussen 1934, 157). Moreover, before permanent market halls were erected during the first decades of the nineteenth century, the square was filled with unsightly stalls and sheds. Finally, as Steen Eiler Rasmussen remarked, it must have

been quite dangerous to walk in the square at night because there was little police protection provided in this district up to the nineteenth century.

Now that it was considered fashionable to live in town residences facing a square, many other residential squares were erected: Leicester Square (1635), Soho Square (1681), Red Lion Square (1684), St. James's Square (1684), Grosvenor Square (1695), and Berkeley Square (1698), to name a few of London's squares built during the seventeenth century. Of course, the residential square was soon found in other cities in the British Isles, such as Edinburgh, none more successful than those built in Bath.

Early in the eighteenth century, Queen Anne stayed at Bath on the advice of her physician. It was a spa that had been popular during the Roman period in England and became fashionable again because of the queen's visit. An architect, John Wood the Elder, acquired a leasehold from a landowner, Mr. Gay, for ninety-nine years on a large property in Bath. Wood undertook a speculative venture that resulted in a large sector of the

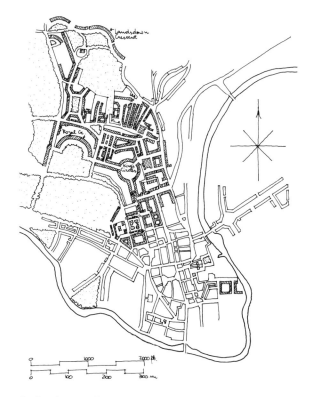

Bath: nineteenth century
(after Walter Ison)

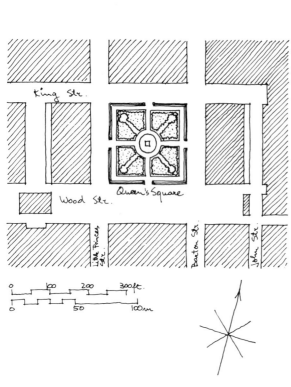

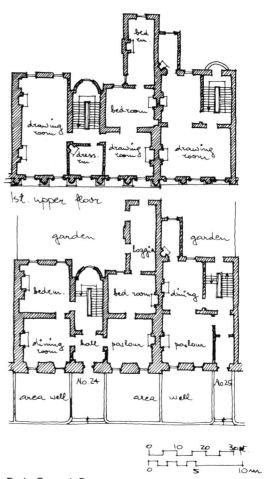

Bath: Queen's Square, John Wood the Elder's original plan
(after Walter ison)

Bath: Queen's Square
(after Walter Ison)

city being wholly built with interconnected residential squares. Wood began with Queen's Square (1727) and, following the trend already established in London, he built a series of town houses whose future residents were to own them as leasehold rather than freehold property. Wood's design approach for Queen's Square emulated a palace forecourt: the principal building occupied the north side and the buildings on the east and west sides formed wings. This ensemble was to be viewed from the south side of the square because only then would the elaborate façade of the north building—benefitting from the light and shade offered by its south aspect—be appreciated.

Queen's Square was built according to Wood's plan except for the west side, which "eventually took the form of a large mansion, set back from the frontage line, with its enclosed forecourt flanked by two equally imposing buildings, each uniting two houses into an elaborate composition" (Ison 1948, 129). But the north front of Queen's Square still dominates the space as Wood intended. "The seven large houses of varying size are grouped so that they form a symmetrical composition, with a central pavilion of five bays, flanked by wings and terminal pavilions of six and three bays respectively" (Ison 1948, 129).

The central square garden of Queen's Square had four wide iron gates in the middle of each side; the garden was divided into four parterres, and in its center was a basin from which rose an obelisk. The pathways were gravel walks, and the parterres were planted with flowering shrubs and espaliered lime and elm trees.

After his success with the development of Queen's Square, Wood continued his speculative

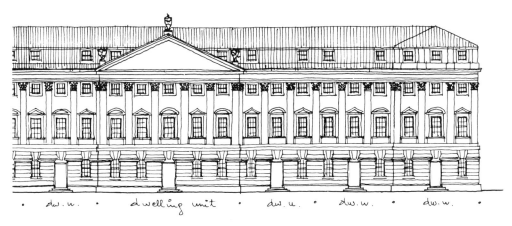

Bath: Queen's Square, north side
(after A. Mowbray Green)

venture along Gay Street to the King's Circus (1754). This circular "square" surrounded by thirty-three attached town houses has three regularly placed entrances with a view towards a concave façade. The façades of the three-storied town houses defining the circus were articulated by three rows of classical columns, one above the other. King's Circus has a diameter of about 320 ft (97 m) and its façade "resembles the façade of a Roman amphitheatre which has been turned outside in and made concave instead of convex" (Rasmussen 1934, 163).

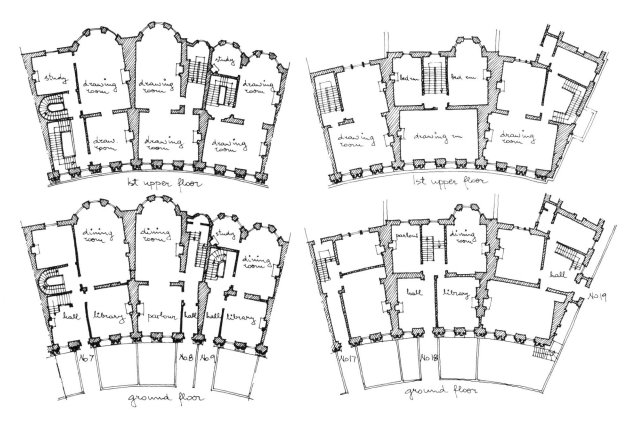

Bath: King's Circus
(after Walter Ison)

Bath: King's Circus

Bath: The Royal Crescent

Shortly after construction began on the King's Circus, Wood died, but his work was completed by his son. John Wood the Younger continued in the tradition of his father, and in 1767 he began to build the Royal Crescent, which took about eight years to complete. This impressive row of thirty stately houses, following the concave lines of a lawn semielliptical in plan, was a palatial housing development that, perhaps more than any other, fulfilled the aspirations of the wealthy concerning housing. The variety of interiors of this row of individual town houses was concealed behind a unified palatial façade with 114 colossal Ionic columns spanning two stories and sitting on a high rustic plinth. Facing an extensive green (a park), the old town of Bath on the banks of the Avon River, and the rolling hills beyond, the architectural ensemble of the Royal Crescent was "royal" not only in name, but also in concept. Although the occupants of this great complex with its magnificent view and physical setting were not royalty, their environment, nevertheless, projected a courtly life.

During the last decades of the eighteenth century and the beginning of the nineteenth century, the Royal Crescent was copied by many builders, and crescents surpassed residential squares in popularity. Camden Crescent (1788), Landsdown Crescent (1789), Somerset Place (1791), and Windcombe Crescent (1805), are some examples of terraced house developments in Bath, and these, of course, influenced builders in other parts of the British Isles. John Palmer's design for Landsdown Crescent is noteworthy because "the concave crescent and its convex wings form a serpentine line of buildings following the curving contours of the south-east slopes of Landsdown, and are one of the most conspicuous elements in the Bath scene" (Ison 1948, 128). The three curves of the building, in accordance with the rise and fall of the land, make Landsdown an interesting example of planning. The natural features of the land were taken into account by the developer without the sacrifice of light and sun exposure in any of the dwellings; in addition, an aesthetically pleasing urban environment was achieved.

Bath: The Royal Crescent (1767–75)

By the end of the eighteenth century London's residential squares, hitherto hard surfaced, began to have a central landscaped enclosure similar in concept to the squares and crescents in Bath. In Sigfried Giedion's opinion, London's claim to high levels of modern planning came about during this period and manifested itself in the harmonious interrelation of residential squares, places, and crescents. "On such sites as Bloomsbury, well-ordered spaces of every shape—oblong, circular, square, elliptical—accumulated to form a new and composite organism. In them the late baroque inheritance was carried on in a completely native manner, perfectly adapted to the conditions peculiar to London" (Giedion 1954a, 626).

The district of Bloomsbury was under development for a period of over one and a half centuries, a period that encompassed the reign of Louis XIV, the French Revolution, and the rise of the bourgeoisie in the wake of free trade. The town planning principles employed in the development of Bloomsbury during this period resulted in a residential urban environment where parts of the Duke of Bedford's landscaped garden survived in squares, crescents, and wide avenuelike "places." But, in contrast to the palatial town houses in Bath, the buildings in Bloomsbury had a less imposing character.

It was again a Duke of Bedford who began to parcel out an estate in the Bloomsbury district of London. Initially, an area of 112 acres (45 hectares) was subdivided into a number of properties along tree-lined streets and squares; the fronts of houses were to face public places, planted with gardens of grass and plane trees. Bedford Square was one of the first squares to be built (1775–1780), followed by others, such as Russell Square, Southampton Square (later called Bloomsbury Square), Torrington Square, Tavistock Square, as well as elongated places such as Woburn Place and Bedford Place. Of course, the Duke of Bedford did not undertake the development of Bloomsbury alone; he leased his lands to speculators and builders. It was they who planned, designed, and built the various projects.

James Burton, a speculator and builder, developed the site of Bedford House, which was pulled down in 1800 and replaced by Bedford Place "with its magnificently coordinated houses. . . . He planted the land behind the houses on Bedford Place, which runs between Bloomsbury and Russell Squares, with lawns and shrubbery. The result was particularly pleasing, for the low mews or stables behind the houses did not obstruct the view, and the openings at the end of the rows of houses linked the parallel areas of greenery so that there were no closed blocks" (Giedion 1954a, 631).

Thomas Cubitt followed Burton's work and built Torrington Square in 1827, an elongated quadrangle

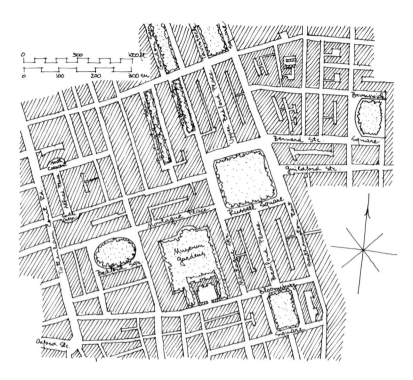

London: Bloomsbury area (nineteenth century)
(after Survey of London)

in form with a long central enclosure landscaped in the naturalistic English tradition of the early nineteenth century.

Of the various squares built in London during the eighteenth century, Bedford Square in Bloomsbury probably best illustrates the typical residential square of this period when town-house living became affordable to a large segment of the middle class. The square's design is attributed to the architect Thomas Leverton, but its execution was left to several builders. The four sides of the square were leased to speculative builders, who erected nearly uniform rows of town houses along them. The land was leased for ninety-nine years, and after the expiration date the land and the buildings on it reverted to the ownership of the Bedford Estate. The original lease for the land of one terraced house is estimated to have been £3 per annum. After the first expiration date the estate renewed the leases for the land and buildings to existing or new tenants, but the lease from then on was much shorter (usually between twenty and fifty years) and the amount as well as the length

of the lease was a function of the size of the property, its state of repair, and the amount that the new leaseholder was willing to spend upon its improvement. The Bedford Estate viewed the resulting staggering of leases as an advantage because the renewal of leases from then on would average out over bad and good years; thereby a wholesale renewal during a period of depression was circumvented. This policy, of course, resulted in the preservation of the square in its original form and prevented any temptation of economic opportunism to redevelop it.

Until the end of the nineteenth century Bloomsbury's approaches from Euston Road and Oxford Street were controlled by gates and "people who had no business in Bloomsbury were not admitted to the quarter. The grocer could not even send his errand-boy across to Bedford Square, he had to bring the goods himself in order to get in" (Rasmussen 1934, 166). This arrangement was not unlike that found in the *close*, the ecclesiastical precinct common throughout England during the Middle Ages until the dissolution of monasteries

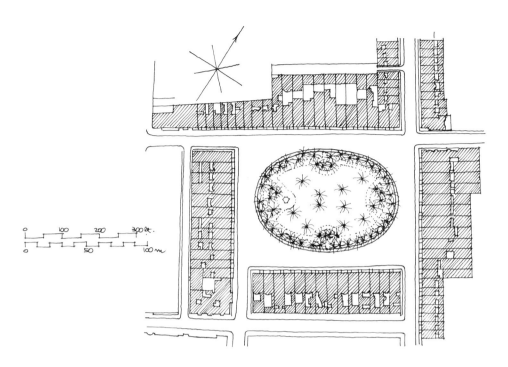

London: Bedford Square (1914)
(after Survey of London)

in the sixteenth century. (The Inns of Court, that is, the Inner and Middle Temples, are a survival of a lay precinct in today's London.) With its controlled access Bloomsbury also resembled the oriental mahalahs, but while Bloomsbury was a purely residential district with a homogeneous population with roughly similar incomes, mahalahs had both residential and commercial land use and were virtually a city within a city, with a population of varied income levels.

Typical of residential squares, the fronts of the Bloomsbury town houses were regimented handsome façades reflecting the fact that they sheltered people of a similar class, with similar values and aspirations. In contrast, the rear of the properties, which were not meant to be seen, contained the stables and service buildings, reached through a back lane, the mews. These were built to the specifications and needs of each owner. A small yard separated the front building from the rear stables; this yard was most often used for outdoor household chores.

Originally, town houses in Bloomsbury and

along Bedford Square had no private gardens, but residents facing a square had access to the landscaped park occupying the central area of the square. This communal outdoor space was surrounded by a street for access to the front entrances of the town houses. The central garden was planted with grass and trees in the English tradition of simulating a natural landscape and was fenced in; access to it was limited to members of a household that possessed a key to one of its small gates. The resident families of Bedford Square were entitled to use their park for outdoor recreational needs, but in full view of the public. This feature of occidental urban living is in antithesis to oriental urban living.

In the Orient, as discussed in Part II, the court garden of a home was a small private outdoor space hidden from both the view of the public and neighbors, and outdoor family recreation was a strictly private affair. In London the courtyards of town houses were merely service yards, and the semipublic landscaped park of the square functioned as oversized court-gardens; instead of being private,

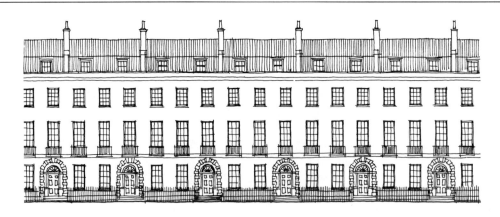

London: Bedford Square, typical town house
(after Steen Eiler Rasmussen)

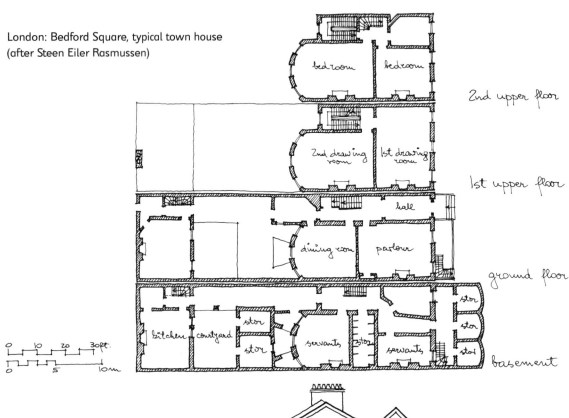

2nd upper floor

1st upper floor

ground floor

basement

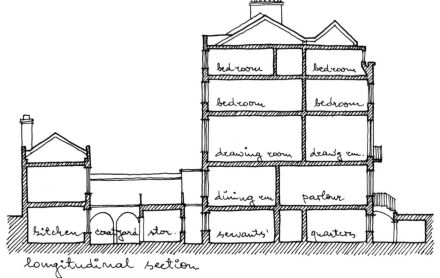

longitudinal section

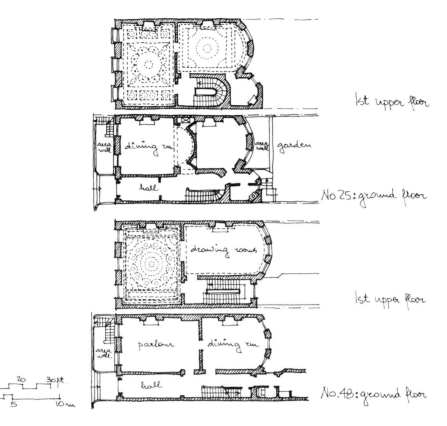

London: Bedford Square
(after Survey of London)

these outdoor spaces were overlooked by the general public, and family recreation in the outdoors thus became a public affair.

Several cities founded in North America incorporated the "square" concept. Cities were laid out in a gridiron street pattern with at least one large square designed as a civic center. In 1683 when Thomas Holme, William Penn's surveyor general, drew up the plan for Philadelphia, he provided, in addition to one central square, four smaller squares for the recreation of the future city's inhabitants. At this time residential squares were already very fashionable in London.

In 1733, when Savannah was settled in the colony of Georgia, James Edward Oglethorpe and his 115 colonists adopted the concept of residential squares for their new city. The original plan for Savannah included six wards, each with a central square. The wards were about 10 acres (4 hectares) in area and the central squares about 2 acres (0.8 hectares) between building lines. Squares were

linked axially to each other by 75-ft (22.8-m) wide avenues, while north-south streets dividing the wards were given a width of only 40 ft (12 m). In the four corners of each ward were two rows of five building lots 60 ft (18.2 m) wide and 90 ft (27.4 m) deep; the two rows of lots were separated from each other by a narrow lane. "Each corner set of ten lots constituted a tithing, so that the whole ward contained forty lots, or four tithings. The total for the city thus came to 240 lots" (Bannister 1961, 48).

To the east and west sides of each square were two "Trustee" lots intended for various public structures and official residences. The six wards were arranged in two sets of three, separated from each other by a wide avenue. The overall area of the six-ward city was 68.8 acres (27.8 hectares), and before 1790 the total number of inhabitants did not exceed 2,000. In anticipation of a possible Spanish attack from the south, Savannah was fortified with ramparts; six gates linked the city with its

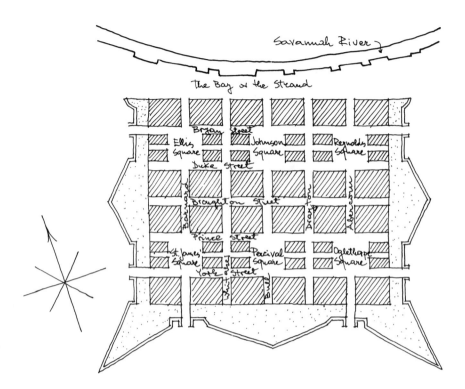

Savannah, Georgia
(after eighteenth-century map [1757])

surrounding countryside. Immediately beyond the ramparts were a burying ground and the "common," both in public ownership.

In 1790, when the city received its city charter, Savannah had to be extended beyond its original limits. As the city grew, new districts were added following the original ward plan until the common land holdings of the community were exhausted. Thus, by 1856 the city possessed twenty-four squares within the city, all but one—Ellis Square, which became the marketplace—landscaped and defined by a barrier chain.

As Edmund Bacon described, the visual effect of the sequential squares in Savannah is very pleasing because each square has its own special character. Since squares are linked to each other along two axes, the spatial urban effects are in great contrast to the monumental single axial plans employed in Paris, Washington, and other cities. The squares of Savannah are tranquil places, and "when one is within any of these squares, one feels entirely removed from the rushing traffic of the surround-ing streets, which crosses but does not parallel the lines of sight" (Bacon 1976, 221).

In keeping with the architectural style of the Georgian era, many dwellings in Savannah were town houses, three to four stories high, built close to the edge of the sidewalk. In contrast to their London counterparts, these dwellings had no basements or cellars because of the heavy vapors given off by the nearby swamps. The first or ground level of the typical town house in Savannah was used for offices, dining room, kitchen, and service rooms. The second or main floor, one story above the ground level, comprised the reception rooms, parlors, and drawing rooms, while the upper floors contained the bedrooms. A steep stairway led to the front door; the doors were usually arched, with a fan transom. The stairways were embellished with wrought-iron handrails and ran parallel rather than at right angles to the sidewalk.

Savannah is a unique example of a city that built residential squares on a citywide basis until the middle of the nineteenth century. The diagrams,

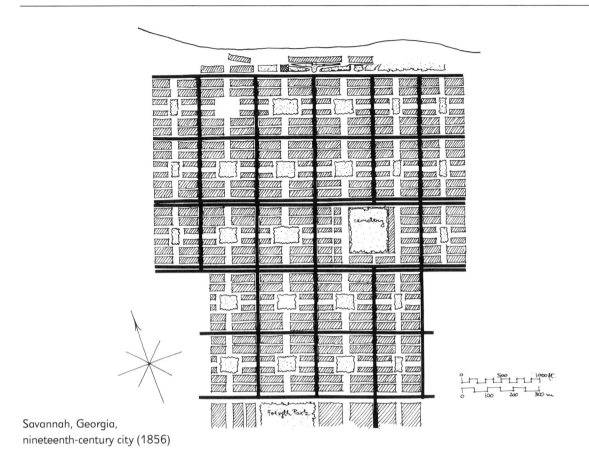

Savannah, Georgia,
nineteenth-century city (1856)

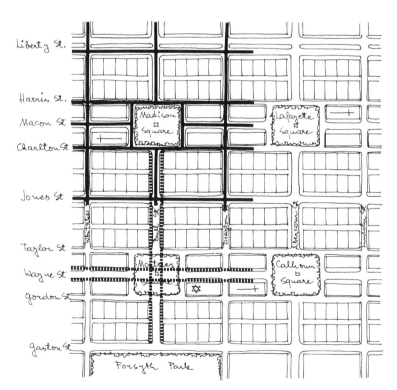

Savannah, Georgia: Grid of wards
(after Stanford Anderson)

based on Stanford Anderson's analysis of Savannah, illustrate clearly that the city's geometric order established two types of hierarchies: one internal to each ward and another that evolved in the additive growth of the city.

THE TOWN HOUSE

In the occident the "private" house evolved as a result of the separation of private and public life. As Mumford (1961) observed, the dwelling became spatially separated from any visible means of income. Thus, a generic building type came into existence for the middle class: the town house.

The town house had its roots in medieval attached urban dwellings, but all commercial and business accoutrements, which were an intrinsic part of the medieval house, were eliminated. Gradually, with the development of residential squares and crescents by large-scale building speculators, the town house evolved as a mass-produced product, at the time not considered to be "real architecture." Nevertheless, it was a refined building type, and developers paid considerable attention to its aesthetic appearance, if for no other reason than that of public appeal. After all, builders of town houses had to sell or lease the buildings. Therefore, they attempted to satisfy the prevailing ideas of beauty; they had to be careful to employ a design and building materials that were acceptable at the time of construction.

The façade of a typical London town house consisted of two window bays and an entrance door. The ground-floor level was a few steps above the sidewalk and was reached through a vestibule. The front section of the house was occupied by a parlor; behind it, overlooking the yard, was a dining room. Both of these spaces were accessible through the stair hall with its curved and spiraling staircase, which was the vertical communication link of the entire dwelling. The parlor functioned as a reception room for visitors other than relatives or close friends of the family. The dining room's position at

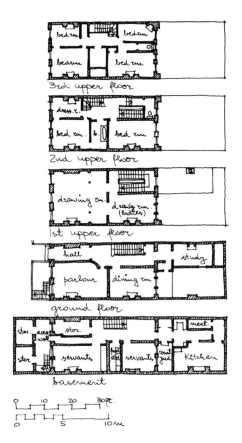

London: Typical 20-ft town house
(after Hermann Muthesius)

ground-floor level was determined by convenience, since all service rooms as well as the kitchen were located below it. The level below the ground floor was partially a basement (at least half its height above grade) and partially a cellar (less than half above grade). That this was so becomes evident when one examines a cross section through a typical Georgian town house. It presents a peculiarity in terms of grade levels characteristic of many town-house developments—namely, the yard level was much lower than the street level apparently because of the gradual buildup over time of the road surface. Hence, the front section of the house had a cellar, while the rear section was either a basement or entirely above the yard level. Between the edge of the sidewalk and the front of the building was an area well with a narrow service stair. Coal bins were dug below the sidewalk, and a small bridge with a few steps spanning the well linked the front door to the sidewalk.

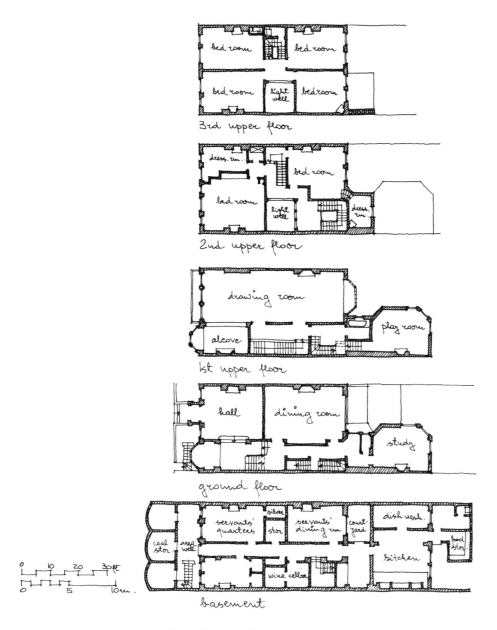

London: Cadogan Square No. 68; R. Norman Shaw, architect
(after Hermann Muthesius)

The second level of a typical town house, known as the piano nobile—a floor with a high ceiling—contained two drawing rooms in addition to the stair hall; a broad room used predominantly by men occupied the entire front of the house, while at the rear a narrower room, where smoking was not permitted, was designed for use by women. The third floor contained the master bedroom as well as children's rooms, while the garret, lit through dormer windows, contained the rooms of the ser-vants. To the rear of the property and abutting a narrow back lane were the stables and related facil-ities. Living accommodation for a coachman was often located above the stables.

Both exterior and interior details as well as the proportions of town houses were classical, but ornamentation was often subdued and, on the front façade, was limited to the main entrance, as exemplified in the town houses in Bedford Square. After the introduction of a window tax, the relative

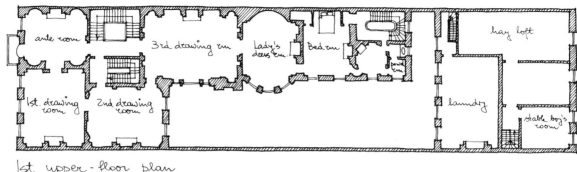

1st upper-floor plan

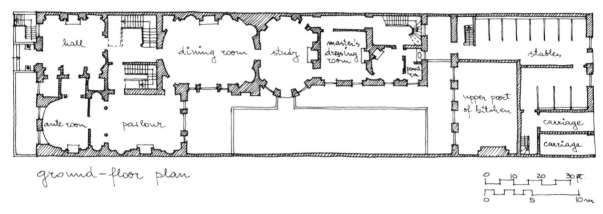

ground-floor plan

London: Grosvenor Square town house by Robert Adam, 1773
(after Hermann Muthesius)

area of the exterior wall in comparison with that of the windows, was increased and the English town house of the eighteenth century emerged as a simple and dignified building with very little ornamentation on its façade.

The separation of the family from everyday business affairs also brought about a change in household organization. Domestic responsibilities, which hitherto had been shared by husband and wife, now became the sole responsibility of the woman and, in a sense, a specialized job. Of course, housework had been a necessary activity since time immemorial; it now became ritualized. Rugged furniture, which had been scoured with lye periodically during the Middle Ages, was replaced with baroque furniture with a mirrorlike finish, which had to be dusted every day and polished often. Metalwork, silver, and brass had to be polished, and a lot of useless but decorative vases and bric-a-brac demanded constant attention. In fact, housework became so time-consuming that

"woman's work was never done." Servants were needed to assist in household cleaning, cooking, and child rearing. And, just as the head of the family supervised his staff at his office, so did his wife hers at home. Wealthy households sometimes employed half a dozen people or more.

While the upper and middle classes in England evolved a new domestic life pattern disassociated from making a living, the majority of craftsmen and workers continued to live as they had done during the Middle Ages. The workshop of a craftsman was still an integral part of his home—the shopkeeper lived above his store.

Town-house living initially was exclusive to the aristocracy and the wealthy bourgeoisie. Eventually, the concept was adopted by others, and by 1830 even some artisans embraced the concept of town-house living. Houses in Munster Square, St. Pancras, London, have in principle a similar arrangement to those in Bedford Square, but their accommodation is smaller and less luxurious.

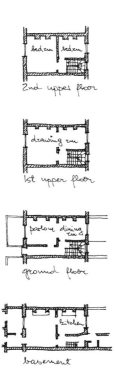

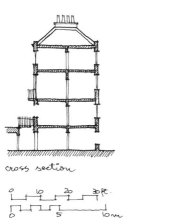

London: Munster House artisans' houses
by John Nash, 1830
(after P. N. Davies-Colley as cited in F. R. Hiorns)

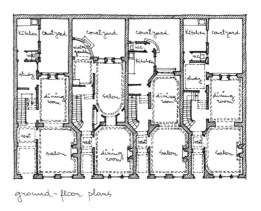

Paris: Typical town houses on Rue d'Offremont

These artisans' homes, designed by the famous architect John Nash, are also narrower, less deep, and not so high as those of the fashionable squares. They have neither a garret nor a coachhouse. The houses were only two bays wide, with one wide window and a front entrance. However, in the functional distribution of spaces within the dwelling these houses followed the tradition established in their predecessors: the kitchen was in the basement, the parlor and dining rooms were at ground-floor level, and the bedrooms were on the upper floors. Although Munster Square had a central fenced-in park that was the semipublic domain of the residents living around the square, the artisans' homes also had gardens in the rear, since a service yard was not required in the absence of coachhouses. The residents, therefore, had a choice between a private garden and a semipublic park for outdoor recreation.

The town-house concept of middle-class housing also found application in many western European countries. Although formality, a characteristic of the nineteenth-century bourgeoisie, was retained in most European town-house developments, continental urban houses differed from their English counterparts in several other respects. First, European town-house developments lacked a collective landscaped outdoor space; instead, many town houses had tiny gardens at the back of the property in the absence of stables and service lanes. Nineteenth-century examples in Paris,

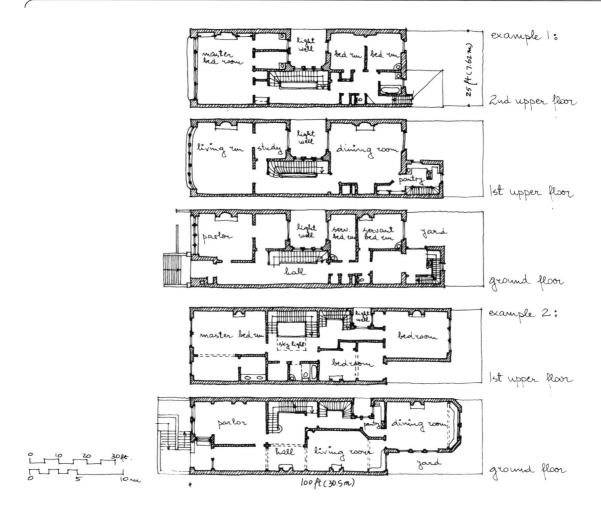

Typical North American town houses
(after J. Stübben)

Brussels, and Cologne illustrate this rear-courtyard treatment. Second, European town houses were not built on the same large scale as they were in London; thus, they lacked the harmony and continuity of Bloomsbury, for example. Finally, the internal arrangement of the servants' quarters, ordinarily at ground-floor level in European houses, made area wells, so characteristic of English terraced houses, superfluous.

In the New World as well, the town house became popular during the eighteenth and nineteenth centuries. Probably Philadelphia was the first American city to adopt this English concept of urban living. According to H. Dickson McKenna, by 1700 brick town houses similar to those built in London were common in Philadelphia. Even today, these urban dwellings are still the most charming

features of Philadelphia around both the Rittenhouse Square and Society Hill areas. High land values as well as the gridiron plan of street layout and the subdivision of city blocks into narrow and deep lots favored the use of attached rather than freestanding urban house forms.

The design of Boston's first town houses, erected towards the end of the eighteenth century, is attributed to the famous architect Charles Bulfinch. Upon his return from a visit to London and Bath, Bulfinch designed several town-house rows; Colonnade Row on Tremont Street facing the Common and Tontine Crescent are best known. Later, during the nineteenth century, several contractors embarked upon speculative ventures erecting groups of ten to twelve attached houses from identical plans and elevations, and many

New York City: Typical town house
(after T. J. van der Bent)

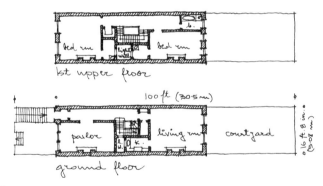

New York City: Small town house
(after J. Stübben)

rows of these town houses have survived in Boston's Beacon Hill area as well as in other parts of the city.

Town-house construction in New York City began toward the end of the eighteenth and beginning of the nineteenth century. In most cases the London town-house plan was used as a model, but in one significant respect the American plan differed: there was no cellar or basement accommodation. Hence, the service entrance was at or near grade level and a stoop or exterior flight of stairs led to the front entrance of the parlor floor.

Calvin Polard, an architect and surveyor, was one of the most prolific designers of town houses in New York City during the first half of the nineteenth century. The standard layout of a typical Polard New York town house consisted of a ground floor with service entrance, servants' parlor, and dining room in the front and a large kitchen in the rear. An intrinsic feature of the kitchen was a stove niche flanked by masonry supports for the fireplace in the room above; "the coal stove fit neatly between the masonry supports and vented into the chimney flue—usually around the clock; it was banked at night, then opened up in the morning to prepare breakfast" (McKenna 1971, 23).

A stoop, reminiscent of early Dutch settlers' homes, led to the front entrance of the house, which in turn led into the vestibule. From the vestibule one entered the stair hall located, as was the entrance door, near the party wall. A parlor occupied the front section of the house; a dining room, the rear section. The dining room was linked through a butler's pantry equipped with a dumbwaiter and a stair to the kitchen below. Both the parlor and the dining room had identical fireplaces, and a central wide opening with sliding doors allowed the two rooms to combine into a single space. In some instances the dining room was placed below the parlor floor, in which case the main-floor level had a double parlor.

The floor above the parlor contained a large master bedroom on the street side and a smaller bedroom facing the rear yard, with a bathroom tucked into the corner behind the staircase. The master bedroom functioned as a bed-sitting room and was usually L-shaped so as to provide clearance for the ascending staircase. Between the bedrooms were the clothes closets, which also acted as an acoustic barrier between the two rooms. The top floor of the typical town house had a similar layout to the main bedroom floor but, instead of the bathroom, an additional bedroom occupied the corner.

The early nineteenth-century town house was designed in the Federal style based on the classical tradition in architecture of the previous century; this style was believed to represent universal principles and forms that appealed in all times and circumstances. Certainly, the Federal style resulted in street façades of a pleasing simplicity that was acceptable to New Yorkers not yet demanding pretentious dwellings. The most elaborate feature of the restrained town-house façade was the front door with a transom light and, frequently, sidelights as well. Usually, windows were modest in scale, small-paned and double-hung, but in some instances the sills of parlor windows were lowered to the floor and iron guardrails protected the lower panes of these triple-hung tall and elegant windows. While back windows were often equipped with exterior shutters, those facing the street were fitted with hinged narrow-panel interior shutters that were folded back and concealed in side niches when not in use.

Many early town houses in America were built of bricks brought to this continent as ballast on ships, but around the middle of the nineteenth century stone replaced brick, in particular a soft sandstone stained evenly by traces of iron ore. These "brownstone" houses became very popular in New York City and were also eventually built in other cities, such as Boston and Chicago and on occasion even in Montreal, although the gray stone house is far more prevalent there.

In cities on the west coast town houses were primarily constructed of wood. Many of these wood town houses were destroyed by fire or demolition, but some have survived, especially in San Francisco.

After 1830, the Federal style was gradually succeeded by a series of Revivalist styles, such as Greek Revival, Gothic Revival, and Colonial Revival, resulting in various degrees of elaborate architectural ornamentation to town-house façades.

The rectangular street layouts and the narrow but deep building lots prevalent in most American cities admirably suited the application of the town-house concept. With the mounting pressure for effective land utilization, town houses became narrower and deeper over time—two 25-ft (7.62-m) lots were divided into three, and a third room (without direct daylight) was inserted between the front parlor and the rear dining room. In middle-class homes this windowless room was used, for example, as a music room; however, in workers' houses it was used as a bedroom. This building practice was later exploited in lower-income housing.

In America, the town-house concept was also copied for worker's housing. Built of wood, two-story row houses were constructed in many mill towns. In larger cities, because of fire hazards, modest town houses were built of brick. These dwellings served a large segment of the working population until the great influx of immigrants created a housing shortage and an opportunity for landlords to exploit the housing market. The "dumbbell" tenements were then invented.

CHAPTER FOUR

THE NINETEENTH CENTURY

INDUSTRIALISM AND URBANISM

The Industrial Revolution was one of the most important and far-reaching periods of modern history. Since industrialization was neither sudden nor violent, it could be argued that the term "evolution" rather than "revolution" would be more appropriate. However, the gradual changes precipitated by industrialization invariably had such an enormous impact upon societies that the term "industrial revolution" is not inappropriate.

As is the case with most other historic periods, the Industrial Revolution occurred at different times in different nations. England was the first to experience it, for it was the only country in the eighteenth century that possessed the preconditions for a change from a basic local market economy to that of an international industrial one. These were stable political institutions with internal free trade, experience in foreign trade (notably with the New World), abundant energy (primarily coal), advantageous climatic conditions (important for the textile industry), and favorable geographic location (England was a maritime nation).

The Industrial Revolution in Great Britain, which began roughly around 1760, was preceded by an agrarian revolution. The Enclosure Acts ensured that common fields as well as common waste land were enclosed and brought under intensive cultivation. This additional land available for farming, coupled with improved agricultural technology, resulted in improved productivity. To facilitate the marketing and distribution of the surplus produce, improved roads and canals provided an unprecedented network of good transportation routes.

In the initial stages of the Industrial Revolution the basic source of energy was flowing water. Thus, most new industries were located by river banks, since the operation of their great machines relied on the latent kinetic energy of the flowing water. The harnessing of water power was accompanied by the construction of industrial buildings in wood and stone. The scale of these early industrial buildings was in harmony with all other buildings in their respective surroundings, and to live near an industrial building was not only acceptable but often considered an advantage, since it meant a desirable proximity to the place of work and to the amenities of the river bank.

Although the industrial community was composed of residential, commercial, and industrial buildings, it was a harmonious urban entity. The interrelationship of homes, public buildings, and factories in this early era of industrialization was marked by compatibility, and all components of a settlement had their roots in a common pool of natural resources. For example, the river was a source of energy for industry; it served as a highway for transport and commerce, and it also provided recreation for members of the community.

Workers' urban houses were very similar to those of the earlier agricultural society. Workers lived in small cottages not unlike those of farm workers, while their employers occupied so-called villas that imitated (on a smaller scale) the manors of the landed gentry. In one respect, however, the working man experienced a considerable change in his domestic setting during the Industrial Revolution—with his removal from the countryside to the city, the worker no longer had a garden to provide him with food, which meant that he was entirely dependent upon his wages for subsistence.

The Industrial Revolution entered its second phase when coal replaced water as a source of energy. The siting of factories necessarily changed to where coal was abundant. Thus, mining regions became the significant areas of industrial development. Although the major rivers lost their initial dominance in determining the location of industry, they retained, for a while, some importance as transportation routes; soon this role was seriously challenged by the invention of the steam engine and the rapid development of the railway network.

The selection of industrial sites was then based upon a number of different and quite complex considerations. For example, many new industrial sites opened in areas to which it was possible to transport coal some distance from the mines; other factors, such as the cost of transporting raw materials for manufacturing goods or the existence of an available labor force, overweighed the cost of coal transport in selecting the site of a factory. Thus, in the second phase of the Industrial Revolution, economic and demographic considerations determined the location of industrial developments.

The use of steam power was accompanied by construction in brick and iron, at first cast- and wrought-iron and later steel. Large-spanned structures were erected for mills, foundries, and factories for the mass production of industrial goods. This new method of industrial construction as well as the evolution of efficient techniques for converting fuels to energy was not, however, matched by similar progress in the building of

homes; the new industrial age had little influence on domestic design, with the possible exception of decorative detail provided by mass-produced ornaments.

However, a number of changes that had a particular urban significance took place simultaneously with the growth of industrialization. In fact, without these changes the Industrial Revolution could not have had as great an impact as it did upon society in some parts of the world during the nineteenth century. Towns and cities grew in size and, as their populations increased, the social problems that derived from outmoded housing also multiplied. Migration from the rural areas was so great that cities could no longer efficiently control their growth, nor could they relieve the ever-increasing burden of providing decent housing. Industrialization and urbanization produced overcrowded slums.

It is true that so-called slum conditions existed to some extent before the Industrial Revolution, but their occurrence in villages and towns that were relatively small seldom provoked the acute problems of mass-produced human misery that occurred in industrial cities.

Before the Industrial Revolution so irrevocably altered the size and character of cities, the open countryside was never far from the center of a community, and this very fact made the meanest slum seem less severe. Similarly, because towns and cities were relatively small, the homes of well-to-do people, public buildings such as the church or school, and shops were close neighbors to the dwellings of the poorest families. The home of the poorer family may have been dilapidated, but it was served by a church, a school, and various shops common to all inhabitants. For this reason, any attempt to limit the dwellings of the underprivileged to a particular part of the town did not mean in effect a true isolation from the rest of the community.

With the expansion of industrial development these mitigating conditions rapidly lost significance. People who worked in factories had to leave their villages: the absence of cheap, quick means of public mass transportation made it imperative to live close to the workplace. Thus housing inevitably grew in the midst of the gray environment of factories and slag heaps that replaced the green fields of another era. Bleak housing developments reached such dimensions that they equaled whole towns in size, forming isolated communities with their own institutions and commercial establishments. The inhabitants of these communities no longer had a heterogeneous socioeconomic background, and they soon became outcasts from their parent communities. The churches of the rich were no longer the churches of the poor, nor did workers' children attend the same schools as the children of well-to-do families, and, of course, shops catered to disparate clienteles.

As the factories prospered and new technological achievements led to both the extension of existing industries and the founding of new ones, people from overpopulated rural areas flocked to the cities. This migration, coupled with a high birth rate, meant that the industrial centers of the British Isles experienced phenomenal population increases. The spectacular growth is illustrated by the following figures:

> Birmingham's population rose from 71,000 in 1801 to 265,000 in 1851 and 760,000 in 1901; corresponding figures for Manchester were 75,000, 338,000, and 645,000; for Leeds 53,000, 172,000, and 429,000; and similar rates of increase obtained in Liverpool, Sheffield, Newcastle, Hull, and other centers in industrial and mining districts (Burke 1971, 127).

The population growth in the entire country during the age of industrialization was equally impressive. From six million inhabitants in 1750, the population in 1800 rose to nine million; in 1850, eighteen million and by 1900, forty million. A large proportion of the population growth was accommodated in urbanized areas. Thus, in 1851, out of 3,336,000 people age twenty years and over inhabiting sixty-two English and Welsh towns (including London), only 1,337,000 had been born in the town of their residence. Naturally, the figures for the labor force reflected the changing economy. For example, in 1818, 57,000 workers were employed in the textile industry; in little more than two decades textile workers numbered 500,000, almost tenfold that of 1818.

Cities and towns were ill-prepared to accommodate the large influx of people seeking employment in urbanized areas. In the new industrial towns as well as in the workers' housing estates on the periphery of established towns, the most elementary traditions of municipal amenities and services were not provided. Despite their foulness, even open sewers represented comparative municipal affluence. And, as Mumford remarked, whole districts were sometimes without access to water and "on occasion, the poor would go from house to house in the middle class sections, begging for water as they might beg for bread during a famine" (1961, 463).

The dire conditions in industrialized urban areas during the nineteenth century were appalling in all sectors: "industrialization, the main creative force of the nineteenth century, produced the most degraded urban environment the world had yet seen; for even the quarters of the ruling classes were befouled and overcrowded" (Mumford 1961, 447).

Under these abominable living conditions mortality rates were staggering. "It appears that in 1840 the general crude death rate was 23 per 1,000; the average age of death was twenty-nine and that one child in six died before the age of one year" (Hiorns 1956, 323). Overcrowded cities also became breeding grounds for epidemics. The cholera epidemic of 1832 spread rapidly through England and scourged people of every rank. Epidemics could not be ignored, and people of conscience (as well as with considerable self-interest) rallied to improve the living conditions in the cities.

Great Britain was the first, but hardly the only, country to fall victim to urban degradation as a result of the Industrial Revolution. Other European countries experienced similar conditions although the extent may not have matched that of England. Not only was the expansion of industrialization less rapid in Europe, but several large cities, profiting from the experience of Britain, took active steps during the early part of the nineteenth century to establish some protective standards for public health. Health boards were created on the continent and in the United States to control the threat of epidemics.

From the middle of the nineteenth century onward, several social reformers called attention to the tremendous impact of the Industrial Revolution upon the city and upon the housing conditions of the working class in Great Britain, and rallied to combat the seemingly inevitable deterioration of urban life. In 1842 Edwin Chadwick submitted his *Report on the Sanitary Condition of the Labouring Population and on the Means of its Improvement*, a document that eventually brought about a reform of the English laws concerning open space around buildings and better ventilation within them. Lord Ashley, the future seventh Earl of Shaftesbury, championed the cause of women and children and was cofounder of the Society for Improving the Condition of the Labouring Classes. This organization advocated (1) the introduction of "allotments into the environs of London, so that working men might grow their own produce," (2) the building of model housing which "combined comfort with economy," and (3) the organization of "well-conducted loan funds" (Tarn 1971, 5). The first and the third objectives of the society were never realized but, with the construction of Model Houses for Families, the society set an example for tenement buildings that was remarkably advanced for its time.

One of the first social realists of nineteenth-century Britain was Octavia Hill. A keen observer of the desperate conditions in London slums, she first deplored the malpractices of slum landlords and the lack of public open spaces in rapidly growing industrial towns. In her first endeavor to improve these conditions, she obtained both spiritual and material backing from her former teacher, John Ruskin, in the development of a model housing project in a slum court in Marylebone, London (1864). These model lodgings for poor tenants were financed by Ruskin, but otherwise the property was managed by Octavia Hill. Her concern with the lack of open spaces eventually led to the foundation of the National Trust (1895) and subsequently to the preservation of many open spaces in crowded urban areas.

As the awareness of poor housing conditions increased, several other reformers set about to try to improve them. Perhaps the foremost of these was Henrietta Octavia Rowland and her husband Samuel Augustus Barnett, a clergyman and social reformer, who devoted their lives to improving the lot of the poor. Barnett was vicar of St. Jude's in Whitechapel, London, and he and his wife carried out most of their work in this parish. The Barnetts' activities included the organization of relief, the coordination of charities, provision of entertainment, and the establishment of adult education for the poor. Their most significant achievements were the building of model dwellings, and the establishment of the Christian Settlements in London (social settlement houses first established in 1884).

Settlement houses in Great Britain were inhabited by university-trained men and women who elected to "settle" among laborers in an industrial area in order to associate themselves as good neighbors with the working classes. The "settlers" were to give lectures in the evenings to their neighbors and to bring about a mixture of the sharply separated classes, to the equal advantage of all.

Dame Henrietta (Mrs. Barnett was honored in recognition of her public service) continued her attempt to bring about a better understanding between the educated and noneducated city dwellers through the settlement experiment, but finally came to the conclusion that the scheme was not effective in existing urban areas. She abandoned the hope of ameliorating conditions in cities and adopted the view advocated by Ebenezer Howard that it would be far better to build new settlements—garden cities—containing houses for all kinds of people, from large villas to the most modest cottages.

By the late nineteenth century, it was apparent that not all workers suffered under the dire urban living conditions created by the Industrial Revolution, and that in some cases their living conditions actually improved, since the reality of rural life was not always the idyllic existence perceived by urban dwellers. This was especially true for workers who were fortunate enough to work for industrialists like Robert Owen in New Lanark, Titus Salt in Saltaire, the Cadbury family in Bourneville, or Viscount Leverhulme in Port

Sunlight. Bourneville (begun in 1879) and Port Sunlight (begun in 1888) became model industrial settlements that went beyond the concept of model homes. In Bourneville, for example, the picturesque streetscape was an explicit aim of its developer "and gardens were to form by statute an inviolate part of the whole" (Choay 1969, 30); perhaps even more important, the homes of the Bourneville settlement were from the start available to the public at affordable rents and were not limited specifically to workers employed in Cadbury's factory. Located near Birmingham, Bourneville thus became a desirable suburb for workers employed in other industries. With other similar settlements, such as Pullman City near Chicago (1867), Krupp's Schederhof in Essen (1872), and Agnetha Park in Delft (1885), Bourneville must have influenced social and urban reformers in their belief that a marriage is possible between urban and rural settlement patterns. The price for this marriage was urban sprawl, and "not a voice was raised against the urban explosion; it would be healthier and that was enough" (Tarn 1971, 36).

The surrender of social and urban reformers to the notion that good housing for workers is only possible to build in suburbs or new towns was unfortunate because it inadvertently acknowledged a defeat, in that it sought to avoid urban housing problems rather than try to find solutions to them.

BACK-TO-BACKS, TENEMENTS, AND BYLAW HOUSING

As we have noted, the great influx of rural people to cities and towns created an unprecedented demand for workers' housing in all countries affected by industrialization. This new demand was partially met by the conversion of middle-class housing into tenements, but to a greater degree by the construction of new housing.

In Great Britain a building process developed for middle-class housing in the seventeenth and eighteenth centuries that became the vehicle for the construction of workers' housing in the nineteenth century with one important change. The high standards of construction previously employed were replaced by shoddy building practices that were justified, no doubt, by the need to meet the ever-growing demand for living accommodation by the new migrants settling in urban areas.

At first, traditional rural and urban housing models were copied by the builders. One model was almshouses, privately financed homes for the city's poor. Other models were the traditional farm laborers' cottages and tenants' housing in rural settings similar to those built toward the end of the eighteenth century. All of these dwelling prototypes were easily adaptable to tightly packed row-house developments. However, "under these congested conditions primitive hygiene and sanitation revealed inadequacies scarcely noticeable before; cesspools overflowed, drainage was either blocked or non-existent, and water supply became polluted" (Pawley 1971, 11).

In contrast to the farm laborer's cottage, which had small gardens back and front, the new version—the worker's cottage—had merely a small courtyard in the rear. Moreover, the rural cottage home, which had evolved over centuries from a single-room dwelling to a two-story house with living room and scullery at ground level and one or two bedrooms on the upper level, regressed in its urban version to a single-room dwelling, which at best was equipped with a box bed in a corner of the room. These reduced standards, aggravated by a lack of the amenities enjoyed by previous generations of laborers, resulted in mean living conditions, often without proper sanitary facilities.

The pressure for greater exploitation of urban land led to the use of the "back-to-back" dwelling, a row-house development where all dwelling units except the end units were attached on three sides to neighboring units. This dwelling form also had its roots in rural housing. The earliest known examples of back-to-back rural dwellings date back to 1706. Generally, back-to-back dwellings

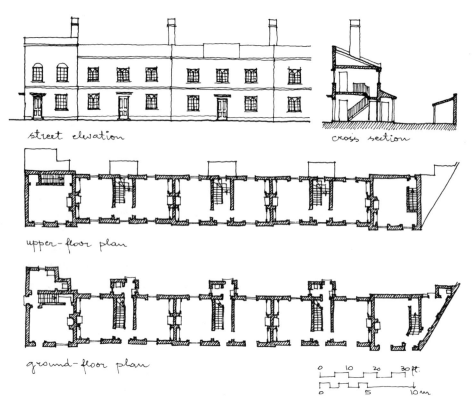

London: 1819–20. Drapers' almshouses, Glasshill Street
(after Survey of London)

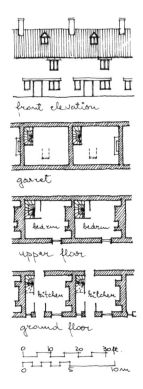

Farm laborers' cottage (1796)
(after M. W. Barley)

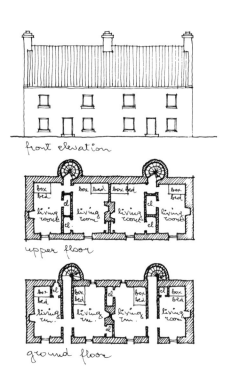

Weavers' tenements (1780)
(after M. W. Barley)

had a living room and a scullery at ground level and two bedrooms on the upper level; they had only one entrance, and all windows were on the entrance side. No cross-ventilation was possible in the dwelling unit. The absence of open space in urban areas, combined with poor sanitary facilities, resulted in very unhealthy living conditions. To maximize land-use efficiency, rows of back-to-backs were frequently built at right angles to the street and were separated from each other by narrow and ill-ventilated alleys or courts. At the rear of the courts were the communal toilets, shared by all the tenants, often at the ratio of seven families to one toilet.

By the end of the nineteenth century and into the twentieth century, considerable sections of residential areas in industrial cities such as Liverpool and Birmingham used the back-to-back dwelling form for workers' housing. In 1913 a council inquiry revealed that Birmingham had 43,366 dwellings of the back-to-back type. There were 200,000 people housed in these cavernous dwellings which mostly lacked individual water supplies or sanitary facilities. The communal outbuildings were probably the dwellings' most degrading features and "inevitably tended to undermine the health and morals of the tenants" (Burke 1971, 129).

During the nineteenth century the housing of single men and women also presented an evergrowing and unprecedented urban problem since hitherto they had been housed by their employers. Before the Industrial Revolution, as described earlier, apprentices and workers as well as maidservants were accommodated on the premises of their respective employers. However, with the emergence of large factories, young people seeking new job opportunities flocked to the cities. Since their employers rarely provided lodging for them, single workers usually had to board with the families of other workers, who already lived in very crowded conditions.

Charitable organizations attempted to meet the needs of these men and women by building common lodging houses. In J. N. Tarn's opinion, social reformers, partly because of the limited financial

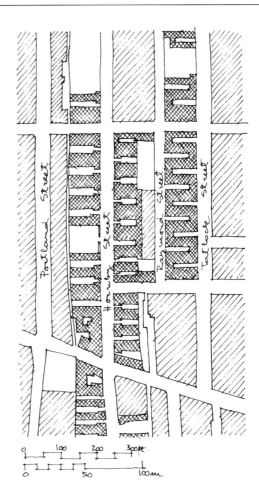

Liverpool: Hornby Street area, back-to-back housing, 1902 (after J. S. Nettlefold)

means of charitable organizations, were at the outset interested only in the lodging house for single workers rather than in the multiple dwelling for working-class families with children. Lord Ashley's society, for example, began the construction of a lodging house for men and boys in 1846 and completed it the next year. The society purchased a small and rather difficult site in St. Giles, London, and built on it a five-story building that could not be lighted from the rear at all except at the point where the staircase occurred. The arrangement of the building was to become typical:

On the ground floor a common room and steward's flat, below it cooking and washing facilities, above two dormitories on each floor,

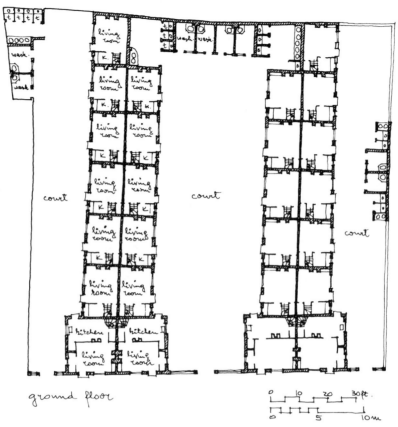

ground floor

0   10   20   30 ft.

0   5   10 m

Birmingham: Courts
(after J. S. Nettlefold)

separated by the stair and divided into cubicles 8-ft. 9-in. [2.7 m] long and 4-ft. 3-in. to 4-ft. 9-in. [1.361.5 m] wide. There were six wash-basins on every floor and one W.C. to every twenty-five lodgers. Because of the impossibility of providing rear windows only half the cubicles had direct natural light and ventilation so there was some well-intentioned critical comment about that planning weakness from interested observers as well as derogatory remarks about the amount of accommodation crammed onto the site (Tarn 1971, 6).

During the middle of the nineteenth century multistoried model tenements for worker families first appeared in the city of London. A corner site at Streatham and George Streets, in Bloomsbury, was acquired by Lord Ashley's society, and architect Henry Roberts was entrusted with the design

of Model Houses for Families. The building, completed in 1850, consisted of a series of flats accessible from an open gallery in the rear. The five-story-high building was U-shaped and enclosed a large courtyard, or drying ground. The open galleries overlooked the courtyard and linked to each other and the street entrance by a wide staircase. A typical dwelling was entered through a narrow hall, which led to the living room; a scullery, a toilet, and a small bedroom had window openings toward the gallery, while the living room and a large bedroom were lit and ventilated from the street side. The flats were self-contained, and the standard of accommodation was very generous for its time. Complementing the traditional London street appearance, the façades of the building were well designed, with brick walls and large double-hung

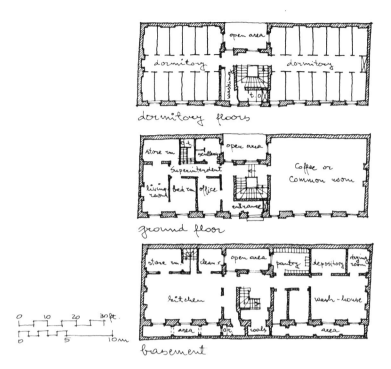

London: Model lodging house
(after J. N. Tarn)

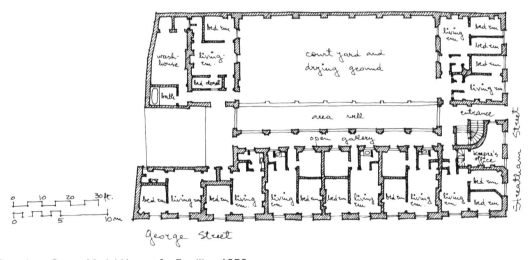

London: Streatham Street, Model Houses for Families, 1850
(after J. N. Tarn)

windows. This building became a model for subsequent tenement buildings, but it was rarely equaled during the nineteenth century.

The Katherine Buildings, in the Whitechapel area of London, were completed thirty-five years after the Streatham Street building and clearly demonstrate that tenement or multifamily housing design, far from having advanced during that peri-od, actually regressed in its spatial dwelling standards. Also employing external balcony access at the rear, the flats of the five-story Katherine Buildings were much smaller than those of the earlier example; five rooms were clustered along a narrow corridor that reached from the gallery to the front of the block, and each room could be let singly or in a variety of combinations. Toilet

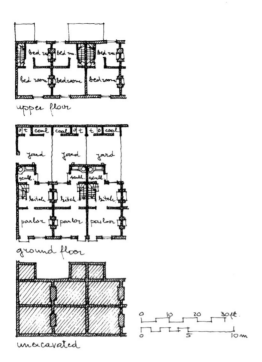

Bylaw housing, Nottingham (1879)
(after M. W. Barley)

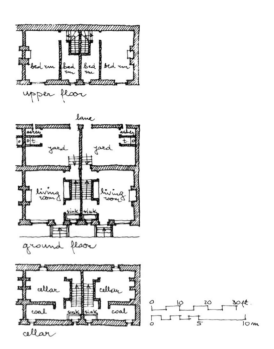

Bylaw housing, Akroydon, Halifax (1853)
(after J. N. Tarn)

facilities within the flats were sacrificed for the sake of rental flexibility and were clustered near the main stair halls linking the various galleries to the street entrances.

During the second half of the nineteenth century local governments undertook to curtail the construction of substandard housing. They enacted model bylaws pertaining to health standards in housing that reflected the spirit of the Nuisance Removal and Disease Prevention Act passed by Parliament in 1855. To comply with these new health regulations, small builders developed two-story row houses with privies and a small yard at the rear of the property. In a sense, these so-called bylaw houses were modeled on Georgian town houses, but their scale was minuscule in comparison. Moreover, the dreary façades of bylaw houses lining the treeless streets, block after block, created a monotonous and uninspiring urban environment, which was in marked contrast to the landscaped Georgian residential squares and crescents.

Bylaw houses were built well, and many survive today in industrial towns in Britain. A terraced housing development built in 1879 in Nottingham serves as an example of typical bylaw housing. The frontage of each row house was 12 ft (3.65 m), in contrast to the 22 ft (6.7 m) of the modest town houses built in Bath. Since there was no entrance hall in the bylaw house, the front door led directly into the parlor, which was lit by a single window facing the street. Across the parlor was the kitchen and the winding staircase that led to the upper floor. Behind the kitchen was the scullery, equipped with a sink and a washing copper. The scullery gave access to the rear yard, where a coal storage shed and toilet were located. The upper floor of the bylaw house had a large bedroom at the front and a smaller one at the rear. An attic space was sometimes provided above the bedrooms.

London, with 4.2 million inhabitants, was by far the world's largest urban agglomeration during the last decade of the nineteenth century. New York, with its satellite cities, came next with 2.7 million, but its rate of population growth was unmatched even by London. In 1812 New York City had fewer than 100,000 inhabitants and grew to over half a million in a mere thirty-five years. The provision of housing accommodation for the great influx of immigrants and the natural growth of its own population was a mammoth undertaking that resulted in the exploitation of poor people by unscrupulous builders and landlords.

In the initial stages of New York's growth large homes abandoned by their former owners were converted into tenant houses. The large rooms of these decorous houses were partitioned into several small rooms without regard to light and ventilation; several dwellings were thus created from a single home. To further increase the profit derived from the conversion of these houses and to respond to the ever-growing demand for additional accommodation, new structures were built at the rear of the properties, replacing the gardens of the former residences. It was not uncommon that a house originally built for a single family became, with its infamous "rear house," a tenement for ten families.

The number of existing large houses vacated by their former owners was inadequate and their conversion to tenant houses could not satisfy the demands for housing. Estate owners and agents of property turned to a new mode of housing construction and ushered in the era of the tenements. On the North American continent many of these early multistory tenements were unventilated, unsanitary buildings that consisted of a living room of 10 by 12 ft (3 by 3.6 m) and a tiny bedroom without access to direct daylight measuring 6 by 7 ft (1.98 by 2.13 m) in size. The construction of dark and unventilated bedrooms persisted for some time until municipal regulations prohibited them.

A typical early form of tenement housing employed dwellings with a series of narrow rooms arranged in line, the so-called railroad flats. These buildings were built on standard 25-ft (7.62-m) wide lots. A central staircase and hall gave access to four flats on each floor level. Each flat was three or even four rooms deep, so only the front living room had direct access to daylight and fresh air.

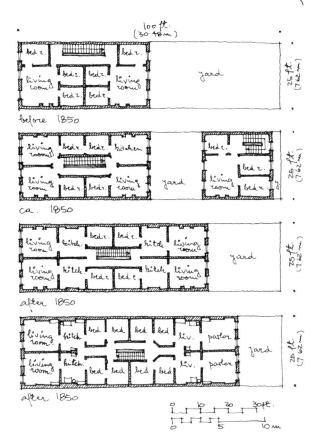

New York City: Railroad flats
(after I. N. Phelps Stokes as cited in J. Ford)

Living conditions in these dingy flats were further depressed because several families frequently shared one flat. In one known instance, five families shared a single room.

Gotham Court, Nos. 36–38 Cherry Street, in New York, was an especially ill-reputed tenement building five stories high with 126 two-room flats. It was a notorious center of disease and crime until it was demolished in 1896. "Although the plan itself was not really bad, except that none of the apartments had through ventilation, the location of most of the rooms, upon two narrow alleys which also furnished light and air to several overcrowded rear tenements on adjoining lots, resulted in particularly unsatisfactory conditions" (Ford 1936, 878). Waterclosets were in a cellar below the side courts and were lit and ventilated through grilles in the pavement.

Restrictions by the New York Health Board and the Tenement House Act of 1867 prevented the

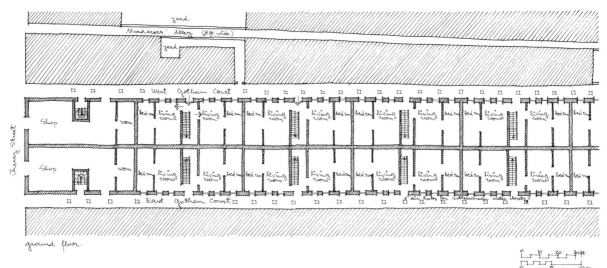

New York City: Gotham Court
(after I. N. Phelps Stokes as cited in J. Ford)

further construction of unventilated rooms and led to the use of the "air-shaft" building. The three-room-deep flat now had its innermost rooms ventilated by means of small windows opening upon a chimneylike airshaft.

Generally, tenements were built five stories high above a basement (at that time, the limit for climb-ing stairs in buildings without elevator service was five stories; today, it is three stories), and their plans varied slightly from one to another. In 1879 a tenement with flats that had pathetically inadequate light in all of its interior rooms was approved by the Board of Health, presumably because its central staircase was lit from the roof. The mean

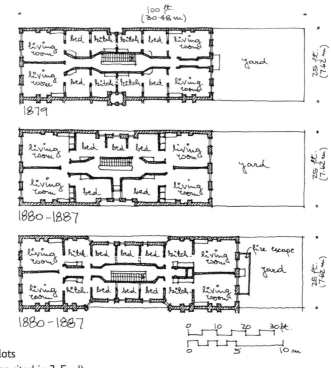

New York City: Air-shaft flats
(after I. N. Phelps Stokes as cited in J. Ford)

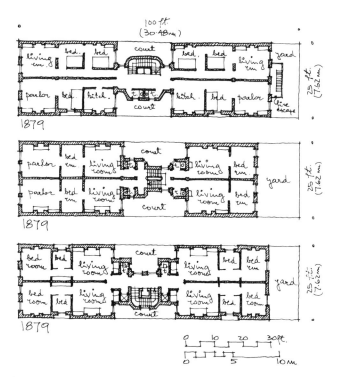

New York City: Competition design,
The Plumber and Sanitary Journal
(after I. N. Phelps Stokes as cited in J. Ford)

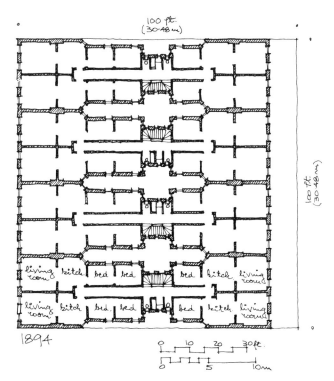

New York City: Dumbbell tenements
(after Roy Lubove)

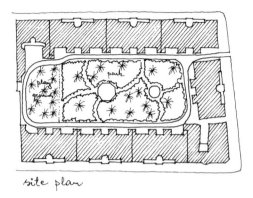

site plan

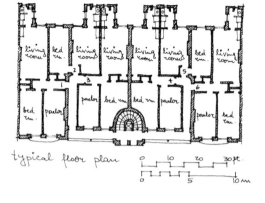

typical floor plan

New York City: Brooklyn Riverside Buildings
(after Jacob A. Riis)

standards of multiple housing can also be seen in the results of a competition sponsored by *The Plumber and Sanitary Engineer Journal*. A number of prize-winning submissions were exhibited to the public in 1879; these plans retained the use of air shafts, but provided larger light wells adjacent to the main stair hall. The configuration of their floor plans eventually earned them the designation "dumbbell" tenements. Dumbbell tenements were built extensively in New York City during the last two decades of the nineteenth century. They were often constructed in clusters of four on a 100-ft (30-m) wide building plot. The New York Tenement House Law of 1901 marked their demise. The last decade of the nineteenth century saw the emergence of the "park tenement," such as the Riverside Buildings in Brooklyn. Their distinction lay primarily in the provision of a large open space or park in the middle of the block of buildings, with the buildings only two rooms deep.

The park-tenement concept of housing was pioneered by I. N. Phelps Stokes (1867–1944), a New York architect who specialized in the planning and design of housing for low-income families. Phelps Stokes was most likely influenced in the direction of his specialization by several philanthropist members of his well-known family including his grandfather, James Stokes, who was one of the founding members of the New York Association for Improving the Condition of the Poor. This organization, however, was helpless in its attempt to counteract the dire living conditions created by the large influx of immigrants to major cities like New York. Perhaps no other account than that of Jacob A. Riis, in *How the Other Half Lives*, describes so unforgettably the misery encountered by immigrants in New York tenements. But, in the light of such bleak housing conditions, park-tenements were windows of hope, and they remained only a hope for far too many.

FROM VILLADOM TO SUBURBS

The town-house concept continued to be used for urban dwellings of all income groups throughout the nineteenth century, but after about the middle of the century the popularity of the town house or row house—"which was seen as a life-style defiled through its adoption by the working classes" (Aston 1976, 189)—began to diminish, first in Great Britain, then in other European countries, and finally in North America. The attached urban town house no longer represented the ideal family home, a role that was gradually usurped by the detached country house, the "villa."

By the end of the eighteenth century some well-to-do families in England had already begun to abandon their town houses in deteriorating cities perceived to be congested, polluted, and crime-ridden. They fled to the countryside. This new trend was also abetted by the fact that to have a landed estate was in reality a prerequisite for advancement in society and a qualification for voting, serving as a magistrate, and entering Parliament, all of which induced a medley of well-to-do merchants, lawyers, bankers, and tradesmen to aquire property for residence in the countryside (Aslet 1985, 98).

Initially, only families who had their own means of transportation could afford to move to the country, and it helped if the profession of the head of the family did not demand his daily presence in the city. With the introduction of the horse tram or omnibus, followed later by electric street cars, then underground and commuter railways, the villa with its own large garden on the edge of the city became affordable to ever-larger groups of people. Moreover, "the downward percolation of modes of behavior which is the most pronounced feature of modern society, steadily reduced the villa in scale, and brought it from the depths of the country first to the suburb, within carriage distance of shop, warehouse or office, and then into the town itself" (Barley 1963, 60). The English adage "a man's house is his castle" was well reflected by the detached villa, and this view may partially explain its immense and immediate popularity in the Anglo-Saxon world.

In its standard form, the villa was a detached two-story dwelling with a central entrance leading to a hall flanked by formal rooms on the first floor; bedrooms, dressing rooms, and bathrooms on the second; and kitchen, scullery, larder, and other domestic facilities in the basement. In contrast to cities, site conditions in the countryside permitted the planning of the house so that all representational rooms (rooms used for receiving or entertaining guests) could occupy one floor level. At times, there was even space for the kitchen and other service rooms at grade level, but these domestic offices were relegated to the rear of the

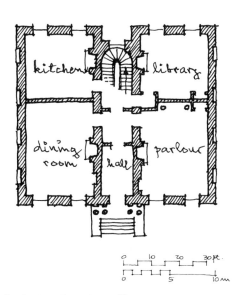

Early nineteenth-century villa

house or to a one-storied rear wing penetrating into the garden and screened by a hedge from view of reception rooms (Quennell 1910, 8).

In its classical form, the villa first emerged as a symmetrical two-story "square house" with concealed roofs, balustraded parapets, and a spacious entrance, either with a pillared porch or an ordered portico towards the street; its simple symmetries of proportion suggested "the smiling repose of a more southern climate" to housing critics (Kerr 1893, 217). Eventually a new fashion emphasizing the picturesque followed, a style that resulted in pretty rather than dignified domestic buildings. Picturesque villas had an asymmetrical plan and affected a "playful character, with a doorway in ambush, high pointed roofs, prominent dormers, and conspicuous chimneys, all suited to more northern latitudes, where the gray fog frowns, the frost bites sharply, and the snow lies deep and long, and where the bricks and tiles appropriately run to red" (Kerr 1893, 217). An indispensable element of the villa was its garden which gave a framework for the building in nature and was perceived as if it were the continuation of the rooms of the house.

The battle of the styles fought during the nineteenth century is also reflected in domestic architecture. During the early decades of the century the

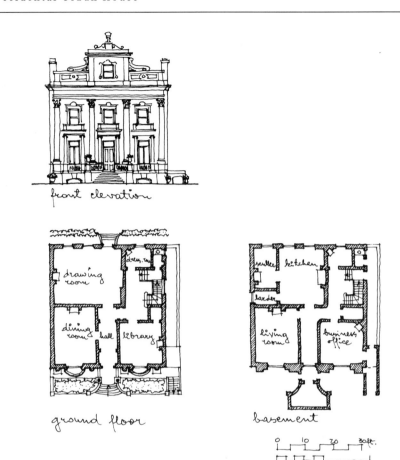

A suburban villa
(after C. J. Richardson)

style in vogue was Greek Revival, which gave way gradually to Gothic Revival, which in turn was replaced by Queen Anne style. Queen Anne style—a misnomer—was an eclectic style influenced by Old English domestic architecture as well as by the chateauesque style of France. In England, Queen Anne style was characterized by a blending of Gothic and Renaissance elements borrowed from picturesque country houses and cottages, while in the United States, colonial-style architectural elements were added to it.

The inauguration of a saner style for English domestic architecture, characterized by a beauty of fitness of purpose, is primarily attributed to Norman Shaw (1831–1912), the architect, and William Morris (1834–1896), the craftsman, but in the thirty years between 1850 and 1880 a lower school of designers "exercised considerable initiative of its own and, in fact, evolved . . . the Victorian 'vernacular'" (Summerson 1948, 63), which consisted of a blending of styles.

By the 1880s the Arts and Crafts movement had emerged, advocating a non-copyist architecture (one not based on copying other styles) that emphasized the importance of craftsmanship and high standards of design, not only in building, but for everyday objects as well. Through the pursuit of simplicity and harmony with nature, English domestic architecture was renowned during the last decades of the nineteenth century and exerted a profound influence upon housing developments in other countries as well.

The popularity of the villa did not escape the attention of builders who were eager to broaden the range of potential buyers. To reduce the cost of the villa and to increase the profitability of the land used for its construction, Victorian builders adopted two devices, one from the Georgian town house and the other from model farm workers' cottages. The first involved the basement kitchen, and the second, the pairing of villas as semidetached dwellings. With the arrival of the small lower-middle-class villa, house-building graphs soared between 1877 and 1887 and "London became ringed round with great blotches of this new villadom: street upon street, most of it lying at right angles to the main roads and consisting of houses either semi-detached or in rows so built as to give a semi-detached impression" (Summerson 1948, 71). Whether detached or semidetached, these "new" dwelling prototypes became the ideal house.

The Englishman's dream was shared by urban dwellers of other nations, and its realization was nowhere more attainable than on the North American continent, where available land for urban expansion was most abundant. One important American proponent of this dream house was Andrew Jackson Downing (1803–1892), a landscape architect from Newburgh, New York. At the age of twenty-nine he was already famous not only in America, but also in England and France. His influence on American taste during the second half of the nineteenth century was profound. He was a gentle and romantic person who advocated the belief that "when smiling lawns and tasteful cottages begin to embellish a country, we know that order and culture are established" (Lynes 1954, 22).

Downing married the great-granddaughter of John Adams, the second president of the United States, and built for himself and his bride a country house along the Hudson River.

> By the standard of its own day it was "a simple house" in what was then called the Elizabethan style, but which we now think of as Gothic Revival. It was built of stone—neatly symmetrical, with slender, octagonal towers at either side of the peaked entrance and matching verandas whose roofs, decorated with ornamental woodwork, were supported by slender columns and shallow arches" (Lynes 1954, 23–24).

Downing's living room overlooked a meticulously manicured lawn with urns filled with flowers. His small estate of five acres was carefully landscaped with trees and flowering shrubs so as to obscure from view a village below his property, but at the same time to retain his Hudson River Valley view.

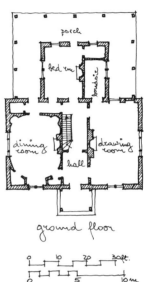

Andrew Jackson Downing: Cottage in bracketed style (after Ettore Camesasca)

Downing lived in a country town, but his activities both as a landscape architect and writer brought him frequently to New York City. Urban dwellers who were longing to leave the grime- and crime-ridden city for a healthier living environment were easily persuaded to adopt Downing's views. Of course, the link with the city could not be entirely broken, for business activities demanded it; at least for the family head, the home had to be within commuting distance from the office in the city.

In his book *Modern Dwellings in Town and Country*, published in 1878, Henry Hudson Holly asserted that for Americans the privilege to build country homes for themselves was already widespread in the 1870s, because "for such rent as they would pay for a flat or tenement in town, they can secure an entire house with sufficient ground for garden and ornamental lawn; and if not immedi-ately in a village, sufficient acres can be obtained to afford the luxury of a horse and cow, the products of the little farm going far toward the support of an extra man, and with good management may be made a source of profit also" (Holly 1878, 21).

Of course, the majority of urbanites who opted for country living did not contemplate hiring help to operate a farm, but more often dispensed with servants altogether, especially when their home was equipped with some modern conveniences. They discovered that with the aid of appliances, housework became less burdensome and the help of servants was not only dispensable, but in fact beneficial. The additional work resulting from the absence of a maid was compensated by greater independence for the housewife and, most of all, by a greater privacy in family life.

In 1878, railroad and steamboat service from Manhattan was so frequent that commuters could reach their homes in the country in about the same time and nearly as cheaply as using the old omnibus ride from City Hall to uptown. More and more New Yorkers availed themselves of the rapid transit systems servicing a radius of twenty miles around the city and built picturesque and cheerful homes in the countryside where the heads of fam-ilies recuperated from the "deleterious effects of the confinement of city life" and, where, with the aid of fresh air and wholesome food, they laid "the foundation for greater strength and increased hap-piness for their children" (Holly 1878, 21).

The exodus of the urban middle class was so pro-nounced that the *New York Herald*, of April 19, 1877, predicted "New York is gradually, year by year, becoming the home of the very rich and very poor" (Holly 1878, 21), an uncanny prophecy of polarization that gained additional momentum during the twentieth century with the introduction of the automobile as a new transportation mode affordable to families of average income. After World War II, the social consequences of the accel-erated trend to suburbanization made possible by moderate-priced cars became alarming, and its repercussions upon life in large American cities nearly catastrophic.

NINETEENTH-CENTURY SUBURBAN DEVELOPMENT

With the popularity of villas and detached dwel-lings in the outskirts of cities, a new residential settlement pattern emerged that offered the best of two worlds: first, a healthy living environment in the tranquil natural setting of the countryside and, second, proximity to a large city, not only allowing breadwinners to commute to their city jobs but also allowing family members to partake in commercial and cultural opportunities.

In contrast to previous eras, when city expansion was carefully planned in order to economize with the necessary defense installations, defense con-siderations no longer constrained city expansion in the nineteenth century. Growth became relatively uncontrolled and haphazard in accordance with the prevailing liberal spirit tempered only by available transportation modes. Residential suburbs for the well-to-do occupied only part of the urban expan-sion area of larger cities, since railway shunting yards, gas works, industries, and crowded industri-al workers' housing also expanded beyond city limits. Thus, traffic congestion, pollution, noise, dirt, and, above all, poverty also found their way into considerable segments of the city's outskirts.

This urban sprawl consumed large areas of agri-cultural land, and productive farmland became increasingly remote from the city center. The sub-urban belt surrounding the city resembled more and more a noose that threatened to strangle it, and its inhabitants looked back with nostalgia to the past when medieval cities offered liberty, safe-ty, and opportunity. Increasingly, city dwellers began to envy the physical setting of those who lived in smaller towns untouched by industrializa-tion, where traditional characteristics were re-tained, including that of close walking distance from any part of the town to the open countryside.

The craving for open space and nature became an obsession with most late nineteenth-century urban dwellers affected by large-scale industrial development. It cannot come as a surprise that many of the middle-class families who could afford to do so strove to live in satellite communities characterized by the attributes of both town and country. Sometimes, the exclusiveness of well-to-do families' residential communities went to extremes, as exemplified by a villa suburb at Haling Park in Croydon, England, where the entrance to the estate was marked by gates tended by liveried gatekeepers who prevented undesirable persons from entry (Aston 1976, 188).

An American example of an exclusive residential development with a gatehouse at its entrance is Llewellyn Park in West Orange, New Jersey. Begun in 1853 on the eastern slope of a mountain within sight of New York City, this community was founded by Llewellyn Haskell, a rich wholesale druggist, who engaged Alexander Jackson Davis to lay out the residential park and to design several of the houses. Jackson built Wildmont, a Gothic revivalist villa with a tower, turrets, oriels, and traceried windows for himself and his bride (Kastner 1981, 82).

The development site of Llewellyn Park, about 400 acres (162 hectares) in area, was landscaped in a picturesque way with curved roads giving access to about fifty fenceless plots ranging in size from 3 to 10 acres (1.2 to 4 hectares). The spine of this residential enclave was a central park strip, almost a mile long (1.6 km) and nearly 60 acres (24 hectares) in area, with a wooded ravine and a brook, traversed by walks. Rustic kiosks, seats, and bridges were provided in appropriate areas in harmony with the natural forest setting; the cost for the park's maintenance was levied proportionately from the residents (Reps 1965, 339).

Llewellyn Park was the first architecturally planned community where buildings, mostly in picturesque Gothic style, were built to complement the rustic environment characterized by clumped trees and craggy slopes. The original gatehouse of unfinished stone masonry walls and shingled roof as well as a castellated villa named Castlewood, both designed by Davis, are still standing. But more surprising is the fact that this development has retained its original character over the years since neither resubdivision into smaller plots nor conversion of large villas into condominium apartments has taken place.

Exclusive suburbs such as Llewellyn Park were relatively rare in comparison with more conventional villa suburbs. These suburbs also featured large detached houses, each with their own large garden that fronted on streets bordered by trees with a gentle gradient for horse-drawn carriages. These ad hoc residential communities were precursors of planned "garden suburbs," conceived not merely as urban accretions, but as suburban entities with their own community facilities. Riverside, west of Chicago, and Bedford Park, near London, are two late nineteenth-century examples of garden suburbs.

RIVERSIDE, ILLINOIS

A dormitory suburb, known as Riverside, was established between 1868 and 1871 about 4 miles (6.43 km) from the outskirts of Chicago. It was a community with a curvilinear street pattern destined to become a model residential suburb for "better" homes. And, "by the latter part of the nineteenth century most large cities could boast of one or more suburban communities or outlying subdivisions planned in curvilinear fashion" (Reps 1965, 348). In fact, it became fashionable to live in communities with winding streets.

The establishment of this community began when the promoter Emery E. Childs acquired a farm called Riverside from David A. Gage and formed the Riverside Improvement Company to guide its development. From the outset this land assembly of 1,600 acres (647.5 hectares) was ideal for residential development because, in contrast to the usual flat, bleak, and windswept prairie of the region, the site consisted of gently rolling well-drained land covered with groves of mature trees along the banks of the meandering and north-flowing Des Plaines River. Moreover, the land was bisected in a roughly east-west direction by the Chicago, Burlington and Quincy Railroad, a commuter line already in operation with a daily service of twelve passenger trains.

The design of this residential community was completed within two years by Olmsted, Vaux and Company and signified a departure from the gridiron street layout so much in vogue at the time on the North American continent. A sensitive landscape architect, Frederick Law Olmsted rejected the traditional practice of imposing a rigid geometric street pattern on the existing topography, and instead respected the contours of the land as well as the amenities offered by the riverbanks in the design of "curvilinear streets winding around natural features and focusing on the river" (Bach 1979, 336).

In his report to the trustees of the Riverside Development Association who gave him the design commission, Olmsted insisted that a general plan should be developed and adhered to, ensuring a distinctly rural attractiveness. Thus, emphasis was placed on retaining the bucolic character of the site, a fact still in evidence today. Tranquillity, leisure, and plenty of open space all characterized Riverside as a desirable place to live in and raise a family. These features were in great contrast to the living conditions prevalent in the noisy, busy, and crowded city.

In Olmsted's plan about 700 acres (283.27 hectares) (almost half of the property holdings) were devoted to parks, walks, and roads, including generous borders along the streets. Moreover, recreation grounds and parks were unfenced to suggest an informality reminiscent of village greens, while streets were provided with spontaneity through the use of roadside trees in irregular clusters. Finally, because Riverside residents were to live in detached houses with a generously treed and landscaped front lawn and large gardens for fruit trees and vegetables in the rear, there was no need for back alleys, a deplored and discredited urban system of property access, which was ridiculed at the time as leading to homes with "the Queen Anne front and the Mary Anne back" (Creese 1966, 186).

The development of Riverside had run into financial difficulties by 1869 and Childs defaulted on his payments to the planners, who were offered lots instead of cash. Moreover, the Chicago fire of 1871 "completely paralyzed the sale of suburban real estate, and the Riverside Improvement Company had to suspend payment" (Roper 1973, 324). However, the suburb was still an attractive place with well-constructed roads and walks requiring almost no upkeep, and by 1877 it grew into a residential community of forty-five families with an efficient organization run by a board of trustees. The "public and private grounds were well kept . . . and speculators and home owners alike were holding their lots as good long-term investments" (Roper 1973, 324).

Riverside had a great influence upon the planning approach to suburban developments and marked the beginning of community-oriented planning that stressed harmonious association and cooperation for a wholesome suburban form of domestic life. But this design approach was also space-consuming and therefore affordable only to a small segment of society. These shortcomings aside, however, Riverside nevertheless remains a good example of sensitive planning resulting in harmony between nature and a man-made living environment.

The houses of Riverside reflected the individualism of their owners, and no particular style of architecture governed their appearance. The unifying element of this arcadian residential setting was provided by the dominance of nature over buildings which was, of course, in vivid contrast to the prevailing urban living environment of the time. Planting and the careful siting of houses in relation to each other and to the public rights-of-way were envisaged as means to secure privacy for the indoor and outdoor domestic activities of residents.

Many noted architects designed the early houses in Riverside. Calvert Vaux, William LeBaron Jenney, Louis Sullivan, and Frank Lloyd Wright, for example, designed homes in this community that still fulfill their original use.

Frank Lloyd Wright built what he called his "best" home (Bach 1979, 339), the Coonley House (1908), at Riverside, although most of his domestic buildings erected in the Chicago area, including his own residence, were in Oak Park, and others still in River Forest. Like Riverside, these twin communities were in essence dormitory suburbs for middle-income and well-to-do families. Although Oak Park and River Forest were established after Riverside, the two communities still featured a traditional street-grid layout rather than emulate the sensitivity towards nature in planning demonstrated just a few years earlier by Olmsted.

Curvilinear streets were also absent in little-known Garden City, a suburban community on Long Island whose name is familiar as the rallying cry of a later urban reform movement. Established in 1869 by Alexander T. Stewart, Garden City was initially a residential community of tenants, since the founder (and after his death his estate) retained "complete ownership of all lands and buildings" (Lewis 1949, 114) until 1895, at which time the estate offered both houses and building plots for sale. Located 20 miles (32 km) east of Manhattan, Garden City was laid out with rigidly rectangular residential city blocks separated from each other by broad streets. The community was well landscaped and featured at its center a large park with trees and shrubbery. Within the park were both the railway station and the club house, the first the economic lifeline and the second the social focus of the community.

BEDFORD PARK, LONDON

A cloth merchant, Jonathan T. Carr, was an early pioneer of the planned "garden suburb" in England. In 1875 he acquired about 25 acres (10.11 hectares) of land at Chiswick, adjoining a Georgian mansion, an orchard, a farm, and a new metropolitan railway line. If developed as a residential estate this tranquil setting promised comfortable living "where the nightingale and skylark could still be heard" (Creese 1966, 87) and yet by railway the commuter time to London was only about thirty minutes.

The name of the community, Bedford Park, derived from the fact that the Bedford brothers were the original owners of the estate prior to its acquisition by John Lindley, a curator of the Royal Horticultural Society Gardens, who in turn sold the land to Carr. For the development of the estate, Carr founded a company to carry out the work, a task that took about six years.

The nucleus of the community was planned near the station and its importance as a destination point is reflected in the layout as several major streets converge towards it. Although the street network of this garden suburb was completely informal and carefully aligned so as to save most of the large trees planted by Lindley, a certain conventional geometry was obtained. The wide streets defined elongated street blocks with building setbacks varying from 15 to 20 ft (4.57 to 6.09 m). The presence of mature trees and the beautiful rustic landscaping of the grounds, rather than the alignment of streets, gave this development a cozy and rural character much admired during the late nineteenth century.

The houses in Bedford Park were built primarily for a middle-class clientele, including people of quite moderate income who aspired to raise a family in the countryside, but whose work demanded easy access to London. Although a few detached homes and also a row of town houses were built, by far most dwellings in this garden suburb were comfortable semidetached houses placed on lots that were 50 ft (15.24 m) wide and 75 ft (22.86 m) deep. Homes were mostly built in red brick with steep red-tiled roofs, massive chimneys, and windows with small panes, thick sash bars, and white-painted woodwork.

Four architects—E. W. Godwin, Norman Shaw, Maurice B. Adams, and E. J. May—were primarily engaged with the design of buildings in Bedford Park. Godwin designed the first eighteen houses, and these were neither Italian nor Gothic, but picturesque houses built of red Suffolk brick characterized by an ingenious play of gables, bays, and dormers, a style inspired by the vernacular of the southern counties. After a dispute over competence—probably unjustified since these houses are considered by many today as the best in Bedford Park—Godwin was replaced by Shaw,

Semidetached villa by R. Norman Shaw

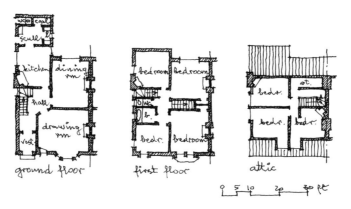

Semidetached villa by R. Norman Shaw, Bedford Park
(after Andrew Saint)

whose influence upon the appearance of this garden suburb was most pronounced.

Although Shaw designed several public buildings, including a church, a clubhouse, stores, and an imitation multigabled wayside inn near the railway station, his influence on residential design was most important. He is attributed with breaking the tradition of placing the kitchen in the basement by bringing it up to the ground-floor level in his Bedford Park houses, thereby achieving not only easy access between the kitchen and dining room, but also providing better daylight and ventilation in the kitchen. In addition, Shaw initiated the practice of placing the sanitary pipes on the outside walls for hygienic reasons and ease of access for repair.

Once again, after a dispute in 1880, Carr replaced Shaw with Adams, Godwin's former assistant, and entrusted him with the design of a church, a parish hall, and the Chiswick School of Art. In his domestic architecture, Adams retained Shaw's ideas, but perhaps did not express them well. Finally, E. J. May was commissioned to design the vicarage, an addition to the clubhouse, and several residences.

By 1881 Bedford Park had almost five hundred homes, every one of them with a garden, and regardless of size each house had a tile bathroom with hot and cold water. Many of the houses, including Carr's own home, were decorated with tiles and wallpapers that had been designed by William Morris. An early protagonist of the Arts and Craft Movement, Morris advocated beauty and usefulness in home furnishings through the application of good craftsmanship, in great contrast to the prevalent Victorian-style rooms cluttered with mass-produced objects (Chambers 1985, 250–52).

Bedford Park acquired a character of its own, pronouncedly different from what was built elsewhere. In spite of the fact that its villas were restrained and had little ornamentation in comparison to other contemporary domestic buildings, they nevertheless had a great influence upon subsequent residential developments in Great Britain and elsewhere. The architect Hermann Muthesius, a special attaché at the German embassy in London, much admired the residential setting of Bedford Park, "where 'small' houses were combined with a pleasant, semi-rural environment, and represented a type that could be applied on a fairly large scale" (Aslet 1985, 220). This community represents the starting point of the smaller family house, which was subsequently copied in suburbs throughout Great Britain.

Another characteristic of Bedford Park was the relaxed formality of its residents' social life. This informality represented the beginning of a new trend in suburban living, and probably derived from the influence of some of its residents, who not only included painters and sculptors attracted to the community by the Art School (Aslet 1985, 221), but also authors, playwrights, and professional people, who moved with their families to this suburb to take advantage of a healthier outdoor life. Many residents met informally at the tennis club, one of Bedford's leading institutions, to try their hand at this relatively new game. Tennis became a popular middle-class activity promoting a heightened interest in salubrious exercise, and its importance was further enhanced by the fact that the gardens of most large houses had room for a private tennis court, which, at a certain social level, eventually became necessity (Aslet 1985, 222).

Apart from physical exercise, many Bedford Park residents also partook in the intellectual life of the community. Such activities as the amateur dramatic society and the ladies' discussion group held in the clubhouse were often reviewed by the popular press, which added another dimension to Bedford Park's prestige.

Perhaps the greatest achievement of the designers of Bedford Park is the fact that this community "has worn well," as Steen Eiler Rasmussen so aptly wrote. It has stood the test of time because of the simple appearance of the brick houses, the tiled roofs, the rustic effects of the weather-worn oak fences, and the landscaping of the ground with mown lawns, flower beds, clipped bushes, and majestic trees. It still is a garden suburb with "a mark of culture" (Rasmussen 1934, 196).

Riverside and Bedford Park were exemplary planned residential communities of the nineteenth century, and laid the foundations for garden suburb developments of the twentieth century as exemplified by Forest Hill Gardens, near New York City, and Hampstead Garden Suburb and Ebenezer Howard's Garden Cities in the outskirts of London.

PARISIAN APARTMENT BUILDINGS

In the wake of an unprecedented urban population growth during the nineteenth century, the expansion of residential areas in large cities of Great Britain evolved differently than on the European continent. In London, for example, where increasing numbers of families opted to live in suburban villas, most residential expansion was horizontal.

On the continent, however, horizontal urban dispersal was curtailed because land was more scarce, and because moving existing defense installations (necessary during wartime) was prohibitively expensive. Most Parisians began to live in urban apartment houses rather than suburban detached villas.

Paris: Apartment building on Ave. de la Grande Armée

By the end of the nineteenth century, Parisian apartment houses evolved into sophisticated urban multistoried buildings that were clearly set apart from mere tenements. With their palatial street façades along tree-lined avenues, generous spatial standards, and mechanical conveniences such as central heating systems and elevators, these new apartments became desirable dwelling alternatives for the gentry as well as the bourgeoisie, the former favouring hitherto the *hôtel particulier* (a commodious town house), and the latter the detached suburban villa.

Several reasons made the acceptance of the apartment house a desirable alternative. First, urban plots for individual town houses—not to mention the excessive land requirements of the spacious hôtel-particuliers preferred by the elite—

became prohibitively expensive after the redevelopment of Paris by Baron Georges-Eugène Haussmann (1809–1891). Second, before the private motor car came into use, many wealthy families found the suburban villa too distant from the urban core. But perhaps the most significant factor influencing the acceptance of apartment-house living by the well-to-do was the profusion of treed avenues, boulevards, *rond-points*, and promenades in so-called *beaux quartiers*, such as Passy, which were also legacies of Baron Haussmann. These spacious and verdant rights-of-way afforded a pleasing prospect for the apartments fronting them, and this feature, combined with generous room sizes in buildings with palatial façades, eventually established apartment living as not only acceptable but fashionable.

As a prototype, the Parisian apartment house underwent considerable changes during the eighteenth and nineteenth centuries, a period when the population of Paris grew unprecedentedly and multifamily rental buildings were erected to house an expanding population within city boundaries rendered inflexible by costly defense installations. The population growth in Paris was staggering; for example, it grew from 640,504 in 1798 to 2,344,550 in 1881, and this growth occurred during a period that witnessed wars and revolutions. A census taken in 1817 revealed that 224,922 families resided in 26,751 houses, which translates into about eight families per house. And, since the population of Paris in 1881 was housed in roughly 76,000 residential buildings (Meyers 1890, vol. 12, 722), i.e., about 31 persons per building, it is quite evident that the *maisons-à-loyer* (rental houses) constituted a significant part of the housing stock. Many of these multifamily dwellings were no doubt crowded tenements inhabited by the underprivileged, but a significant number were apartment houses that during the *belle époque* of the late nineteenth and early twentieth centuries blossomed into the palatial apartment buildings so characteristic of Paris.

According to Viollet-le-Duc, the custom of building maisons-à-loyer "for the express accommodation of several families does not go back further than the seventeenth century" (White 1875, 1101). It is recorded, for example, that during the reign of Louis XIV, some residential buildings with two levels of dwellings in addition to a habitable attic floor were erected over a row of shops with mezzanines above, which appears to be a continuation in spirit of medieval shopkeepers' dwellings. The architect Monnicault built such buildings on Rue de la Ferronnerie; each originally had a single occupant but later were let as flats. These buildings may have influenced the architect Victor-Thierry Dailly to erect several similar buildings between 1715 and 1730, during the reign of Louis XV, on Rue Childebert in Saint-Germain-des-Prés. These were designed as maisons-à-loyer, with pilastered upper stories above an alternating rhythm of shops and entrance doors at ground level; unfortunately these buildings were demolished to make way for the Boulevard Saint-Germain (Gallet 1972, 66).

By the early 1800s, apartment houses in Paris acquired a standard spatial organization rooted in precedents from the previous century. They were based on a mixed land-use pattern, primarily residential but with a commercial component at ground-floor level. A typical building, erected on a corner site of Place de la Madeleine and Rue de Trouchet and still standing, portrays the intrinsic features of an early nineteenth-century apartment building (Fils 1837, plates 6–10).

Typically, apartment houses were built upon a vaulted cellar with numerous storage compartments, and the ground-floor area fronting the street was usually designated for commercial use with the exception of the main entrance or porte cochere (covered carriageway); apart from giving protection from rain to tenants and guests disembarking from carriages, the porte cochere also allowed vehicular access to the courtyard and hence to stables and coach houses in the rear.

The main entrance was always supervised from a loge or lodge by a concierge. Originally the designation "concierge" was reserved for the manager or administrator of a royal house, and was first appropriated by the portiers (doorkeepers) during the nineteenth century when they became the collectors of rent for the proprietors of apartment buildings (Hautecoeur 1955, 126). Nevertheless, they still had to do the jobs of former portiers, namely to clean the staircases and the sidewalk in front of the building, to distribute the mail and parcels delivered by the postman, and to supervise the entrance to the building from an often dingy and cramped lodge.

Closely linked with private staircases to the commercial ground-floor area was an intermediate floor or mezzanine, called entresol, containing spaces that could be used for workshops or even living accommodation by the merchants who rented the shops below.

The first floor, or bel étage, was the most desirable floor level before the introduction of elevators. Since it was raised well above street level, the first-floor apartment offered privacy from passersby, but was still reasonably accessible through a gentle flight of stairs. Frequently, this first-floor level was occupied by the landlord himself or a principal tenant, "who took the whole house on lease and sublet the other stories" (Gallet 1972, 64).

Above the bel étage, typical floors usually contained only two apartments on the street side of the building and additional dwelling units in the rear if the depth of the lot permitted. Of course, the two front apartments were the most desirable and were accessible from the main staircase, the grand escalier. The ceiling and window heights decreased towards the top of the building, and so did the rental value of these walk-up apartments.

Finally, the attic space was divided into numerous bedrooms strung along a central corridor. The attic-floor bedrooms were allocated to the servants of the tenants, and it was customary to provide about two servant bedrooms for each apartment unit. Service staircases linked the attic space to the kitchen doors of the various apartment floors. Two compartments in the cellar were also allocated to each apartment: one served for the storage of wine and the other for wood and coal.

In the classical tripartite composition of the street façade, the ground floor and mezzanine levels were expressed as the base; the first, second, and third floor levels as the main body; and the fourth and attic floor as the crown of the building. The base was usually rusticated and the entrance portal emphasized. The main façade was most often plain with pedimented windows, but, on occasion, pilasters between windows were used as additional decorative features. The crown of the building was marked by a pronounced projecting cornice at the windowsill level of fourth-floor apartments; the attic floor bedrooms were hidden behind a steep mansard roof.

The buildings were constructed along traditional lines; a typical workforce was about twenty-five men for a medium-sized apartment building. The workers were supervised by a *contre-maître*, or foreman, who did no physical labor himself. The construction workers consisted of about six *compagnons*, or journeymen masons; ten *garçons*, or assistant masons; two to four *tailleurs de pierre*, or stone carvers; and about four men whose work was to raise stones and mortar from the ground to the scaffoldings by means of a winch and place them where they were required.

Masons worked an average of ten hours every day during the summer and eight hours in winter, with one Sunday off a month in addition to the recognized *fête* days. The best paid workmen were the stone carvers who ornamented the façade after the structure was built in the rough. Masonry work on a medium-size building was usually commenced late in the spring and finished before Christmas, when the plasterers and carpenters took over.

The French-born American architect, Philip A. Hubert (1830–1911), described in an essay—unfortunately without plans or sections—the physical organization and tenant mix of a typical Parisian apartment building (Hubert, Pirsson & Hoddick 1892, 55–64); although this description dates from the late nineteenth century, the building he described must have been an early example of a maison-à-loyer because its sanitary installations were rather primitive.

Located on a quiet street south of Rue Saint-Honoré, the apartment house had a street frontage of about 100 feet and was six stories high "without the least pretence to architectural features or orna-

mentation." A central arched passageway paved with stone connected the street with the building's courtyard and could be shut off at night by a strong iron grill portal. At the rear of the courtyard were low buildings: half were used for stables and the other half as a shop for a piano maker.

Opening upon the arched porte cochere was a small ground-floor shop with living accommodation in the rear; this lodge was occupied by the concierge, a repairing tailor by trade with a sign to that effect on the front window. Also from the passageway opened a large common vestibule that led to a stair hall, which in turn gave access to the various floor levels. Except on very cold days the swinging doors of this vestibule were kept open throughout the year.

The covered carriageway, the unheated vestibule and stair hall were all perceived by the occupants of the apartment building as a semipublic continuation of the street and were treated accordingly. Although swept once a day and mopped once a week, the stone staircase, or "ascending street," did not appear attractive, since its walls and ceilings had, according to Hubert, "that indescribable color upon which time ceases to have an effect."

The masonry walls and floors of the apartment house were solidly built to exclude the penetration of sound, smells, or insects from one apartment to the other. Individual apartments were entered directly from a stair landing through a strong but plain front door. Generally, dwellings were on the large side, with generous windows opening on the street or courtyard and so arranged that a reasonable privacy in the apartments could be enjoyed.

The kitchen was tiled with brick, and its only built-in features were a cupboard, let into the wall, and a sink without connection to municipal water supply. Water used in the apartment had to be brought up in pails by water carriers; there were 20,000 water carriers patrolling the streets of Paris at mid-nineteenth century (Giedion 1954, 645). Devoid of any fixtures, the bathroom too was tiled like the kitchen, and tenants were expected to furnish it with a portable bathtub.

Reminiscent of medieval practices, the toilet arrangement consisted of a 10-ft (3-m) diameter stone tower built on the courtyard side about 12 ft (3.65 m) away from the main structure and connected to every stair landing with a covered bridgeway; at every floor level there was a small privy so arranged that "the matter fell directly down into a vault below, without ever touching the sides." Paid for by the landlord, the cesspool had to be emptied periodically, but in the absence of water closets—which use an abundance of water—this did not have to be done too frequently.

The occupants of this apartment house represented a wide spectrum of income groups. On the ground floor lived the concierge and the piano maker and their families. The entire first floor was occupied by the landlord, an old gentleman from a grand but untitled family from Brittany.

On the second, third, and fourth floors were two apartments each. Two wealthy families with their servants occupied the second floor; the family of a doctor and another professional man lived on the third; a retired army officer, and a widow with an unmarried daughter and a government-employed son lived on the fourth floor. Finally, the fifth or attic floor was divided into four dwellings, each occupied by people of a lower income group; one of these tenants was a toy maker. The families on the top floor had several children, but they were seldom seen or heard.

The rents of the various apartments decreased in proportion with their respective distance from the bel étage, which would have fetched the highest rent if it were not occupied by the owner himself. The two second-floor apartments were assessed at half, the two third-floor apartments at a third, the two fourth-floor apartments at a quarter, and the four top-floor dwellings together at a mere sixth of the value of the owner-occupied floor.

The apartments were seldom empty since people generally lived in the same dwelling for many years. Tenants were required to attend to internal repairs as well as to pay the municipal tax allocated to their dwelling, but the latter seemed "absurdly small" to an American like Hubert. Loss of rent through nonpayment was rare, because in the case of sickness or other trouble the landlord was quite generous with the poorer tenants. His instructions

to the concierge collecting the rent were to reduce or forgive it on such occasions.

Two land-use characteristics of this early apartment building seem significant: first, the presence of some commercial activity at ground-floor level, and, second, the heterogeneous mix of income groups represented by the occupants. The mixed land-use concept of development was a continuation of a heritage from the Middle Ages; it assured a good urban land-use efficiency, convenient access to shops, and a lively urban street life.

The heterogeneous tenant mix was a natural reflection of Parisian society: nobility, bourgeoisie, merchants, artisans, and laborers who found it expedient in economic terms to share the same building. Certainly there was no conscious effort to create a balanced social cross section in the building. In fact, tenants rarely had social intercourse with neighbors above and below except, of course, a polite greeting when they met each other on the common staircase or in the porte cochere.

During the seventeenth and eighteenth centuries, the hôtel-particulier was the traditional dwelling preferred by the aristocracy and the very well-to-do as their urban residence. The spatial organization of these noble mansions—*entre cour et jardin* (between courtyard and garden)—may be exemplified by a rather modest Parisian hôtel on Rue Saint-Dominique (Guicestre 1839–1911, 210).

In accordance with traditions, the *corps-de-logis* (or main residential building as distinct from the wings or pavilions) of the hôtel was set back from the street and was entered by a porte cochere flanked by stables and coach houses followed by a *cour d'honneur* or courtyard. With windows opening upon the street, the stables served as a buffer between the street and the entrance courtyard, which indicates that seventeenth-century streets were neither clean and quiet nor wide and pretty enough to be held in high esteem.

Occupying the central part of the narrow and deep medieval urban lot, the corps-de-logis was entered through a centrally placed vestibule. This entrance hall was slightly elevated and from it opened on one side a dining room and on the other

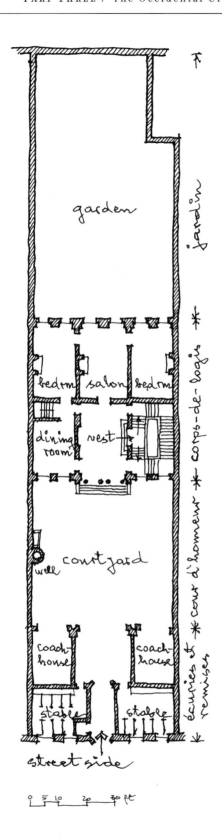

garden

jardin

bedrm | salon | bedrm

dining room | vest

coach-house | coach-house

stable | stable

well | courtyard

écuries et remises * cour d'honneur * corps-de-logis

street side

0 5 10   20   30 ft

Paris: Hôtel-particulier on Rue Saint-Dominique
(after G. Guicestre)

a grand escalier, the latter giving access to the upper floors. These three principal spaces on the courtyard side of the mansion were complemented by a similar tripartite division of spaces on the garden side, with a central *salon* designed in axial continuation of the hall, and flanked by chambers, all three rooms fronting on a formal garden. Wedged between the dining room and one bedroom was a secondary staircase for servants' access to the adjoining rooms.

After the introduction of wide avenues and boulevards in Paris, newly constructed hôtel-particuliers departed from the traditional entre-cour-et-jardin organization and, in a sense, inverted the position of the house with the stables. This becomes evident from a closer examination of a hôtel on Avenue du Bois-de-Boulogne (Rumler 1839–1911, 170).

Designed as a mansion, this luxurious hôtel-particulier featured a grand entrance sequence of a vaulted porte cochere, a large vestibule, and an escalier d'honneur. The main staircase led to the bel étage and opened into a wide gallery placed between the *grand salon* on the street side and a *serre* or winter garden on the courtyard side. A *cabinet de travail* (study) and a *bibliothèque* (library) was on one side of the grand salon and a *petit salon* and a *boudoir* on the other; the first two reception rooms were used by the master of the house, the other two by his wife. The *salle à manger* (dining room) faced the courtyard and was served from a kitchen located below it.

Formality and convenience dictated the sequence of principal spaces of this hôtel in conformity, of course, with a set of traditional rules that later also found application in luxury apartment house construction.

The porte cochere enabled guests and occupants of the mansion to enter the building under cover. In northern countries the porte cochere was quite common before it became fashionable in Paris and was valued because it provided protection in bad weather to elegantly dressed guests disembarking from their carriages.

From the porte cochere one entered a vestibule with decoration in carved stone similar to the

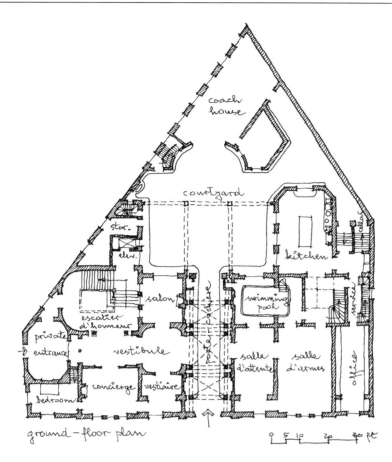

ground-floor plan

Paris: Hôtel-particulier on Avenue du Bois-de-Boulogne
(after E. Rumler)

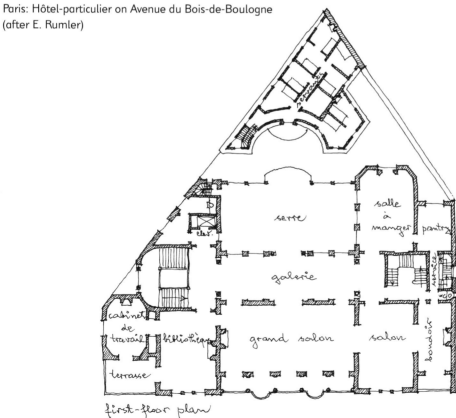

first-floor plan

exterior façade—instead of wood paneling, for example—because this anteroom still echoed the design of the entrance to the building. A concierge supervised the vestibule from the lodge opening on it.

Normally, the entrance sequence continued through the escalier d'honneur, if possible placed to the right of the vestibule, the direction that visitors would instinctively take. The principal staircase was also a reception space; the host often greeted his guests from the piano nobile landing. Usually, flights of stairs were arranged around an open newel or central void to afford the stair hall a certain splendor.

The reception rooms of the bel étage were also designed in accordance with traditional rules that distinguished three categories of rooms—formal reception rooms, informal rooms for intimate conversations, and private rooms for personal life. The grand salon and the gallery as well as the dining room were formal reception rooms; the library, the little salon and the boudoir were informal rooms; and the study and bedchambers, the latter combined with dressing rooms and bathrooms, were dedicated to family life.

There is little doubt that the spatial organization of the aristocratic hôtels-particuliers, as described above, influenced the design of apartment buildings. This should not be surprising since the bourgeoisie often tried to emulate the residential design of the aristocracy, usually at a diminished scale proportionate to their income.

The salient features in apartment-building design adapted from the hôtel-particuliers were mainly the entrance sequence consisting of the porte cochere, the vestibule off this passageway, and the staircase giving access to the upper-story apartments; the stair hall of apartment houses was not only generous in size and well lit, but the flight of stairs was often curved, which gave it a monumental appearance similar to the escalier d'honneur of the hôtel-particuliers. Since the entranceway of apartment houses served several dwellings, a lavish treatment of the vestibule and curved "dancing stairs" (so named for their fanciful design) was considered justified.

Additional similarities can also be discerned in the arrangement of the concierge's lodge close to the vestibule, and the location of the stables and coach houses at the rear of the property.

Finally, a striking similarity is apparent in the typical apartment unit layout with its en-suite string of salons and master bedrooms linked axially to each other on the street side, the dining room on the courtyard side, and secondary bedrooms together with domestic offices including kitchen in a side wing reaching towards the rear. The dining room was the only reception room with a view toward the rear because a view during a sit-down dinner was not considered essential, and its proximity to the pantry and kitchen was convenient for service. After dinner the family and their guests always moved to the salon or other formal reception rooms. At the height of the belle époque, in the late 1800s, even the galleries of luxurious hôtels were copied by the bourgeoisie to replace the corridors that separated the main reception rooms along the street side from those of the courtyard side.

Apart from the salons, both the boudoir and the lady's bedchamber also occupied a principal location along the street façade. Spending many hours daily in her chamber, the mistress of the house viewed her bedroom suite as "the home of the home" and decorated it to her taste alone; a dressing room, or cabinet de toilette, adjoining the bedroom facilitated the latter's tidiness. The boudoir's function was that of an intimate and elegant small reception room, and it was viewed as a privilege to be admitted there; to those permitted to enter the boudoir, the lady of the house was always at home. Friends of the "second degree" were officially received in the petit salon, and only at certain times of the week. The grand salon was used periodically for social gatherings that included, in addition to friends (of the first and second degree), acquaintances of third-degree importance in the hostess's social circle.

Invariably a suite of rooms was designed so that doors allowed communication between them, but seldom at the expense of their potential independent use, since they also were accessible through a

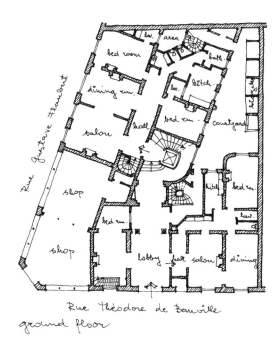

Rue Théodore de Banville
ground floor

typical floor plan
(1st, 2nd, 3rd and 4th upper levels)

Paris: Apartment building
(after Sydney Perks)

hall or corridor. Not only did this arrangement allow an attractive en-suite use of representational rooms on festive occasions, but it also enabled the use of adjoining rooms in various combinations of smaller suites.

Notwithstanding the flexible access from one room to the other, apartments were also divided into three distinct zones: a "social" zone, consisting of the salons and dining room; a private or "personal" zone of bedrooms, boudoirs, study, and bathrooms; and a "service" zone of the pantry, the kitchen, and servants' bedrooms.

During the second half of the nineteenth century, modern mechanical and sanitary installations were introduced in Parisian apartment houses. Kitchens, equipped with a large fireplace with a turn-spit or hooded stove, and a large table and racks for utensils, now were also supplied with running water. These new buildings were designed to cater to well-to-do people, thereby abandoning the tradition of mixed tenancy but retaining for a while some component of commercial use.

A typical apartment house situated on the corner of Rue Théodore de Banville and Rue Gustave Flau-

bert, designed by L. C. Lacan (Perks 1905, 183), demonstrates the design features of a mixed-use building intended primarily for middle-class occupancy. While the size of the building itself was relatively small by today's standards, the dwellings were quite large. Governed by a restriction limiting the maximum height of apartment houses to about 65 ft (20 m), the building had six stories, including the attic floor. A well-enforced municipal building code also controlled the cornice line and the shape of the roof.

The main entrance of this building was located on Rue Théodore de Banville and led to an elaborately adorned lobby supervised from the lodge by the concierge; at the end of the lobby was a grand stairway, with an elevator in the stairwell giving access to the various upper levels. Also at ground level was a large commercial space, which could be let as one or two shops; in addition, two apartment units, a smaller one entered directly from the lobby, and a larger one off the stair hall were also at ground-floor level.

The upper floors each had two large apartment units with all principal rooms, including the dining room, facing the street. Since a hall ran parallel with the main rooms, each principal room could be used independently, but the en-suite arrangement of the reception rooms also allowed intercommunication between them if so desired; thus, the flexibility existed to create, for example, a master bedroom suite, by using the small salon of the corner apartment as a boudoir for the lady's bedroom. Smaller bedrooms, kitchens, and bathrooms faced the courtyard, and ancillary rooms, such as toilets and dressing rooms, were lit and ventilated from light shafts. Each apartment had access to a service stair near the kitchen; these stairs also gave access to servants' toilets and led to the attic floor where the servants' quarters were located for all apartments. This corner apartment house had neither a porte cochere nor facilities for stables or coach houses, since the building lot was very small.

Fashionable apartment buildings became stereotyped during the belle époque, an era of optimism and prosperity that came to a sudden halt with the outbreak of World War I in 1914. Many luxury apartment buildings built then catered exclusively to the elite, and in these buildings commercial activity was no longer permitted. Thus, apartment houses built along prestigious avenues became pure residential buildings for upper-income groups only, apartment units conformed to a design pattern used in the hôtel-particuliers built for the aristocracy.

The principal apartments, namely those above the ground floor but below the attic floor, were usually arranged in a traditional way, with the salons and master bedrooms facing the street, and the dining room, secondary bedrooms, and the kitchen with its ancillary spaces fronting the courtyard.

The architect Fernand Mazade described a luxury apartment house located on Avenue Henri-Martin, one of the most fashionable avenues in Passy (*The Architectural Record*, vol. 13, 1903). It was designed by Émile Vaudremer (1829–1914), a native Parisian who was a member of the Architects' Institute and whose influential atelier was frequented by Louis Sullivan, among others.

Planted with four lines of chestnut trees, Avenue Henri-Martin was not an avenue by name only; rows of trees bordered the curbs of two sidewalks and two carriageways, and a broad median strip was reserved as a bridle path. The avenue ran from Place du Trocadéro to Bois-de-Boulogne, and was bordered by well-kept private residences and apartment buildings, many of them set back from the street line so as to provide space for a front garden. From shops in adjacent streets supplies of provisions for housekeeping were easily procured, but equally frequent was the practice of purchasing supplies from merchants who called every morning for orders to be delivered to the house. Avenue Henri-Martin formed part of a beaux quartier whose residents were within walking distance of the Champs Élysées, the Bois-de-Boulogne, the Seine River promenade, and close to a subway as well as the Girdle Railroad station, streetcar stops, and cab stands.

This apartment complex, built in 1898, consisted of three buildings with two interior courtyards. The front building was seven stories high, the top floor being a garret; the building between the first and second courtyard was eight stories high with garrets on the two top floors; the rear building fronting the second court and abutting the rear boundary of the deep lot was four stories high; finally, the last building, entered through the east wing of the third building, fronted on a third court, a service court containing stables, haylofts, and coachmen's lodgings. Arched passageways linked the courtyards with each other, and the driveways of the two porte cocheres below the first two buildings were lined with thick linoleum, in order to deaden the noise of carriages and horseshoes as well as to reduce vibration.

The front building had the most prestigious apartments, with two dwellings per floor above ground-floor level; they were reached through a stair hall which also had an elevator. In these large apartments, reception rooms, such as the grand and petit salons, and two bedrooms faced the street, while the dining room, additional bedrooms, kitchen, and ancillary domestic offices faced the courtyard. All rooms were equipped with

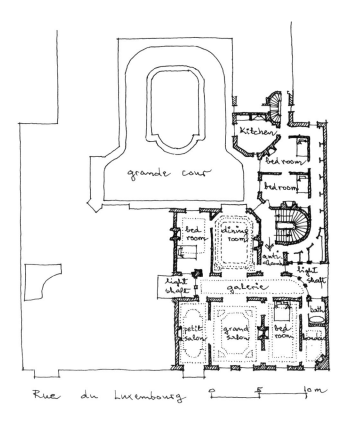

Paris: Luxury apartment building

fireplaces, and the masonry dividing walls containing the chimneys were 14.5 in (36.8 cm) thick. A wide gallery, reasonably well lit from both ends through *courettes* or light shafts, separated the front rooms from the principal rear ones, while a corridor reached back to the kitchen and service stair at the end of the side wing.

The second building had three apartments per typical floor and was served by two staircases so that a maximum of only two apartments were allowed to open upon a single stair landing. These rear apartments were considerably smaller than the front units, but were still comfortable five-room apartments excluding the kitchen, butler's pantry, and bathroom. The sixth floor of the second building contained three large artist's studios complemented by living accommodations, and the top garret floor contained servants' rooms.

The ground floor of the third building consisted of coach houses, harness rooms, and bicycle storage, and each of the three floors above contained a four-room apartment unit.

In contrast to the plain façade of the older apartment house described by Hubert (page 314), this building had a handsome hewn stone street façade enlivened with bay windows and granite balconies with cast-iron railings, and the large French windows were provided with folding iron shutters. Hewn stones were also used for the ground-floor section of the interior façades; the white brick courtyard walls above the ground floor were adorned with intermittent bands of red brick with cast-iron railings for French doors and keystones in the arched lintels.

The floors of all principal rooms were parqueted and their walls papered; reception rooms were decorated with a false wainscoting and painted a light color. In keeping with French custom, principal rooms were linked with adjacent rooms to allow direct communication between them, but they also were directly accessible from the gallery or corridor so as to enable their private use when so desired. Electricity and gas were provided for each centrally heated flat. The stair halls were also heated, and they were lit until midnight. Daytime supervision was the responsibility of the concierge, whose lodge was located in the first porte cochere fronting the main entrance to the vestibule leading to the main stair hall. Everybody entering or leaving the apartment complex had to pass in front of the concierge's window. At night, after closing hour, he had to be summoned to open the gate.

An unusual feature of this apartment complex was that its east side abutted the old and closed Passy cemetery; this permitted window apertures along the party wall, considerably enhancing the brightness of the east apartments. The complex was owned by the Vicomtesse de Tredern, a celebrated society singer of the era. Mazade considered the building to be a good investment and estimated a return of at least 5 percent, i.e., 2 percent higher than the normal rate at the time.

Although Mazade did not include a list of tenants, he nevertheless referred to the fact that residences along Avenue Henri-Martin were "occupied by people of the very best class—members of the Institute, noblemen, generals and so forth." As a tenant, Mazade prided himself on being a neighbor of Prince de Chimay and the Princesse de Polignac, and confessed: "Without turning up my nose at the poor quarters, . . . I vastly prefer to be here than to live in a dirty street where one would be constantly exposed to being jostled by unmannerly boys or drunken laborers" (Mazade 1903, 357).

Well-appointed apartments were also constructed on the Left Bank. Being close to the university, these buildings were mostly occupied by university teachers and learned members of the Institute and their respective families.

Late nineteenth-century Parisian apartment houses were much admired by American architects, and their descriptions in architectural journals influenced greatly the design of multistory residential buildings in large American cities, with, of course, some modifications such as extra bathrooms and servants' bedrooms included in the suite. American builders and tenants referred to their apartments as "first-class French flats" with pride.

Three general characteristics of Parisian apartment buildings contributed to their viability. First, Paris was a unique city with many treed thoroughfares which presented attractive building sites for apartment houses with a pleasant street prospect. Second, the maximum height of apartment buildings was limited to about 65 ft (20 m) which, through the use of generous ceiling heights, resulted in buildings rarely exceeding six stories; these medium-high buildings were appropriate in scale to the width of avenues and boulevards and assured reasonable access to light, air, and sunshine for most apartment dwellers. Moreover, apartment buildings, with the exception of luxury ones, were seldom purely residential buildings, since commercial land use was frequently incorporated in them, mainly at ground-floor level; the mixed land-use concept of development ensured a greater degree of urban efficiency than twentieth-century single-use zoning would later allow. Finally, an important characteristic often overlooked by contemporary students of nineteenth-century urban housing is the fact that the socioeconomic mix of occupants of Parisian apartment buildings, with the exception of the most luxurious ones, represented a wide range of income groups.

The mixed land-use concept used for Parisian apartment houses offended some leading architects and town planners of the twentieth century, including Le Corbusier. While some of their objections were justified, others were not. It is undeniable that some aspects of Parisian apartment houses were undesirable, such as their congestion on small plots, which required small courtyards and light wells to light and ventilate rear rooms. Relegating servants to the crowded attic floor and the concierge to a dingy lodge was far from ideal, but these conditions improved at the turn of the century when servants were accommodated in the apartments where they worked, and the concierge was provided with a better ground-floor apartment.

Most surprising is the criticism of the mixed use of these buildings by Sigfried Giedion, an influential spokesman for the Modern movement. For example, he stated that the Parisian apartment houses "artificially bring together functions which, in an industrial society, should be kept strictly separate," because "it is absurd in an age of industrial production to permit residence, labor, and traffic to intermingle" (Giedion 1954, 672). Fortunately, this simplistic view is no longer shared by urbanists who have witnessed the negative results of single-use zoning. Urban housing is compatible with many urban functions and mixed use buildings with a housing content not only present social and economic advantages, but also promise a lively and exciting urban living environment. This concept represents the only hope for the rejuvenation of those cities that have unfortunately become "suburbanized."

APARTMENT BUILDINGS IN GREAT BRITAIN

While apartment living became quite common in large European cities during the nineteenth century, in the British Isles it was still relatively rare. It is estimated that "in 1911 only one dwelling in thirty was a flat in England and Wales" (Sutcliffe 1974, ix). This variance is primarily attributed to the fact that in England the middle-class ideal was to live in a suburban detached or semidetached villa, or, as an alternative, in an urban town house.

As city life deteriorated during the nineteenth century, due to overcrowding in the wake of the large influx of people seeking employment in industries, it is not surprising that well-to-do families began to move to the arcadian suburbs or countryside. Such an urban dispersal could occur in the British Isles because cities were relatively safe from military attack, and horizontal expansion of urbanized areas was not curtailed by maintenance or construction of costly fortification systems to protect city dwellers.

An exceptional position with respect to multiple housing, however, is held by Old Edinburgh, because apartment houses known as "lands" were quite common there not only during the nine-

teenth century but before. Apparently apartment house construction in Edinburgh dates back at least to the sixteenth century, as substantiated by many descriptions of tall residential buildings, ten and even twelve stories high, in the Old Town and within the confines of the Flodden Wall, which dated from the early 1500s. The development of the land or block of flats—commonly only five or six stories high including the attic—is attributed to the crowded conditions of this medieval walled town.

In Scotland, the custom of erecting a building, frequently for the well-to-do, with self-contained private residences on successive stories was not only inherent to Edinburgh but also to Glasgow and even smaller towns. These private suites of apartments were called "flats," derived from the Scottish word "flaet" which dates back to the twelfth century and means "floor" or "story."

Usually a single flat occupied the entire floor of a multistory building. Owned independently of its neighbors, it was called a "house." The term "common interest," peculiar to Scots law, was applicable to the rights of proprietors of the different flats contained in a single building and conveyed certain rights to them over every part of the building other than the flats of which they were proprietors (Perks 1905, 4–5). This law considerably antecedes those of both cooperatives and condominiums enabling ownership of self-contained dwelling units in contemporary apartment houses.

Edinburgh: Riddell's Court
(after Sydney Perks)

Gladstone's Land, 483–489 Lawnmarket, is perhaps the most authentic example of a seventeenth-century apartment house. It was occupied at the time of the Stent Roll in 1635 by five distinct households, two of which were headed by landlords: Thomas Gladstaines and David Jonkin, both merchants. The lower half of this six-story building was owned by Jonkin, and the upper half by Gladstaines. Jonkin occupied the first floor and leased to Andrew Pringle the ground floor, consisting of a street-front shop with a low tavern below and a dwelling in the rear, while the second floor was leased to Andrew Hay. Gladstaines's dwelling was on the fifth and attic floors, and he collected rent from his tenant John Adamson, who lived on the fourth floor (Robinson 1982, 40).

Gladstone's Land is the last apartment building left in Edinburgh with an arcaded front. The main entrance, located at first-floor level above the arcade, was reached by an external stair and led to the spiral staircase that linked the floors above.

From the sixteenth century onwards, the external walls of Edinburgh apartment houses were built of stone. Their thickness varied from 2 to 3 ft (0.61 to 0.91 m), decreasing proportionately towards the top. The underside of floor boards and the open joists were usually exposed in the ceiling and were decorated with floral designs. In Gladstone's Land, the boarding of a painted ceiling as well as a decorated frieze is preserved in the interior of the first-floor dwelling. (Ornamental plaster ceilings came into vogue later and were used extensively during the eighteenth century.)

Access to the various floors of apartment houses was usually provided through a circular staircase turret known as a "turnpike stair" and built of stone, with a solid newel and a gentle rise of about 6 in (15 cm) for every step. While the external entrance to these winding staircases was open, doors fitted with a "twirling pin," a manually operated bell, marked the entries to the various apartments. As an alternative to the turnpike stairs, internal wooden staircases with a well hole were also sometimes used.

Riddell's Court may serve as an example of a pre-nineteenth century turnpike-stair apartment house and Wardrop's Court and James' Court as examples with interior staircases. Characteristic features they shared were the so-called bed presses or bed boxes resembling a large cupboard hiding the bed. The Edinburgh bed press with doors made to slide on runners or hinged in the ordinary way closely resembles the French closed berth called *lit clos*, which is still used in old buildings of Brittany. In the kitchen of the James' Court building is an unusual double bed press divided by a shelf about halfway between floor and ceiling—the lower berth for a maidservant opens off the kitchen and the upper berth for a manservant faces the hall. This building has also the distinction that the son of Lord Auchinleck, James Boswell (1740–1795), Scottish lawyer and biographer, was one of its residents, occupying a two-story house or duplex apartment with a private internal staircase.

Another characteristic of Edinburgh flats are the small garderobes or closets in the corner of bedrooms containing an earth closet (toilet) and ventilated directly to the outdoors. Fireplaces in most large rooms were used to heat the flats, and coal was often stored below the bed.

In his book *The Social Life of Scotland in the Eighteenth Century*, Henry Grey Graham describes the lofty houses of Old Edinburgh that were built both in narrow lanes and along the High Street. He asserts that their narrow staircases were really upright streets, and therefore similar in interpretation to the staircases of Parisian apartment houses. Moreover, the similarity with Parisian apartment buildings is also discernible in the heterogeneous nature of the occupants inhabiting these structures. Graham writes:

> In the same building lived families of all grades and classes, each in its flat in the same stair—a sweep and caddie in the cellars, poor mechanics in the garrets, while in the intermediate stories might live a noble, a lord-of-session, a doctor, a city minister, a dowager countess, or a writer. Higher up over their heads, lived shopkeepers, dancing-masters, or clerks" (Perks 1905, 15).

Old Edinburgh was the historic city on Castlehill, and apart from its famous spinal thoroughfare called the Royal Mile or Via Regia, which linked the

Castle with Holyrood Palace, it had few streets or "gates," the latter derived from the word "gait" which means in Scots a way or road. Instead of streets, this typically medieval city had many "wynds," "vennels," and "closes." Wynds and vennels were often narrow and steep public thoroughfares unfit for wheeled traffic; vennels (from the French *venelle*, i.e., slip away), were usually dirty alleys in the poorer part of the town (Lindsay 1938, 87). Although equally narrow, closes enjoyed a more distinguished status not only because they were usually private passages, but also because these cul-de-sacs were very picturesque as they passed under buildings through so-called pends (passages for pedestrians) and led to courts from which one or two lands were accessible.

Multistoried lands were also built in Glasgow, as exemplified by two arcaded buildings that stood at 17 and 27 High Street before their demolition in the 1870s. Crowned by steeply pitched and crowstepped gables, both buildings were built during the early seventeenth century and were four stories high, excluding the attic floor. Each floor was reached by a turnpike stair. The original layout of these "houses" consisted of a large hall with windows facing the street and a smaller chamber in the rear. At a later date the floor plans were altered, when the halls were divided by wooden partitions into smaller rooms (Worsdall 1979, 64–65).

After the union of Scotland with England (1707) there was no longer any reason to contain residential development within the walls of Old Edinburgh and in 1760 extensive building operations for the New Town began north of the steep-sided valley in which the railway now runs. This was a deliberate attempt at a new beginning. First, fashionable terraces of single-family attached town houses were built, as in other parts of Britain, but eventually their design was adapted to a unique form of multiple dwelling consisting of stacked units known as "main door houses," confirming the persistence of a tradition of multiple dwellings.

A typical eighteenth-century main door house in Edinburgh was built on Castle Street and consisted of four dwelling units, two lower ones with their own street address and two upper ones reached through a central staircase. Sir Walter Scott (1771–1832) lived in one of these lower dwellings from 1798 to 1826. As in Georgian town houses, the kitchen and servants' quarters of the lower units were in the basement; the entrance, parlor, and dining room were at ground-floor level, and the drawing room at the first upper level. Limited to three floor levels, this dwelling had bedrooms both on the ground floor and upper floors, a departure from the town house norm of bedrooms on upper floors only.

The two smaller upper units were entered at the third floor, from the public staircase, and above this level a private interior stair connected the two floors of these dwellings. The kitchen, dining room, a bedroom, and a drawing room were on the entrance level, while bedrooms occupied the attic (Perks 1905, 12).

Another example of main door houses with flats above was built in the 1830s at 1–5 Abbotsford Place, Glasgow, but, unfortunately, this building was also demolished. While the main door houses were entered from the front, the flats were reached by traditional circular turnpike stairs from the rear yard, the latter connected to the street by a pend. The flats in this building had a very sensible plan with a drawing room, dining room, and one bedroom lit from the street side, and two additional bedrooms and the kitchen from the yard. A central

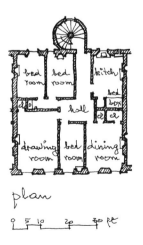

Glasgow: Abbotsford Place
(after Frank Worsdall)

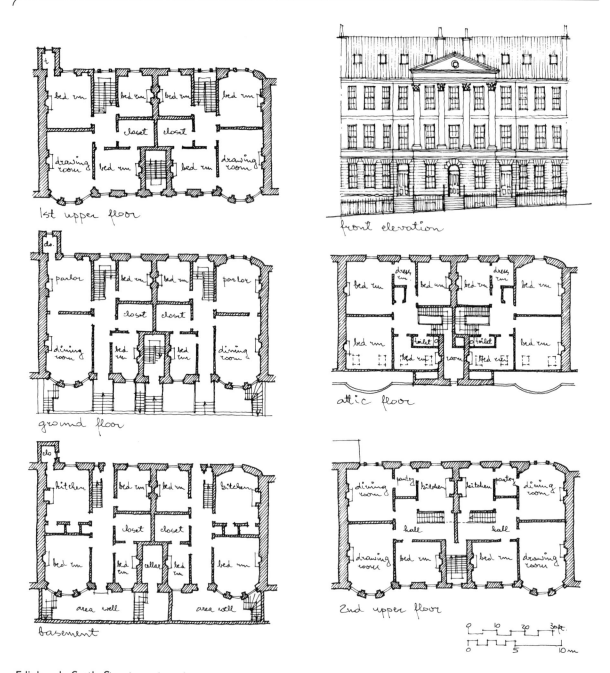

Edinburgh: Castle Street apartment
(after Sydney Perks)

lobby acted as a pivotal axis of the flat, and a short bedroom hall with a toilet at the end gave some privacy to two bedrooms. Typically, the kitchen had a bed press for a maid in one corner of the room (Worsdall 1979, 79–80).

In the middle of the nineteenth century whiskey distillers built model housing for their workers in Edinburgh. These Scottish versions of terraced flats were in fact stacked dwellings with the downstairs flat entered from grade level and the upstairs through a generous outside stair that gave "the row a great deal of character" (Barley 1963, 65). An example of such a development is a row of main door houses known as the "colonies" off Glenogle Road, with ground-floor and first-floor flats entered from opposite sides.

By the end of the nineteenth century many flats in Old Edinburgh, originally occupied by the well-to-do, were abandoned and subdivided into smaller units to be occupied by the very poor and rented even as single rooms licensed for a fixed number of people. Sir Patrick Geddes (1854–1932), the noted botanist, regionalist, and city planner, moved in 1887 to the Old Town of Edinburgh in an attempt to conserve many old buildings near the Royal Mile and "to play a more direct role in the social and physical regeneration of the old Town, in part through developing it as an academic/residential quarter, with the first halls of residence for students of the University" (Cornforth 1981, 573). Riddle's Close, Wardrop's Court, and Nos. 3 and 5 James' Court were restored or rebuilt by Geddes in collaboration with Stewart Henbest Capper and Sydney Mitchell, both architects.

Capper also designed a picturesque cluster of blocks of flats incorporating the octagonal house of the Scottish poet Allan Ramsay into the complex. This five-story apartment house, called Ramsay Garden, was located on the slope below Castle Esplanade, near the west end of the Royal Mile. Operated on a cooperative basis, Ramsay Garden was "commissioned, conceived and financed in part by Sir Patrick Geddes" (Sinclair 1984, 58), who also occupied one of its large apartment suites after the building's completion in 1893.

The native tradition of building flats persisted into the twentieth century and, before the First World War, was also used for semidetached so-called flatted villas that also had a recess in the kitchen for a servant's bed; even after the Second World War flatted villas were built in Corstorphine, Edinburgh (Barley 1963, 61). The householder in the upper dwelling could open the locked front door for a visitor without going downstairs by an arrangement of chains and pulleys.

The Inns of Court, or the Inner and Middle Temples, a cluster of buildings provided with housekeeping services, where lawyers slept, dined, and studied, may represent one of the earliest catering flats in Great Britain. Its members lived in "chambers" consisting of a room to sleep in, a study for business, and a dark passage or anteroom where an attendant was stationed. The chambers were cleaned by a "victuler" or a laundress (who was not allowed to be younger than forty years of age), and meals were served in a common dining hall.

The self-contained precinctual community of the Inns of Court dates back to the Middle Ages, when lawyers established their halls, libraries, dwellings, and outdoor recreational facilities on the secluded and deserted grounds of the Templars, just outside the city wall. Lincoln's Inn and Gray's Inn were similar institutions.

During the nineteenth century, a multiple-dwelling form evolved in London resembling in principle the domestic organization of the Inns of Court. Known as catering flats, these buildings were to offer residential accommodation to affluent people, mostly singles and childless couples, who sought the homelike quality of a luxurious apartment building combined with the household services of a hotel (Perks 1905, 54).

The development of this new building type was attributed to the increasing difficulty in obtaining good servants, but another reason was the demand for an agreeable form of dwelling for nontraditional households of well-to-do people who could and were willing to pay for the housekeeping conveniences they obtained.

Catering flats consisted of a number of self-contained suites of various sizes, usually with a pantry but without kitchens and servants' rooms. Cleaning and other household services, including meals, which were served either in the common dining room or in the privacy of the apartment, were rendered at request and paid for at fixed charges, whereas all other amenities, such as the use of common reception rooms and billiard rooms and the like, were included in the rent.

Early examples of catering flats emulated the Georgian town house in spatial organization. A good example is Campden House Chambers, designed by E. J. A. Balfour and Thackeray Turner, and built around the turn of the century. This block of catering flats consisted of suites ranging from two to four rooms, each with an open fireplace. Tenants in the building had access to a common dining room located, like the kitchen and all nec-

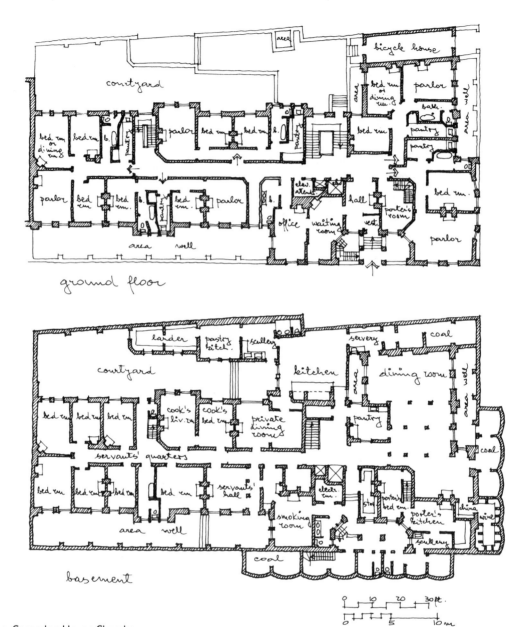

London: Campden House Chambers
(after Sydney Perks)

essary accommodation for the staff, in the basement, which was lit through area wells.

As a rule, catering flats for bachelors were designed without common rooms, and since these tenants used their clubs for lunch and dinner, breakfast was the only meal served. Such buildings were relatively small, four to five stories high, with two suites per floor, each containing a sitting room, bedroom, and bathroom. Nos. 104–112 Mount Street, designed by Ernest George and Peto,

and the Bachelors' Chambers on Park Lane West, designed by Alfred Waterhouse, are examples of intimately scaled catering flats. In the former building, the caretaker's rooms and kitchen were on the top floor; in the latter, the caretaker occupied the basement.

For independent single women, such as authors, artists, and nurses, the Ladies' Residential Chambers, with adjacent suites sharing a pantry and toilet, was built on York Street, in West London. In contrast to the bachelor chambers, however, this four-story building, with an additional garret floor, was designed with a common dining room in the basement. Designed by Balfour and Turner, the domestic offices and servants' rooms were all located in the basement, an arrangement similar to that of Campden House Chambers.

A corner building, Marlborough Chambers on Jermyn Street, also in London, was a larger structure with seven rented shops at sidewalk level in addition to an entrance lobby on each of the bordering streets. Above the shops were four floors of apartments ranging in size from two to five rooms, flats that were considered at the time to be "some of the best and most expensive suites in London" (Perks 1905, 155). The kitchen and various living accommodations for the staff were in the garret, and meals were served from there to tenants in the privacy of their chambers.

One of the largest blocks of catering flats in London was Queen Anne's Mansions, in Westminster. The construction of this palatial building (now demolished) was commenced in 1873 by Henry Alers Hankey and completed in 1889 with the participation of E. R. Robson, architect. In addition to their private luxury suites, the tenants also had access to a number of well-appointed common rooms, including several dining rooms, parlors, and a large two-story drawing room with a stage. A recreational area for tenants was built on part of the roof of this eight-story building.

Following the American model of apartment hotels, the Savoy Hotel in London built an extension containing suites with varying numbers of rooms for long-term residents that were let at a yearly rental in every way like catering flats. Meals were either served in the private rooms or in the public dining room of the hotel.

Serving an affluent clientele with a high living standard, catering flats on the whole were economically quite successful, but in the total housing stock of pre–World War I, they represented but an oddity in a nation that tenaciously adhered to the privacy of a family home.

At the beginning of the nineteenth century, York House, a London property on Piccadilly, was converted into freehold flats with two new rows of suites built along the two sides of its deep garden. A covered walk ran down the middle of the garden and entrance to the suites was through a stair hall shared by flanking suites. Each suite consisted of two lofty rooms in the front, an entrance hall, and a small room and toilet in the back. Renamed "The Albany," this multifamily building was inhabited by many celebrated men, including poet Lord Byron, writer and statesman Lord Macaulay, military commander Lord Clyde, and statesman William Ewart Gladstone (Perks 1905, 20).

Between 1804, when York House was converted, and 1880, there appear to have been very few blocks of flats constructed in England. In Dickens's *Dictionary of London*, published in 1879, reference is only made to Queen Anne's Mansion, a few blocks of flats along both Victoria Street and Cromwell Road, and to a single apartment block on George Street.

If the Victoria Street flats in Westminster represent the state of the art in English apartment house design of that era, the layout of these suites can hardly be compared in comfort and grandness to their continental counterparts. In one respect, however, these buildings were advanced. They were both fire- and soundproof, which was assured by a complex three-layered floor system with a noncombustible core composed of iron girders and brick arches, and with a joist-supported ceiling below and wood floors above.

The first blocks of upper-class flats on Victoria Street were built in 1853 by a builder called MacKenzie, but in spite of the fact that this novel form of residence was praised in the press as being reasonable and comfortable to live in, the insular and conservative society of London resisted the concept of multifamily living.

During the nineteenth century, English society was rather reluctant to embrace the flat as an integral part of British life, especially if flats were built over shops along a main street. In contrast to their continental counterparts, the well-to-do English family preferred the quiet of a residential side street to the bustle and vivacity of a main thoroughfare.

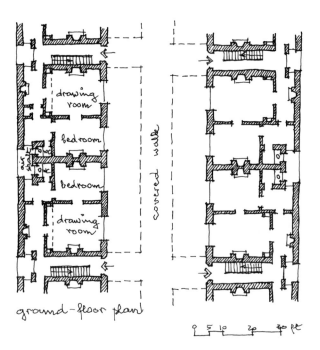

London: The Albany
(after Sydney Perks)

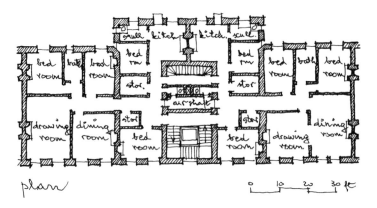

Westminster: Victoria Street apartments
(after Sydney Perks)

A major initial objection to flatted dwellings was based on the fear that infectious diseases would spread more rapidly with several families living under one roof. In a paper delivered at the general meeting of the Royal Institute of British Architects in 1894, Professor Robert Kerr, an architect and cofounder of the Architectural Association, admonished that "the doctors are telling the dwellers of flats plainly that the absence of fresh air for themselves, and the presence of polluted air with their neighbours, not only must be expected to produce ill-health, but must be taken to be realising that disagreable expectation already" (Kerr 1893/94, 222). While it is true that Kerr did not discuss this issue in depth and even suggested waiting until a more substantiated pronouncement was made by the medical profession, he nevertheless planted a seed of caution in the minds of many. Additional objections to multifamily residences included noise in the flat above or below, servant problems engendered in the untraditional flat, and the greater risk of burglary.

Since most of these objections were not very well substantiated, apartment living eventually gained wider acceptance, but the majority of urban dwellers in England continued to accept much less readily than the Scots, or the French, the concept of making a home in a multistoried apartment house. The building industry was even more conservative and responded very slowly to an anticipated need for rental flats. As late as 1892, the *Spectator* stated that the demand for flats was greater than the supply.

Perhaps the most significant encouragement for the acceptance of this new domestic arrangement, especially as a second home in the city, was derived from the very well-to-do segment of society, whose members began to travel more extensively in Europe and became familiar with good examples of apartment dwellings.

Some distinguished architects, such as Norman Shaw, also attempted to add respectability to this form of architecture by designing some prestigious blocks of flats. One such group of residential buildings, Albert Hall Mansions, erected in Kensington between 1879 and 1886, had an exceptional design. Usually, flats were designed on a single floor level, but in the Albert Hall Mansions, Shaw introduced multilevel dwelling units in order to juxtapose two lofty stories of principal rooms in the front of the building, with three lower stories for bedrooms and domestic offices in the back. Such an arrangement resulted in a better distribution of building volume, but also in a complicated structure necessitating several private internal staircases. The lower floors of the Albert Hall Mansions consisted of three-level "maisonette" units, with reception rooms and some bedchambers at ground-floor level, bedrooms above, and kitchen and a maid's room in the basement.

While Shaw's arrangement of these multilevel dwellings resembles the traditional English town house more closely than the single-level French apartments do, his ingenious layout was not duplicated in many subsequent buildings in London, but it may have inspired the duplex apartments of New York City. However, for many years the dwellings of the Albert Hall Mansions were considered some of the best that were built in England.

Conventional English flats were obviously inspired by French apartments, but they never developed the sophistication inherent in the latter. A typical early English flat usually had an entrance hall, small and badly lit, and an awkward corridor that was narrow, long, and dark. The principal rooms, as well as some bedchambers, lacked the flexibility offered by the en-suite arrangement so familiar in Parisian flats. Nevertheless, several attempts were made by architects in London during the last decades of the nineteenth century to approximate the luxury of both Parisian and New York City apartment houses.

One example was Cleveland Row on St. James's Street, a block of flats designed by W. Woodward, wherein each stair landing opened onto two large suites. The entrance hall and the three principal rooms opening from it were generous in size, but no doors were provided between the formal rooms to facilitate their combined use during a reception. Besides the main stairway with an elevator in the well, this block of flats also had a service staircase in the rear.

American influence probably shaped the design of a block of flats designed by Amos F. Faulkner on Sloane Square. With four large flats to each floor, two main staircases, each with an elevator, were used in order to reach two flats only from each stair landing. The location of the dining room on the street side of the building resulted in an awkward service connection with the kitchen, a problem cleverly avoided in French apartments with the dining room traditionally on the courtyard side.

Infrequently, apartment buildings above commercial establishments were also built in London. Gloucester House, on the corner of Piccadilly and Park Lane, and St. George's Terrace, on Gloucester Road, were two examples.

Designed by the architects T. E. Collcutt and Stanley Hamp, Gloucester House had at grade level several shops and a bank, as well as a noble entrance hall with a fireplace and a grand stairway with an elevator in the stairwell. At each landing there was only one large and luxurious flat reached

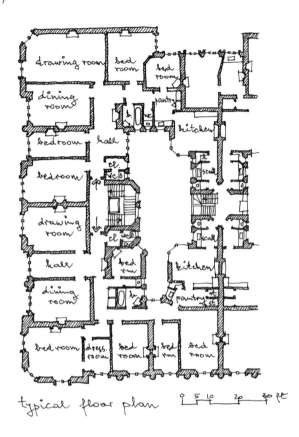

typical floor plan

London: Sloane Square apartments
(after Sydney Perks)

through a vestibule with a coatroom and toilet. On one side of the vestibule, the formal section of the apartment clustered around a generous hall, also with an open fireplace, that gave access to an interconnected drawing room and boudoir, as well as a dining room and a master bedroom suite, the latter with a private dressing room and bathroom. On the other side of the vestibule were six additional bedrooms, bathrooms, and toilets, a smoking or billiard room, and domestic offices, all reached off a long central corridor. A service staircase with a service elevator served the domestic side of the flats.

St. George's Terrace was a group of buildings containing five blocks of flats, each block with two apartments per floor, arranged so that they could be united into one large family suite. Paul Hoffmann, the designer of this structure, provided commercial outlets at sidewalk level.

Apart from rich people who desired a second home in the city and, of course, well-to-do single persons, apartment living was not viewed by Londoners as an acceptable alternative to the suburban villadom enjoyed by the middle class. By the end of the nineteenth century "the Englishman was more firmly wedded than ever to the concept of his house with its patch of garden and he appears to have gritted his teeth against the growing problem of commuting, recognising it as a necessary evil" (Tarn 1974, 38).

NEW YORK CITY APARTMENT HOUSES

During the second half of the nineteenth century, apartment house living was introduced in New York City, and it became a viable urban residential alternative to traditional row-house dwelling for middle- and upper-income families. Since the concept of multiunit living was mainly propagated by American artists and architects familiar with Parisian lifestyles, the influence of French apartment house prototypes is pervasive. In spite of some severe criticisms leveled against this foreign dwelling form, apartment house living appealed to many, and over the next decades not only resulted in the establishment of several apartment houses but also gave rise to several hybrids, such as the cooperative apartment, the studio apartment, the apartment hotel, and the luxury apartment house with duplex or two-storied maisonette units. During the twenties and early thirties, the latter building type was unmatched as the height of residential luxury.

While New York City building regulations made no distinction between a tenement and apartment building—both were defined as multiunit housing types with accommodation for three or more families living independently from each other—there was nevertheless a great difference between the two.

In contrast to dwelling units in tenements, which were designed to barely meet the minimum spatial standards required by law with few provisions for communal services, dwellings in apartment houses were much more commodious. Their tenants had access to several centralized services. Apart from passenger and goods elevator service that facilitated access to apartments in the upper floors of the building, the central heating of apartments as well as centralized refrigeration in kitchens were the most significant amenities, since they made it unnecessary to haul coal or ice to individual dwellings. The boiler room for the central heating system and the central refrigeration plant were usually located in the basement, both attended by a resident caretaker. The individual meters for gas used in kitchen ranges and electricity for general lighting were also housed in the basement.

Another conventional collective convenience provided in apartment houses was a laundry with access to open-air drying. An adequate number of laundry rooms, each with a steam dryer, was usually provided so that each family had weekly access to one laundry room for two consecutive days. These facilities were usually lodged on the roof and either an elevator or a dumbwaiter was extended to the roof level for the delivery and return of linen.

Luxury apartments, of course, had a doorman in attendance to admit tenants and guests to an elegant entrance lobby from which the elevator lobby and grand staircase were reached. Various public rooms, such as a waiting room or a women's receiving room, opened off the lobby, and the proper operation of the building was supervised from a clerk's office nearby. The management and supervision by a concierge, so familiar from Paris, never gained acceptance by American apartment house tenants.

Richard Morris Hunt (1827–1895), the Paris-trained American architect, is credited with the design of one of the first apartment houses built in New York. Located on the south side of East 18th Street, between Third Avenue and Irving Place, this early prototype was built in 1869 and was financed by Rutherford Stuyvesant. For many years the Stuyvesant Building was popularly referred to as "the French Flats" (Israels 1911, 477); the term

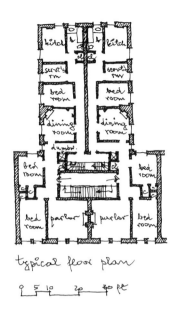

typical floor plan

New York City: The Stuyvesant, Richard Morris Hunt

"apartment" was not in common use before the last quarter of the century.

Initially, Hunt's apartment building was the center of much controversy as critics stated that it was both wicked and immoral to house several families under one roof, a domestic arrangement only suitable for low-income families in tenements. But in time, adverse criticism of apartment house living for middle- and upper-income families became more subdued and the concept gradually gained acceptance.

Although influenced by Parisian apartment houses, the Stuyvesant did not project the formal elegance of its continental precursors, not only because of the simple decor and diminished size of its reception rooms, but also because principal rooms were not interconnected and could only be reached individually from a long, narrow, and crooked corridor stretching from the parlor to the kitchen in the rear. Thus, in the absence of an en-suite arrangement, these dwellings did not offer the flexibility of most Parisian flats, which could be subdivided further into private apartments.

The Stuyvesant Apartments, which also contained a few commodious studio apartments for artists on the attic level, was targeted for the "better class" tenant. From the very outset this building venture was a success in spite of the fact that the five-story structure had no elevator service.

Two years after its completion, the success of the Stuyvesant led to the construction of another apartment building by Hunt: the Stephens Apartment House (later converted into the Victoria Hotel). In order to appeal to even wealthier tenants this building was provided with many conveniences including elevator service, and, with its three-story mansard roof, it had a decidedly Parisian look to it.

The main deficiencies of the first apartment house were gradually corrected in subsequent buildings such as the Osborne, which was designed by the builders Duggin and Crossman and completed in 1876. Situated on Fifth Avenue between 52nd and 53rd Streets, this six-story apartment house offered large dwelling units reflecting "taste and elegance" as well as "solid comfort and convenience" (Boyer 1985, 155). Accordingly, the two street-fronting reception rooms of each apartment, the library and the parlor, had an en-suite arrangement which extended to the master bedroom opening towards the rear; of course, to enhance the flexibility of their use, these rooms were also accessible from the corridor. As in French apartments, the dining room was placed in the rear of the apartment and separated from the kitchen by a butler's pantry, which acted as a buffer against kitchen odors. Two large apartments were accommodated on each floor level of the Osborne, with a formal staircase and elevator service in the front part of the building, and a rear stairway with a dumbwaiter so that provisions could be brought in by the rear entrance.

Other examples of commodious apartment houses in the 1870s were the Bella, at the corner of 26th Street and Fourth Avenue; the Florence, at the corner of 18th Street and Fourth Avenue; the Elise, on Eighth Avenue near 57th Street, with its seven-room apartment suites, each equipped with electric bells, speaking trumpets (before phones, these tubes enabled people to converse with others in different rooms) and elaborate bathrooms; and the large and very successful Vancorlear apartment building, on Seventh Avenue between 55th and 56th Streets, that offered six large fashionable suites per floor and was designed by Henry Janeway Hardenbergh (1847–1918). Its rear rooms were also well lit, since they opened on a large courtyard, a design concept subsequently repeated by its owner, Edward Clark, who was the architect for The Dakota apartment building.

The rapid acceptance of apartment house living is evidenced by the fact that in 1875, six years after the Stuyvesant Apartments were built, 112 apartment houses were built in a single year, a trend that continued during the following decades so that "by 1900 thousands of these structures had filled out the city" and between 1902 and 1910 an additional 4,425 new apartment houses were erected in Manhattan alone (Boyer 1985, 154, 220).

In addition to Richard Morris Hunt, another early pioneer of American apartment house design was Philip G. Hubert, of the firm Hubert and Pirsson (after James A. Pirsson's death known as Hubert, Pirsson and Company). Born in France in 1830, Hubert came to the North American continent as a young man in 1849. After a few years pursuing a teaching career, Hubert settled in New York and devoted himself to the practice of architecture, which he had studied with his father in France.

Hubert was an innovative architect and devoted much attention to improving apartment house construction and design. Thus, for example, he was much concerned with devising a construction method so nearly fireproof that the entire contents of a single apartment unit might burn to ashes without endangering the occupants of neighboring units. To achieve such aims he introduced sheathing of steel beams with fireproof plaster blocks or cement, and substituted wood joist flooring with a noncombustible floor system. Hubert is credited with having first provided running water, both cooled and filtered for drinking, to individual apartment units; moreover, he equipped apartment kitchens with refrigerators cooled from a central plant.

Hubert was also the originator of the New York City cooperative apartment house (popularly known as Hubert Home Clubs), and one of the first architects to design duplex apartments. The latter arose from the realization that subordinate rooms, such as bedrooms and housekeeping offices, would not be impaired by a reduced ceiling height, thus enabling three stories of such rooms to correspond to two stories of formal rooms with high ceilings, with, of course, a split-level floor arrangement. Eventually, the term "duplex apartment" came to designate two-story apartments with an internal private staircase, no doubt to simulate the ambiance of traditional private houses, which were seldom single-storied before the advent of the bungalow.

The cooperative apartment house was pioneered by Hubert in order to create an alternative method of financing as well as to ensure their sound construction, which unfortunately was a rarity before strict building codes were in effect, and the builders' prime objective was to build, sell, and make a quick profit.

Essentially, a cooperative was a corporation that owned the entire building and its members received stock certificates in proportion to their down payment, which entitled them a lease to an apartment in perpetuity. A member "could occupy, sublet, or even sell his apartment, depending on the regulations of the association" and the only monthly expense was a sum to cover the running costs of the building (Handlin 1979, 267).

Cooperatives did not enjoy the popular support that Hubert envisaged. First, the general public did not like the connotations of a "cooperative," although Hubert was careful to refer to it as a "Home Club" (a later designation was "private apartments"). Second, the number of people with adequate cash for a down payment in a cooperative was rather limited. Finally, members of cooperatives had little experience in either financing or managing real estate, not to speak of the problem of safeguarding the value of their investment, which could easily be impaired if "undesirable" people succeeded in becoming coproprietors.

In 1882, Hubert designed a building complex, the Central Park Apartments, which was erected on Seventh Avenue at 58th and 59th Streets. At the time, this cluster of eight apartment houses—the

Madrid, Cordoba, Granada, Valencia, Lisbon, Barcelona, Saragossa, and Tolosa—were said to be the finest and largest of their type in the world, and with their lavishly decorated spacious rooms, they served for many years as models of what a luxurious and well-appointed apartment house should be.

Also called the Navarro Buildings (named after their builder Juan de Navarro) or Spanish Flats, this residential complex was initially planned as a cooperative venture, but shortly after completion was converted into a conventional rental arrangement. Each building contained thirteen apartments; some were duplex apartments with a split-level arrangement allowing for a reduced ceiling height in the kitchen and servants' wing. A vehicular service tunnel facilitated the servicing of the buildings through their basements (Price 1914, 74–76). The buildings were demolished in 1927, and the only reminder of their former existence is the nearby Navarro Hotel.

Hubert built several other cooperative apartment houses in New York City, including the Hawthorne, the Hubert, the Rembrandt, and the Mount Morris, as well as apartment houses at 80 and 121 Madison Avenue.

Built in 1883, the 121 Madison Avenue building was one of the original Hubert Home Clubs. It contained five duplex apartments on every second floor. The apartments were relatively large and compact, but they had only one bathroom per apartment in addition to a toilet for servants.

Rental apartment houses received a boost from those builders who realized the long-term benefits to be derived from well-constructed buildings. This trend was obviously more prevalent in the construction of luxury multifamily dwellings.

Perhaps the most famous of luxury apartment buildings in New York was built in 1884 on Central Park West between 72nd and 73rd Streets and designed by Hardenbergh. Like the Vancorlear, this chateauesque apartment complex was initiated by Edward Severin Clark, head of the Singer Sewing Machine Company, who bought a large plot adjacent to Central Park before the landscaping of the park was completed and who foresaw the site's potential for future residential development. The

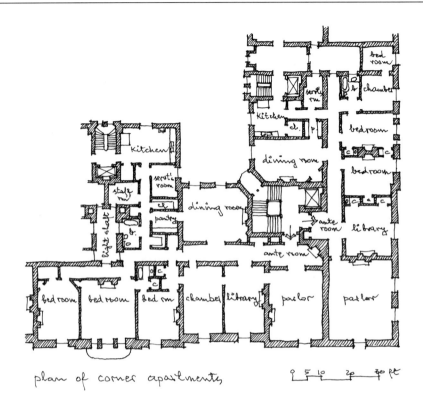

plan of corner apartments

New York City: The Dakota apartments

building site on West 72nd Street was at a considerable distance from the center of the city, which prompted one skeptic to label it as far from civilization as the Dakota Territories. This comment caught Clark's fancy and he named the building the Dakota.

In compliance with the official distinction made between an apartment house and a tenement, the Dakota's sixty-five suites, ranging in size from four to twenty rooms, had access to a full range of centralized services including electricity generated in its own power plant, central heating, and elevator service. To stress the luxurious nature of the building, an additional array of amenities was introduced: a baronial dining hall serving a daily table d'hôte for tenants and their private parties, complemented by a well-stocked wine cellar that supplied wine to the communal or private dining rooms upon request. A playroom and a gymnasium were provided under the mansard roof for tenants' children and, since the original site of the Dakota extended beyond the building proper, a lovely pleasure garden as well as croquet lawns and

private tennis courts were also provided. To prevent the odor of horses from bothering the Dakota's tenants, their stables were located at an acceptable distance from the building, on the southeast corner of 75th Street and Broadway.

The general layout of the apartments was improved with an en-suite arrangement parallel to a corridor access. Parlors, libraries, and principal bedrooms faced the street, while the dining room, not unlike its French counterpart, as well as secondary bedrooms, kitchens, and ancillary spaces including servants' rooms opened upon a large central courtyard. This courtyard provided both unity and privacy to the building and gave adequate light and air to rooms facing it.

Vertical access to the apartments was gained through a staircase and an elevator appropriately located in each of the four corners of the courtyard, while service stairs and service elevators at mid-block served kitchens.

The reception rooms and principal bedrooms were generous in size and paneled and wainscoted in hard wood in a pleasing design; the ceiling height throughout the apartment was in excess of 13 ft (3.9 m).

The Dakota was built as a fireproof structure with solid 28-in (71-cm) thick masonry walls on the lower floors diminishing to 12 in (30 cm) on the upper ones. These load-bearing walls supported soundproof floors resting on iron beams 3 to 4 ft (91 to 121 cm) on center.

The design of the seven-story building's façades was reminiscent of a Renaissance chateau with a steep roof, gables, dormers, oriels, finials, and other ornaments that took master mason John Banta four years to complete. The main entrance to the building was from 72nd Street through a porte cochere leading to the courtyard and was guarded by a doorman in a brass sentry box.

With all dwellings rented prior to opening day, the Dakota was an instant success and the long list of would-be tenants—still the case today—was a measure of its prestige. The Dakota's success prompted the construction of many other residential buildings in New York and even its name was emulated in apartment houses such as the Nevada on Broadway at 69th Street, the Iroquois at 53 West 44th Street, not to mention the Mohawk and the Minnewaska, both at the corners of 88th Street and Central Park West.

Central Park West, with its nearly 2-mile (3.2-km) long frontage on the park, was developed as an almost continuous row of apartment houses before the dawn of the twentieth century. Most of these buildings, however, were far inferior to the Dakota and often featured a U- or H-shaped plan with a deep and narrow "slot" towards the street, presumably to increase the frontage of the building with a view on the park. Rooms opening upon the slot were usually dark and had but a very oblique view to the park if one stood at the window. Characterized by the frequent use of bay or bow windows on their façades, these buildings rarely exceeded eight stories in height.

The interior courtyard of ample proportion, as exemplified in the Dakota, was also later copied by designers of large apartment buildings. Examples are the Graham Court, with its landscaped courtyard and a fountain in the center (built in 1900 on

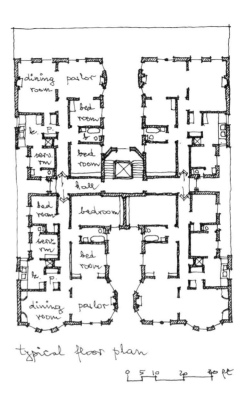

New York City: "H" plan apartment house (after C. Israels)

Seventh Avenue between 116th and 117th Streets; Clinton and Russell, architects), the Belnord (built in 1908 and occupying the entire city block between Broadway, 86th Street, Amsterdam Avenue, and 87th Street; H. Hobart Weekes, architect), and the Apthorp (built by the Astor Estate, also in 1908, on Broadway between 78th and 79th Streets; Clinton and Russell, architects).

As in the Dakota, the main staircases and passenger elevators of the Apthorp were at the corners of the courtyard. The building was designed as a twelve-story fireproof luxury apartment house with 110 self-contained apartments, seven of them duplex apartments. Both duplex and simplex units had exceptionally large reception rooms. "The decoration in the apartments showed great diversity, running the gamut from Elizabethan to Adams to Colonial, from Francis I to Louis XVI, with Louis XIV and XV thrown in for good measure" (Tauranac 1985, 241). Radiators below windowsills and hidden behind wainscoting, ice-making machines in kitchens, and mail chutes on stair landings were

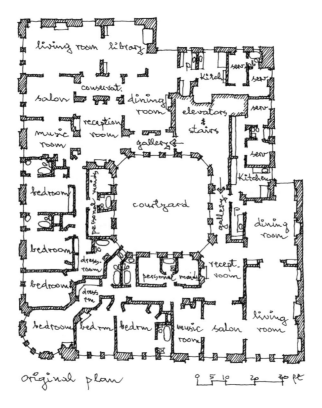

New York City: Alwyn Court
(after A. Alpern)

new amenities introduced in this building. Serviced rooms on the twelfth floor were available for tenants' houseguests, and a large playroom for children was provided on the roof (Handlin 1979, 220).

The courtyard of the Apthorp was landscaped with flower beds, two fountains, and several benches; in addition, the building also had a roof garden with a pergola-shaded promenade from which tenants and guests alike could enjoy spectacular vistas of Manhattan as well as views across the Hudson River to New Jersey.

An unusually handsome thirteen-story luxury apartment house, with a small interior courtyard, was built in 1907 by Alwyn Ball Jr. at 182 West 58th Street, on the southeast corner of Seventh Avenue. Designed in French Renaissance splendor by the architects Harde and Short, the Alwyn Court originally contained twenty-two exceptionally spacious fourteen-room apartment units with five baths, two apartments to a floor. Decorated with

marble and hardwood paneling, most principal rooms faced the street, while secondary rooms opened upon the interior courtyard; kitchen windows as well as those of servants' rooms faced light shafts.

In addition to large living rooms with wood-burning fireplaces and paneled dining rooms, many apartments also featured libraries or billiard rooms, salons, reception rooms, music rooms, conservatories, and a Paris-inspired gallery instead of a hall. Principal bedrooms, some with white enameled woodwork and silk wall hangings, were designed as sumptuous retreats with private baths and dressing rooms, the latter with large storage closets and full-length mirrors. Each apartment also had access to a central wine cellar.

Following the Depression the number of tenants who could afford such luxurious accommodation diminished considerably and necessitated the conversion of the building into smaller apartments. Edgar Ellinger, the building's new owner, gutted Alwyn Court and resubdivided it with the financial assistance of the Drydock Savings Bank. The original twenty-two apartment suites were replaced by seventy-five smaller units ranging in size from three to five rooms (Alpern 1975, 54).

More recently, Alwyn Court experienced yet another conversion. In the beginning of the 1980s the building's ornate façade was cleansed of the grime and dirt accumulated over the decades and its damaged ornaments were painstakingly restored. The courtyard was covered with a glazed pyramidal skylight and converted into an enclosed atrium, not only to beautify a former gloomy air-shaft, but also to conserve energy. The walls of the atrium were painted in gray tints to represent architectural elements in relief. This grisaille mural, in conjunction with a new marble paved floor, transformed the former grimy court into a beautiful space in keeping with the luxurious appearance of its street façade and interior decor (Beyer, Blinder & Belle 1984, 37–38).

STUDIO APARTMENT HOUSES

At the turn of the century a need for studio apartments was expressed by some New York City artists, who wanted a building that combined working studio space with comfortable living quarters. In fact, such a studio building, specifically for artists, had already been built in 1857 at 51–55 West 10th Street by Richard Morris Hunt for James Boorman Johnson. The architect himself occupied space with his extensive library in the Studio Building and conducted his atelier-based architectural instruction from there. Although this building became the center of the city's artistic life, it took several decades before demands for new studio buildings were voiced.

The landscape painter Henry W. Ranger rekindled the studio apartment house concept as a cooperative venture and succeeded, with ten artists and the builder William J. Taylor, in raising the required capital to realize his dream. Designed by

Pollard and Steinman, Ranger's studio apartment house, at 27 West 67th Street, became a success from the very outset, not only in terms of meeting the desired residential and studio needs of his artist partners, who occupied half the building, but the rent generated from the other half of the apartment building produced a handsome 23 percent return on their investment.

The architects had designed a fourteen-story building with each set of two floors containing one corner duplex unit and six studio apartments. All studios, 18 ft (5.5 m) high, had northern exposures and abutted the two-story living quarters of their occupants, with a parlor and dining room at the lower level and bedrooms above. To prevent blocking the ideal lighting of their studios, the cooperative also acquired adjacent lots where multistoried buildings, if developed, could interfere with the proper illumination of their workplaces.

In 1906, after the completion of the building, Taylor embarked on a similar building project for another group of cooperative members at 131–135 East 66th Street, on the northeast corner of Lexington Avenue. Charles A. Platt, whose designs for private residences were much admired by the artists of this cooperative, was the architect. Platt designed an Italian Renaissance palazzo-inspired façade and kept an apartment in the building for himself (Tauranac 1985, 170–71).

Two years later another cooperative studio apartment house with a heavily ornate neo-Gothic façade was built at 44 West 77th Street. The architects Harde and Short adopted an H-shaped plan for this building, which accommodated two apartment units on each typical floor. Studios with lofty ceilings occupied the central bays with the largest studio, 25 ft by 44 ft (7.6 by 13.4 m), on the top floor. Staggered floors account for the side bays of the main façade being fourteen stories high in comparison with the eight stories of the central bays. Although the building still stands, it is hardly recognizable because much of its façade adornment was removed because of deterioration caused by air pollution (Alpern 1975, 60–61).

A building venture that is a financial success invariably breeds imitation. And this was certainly

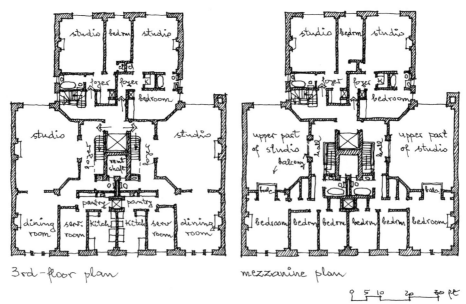

3rd-floor plan

mezzanine plan

New York City: Studio apartment house
(after David P. Handlin)

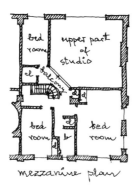

mezzanine plan

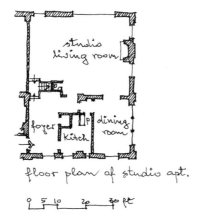

floor plan of studio apt.

New York City: Hôtel des Artistes
(after A. Alpern)

the case with studio apartment buildings. But in addition, the success of this building type was further enhanced by the fact that its unusual interior spaces caught the fancy of tenants other than artists, who realized that the two-story studio space, with the added romantic touch of balconies at mezzanine level, was equally attractive as a room for soirees and other entertainments. Thus, it also became chic for well-to-do literati and connoisseurs of art to live in studio apartments, but in contrast to artists, these tenants preferred windows with a southern orientation. And builders responded to the new demand.

Perhaps the most famous cooperative studio apartment house in New York City is the Hôtel des Artistes, located at 1 West 67th Street. Built in 1916, this building was designed by George Mort Pollard and combined features of an apartment hotel and studio apartment house. A communal kitchen, restaurant, theater, ballroom, swimming pool, and squash courts were the collective amenities accessible to the occupants. Most apartments had fireplaces in their double-height studios and featured balcony bedrooms at the upper level. The decor was primarily English Gothic in the interior as well as on the street façade, the latter with carved stone figures representing the arts (Alpern 1975, 90–91).

Some of the original collective facilities are now converted into small apartments and the ballroom and theater serve as television studios. The restaurant is still in use as the chic Café des Artistes.

APARTMENT HOTELS

In the late nineteenth and early twentieth centuries, apartment hotels—North American counterparts of the English catering flats—enjoyed great popular appeal in New York. There were many reasons for the attraction of these apartment-house hybrids.

First, American hotels gained great respectability during the nineteenth century when luxurious Palace hotels (named after the famous Palace Hotel in San Francisco, which cost $5,000,000 and had 1,000 rooms and 500 baths) were built in most large cities. No longer associated with crowded inns, hotels offered their guests sumptuous accommodation, impeccable service, and mechanical ingenuity. When the Plaza Hotel opened in New York, for example, several millionnaires, including Alfred G. Vanderbilt, George G. Gould, C. K. J. Billings, and Mrs. Oliver Harriman, rented corner suites with a view over Central Park South and Fifth Avenue as their permanent residence.

Second, as it became increasingly difficult to hire reliable domestic help, especially in large cities where many rewarding employment opportunities existed, the apartment hotel solved the "servant problem." Since apartment hotels introduced a domestic organization with service provided by personnel responsible to management, they had no problem recruiting help, because it was felt that the degrading social status of "servant" did not apply to service employees.

Third, many well-to-do people whose permanent residence was in the countryside desired to maintain a smaller city residence for the social season, without the burden of having to staff it.

Apartment hotels were ideal for a second home or a pied à terre in the city with perfectly trained servants at instant call.

Fourth, by the late nineteenth century an increase in the number of nontraditional households, such as well-to-do singles, affluent childless couples and wealthy retired people, created a demand for a new residential building type which offered the conveniences of a hotel, but where the occupants were long-term residents rather than transient guests.

Finally, due to the interpretation that dwelling suites in apartment hotels were not self-contained because they lacked individual kitchen facilities for preparing meals, they were not subject to the city's strict tenement house law. Instead of kitchens, hotel apartment suites usually had a service pantry equipped with storage cabinets, refrigerator, and sink, but no stove. Moreover, the law was also more lenient in hotel construction with respect to the location of bathrooms, which, in contrast to regular apartment units or even tenement dwellings, could be interior spaces without direct access to daylight or ventilation. Hence, it is not surprising that many real estate speculators and builders took advantage of the existing demand for apartment hotels as well as the leniency of the law governing them, to erect many of these new building types in New York City. By the early 1930s about 15,000 families lived in 150 apartment hotels in New York City alone (Ruttenbaum 1986, 99).

Initially, apartment hotels such as the Arlington, designed by the architectural firm Israels & Harder, were relatively small buildings on two typical New York City lots with a combined frontage of 50 ft (15.25 m) and were modeled on London catering flats with apartments ranging from one bed-sitting room to three-room suites in size. Other buildings such as the Chelsea, at 222 West 23rd Street, however, were much larger structures.

Designed and built in 1883 by Philip Hubert, the Chelsea was an apartment hotel operated primarily as a cooperative. One-third of the ninety original apartments were rented, as well as the commercial spaces at ground-floor level, but the rest of the

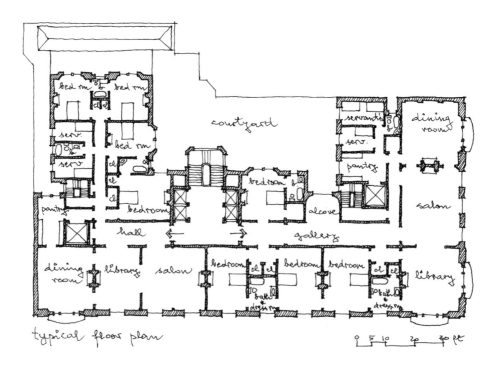

typical floor plan

New York City: Astor apartment hotel
(after C. Israels)

apartments were occupied by members of the cooperative. Apartment units ranged in size from three to nine rooms, and many had no kitchen facilities, since occupants were expected to use the large public or smaller private dining rooms operated by a restaurant on the ground floor. Apartment hotels like the Chelsea and the Sevilla on 58th Street were "intended to meet the wants of people who desired to combine the freedom from care of a hotel life with the comforts and privacy of an individual home" (Price 1914, 75).

By far the most palatial apartment hotel built in the first decade of the twentieth century was the Ansonia, at 2107 Broadway between 73rd and 74th Streets. It was indeed built to combine the comforts of a hotel with the privacy of a home for affluent people.

William Earl Dodge Stokes, its builder, hired the French-trained architect Paul Émile M. Duboy to design this New York landmark evoking the grandeur of Parisian belle époque architecture. Its façades were covered with ornament and the two street corners marked by exquisite towers.

Erected in 1903, the sixteen-story Ansonia represented the ultimate luxury apartment hotel living in a fireproof and soundproof building. Filtered hot, cold, and ice water, as well as filtered heated air in winter, and cooled air in summer, were provided to all dwelling suites. The suites ranged in size from one to eighteen rooms, the latter with three bathrooms and four toilets. The 122 large suites were known as housekeeping apartments and their occupants had their own kitchens, while tenants in the 200 bachelor apartments (some of which were furnished) were expected to use the catering facilities. Meals were served either in the privacy of the suites or in one of the restaurants.

After its completion, the Ansonia was hailed as the largest and best equipped residential hotel. Electric power, for example, was generated in the cellar of the building and supplied power to 2,710 rooms and domestic offices in addition to the public spaces. House telephones connected each dwelling unit to a central switchboard, and pneumatic tubes linked the apartments to the manager's office.

The principal communal spaces on the ground floor consisted of a large Louis IX–style dining room with a seating capacity of 550 guests, a grill room with a cafe, and an assembly room with a palm court garden. A bank, a drug store, and a flower shop were the building's commercial outlets at sidewalk level. On the sixteenth floor was a banquet hall that could accommodate one thousand diners at large tables. And part of the roof level was landscaped as "a garden where orchestras played on long summer nights" (Tauranac 1985, 237). In the basement were the kitchen, the laundry, cold-storage room for furs, safe-deposit vaults, a 100-ft (30.5-m) long swimming pool, Turkish baths, a car repair shop, and a series of commercial outlets such as a grocery store, barbershop, and manicuring parlor. Finally, there were billiard rooms and private dining rooms in the building for the exclusive use of tenants. The management of all these facilities was entrusted to Gurnsey E. Webb, who was induced by Stokes to leave the Plaza Hotel, to ensure smooth operation of his building.

Stokes's own luxurious apartment was on the sixteenth floor, close to a minifarm he installed on the roof, where he raised chickens and goats; "the chicken eggs he sold at discounted prices to tenants, the goat's milk he kept for himself to drink and make cheese" (Tauranac 1985, 237).

Concurrently with the Ansonia, other apartment hotels were built on the Upper West Side, usually in the baroque style. A brownstone apartment hotel, called Hotel Lucerne, located at 201 West 79th Street and designed by Harry B. Mulliken, was an exception. But it was decades before an apartment hotel approximated either the luxury or the size of the Ansonia.

Not everybody was enchanted with the concept of apartment-hotel living. The large ones, such as the Ansonia, were especially subjected to severe criticism. Their foes claimed that these buildings were patronized by bohemians, that they fostered domestic irresponsibility, destroyed everything implied by "home," and therefore represented the most dangerous enemy of American domesticity (Handlin 1979, 403). In spite of these accusations, apartment-hotel living continued to enjoy popular support and attract many urban dwellers who appreciated the affordable housekeeping services available to them.

CHAPTER FIVE

TWENTIETH-CENTURY HOUSING: 1900–1950

DOMESTIC REVIVAL IN GREAT BRITAIN

With the death of Queen Victoria in 1901, the Victorian Age did not come to a sudden halt, but continued, slightly modified, as the Edwardian Age. The transition in domestic design from the nineteenth to the twentieth century was bridged by the Arts and Crafts and Garden City movements, which were both rooted in the nineteenth century. The Arts and Crafts movement that initiated the Domestic Revival reached its golden age at the turn of the century and continued well into the twentieth century. The Garden City movement also did so; it was essentially a confirmation of a trend that existed decades before the turn of the century, when many well-to-do families abandoned their homes in the city for new ones in the countryside.

In 1884 a talented group of young architects, devoted to the prophets of the Arts and Crafts movement and committed to the improvement of domestic design, formed the Art Workers' Guild. Instead of following classical and medieval architectural styles, they sought design inspiration from indigenous rural buildings in Britain and they became known as "free-style" architects. Ernest Newton and Ernest Grimson, among other members of the guild, designed new homes that were, at

times, difficult to distinguish from old indigenous cottages.

Domestic Revival is characterized by simplicity, informality, wholesomeness, good craftsmanship, honest use of building materials, and a healthy respect for the physical environment. Gabled and half-hipped tiled roofs, high chimney stacks, tile-hung walls, dormers, oriels with glazing bars, and windows with glazing bars were some typical design features borrowed from indigenous rural cottages.

At the turn of the century, the English house became a synonym for the "exemplary" home and was publicized by Hermann Muthesius in his three-volume work *Das englische Haus* (1903). English domestic architecture influenced residential work throughout Europe, but its impact was most significant in North America, where the availability of inexpensive land encouraged country living, and where the flight of city dwellers to the "suburbs" had already begun.

The practice of free-style architecture was not limited to members of the Guild, as exemplified by the work of Charles F. A. Voysey, M. H. Baillie Scott, Charles Rennie Mackintosh, and Edwin Landseer Lutyens. These four architects, although not members of the Guild, were notable practitioners of free-style architecture.

Voysey's commissions involved primarily the design of moderate-sized country houses for clients of the upper-middle income group. His

Somerset Cottage
(after A. Quincy)

Gloucestershire Cottage
(after H. Allingham and S. Dick)

Stoneywell Cottage, Ulvercroft (1898–99), Ernest Gimson
(after A. Service)

buildings, usually two stories, had simple volumes with steeply pitched slate roofs and walls finished in white roughcast. The window openings, with stone reveals, were often grouped horizontally, and he playfully used various building elements indigenous to rural cottages, such as buttresses and hood-molds (moldings above windows that repel water), to enliven the façades. Nevertheless, his homes were essentially ornament-free and sparsely furnished, projecting a peaceful image in both form and color. He paid special attention to the fireplace area, or "inglenook," and favored untreated oak paneling and oak furniture wherever possible.

Instead of the customary 10-ft (3.05-m) ceiling height, Voysey used relatively low ceilings; he preferred 9 ft (2.75 m) for principal spaces, and 8 ft (2.44 m), or even 7 ft 9 in (2.36 m) for other rooms. Apart from obvious economic considerations, he felt that the lower ceilings enhanced the comfort of rooms; lower ceilings not only made rooms seem cozier and larger, they made them

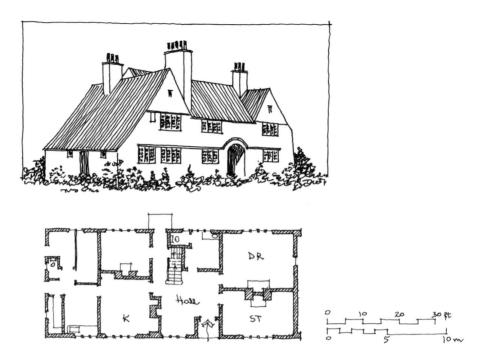

The Orchard, Chorley Wood (1899), plan and perspective, C. F. A. Voysey
(after A. Service)

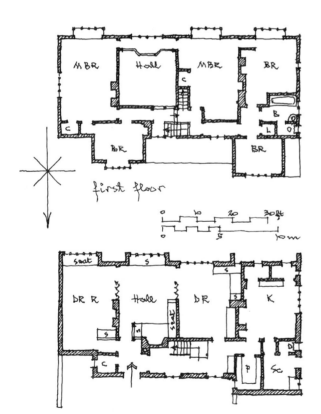

An Ideal Suburban House (1894–95), two plans,
M. H. Baillie Scott
(after Peter Davey)

easier to heat in winter. So consistent was Voysey's interior design vocabulary that in Nikolaus Pevsner's opinion, if one saw one of his houses, one saw them all.

Voysey's contemporary, M. H. Baillie Scott, published an article entitled "An Ideal Suburban House" (1894–95) in *The Studio* (an influential arts periodical of the time), and in it presented a new design for a two-story house with all principal rooms facing south. Adhering to deep-rooted medieval traditions, a lofty two-story hall with an inglenook and large open fireplace was envisaged as the central gathering place of the home, the main family room. At the ground-floor level the hall linked the drawing room to the dining room, while its lofty upper part separated two master bedrooms; however, in keeping with medieval design traditions in hall-type urban houses, a gallery linked these bedrooms to each other.

A famous Scottish architect of this period was Charles Rennie Mackintosh, married to Margaret Macdonald, an artist in her own right. In great contrast to the typical dark, overcrowded interiors of the time, with papered walls and somber upholstery,

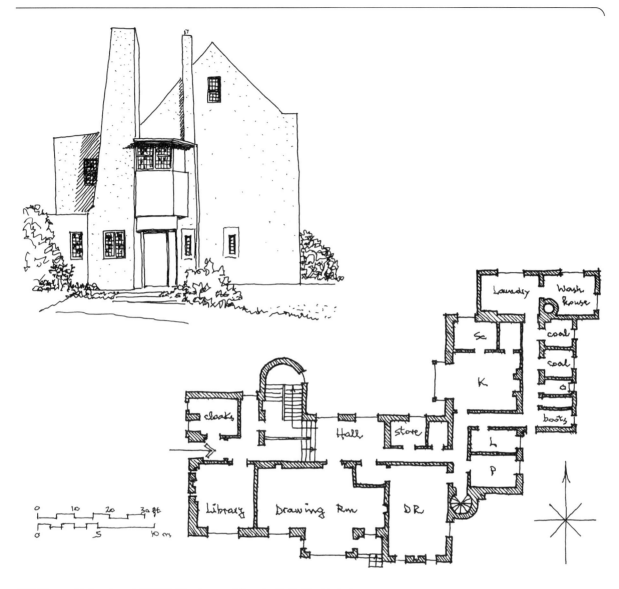

Hill House, Helensburgh (1902–5), plan and façade, C. R. Mackintosh
(after R. MacLeod)

the Japanese-inspired Mackintosh dwelling was airy, with white painted walls, white carpets, and a whitewashed fireplace. The exquisite furniture appeared to have been made more for art than comfort, nevertheless numerous visitors to their Glasgow dwelling were awed by the ambience.

In keeping with Scottish tradition, Mackintosh's domestic buildings had steep roofs, pronounced gables, and massive chimney-stacks. The stone walls were finished externally with "harling" (Scottish stucco or plaster) and, in response to the harsh climate, the windows were relatively small. The interiors of his buildings were reposeful and charming in a very original way and, like Voysey, Mackintosh also sought to achieve unity between the spaces he designed and the furniture they contained.

Edwin Lutyens emerged as yet another inventive turn-of-the-century architect whose buildings were Arts and Crafts–inspired. With the sympathetic use of textured gables (at times built of secondhand bricks), dominating chimneys, and steep roof planes built of traditional materials, all complemented by a pleasant landscape setting, Lutyens's work evoked a romantic appreciation of the vernacular. Not only were the exteriors of his

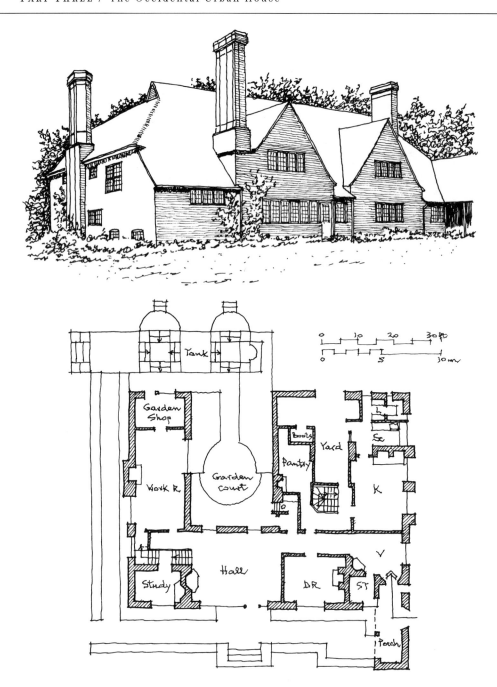

Munstead Wood, Godalming (1897), plan and perspective, Edwin Lutyens
(after D. O'Neil)

buildings appealing and comfortable, but so were the principal rooms of his houses, which often had matte gray rather than shiny oak paneling.

In collaboration with landscape architect Gertrude Jekyll, Lutyens built several homes distinguished by a heretofore unparalleled relationship between house and garden. Jekyll's own house, Munstead Wood (1897) at Godalming, Surrey, and

Deanery Garden (1902) at Sonning, Berkshire, designed for Edward Hudson, the founder of *Country Life* magazine, are but two examples of Lutyens's free-style work before he became more eclectic in his style.

Two additional architects, Richard Barry Parker and Raymond Unwin, contributed to the popularization of the Arts and Crafts movement, especially

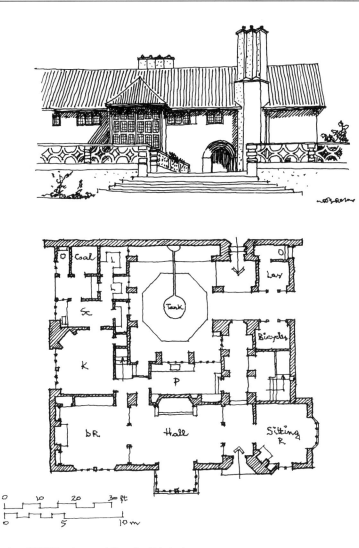

Deanery Garden, Sonning (1902), plan and façade, Edwin Lutyens
(after D. O'Neil)

in the domain of town planning and in the design of small servantless houses and moderate-sized middle-class dwellings built in garden cities and garden suburbs. Inspired by traditional English village greens with houses set well back from the roadway, Parker and Unwin introduced a common green space, the "close," to residential neighborhoods.

Characteristically, the domestic interiors of houses designed by Parker and Unwin reflected simplicity, with few pieces of furniture, uncarpeted floors, and plain walls enlivened only by the play of light and shade on their surfaces. In contrast to this general plainness, a cozy recess, or inglenook, with a brick-lined hearth, copper hood, and wood-

en benches, invariably formed the "homey" part of the house. The exterior of their cottage-style houses, with low bay windows, was informal, asymmetrical, and usually picturesque. Parker and Unwin's design and planning principles are clearly defined in *The Art of Building a Home* (1901).

In the wake of the Industrial Revolution, a craving for nature, elbowroom, and wholesomeness obsessed most city dwellers, and a marriage of town and country became a logical objective. This ideal was achieved by Ebenezer Howard's Letchworth Garden City and Dame Henrietta Barnett's Hampstead Garden Suburb—two turn-of-the-century communities featuring exemplary urban design and domestic architecture, much of it

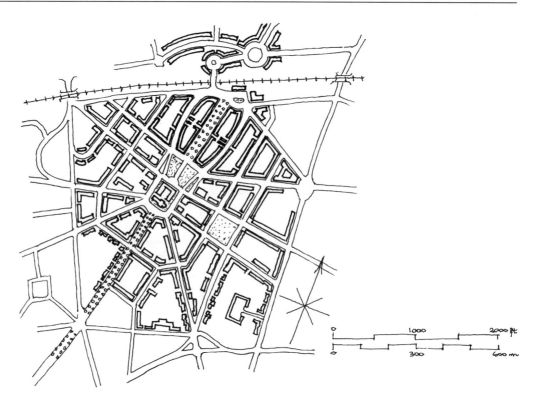

Letchworth Garden City (1904), Parker and Unwin
(after F. Jackson)

attributed to Parker and Unwin. Unfortunately, the majority of people seeking a home in a town and country environment had to settle for suburbs rather than garden cities.

LETCHWORTH

Letchworth was the first garden city built according to the tenets developed by Ebenezer Howard. An idealist and a keen observer of the social struggle that followed industrialization, both in England and in North America (he lived in Chicago from 1872 to 1876), Howard proposed a new town policy of "garden cities" to relieve the pressure that had brought about overgrown urban centers, congested living, and, worst of all, the impoverishment of the human spirit.

Howard formulated three important planning principles for the Garden City movement. First, to prevent the speculative spiral of increased land values, permanent ownership of the entire urban development area was to be held by the municipality and turned over to private lands by means

of leasehold only. Second, the compact self-contained urban community's population was to be restricted to about 30,000 inhabitants. Third, the interdependence of urban and rural development patterns, a marriage of "town and country," was to offer the best of two worlds. Howard's town planning ideas were not attributable to any single influence, but arose from many unrelated sources, including Henry George's economic theories and Edward Bellamy's utopian romance *Looking Backward*. A famous quote attributed to Howard reads: "I have taken a leaf out of the books of each type of reformer and bound them together by a thread of practicality" (Purdom 1949, 387).

The main feature of Letchworth's master plan was a radial road network with a broad avenue linking the town center with the railway station. At the outset, before the trees matured, streets looked rather barren, but today its residents truly live in a garden setting. Especially charming are the smaller residential streets, like Rushby Mead, which "capture the originally intended balance between nature and architecture, with the plain gables

Rushby Mead, Letchworth
(after W. L. Creese)

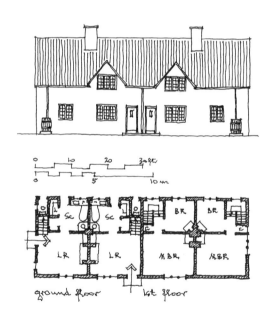

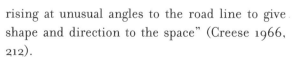

Small four-room cottages, Letchworth (1904–5),
Parker and Unwin
(after F. Jackson)

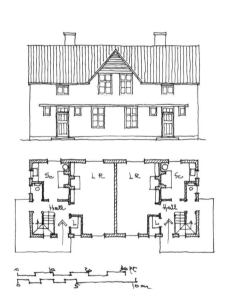

Sycamore Avenue Cottages, Eastwick (1905), R. Unwin
(after F. Jackson)

rising at unusual angles to the road line to give shape and direction to the space" (Creese 1966, 212).

Heeding Unwin's admonishment "nothing gained by overcrowding," Parker and Unwin introduced an array of sensitive, low-density, housing clusters, often grouped along green common spaces. Typically, cottages were built with prominent gables and steep roofs with dormer windows, features that gave a pleasing rhythm and unity to residential areas. The layout of the Pixmore Hill area (1905), for example, with clusters of cottages facing a common green in front and allotment gardens in the rear, anticipates the "superblock"

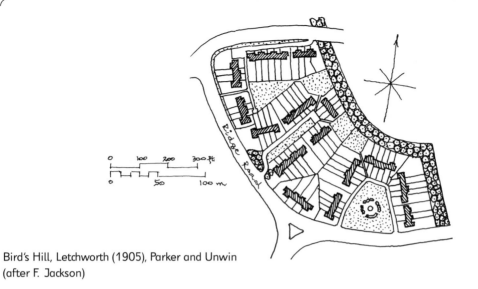

Bird's Hill, Letchworth (1905), Parker and Unwin
(after F. Jackson)

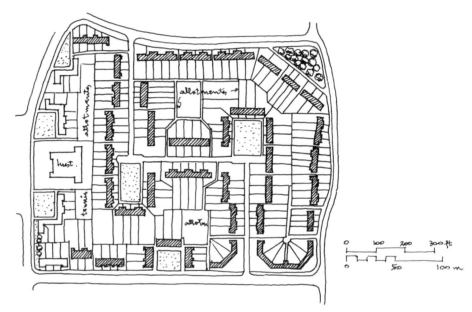

Pixmore Hill, Letchworth (1905), Parker and Unwin
(after F. Jackson)

concept introduced by Henry Wright and Clarence Stein decades later.

Few people could afford the detached villa. Semidetached houses, quadrexes (rows of four attached houses) and conventional attached cottages, or terraced houses, were more affordable dwelling types that allowed a broader range of income groups to enter the housing market. A cluster of smaller four-room cottages, designed by Parker and Unwin, exemplifies the more modest home available to moderate-income families of the garden city.

Conceived by Ebenezer Howard, low-rise cooperative housekeeping quadrangles were also built in Letchworth. Homesgarth (1909–13) and Meadow Way Green (1915–24) are two examples of these quadrangles whose residents had access to food-catering services in a common dining room and house-cleaning service by in-house staff in their private dwellings. These residential quadrangles were designed for well-off, childless, or elderly residents to ease the burden of housekeeping while still providing self-contained private dwellings.

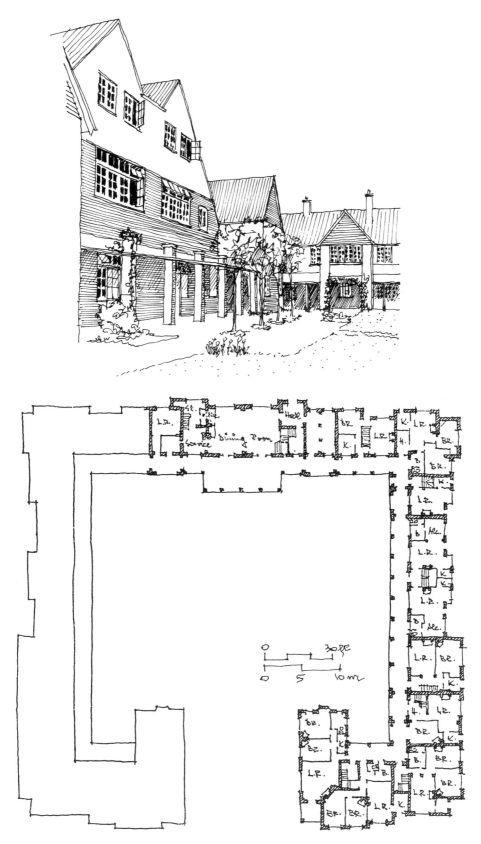

Homesgarth, Letchworth (1909–13), plan and perspective, A. Chapham Lander
(after C. B. Purdom)

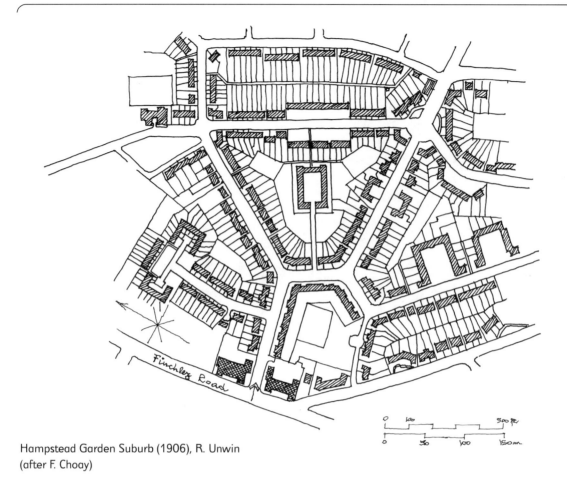

Hampstead Garden Suburb (1906), R. Unwin
(after F. Choay)

HAMPSTEAD GARDEN SUBURB

Three late Victorians—Dame Henrietta Barnett, Sir Raymond Unwin, and Sir Edwin Lutyens—were credited with the establishment of Hampstead Garden Suburb, but its inception is mainly due to Henrietta Barnett's efforts to build a garden suburb where desirable homes, including villas and modest cottages, would be available to a broad segment of society. The community was conceived to be in harmony with nature, with homes reflecting a "cottage" style of domesticity. The two principal design objectives of Unwin's master plan were, (1) to afford vistas from every part of the community towards the open countryside and, (2) to design the street network of the community for the benefit of those living there rather than for people merely passing through. Work on the construction of the community began in May 1907.

The urban design concept of Hampstead Garden Suburb reveals some influences derived from the

Artisan's living room (1902), R. Unwin
(after F. Jackson)

work of Camillo Sitte, whose *City Planning According to Artistic Fundamentals* was familiar to Unwin. Translated into several languages, Sitte's book had an unequivocal impact upon fin de siècle architects and town planners.

Meadway houses, Hampstead Garden Suburb (1908–9), M. H. Baillie Scott
(after W. L. Creese)

Lucas Crescent, Hampstead Garden Suburb (c. 1906), T. G. Lucas
(after W. L. Creese)

Inspired by William Morris and the Arts and Crafts movement, Sitte, an Austrian architect, profusely illustrated his manuscript (made during his extensive travels in European countries) with numerous sketches of pleasant urban spaces. He discovered, for example, that dramatic effect in medieval or Renaissance urban squares was achieved through sensitivity in spatial formation rather than through imposing dimensions, the latter a design approach often used during the nineteenth century.

Designed by Lutyens, the formal landscaped square of Hampstead Garden Suburb, with two churches and a large public building, was conceived as the center of the community—an antithesis of Sitte's teachings. Sited at the highest point of the development site, this windswept, shopless, and publess public space failed to give the community an animated focus. In contrast, Unwin's arcaded commercial buildings, at the Finchley Road entrance to the suburb, was in the spirit of Camillo Sitte. Other buildings designed by Unwin were the clubhouse, a quadrangle for older people called The Orchard, and several domestic designs. Unwin moved his family and office to the edge of Hampstead Heath to be closer to his work and occupied Wyldes Farm, a large seventeenth-century house with outbuildings and a huge barn.

The two garden communities, Letchworth and Hampstead Garden Suburb, popularized low-density housing unobtainable in traditional cities, and the two communities became so seductive that they inspired similar development elsewhere on the continent. Examples are the *cité-jardins* Epernay and Rosny, near Paris; Le Logis, near Brussels; Hellerau, near Dresden, and Buchschlag, near

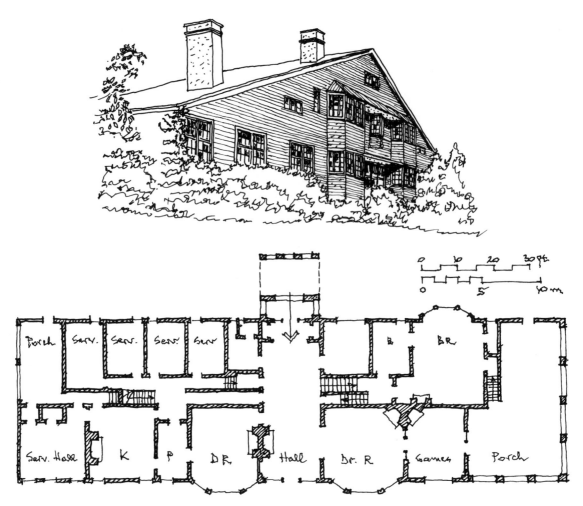

W. G. Low House (1886–87), plan and perspective, McKim, Mead, and White
(after Vincent Scully)

Frankfurt am Main; Käpylä Garden Suburb, near Helsinki; and Wekerle Telep, near Budapest. In fact, several decades after the initiation of the Garden City movement, the prefix "garden" or "cité-jardin" had to be used by protagonists of new planning concepts, such as Soria y Mata's *cité-jardin linéaire* or Le Corbusier's *cité-jardin verticale*, to have a chance for popular acceptance.

ARTS AND CRAFTS IN NORTH AMERICA

The desire for an architecture liberated from the aesthetic rules of the past had already begun in the 1870s and 1880s when, inspired by the East Coast vernacular, several architects designed houses in the Shingle style, a name derived from their external cladding. William Ralph Emerson's country houses, for example, were typical Shingle-style homes with open-plan interiors, built with great sensitivity to their natural surroundings. Other noted architects, such as Henry Hobson Richardson and Charles Follen McKim, also designed remarkable shingle-clad country houses. The Shingle style was also part of the architectural vocabulary used by Bruce Price in his domestic buildings for the resort village of Tuxedo Park in Orange County, New York.

Calvin Milton Woodward, an American educator who studied the work of William Morris in England, founded, in 1880, a manual training

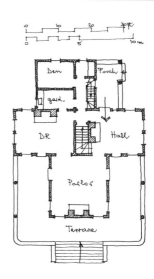

William Kent House, Tuxedo Park, plan and perspective, Bruce Price
(after Vincent Scully)

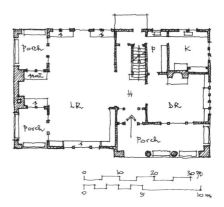

Craftsman House, plan and façade, Gustav Stickley
(after G. Stickley)

school in St. Louis, Missouri, under the administrative direction of Washington University with a curriculum based on Arts and Crafts training. Another milestone in Arts and Crafts development occurred in East Aurora, New York, in 1894, when Elbert Hubbard, with his flat porkpie hat, cape, and flowing tie—an attire also affected by Frank Lloyd Wright years later—founded the Roycroft Press, which, a year later, published the magazine *Philistine*. Emulating William Morris and his disciples, Hubbard praised the fine craftsmanship of articles made before the Industrial Revolution and hoped to banish cluttered bric-a-brac, dust-collecting tasseled draperies, flowered carpets with fringes, and overstuffed ornate furniture from the musty rooms of American homes.

Gustav Stickley, a furniture manufacturer, self-styled architect, and editor of the monthly period-

Inglenook of Craftsman house, Gustav Stickley
(after G. Stickley)

ical *The Craftsman*, visited England in 1898. Upon his return, he tried to persuade Americans to be more sensible in their home designs and to pay greater attention to the objects with which they

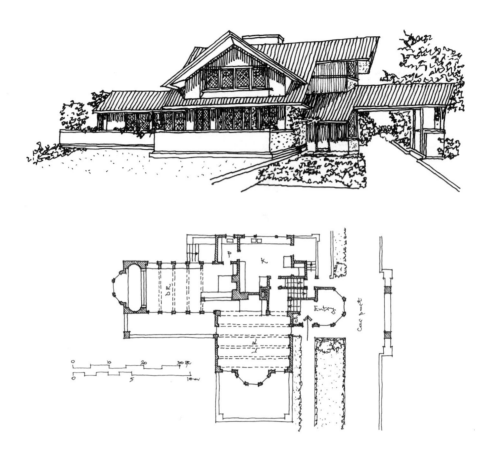

"A Small House with Lots of Room in It," plan and façade,
Frank Lloyd Wright's second design for the *Ladies' Home Journal*

surrounded themselves. He believed in the sanctity and wholesomeness of the home, as well as in the virtues of outdoor life. Stickley, too, rejected both the luxury and clutter of Victorian dwellings, arguing that simple and useful houses were the kind in which children enjoyed growing up and would remember, later in life, with fondness as "homes." His own Mission-style furniture (similar to Shaker furniture) was simple and functional; it can be considered a forerunner of modern chairs, tables, and sofas.

Edward William Bok, editor-in-chief (1889–1919) of the popular *Ladies' Home Journal*, also abhorred lavish interiors. He turned his attention to "wretched" Victorian houses with useless turrets and filigree work erected by builders for people who could not afford to hire an architect. His first attempt, in 1895, to persuade the architectural profession to provide well-designed plans and elevations of small houses through his magazine was fruitless. Eventually, Bok found one architect, William L. Price, who supplied him with a series of drawings for pleasant and affordable homes, and these were published. Later, other architects also prepared house plans for the *Ladies' Home Journal*, including Frank Lloyd Wright, who submitted three designs. The public's response to these designs was positive, and the plans were actually used for the construction of new houses throughout the country. These homes were unique because they had living rooms rather than parlors—Bok considered the latter useless extravagance.

Wilson Eyre's numerous comfortable homes, in what was known as "the Philadelphia residential style," were influenced by the unaffected craftsmanship of the Pennsylvania farmhouse, the Shingle style, and the Arts and Crafts movement. In Chestnut Hill, a suburb of Philadelphia, Eyre

C. A. Potter House, Chestnut Hill (c. 1881), Wilson Eyre
(after Vincent Scully)

designed the Charles Newhall house (c. 1881) with an impressive two-story entrance hall with a grand staircase and a gallery on three sides. In 1901, Eyre founded the magazine *House and Garden* and served as editor until 1905.

The interiors of American homes changed as a consequence of the influence of Hubbard, Stickley, Bok, and Eyre, and the contribution made by Elsie de Wolfe, one of the first professional decorators in America. Stuffy parlors were replaced by living rooms in midsize houses and apartments. In the absence of air conditioning, the use of verandahs and sleeping porches during the hot and humid summer months was quite common, and in warmer climates they were used year-round, often with bamboo and wicker furniture. As homes became more informal at the beginning of the twentieth century, a new feeling of airiness also became evident, and with the founding of the first American Society of Arts and Crafts in Boston, the British Domestic Revival movement officially reached the American continent. Later, chapters of the society were established in other cities, including Chicago, where Frank Lloyd Wright became a member.

Wright's own modest house, built in 1889 in Oak Park (a suburb of Chicago), has many features that resemble the early American Shingle style as well as the free style of British Domestic Revival. His house, a simple unadorned building with a dark brown shingle-clad steep gable facing the street, is strikingly similar to the W. Chandler House designed by Bruce Price in Tuxedo Park; his low Voyseyesque ceilings and traditional inglenook off the living room, with benches facing each other, are typical features of English Domestic Revival designs. Like his English Arts and Crafts contemporaries, Wright believed in the total-work-of-art,

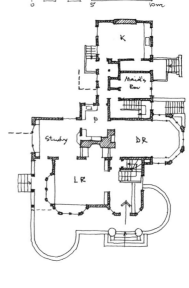

Wright's Oak Park Home (1889), plan and elevation,
(after Y. Z. MacDonough)

Wright's inglenook
(after Y. Z. MacDonough)

Wright's master bedroom
(after Y. Z. MacDonough)

which meant that he designed most of his furniture as well. He preferred the informal life associated with the rural homesteads that he knew from his childhood in Wisconsin, an informal hominess that he strove to recreate in his designs for servantless homes with an open plan and a "workspace" instead of a kitchen.

Charles Sumner Greene, Henry Mather Greene, and Bernard Ralph Maybeck were the most admired West Coast Arts and Crafts architects. The Greene brothers moved to California and designed mostly domestic buildings that reflected not only Arts and Crafts and Shingle-style principles, but also a Japanese design approach. On the way to visit

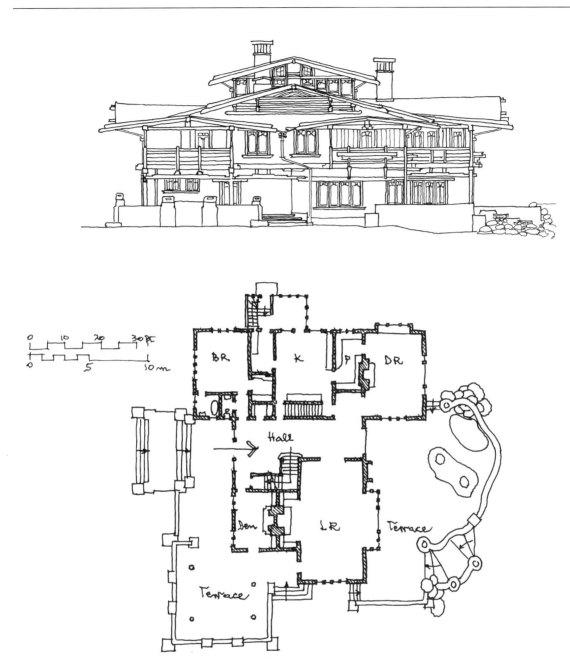

Gamble House, Pasadena (1909), plan and façade, Greene Brothers
(after Esther McCoy)

their parents in Pasadena, the two brothers stopped in Chicago to see the 1893 World's Columbian Exposition, which brought arts and crafts from remote corners of the world to America. Of all the buildings of this exhibition the one that most profoundly affected the Greene brothers was the Japanese pavilion. They were impressed by both the superb craftsmanship and the structural and aesthetic integrity of the building, which embodied the Arts and Crafts principles taught to them in St. Louis by Woodward.

Enchanted by the beautiful landscape of the West Coast, its gentle climate, and the vitality of its people, the Greene brothers permanently settled in

California. Built mainly of wood, the Greene brothers' elaborately detailed homes, in combination with their furniture and landscape design, formed an impressive unity. This is best illustrated by the much acclaimed David B. Gamble House (1908). Less spectacular, but perhaps of greater importance, were the dozens of homes designed for families of more modest means—small flat-gabled wooden bungalows with wide projecting roofs, a house form said to have complemented the more casual domestic lifestyle identified with the West Coast.

Bungalows originated in India and were adaptations by British colonial officers of indigenous Bengali huts called *bangala* for their own use. Admirably suited for a hot and humid climate, other colonies soon adopted them. The main characteristic of this building type was a high-ceilinged double living and dining room, lit and ventilated by clerestory windows; two large shaded verandahs, front and back, served as outdoor extensions of these two principal rooms. Both the living and dining rooms were flanked by bedroom suites, also lit and ventilated from above, each with a set of private dressing and bathrooms; the latter had an outside entrance to allow easy access for servants. This unique arrangement protected the walls of principal rooms from being heated excessively by the sun; the dressing and bathrooms shielded the bedroom from the sun, just as the bedroom shielded walls of principal rooms from the sun. To avoid cooking odors in the house, the kitchen was invariably placed in a separate building, at the rear of the property and next to the servants' quarters.

Upon their return to England, colonial administrators first built bungalows as second homes near the seaside, and soon realized that bungalows were convenient and particularly well-suited for elderly retired couples in contrast to conventional two-level cottages and town houses. Thus, by the end of the nineteenth century, bungalows were also built as permanent homes in England's suburbs. In the United States, the first documented use of a bungalow was as a summer house (1880) on Cape Cod, Massachusetts (Duchscherer 1995, 11). Within a decade, bungalows had become so popular that

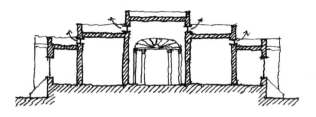

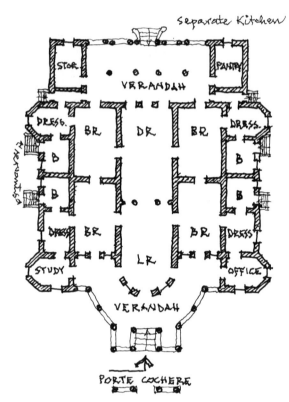

Bungalow, Bangalore, India,
plan and section
(after Janet Pott)

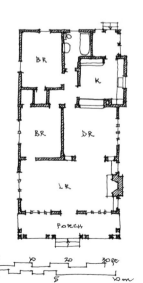

Craftsman-style bungalow,
California, c. 1909,
Henry Wilson
(after P. Duchscherer
and D. Keister)

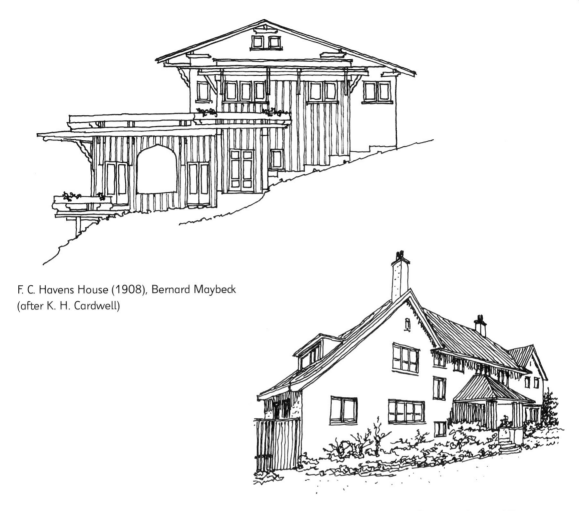

F. C. Havens House (1908), Bernard Maybeck
(after K. H. Cardwell)

W. F. Hunting House, Vancouver (1911), Maclure and Fox
(after H. Kalman)

they were used in several residential neighbor-hoods of California.

Bernard Ralph Maybeck was another Arts and Crafts architect whose homey domestic designs complemented the informal Californian lifestyle. Educated at the Beaux-Arts in Paris, he returned to the United States in 1890 and got a job in San Francisco in the office of A. Page Brown. With his colleagues Willis Polk and A. C. Schweinfurth, Maybeck is credited with designing pleasant unpretentious houses expressive of their wooden structure. His greatest contribution to domestic design was a humane approach that resulted in a unique San Francisco Bay Regional style carried on today by a younger generation of California architects.

Samuel Maclure, a self-educated West Coast architect who studied art for a brief period at the Spring Garden Art School in Philadelphia, was one of the first Canadians to design homes in the spirit of both the English Arts and Crafts and American Shingle style. His initial buildings were probably inspired by Wilson Eyre's houses, but later, in partnership with Cecil Croker Fox, who apprenticed with Voysey before emigrating to Canada, his residential buildings were more Voyseyesque, as exemplified by the Hunting house (1911) in Vancouver, with a whitewashed roughcast front facing the street.

Maclure's Ontario counterpart was Eden Smith, born near Birmingham, who settled in Toronto after unsuccessfully homesteading in Manitoba.

Eden Smith house, Toronto (1896)
(after H. Kalman)

After working for an architect and passing the prescribed examinations, he built his family home (1896) near Toronto's High Park. The front of the house, with a projecting cross-gable, was typically English inspired; the shingled west side, featuring a verandah, resembled the American Shingle style. A two-story oak-paneled hall with a staircase formed the core of the house.

Eden Smith was a prolific architect who designed hundreds of homes in the Toronto area, many for the well-to-do. However, for the typical, and more affordable, 25-ft (7.6-m) narrow Toronto building lot, he introduced the so-called "inverted" house, where the living and dining rooms faced the rear garden rather than the street (especially beneficial if the garden had a southern exposure). Another unusual feature of Eden Smith's houses was that they often had a side entrance, which was most unconventional in Toronto, since main rooms and the front door traditionally faced the street.

Several distinguished Montreal architects also built large homes and country houses for well-to-do clients in the Domestic Revival style. In Senneville Robert Findlay designed the Harry Abbott House (1892), a multigabled and half-timbered country house, while Edward Maxwell, a contemporary of Findlay, was responsible for the restora-

tion in the free-style spirit of the John J. C. Abbott country house (1898). Both Charles J. Saxe and John Smith Archibald designed the half-timbered Minnie Louise Davis house (1902) in Westmount.

Percy Nobbs, in partnership with George Taylor Hyde (one of the first McGill University graduates in architecture), built several homes in the Montreal area that unmistakably reflect Lorimer's simple and plain architecture. Nobbs believed that all façades of a home should be given equal design consideration in order to ensure that rear views of buildings were as pleasing as the front views. This design approach is evident in his own family home (1913–15) as well as in a cluster of five houses that Nobbs and Hyde built in the early twenties.

Throughout the twenties and thirties, beautiful homes inspired by Arts and Crafts designs and by traditional rural dwellings of Quebec—the latter influenced by Ramsay Traquair's survey of Quebec's indigenous architecture—were designed by McGill graduates. It is remarkable how well many of these buildings survived, proving the advantage of solid masonry construction, good craftsmanship, and the use of time-tested building materials.

While many upper-income people resided in Arts and Crafts dwellings, more moderate- and low-income Montrealers lived in so-called duplexes and multiplexes, typical multifamily urban housing indigenous to Quebec cities. Already popular alternatives to single-family houses during the nineteenth century, these duplexes are homes for two families in a single building, one above the other, each dwelling with a private entrance and a separate street address. Multiplexes evolved from duplexes, first, by stacking three dwellings to make triplexes, with private street entrances made possible through the use of external staircases leading to a second-story balcony. Around the turn of the century, the number of dwellings in multiplexes increased to four, and then to five, a quintuplex, often with the landlord occupying a large ground-floor flat. On top of the owner's dwelling were stacked two narrow flats for rent on the second- and third-floor levels, self-contained "cold" flats heated by tenants themselves. A sixplex is a

Percy Nobbs house at 38 Sunnyside Avenue, Westmount (1913–15),
P. E. Nobbs and G. T. Hyde

Two small houses from a cluster of five, Westmount (1921–25),
P. E. Nobbs and G. T. Hyde
(after S. Wagg)

variation of the quintuplex, but has two flats at ground level.

The layout of the multiplex narrow upper flats usually consisted of a double parlor in the front, a similar deep room in the rear, with a bedroom and bathroom in between. The back section of the double parlor, often screened off by a curtain, served at night as a bedroom. The deep room in the back of the flat was a combination kitchen/dining/living room, and a part of it was often used by large families as an additional bedroom at night. The two narrow multiplex flats are reminiscent of a pair of New York City railroad flats, but since multiplex flats are through units only in three-story buildings, living conditions in them are superior to the infamous dumbbell dwelling units.

Rows of brightly colored ornate external staircases led to balconies to create unique and

Typical Montreal multiplexes with staircase access

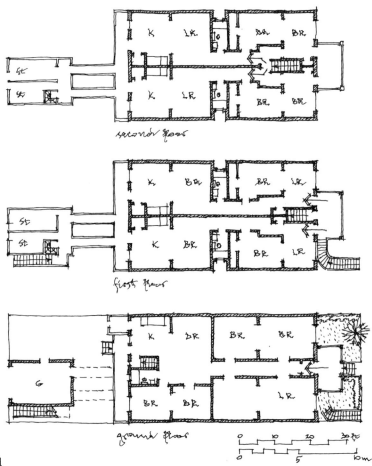

Quintuplex, Montreal
(after Jean-Claude Marsan)

picturesque streetscapes. Not only do these open stairs feel safer than unsupervised internal stairs, but they make a contribution to the animation of Montreal's streets. External stairs function as tiered seats of a viewing platform from which street life can be observed, especially during the summer months.

FOREST HILLS GARDENS

As noted earlier, many years before Ebenezer Howard's Garden City concept was introduced in Great Britain, a model town called Garden City (1869) had been built on Long Island, New York. Originally intended only for tenants of modest means, this community was established by Alexander Turney Stewart, a merchant who had emigrated from Ireland. At the outset, Garden City was an exclusively residential suburb with broad streets and a central landscaped park with a clubhouse and a railway station. Only years after Stewart's death were houses and plots of the estate offered for sale (1895).

The first American planned garden suburb, Forest Hills Gardens, emulated its English predecessor. From the very outset, this community (which could be reached within fifteen minutes by rail from Pennsylvania Station) was envisioned by its founding company (a subsidiary of the Russell Sage Foundation), to serve as a model community for families of moderate means, but also as a business venture with an educational purpose. American planner Clarence Arthur Perry's "neighborhood unit" planning concept, with its six essential characteristics, was first introduced in this community. First, the population had to be large enough to sustain its own elementary school; second, the boundaries had to be well defined by arterial streets; third, several small parks had to be distributed within the community; fourth, public institutions, such as the elementary school, had to be located near the center; fifth, shopping facilities had to be sited along the periphery, preferably at the junction of major traffic routes; sixth, the street network had to be adequate for circulation within the community, but at the same time

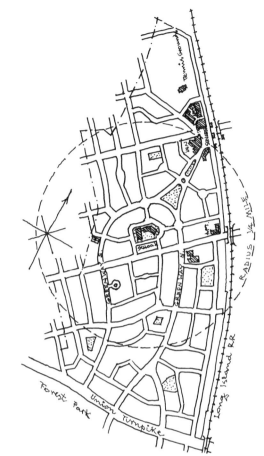

Forest Hills Gardens, Queens (1911),
Frederick L. Olmsted, Jr.
(after H. M. Lewis)

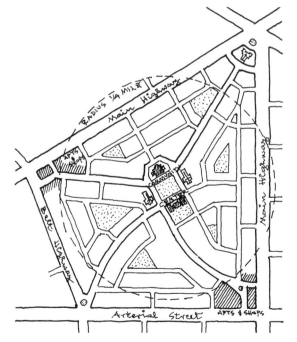

Neighborhood Unit Principles, Clarence A. Perry
(after H. M. Lewis)

Forest Hills Gardens Houses (1912), Grosvenor Atterbury
(after Robert A. M. Stern)

Commercial Center, Forest Hills Gardens, Queens,
Grosvenor Atterbury
(after H. M. Lewis)

discourage through traffic. Frederick L. Olmsted, Jr., the planner and landscape architect of Forest Hills Gardens, adhered to most of these principles.

Similar in concept to its counterpart in Hampstead Garden Suburb, the commercial center of Forest Hills Gardens was also planned as a gateway and located close to the railroad station. Designed by Grosvenor Atterbury in partnership with John Tompkins, a cluster of buildings, with shops along arcaded colonnades, defined three sides of a brick-paved public square, and the railroad station the fourth. In contrast to the undifferentiated and monotonous grid street pattern of neighboring communities, Forest Hills Gardens' local streets were curved, lavishly planted, and, to meet specific traffic needs, varied in width. Curved twin roads, Greenway South and Greenway North, formed the spine of the community, converging into a wide avenue as it approached the commercial center.

The development company erected several residential model homes, designed by Atterbury, that were distributed at various locations on the site. These clusters of houses not only formed picturesque streetscapes of solidly built and beautifully textured homes, but also established the community's standards for domestic architecture. In 1910, Atterbury began to build houses at Forest Hills Gardens using a precast concrete system, one of the first practical precast concrete systems in America. Precast concrete panels that formed the walls, floors, and roofs of the house were fixed together by tongue-and-groove joints bedded in mortar. The exterior surfaces of the panels were worked with a wire brush to expose the texture of the gravel aggregate and, after completion of landscaping, the houses did not have a mass-produced appearance, but resembled the typical homes of English garden suburbs.

Although freestanding houses were most popular, semidetached and rows of attached houses were also built, and in retrospect, it is these clustered attached houses that are responsible for the charm and the variety of street scenes in the community. An additional benefit of the attached homes was their affordability, making it possible for moderate-income families to acquire houses with an "enduring value at a low price" (Koestler 1915, 188). Finally, three apartment houses were also constructed in the community, two buildings adjacent to the grounds of the West Side Tennis Club, and the third at a major street intersection along the eastern boundary.

Forest Hills Gardens was not only an attractive residential community but also a successful business venture. In 1923, a corporation whose membership consisted solely of property owners in the suburb took over the management and enforcement of deed restrictions of the community property. Although at times the socio-economic homogeneity of its residents has been considered a shortcoming, this suburban community is more often cited as an example of a high degree of social interaction, good management, and the neighborhood unit design concept. Although engulfed today by nondescript development, Forest Hills Gardens is one of the few residential areas in New York City that have resisted obsolescence for nearly a century.

AVANT-GARDE MOVEMENTS OF EUROPE: ART NOUVEAU, JUGENDSTIL, SECESSION, NATIONAL ROMANTICISM, AND NIEUWE KUNST

A fascination with organic forms, particularly the sinuous and slender stems of plants supporting delicate blossoms with iridescent colors, shaped Art Nouveau. At the outset, it was a decorative style characterized by flowing, undulating, and entwined lines; it influenced the design of jewelry, book covers, and illustrations, as well as many household objects and furniture.

Two Belgians, Henry Clemens van de Velde and Victor Horta, are credited as the first architects who adapted Art Nouveau to domestic design. Inspired by William Morris, van de Velde believed in an uncompromising design unity in domestic architecture, and, hoping to demonstrate the viability of such a harmony, he built Villa Bloemenwerf (1894–95), in Uccle, a suburb of Brussels. He designed everything in his house, including hardware, furniture, carpets, curtains, table service, and even his wife's dresses. With a polygonal floor

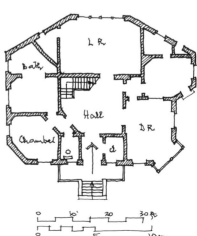

Bloemenwerf, Uccle (1895), plan and façade, Henry C. van de Velde (after Maurice Culot)

Edmond van Eetvelde House (1895–98), octagonal hall,
Victor Horta
(after K-J. Sembach)

"Zonnebloem" House,
Cogels-Osylei, Jules Hofman
(after Gaert Bakaert)

plan, stuccoed walls, and large windows—small paned and shuttered—the villa was both original and functional. The originality of his design caught the attention of several art historians and art dealers, which led to a commission to design several rooms in Samuel Bing's Parisian art gallery, La Maison de l'Art Nouveau.

Art Nouveau reached its first eminence in domestic architecture with buildings designed by Victor Horta, whose contribution to residential design went beyond mere decoration and included the imaginative use of iron and glass in new structural forms. By using a broad top-lit staircase as the main circulation space to reach rooms at different levels, Horta tried to avoid dark corridors in his dwellings and to bring cheerful brightness to the center of the house. The Edmond van Eetvelde House (1895–98), for example, featured an octag-

onal hall with a colorful glazed domed skylight flooding the interior with daylight. Horta's influence was not limited to Brussels alone. Beautiful examples of this new style were also built at Cogels-Osylei, a suburban residential area developed at the turn of the century for the bourgeoisie of Antwerp.

One of the most accomplished French Art Nouveau architects was Hector Guimard, famous for his Paris Métro entrances (1899–1904). He also designed Castel Béranger (1897–98), an impressive six-story Parisian corner apartment building, built as a revenue-producing building for a widow, Mme. Fournier. Although this apartment house featured some eclectic details on its façades, its green iron railings and gates, as well as its stained glass windows, were pure Art Nouveau. Every detail in the interiors of this building's thirty-eight

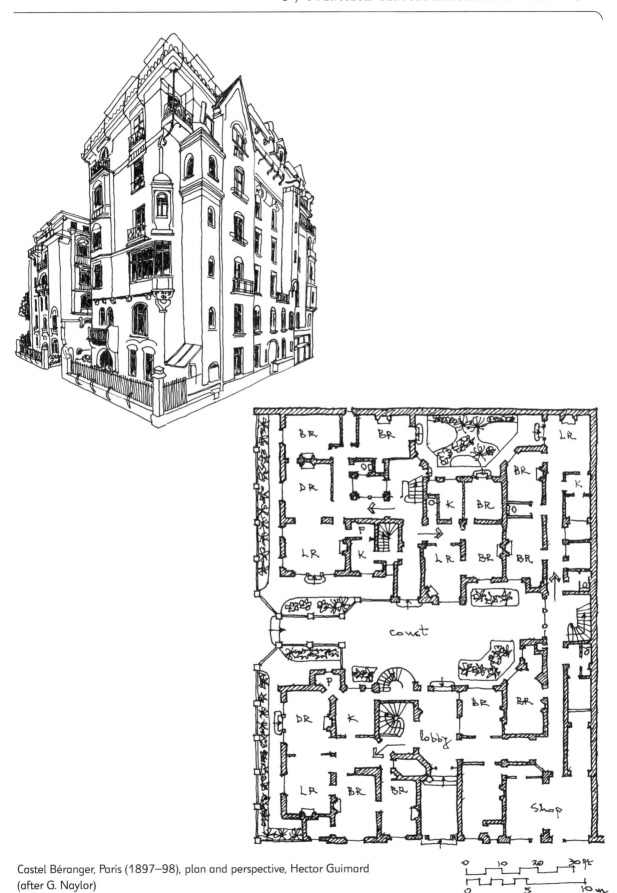

Castel Béranger, Paris (1897–98), plan and perspective, Hector Guimard
(after G. Naylor)

Casa Milà, Barcelona (1906–10), Antonio Gaudí
(after Nikolaus Pevsner)

apartment units was designed by Guimard himself, including the ground-floor space he rented for his professional office.

Perhaps the most individualistic and original Art Nouveau architect in Europe was Antonio Gaudí y Cornet, a Catalan, whose mature buildings were counter to all accepted principles of architecture. Apparently he was influenced by Eugène-Emanuel Viollet-le-Duc and John Ruskin, as well as by the Mujedar architectural traditions of his native country, but the buildings he designed were unique and unmistakably personal. And, in contrast to many of his contemporaries who at a later date abandoned Art Nouveau and embraced the international Modern movement, Gaudí persisted until his death in building in his unique and imaginative way.

Gaudí's most impressive residential building was Casa Milà (1906–10), a six-story corner apartment house complex in Barcelona. Nicknamed La

Pedrera (the stone quarry), Casa Milà offered large apartment suites with odd-shaped enfilade reception rooms along the treed boulevard, while secondary rooms opened on irregularly shaped interior courtyards. The design of the individual apartment units is playful, with light intensity constantly changing and architectural details perpetually presenting new surprises. The façade of this apartment complex is horizontally articulated, and balconies with metal railings—resembling tangles of seaweed—bulge in and out from the undulating façade. Other building features, unusual at the time, were an underground garage, a developed attic space, and a roof terrace—the latter is a ceramic tile landscape of various levels with chimneys and air ducts.

In contrast to Gaudí's Spanish Art Nouveau, the German Jugendstil was not only more measured, but more closely related to the British Arts and Crafts movement. When Hermann Muthesius returned to Berlin from England, he not only published his work on the English house but also built his own country house, Freudenberg (1907–8), in Berlin-Nikolasee. Unquestionably inspired by the so-called butterfly plan of Edward S. Prior's house, The Barn (1897) in Exmouth, Devon, Muthesius's house, although larger than The Barn, was less homey. More in keeping with the scale of a single-family detached dwelling was the Haus de Burlet (1911), at Berlin-Schlachtensee, and the attached dwellings designed by Muthesius for the German garden city Hellerau, emulating British prototypes, but using a traditional German design vocabulary.

After the 1906 Exhibition of Arts and Crafts in Dresden, Muthesius criticized the prevalent state of applied art in Germany and antagonized some of his conservative colleagues, but, with the help of those colleagues who were inspired by his criticism, Muthesius founded the Deutsche Werkbund, an organization that focused its interest on both craftsmanship and methods of mass production to further the cause of good design.

At the end of the nineteenth century, Vienna, the capital of the Austro-Hungarian monarchy, was a city receptive to new ideas. In 1897, several prominent artists renounced their membership in the

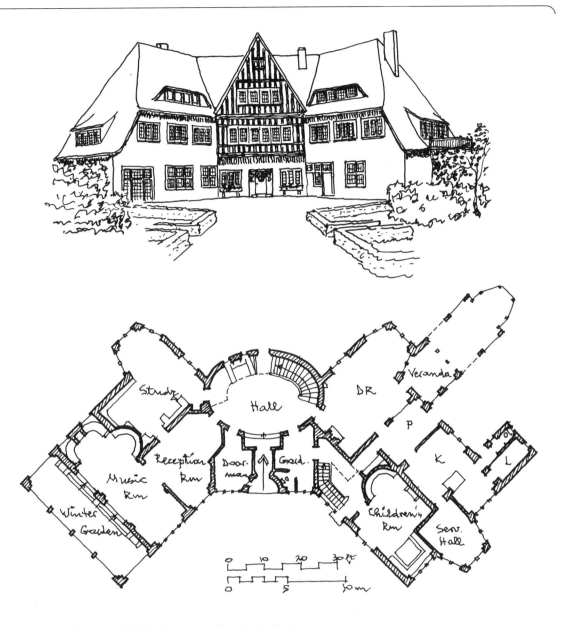

Freudenberg, Berlin-Nikolasee (1907–8), plan and façade, H. Muthesius
(after Julius Posener)

Viennese Art Academy and founded a new association, known as the Viennese Secession. The new Secessionist movement received moral support from young writers and journalists as well as backing from several private patrons. Private financial support enabled the Secessionists to build their own exhibition building, Das Haus der Secession, in close proximity to the Academy of Fine Arts, but with its back turned towards it. The designer was Joseph Maria Olbrich, a talented and avant-garde architect, one of the founders of the Secession.

Olbrich designed a villa for Max and Johanna Friedmann (1899) in Hinterbrühl bei Wien, a house with its "omega"-shaped porch immediately recognizable as an Olbrich design. As a *Gesamtkünstler* (total artist), he designed everything in the interior of the house: wall decorations, furniture, hinges for cabinets, and even the letter box. Floral patterns were used everywhere, on walls, windows, doors, railings, and furniture, while the walls of the master bedroom depicted a forest scene.

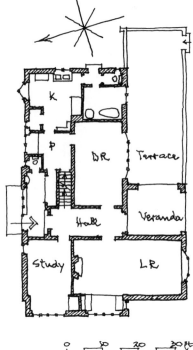

Haus de Burlet, Berlin-Schlachtensee (1911),
plan and perspective, H. Muthesius
(after Julius Posener)

Two years later, having attracted the attention of Queen Victoria's grandson, the Grand Duke Ernst Ludwig von Hessen und bei Rhein, Olbrich was asked to establish an artists' colony in Darmstadt, Germany. The Grand Duke was familiar with the British Arts and Crafts movement and, in 1896, commissioned Baillie Scott to design two rooms in his new palace. Now he aspired to lay the economic foundations for a similar creative craftsmanship in Hessen, and invited seven young artists—among them Peter Behrens—to live in the colony, offering each of them a monthly stipend to ensure their financial independence, so that they, in turn, could devote themselves entirely to creative pursuits.

In the center of the artists' colony, *Mathildenhöhe*, Olbrich designed the Ernst-Ludwig House (1901), a building with six individual studios in a row, each lit by north-facing glazed roofs. Scattered nearby were the resident artists' villas, including a house for the colony's manager. All homes were designed by Olbrich, with the exception of one, Behrens's own house. Three of the villas, including the one Olbrich built for himself, were essentially traditional German house types: white stuccoed homes with semihipped red tile roofs. What made them different, however, was their colorful ornamentation and their playful fenestration, including bay windows and, on the exterior of Olbrich's house, flower rails suspended from the eaves. With its "omega"-arched recessed entrance porch, Deiters House, the villa designed for the manager of Mathildenhöhe, is a most charming Art Nouveau home; other villas, with flat or barrel roofs and cubic in form, anticipated the Modern movement.

Finally, Behrens's house was the most striking and original. It too was a white stucco building, but pilasters of dark ceramic tiles emphasized its corners while similar ceramic tile ogival "lisenes" (pilaster strips) framed its gables. Behrens was the only artist of this colony—apart from Olbrich—who had the courage to design both the exterior and interior of his home. The new style of Mathildenhöhe was not universally admired; traditionalists rejected the architecture of the artists' colony.

Unfortunately, the Mathildenhöhe colony suffered damage from a bombing raid in 1944; after

Villa Friedmann, Hinterbrühl (1899), J. M. Olbrich
(after Ian Latham)

Olbrich House, Darmstadt (1901), J. M. Olbrich
(after J. M. Olbrich)

Deiters House, Darmstadt (1901), J. M. Olbrich
(after Ian Latham)

Behrens House, Darmstadt (1901), Peter Behrens
(after Peter Davey)

the war some buildings were restored, others altered unrecognizably, and still others disappeared altogether.

Heinrich Krebs, a German salesman, bought Howard's book on the garden city concept while visiting England in 1902, got it translated, and with the help of others—including Peter Behrens—founded a garden city association in Germany. In fact, this movement was enthusiastically embraced by industrialists in the belief that it was respon-

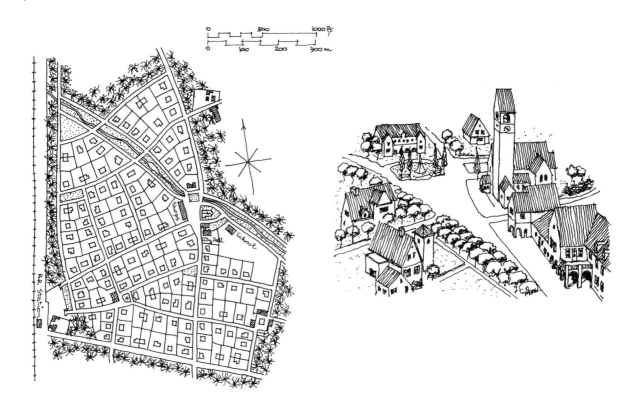

Buchschlag, near Darmstadt (1905), F. Putzer
(after C. Mohr)

Town square project, Buchschlag (1905)
(after C. Mohr)

sible for good British industrial labor relations. The advertising booklet from 1905, for Buchschlag, a garden suburb built between Darmstadt and Frankfurt am Main, outlines the raison d'être for its construction: to enable people who worked in nearby cities the ownership of a home with a garden, close to nature, in peaceful surroundings with fresh air, and away from the hustle and bustle of city life. Friedrich Pützer, an architect and teacher, prepared the master plan for this garden suburb.

Villenkolonie Buchschlag was initiated by Jakob Latscha, a Frankfurt businessman and social reformer, who, in 1904, acquired from the Grand Duke Ernst Ludwig a site with the understanding that land speculation would be prevented. Accordingly, building plot purchasers had to commit themselves to build a single-family detached house within three years. The planned town center, a square surrounded by a church, city hall, and arcaded buildings with shops, resembled the center of a typical German small town; it was never built.

All buildings in the community were of masonry construction, often with a stone base, and had roughcast or colored stucco finish above. In domestic buildings polygonal bay windows were frequently used, and windows were usually small-paned and shuttered. Most roofs were tiled, with the color red prevailing. Great attention was given by all homeowners to the landscaping of their property, invariably defined by picket fences. The overall pleasing impression of this community was that of neatness, ease, and comfort.

The principal space of most homes was a hall-type family room or Diele, with a *gemütlich* corner or alcove. Usually an oak staircase led from this room to the second-floor bedrooms and bathrooms, as well as to the guest room and maid's room on the third level; both upper levels were accommodated in the cavernous attic space under a steep tiled roof. Ceramic tile ovens, or Kachelofens, augmented at times by central heating, heated the rooms.

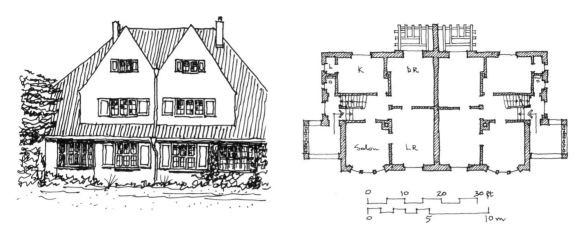

Semidetached house at 6–8 Falltorweg, Buchschlag, plan and façade, W. Koban
(after C. Mohr)

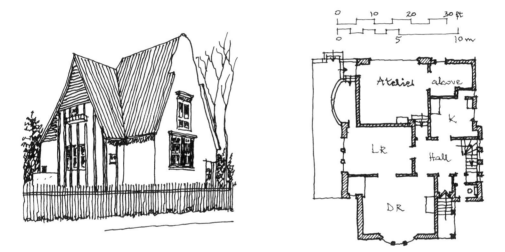

Detached house at 15 Kohlseeweg, Buchschlag, plan and façade, C. F. W. Leonhardt
(after C. Mohr)

Like many of his avant-garde contemporaries, Henrik Petrus Berlage rebelled against historicism and, inspired by the Arts and Crafts movement, he began to use traditional Dutch building methods with craftsmanlike exposed brickwork on masonry walls instead of the pervasive stucco. In the Netherlands, in contrast to Britain, detached and semidetached houses were considered a wasteful use of land and economically unsustainable. Hence, Berlage—the intellectual leader of the Amsterdam School—adopted the closed block pattern of perimeter development, which after widespread application throughout his native country led to the successful *hofje* (court)

pattern. Families preferred the closed block pattern, because their children could play safely in a protected communal space, or garden, in the center of the block. In collaboration with J. Gratama and G. Versteeg, Berlage built the large municipal housing estate of Transvaal Neighborhood (1919). This housing project shows urban design influences from both Camillo Sitte and Raymond Unwin.

Another leading member of the so-called Amsterdam School was Michel de Klerk, whose most significant domestic architecture was the workers' housing blocks in the Spaarndammerbuurt (1913–15), built for Eigen Haard, a housing

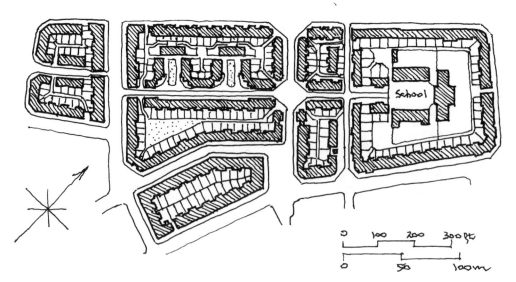

Transvaal neighborhood, Amsterdam (1919), H. P. Berlage, J. Gratama, and G. Versteeg
(after D. I. Grinberg)

Eigen Haard, Spaarndammerbuurt, Amsterdam (1913–15), Michel de Klerk (after
Peter Davey)

association. Protected now as a historic monument, the individualistic brick buildings, with unusual window shapes and eccentric parabolic gables, were probably inspired by Olbrich.

Another remarkable housing development in the Spaarndammerbuurt was Zaanhof, built for Het Westen, another housing association. This Sitt-esque housing estate, reminiscent of a medieval

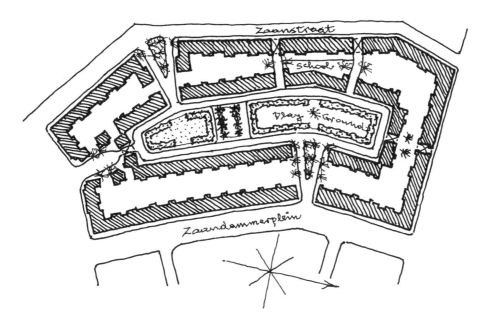

Zaanhof, Amsterdam (1919), site plan and perspective, H. J. M. Walenkamp
(after D. I. Grinberg)

town, was designed by H. J. M. Walenkamp, each house identified by a gable facing the public space. The design concept of this development entailed two annular parallel closed-block developments with a well-defined public urban space in the center.

Nurtured by millennial celebrations held in 1896, a national consciousness provoked Hungarians to search for an architectural style that would reflect their own heritage. While working in Paris (1875–78), Ödön Lechner visited England and, after his return to Hungary, pursued a life-long search for a Magyar national style. Just as members of the Art Workers' Guild studied ver-nacular architecture rooted in the English countryside, Lechner, too, turned to rural folk art for inspiration. He also explored the possibilities offered by new building materials, including the use of polychrome glazed terra cotta for both external and internal use.

With the motto *Régiben az Ujat!* (In the Old the New), a group of architects known as the "Young Ones" set out to survey Transylvanian folk architecture. They shared the conviction that great insight would be gained from the study of indigenous rural buildings. Károly Kós, the most outspoken member of the group, attempted to go beyond

Gateway, Wekerle-telep, Budapest (1908–13)
(after J. Gerle)

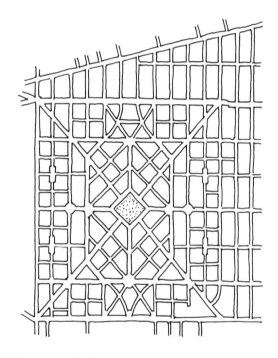

Wekerle-telep, Budapest (1908), Ottmár Györi
(after Z. Jékely, et al.)

the initial stages of the "tulip decorated" Hungarian style, seeking inspiration from the structural elements of Transylvanian vernacular buildings.

In the workers' settlement Wekerle-telep (1908–13) at Kispest, on the outskirts of Budapest, the influence of Transylvanian vernacular architecture is pervasive. Ottmár Györi's planning concept for this garden community with 4,140

dwelling units shows some influence of Howard's Garden City movement, but its urban design is proof of an even greater familiarity with Camillo Sitte's design principles. Vehicular and pedestrian traffic to the central square had to pass through gateway structures reminiscent of the large portals of farmsteads common in Transylvanian villages. In his autobiographical notes, Kós acknowledges the great influence of the Arts and Crafts movement upon his architectural outlook. He also paid tribute to the work of Eliel Saarinen and Aksel Gallén-Kallela, both engaged in the development of a new Finnish identity.

At the turn of the century, an awakened national consciousness in Finland, accompanied by a struggle to gain independence from Russia, brought about a reform movement led by a distinguished group of artists and architects. Inspired by *Kalevala*, the Finnish national epic, and influenced by Karelian folk architecture, painter Aksel Gallén (Gallén-Kalela) built for himself and his family a combination atelier-dwelling called Kalela (1895). It represents one of the first buildings in Finland termed "National Romantic" in style. His new home was surrounded by nature and built on a lake's rocky peninsula. The central space of the building was a lofty studio/living room with a large north window, a skylight, and a fireplace.

The Hvitträsk Studio House (1902) at Kirkkonummi, near Helsinki, is another building in the

Hvitträsk, Kirkkonummi, near Helsinki (1902), Gesellius, Lindgren and Saarinen
(after Kenneth Frampton)

National Romantic style. Designed by Herman Gesellius, Armas Lindgren, and Eliel Saarinen, this building was to contain not only three family homes, but also a common workshop and studio for the three architects. In the best Arts and Crafts tradition, building materials used were identical with those of vernacular buildings in the region. The ground-floor walls were built of rough stone, partly stuccoed, and the upper floor was shingled, and a steep pantiled roof sheltered the whole complex.

Although this movement heightened a sense of national pride, it did not influence events on the Continent, with the exception of Hungary—as mentioned earlier—but it did inspire the reform movements of the other three Scandinavian countries. Norway only gained its independence from Sweden in 1906, but suburban homes were built in Norway, too, with the techniques of traditional timber farm building. Professor Kay Fisker, a Danish architect, recalled that "Finnish avant-garde architecture, i.e., National Romanticism, was considered to be so revolutionary that attempts were made to prevent Danish students of architecture from reading the Finnish architectural publications" (Salokorpi 1970, 8–9).

Like Finland, the other three Scandinavian countries also studied their respective heritage in search of a nationally identifiable architecture. This search resulted in a distinct Danish, Swedish,

and Norwegian variety of National Romanticism. After Denmark lost Slesvig-Holstein, in 1864, it was the first Scandinavian country that not only built country houses in a National Romantic style, but also public buildings. In *Arts and Crafts Architecture: The Search for Earthly Paradise*, the author, Peter Davey, made the observation that Scandinavian architects—in contrast to their English counterparts—often received commissions for public buildings "precisely because their work was identified with national aspiration" (Davey 1980, 196). For example, Martin Nyrup designed the Copenhagen town hall (1892–1905); Ragnor Östberg the Stockholm town hall; and Gesellius, Lindgren, and Saarinen the Finnish National Museum (1905–12), Helsinki.

Searching for design inspiration in indigenous architecture not only brought about a greater regional and national consciousness, but also various avant-garde design trends, all influenced by the Arts and Crafts movement. The variations of the home-grown national styles, as represented by Art Nouveau, Jugendstil, Secession, National Romanticism, and Nieuwe Kunst, came to a halt with the emergence of the Modern movement, which, in contrast to the previous idiosyncratic regional styles, had advocated a rational approach to design by objecting to the notion of "style"; nevertheless, eventually, it became identified as the International style.

HOUSING BETWEEN THE TWO WORLD WARS

In both Europe and North America, private housing construction was at a standstill during World War I; the critical shortage of dwelling accommodation existing prior to 1914 became even more severe. A lack of funds, and a deficit of building materials and skilled construction workers, continued to hamper access to affordable urban housing for most returning war veterans.

The general belief that an opportunity existed to "build a better world" prevailed. To sustain people's optimism, governments enacted social building programs designed to ease housing shortages. Most governments introduced rent control as a temporary measure to curb profiteering, and subsidized housing construction through low-interest loans to municipal governments or to nonprofit housing societies. The latter policy was so successful that approximately seven and a half million low-rent homes were built in Europe between 1919 and 1939 (Reed and Ogg 1940, 36).

During the postwar years, health considerations were paramount in housing design. Proper sun orientation, adequate sun exposure, and good ventilation, in addition to hygienic improvements—running water and a private toilet in each dwelling—were the means for a concerted effort to fight tuberculosis and other maladies. Finally, the efficient layout of dwellings with compact kitchens, small bedrooms, but spacious living rooms, complemented by easy access to an outdoor space for play and recreation, were new standards desired by homeowners and tenants. Functionalism, practicality, and a new ornament-free aesthetic inside and outside of dwellings became the legacies of the Modern movement.

UNITED STATES

The trend of the well-to-do to move from attached urban dwellings to detached homes in the outskirts of cities continued after World War I. With the great increase of private car ownership, suburbs became more accessible, and the opulent detached residences built in communities like Oyster Bay (near New York City) or Lake Forest (near Chicago) acquired a social distinction previously held only by urban mansions of the well-to-do.

People with a moderate income also joined the flight to the suburbs. Builder-designed tracts of inexpensive, small, but colorful stuccoed bungalows were built in West Coast suburbs. Also indigenous to California were the so-called bungalow courts, consisting of a cluster of freestanding single-story houses around a common landscaped entrance court. Initially, these bungalow courts were built as vacation homes, but this design concept was later adopted for permanent residences. Owner-occupied dwelling units increased substantially across the nation because of the small and inexpensive prefabricated bungalows offered in the twenties by several manufacturers.

The proliferation of the private motor car drastically changed the size of pre–World War II dormitory suburbs. The width and breadth of the early suburbs, usually spaced from three to five miles apart along a rail line, were defined by tolerable walking distances from the station. Thus, green belts invariably separated one suburb from another, but as soon as the use of cars became widespread, the walking distance constraint limiting the size of suburbs no longer applied. "The suburb ceased to be a neighborhood unit: it became a diffused low-density mass" (Mumford 1961, 505), enveloped by a continuous network of urban communities, now referred to as conurbation.

On the East Coast, the upward mobility of first-generation immigrants who came to North America prior to World War I, and who lived under appalling conditions in railroad flats, created a demand, in the twenties, for affordable housing with more pleasant surroundings, far away from crowded tenements. In New York, for example, builders responded to this new demand by constructing four- to six-story garden apartments in outlying boroughs, with wholesome dwellings that were well lit and well ventilated. A landscaped narrow strip of land along the street, and a semi-

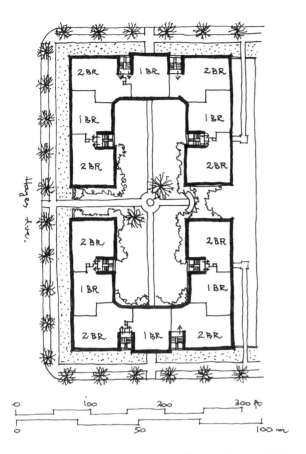

Hayes Avenue Garden Apartments, Jackson Heights, N.Y.
(c. 1922), Andrew J. Thomas
(after Richard Plunz)

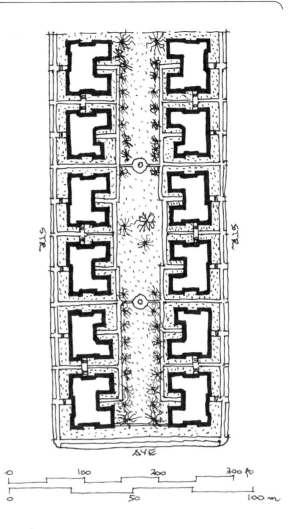

public landscaped courtyard, often both served as entrance courts.

It was probably Andrew J. Thomas, a self-educated architect, who introduced the term "garden apartments" for residential buildings constructed in New York City's outlying boroughs. The landscaped garden setting of these four-story walk-ups maintained the illusion, if not the reality, of the house in the garden, as historian Richard Plunz observed (1990). The popularity and economic success of garden apartment buildings induced a few developers to employ similar design principles in midtown developments, but with higher densities and elevator service. Garden apartments attracted the attention of workers' unions, and the Amalgamated Clothing Workers of America initiated a cooperative garden apartment development for its members in the Bronx.

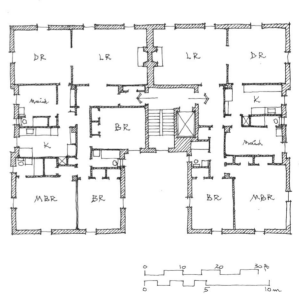

The Château Garden Apartments, Jackson Heights
(1922), two plans, Andrew J. Thomas
(after Richard Plunz)

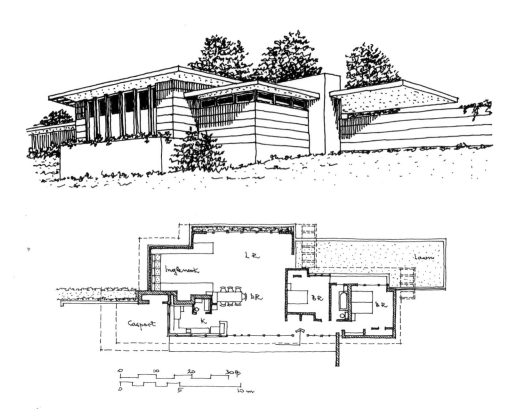

Goetsch-Winkler House, Okemos, Michigan (1939), plan and perspective, Frank Lloyd Wright
(after F. L. Wright, 1963)

Undoubtedly, the most influential American architect of the interwar period was Frank Lloyd Wright, and during this period he crystallized his ideas on the servantless home. His "Prairie style" houses were soon recognized as homes in harmony with their natural surroundings. In contrast to his early work, most of his later dwellings had an open plan with a generous living room, a well-defined dining area, small compact private bedrooms and bathrooms, little wasted circulation space, and a centrally located kitchen where the housewife would be "now more hostess 'officio,' operating in gracious relation to her home, instead of being a kitchen mechanic behind closed doors" (Wright 1963, 107). Wright's domestic architecture popularized the rambling single-story detached home flooded with sunlight. He viewed the house essentially as a broad shelter in the open, rather than a cave, a house with vistas without and within. To increase the sense of interior space he often wrapped windows around the building's corners and used a continuous band of narrow windows to separate the roof from the walls.

An early proponent of the open plan, Frank Lloyd Wright improved the spaciousness and livability of the house through the elimination of the traditional cellular sequestration whereby each domestic function was properly conducted room to room, or "box to box" as Wright called it. "Scores of unnecessary doors disappeared" (Wright 1963, 34).

By definition, no two Wright-designed houses could be the same because the house expressed the individuality of its owner; thus, the Malcolm Willey House (1934) in Minneapolis, the George D. Sturges House (1939) in Brentwood Heights, near Hollywood, and the Goetsch-Winkler House (1939) in Okemos, Michigan, were all different, yet in harmony with nature.

Wright's design grammar also shaped the design of homes so that existing climatic conditions were complemented by building elements that ensured comfort for their occupants throughout the year.

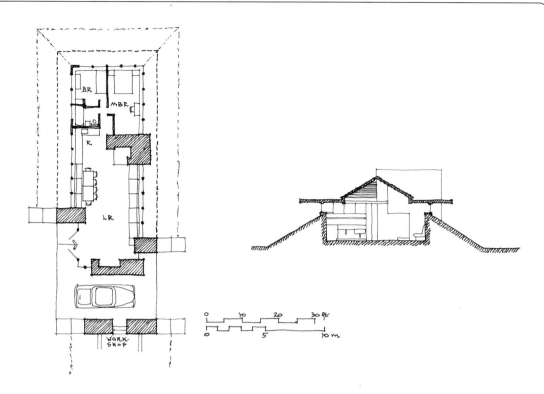

Berm-house, Detroit, Michigan (1942), plan and section, Frank Lloyd Wright
(after F. L. Wright, 1963)

The opportunity for proper cross-ventilation was always provided. Moreover, for indoor comfort, Wright skillfully used solid masonry walls as a thermal mass in order to even out the diurnal flux of temperatures (especially beneficial in the Southwest and Southeast of the U.S.). And the projecting eaves of Wright's houses, a well-recognized trademark, allowed the sun to penetrate in winter when it was lower on the horizon, but shaded the house in summer.

Frank Lloyd Wright's concern for climate is perhaps best illustrated by his berm-type house (1942) designed for Detroit auto workers. Envisaged as part of a project for self-supportive "cooperative homesteads," the house used the excavated material from the construction site to form earth banks rammed up against the house; these sodded berms were to deflect the wind from the house and to insulate the exterior walls. This small and economical house also illustrated the essential planning approach and discipline imposed by a modular grid.

Most Frank Lloyd Wright–designed houses had neither an attic nor a basement, a characteristic shared with bungalows; he disliked attics because this "waste space" prevented the use of clerestory windows and skylights, and he considered basements unhealthy because of their dampness. Oddly, the Wright house rarely had a vestibule or any other form of air-lock device at the front door, a feature that was inconsistent with his climate concerns, but shared with most early bungalows.

During the interwar period a new emphasis was placed on the complementary relationship between house and garden, partly attributable to Japanese influences and partly to the increasing use of glass in domestic architecture. Wright was one of the most successful interpreters of this new trend "to bring nature into the house and the house to nature." As a proponent of the "natural house," Wright suggested that the true integration of a house with its building site is achieved when the boundaries between the garden and the house are difficult to define (Wright 1963, 46–47).

Wright's belief that a community that was close to the soil could surpass all adverse effects of the Industrial Revolution led him to advocate proposals for urban decentralization. His concept of urban reform was crystallized in the early thirties and published in his book *The Disappearing City* (1932). Convinced that individuality is of paramount importance in human development as well as for freedom, Wright proposed a new city structure, the "Broadacre City," which was to render a minimum one-acre plot to a self-sufficient homestead, with enough land to grow at least some food for the family. He also made an allowance for "quadruplex" houses sharing a two-acre lot for those with lesser means.

Wright's urban reform concept had an affinity with the allocation of land in quarter sections of a one-mile grid used in the midwest for homesteaders of a previous era. In fact, Wright retained the mile grid as the skeleton of his proposed Broadacre City. A reconciliation of town and country was clearly implied by Wright, just as Ebenezer Howard and Soria y Mata promised it before him.

Wright's concept was worked out on a four-square-mile area with an anticipated total population of some 1,400 families, which amounted to a gross density of only 0.54 dwellings per acre (1.33 dwellings per hectare). A three-dimensional grid of air corridors was planned for the future use of "aerotors" (helicopterlike aircraft) to complement the road network.

This concept was never realized and was "dismissed as impractical utopianism" by someone who loved the countryside and disliked the city, but as John Sergeant so aptly observed, following his study tour of Wright's architecture, "in all those weeks on the highway I was constantly traversing roadside commercial strips and farflung residential areas that seemed very close to Wright's predictions" (Sergeant 1975, 12).

The increased ownership of cars, which reached 21,308,159 registered automobiles in 1928 (Stein 1957, 41), brought about legitimate concerns for children's safety on streets, especially in the case of through traffic in residential communities. The design challenge to alleviate these concerns was

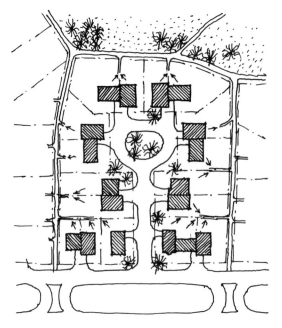

Burnham Place, Radburn, N.J. (1929), Clarence Stein and Henry Wright
(after C. Stein)

met in Radburn, New Jersey, an experimental community within commuting distance of New York City. Designed by Henry Wright and Clarence S. Stein, the Radburn development pattern was based on a horizontal separation of vehicular and pedestrian traffic by means of a series of cul-de-sac streets for vehicular access on one side of houses, and an interconnected network of walkways for pedestrians on the other side. Pedestrian paths were continuous and never interrupted by car traffic within the superblock of 35 to 50 acres (14.16 to 20.23 hectares). Children visiting neighboring friends, including those living in adjacent superblocks reached by pedestrian underpasses, or walking to the playground and school within the superblock, were assured of safety from traffic accidents. Most dwellings in Radburn were single-family homes, but a few rental units in garden apartments also were provided.

Before the Great Depression stopped the building boom, only two superblocks were completed in Radburn by developer Alexander Bing. However, the Radburn concept found application in such communities as Greenbelt, Maryland, a government-funded New Deal development with the goals of providing work for the unemployed and building low-rent housing. In 1935, the government's Resettlement Administration started the construction of several additional residential communities with a Radburn-type horizontal traffic separation: these were Greenhills, near Cincinnati; Greenbrook, between New York City and Philadelphia; Greendale, near Milwaukee; and Baldwin Hills Village, in Los Angeles.

Before the Great Depression, developers had also begun the construction of luxury apartment houses. With their height no longer limited to twelve floors, the New York luxury multifamily trendsetters were the Park Avenue and Central Park West high-rise apartments. These buildings also featured many double-floor (duplex) apartment units with an interior stairway to simulate the internal arrangement of spacious town houses.

A preeminent New York designer of luxury apartment buildings was Emery Roth, a self-educated architect and Hungarian émigré. He paid particular attention to the improvement of the layout of apartment dwellings. One device was the design of hallways or foyers as pivotal axes for better communication between rooms; another was the careful location of both windows and doors to optimize a room's potential for attractive furniture layouts. He also enlarged the size of master bedrooms and provided them with adequate closet space, a rarity at the turn of the century. Finally, it was Emery Roth who initiated the concealment of water tanks and elevator penthouses in masonry towers, derisively called "Roth's Towers." Prior to their concealment, unsightly water tanks mounted on iron stilts marred the roof lines of otherwise attractive buildings (Ruttenbaum 1986, 51).

Two famous turreted rental apartment complexes built between 1928 and 1930 were the San Remo Apartments and the Beresford Apartments, both on Central Park West. The twenty-seven-story twin-towered cathedral-like San Remo, crowned with a colonnaded Roman-style temple, and the twenty-two-story Beresford with its three illuminated towers, were an embodiment of opulence in apartment living that would not be surpassed for many decades.

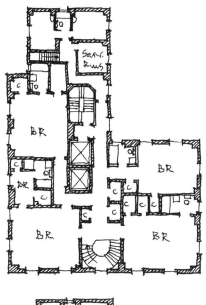

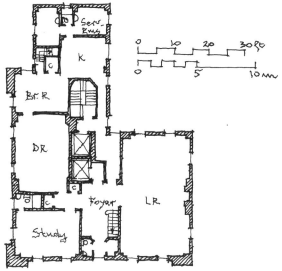

San Remo duplex apartment (plans of twenty-sixth and twenty-seventh floors), Emery Roth (after S. Ruttenbaum)

To reduce the length of corridors, Roth designed both buildings with multiple vertical-access cores, which also had the advantage that only one or two apartment suites were entered at each floor level from their respective elevator lobbies. Roth's buildings contained several duplex apartments, but those in the towers of the San Remo had the added advantage of no lateral neighbors; hence they were lit from all sides and represented veritable "mansions in the clouds" (Ruttenbaum 1986, title page). Most apartments had large dining and living rooms, the latter with an open fireplace. A special feature in the San Remo Towers was a dressing room off the large master bedroom.

By romanticizing the past and advertising the twin-towered San Remo complex as "the aristocrat of Central Park West," its developers successfully attracted "old money" tenants and set the stage for emulation. In quick succession three additional twin-towered apartment buildings were constructed along the west side of Central Park: the El Dorado (Margon & Holder, with Emery Roth as associate architect), the Majestic, and the Century (both by Irwin S. Chanin, architect). In contrast to the San Remo, these three Art Deco buildings celebrated the future—as people saw it then—and were targeted for "new money" tenants.

During the interwar years, luxury apartment houses were also built in other large cities, notably Chicago, on Lake Shore Drive. In 1917 one of the first penthouse apartments was built on Lake Shore Drive. Engaged in the design of a luxury eight-story apartment house, the architect William E. Walker conceived a twelve-room "bungalow-on-the-roof" to build for himself. After Walker occupied the penthouse he discovered that such a dwelling unit offered several additional advantages over and above a grand view: more privacy, greater security, better air, and, since the penthouse was above the fly belt and mosquito line, there was no need to install window screens. While it would have been economically inconceivable to build a bungalow at grade level on Lake Shore Drive, a bungalow-on-the-roof was viable (Moulton 1917, 149).

The crash of the stock market in 1929 and the Depression arrested further development of luxury apartment houses and forced many owners to convert large dwellings into smaller ones that would be affordable to a new generation, whose servantless households were smaller and their lifestyle less formal.

While a new program to aid moderate- to high-income families through Federal Housing Administration (FHA)–insured home mortgages with lower interest rates was a decided success, the provision of low-rental housing only really got underway in 1937 when the United States Housing Authority (USHA) was established. This permanent agency was empowered to lend and grant public funds to local government housing authorities and to establish minimum standards for the construction and maintenance of public housing. Although many municipalities took advantage of this program, the newly constructed low-rental housing units were not enough to meet the demand. The housing census of 1940 showed that about 19 percent of the existing housing stock needed major repairs; 46 percent of all dwelling units had no private bath; 22 percent had no gas or electricity; 30 percent lacked a refrigerator; and 12 percent had no central heating or stoves (Carskadon 1944, 2).

GREAT BRITAIN

As in North America, most dwellings constructed in Great Britain during the interwar years were in the suburbs. Since the majority of the public preferred Arts and Crafts parlorless homes, builders continued to build Edwardian-style cottages with a living room, essentially a large family room with windows towards the street and the garden. Conceived as the heart of the house, this living room had to be well designed, with traffic lines that did not interfere with the dining area or seating for conversation near the fireplace, the latter ideally in an inglenook with built-in seats. With the staircase leading to the upper-floor bedrooms also part of the family room, this design represented in early twentieth-century domestic architecture the British version of the open plan. The suburban housing boom peaked in the thirties, with 275,000 houses built in a single year.

Introduced by Lloyd George's government, the Housing and Town Planning Act of 1919 enabled land to be purchased for garden suburbs and facilitated the construction of low-rent housing. Most local authorities, including the London County Council (LCC), favored suburban development. Gardens and green open spaces were not only considered beneficial for health, but also a likely

Cottages at Norbury Estate, Croydon (1906), London County Council
(after *Home Sweet Home*)

Bellingham Estate, Lewisham (1921), London County Council
(after *Home Sweet Home*)

deterrent to bring about radical changes in society by workers cultivating their own gardens. Modeled on Raymond Unwin's cottage prototypes at Hampstead Garden Suburb, several homey cottage estates with two- to three-story terraces and semi-detached houses were built in the outskirts of London. Between the two world wars, the LCC provided new cottages for 59,591 families (Walters 1976, 40).

One of the most successful housing estates that approximated the Garden City ideal was Roehampton. Opened in 1921 and completed six years later, this estate comprised 1,118 cottages and 94 flats on a treed parkland site. Another LCC cottage estate of

Becontree Estate, Dagenham (1921–27), London County Council
(after *Home Sweet Home*)

this period was Becontree, hailed in the twenties as the largest municipal housing estate in the world (Walters 1976, 32); indeed, by 1945, this estate had over 14,000 family dwellings. The predominant style for cottages was neovernacular, with brick walls, tiled roofs, prominent chimneys, dormers, and white-trimmed multipaned windows. With beautifully landscaped lawns and gardens, shaded by mature trees, these cottage estates acquired a timeless quality of domestic charm.

By the late twenties, and early thirties, attention was focused on the inner urban areas. Since legislation no longer allowed the construction of densely occupied apartment blocks built around courtyards, a slum clearance drive was necessary to create land for blocks of flats in green spaces. Acres of the notoriously dingy back-to-back slum dwellings of the nineteenth century were cleared and replaced by flats with balconies in close proximity to green open spaces. The Ossulton estate (1929), St. Pancras; the China Walk estate (1929), Lambeth; and the Stamford Hill estate (1931), Hackney, are three examples. While these housing estates reflected a traditional domestic style, the design of the Oaklands estate (1936) in Lambeth, with its flat roofs, rounded corners, streamlined balconies, and horizontal window bars, showed the clear influence of "continental modernism" (Walters 1976, 40).

The improvement in public health during the three decades between the two world wars was to a large extent attributable to better housing and better nourishment, a fact manifested by the comparative percentage figures of military conscripts ranked as 36 percent in first-class health in 1917–18 versus 83 percent in 1939. In spite of the great effort to relieve the housing shortage during the interwar period, by the start of World War II in 1939, large numbers of low-income residents of London and other large cities still suffered from overcrowding and all too many still lived in slums.

FRANCE

Following World War I, the Garden City (cité jardin) movement influenced the rapid expansion of suburban developments in France. Other contributing factors were improved commuter rail transportation and the eight-hour working day (legislated in 1919), which allowed more time for long-distance commuting. While, at the outset, suburban development was characterized by single-family houses, later, for economic reasons, apartment blocks became more prevalent.

The first priority was the rebuilding of the northern regions of France devastated in the war. Only with the passing of the Loucheur Act in 1928—authorizing long-term, low-interest government loans of up to 90 percent of the cost of housing for war veterans and low-income families—did the housing industry switch into high gear, erecting about 180,000 low-rent and 15,000 medium-rent dwellings during the next four years. This housing boom was shortlived because rearmament commitments from 1932 onwards once again limited the resources for subsidized housing.

The largest cité jardin of the Seine department was Plessis-Robinson, southwest of Paris, a community with 5,500 dwelling units mostly in rows of four- to five-story apartment blocks separated from each other by spacious courtyards. Cité de la Muette (1930–34) in Drancy was another Seine department town near Paris, that is an example of high-density development, with 1,060 dwelling units. Erected between 1930 and 1934 and designed by Eugène Beaudouin in collaboration with Marcel Lods, it was a mixed residential estate with rows of walk-up apartment blocks and five identical elevator-serviced sixteen-story apartment towers, or point blocks, the latter quite visionary for the time. The walk-up apartments were designed with direct stairway access to two flats per landing to ensure reasonable privacy, cross-ventilation, and at least two orientations for each dwelling.

During the interwar years, Charles Edouard Jeanneret, or Le Corbusier (1887–1965), formulated the housing design and planning concepts that so radically influenced the Modern movement in architecture. With Paul Dermée, in 1920, Le Corbusier founded the magazine *Esprit Nouveau*, and from 1922 onward he had an architectural practice—initially in partnership with his cousin Pierre Jeanneret. Le Corbusier's architecture was

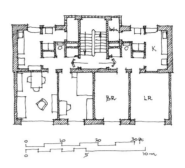

Cité-jardin apartments, Chatenay-Malabry (1933), Bassompierre, de Rutté, Sirvin and Avfridson (after Otto Völkers)

both emulated and plagiarized, and his writings influenced the work of countless twentieth-century architects and planners.

It is said that one day Le Corbusier, in the company of his cousin, discovered a small bistro in the center of Paris which had a mezzanine in the rear and a lofty ceiling in front. Impressed by the spatial quality of this bistro, the two architects amused themselves with its potential application in house design. In fact, Le Corbusier applied this concept in the Maison Citrohan (1920), a Villas Apartment project (1922), a villa (1927) at the Weissenhof colony (Bruckmannweg 2), and in the mezzanine apartments of Unité d'Habitation.

Unlike Frank Lloyd Wright, Le Corbusier loved the city, "believing it to be the highest expression of civilization, out of which man's loftiest contributions had emanated throughout history" (Grossman 1962, 131). But he was also concerned with the appalling conditions that many urban dwellers had to endure "without hope, without sky, without sun, without verdure." Le Corbusier anticipated a shorter working day and therefore an increase in leisure time—changes that would eventually demand a new order of life with more open space for recreational opportunities. To create more space in congested cities would necessitate bold action, such as the demolition of large segments of existing cities to make room for new developments with recreation space at one's doorstep.

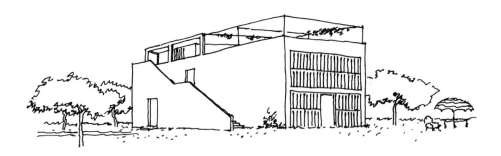

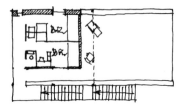

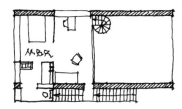

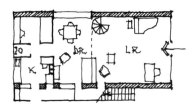

Maison 'Citrohan' (1920), three plans and perspective,
Le Corbusier
(after W. Boesiger and H. Girsberger)

Le Corbusier did not dismiss the city as readily as older reformers did, because urban living conditions resulting from the Industrial Revolution were no longer as hopeless as they once appeared to his predecessors. Because city governments were engaged in building workers' housing, the hope for a better future for cities did not appear beyond reach. This is not to say that Le Corbusier did not witness the plight of the urban poor, but by the time he reached maturity the worst was over. Le Corbusier's generation was not so much concerned whether cities would be regenerated, but rather how.

Both new garden cities and traditional congested city blocks were equally disastrous in Le Corbusier's view. The two extremes represented the dichotomy of urban living conditions and demanded a resolution. Le Corbusier found a solution in the reconciliation of the desire to be both close to nature and at the same time to be able to enjoy the proximity of all amenities that great cities offered.

In the twenties, Le Corbusier proposed a grandiose plan for a "vertical garden city," which he called *Ville Radieuse*, or Radiant City, where "a pact is sealed with nature, [and] nature is entered in the lease" (Le Corbusier 1948, 52). In essence, the required high density of large cities was resolved by high-rise buildings for both business and habitation with a land coverage of merely 18 percent. The Ville Radieuse proposal was exhibited in 1925 as a schematic plan for a verdant city of three million inhabitants. Remarkably symmetrical and geometrical in its design, this proposed city's core was envisaged to consist of twenty-four cruciform skyscrapers, each accommodating 10,000 to 50,000 employees; at the foot of these commercial office towers were the extensive parks and gardens with restaurants, café, luxury shops, theaters, and car parking facilities.

The residential zones of the Radiant City, running parallel both to the north and south of the city core, featured two distinct residential quarters although the projected population densities of both were supposed to be approximately the same. The first of these residential areas featured a linear

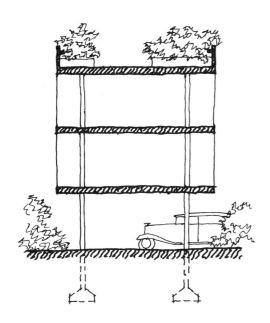

Independent Framework (1942), Le Corbusier
(after Le Corbusier and de Pierrefeu)

design with high-rise apartment slabs that straddled streets and parklike city blocks; the second area was more conventional, with apartment blocks sited along the perimeter of city blocks. Beyond the residential zones was envisaged a green belt, a free zone of woods and fields, followed by a belt of low-density suburbs.

The absence of a large-scale comprehensive development along the lines of Ville Radieuse should not be interpreted to mean that Le Corbusier's ideas of urban reform failed, since many urban renewal developments and projects built after the publication of Ville Radieuse reflect Le Corbusier's ideas, and led to the popular "tower-in-the-park" design concept. Williamsburg Houses (1938) in Brooklyn and Stuyvesant Town (1943–49) on the Lower East Side of Manhattan were both designed in accordance with the concept.

Although Le Corbusier disapproved of the detached house, he was not blind to the fact that it represented the desire of countless urban inhabitants. Although he objected to the land-use inefficiency intrinsic to detached single-family house developments, he did accept several commissions to design villas. Le Corbusier introduced five design principles for villas, which entailed (1) the use of pilotis (see drawing at left) to free the ground and lift the dwelling above the dampness of the earth, with better access to sun and air; (2) the utilization of roof terraces and roof gardens not only as additional outdoor extensions of the dwelling, but also as an insulation retarding the temperature changes that roofs are exposed to; (3) the elimination of the design constraints imposed by load-bearing walls by replacing them with a structural frame that provides greater freedom of design; (4) the use of ribbon windows to optimize daylighting indoors; and (5) the liberation of the façade from load-bearing functions, enabling a departure from traditional design constraints. By 1914, Le Corbusier had already demonstrated the advantages of these design principles with the Domino House project and, thereafter, most of his villas built during the interwar period employed pilotis to free a considerable area of the ground beneath the buildings.

Le Corbusier's main interest in housing focused on the development of viable and affordable multiple dwelling forms. He perceived high-density and high-rise housing as a necessity in large cities for three reasons: (1) to reduce traveling distance between places of work and home, (2) to free the ground area around buildings for recreational use and traffic arteries, and (3) to ensure good views and access to ample sun and air for each dwelling.

Germany

After World War I, the defeated nations experienced harder times than their victorious or neutral counterparts. The threat of starvation, accompanied by an unprecedented inflation, delayed housing programs devised to alleviate a desperate housing crisis. Eventually, with investment loans from abroad, both Germany and Austria rallied their forces and built municipal housing estates on a scale that was much admired and emulated by other nations.

With foreign loans, the economic climate in Germany improved to such a degree by the mid-twenties that city governments were able to

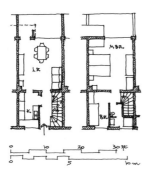

Römerstadt housing estate, Frankfurt-am-Main
(1926–30), Ernst May
(after Leonardo Benevolo)

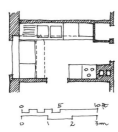

Frankfurt prototype kitchen (1931), Grete Lihotzky
(after K.W. Schmitt)

considerably alleviate overcrowding in dwellings. A pragmatism, known as *Neue Sachlichkeit* (New Realism), prevailed, emphasizing standardization and mass production of building elements, in order to reduce building costs and thus enable the provision of affordable and healthy dwellings with ample access to sun and air.

As in England's housing developments, nurseries and kindergartens as well as recreational spaces were viewed as an intrinsic part of residential projects. There was, however, an important distinction between England and Germany with respect to dwelling types in residential developments. While in England the small single-family house or cottage—detached, semidetached, or as row houses—prevailed, in Germany the low-rise, three- to four-story apartment house was favored. Before 1930, Germany produced over two million dwellings of a pleasing design in low-income housing estates with extensive communal facilities.

A first-rate example is the housing built in Frankfurt-am-Main by Ernst May, an architect and the city's building councillor. Between 1925 and 1930, he was responsible for about 90 percent of all housing construction in that city and, having worked with Raymond Unwin in England, May became a strong advocate of the Garden City movement and the attached single-family dwelling, as demonstrated in his Römerstadt housing estate in Frankfurt (1926–30). It was also during this period that the Frankfurt kitchen, an efficient prototype for a small dwelling, was designed by Grete Lihotzky (1931).

Equally exemplary were several suburban housing estates built in Berlin, such as the Hufeisensiedlung (horseshoe-settlement) adjacent to a pond in Britz (1927), and the Zehlendorf housing estate, sited in a pine forest (1926–31). Both projects were designed by Bruno Taut: the Britz walk-up apartment development in partnership with Martin Wagner, and the Zehlendorf estate with three-story town houses in collaboration with Otto Rudolf Salvisberg and Hugo Häring.

A large housing development in Berlin-Siemensstadt (1929), featuring parallel rows of apartment blocks in a park setting, introduced the so-called Zeilenbau design approach, with buildings planned in parallel rows with a north-south axis to give a western exposure to living rooms and an eastern one to bedrooms and kitchens. This rigid concern with sun orientation brought about a certain monotony, especially in large-scale residential developments.

The Berlin four-story walk-up apartment blocks were separated from each other by wide wooded spaces to provide ample outdoor areas to residents. The larger apartment units were entered directly from the stairhall landing, while one-bedroom units had outdoor gallery access. Although most apartments were rather small in comparison with today's standards, they all had a private balcony, a bright kitchen, and a private bathroom. Moreover, cross-ventilation and central heating were new amenities, previously unavailable in crowded tenements built during the nineteenth century. Berlin-Siemensstadt represents the collaborative

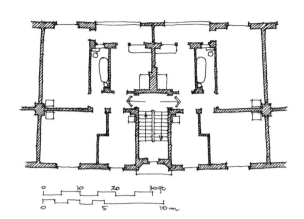

"Hufeisensiedlung," Britz, Berlin (1925–27),
B. Taut and M. Wagner
(after Maria Berning, et al.)

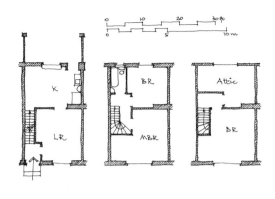

Housing estate, Zehlendorf, Berlin (1926–31),
Bruno Taut, et al.
(after Maria Berning, et al.)

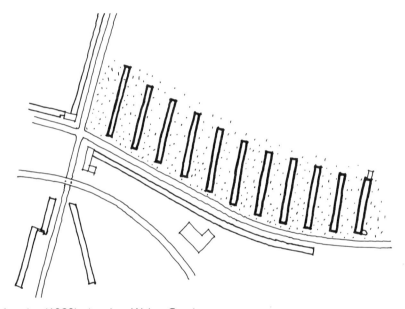

Berlin-Siemensstadt housing (1929), site plan, Walter Gropius
(after S. Giedion)

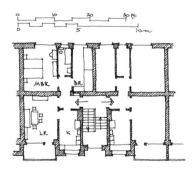

Berlin-Siemensstadt apartments (1929), Walter Gropius
(after S. Giedion)

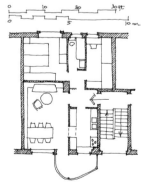

Berlin-Siemensstadt minimum standard apartment
(1930), Hugo Härig
(after K. W. Schmitt)

Weissenhof Colony walk-up apartments, Stuttgart (1927),
Ludwig Mies van der Rohe
(after J. Joedicke and C. Plath)

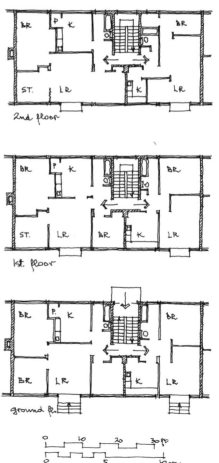

efforts of several noted architects, such as Walter
Gropius, Hans Sharoun, Hugo Häring, and Fred
Forbat, as well as Henning and Otto Bartning.

Perhaps the greatest influence upon the evolution of housing design in this period was exerted by
the city of Stuttgart when, prompted by the
Deutsche Werkbund, it constructed the Weissenhof Colony (1927) under the direction of Mies van
der Rohe, with the participation not only of selected German architects but also architects from
neighboring countries, who made a contribution to
housing design. The aim of this international
exposition was to demonstrate to the public the
"New Home" with sound living conditions.

Nestled on a southeast-facing sloped site, the
Weissenhof Colony represents a milestone in
domestic architecture built between the two world
wars. The original design criteria called for middle-
sized dwelling units suitable for families with

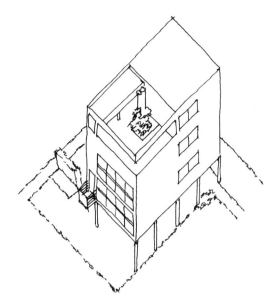

Weissenhof Colony villa, Stuttgart (1927), Le Corbusier
and Pierre Jeanneret
(after J. Joedicke and C. Plath)

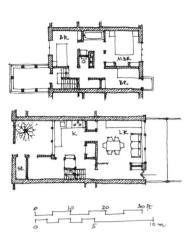

Weissenhof Colony row houses, Stuttgart (1927),
J. J. P. Oud
(after Leonardo Benevolo)

restricted incomes. This was observed only by Mies van der Rohe, Gropius, Le Corbusier, Behrens, Schneck, Oud, and Stam; other architects chose to design homes more suitable for the upper-middle class. The open-plan design approach, with the living room and dining room combined into a single space, was generally employed by most architects in order to provide spaciousness in their houses, and all architects used new construction methods and new building materials.

The fact that all buildings had flat roofs and plain white stucco walls led to the criticism that the colony did not respect German traditions. Hermann Muthesius, for example, criticized (1) the absence of roof eaves, which traditionally protected walls from the rain; (2) the open plan, which prevents the use of a room for study in privacy; (3) the over-dimensioned windows, which would be unpleasant during the cold winter months; and, (4) the flat roof spaces, indigenous to climates where they are used year round. These were not flattering comments in the late twenties, and, indeed, in 1938, under the Nazi regime, these "degenerate" buildings were ordered to be demolished. Although the order was never executed, several Weissenhof buildings were eventually destroyed during bombing raids.

The three houses designed by Le Corbusier—one detached and two semidetached—were typically based on his five design principles. Walter Gropius's two steel-framed houses, with asbestos cement sheeting on the exterior, demonstrated the viability of dry assembly construction methods, and his use of a modular grid demonstrated the feasibility of standardization. J. J. P. Oud's cluster of five two-story town houses were planned with a southern exposure for a large living room on the ground floor, and two bedrooms on the upper level, all fronting on a private garden; the main door was reached through the front garden, while the rear service entrance led through a walled courtyard. The wet core (all plumbing) was in the center of the house and, with the staircase acting as the main traffic distributor, corridors were avoided on the main floor.

Although not an exceptionally innovative solution, Mies's walk-up apartment strip with four vertical-access staircases, each serving two flats per floor, demonstrated "how flexible apartments can be if the structure itself is a skeleton building" (Hilberseimer 1956, 63). While the stair halls, kitchens, and bathrooms were by necessity fixed, all other spaces of the dwellings were left free to be subdivided by means of movable partitions or walls

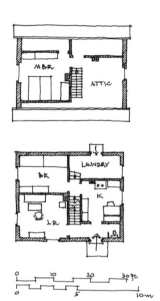

Village-like colony near Rottweil (1937–40), two plans and perspective
(after Leonardo Benevolo)

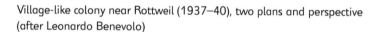

according to the needs of those who would inhabit them. A great variety of layouts was offered for the two apartment sizes contained in the building; consistently, all living rooms faced southeast with large horizontal fenestration. Communal laundries, drying rooms, storage areas, and large sun decks were placed on the roof level, the latter partially shaded by a cantilevered roof. Le Corbusier's houses, Oud's town houses, and Mies van der Rohe's walk-ups, with a few other restored buildings in this colony, are now preserved as historic monuments.

After the completion of the Weissenhof Colony, Mies continued his pioneering work in domestic architecture, first with the construction of the much acclaimed Tugendhat House (1930) in Brno, the Czech Republic; then a house for the Berlin Building Exposition of 1931 and a project for a Courtyard House with three courts (1934).

Shortly after the Great Depression of 1929, after foreign loans were called in, Germany once again plunged into economic chaos and, as a result, the political scene shifted to the right. The emigration of German architects commenced: Ernst May, Fred Forbat, Gustav Hassenpflug, Hans Schmidt, Walter Schwagenscheidt, and Mart Stam left for the Soviet Union to work on the new town Magnitogorsk in the Urals. They were followed by Bruno Taut,

Arthur Korn, Hannes Meyer, Hans Albers, Walter Gropius, Marcel Breuer, Ludwig Hilberseimer, Laszlo Moholy Nagy, Lyonel Feininger, and, finally, Mies; many of them eventually settled in North America.

With the departure of the most renowned architects, and after the national socialist seizure of power, the official housing policy of Germany changed radically. Single-family detached one-story stuccoed gabled houses with bedrooms tucked below steep red-tiled roofs—houses having the "German look"—were built in villagelike colonies in the city outskirts. The colonies resembled an early suburban sprawl, with an important difference: residents only had the promise of a car in the distant future.

AUSTRIA

After the loss of large territories, the postwar Austrian government was forced to dismiss more than 80,000 government employees, a catastrophe for the middle class, which already lost much investment in war bonds and was hard-hit by inflation. Vienna, the former hub of the Austro-Hungarian monarchy, was hardest hit. In spite of many adversities, however, Vienna, with its social democratic government, soon emerged as an exemplary municipality, building about 64,000 dwelling units between the end of World War I and 1934, increasing the number of dwelling units by 10 percent. Two design approaches were used for the new housing stock. One was the construction of suburban cottages in garden colonies, and the other the building of superblocks, consisting mainly of four- to six-story walk-up apartments built around large garden courts.

Initially, garden colonies of detached houses were built on vacant land owned by the city and managed by housing cooperatives. The simple houses had neither running water nor sewer connections, but since their lots were deep, the occupants could grow vegetables, plant orchards, and keep goats, pigs, or chickens to supplement their meager food supply during the inflationary postwar years.

In 1920, Adolf Loos became the chief architect of the municipal housing department of Vienna. Loos continued to build garden colonies, but with attached dwellings built in rows on narrow-fronted deep lots. His Heuberg model estate featured an economical and ingenious terrace house design, with greenhouses in the front and gardens in the rear. The economy of these dwellings derived from using the cross-wall structural system, spanning 18 ft (5.50 m) from firewall to firewall. With this system, the front and rear façades were suspended from floors rather than supported on foundations, and neither a cellar nor attic space was provided. At Heuberg, Loos attempted to create a closer link between workers' dwellings and allotment gardens, the latter traditionally on leased land at the outskirts of cities.

Allotment gardens were introduced during the mid-nineteenth century by a German physician, Daniel Gottlieb Moritz Schreber, with the aim of giving workers and their families in crowded tenements access to a green piece of land for both cultivation and recreation. These allotment gardens soon sprouted little gazebolike shelters, and once-derelict urban land was transformed into little green colonies. Schreber's idea was so enticing that several industrialized countries adopted the concept in spite of the inherent shortcoming that

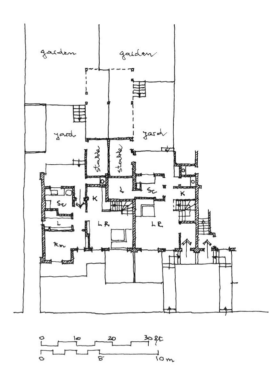

Heuberg model estate, Vienna (1920), Adolf Loos (after L. Münz and G. Künstler)

considerable time was needed for public transit to reach these colonies.

After 1923, the City Council of Vienna adopted a new housing policy, and began to build walk-up apartment buildings for low-income families. Entered through monumental arched gates that led to landscaped courtyards, these "public housing palaces," called *höfe*, were veritable cities within a city. While they gave the impression of spaciousness, in reality the individual apartments were very small (410–620 sq ft or 38–57 m^2). Moreover, three to four dwelling units were entered from each staircase landing, which forced a back-to-back arrangement of dwellings and, therefore, loss of cross-ventilation. Each apartment was heated individually by kachelofens, the typical ceramic stoves indigenous to this region. Apartment

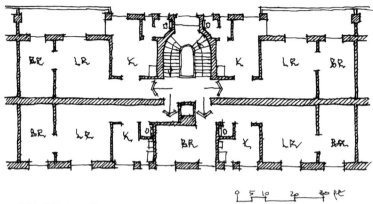

Karl-Marx-Hof, Vienna (1926–30), Karl Ehn
(after Y. Ashihara)

dwellings had neither hot water, showers, or bath-tubs, but residents had access to many excellent community facilities, including bathhouses, mechanically equipped laundries, kindergartens, clubrooms, gymnasia, and cooperative food stores, as well as outdoor playgrounds and recreational areas.

Designed by architect Karl Ehn, Karl-Marx-Hof (1926–30), with 1,382 apartment units, was one of the largest of these housing complexes. Rents were low, around 5 percent of a skilled worker's average wage. The municipality subsidized the rents through taxes collected from betting on horse races, the consumption of alcoholic beverages, movie tickets, and a tax collected from residents of apartments with private bathrooms and those employing servants. In the mid-thirties, with the emergence of national socialism, the social demo-cratic party fell into disfavor, and after their expul-sion from power following the German occupation in 1938, social housing programs in Austria ceased abruptly.

THE NETHERLANDS

The Netherlands occupied a singular position in housing design since, by 1902, it already had a Housing Act designed to facilitate the construction of low-rent housing, enable the clearance of slums, and make improvements in town planning. Although garden suburbs were built, their design was invariably governed by efficient land-use considerations to preserve as much agricultural land as possible. Thus, suburban homes were mostly one-family row houses with narrow street frontages, and small gardens. Shaded by trees, res-idential streets were narrow and usually had a sidewalk only on one side. Low-density develop-ment peaked in 1922 and was gradually replaced by medium-density housing estates.

Dutch architect-designed multiple housing built during the interwar period was of exceptional quality. In Rotterdam, Michiel Brinkman's munic-ipal residential development Spangen (1919–21) featured stacked dwelling units in continuous four-story buildings around the perimeter of a city block. A two-bay three-bedroom flat on a single plane with direct access from the landscaped court occupied the ground floor; a similar apartment was superimposed on the floor above and was reached from the court through a private staircase. The third and fourth floors contained rows of two-story units accessible from an outside third-floor gallery, a "street in the air." The upper units, each a single bay wide, had the living room, kitchen, and toilet on the lower level and three bedrooms above, simulat-ing the arrangement of conventional row houses.

A more traditional design approach for munici-pal multiple housing developments in Rotterdam was used by Jacobus Johannes Pieter Oud, exem-plified in his Tusschendijken (1920–23). Oud pro-vided direct street entrances for ground-floor units, and staircase access with only one flat per landing to the upper flats in his first scheme, and more traditional shared staircase access with two flats per landing for the two-story upper dwellings in his second project. Both these housing estates used a Sittesque closed block, characterized by a continuous mass of building along the street broken only by entrances to an interior garden.

Oud's best known housing project was built in Hoek van Holland (1924–27), a stacked-unit housing development of two rows of identical terraces with rounded end units. All dwellings, which ranged from one- to three-bedroom units, had their own private street entrances; ground-floor units had access to a garden in the rear, while upper dwellings had balconies both in front and

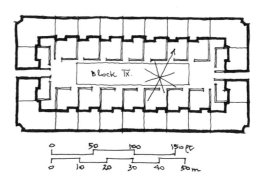

Spangen, Rotterdam (1919–21), J. J. P. Oud
(after D. I. Grinberg)

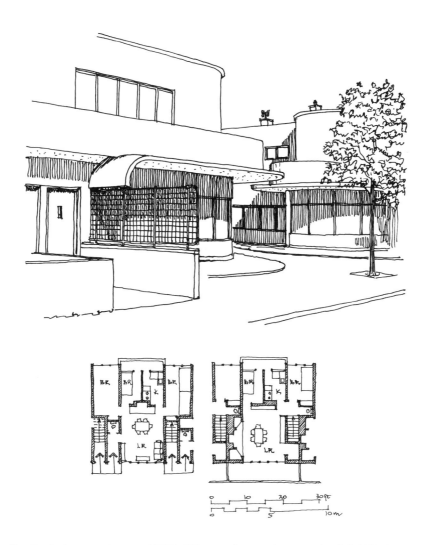

"Hook of Holland"—Stacked terrace-houses (1924–27), two plans and perspective, J. J. P. Oud
(after Leonardo Benevolo)

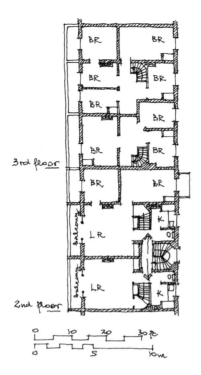
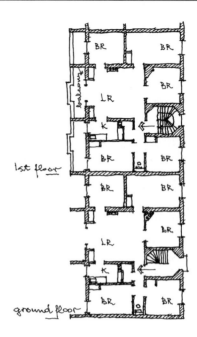

Tusschendijken, Rotterdam (1920–23), J. J. P. Oud
(after D. I. Grinberg)

back. This housing scheme represents a transition from the *De Stijl* movement to the *Nieuwe Zakelijkheld*, or New "Sachlichkeit," (New Objectivity) and is characterized by the extensive use of white plastered walls.

By the mid-thirties the influence of the German Zeilenbau resulted in a departure from perimeter planning, and the adoption of parallel rows of walk-up apartment buildings separated from each other by green areas. Called *Strokenbouw* in Dutch, this new planning approach advocated the opening-up of the block. Large housing estates of four-story buildings in the outskirts of Amsterdam bear witness to the monotony created by these new residential environments as well as to the loss of the territoriality that was inherent in the defined inner garden spaces of closed residential blocks.

SCANDINAVIA

Despite its neutrality, Sweden also experienced a housing shortage immediately after the war; almost half (47 percent) of all households lived in overcrowded dwellings. Rent control, as well as housing subsidies to municipalities, and nonprofit housing cooperatives had to be maintained until 1923 when the shortage abated. Thereafter, government loans for housing developments were given exclusively to cooperatives, which had proven themselves to be most efficient in providing high standards of design. Between the two world wars, these cooperatives built about 36,000 urban dwelling units.

The 1930 Stockholm Exhibition on the island of Djurgården was a milestone in Scandinavian architectural development. Several Swedish architects designed residential buildings for the exhibition, with the aim of presenting economic design solutions for low-income housing. Sven Markelius, an architect and town planner, and Kurt von Schmalensee designed detached houses demonstrating the advantages of the open plan; Uno Ahren and Oswald Almquist presented a well-designed row-house scheme; and Gustaf Clason attracted much attention with his flat with strict zoning of activities for a family of three to four members.

Multiple-dwelling standards were much improved as a result of the Stockholm exhibition. The

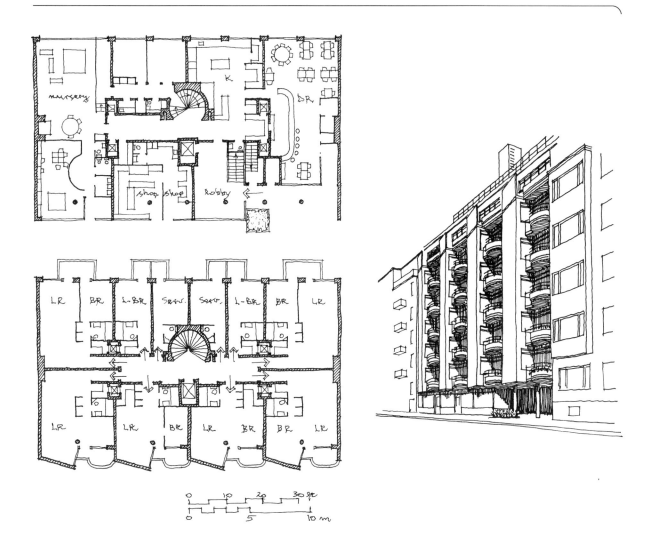

Kollektivhus, Stockholm (1935), two plans and perspective, Sven Markelius
(after B. Waagensen and J. Rubin)

majority of cooperative urban dwellings construct-ed after the exhibition were blocks of apartments, built as a rule in rows, with gardens and play-grounds in between. The Kristineberg housing development, built in one of Stockholm's suburbs, illustrates the housing standards of the early thir-ties. The apartment units were comfortable and well equipped, consisting of a living room, two bedrooms, a kitchen, a bathroom, and a balcony. All rooms were well proportioned and well lit through the use of large windows and glazed doors leading to the balcony. The kitchen had built-in cabinets, a refrigerator, a gas stove, a stainless steel sink, and running hot and cold water. Apartments were centrally heated, and occupants had access to

a garbage chute for an incinerator. Communal laundries had electric washing and wringing machines next to a steam-heated drying room.

Apartment blocks had plenty of open space around them. In addition to gardens and play-grounds, other communal facilities included a community nursery, where mothers could leave their small children in the care of trained nurses; in addition there was a kindergarten and an infir-mary where children were cared for when sick. Finally, a gymnasium and several social rooms were at the disposition of the tenants.

In the early thirties the merits and demerits of collective services received much attention from housing reformers, and the turn-of-the-century concept submitted by Otto Fick of a *Kollektivhus* or "collective house"—an apartment house with centralized household services, including meal service—was revived. Most reformers agreed that working-class women needed help because household chores were particularly burdensome. In fact, collective habitation was most often requested by single working men and women, who not only looked to ease their household chores, but also wanted the social interaction these buildings offered to their residents. In the general discourse on collective habitation, sociologists Alva and Gunnar Myrdal emerged as protagonists of these building types, arguing that liberating women from housekeeping would lead not only to their emancipation but, eventually, to equal opportunities in the work force.

After several attempts, Sven Markelius succeeded in 1935 in building a relatively small Kollectivhus, at 6 John Ericsonsgatan in Stockholm, with fifty-seven apartment units for families. Most of the dwellings were one-bedroom or bed-alcove units, and all had balconies. Dumbwaiters, each serving a set of two apartments on each floor, linked the butler's pantries of the kitchenless dwellings to a service corridor adjacent to the central kitchen. A self-service restaurant, a combined nursery and kindergarten for twenty preschool infants, and a small convenience store were additional amenities at ground-floor level.

To the disappointment of both Myrdal and Markelius, the utopian ideal of working-class families living in collective apartment buildings did not materialize. Only professional and self-employed people took advantage of this new house form, in spite of the fact that the dwellings were designed to be affordable to low-income families. A further disappointment—one that no one foresaw—was that families whose children had grown up were reluctant to move out of the collective apartment buildings and, in consequence, both the nursery and the kindergarten were underused. With a decreasing resident population, other collective services were also threatened, and eventually it became necessary to convert the laundry service and restaurant into commercial operations, and to allow the use of child-care facilities by children living in the neighborhood, so that revenue received from nonresident users could sustain these facilities.

Before these economic woes surfaced, Markelius's collective house received favorable newspaper coverage, which, in turn, led to the establishment of several similar projects in Stockholm, but mostly for single women and childless couples.

A serious housing shortage in Denmark during the first decade of the twentieth century was further aggravated after World War I by high inflation and a rapidly growing urban population. The idea that workers should take matters into their own hand and combat both housing shortage and unemployment through the establishment of cooperative building societies gained strength. While the yearly housing construction by building societies accounted for 10 percent before World War I, by 1945 it reached 77 percent.

Following the Stockholm architectural exhibition, Danes were influenced by trends in modern architecture, but—as has always been the case—modified them to suit their own values. In the twenties a significant milestone in the construction of multiple dwellings was a change in the building code permitting a single staircase access to multiple dwellings in fireproof buildings, provided that each flat also had a balcony from which tenants could be rescued in case the staircase became impassable because of smoke or fire. At first, balconies were small and offered little privacy, but by the thirties more attention was given to both size and privacy, and by the forties they were recessed into the building mass. Balconies became veritable outdoor rooms with flower boxes along their railings.

The most frequently built multiple-housing form of this period was the three- or four-story apartment building with two dwelling units per stairway landing, an arrangement that allowed for a reasonable degree of privacy and good cross-ventilation for each unit. Although dwelling sizes gradually increased, they were still too small to form the ideal setting for family life.

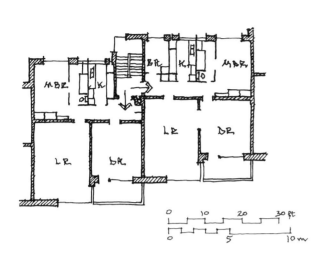

"Bellavista" housing estate, Klampenborg, Copenhagen
(1933), Arne Jacobsen
(after J. Pedersen)

Chain houses, Gentofte, Copenhagen (1943),
Arne Jacobsen
(after J. Pedersen)

Designed by Arne Jacobsen, the Bellavista housing estate (1933) in Klampenborg represents the best in multiple housing of the period. The U-shaped site plan of these walk-up apartments affords all residents an unobstructed view. A white brick building with a flat roof, large metal corner windows in the living rooms, and recessed balconies reflect the influence of the Modern movement. At first apartment buildings were built around the periphery of city blocks with the center landscaped like a garden, but in the thirties, the German Zeilenbau planning approach was adopted.

Single-family detached houses, called *parcelhuse*, also received state funding and were built in large numbers in the outskirts of cities and large provincial towns. In contrast to prewar houses with all rooms similar in size, these new homes featured large living rooms and smaller bedrooms; direct access from the living room to the outdoors altered the perception of the garden as a mere ornamental part of the house instead of an integral part of the living space.

Arne Jacobsen designed an interesting "chain house" development in Gentofte, a suburb of Copenhagen. This development consisted of single-family houses with all the virtues of a detached house, but because they were linked to each other by masonry walls, their gardens received more protection, and hence children were safer when playing in them.

Danish housing construction during the interwar period was so effective that a surplus of dwellings was created by the late thirties. However, this housing reserve was not adequate to satisfy housing needs during World War II, and Denmark once again experienced a housing scarcity.

With the opening of Mies van der Rohe's Weissenhofsiedlung exhibition in Stuttgart in 1927, modern functionalism in domestic architecture also reached Finland and, three years later, it got another boost from Gunnar Asplund's Stockholm exhibition.

The English garden suburb concept, too, influenced housing developments in Finland, as exemplified by the Käpylä garden suburb (1920–25). The master plan, drawn by Birger Brunila and Otto-Iivari Meurman, with the grouping of houses around small open spaces, clearly reveals the influence of British planners. The houses designed by Martti Valikangas reflected the "organic ratio-nalism" of domestic architecture at the beginning of the century. "The basic plan of the houses does away completely with classical axial symmetry . . . and results in dwellings that are particularly com-fortable to live in. Today the residential environ-ment of Käpylä is one of the most pleasant and most unspoiled in Finland" (Salokorpi 1970, 15–16).

RUSSIA

After the Russian Revolution of 1917, and under the new Soviet rule, it was generally accepted that Russian society would change radically. The lead-ership felt that during a period of social change it was necessary to look beyond bourgeois villas and apartment houses to find a housing solution. New house forms had to be developed that would not only reflect socioeconomic changes in society, but also be economical and function as "social con-densers." One solution was suggested in "housing communes" or domkommunas, which, in their organization, were very similar to the Danish Kollektivhuse. They entailed apartment buildings with kitchenless small apartment units, but with access to numerous collective services including central food catering, a concept introduced at the turn of the century by Otto Fick.

Collective habitation met several criteria set forth by the Russian leadership. First, it justified the construction of smaller and more economical dwelling units, depending on collective household services; second, it helped discredit traditional individualism by linking dwelling comfort to com-munal living; third, it liberated women from domestic work to be gainfully employed in labor-short industries and allowed them to partake as equal partners with men in the rebuilding of their homeland.

Domkommunas were very much in the spirit of Communism and complemented Lenin's idea that the true emancipation of women would come about only when the "micro-economics" of the private household were replaced by the "macro-econom-ics" of the socialist state. It was hoped that through

communal living with everyday housekeeping needs satisfied by collective services, inhabitants of the domkommuna would have the opportunity to improve and educate themselves in order to make a maximum contribution to their society. It was also expected that this new way of life would dis-courage the self-centeredness of individuals and the materialism manifested by capitalists.

As early as 1919, the management of a large Soviet state industrial plant prepared specifica-tions for the construction of apartments of the "hotel" type. This project contained the germ of an idea that later led to the development of the domkommuna concept, contained in the 1925 pro-gram of a housing design competition announced by the Moscow Soviet. After a series of "fraternal competitions," a research and design group was formed, which published drawings of five proto-type dwellings known as "stroikom units." One of these prototypes featured an innovative design of two superimposed one-bedroom units: each had a one-and-a-half-story living room facing south, and was serviced from the north side by a single loaded corridor at mid-level which wedged between the bedrooms of the two apartments. Thus, each apartment was a through unit, allowing both cross-ventilation, and, during the long winter months, a deep penetration of sunlight in the liv-ing room, which was possible because of its unusu-al ceiling height.

In a slightly modified form, this innovative design was also used by Moses Ginsburg, who headed a team of architects engaged in the design of the Narkomfin apartment building on Novinsky Boulevard in Moscow. Built between 1928 and 1929 for the People's Commissariat of Finance, this building contained several collective facilities that were accessible to its residents: a central kitchen and dining room, day nursery, library, meeting rooms, laundry, and a roof garden. It may be of interest to note that the mezzanine-bedroom arrangement of the Narkomfin dwellings resem-bles a design by the British architect D. G. Hoey submitted for "Improved Dwellings for the Poorer Classes," in 1889. Also, the well-known cross sec-tion of the Unité d'Habitation at Marseilles is in

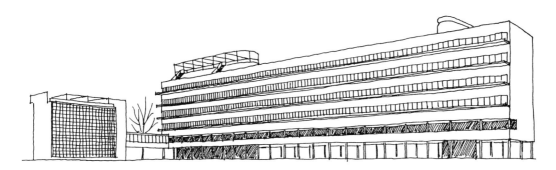

Narkomfin, Moscow (1928–29), perspective, M. Ginsburg, I. Milinis, and S. Prokhorov
(after Anatole Kopp)

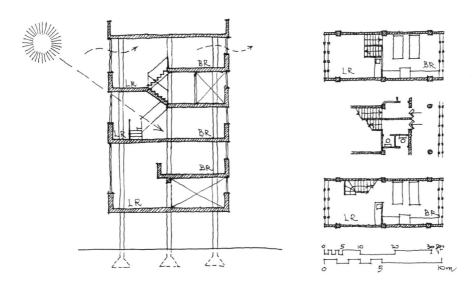

Narkomfin, Moscow (1928–29) three plans and cross section, M. Ginsburg, I. Milinis, and S. Prokhorov
(after Anatole Kopp)

essence a larger version of the cross-over two-level dwellings wrapped around an "interior street" submitted by I. Sobolev, in 1927, as a design proposal in another fraternal competition exploring new house forms.

Between 1926 and 1930 close to 30 percent of newly erected dwellings were in housing communes; a typical domkommuna had 400 to 800 residents. In the northern part of the country, enclosed corridors gave access to the various dwelling units, while in the south, open galleries served the same purpose.

The domkommuna building program, however, did not live up to the idealistic expectations of Russian housing reformers, and by 1932 this program was discontinued. The abandonment of Russia's collective habitation experiment is attributable to four reasons. First, the housing shortage was so acute that compact one-bedroom dwellings were often occupied by large families or, in extreme situations, by more than one family. Second, the acute housing shortage often necessitated the postponement of collective facilities in order to free labor and building materials for more essential additional dwellings; the promise that the omitted "nonessential" services were to be installed at some future date did not prevent daily discontent. Third, incompetent management of

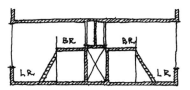

D. G. Hoey, 1889

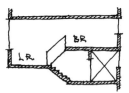

M. Ginsburg, 1928

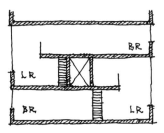

I. Sobolev, 1927

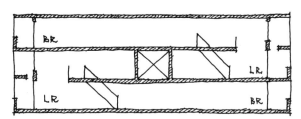

Le Corbusier, 1944

Cross sections of two-story apartment units

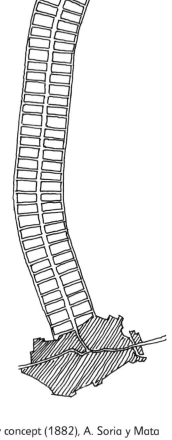

Linear City concept (1882), A. Soria y Mata
(after F. Choay)

collective apartment houses resulted in large-scale dissatisfaction. Fourth, the concept of collective habitation presupposes a considerable degree of sophistication and affluence on the part of the users; Russia, at the time, was in transition from an agrarian rural society to an industrialized urban society, hardly an ideal condition under which to test a new housing concept.

In the domain of town planning, Soria y Mata's linear city movement as well as Garnier's vision of the future city greatly influenced planning policy in the Soviet Union. The plan of the Association of

Modern Architects (O.S.A.) for Magnitogorsk (1929) and N. A. Miliutin's plan for Stalingrad (1930) are two good examples of the Soviet linear city structure, represented by a development of six parallel zones along a riverside. The first zone, adjacent to the river, was planned as a recreational park; the second zone for residential development; the third zone as a park belt, at least 1,640 ft (500 m) wide, with a main arterial highway running through it; the fourth zone was designated as an industrial area; the fifth zone contained the railway line; and, finally, the sixth zone was reserved for agriculture.

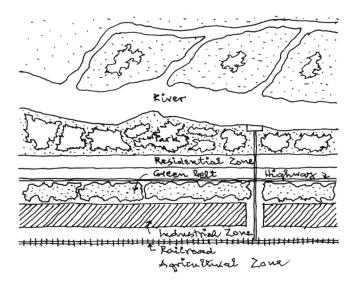

Magnitogorsk, Russia, (1929), N. A. Miliutin
(after A. Korn)

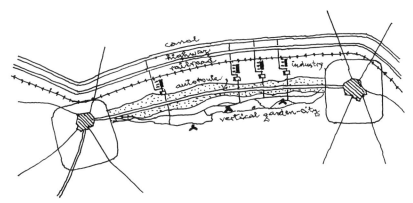

The linear industrial city (1942–43), Le Corbusier

The park zone, adjacent to the river, also contained administrative and social buildings, such as clubs, concert halls, sports palaces, and other institutions. These facilities were deliberately placed in the park not only because of the inherently pleasant surroundings, but also to force workmen leaving their industrial plant to pass through the residential neighborhood (and go home) before going to the recreational and social zone.

In addition to housing, the residential development area also contained nurseries, kindergartens, schools, restaurants, catering kitchens, and administrative and communal buildings. Technical schools, however, were located in the industrial zone, in close proximity to industry, to facilitate the sharing of libraries, laboratories, lecture rooms, and workshops. Excluding the agricultural zone, a linear city for a population of 50,000 inhabitants was planned to be about 3.1 to 3.7 miles (5 to 6 km) long and 1.2 to 1.8 miles (2 to 3 km) wide.

The construction of Stalingrad was proposed to form part of the first "Five Year Plan" and, in accordance with the linear city concept, was designed as an urban settlement for a population of 75,000 to 90,000 inhabitants—a linear city stretching many miles along the Volga River. The residential sector of Stalingrad had several collective apartment buildings with a centralized catering service provided by "communal cooking laboratories."

The city of Magnitogorsk was an urban ribbon 18.6 miles (30 km) long that united an industrial center with collective farms. The planning of this city was initially entrusted to a German design "brigade" headed by Ernst May, who left Germany before the national socialist takeover. As could be expected, this design team followed a residential housing concept familiar to them from the many residential developments they designed in Germany. In 1931, Magnitogorsk's housing stock consisted of 75 percent single-family dwellings and only 25 percent collective and communal dwellings. After May's departure from the Soviet Union, residential plans were modified to de-emphasize single-family houses and revert to more traditional multifamily housing standards.

LATIN AMERICA

In 1936, having been commissioned to design the new Ministry of Education and Health of Brazil, a group of architects including Lucio Costa, Oscar Niemeyer, and Affonso Eduardo Reidy, invited Le Corbusier to visit Rio de Janeiro as a consultant. Although Le Corbusier only stayed three weeks with the design team, his subsequent influence upon Latin American architecture was unrivaled by any other master-architect of the Modern movement. The new ministry building introduced the concept of pilotis to lift the building off the ground to enhance the circulation of air, as well as the use of the *brise-soleil*, external shading devices that protected windows from direct solar heat. These two design features were tailor-made for the climate of most South American countries. Although Le Corbusier proposed sunshades in some of his projects prior to his Rio visit, it was the Brazilians that first demonstrated their practical use in various forms: horizontal, vertical, fixed, or moveable. Apart from obvious advantages, sunshades were also favored by the public because of their extra function as privacy screens to domestic life—a feature that was innate to traditional Brazilian patio houses.

The first beneficiaries of modern domestic design were the affluent, whether living in single-

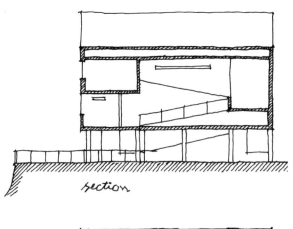

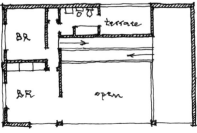

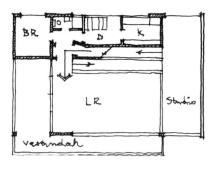

Oscar Niemeyer house, Rio de Janeiro (1942)
(after Philip L. Goodwin)

family homes or apartment houses. Bernard Rudofsky, who arrived in the late thirties, designed the Joao Arnstein House (1941) in Sao Paolo, a splendid, introverted modern house built around five walled gardens: three private and two semiprivate outdoor spaces. The latter two gardens were screened from the street to allow the merest glimpses of their lush growth. In contrast, Oscar Niemeyer's three-story reinforced concrete–frame extroverted house was built on pilotis on a steep south-facing site with a wonderful view and, as in Le Corbusier's Villa Savoye at Poissy (1929–31),

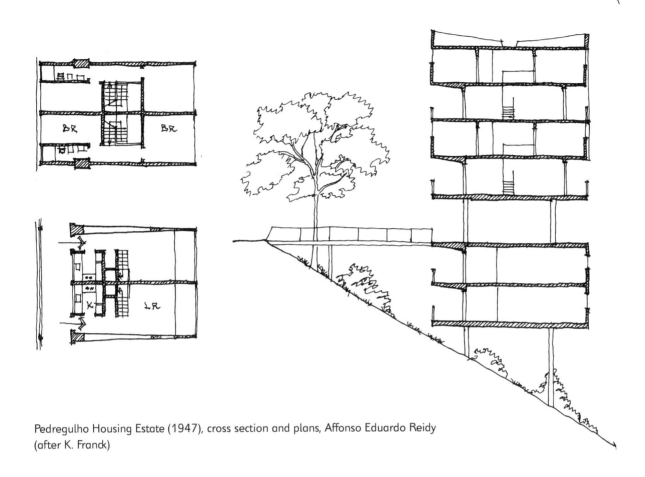

Pedregulho Housing Estate (1947), cross section and plans, Affonso Eduardo Reidy
(after K. Franck)

ramps took the place of stairs. A modern elevator-serviced high-rise apartment house at 322 Praia do Flamengo, along the most expensive section of Rio de Janeiro's waterfront, had windows with a projecting frame enabling interchangeable panels of glass and shutters.

Four-story open gallery access walk-ups were used for the Realengo Workers' Housing (1942), a low-rent residential development built by the Institute of Industrial Insurance. The cross-ventilated dwellings had only their hallways, kitchens, and bathrooms located next to the access gallery, thereby protecting the privacy of the main habitable rooms. An epitome of Rio's modern apartment house is the Pedregulho Housing Estate (1947), an 853-ft (260-m) long seven-story-high curved building on pilotis following the contours of the hillside. Designed by Affonso Eduardo Reidy for lower-paid municipal workers, the main structure with 272 apartments has gallery-access corridors to enable through-ventilation of dwellings.

Accessed by bridges to the third level, the building has smaller flats below and duplex apartments above the entry level. This housing estate has additional apartment houses as well as amenities, such as a nursery, a kindergarten, an elementary school, a gymnasium, swimming pool, playgrounds, a health center, and a shopping center.

A total commitment to the Modern movement's architectural design tenets and planning concepts was exemplified later in Brasilia (1956), the new capital of Brazil. Entrusted to Lucio Costa, the monumental master plan of the city with public buildings and residential superblocks, or *superquadras*, was distributed in a vast public open space setting. Conceived primarily for motorcar traffic, the scale of the city is congruent with autoroutes rather than pedestrian streets. Freestanding high-rise buildings and the lavish use of open spaces created an urban environment in Brasilia that is diametrically opposed to the urbanity prevalent in most Latin American cities, where social interaction traditionally occurred around a central plaza. Built in the wilderness, at a great distance from the urbanized coastal region, the planned city of Brasilia evolved over the years as the center of a shapeless large urban agglomeration fed by a population explosion (Cohen 1998).

In the forties and fifties architects believed that with rational design and mass production, the housing crisis in Latin American countries would be resolved. This did not materialize, primarily because population growth throughout Latin America was so impressive that neither private enterprise nor government was able to keep pace with housing demands. A stream of rural migrant families flocked to cities in search of employment, and since most of them could not find affordable housing, they resorted in desperation to temporary shelters that they built from discarded materials on empty land.

Over time—if the squatters' makeshift shelters were allowed to remain standing—their owners gradually improved them by converting them into more substantial dwellings constructed of solid building materials. Squatter settlements built in Lima, Peru are called *barriada*; in Rio de Janeiro, *favela*; in Venezuela, *ranchos*; and in Salvador, when built over water, *alagados*. Although there is a tendency to view these communities as shanty-towns or slums, in reality they are neither. The majority of dwellings are not shanties and, in great contrast to slum tenements that are rented, they are mostly owner-occupied.

By definition, a squatter settlement is an unplanned site. Their layouts are thus structured organically and informally, with pedestrian circulation made possible by a network of pathways with staircases inserted here and there on hilly sites. The settlements are reminiscent in their patterns to that of a Dogon "cliff-debris" village or the narrow alleyway network of old medinas. Most residents of squatter settlements prefer their communities to that of public housing estates, but, in spite of this strong sense of belonging, residents of *barrios* lack access to municipal infrastructures for sanitation as well as to municipal services, including garbage collection and police protection.

In several Central and South American cities serious attempts were made to force squatters to move into social housing estates. In Mexico City, for example, Mario Pani built thirteen-story tower blocks for 5,000 residents at the Presidente Alemán public housing complex (1950); ten years later, he designed a new residential district, Nonoalco-Tlatelolco, to house about 70,000 people in buildings ranging in height from four to twenty-two stories with half the site devoted to open space. A significant design objective of this large project was to provide dwellings that enabled different social classes to live next to each other.

The rapid growth of the urban population of Caracas during the early postwar years necessitated the construction of large housing estates, such as El Paraiso (1954) and 23 de Enero (1955–57). Carlos Raul Villanueva, chief advisor to both developments, formulated the program and inspired his architectural collaborators in the design of these "modern" estates set amongst squatters' improvised homes in the outskirts of Caracas. Critics from home and abroad referred to these high-rise blocks as "ugly boxes" built in a beautiful valley and accused the designers of cramming poor children of the wilderness into "filing cabinets" (Moholy-Nagy 1964, 143).

Aware of the extreme difficulty in solving the housing needs of lower income groups through the construction of high-rise public housing, a new generation of young Latin American architects, who studied the residential environment of poor people living in squatter settlements, advocate the use of simple building techniques suitable for low-rise dwellings. A sites-and-services design approach, entailing small plots of serviced land allotted to migrants, complemented by assistance to help residents build a home on the site, promises relief from both the acute housing crisis and sanitary problems, although the spontaneity of the existing organic pedestrian network will have to be sacrificed.

CHAPTER SIX

TWENTIETH-CENTURY HOUSING: 1950–2000

DECLINE OF AMERICAN CITIES

North American cities thrived at the end of World War II. Populations increased dramatically, not only because war industries attracted thousands of workers from rural districts and small towns, but also because thousands of urban immigrants from war-ravaged countries flocked to American cities. This population increase, along with consumer demand after the war-imposed shortages of the forties, ensured sustained economic growth throughout the fifties.

A characteristic of the traditional city was the distribution of residential development over its entire urbanized area, with the exception, perhaps, of a relatively small central business district (CBD). Residential densities were usually highest near the city center and decreased gradually towards the periphery. While it is true that some segregation of similar income groups was identifiable in certain neighborhoods, chances were that all residents were likely to meet in shops, cinemas, baseball parks, etc., and, even more significantly, rich and poor children often attended the same elementary and high schools in mid-sized cities.

Cities were crowded after the war, and the baby boom that followed triggered an acute housing shortage. This forced an increasing number of young families seeking a home environment to leave the cities for the suburbs. Government policies aided this exodus, but what began as a trickle soon turned into a flood. Cities were short-changed by this flight from the city and it is now clear that they could not afford the loss of young and relatively well-to-do families whose income potential was to improve over the years. But at the time cities were composed primarily of commercial, manufacturing, and institutional development.

The negative consequences of an urban policy neglecting residential land-use were only realized when commerce began to follow the suburbanites, first, to commercial strips along major roads leading out of the city, then to small shopping centers, usually with a supermarket and a department store, and impulse shopping in between. Still later, shopping centers were upgraded to "malls" with at least two supermarkets and two department stores to enable comparison shopping. Eventually, malls were transformed into shopping plazas with climate-controlled atria adorned with fountains and exotic plants. Complemented by gleaming office buildings and entertainment centers, these plazas emerged as suburban hubs that drained even more commercial activities from the inner city. With commercial offices and corporate headquarters relocating in suburbs and light industry moving to industrial parks, urban dispersal was, and continues to be, ongoing.

Many architects and planners see no danger in this development. Peter Rowe, for example, sees the emergence of a "middle landscape," as neither town nor country. This new environment, "still very much under development in both a physical and cultural sense," is the "real locus of growth and innovation in our society," and in Rowe's opinion is replacing "the functional specialization, diversity, and social heterogeneity of the traditional city with dispersed, disurban, and almost rural patterns of small town, country life" (1991, 289–91). While the "middle landscape" emerges, the socioeconomic and environmental effects of a continued unregulated suburban sprawl, accompanied by an increasing rate of car ownership, is making America a nation of suburban dwellers, dependent on the private automobile for all transportation. The adverse environmental effect of increased reliance on private automobiles is the continuation of a severe degradation of air quality in cities and suburbs alike.

The flight to the suburbs by large numbers of city dwellers in pursuit of the American dream created a nightmare for the parent city. This nightmare is well illustrated by the decline of Detroit, a city that paradoxically based its economic future on the mass production of the cars that enabled suburban sprawl. Motown, as Detroit was affectionately known, was the motor and music capital of North America, but after the exodus of mainly white citizens to the suburbs, the city's population decreased from 1,849,568 in 1950 to 1,027,924 in 1990—a loss of over 40 percent (Rusk 1993, 14). With abandoned buildings, empty skyscrapers, and garbage-strewn demolition sites, the city became a ghost town and one of the worst examples of urban racial segregation in the United States. While Detroit's suburbs flourished, a desolate city was ailing in their shadow.

Federally subsidized "urban renewal" interventions were introduced as a means to rejuvenate cities. In the name of progress, megadevelopments of new office buildings were complemented by the construction of new traffic arteries, followed by the wholesale destruction of existing urban fabrics—an abrupt disruption of continuity. Slum areas were razed and their residents housed in modern high-rise tenements. While the physical and sanitary aspects of their new homes were much improved, social conditions were not. Heavy-handed interventions destroyed the familiarity that had existed in former communities and contributed to the alienation that became so prevalent in urban renewal projects.

It is spine-chilling to realize how accurate Jane Jacobs was when she pointed out, four decades ago, how we wasted public funds, and what we built: "Low-income projects that become worse centers of delinquency, vandalism and general social hopelessness than the slum they were supposed to replace. Middle-income housing projects which are truly marvels of dullness and regimentation, sealed against any buoyancy or vitality of city life. . . . Expressways that eviscerate great cities. This is not rebuilding of cities. This is the sacking of cities" (Jacobs 1961, 4).

In the past, housing was an essential component of the inner city, but, apart from a few gentrified pockets, residential land use was allowed to be crowded out by commercial development. Without housing, the liveliness and security of street life in the inner city diminished, especially in the evening when shops close and office buildings are deserted. The greatest concern of inner-city dwellers, today, is security in the home and safety on the streets. Essentially, only two groups of residents still live in the inner city: those who have no choice, and those who can afford to pay for their security. While the well-to-do seek security in guarded luxury high-rise buildings or "gated" communities, the poor and the helpless live in unsupervised tenements, in roach- and vermin-infested dwellings, where both entering and leaving the building is a dreaded challenge. More and more, the American inner city has become the domain of the very rich and the very poor, as foretold by the *New York Herald* over a century ago (April 19, 1878).

Ideally, a city and its suburbs form an economic urban entity, with each component part complementing the other. Regrettably, this is seldom the case. Frequently, the parent city and its suburbs compete with each other for the very same human activities and resources. This competition is reflected in the paradox that while the city is being suburbanized, its suburbs strive for the same urban features and infrastructure standards intrinsic to cities. Just as low-rise, low-density housing projects and suburban spatial standards are incongruous in the inner city, so are high-rise buildings in the suburbs. Both the city and its suburbs have their respective innate attributes, and, similarly, various dwelling prototypes have their inherent characteristics as well as their ideal settings, with some performing best in the city, others in the suburbs.

North American Suburban Sprawl

The relative abundance of land, widespread automobile ownership, a government policy favoring home-ownership, and, above all, a rosy outlook with respect to the future, created the conditions for an unprecedented expansion of suburban development in North America. The post–World War II rise in family income coupled with Federal Housing Act (FHA) loan insurance and the Veterans Administration (VA), which guaranteed and insured loan programs, enabled large numbers of families to become home owners. By 1958, about 5.3 million veterans had obtained GI loans, 95 percent of which were for homes. Veterans proved to be excellent loan risks: fewer than 1 percent of them defaulted on their payments. Home ownership of nonfarm dwelling units increased from 41.1 percent in 1940 to 66 percent in 1970, and most new homes were built in suburbs, sprawling over the countryside adjacent to large cities.

Automobile ownership, an obvious corollary to suburban home ownership, also rose in the post-war years. Three out of every four American families owned a car in the early fifties, but by 1955 the ratio of one car per family was reached. Today, two cars per suburban household no longer seems a luxury but a necessity. While most suburbs grew by accretion, a few were conceived and built as planned communities employing a mass produc-

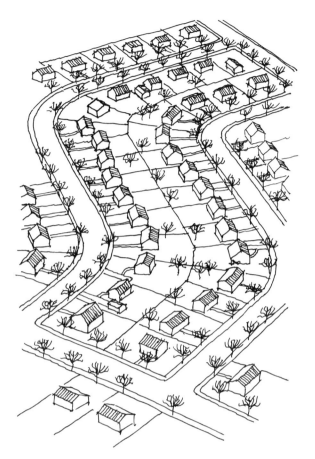

Levittown, Long Island, N.Y. (1949)
(after M. T. Kaufman)

tion building technology perfected during the war years for the construction of housing for workers engaged in the manufacture of ships, tanks, and airplanes.

In the late forties, one of the most successful entrepreneurs of "instant suburbia" was Abraham Levitt, who with his sons William and Alfred established a new town on Long Island. Now known as Levittown, this low-density (three dwelling units [d.u.]/acre or 7.7 d.u./hectare) community with rows of nearly identical Cape Cod–style and ranch-type houses, mostly on 60- by 100-ft (18.28- by 30.48-m) lots, attracted families by the thousands; they queued up in front of the sales offices to become owners of homes built on former potato fields. Homes fronted on wide curvilinear streets, a pattern not derived from any natural contours on the site, but designed to be picturesque. Sites for schools and a "village green" shopping area, as well

Model house, Levittown (1949)
(after B. Kelly)

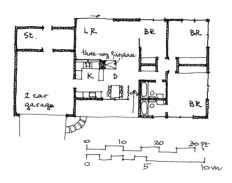

Model house "Landia," Levittown (1951), Alfred Levitt
(after "Landia")

as land for parks and public swimming pools, were donated by the builders to the community—marketing features that ensured not only quick growth but also financial success for Levitt and Sons.

The Levitt home was relatively small (800 sq ft or 74.32 m² for the Cape Cod, and 900 sq ft or 83.61 m² for the ranch) and conservative in its design. The attic in these asbestos-sided homes was envisioned as an expansion space for a growing family. Each house was equipped with basic household appliances, including a washing machine, as part of the standard equipment; later, the list of appliances was extended to include a television set as well and, in order to qualify for inclusion in the home mortgage, the television was built into one of the walls of the living room.

An added attraction of Levittown was the provision of paved roads and sidewalks—features hitherto associated with urban rather than suburban development. The landscaping of the outdoor areas originally consisted of sodded lawns and a few saplings and bushes, but during the following decades Levittowners nurtured this sparse landscape, with the result that the community no longer projects the starkness that confronted the pioneering homemakers. The critics of Levittown who predicted slum conditions in a few years were wrong.

Prior to pseudo-urban Levittown, suburbanites fully accepted the tradeoff of urban amenities for a new but rustic lifestyle close to nature, which frequently meant an absence of sidewalks, street lighting, municipal sewage systems, water lines,

and, at times, even unpaved roadways. Without municipal infrastructure, many suburban homes in the fifties and sixties had septic tanks and individual water wells, both necessitating large building lots. Clean air, nature close at hand, lots of elbow room, clean snow cover in winter, friendly neighbors, and a safe environment for children more than offset the loss of urban amenities and the inconvenience of increased commuting time necessary for work in the city.

Aware of the importance of good education and the value of good teachers, suburbanites emphasized the establishment of excellent schools in their child-oriented communities. The service area of an elementary school, in fact, determined the size of the minimum planning unit of a suburb, the "neighborhood," with a maximum of 1/2-mile (0.8-km) walking distance from the farthest dwelling to the centrally located school.

The word "street" with its urban connotation was avoided in most suburbs, and the terms avenue, boulevard, crescent, or drive were used instead. Initially, the standard width of a suburban public right-of-way was a "chain" (66 ft or 20.11 m). With minimum setback requirements of 20 ft (6.09 m) from the right-of-way, the visual width of streets, from house front to house front, added up to 106 ft (32.30 m), a width in excess of that of Fifth Avenue in New York, which is 100 ft (30.48 m) wide. Both Shaftesbury Avenue in London and Boulevard Haussmann in Paris—wide tree-lined urban thoroughfares with multilevel buildings on both sides—

are narrower than the typical North American suburban street. Neither traffic intensity nor aesthetic considerations justify the amount of land set aside for streets in suburban development.

Since many suburban residents had managerial skills, they elected a mayor and council members from their own ranks who could effectively run municipal affairs. The local council discovered early on that the suburban population, consisting primarily of young married couples with children, had fewer social liabilities than city dwellers. Generally unburdened by crime or welfare payments to the elderly, unemployed, or underprivileged, and with light traffic and no subsidy to mass transit systems, suburban municipalities could levy taxes that were very low in comparison to those paid by city dwellers. These favorable circumstances meant that suburbs enjoyed good borrowing power, which was soon put to use to obtain loans for the upgrading of municipal services to match, or even exceed, those of the city. These works were financed with borrowed money amortized over several decades, and paid for through the levy of local improvement taxes. Suburbanites rightfully considered themselves very fortunate since they could now enjoy the best of two worlds: country living with urban amenities.

Whereas the majority of suburbanites opted for residential developments with urban amenities, a few well-to-do families adhered to the original objective of country living, which often implied living at a greater distance from the parent city. These "exurbanites" were willing to do without standard urban amenities in exchange for more space in a bucolic landscape.

A small residential enclave called The Five Fields in Lexington, Massachusetts, was such a departure from typical monotonous suburban subdivisions. Designed by The Architects Collaborative (TAC) and begun in 1951, this 80-acre (32.37-hectare) tract of gently rolling and partially wooded land derived its name from the farmers' fields whose stone-walled boundaries were in great part allowed to remain.

As in Riverside, near Chicago, both the roads and the siting of freestanding houses complement the

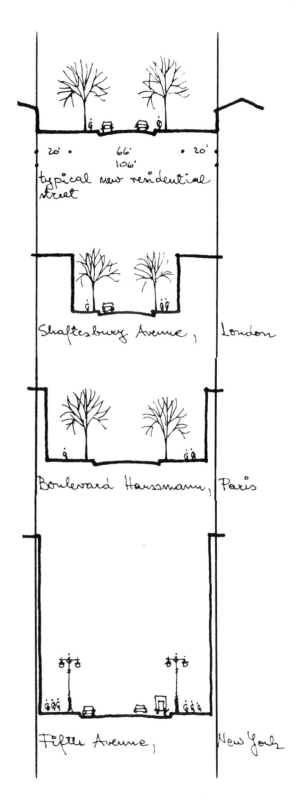

Street cross sections
(typical suburban street; Shaftesbury Avenue, London; Boulevard Haussmann, Paris; Fifth Avenue, New York City)

existing topography, a conscious attempt not to interfere with the natural formation of the landscape. In keeping with New England tradition, a 20-acre (8.09-hectare) area was set aside in the center of the development for a common green.

The discomfort of commuting on clogged highways in the fifties and sixties was even then an annoyance but as suburbanites and exurbanites increased in number, they acquired political clout which enabled them to lobby effectively for new expressways to alleviate traffic congestion. In fact, their influence was so strong that new autoroutes were even extended to the city's downtown area to facilitate rapid access for white-collar workers employed in the heart of the city.

Although suburbanites now had easy access to their workplace, their demand for inexpensive parking areas entailed the creation of large parking lots—mostly on demolished building sites—in the inner city, a wasteful use of urban land serviced by an expensive infrastructure. Improved access to the city core via limited-access autoroutes or expressways created the anomaly that made travel time from suburbs to downtown shorter than from many residential districts of the city proper, whose residents had to wind through a myriad of streets with traffic lights to reach the same destination.

In the early seventies, during the energy crisis, the rapid expansion of suburbs appeared to be slowed by higher fuel costs affecting both transportation and home heating. But this was only short-lived. First, a changeover from large gas-guzzling cars to smaller compact cars eased transportation costs. Second, many homes were retrofitted with increased insulation to reduce heating costs in winter and air-conditioning costs in summer. When oil prices slumped after a few years, life in auto-intensive suburbia in the eighties and nineties once again became desirable and affordable, not only for child-oriented families, but for all types of households.

Nevertheless, the energy crisis left an impression of vulnerability in the public's mind and it prompted some architects to experiment with the design of energy-efficient houses by exploiting solar energy through optimized orientation of dwellings towards the sun. Other measures, such as the active collection of solar energy through solar panels and earth shelters that promised warmth, quiet, and energy efficiency in subterranean dwellings, proved to be either too expensive or too radical a solution for the public at large.

It was also a heightened concern with energy conservation that led in the eighties and nineties to the reassessment and gradual public acceptance of more energy-efficient cluster- and town houses as viable suburban dwelling alternatives to the hitherto unchallenged dominance of the detached home. An attached two-story town house, for example, saves nearly half (45 percent) of the energy required for heating or cooling a detached single-story bungalow.

In the nineties the process of suburbanization continued and the dream of living in the countryside with urban amenities was as strong as ever. According to the U.S. Bureau of the Census, the suburban proportion of metropolitan development reached about 65 percent in 1980, and there are no indications that this trend will diminish.

The American Dream House

The concept of a house in a garden has almost universal appeal and represents the ideal house for many Americans. Nowhere is the possibility of owning such a house more within reach than on the North American continent, where land and home construction are relatively inexpensive and car ownership accepted as a necessity rather than a luxury. After World War II, the most popular house form in America was the one-level bungalow, but of "modern" rather than Arts and Crafts design.

The use of bungalows spread throughout the continent, including the subarctic regions of Alaska and Canada. In colder climates, bungalows needed foundations reaching below the frost level. A basement and the raising of the ground floor just above the average snow level were inexpensive by-products of the need to dig foundations. A typical countryside version of a large bungalow was the rambling ranch-type house with a two-car garage. Split-level houses were the rage of the late fifties

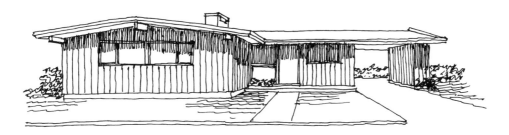

Bungalow with carport (1958), Andrew Chomick
(after *Small Home Design*)

Split-level house (1958), M. G. Dixon
(after *Small Home Design*)

One-and-a-half-story house (1958), Earl R. Dunlop
(after *Small Home Design*)

and early sixties, with a garage at grade, bedrooms and bathroom above the garage, and living/dining room, kitchen, and main entrance at mid-level between the two. One advantage of split-levels was that they required narrower building lots than bungalows. One-and-a-half and two-story houses, so prevalent before World War II, are the most economical freestanding dwellings; two-story houses were built during the postwar period, and recently, since the early eighties, they are once again much favored, especially if "neo-traditional" in style: looking old on the outside and new on the inside.

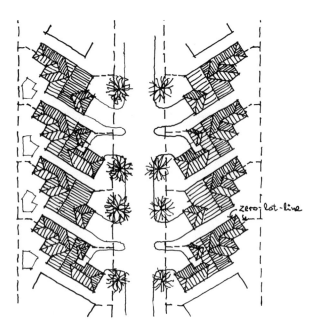

Two-story (Ashley) House, Seaside, Louis Hiett
(after D. Mohney and K. Easterling)

Zero-lot-line subdivision, Orlando, Florida, The Evans Group
(after Philip Langdon)

Today, as in the past, land economy through smaller and more affordable building lots has led to the use of some semidetached bungalows, but more often to semidetached split-level and two-story homes. So great is the desire to live in a detached home that suburbs use such planning ploys as "zero-lot-line" (i.e., without one side yard) subdivisions to reduce the size of lots and make them more affordable.

The obsession with freestanding houses is not a new phenomenon. During the nineteenth century, people of more moderate means displayed great ingenuity in making detached homes affordable. Some examples are the "shotgun" and "camelback" houses built on narrow city lots in New Orleans, Louisiana. Predating trailer homes, these two dwelling types are only 12 or 14 ft (3.65 or 4.26 m) wide, a constraint that forced the design of rooms aligned one behind the other, a layout not dissimilar to the nineteenth-century railroad flats in New York City tenements.

The shotgun house is a single-story dwelling, its name allegedly derived from the notion that a person could shoot a gun from front to rear and not miss a single room. The camelback house is similar, except that it has a single-story front and a two-story back, with a bedroom above. Apparently, camelbacks originated when municipal taxes were levied according to the street-frontage building height. To further enhance their affordability, shotguns and camelbacks were built semidetached or even as row houses. Both of these dwellings are popular in New Orleans for people with modest incomes.

A single-family detached house is inherently ground-related, with easy access to garden or backyard. Moreover, it complements the basic social unit—the family—and is viewed as the ideal home in which to raise children. A "zoned" single-family dwelling complements the requirements of both the adults and children of a family.

Cross-ventilation is an inherent property of detached homes and so is the open-ended possibility of favorable orientation, in theory if not in practice, since side yards are seldom wide enough to allow living-room windows to open upon them. As a low-profile dwelling prototype, the single-family detached house is easily integrated into a natural setting and enjoys a privileged status in municipal zoning considerations. It is eminently

Shotgun house

Camelback house

"Shotgun" and "camelback" houses, New Orleans
(after I. Sanders and C. Schoenberger)

suited to wood construction, whether built in situ or assembled of prefabricated components on the site. Finally, with lot boundaries clearly defined, detached houses are easily mortgagable and they project the image of unencumbered ownership.

In public perception, the advantages of the detached house outweigh its innate disadvantages: the most obvious is low land-use efficiency resulting in waste of precious land and very expensive municipal infrastructure costs. The street frontage (60 ft or 18.28 m) of a bungalow lot is three times that of a town house, which means that road construction, water mains, storm and sanitary sewer pipes, electric, telephone, and TV cables, gas lines, and street lighting are three times more expensive for bungalows than for town houses. Since the cost of postal service, policing, fire protection, street cleaning, and street maintenance are also functions of linear frontage per household, these

services are more expensive too. Finally, a low-density community makes public transit uneconomical, but as distances to schools, shopping centers, community facilities, and recreational areas in spread-out communities are usually too great to reach on foot, many families need two private cars to ensure freedom of mobility.

While the energy greediness of the detached house in comparison to other house forms is incontestable, other shortcomings, especially those within the social realm, are more controversial. It stands to reason that the single-family self-sufficient freestanding house has an isolating influence upon its occupants. Going to the movies, concerts, picnics, and community swimming pools—activities that hitherto lured adults and children away from their home and brought them in contact with other people—are no longer common. With TVs, VCRs, CD players, and computers in the home, and swimming pools and barbecues in the backyard, families have increasingly isolated themselves from the community. With telephones, faxes, and e-mail, physical isolation no longer implies seclusion as it once did. Paradoxically, however, telecommunication devices have also enabled "cocooning," the phenomenon of individual withdrawal from physical social contact, but continuing social interaction by electronic means.

With windows of principal rooms facing the street or the rear of the property, owners of detached homes are very concerned with who their neighbors are and how they maintain their property. While few neighbors object to having a view of a more expensive neighboring home, the opposite is rarely the case. This bias and intolerance results in residential neighborhoods, districts, and, frequently, entire suburbs having the same type of homes, more or less equally priced, and inhabited by people of the same income group.

After the turn of the twentieth century, the size of middle-class households decreased consistently. Households of five or more persons represented 63 percent in 1900, a fact reflected in the multi-bedroom Victorian houses of the turn of the century. In 1949, families with more than five persons accounted a mere 24.5 percent. The trend towards smaller families and households continued during the postwar years. In spite of these demographic changes in society, the single-family detached suburban home has retained its universal appeal.

The obsession with freestanding houses is not a new phenomenon, but the fact that there are other low-rise and low-density prototypes of single-family house forms that are reasonable alternatives to the detached house is a well-kept secret. Nevertheless, many of these alternatives offer not only similar characteristics but at times even exceed the advantages associated with detached homes. The most obvious alternatives are court-garden houses and town houses.

COURT-GARDEN HOMES

As a viable alternative to the single-family detached house, the courtyard, or court-garden, house was used during the late twenties in Germany by Hugo Häring (1928), Hannes Mayer (1929), Ludwig Mies van der Rohe (1931), and Ludwig Hilberseimer (1931), but their true application in residential development had to wait until the post–World War II period, when they were built in cluster-form in Scandinavia, Germany, and Great Britain. Appropriately, the twentieth-century courtyard house is not a mere replica of the Roman domus with its small atrium, but an adaptation of the same principles to suit a northern climate. This resulted in an L-shaped one-story house form with a relatively large court garden to allow the low-altitude winter sun to penetrate the house.

The best-known L-shaped attached court-garden house development is Kingohusene in Elsinore, Denmark. Designed by Jørn Utzen, this model residential enclave built for middle-income families was completed in 1960. The inherent land-use efficiency of the courtyard house enabled the provision of a large common park space with tentacles, as in Radburn, New Jersey, reaching the rear of each home so that children need not cross vehicular traffic lanes. In spite of the generous park area provided for the sixty-two homes, the

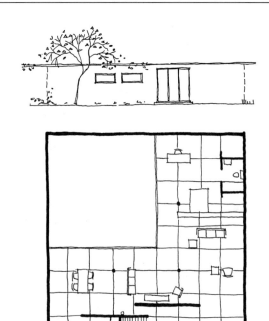

Courthouse project (1931), Ludwig Mies van der Rohe (after D. Macintosh)

density was still 25 percent higher than that of a conventional subdivision with an equal number of single-family detached houses. As Denmark is a northern country, the architect oriented each house with its 33- by 33-ft (10- by 10-m) court garden for optimum sunlight exposure. Moreover, since each private garden is separated from the neighboring garden by a building wing, not only visual but also acoustic privacy is assured to the occupants.

The site plan of Kingohusene may serve as an example of sensitively planned and designed courtyard dwelling clusters, each with a garage accessible from a safe cul-de-sac that does not lend itself to high-speed traffic. A few years after the completion of Kingohusene, Jørn Utzen designed another courtyard house development at Fredensborg (1962–63), near Copenhagen, with similar attributes.

One of the largest attached courtyard house developments in northern Europe for lower-income families was built between 1966 and 1968 at Albertslund, a suburb of Copenhagen. Financed by two nonprofit housing associations and forming

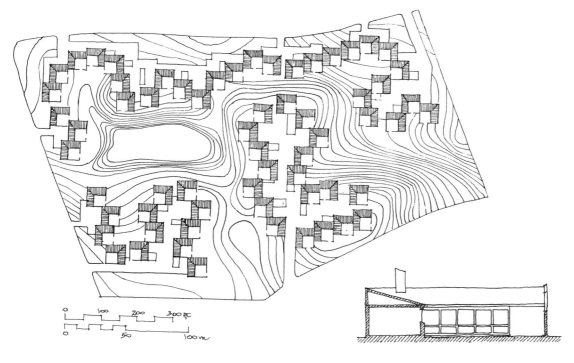

"Kingohusene," Elsinore (1959), site plan and plan,
Jørn Utzon
(after Roar Bjørkto)

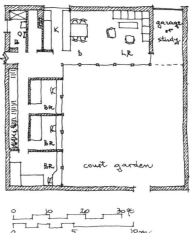

part of a large comprehensive residential development including other house forms, the first stage of Albertslund contained 986 courtyard dwellings constructed of prefabricated concrete building elements. Designed by the architects Viggo Møller-Jensen, Tyge Arnfred, Mogens J. Pedersen, and Jørn Ole Sørensen, dwelling units in this project were downsized to 990 sq ft (92 m^2) with their courtyards measuring about 23 by 26 ft (7.2 by 7.8 m). The residential neighborhood of this court-garden house development has an urban rather than a suburban character.

A few years after the completion of Albertslund, architects J. P. Storgård, J. Ørum-Nielsen, H. Marcussen, and A. Ørum-Nielsen designed the moderate-income residential development Galgebakken (1972–74), outside of Copenhagen. With 156 one-story courtyard houses and 414 one-and-a-half-story attached town houses, this attractive community provided its residents a favorable environment for neighborly contact, but not at the expense of loss of privacy in the home or garden. The cruciform houses, with two courtyards, were designed with a built-in flexibility enabling their occupants to sublet, without any inconvenience, a part of the house with its own private garden.

Attractive and popular court-garden residential communities were also built in Sweden (Stig Ancker's vacation homes at Haverdal, 1953), Norway (M. and G. Kollandsrud's Solvang, near Oslo, 1963), and Finland (T. Korhonen's courtyard homes at Esbo, 1963). Court-garden houses were also used successfully in England (M. Neyland's Bishopsfield houses at Harlow, 1960), France (J.

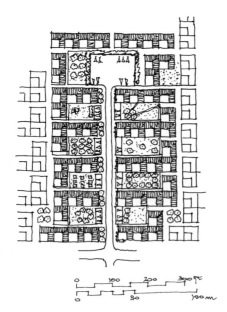
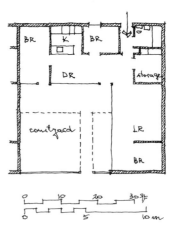

Albertslund, Copenhagen (1966–68), site plan and plan, Møller-Jensen, Arnfeld, Pedersen and Sørensen (after Roar Bjørkto)

Fehmerling's housing at Franconville, 1963), Germany (Interbau '57 courtyard houses in Berlin, by Arne Jacobsen, E. Ludwig, and Günter Hünow), Austria (Roland Rainer's courtyard dwellings at Puchenau, 1970), and Switzerland (Ulrich Low and Theodor Manz's In den Gartenhöfen community at Reinach near Basel).

So far, the North American home buyer has not favored the courtyard house in spite of the fact that prominent architects working in the U.S., such as Serge Ivan Chermayeff and José Luis Sert, demonstrated through design projects the feasibility and attractiveness of these dwelling types. In fact, Sert built in Cambridge, Massachusetts, a court-garden house for his own use, with three patios, as a testimony to the livability of this dwelling type in climates more northerly than that of Spain, his native country. In an interview reported by *House and Home* in its October 1958 issue, Sert (then Dean of the Graduate School of Design at Harvard University) commented that the reasons for selecting a patio house for his own dwelling were simple: "By pushing the enclosing walls out close to the lot line better use is made of expensive land. Both indoor and outdoor living space is private and serene. Every room can have pleasant views regardless of what is beyond the walls." He further

reasoned that "as long as the façade of the patio house reasonably conforms with its neighborhood, the owner—within its enclosing walls—need not conform to the life or tastes or traditions of his neighbors." In a capsule, these are the significant advantages of the patio house.

An enclosed garden or patio is an ideal outdoor extension of a home and gives its occupants true visual and acoustical privacy; this sheltered outdoor space also provides favorable microclimatic conditions, in summer and winter. Its land-use efficiency translates into savings in municipal infrastructure and service costs. Finally, the sociological implications of court-garden dwellings may prove helpful in diminishing the segregationist tendencies in our residential neighborhoods. It is a documented fact that in countries where the inward-oriented courtyard house is indigenous, the stratification of similar income groups in homogeneous residential neighborhoods is less prevalent than in countries where the outward-oriented dwelling is favored.

The most financially successful West Coast patio house development is Rancho Verde in Sunnyvale, California. This project was built by Joseph Eichler and designed by Jones and Emmons in partnership with Claude Oakland. While all Eichler homes had

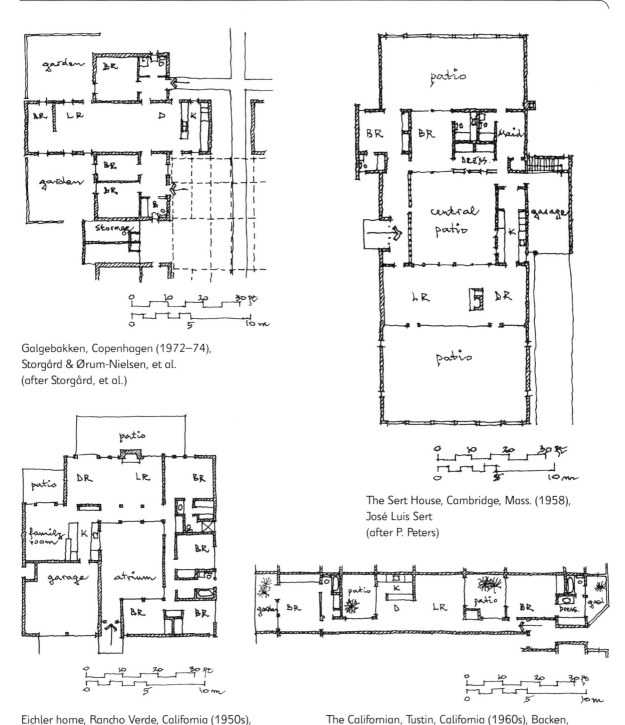

Galgebakken, Copenhagen (1972–74),
Storgård & Ørum-Nielsen, et al.
(after Storgård, et al.)

The Sert House, Cambridge, Mass. (1958),
José Luis Sert
(after P. Peters)

Eichler home, Rancho Verde, California (1950s),
Jones and Emmons, and C. Oakland
(after advertisement brochure)

The Californian, Tustin, California (1960s), Backen,
Arrigoni and Ross
(after Sam Davis)

a central atrium, they were also "detached" bunga-lows, which must have enhanced their acceptabili-ty by home buyers.

A more recent West Coast development is The Californian in Tustin. Designed by Backen, Arri-goni and Ross, this interesting residential enclave consists of single-story narrow-front patio homes, clearly inspired by Chermayeff's design. Aimed at the adult housing market, these homes have internalized courtyards, accentuating the private domain, while narrow walks and small open spaces serve as the public realm.

With a traditional distaste for fences and enclosures, the American public did not embrace clustered patio houses, but this may change when people discover that inward-looking homes give greater security to their residents than outward-looking ones. The court-garden house's 6,000 years of history attest to its viability and inviolability.

ATTACHED TOWN HOUSE DWELLINGS

Street-oriented and outward-looking, the traditional town house is the opposite of the introverted court-garden house. Town houses were rarely built during the first decades of the postwar period in suburban developments, probably because of their association with the squalid row houses of the nineteenth century. Indeed, the first town houses built in North America during the postwar period had mostly undersized rooms and had no redeeming features that would have made them attractive, so they were viewed as mere low-income row house developments. However, as soon as the spatial standards of the detached house were applied to row houses, they became more acceptable and were referred to as "town houses."

An early example of a contemporary urban townhouse development that revived the spirit of the Georgian town house was built in one of the oldest areas of central Philadelphia—Society Hill—and formed part of the Washington Square East redevelopment project of 1958. Designed by I. M. Pei and Associates, and completed in 1965, the individual town houses in this development were spacious, and the interior arrangement, with a curved staircase linking the three floor levels, was reminiscent of their Georgian antecedents. Two living rooms occupied, in the English manner, the piano nobile; the kitchen and dining room are on the ground floor, and bedrooms are above the living

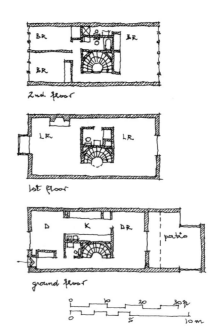

Washington Square East town houses, Philadelphia (1958), I. M. Pei and Associates
(after "Philadelphia Town Houses")

rooms. In one respect this development was disappointing, because it did not provide indoor parking and relegated cars to an open parking lot behind the walled-in patios.

One of the most difficult design tasks in townhouse development is the car storage problem, a consequence of the narrow street frontages. Only single garages could be accommodated on the street side, while placing garages in the rear requires lanes or alleys, which are disliked by municipal authorities.

An ingenious solution of the car storage problem was submitted by a team of architects in a design competition held in 1959 by the Mastic Tile Division of the Ruberoid Company. Probably inspired by Mayfair Lane, an Arts and Crafts residential enclave built in Buffalo in the late 1920s, Paul A. Kennon, Chartier Newtown, Heinz-Henning Huth, and Philip J. Kinsella—all from the office of Eero Saarinen and Associates—won the third prize with their submission of a cluster development of homes around a slightly elevated pedestrian entrance plaza with a communal garage below. Although their project was never realized,

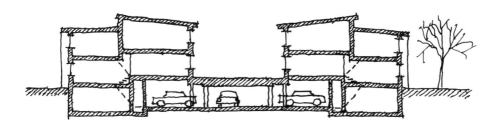

Flemingdon Park, Toronto (1960s), Irving Grossman
(after "Housing at Flemingdon Park, Ont.")

a few years after the competition the concept was successfully applied by Irving Grossman in a town house development at Flemingdon Park in Toronto. With pedestrian circulation at the upper level and vehicular storage underneath, a vertical traffic separation was created in the immediate vicinity of the homes, which was widely publicized in the sixties as the "Flemingdon Park concept." In the Toronto area, several Canadian architects emulated this arrangement with success in subsequent town-house developments.

Two popular European town-house prototypes are conspicuously absent in North America, namely the single-story, or "bungalow," town house, and the split-level town house, while the "linked" town house and the narrow-front town house are becoming popular.

As an attached unit, the single-level town house has distinct merits especially for the elderly; the split-level town house is an adaptive house form that can easily respond to changes occurring over time in traditional households. An outstanding example of a split-level town-house development is in Galgebakken, a residential community previously mentioned. The 414 split-level town houses are aligned with their single-story fronts along a narrow pedestrian path. On the two-story garden side of the dwellings are private outdoor spaces and beyond, a semiprivate community area. The designers used skylights to flood the family room of each home with daylight, and units were designed to be flexible to accommodate both the expansion and contraction that normally occur in the life cycle of families. These homes can function as single large dwellings before children reach adulthood, but they also can be subdivided into

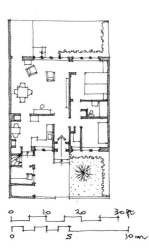

Single-story town house, Stockholm (1930),
Oswald Almquist
(after Otto Völckers)

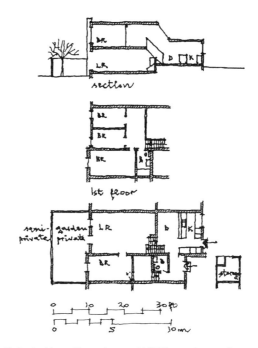

Galgebakken, Copenhagen (1974), section and two
plans, Storgård & Ørum-Nielsen, et al.
(after Storgård, et al.)

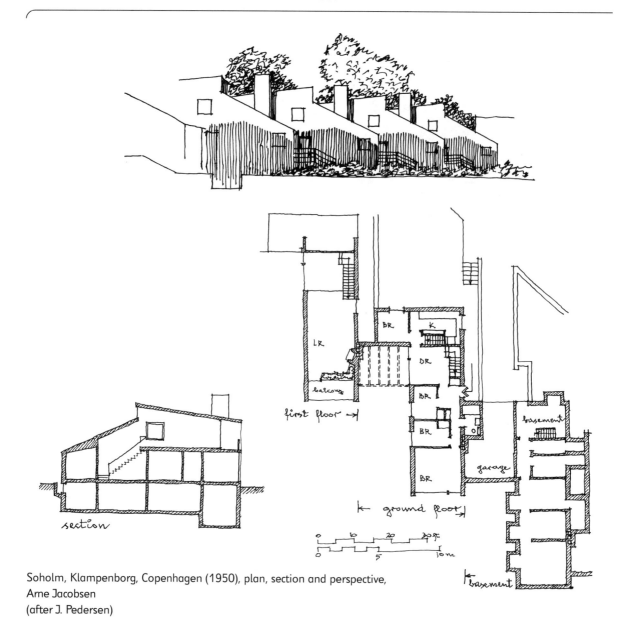

Soholm, Klampenborg, Copenhagen (1950), plan, section and perspective,
Arne Jacobsen
(after J. Pedersen)

self-contained smaller units, one of these as a pos-sible rental unit when children leave home.

The linked town house, or *kædehus* in Denmark, is a house form closely related to the town house, with the distinction that neighboring dwelling units are attached to each other only by garages, with the benefit that occupants of these dwellings have the same acoustical privacy enjoyed by those living in detached homes. Linked town houses may be single-story, two-story, or split-level dwellings and, in terms of land-use efficiency have similar advantages to traditional town houses. Arne Jacob-sen's Soholm development, built in 1950 in Klampenborg, near Copenhagen, has several clas-sic split-level kædehuse, one of which he and his family occupied.

An attractive American example of a linked town house residential neighborhood was designed recently by architect-planners Andres Duany and Elizabeth Plater-Zyberk on a 16-acre (6.48-hec-tare) site in Boca del Mar, Florida. As the name of the development implies, the Charleston Place town houses were inspired by traditional southern hous-es with side courtyards and porches. The sideyards of these Boca del Mar two-story town houses are shielded from the street by a one-story structure, most frequently used as a garage. Behind the garage is a porch facing the courtyard which, in turn, is

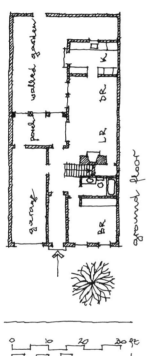

Charleston Place, Boca del Mar, Florida,
plan and elevation, A. Duany and E. Plater-Zyberk
(after Philip Langdon)

screened by a wall and a gate giving access to a brick-paved pedestrian lane with rose arbors. Painted in pastel hues, the 111 condominium homes are charming and, with all the attributes of court-garden houses, may set a precedent for others to follow.

The narrow-front town house, with a street frontage of about 14 ft (4.26 m), also has historic antecedents in the two-bay-wide town houses built for artisans in the nineteenth century. The contemporary version, however, is designed most

often for moderate- to middle-income families.

A trendsetting narrow-front town-house development with two- and three-story dwelling units is Siedlung Hallen, a housing estate near Bern, Switzerland. Designed by Atelier 5, and inspired by Le Corbusier's unrealized housing project Roq et Rob à Cap Martin (1948), Siedlung Hallen's seventy-five dwellings were built between 1955 and 1961 on a wooded hill site, with about half the site conserved as woodland.

Another design approach in narrow-front town houses is the split-level arrangement of the floor plan. LeBretton Flats, a Canada Mortgage and Housing Corporation (CMHC) demonstration project of eight narrow-front town houses, built in Ottawa in 1976, illustrates well the openness and interesting spatial quality that can be achieved with a split-level design. Subsequently, Ian Johns, designer of the CMHC project, built Cathcart Mews (1978) and Springfield Mews (1980–90)—both successful Ottawa residential developments where he reused his design for narrow-front town houses among other building types.

A charming award-winning narrow-front town-house cluster was designed by James K. M. Cheng and the Coal Harbour Architectural Group in 1980 for the False Creek area of Vancouver, British Columbia. Consisting of only fourteen three-story houses, the Willow Arbor homes are distinguished by having their living area on the top floor with access to a roof deck to take advantage of the impressive harbor view and the downtown skyline with its backdrop of distant mountains. The entrance doors and lower floors of this small

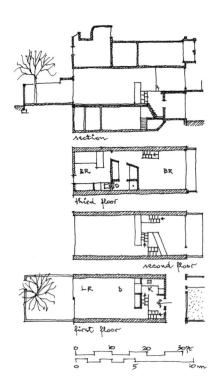

Siedlung Hallen, Bern (1961), three plans and section,
Atelier 5
(after Y. Ashihara)

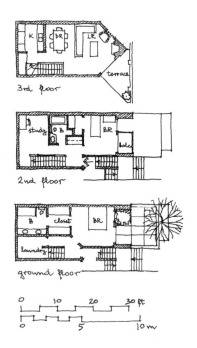

Willow Arbor, Vancouver (1980), three plans,
James K. M. Cheng and Coal Harbour Arch. Group
(after Cheng et al.)

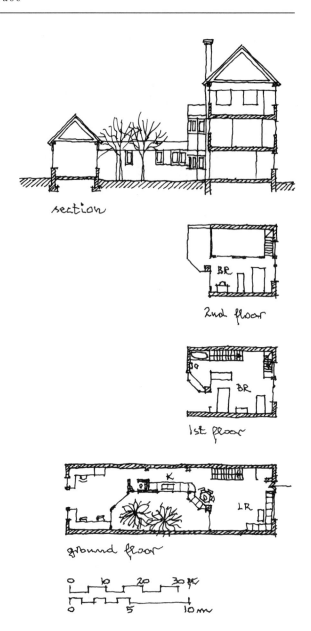

The "New American House" (1984), three plans and
section, Troy West and Jaqueline Leavitt
(after J. Leavitt)

project face a semiprivate courtyard, and entry is
through a gate from the street.

In a competition for a New American House held
in 1984, Troy West and Jacqueline Leavitt, an
architect/planner team, were awarded the first
prize for their cluster of six narrow-front town
houses. The distinguishing feature of their design
submission is the concept of joining a workplace
with the dwelling. A single-story structure on the
street side, designed as an office, workplace, or

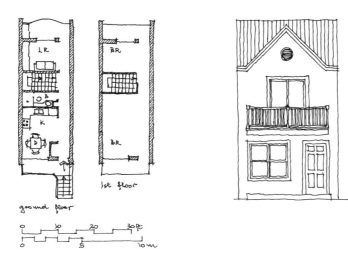

The "Grow Home" (1990), two plans and elevation, Rybczynski, Friedman and Ross
(after Rybczynski et al.)

Sea Ranch, Sonoma County, California (1965), Moore,
Lyndon, Turnbull, Whitaker
(after W. Turnbull)

studio for paid work, is linked to the three-story dwelling behind by a low and narrow kitchen wing. An enclosed courtyard next to the kitchen is a protected and private outdoor space, complemented by a larger common green in the back.

In 1990, another Canadian narrow-front townhouse concept was advanced by Witold Rybczynski, Avi Friedman, and Susan Ross. Called the "Grow Home," these stripped-down versions of two-story row houses, with unfinished second floors, were proposed to make them affordable to low- and moderate-income families. Several Montreal builders adopted Avi Friedman's revised version of these building types, enabling many former tenants to become home owners. A survey made in Montreal by the Affordable Homes Program of the School of Architecture, McGill University, indicated that the gross annual income required to buy a Grow Home is about 30 percent less than for a standard starter home.

Finally, clustered attached homes are also essentially town-house developments. Sea Ranch, built on a grassy, windswept field bordering the California seashore, is one of the most famous prototypes. Designed by MLTW (Moore, Lyndon, Turnbull, Whitaker) and built in the sixties, each condominium unit is different in design from its neighbor, but similar redwood siding and building massing lend harmony to this development. Each home has an ocean view, access to common ground, good orientation, protection from the wind, and screening from the highway. MLTW succeeded in making a real community with this cluster of dwellings.

Town-house clusters have also gained respectability in several East Coast communities. A sensitive clustered development called Windswept, built in the eighties on the South Carolina coast, was designed by Sandy & Babcock. All ninety condominium units have a good view of the sea and the shore, but do not encroach upon the dunes. The staggered siting of the town houses gives better privacy and protection to the decks and balconies and, in addition, breaks up the scale of the building mass. In their beautiful landscaped setting, these dwellings with cedar-shingled walls and copper roofs have a picturesque appearance.

The town house is a good alternative to the detached house. Being attached on two sides means the energy requirement of a two-story town house is only about 55 percent of a bungalow. Even when compared with a two-story detached house, savings in energy costs approximate 30 percent. Smaller lot sizes and narrower street frontages mean greater affordability and, cumulatively, a reduction in transportation costs, not to mention ecological benefits of the diminished rate of urban sprawl and conservation of land.

HIGH-RISE LUXURY APARTMENTS

For the affluent American, luxury high-rise apartment living (e.g., the San Remo with its cathedral-like silhouette in New York City) predates World War II. The design of the new luxury apartment buildings in the postwar era conformed to the tenets of the Modern movement. Accordingly, the massive façades of prewar apartment houses adorned with neoclassical or Art Deco details gave way to building volumes that were wrapped with a thinner transparent enclosure consisting of reticulated patterned planes of sheets of glass held in place first by metal and later by concrete frames.

The typical layout of modern apartment units also changed in response to a generally servantless postwar society, when sculleries, butlers' pantries, and service corridors became redundant. Ornamentation, too, in apartment interiors was considered superfluous and was replaced by pristine (and easy to clean) architectural details. Finally, with increased informality, the day-to-day comfort and convenience of apartment dwellers was more important than a formal setting designed to impress occasional visitors.

The Victorian formality of separate parlors and dining rooms in conventional prewar apartment layouts was replaced by the informality of principal living spaces flowing into each other, as exemplified by the open plan of an L-shaped living room, with the short leg of the L serving as a dining area that adjoins a tight but well-equipped galley-type kitchen. Typically, a central entrance hall gave access to the living room, kitchen, and a bedroom corridor serving the private zone of the dwelling unit. The design of apartment units followed the design principles adopted in suburban houses, but in a significant way apartments differed from houses in that windows usually faced in one direction only, which also meant the absence of cross-ventilation.

High-rise apartment houses complement urban lifestyles by enabling residents to walk to nearby shops, restaurants, entertainment, and cultural establishments, and sometimes even to work. Moreover, their land-use efficiency, based on small ground coverage and increased population density, made them desirable in inner cities.

Mies van der Rohe's 860 Lake Shore Drive Apartments (1950–51) in Chicago represent an important milestone in American postwar high-rise housing design. Built on one of Chicago's choicest sites, both geographically (adjacent to Lake Michigan) and socially (in close proximity to the Gold Coast), these twin twenty-six-story steel-and-glass cooperative apartments inspired many residential buildings throughout North America and beyond.

As an early prototype of a modern double-loaded-corridor high-rise apartment building, Lake Shore Drive Apartments was beset from the outset with excessive elevator waiting time, especially in the more densely occupied North

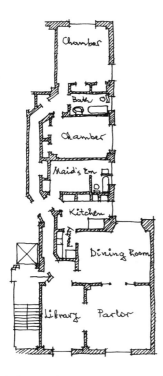

Typical nineteenth-century apartment layout

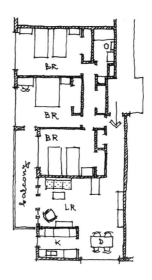

Typical L-shaped living room
apartment layout

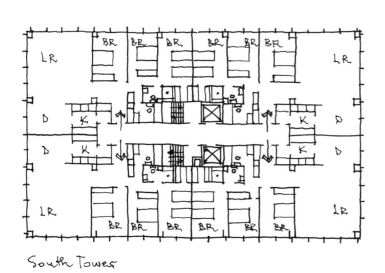

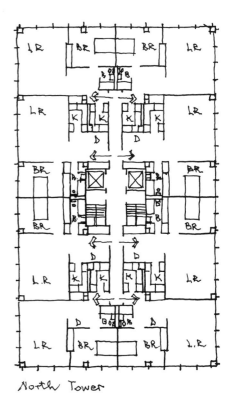

Lake Shore Drive Apartments, North Tower and South Tower,
Chicago (1950–51), Ludwig Mies van der Rohe
(after F. R. S. Yorke and F. Gibberd)

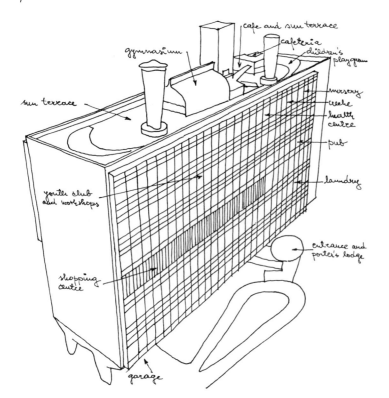

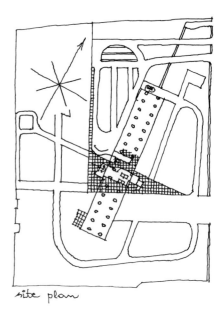

Unité d'Habitation, Marseilles (1952), site plan and axonometric drawing
(after D. Procos)

Tower, which has eight three-and-a-half-room apartments per floor, in contrast to the South Tower's four six-room suites. There were only two self-service elevators in each tower, and this proved to be inadequate for a twenty-six-story building; today's standards demand at least two zoned elevator banks with two cabs each, one bank serving the first thirteen floors, and the second the balance.

As one of the first modern American residential towers sheathed entirely in glass, the building's heat gain from the summer sun, particularly on the west side, was also a problem and had to be corrected through the addition of roller shades set close to the glass and several air conditioners set in the movable low pane of the windows. To maintain the pristine external appearance of the building, the air-conditioning units were installed projecting into the apartments. Since glass as a building material was relatively inexpensive, the construction costs of the twin towers, with their lofty and elegantly furnished entrance lobbies and uniform drapes installed in every dwelling unit, was very reasonable, in spite of the fact that the towers' foundation work was difficult.

Not as well known as Lake Shore Drive Apartments, and not as impressive, is Mies van der Rohe's Colonnade Apartments (1958–60) in Newark, New Jersey. This twenty-two-story glass and aluminum slab block, a double-loaded-corridor building with windows designed to be inoperable, contains 560 rental apartment units for middle-income tenants. Fresh air is supplied by a central ventilation system, and metal enclosures are provided for the placement of air-conditioning units at the option of the tenant. Incredibly, most of the 7-acre (2.8-hectare) site on the southeast side of the Colonnade Apartments is devoted to a parking lot—a land use not envisaged as part of the tower-in-the-park design concept.

Another milestone in high-rise residential development is Le Corbusier's Unité d'Habitation at Marseilles, a 541-ft (165-m) long, twenty-story building, completed in 1952. With all 337 two-story apartments in a single block, lifted well above the ground by huge pilotis, no residents have direct access from the dwelling to a patio or garden, but all have balconies. The nearly 1,800 residents have internal access to a shopping center, day-care nursery, kindergarten, exercise room, and a roof terrace with swimming and wading pools. The narrow dwellings have good acoustical privacy from their neighbors and, most being through-units, they afford good cross-ventilation and exposure on two sides. In keeping with the typical compromise of the Modern movement, most apartments face east and west, and only a few dwellings—located on the south gable-end—have a southern exposure, but no cross-ventilation; to the architect's credit, none face north. Three floors share a double-loaded corridor—an internal street with apartments wrapped around it. The epitome of the tower-in-the-park design concept as well as of the vertical garden city concept—advocated by Le Corbusier many years prior to its construction—the Unité d'Habitation is a beautifully and variously articulated freestanding building on a large site. All its residents can enjoy a spectacular view from their dwelling and from most communal areas.

Le Corbusier's and Mies van der Rohe's concepts of high-rise apartments built as freestanding slab blocks or towers gained respectability throughout the world in the fifties and sixties, especially in context with large-scale urban renewal schemes.

Kips Bay Plaza (1960–65), designed by I. M. Pei and Associates, is a good example of a slab block development of the fifties in New York City. Two twenty-story high-rise luxury residential blocks, typically at right angles to the bordering avenues, with a private park in between, were its main elements. As historian Richard Plunz rightly observed, the façades of these slabs were "large undifferentiated grids of precast concrete and glass"(Plunz 1990, 288)—a design approach that was common in that era—and the park was but a planted garden over the parking garage. Nevertheless, this private plaza provided its users with a safe feeling since commercial buildings, which were part of the development, provided additional definition on the avenue sides to the plaza.

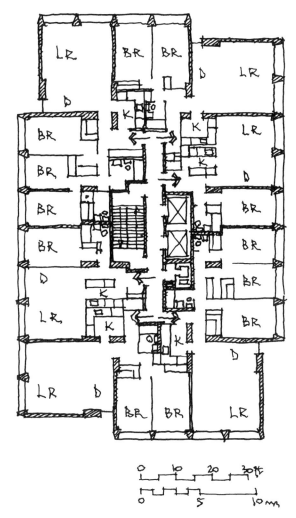

Silver Towers, New York City (1967),
I. M. Pei and Associates
(after Y. Ashihara)

University Towers—now called Silver Towers—is another New York City high-rise project by I. M. Pei and Associates. It consists of three thirty-story concrete towers arranged in pinwheel fashion around a plaza with a Picasso sculpture as its centerpiece. These towers, too, have a plasticity derived from the deep reveals of the wafflelike concrete grid of the façade. The reveals provide apartments with some protection from the sun, but also give their occupants the impression of secure enclosure which thin exterior skins do not.

Greater sophistication in structural design and in construction technology, new types of lightweight building materials, and mechanical improvements such as high-speed elevators, artificial pressurization, and air-conditioning, made it possible to build ever-taller residential towers. These new skyscrapers are awe-inspiring as technological achievements, but a closer examination will reveal that they have many shortcomings in the social, economic, and environmental realms.

High-rise housing is best suited for upper-income residents, who can afford to pay for the upkeep of in-house conveniences—air-conditioning, swimming pools, saunas, recreation and work-out rooms, and 24-hour doorman service, complemented by electronic survey and security systems. High-rise housing is less than ideal for families with young children, because parents tend to restrict child play within the apartment and are reluctant to let young children use elevators, corridors, and the playground on their own. A socioeconomic mix of tenants may be desirable, but in practice is rarely attainable.

Manifestly, increased building height is accompanied by increased building costs. The taller the building, the greater the wind and live load to be transferred to the ground. Since standard fire ladders do not reach beyond nine floors, standpipes on each floor and a sprinkler system have to be installed. Moreover, artificial pressurization becomes necessary to counteract the stack effect of chimneys in buildings higher than forty stories. Without pressurization by mechanical means it is not only difficult to maintain uniform temperatures and humidities in buildings, but also near impossible to prevent the spread of dust, odors, obnoxious fumes, and smoke, in case of fire. The cost of elevator service, too, is a function of building height, since banks of elevators, each bank with at least two cabs, serve ideally between ten and twelve floors only. Buildings in excess of sixty stories require high-speed elevators as well as transfer elevator lobbies, called "sky lobbies," as employed in the one-hundred-story John Hancock Center (1970) in Chicago.

Urban environmental considerations disfavor high-rise buildings. Pedestrians who frequent the modern high-rise core of American cities are all too familiar with the unfavorable microclimatic

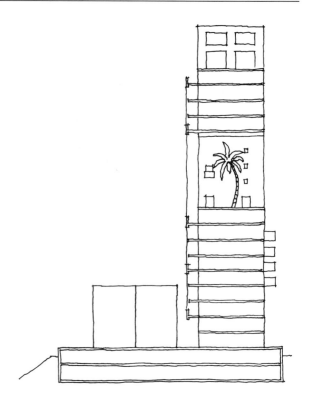

The Atlantis, Miami, Florida (1982), Arquitectonica (after Arquitectonica)

conditions (unpleasant eddies and wind turbulence) associated with tall buildings. Even more detrimental than the wind is the perpetual shadow that tall buildings cast on adjacent properties; to be legally permitted to block someone from the sun—a life-giving force of nature—is in itself astonishing. Surprisingly, postmodern architects who criticized the bland appearance of modern apartment houses with some justification and demonstrated that high-rise buildings could be more attractive, failed to realize that the shortcomings of tall buildings are not functions of their appearance, but of their height.

Arquitectonica's Palace (1980) and the Atlantis (1982), two attractive buildings designed by Laurinda Spear and Bernardo Fort-Brescia for Biscayne Bay in Miami, Florida, perpetuate the notion that high-rise buildings, in spite of all their inherent disadvantages, are all right. The Palace, a forty-one-story slab intersected, at a right angle, by a sixteen-story masonry building resembling a gigantic staircase cascading down towards the sea

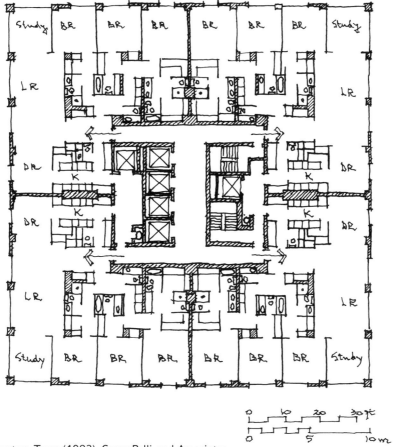

Four-Leaf Towers, Houston, Texas (1983), Cesar Pelli and Associates
(after C. Pelli and Assoc.)

shore, is a luxury condominium apartment complex with 254 dwelling units. The Atlantis, a beautifully designed structure that mirrors adjacent buildings on its glazed smooth north face, is also a condominium, but with only ninety-six apartment units in a twenty-story building. A large 50-ft (15.24-m) cube was carved out of the building at the tenth floor, a void that is used as a sky patio with a Jacuzzi and a palm tree. With the fronds of an orphaned palm tree outlined against the sky, the large "hole" on its shimmering façade is like a mirage in the desert.

Another contemporary high-rise luxury residential building is the Four-Leaf Towers project built in an elegant old neighborhood of Houston, Texas. The two forty-story towers, completed in 1983, were designed by Cesar Pelli and Associates, another renowned American architectural firm. The two towers have 400 apartments including

four two-story penthouse units with corner terraces below the truncated pyramidal roof; there is a 700-car underground garage and seventy surface parking spaces. With tinted glass curtain walls supported by a fluoropolymer-painted aluminum frame, the two towers are colorful and shiny landmarks visible for miles.

HIGH-RISE TENEMENTS

The adoption of high-rise buildings for public housing has led to many disappointments, not only in North and South America, but in many European countries as well. This failure is attributable primarily to the lack of security and safety as well as to poor maintenance of the few collective amenities provided in these buildings.

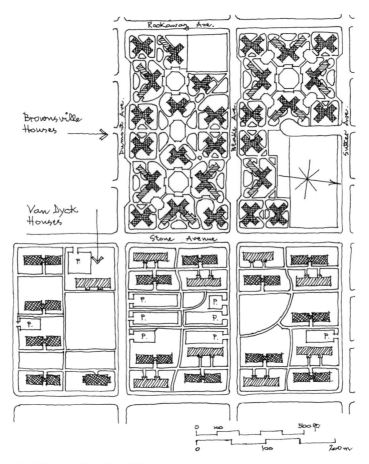

Brownsville and Van Dyck Houses, Brooklyn, N.Y.
(after Oscar Newman)

Oscar Newman, in his book *Defensible Space*, asserts that there is statistical evidence that the physical form of a residential environment plays a significant role in the incidence of crime. His three-year study of crime prevention, mostly in New York City Housing Authority's (NYCHA) public housing projects, revealed a correlation between building height and the occurrence of crime in buildings. He found that in three-story buildings the mean felony rate was nine per 1,000 population, while in buildings thirteen stories and higher, it was more than double, twenty per 1,000. It is interesting to note that in dwelling units themselves, the felony rate in both the three- and thirteen-story buildings was about the same, which implied that the increase of crime frequency occurred in public areas, elevators, halls, lobbies, stairwells, and roofs.

These findings led Newman to the conclusion that the most vulnerable areas were those lacking surveillance. This was substantiated by his discovery that 31 percent of all robberies in high-rise buildings occurred in elevators, notably unsupervised public areas that had to be used to reach dwelling units on upper floors. Just as revealing was the fact that 79 percent of serious crimes, such as robberies, burglaries, rape, and felonious assaults, were committed in common interior spaces of the buildings, rather than on the project grounds, because apprehension was less likely in the complex maze of corridors, stairwells, and elevators of a high-rise building. Statistically, twice as many criminals were apprehended committing a crime outdoors in public housing projects as indoors, odds that probably did not escape the attention of criminals.

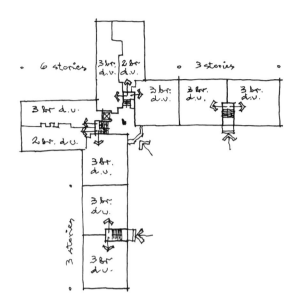

Brownsville Apartments, Brooklyn, N.Y. (1948),
Frederick G. Frost
(after Oscar Newman)

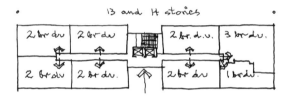

Van Dyck Apartments, Brooklyn, N.Y. (1955), Isadore and
Zachary Rosenfield
(after Oscar Newman)

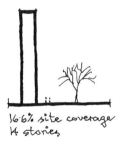

Van Dyck Houses: 16.6% site coverage = fourteen stories;
50% site coverage = four stories

To Newman's surprise, the lower felony rate in low- and mid-rise public housing developments, compared to that in high-rise projects, was not attributable to a lower density, nor to a variance in family composition, background, or socioeconomic characteristics of their respective tenants. This fact emerged from an in-depth study and comparison of two adjacent public housing projects in Brooklyn, New York—Brownsville Houses, designed by the architect Frederick G. Frost, and Van Dyck Houses, designed by Zachary Rosenfield. The former is a mix of three-story walk-ups and six-story elevator buildings; the latter, a mix of three-story walk-ups and fourteen-story high-rise slabs. Both projects house approximately 6,000 people each—populations with identical social characteristics—yet the incidence of robberies is over two and a half times higher in Van Dyck, the high-rise project.

In walk-ups and mid-rise projects, where fewer families share the public areas of a building, self-policing is an important factor in lowering the crime rate. In contrast, the natural surveillance inherent in smaller buildings, where most people know each other at least by sight, is either absent or unreliable in large projects. As noted by Newman, safety in the Van Dyck project is further diminished by the fact that all tall buildings are entered from a private project path network instead of directly from the public street. The desire to free land led to a low building site coverage of only 16.6 percent for Van Dyck Houses, which necessitated an unreasonable building height; a 50 percent site coverage would have resulted in four-story buildings instead of a high-rise.

When two public housing projects—Pruitt-Igoe (1955) in St. Louis, Missouri, and Lafayette Courts (1955) in Baltimore, Maryland—opened their doors to their first tenants, they were praised as "ideal" housing for low-income people and families on welfare. Indeed, those "lucky" tenants who were allowed to move into the new eleven-story buildings agreed that they had never lived in better housing.

Eventually, however, Pruitt-Igoe became a tragic symbol of failed public housing. Designed by Minoru Yamasaki with a skip-stop corridor system

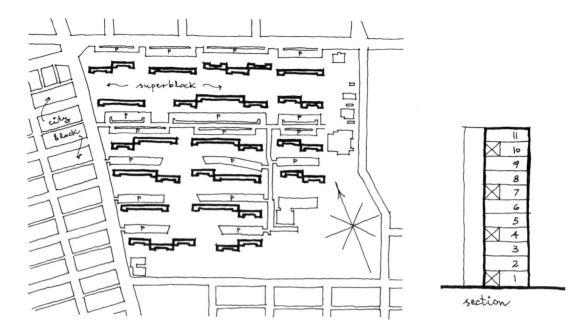

Pruitt-Igoe, St. Louis, Mo. (1955), site plan and section,
Minoru Yamasaki and Associates
(after Oscar Newman)

(corridors and elevator service on only every second and third floor), the widely spaced buildings contained 2,764 dwelling units with an anticipated population of 15,000 persons, but were built without a basic social infrastructure, such as day-care nurseries, kindergartens, schools, or recreational facilities other than playgrounds in close proximity to parking lots. At the beginning, tenants were not worried about break-ins, and their children could be left safely to play outdoors. But, in the absence of building surveillance, entry to the project was open to anyone and tenants became vulnerable to crime and vandalism. When mailboxes, lobbies, stairwells, and elevators were vandalized, and criminals discovered security in the labyrinthine corridor system of the building, the vacancy rate increased. A vicious cycle was set in motion that could not be stopped without demolishing all thirty-three buildings of Pruitt-Igoe in 1976.

As at Pruitt-Igoe, when drug dealing spilled over into the Lafayette Courts project in the seventies, the quality of life deteriorated, and building maintenance was neglected; pipes leaked, roaches and rodents thrived, and vandalism was rampant. In 1992, vandalized elevators alone in the six high-rise buildings cost $15,000 a month to repair. Lafayette Courts was eventually torn down and replaced by a town-house development.

The failure of high-rise apartments is also familiar to the New York City Housing Authority. Both the twenty-two-story Langston Hughes Houses, in Brownsville, and the thirty-story towers of the Polo Grounds Towers, in Harlem, exemplify the total degradation of life of the underprivileged in high-rise buildings. Initially, these projects were built to provide well-ventilated sunny apartment units in fireproof buildings to former tenants of unsanitary, dilapidated, and overcrowded tenements. Unsupervised, the buildings deteriorated rapidly. Vandalism and violence became common in public areas, and overcrowding, through unauthorized sharing of dwelling units, became prevalent, as did homeless people squatting overnight on stair landings, rooftops, and even in elevators.

The failure of high-rise projects for low-income people is not restricted to North America. Similar problems have also beset high-rise projects in Great Britain. In Killingworth Township, near Newcastle, twenty-seven residential towers with a

Perseigne, Alençon (1978–79), atelier Lucien Kroll
(after L. Kroll)

total of 740 dwelling units, built between 1969 and 1972, were demolished in 1987. Another project in Northaird Point, Hackney, had a similar fate. And Sir Basil Spence's Hutchesontown-Gorbals Area "C" blocks, with 400 dwelling units, were blasted to rubble on September 12, 1993. These events contrasted greatly to the enthusiasm with which high-rise housing was welcomed in the fifties and early sixties.

British disappointment with high-rise buildings came about with the realization that these buildings were not only very expensive but did not save land or prevent urban sprawl, as promised. In addition, criticism, on both social and aesthetic grounds, was leveled against high-rise flats by their tenants. As a result of a universal distaste for living in high-rise buildings, their construction was much curtailed, especially for low-income tenants. While, at the outset, tall blocks of flats were seen as prestige symbols in the spirit of the vertical garden city or the tower-in-the-park housing concept, by the seventies they had lost their initial attraction. Instead, greater attention began to be paid to alternative planning concepts for housing, such as mid-rise developments.

In France, instead of demolishing unpopular rows of modern apartment blocks in parklike settings, an attempt was made to improve the area through "humanized" rehabilitation. This procedure involved breaking up the homogeneity of the project by adding new low-rise in-fill housing with improved landscaping, and, at the same time, enhancing and modifying the appearance of the existing buildings through the addition of balconies, roof terraces, penthouse units, and redesigned windows and entrances. Atelier Lucien Kroll's exemplary work for both the Perseigne neighborhood of Alençon (1978–79) and the Champvallon district of Montbéliard-Béthoncourt (1990–95) illustrates the sensible approach of improving undesirable housing developments, rather than expunging them altogether.

High-rise public housing developments in Hong Kong seem to be devoid of the negative connotations plaguing their western counterparts. Apart from the absence of a negative stigma usually attached to large housing estates, effective tenant management in Hong Kong is credited with the low incidence of vandalism and crime. Building managers, who are also residents, know tenants

"Before"

"after"

Champvallon, Montbéliard-Béthoncourt (1990–95),
atelier Lucien Kroll
(after L. Kroll)

personally and respond quickly to their needs; they assist tenants to get required social services and involve them in the maintenance and security of the housing estate. Since public dwelling units in Hong Kong are handed over to new tenants with bare concrete floors, bare walls and ceilings, and only the most basic bathroom and kitchen fixtures, their occupants invariably make improvements, mainly through sweat-equity, and personalize the units in the hope that one day they will own their apartment. This is made possible through a home ownership scheme, offering dwelling units for sale at cost.

POINT BLOCKS

An early experimental housing project, designed in 1927 by Wassili and Hans Luckhardt for Berlin, revealed several advantages of this new concept for multifamily dwellings. These four-story detached "tower-houses" (as point blocks were called at the time), featured four two-bedroom apartment units on each floor, wrapped pinwheel-fashion around a central stairwell. The dwellings were buffered from their neighbors by secondary rooms and built-in closets. However, the design potential for good daylighting from two sides, as well as for diagonal cross-ventilation, was not explored.

Another early example of point-block development was built in Cité-de-la-Muette at Drancy, north of Paris. Designed by Eugène Beaudouin in collaboration with Marcel Lods, five identical sixteen-story elevator-serviced point blocks were constructed in the early 1930s, each tower with two one-bedroom and two efficiency apartments per floor.

A conscious search by Swedish architects for a new prototype for multiple housing that allowed residents more than a single sun orientation led to the development of a detached structure known in Scandinavian countries as a *punkthus*. An early example, dating from 1943, was designed by Olof Thunström for Midsommarkransen, a housing estate near Stockholm. With four small dwellings on a typical floor, these four-story apartment buildings were sensitively designed to avoid any northern exposure of habitable rooms.

During this period, Thunström also experimented with a design that would enable every apartment unit to have windows face four directions, rather than only two. His ingenious design solution took the form of two tiers of apartments linked at one corner by a common vertical circulation core, and where each dwelling had sun exposure on four sides, a feature normally inherent only in detached houses. A few miles outside of Stockholm, at Gustavsberg, Thunström built several point blocks which had the appropriate scale for a residential development in a small community.

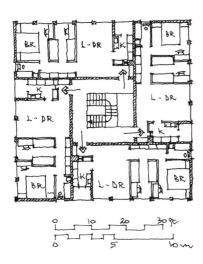

Tower-house project, Berlin (1927), Wassili and
Hans Luckhardt
(after Leonardo Benevolo)

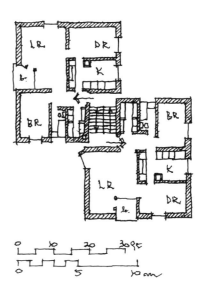

Point block, Gustavsberg, Stockholm, Olof Thunström
(after Thomas Paulsson)

It soon became evident that the Gustavsberg design for multifamily buildings was only economically feasible as a walk-up, since buildings that exceeded four floors in height required elevator service. Because the cost of elevators was too expensive to be borne by two dwellings per floor, economic considerations dictated that elevator-serviced point blocks should have at least four dwellings on each floor. With four dwellings around a compact circulation core, each point-block apartment now had windows on two sides only. This building form became the Swedish prototype for point blocks.

Perhaps the first noted Swedish point-block project was Stockholm's Danviksklippan (1945), designed by Sven Backström and Leif Reinius. Built on a rock outcropping, the nine concrete apartment buildings—eight and ten stories high—have four corner dwellings on each floor level. Most living rooms, some with a fireplace, occupied the corner to benefit from windows on two sides. Access to dwellings is through a central core with a semicircular staircase and one elevator (ten-story buildings have two elevators).

During the following decades Swedish architects experimented with various plan shapes, including triangular ones, but eventually the square and

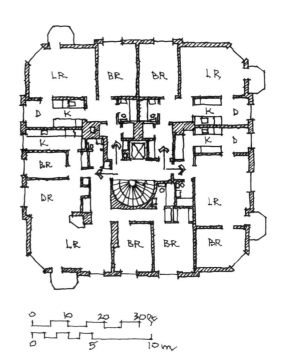

Point block, Danviksklippan, Stockholm (1945),
Sven Backström and Leif Reinius
(after P. Peters)

rectangular plans prevailed and with the acceptance of the punkthus idea in Sweden, they became popular in neighboring countries as well. Designed by Mogens Irming and Tage Nielsen, the high-rise housing development of Bellahøj (1950–52), in

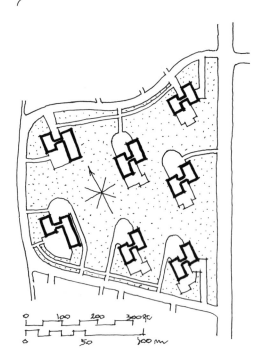

Tower-in-the-park housing estate, Bellahøj,
Copenhagen (1950–52), Mogens Irming
and Tage Nielsen
(after Esbjørn Hiort)

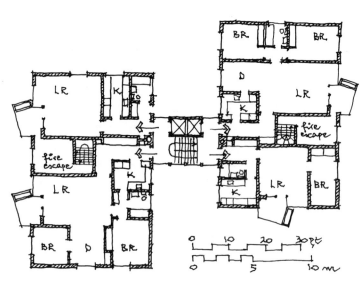

Point block, Bellahøj (1950), Eske Kristensen
(after G. Hassenpflug and P. Peters)

Bronshoj, Copenhagen, for example, has a classic tower-in-the-park estate setting and accommodates about 12,000 apartment units. The eleven-story point blocks were conceived as twin towers, each with only two dwellings per floor, joined to each other by a glazed staircase with two elevators.

Numerous point-block developments were also built in Great Britain. The most noteworthy of the London City Council's early developments was the Alton Estate, Roehampton. To comply with the fire code, two staircases with mandatory exterior walls and one elevator served four dwellings on each typical floor.

Today, high-rise point blocks no longer enjoy the popularity they once had in Great Britain. Disliked by many tenants, primarily because of their height, point blocks, like high-rise slab-blocks, no longer receive funding from public authorities. Point blocks, however, deserve consideration in contrast to high-rise slab-blocks, which are characterized by long double-loaded corridors and dwellings with exposure only on one side; dwellings in slender

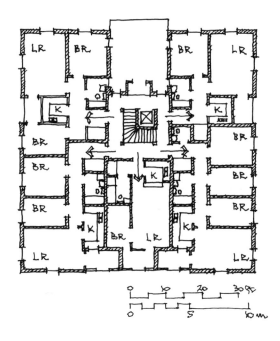

Point block, Rauchstrasse, Berlin-Tiergarten (1985),
G. Grassi and E. Guazzoni
(after Maria Berning et al.)

point blocks not only have two exposures and diagonal cross-ventilation, but also better self-policing of an intimate circulation core. These innate advantages have made point blocks popular with architects and the housing authorities of the former USSR and its satellites. Although usually drab looking, numerous point blocks were built in these countries. The most frequent reason for their unpopularity was that they were poorly maintained.

More than half a century after the Luckhardt brothers made their proposal of four-story "tower houses" for Berlin, Robert Krier won the first prize in a housing competition with similar four-story point blocks for the redevelopment of Rauchstrasse in Berlin-Tiergarten. In 1980, Krier received the commission to realize his scheme, and between 1983 and 1985 six point blocks, each designed by a different architect, were built on the site. At the outset, each building was to have four dwelling units per floor, but, later, financial constraints imposed a change to five dwellings.

Mixed-use Buildings

Most inner cities that are considered attractive, lively, and safe either have residents living downtown or a sizable resident population in close proximity to the city center. Since residential land-use ensures the continuous presence of people, streets are not only more animated throughout the day, but the quality of the urban living environment becomes more of a public issue and the practice of self-policing by residents a corollary. In contrast, a downtown exclusively composed of office buildings basically provides a nine-to-five working population, with the result that after working hours streets are deserted and unsafe.

Zoning prescribing a single land use for a particular area is a planning tool that first became popular during the nineteenth century, when life in cities affected by the Industrial Revolution deteriorated and a new urbanity was sought, isolating residential districts from other activities. The adverse social and economic repercussions derived from single-use zoning practices are being recognized today, and the advantages of mixed land use rediscovered. The most eloquent postwar advocate of mixed-use development is Jane Jacobs who, in her book *The Death and Life of Great American Cities*, outlined the failure of simplistic zoning and advocated a return to diversity. She reminded architects and town planners that cities were innate agglomerations characterized by diversity, and that mixed land use was an intrinsic part of this diversity.

Frank Lloyd Wright's Price Tower in Bartlesville, Oklahoma, is a significant post–World War II example of an early mixed-use development in North America. Completed in 1955, the nineteen-story air-conditioned tower was, at the time, the only high-rise building in this midwestern town, in keeping with Wright's belief that a skyscraper is fit for human occupancy only when standing free, with ample light and air around it. Wright despised the "forest" of skyscrapers that jammed American inner cities, and viewed his Bartlesville tower benignly as "the tree that escaped the crowded forest" (1956, 3)

Price Tower was supported by an immense cruciform reinforced concrete column supporting cantilevered slabs and dividing the building into four quadrants; three were for office spaces and the fourth, the southwest quadrant, for dwellings. As all quadrants looked outward, the occupants of offices and dwellings were assured visual privacy, and the heavy concrete columns between the quadrants afforded good acoustical privacy. The dwellings were designed by Wright as duplex apartments, with living/dining room, kitchen, and powder room at the main level, and two bedrooms and a bathroom at an angled mezzanine, with access to a triangular outside balcony. With the exception of the living/dining room, most spaces in the dwellings were defined by partitions at odd angles and had Wright-designed built-in furniture. Since each quadrant was served by a self-service elevator, apartment dwellers had their own elevator open directly into the hallway of their duplex unit.

Perhaps the most ingenious feature of Price Tower was the design of its outer envelope, which

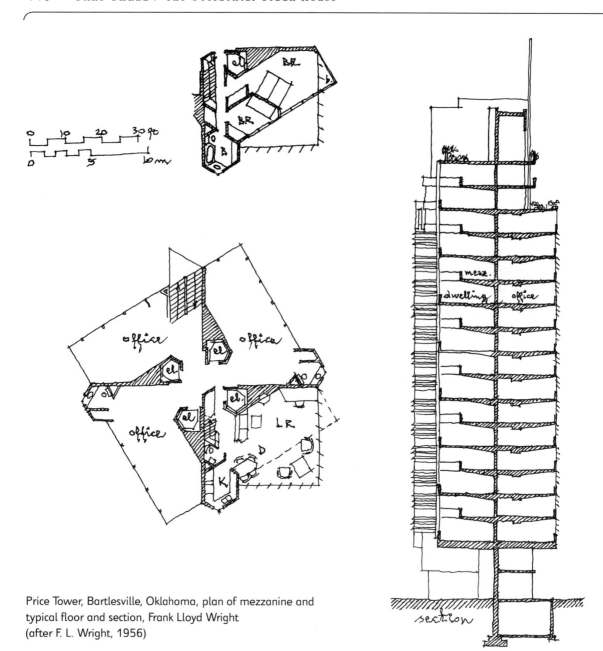

Price Tower, Bartlesville, Oklahoma, plan of mezzanine and
typical floor and section, Frank Lloyd Wright
(after F. L. Wright, 1956)

included copper-sheathed louvers shading the
windows. Horizontal louvers were used for office
windows, while upright copper fins shaded apartments "so that as the sun moves, shadows fall on
the glass surfaces and afford the protection necessary for comfort"(Wright 1956, 16). By designing
the façades of the dwelling quadrant in a different
way from those of the offices, Wright not only
expressed the mixed-use tenancy of the building
but also optimized daylight conditions, creating an
astonishing and pleasing building. Unfortunately,
the apartments of Price Tower were subsequently
converted into offices.

Almost a decade after the completion of Price
Tower, Marina City (1964), a mixed-use building
complex in Chicago, introduced the concept of a
city within a city. Designed by Bertrand Goldberg
Associates, the complex includes apartments,
offices, shops, restaurants, a television theater, an
ice-skating rink, and a marina, but the twin cylindrical residential towers, sixty-two stories high,
are its landmarks.

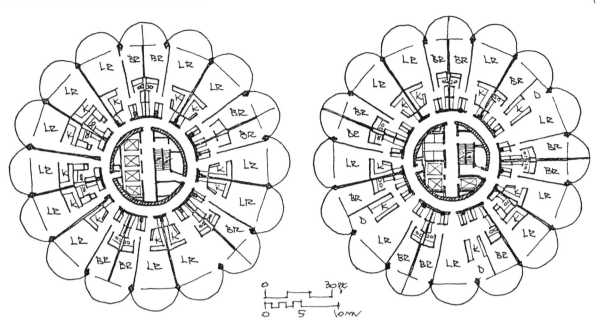

Typical floor plan, 21st–52nd floors

Typical floor plan, 53rd–60th floors

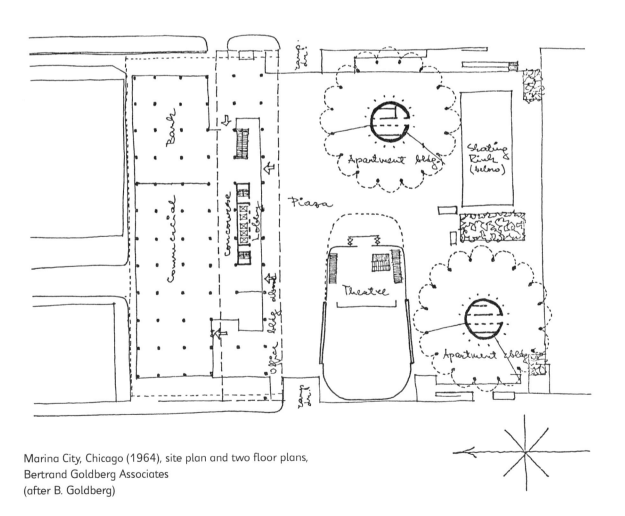

Marina City, Chicago (1964), site plan and two floor plans,
Bertrand Goldberg Associates
(after B. Goldberg)

The Marina City complex has a three-story base consisting of the marina, shopping center, and recreational facilities. On the north side, the base is surmounted by an office building, while the twin towers are sited on the south side, along the edge of the Chicago River. Each cylindrical tower sits on an eighteen-story spirally ramped garage with one parking space allocated to each apartment. The 896 apartment units are raised well above the dirt and noise of city streets, each has access to a semicircular cantelivered balcony. These balconies surround the towers, giving both buildings a striking appearance.

Marina City's elevators, elevator lobbies, and scissor-type fire escapes are accommodated within the central core, and the pie-shaped apartments, ranging from studio-size to multibedroom units, are reached from a single-loaded annular corridor; all dwellings are heated electrically and supplemented by a heat pump above the balcony door. To maximize acoustical privacy no central duct system for ventilation was employed; instead, kitchens and bathrooms are ventilated directly to the outside.

An interesting characteristic of Marina City is that, in spite of the fact that every apartment has access to a parking space, only about a third of the tenants own a car, presumably because 80 percent of them work within walking distance from their apartment. This fact alone demonstrates the important advantage derived from mixed-use developments in city centers. Reduced car ownership in the inner city translates into diminished car traffic and improved air quality.

Developed and financed by the Building Service Employees International Union, Marina City was a good investment, and with its residential occupancy at 100 percent, it became a trendsetter. Bertrand Goldberg Associates wanted to duplicate this feat with another "instant community," River City, near the South Loop of Chicago. The residential component of River City's first phase consists of 446 dwellings, some of them apartments and others town-house or penthouse units. A top-lit meandering ten-story horizontal interior street, with scattered park benches and street lamps, serves as the pedestrian spine of the S-shaped apartment building.

By far the tallest American mixed-use complex with a housing component, also a Chicago landmark, is the 100-story John Hancock Center (1969), towering more than 1,000 ft (304.8 m) above the city. Designed by architect Bruce Graham of Skidmore Owings & Merrill, the top of this steel megastructure, with giant cross-bracing steel members on all four sides to give it stability in the Windy City, "may sway anywhere from 10 to 15 in [25.4 to 38.1 cm]—though those inside would not be aware of it!" (Bach 1979, 94).

At the base of the building, five floors are designated for commercial use and are surmounted by a seven-story parking garage. With intermittent mechanical floors, the next twenty-seven stories are leased as office space, while the following forty-seven are condominium apartments. The building's top section contains an observatory and two restaurant floors, in addition to a television studio and mechanical rooms. The 705 apartment units range in size from studio apartments to four-bedroom luxury suites, with the largest units located exclusively at the uppermost levels. The excessive height of this building made it necessary to have two apartment lobbies, one at ground floor level and the other on the forty-fourth floor, the "sky lobby," where residents have to change elevators. Here, residents also have access to additional amenities, such as a lounge, commissary, restaurant, health club, and swimming pool.

To everyone's amazement, this gigantic mixed-use building, with about 4,000 workers and 1,700 residents in addition to 4,000 visitors, does not generate surges of rush-hour traffic. The benefits of mixed-use urban development were so convincing that the New York City administration introduced bonus incentives if retail space along the sidewalk level and a significant housing component above formed part of new inner-city office building developments. As a result of incentives given in the form of increased floor area ratios, several mixed-use high-rise buildings were erected on Fifth Avenue, a street that for a long time was one of the most prominent retail centers of

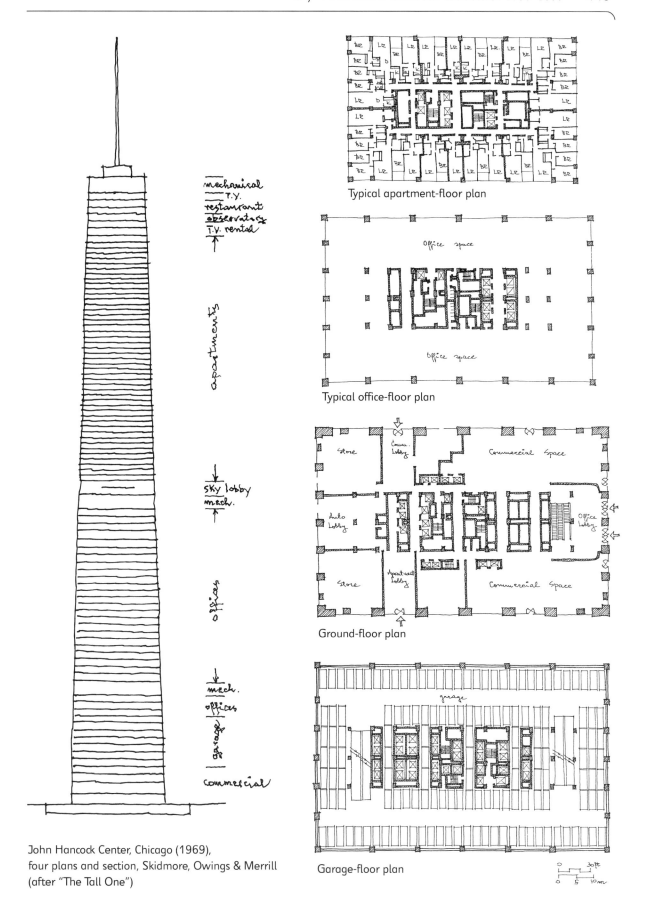

Typical apartment-floor plan

Typical office-floor plan

Ground-floor plan

Garage-floor plan

John Hancock Center, Chicago (1969),
four plans and section, Skidmore, Owings & Merrill
(after "The Tall One")

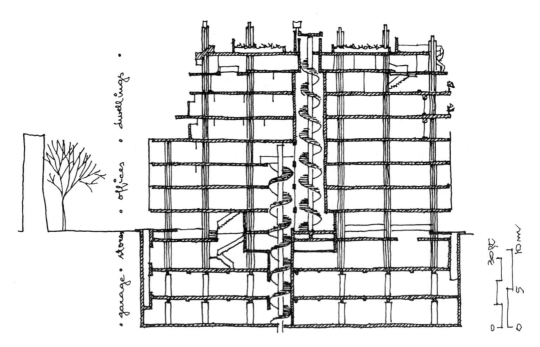

Edificio Pluriusi, Rome, Vicenzo, Fausto, and Lucio Passarelli
(after G. de Carlo and B. Zevi)

America, but by the seventies had begun to show signs of decline after high land values and rents gradually forced out both retail stores and housing. The fifty-two-story Olympic Tower (1976), by Skidmore Owings & Merrill, and the more recent fifty-two-story Trump Tower, designed by Der Scutt of Swanke, Hayden, Connell and Partners, are two examples of mixed-use complexes built after the introduction of bonus incentives. Since both buildings are out of scale with neighboring buildings along Fifth Avenue, they have few redeeming features other than being mixed-use developments.

Although the previously cited examples of mixed-use urban developments all entail high-rise buildings, or megastructures, mixed occupancy is just as advantageous in mid-rise projects, if not more so. An exquisite Italian example of a medium-size building is the Edificio Pluriusi in Rome, built on a corner lot at Via Campania and Via Romagna. Designed by architects Vicenzo, Fausto, and Lucio Passarelli, this reinforced concrete building has three floors below grade and eight above, topped by a roof garden. The ground floor, with recessed glass fronts, was designed for retail outlets, which extend to the first basement level. The three floors above the ground floor were designated as office space behind a curtain-wall façade of tinted glass between enameled steel mullions. The top floors contain apartments, both single-level dwellings and duplex units. An underground garage with a spiral ramp is accessible to tenants and office workers alike.

In contrast to the curtain-walled office section, the residential segment of the building is a highly articulated concrete structure with a series of hovering penthouses. With their exposed clustered columns, pergolas, awnings, and flower boxes bursting with lush plants, the top-floor dwellings are most striking. With multiuse buildings indigenous to Rome, Romans prefer the "hovering villa" on the rooftop in the city to a luxurious suburban bungalow.

Two interesting Canadian examples of mid-rise mixed-use buildings with a housing component were built in Toronto: Hazelton Lanes (1977), designed by Webb Zerafa Menkes Housden Partnership, and The Oaklands (1982), by DuBois Plumb & Associates. Hazelton Lanes consists of fifty-five condominium apartment units in twin

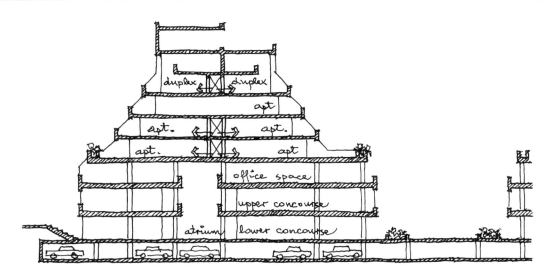

Hazelton Lanes, Toronto (1977), Webb Zerafa Menkes Housden Partnership

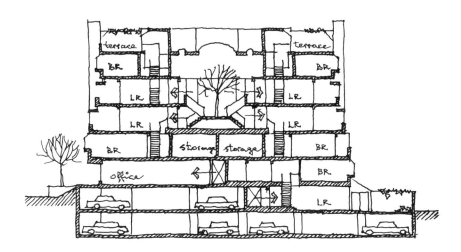

The Oaklands, Toronto (1982), DuBois Plumb & Associates
(after "Apartments with Inner Street")

five-story residential pyramid blocks built on top of a base with a two-level concourse of specialty shops and one office floor; the courtyard space between the two residential blocks is used as an outdoor restaurant in summer, and in winter as a skating rink.

The smaller Oaklands project has nine professional office suites and five apartments (some of them penthouse units) in the main building and eight town houses in the rear of the property. All apartments are entered from a landscaped atrium-like internal street with skylights. To achieve a traditional, homelike atmosphere, apartments are on two levels, each with a fireplace and access to a terrace.

The argument that an ideal urban environment is attainable through the separation of residential and commercial land is no longer tenable, either from a social or an economic point of view. Diversity in land use prevents monotonous urban environments and ensures a more balanced continuity of development. The benefits of sharing costly urban infrastructure and municipal services is also obvious. Finally, mixed-use developments make public transit systems more viable and economical, since the flow balance is more even in mixed land-use areas with around-the-clock occupancy of buildings. The concept of a balanced and conjoined land use has served cities well in the past, and there is no reason to believe that it will not continue to do so in the future.

MID-RISE HOUSING

At the turn of the century, multilevel medium-rise apartment houses were common in most large cities, since building height before the invention of the elevator was restricted to how many stories people could be expected to climb. In Paris, still a quintessentially mid-rise city, the typical apartment house had seven stories, including mezzanine and attic space. After much experimentation with modern high-rise housing outside the protected historic areas of Paris, French architects reverted to the time-proven mid-rise apartment houses.

A traditional perimeter design approach, rather than the tower-in-the-park concept, was used for London's Lillington Street housing development, a milestone and trendsetter for medium-rise housing in England. Designed by architects J. Darbourne and G. Darke for an open competition held in 1961, this Westminster City Council housing estate was built in three stages, and consists of 777 dwelling units in a central built-up residential area of London.

The first- and second-stage developments had a range of one- to seven-person dwelling units distributed in three-, six-, seven-, and eight-story buildings, surrounding a green space overlooked by most. By building close to the boundaries of the site, the open outdoor space represents 62.6 percent of the site. While in the first-phase development only 5 percent of dwellings had a garden; in the third phase, in predominantly five-story buildings, the ratio of ground-related dwellings increased to 36 percent through the use of back-to-back scissor-type maisonettes, all large family units with access to an enclosed private garden or patio. Reached from an open "roof street," accessi-

ble by elevator, smaller dwellings occupied the two top floors.

A growing awareness of the advantages inherent to perimeter mid-rise developments led to a change in England's housing policy, and with buildings sited along the edge of a city block, public streets obtained a better definition. In its contemporary interpretation, with the center of the block devoted to green space, perimeter mid-rise apartment houses offer residents the advantage of both an urban street front and a sheltered green haven at the rear. To visualize the advantages of this design approach, one has to look at a grid seven modules wide and seven modules deep; the annular perimeter area, one module wide, is about equal in area to the remaining area ($7 \times 7 = 49$; $5 \times 5 = 25$; $49 - 25 = 24$, the difference being only one square module). It becomes quite evident from the diagram that the inner area used for outdoor space is more effective than the outer ring—a mere front lawn—yet the two areas are about the same size.

Not all medium-rise housing estates built in Great Britain are as successful and attractive as the Lillington Street project. For example, James Stirling's "futuristic 1,350-dwelling Southgate housing estate at Runcorn in Cheshire, built in 1975," was less successful. In Rod Hackney's opinion, "it was soon nicknamed 'Legoland' by its occupants because of its excessive use of glass, reinforced plastic and 'Toytown'-style designs with porthole windows" (Hackney 1990, 96). This large housing development consists of five-story buildings at a density of 117 persons per acre (295 persons per hectare), about half of Lillington Street's density. The living areas of all four-bedroom two-story family dwellings are at ground level and have access to private patios; balconied three-bedroom units, also two stories high and accessible from an elevated open corridor, occupy the second and third floors. Single-level one-bedroom units with small roof terraces—by far the most intriguing—are on the fourth floor. The open access corridor at the third level, linked to the ground by a series of staircases, was conceived as a public pedestrian path bridging streets and connecting all buildings with each other.

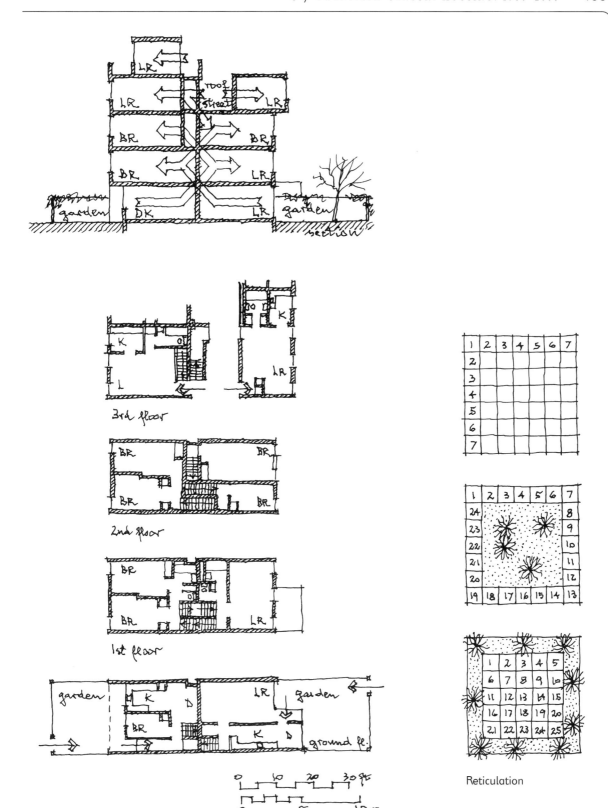

Reticulation

Lillington Street, Phase 3, Westminster (1972), four plans and section,
J. Darbourne and G. Darke
(after David Crawford)

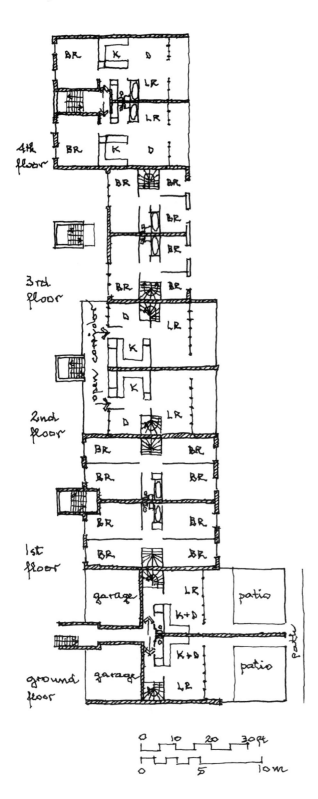

Southgate, Runcorn (1975), James Stirling
(after J. Stirling)

The orientation of all habitable rooms is very sensitive throughout the project, and all dwellings overlook a common green area. However, experimental building materials used in construction decayed prematurely and the annual repair bills were so huge that, in 1989, the Runcorn Development Corporation considered demolishing the entire project. A rescue package for repairs averted demolition.

In Scandinavia too, the advantages intrinsic to medium-rise housing developments were rediscovered. In one Danish housing estate, Farum Midtpunkt, the architects introduced stacked courtyard dwellings, with near total privacy in their indoor and outdoor spaces. Owned by two nonprofit housing associations, and designed by Jørn Ole Sørensen, Viggo Møller Jensen, and Tyge Arnfred, the Cor-Ten-clad concrete buildings of this housing estate contain close to 1,600 dwellings. The majority of these units are accommodated in terraced four-story blocks. The grade level of the development is devoted, unfortunately, to an open garage. The main-floor level of each block has a wide corridor running through the block giving access to all dwellings. On the corridor level are large L-shaped courtyard dwellings on the terrace side, with another set of similar courtyard dwellings above, the latter with a setback to leave courtyards open to the sky. The uppermost dwellings are two-story town houses with a generous terrace. Intermittent staircases in the spine corridor give access to the two units above the corridor. As is customary in Scandinavian housing estates, Farum Midtpunkt has many common service facilities, including day-care nurseries, kindergartens, playgrounds, party rooms, club rooms, hobby rooms, and a small guest hotel.

Mid-rise residential developments have also been built in many parts of Germany. Two residential examples were built in Berlin: Robert Krier's Ritterstrasse-Nord, and Moore, Ruble and Yudell's Tegel Harbor.

The four-story Ritterstrasse-Nord development is the result of an architectural competition based on Krier's urban design studies. With the participation of several architectural firms he successfully

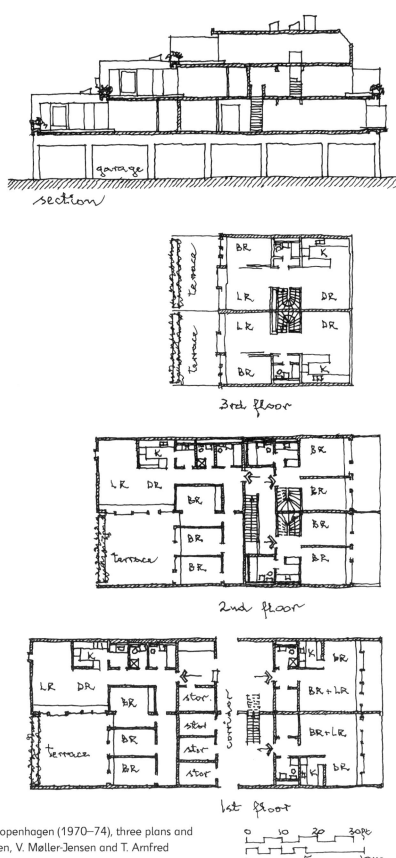

Farum Midtpunkt, Copenhagen (1970–74), three plans and
section, J.O. Sørensen, V. Møller-Jensen and T. Arnfred
(after M. Kjeldsen)

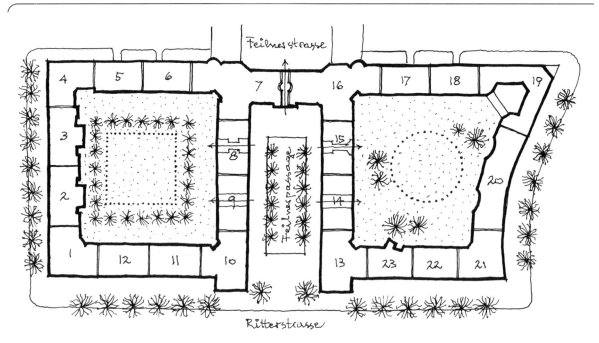

Ritterstrasse-Nord, Berlin (1982–89), Robert Krier
(after Maria Berning et al.)

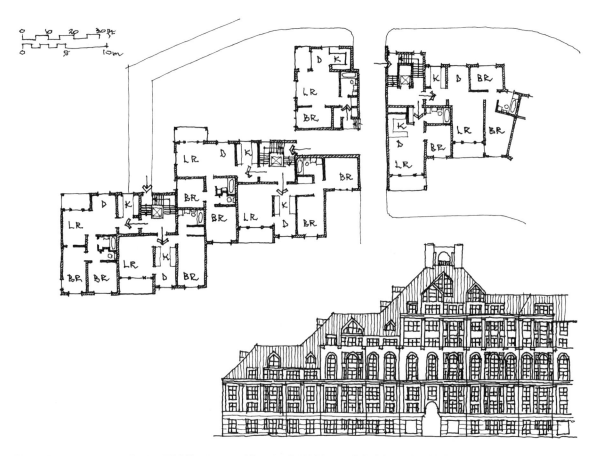

Tegel Harbour housing, Berlin (1980), plans and façade, C. W. Moore, J. Ruble and B. Yudell
(after O. R. Ojeda et al.)

revived old classical urban forms abandoned by the Modern movement, and using the closed city block pattern for his housing development (1981), Krier demonstrated the viability of perimeter block development with enclosed landscaped inner courtyards. A third of the dwellings are designed for families with children, and the high quality of design is praised by the residents.

The Tegel Harbor housing development was also built as the result of an international competition won by three American architects—Charles W. Moore, John Ruble, and Buzz Yudell—in 1980. Forming part of a 26-acre (10.52-hectare) site near lakes and canals, this 170-unit social housing complex, five to eight stories high, is another attempt to build dwellings that are urbane and playful. Although in accordance with social housing norms, most dwellings are relatively small. With its stucco walls, precast pilasters, and dormer windows affording views of landscaped commons and the harbor, Tegel Harbor is one of the most sought-after housing accommodations in Berlin today.

Rogelio Salmona, a celebrated Colombian architect, designed the Nueva Santa Fe Housing Complex (1985–87) in collaboration with architects Pedro Mejia and Arturo Robledo. This large mid-rise housing estate contains 1,800 apartment units distributed within ten city blocks which are a continuation of the gridiron pattern established during the colonial period. Built on a hillside, the red masonry walls are simple, and the buildings create a very pleasant impression. They have a varied fenestration of large French living-room windows, small square bedroom windows, and a row of round apertures off the access gallery. With apartment blocks built around a landscaped courtyard, a beautiful domestic environment was created, harmoniously and serenely blending two landscapes: one of plants and one of brick and mortar.

In Austria, Friedensreich Hundertwasser, an "eco-oriented" artist and ardent opponent of impersonal high-rise housing, designed an unusual medium-rise public housing project for Vienna. Completed in 1985, Hundertwasser House is a colorful, individualistic, and romantic apartment house which, to the dismay of its residents,

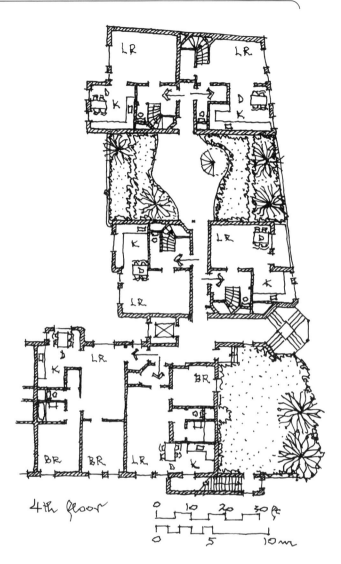

Hundertwasser House, Vienna (1985), F. Hundertwasser and W. Pelikan
(after Y. Ashihara)

has become a most popular tourist attraction. Because Hundertwasser insisted that each tenant's apartment should be identifiable from the street, dwellings throughout the stucco building were painted in different colors and hues, and windows, balconies, and loggias were designed in various sizes and shapes. This luxury of variety—usually reserved for the very well-to-do—was achieved through the selective use of off-the-shelf technology, mass-produced and therefore inexpensive items available in the marketplace, such as ten different kinds of windows, doors, doorknobs, plumbing fixtures, etc.

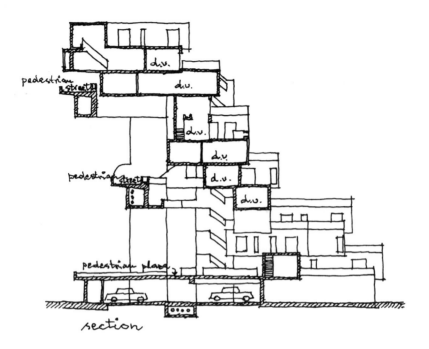

section

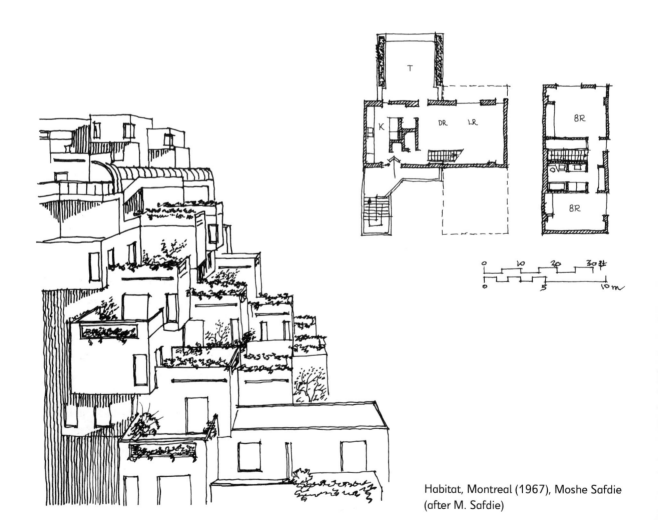

Habitat, Montreal (1967), Moshe Safdie
(after M. Safdie)

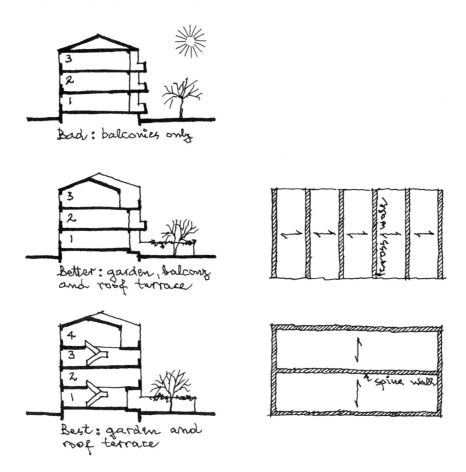

Mid-rise design potentials, three sections and two plans

Built in the inner city, this unusual building distinguishes itself not only by its colorful façades, but also by its many trees and lush plants that sprout all over the building in windows, on balconies, terraces, rooftops, and on the ground. The green plants of this apartment house suggest an opulence formerly associated with palatial urban dwellings of the aristocracy. Aware that trees provide shade, ornament, color, and clean air, Hundertwasser originally wanted to use recycled waste water to fertilize plants and trees of his building, but the city reneged on its permit.

Almost two decades before Hundertwasser House, Moshe Safdie's Habitat, at Montreal's Expo '67, also brought instant fame to its architect, and it, too, became a tourist attraction. With its 354 stacked modular prefabricated concrete boxes, forming 158 dwellings and numerous roof terraces, Habitat is a dramatic and well-articulated ten-story building. Its houses are accessible by sheltered, but open, upper-level streets linked to vertical circulation cores with skip-stop elevator service. This circulation system sometimes requires that dwellings be one story above or below the access street, which is reminiscent of the staircase access of Montreal's indigenous multiplex dwelling. Habitat is sited on Cité du Havre, adjacent to the harbor, so the occupants of every dwelling unit enjoy views in several directions—the skyline of downtown Montreal with a mountain backdrop, Nuns' Island, the busy harbor, or the swift flowing St. Lawrence River with the south shore beyond.

Architects of multiple residential buildings made a long detour during the twentieth century to arrive at the realization that medium-rise apartment houses are socially, environmentally, and economically more advantageous than high-rise apartment buildings. Not requiring sophisticated structural systems, pressurization, water tanks or pumps ensuring adequate water pressure, sprinkler systems, and zoned banks of high-speed elevators translates into greater economy.

Through skillful design, it is possible to have two-thirds of all dwellings of a mid-rise structure either at grade level or at penthouse level, with private gardens at the base or terraces at roof level. The most advantageous construction method for mid-rise buildings is the cross-wall system of load-bearing walls, a departure from the traditional spine-wall system. Cross walls, built in concrete or masonry, have very good acoustical properties and provide the best acoustic privacy between adjacent dwellings. Since external walls are not load-bearing, window sizes and thermal insulation can be optimized without structural constraints.

Environmental considerations also favor midrise buildings because microclimatic conditions adjacent to them are more favorable. They are better protected from the wind, and being more uniform in height, they are bypassed by air streams and devoid of eddies at sidewalk level. They also cast less shadow on the ground and on neighboring property.

Medium-rise housing developments are eminently suited to provide affordable dwellings in the inner city to a wide range of income levels and households, from single persons to families with children. Because self-policing is more effective in these buildings, they provide a feeling of security for their occupants, and, since no dwelling is at a higher level than mature tree tops, each dwelling has a visual contact with verdure, and can be reached by standard firemen's ladders.

COLLECTIVE HABITATION AND COMMUNAL DWELLINGS

In Denmark and Sweden the concept of collective habitation most closely evolved from a utopian ideal to reality. The most compelling proof that collective habitation is desirable is the fact that in the late 1970s, 13,000 Stockholm residents were waiting for accommodation in a "service house"—a more recent Swedish name for the collective house. Collective habitation is an attractive proposition to many families and households. A young working couple would find it very convenient to move into an apartment building where food catering and house cleaning is available on request. Similarly, a new family, transferred from their hometown to an unfamiliar city, would find security in a collective house. Working single parents with preschool children would benefit greatly from using the in-house day-nursery or kindergarten. Elderly couples and retired people, too, can benefit from collective services offered in these buildings. In particular, single people—whether young, middle-aged, or elderly, divorced, or widowed— are all potential collective house residents who want to live in comfort without sacrificing their privacy. To meet an increasing demand and to ensure economic viability, many postwar collective housing projects have been built too large, often resulting in high-rise buildings, which acquired an undesirable institutional atmosphere instead of a homelike ambiance.

One of the first postwar Danish collective houses, Høje Søborg (1951) designed by architects P. E. Hoff and B. Windinge, was built in a Copenhagen suburb, Gladsaxe. The 120 dwellings of this five-story elevator-serviced building ranged in size from one to four rooms. Apart from a doorman, collective services included a common dining room with central kitchen catering, housekeeping services, a children's center serving all age groups, two guest rooms for tenants' visitors, and, at the roof level, common party and meeting rooms with access to a terrace-garden.

If Otto Fick were alive today, and he visited an American family living in a luxury apartment complex like Chicago's River City, a building with 24-hour doorman service and amenities such as swimming pool, sauna, exercise room, rooftop party room, and roof gardens as well as food delivery from an in-house restaurant, he would insist that River City is a Kollektivhus, although in reality it is a mixed-use development. In fact, most American luxury apartment buildings offer services to their residents that are similar to those of

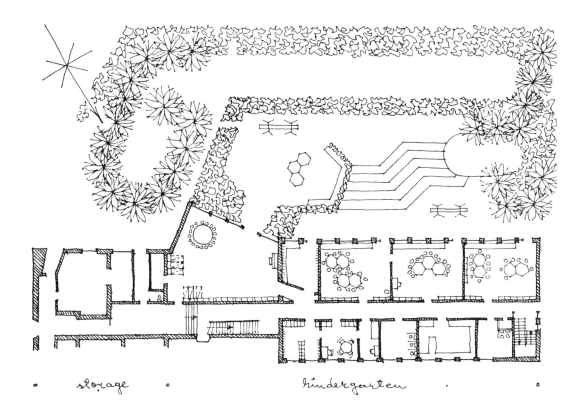

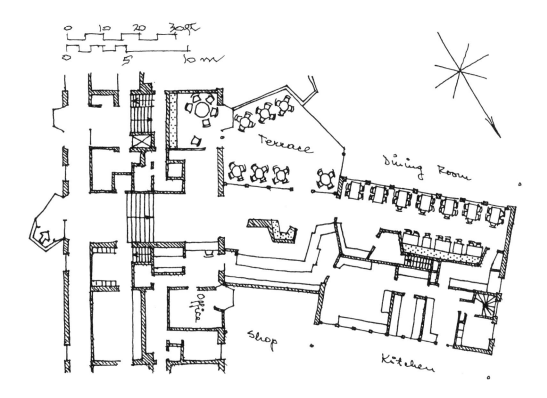

Høje Søborg, Copenhagen (1951), two plans (children's center and communal
dining room section), P. E. Hoff and B. Windinge
(after "Kollektivhuset Høje Søborg")

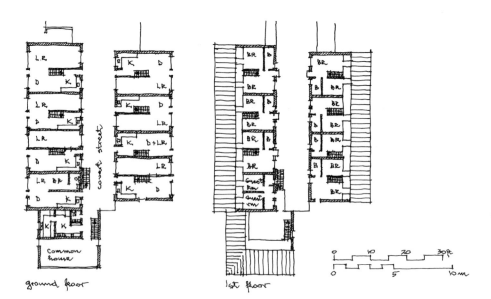

Drivhuset, Randers (1984), two plans, Niels Madsen
(after Vedel-Petersen et al.)

collective habitation. But Fick's original intention of making similar services accessible to moderate- and lower-income groups remains just a dream.

Experience shows that the moderate-size collective house, with 60 to 100 dwellings and collective services limited exclusively to residents, may be desirable from a social point of view but unrealistic economically. Moderate-size collective habitation is only viable if the residents are willing to operate it communally, as is the case in low-rise communal houses called Bofaellesskaber, in Denmark, or in a mixed-use apartment building where collective services are provided by in-house commercial outlets.

The concept of communal dwellings evolved in Denmark, and its genesis is attributed mainly to three forces: (1) the ideological tenets of the counterculture movement of the sixties that gave rise to communal living, (2) the popularity of small-scale low-density, low-rise housing developments, and (3) the new pressure exerted upon the family as an institution in the wake of demographic and socioeconomic changes in society. Like the collective apartment houses that preceded these low-rise dwelling clusters, communal housing was designed to facilitate and enrich the daily lives

of their residents by providing access to several collective services, such as communal dining and child care, the latter especially attractive to working parents. Moreover, these communal dwellings were intended to complement the changes in family composition that arose from new lifestyles, new sex roles, and new household formations. The first communal residential community was built in the early seventies, but since that time over one hundred similar communities have been established in Denmark and many more are in the planning stage. Geographically, these residential enclaves are distributed throughout the country, but are most often found in the vicinity of large cities.

Typically, communal housing consists of a group of independent self-sufficient homes, like those found in any contemporary residential development, but with the distinction that its resident families live in a territorially defined neighborhood and have access to communal facilities and outdoor recreational areas. The community building usually has a common dining room for all residents and a day-care center for children, in addition to other common rooms. Since most of these communities were planned and designed with the

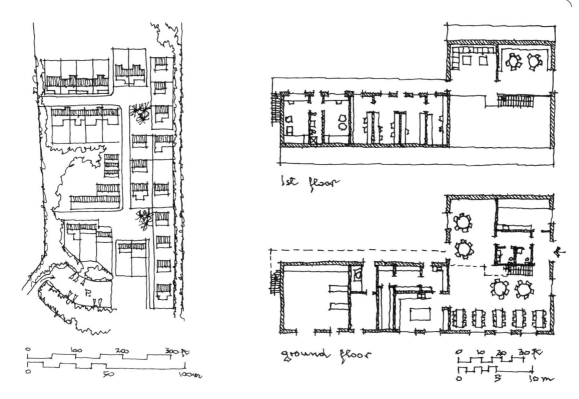

"Faelleshus," Sol og Vind, Beder, Jutland (1980) two plans and site plan, Regnbuen
(after Vedel-Petersen et al.)

participation of their future residents, tenure, size, and organization of the community varies from project to project. However, the complement of private home and communal facilities are shared by all. Most early communal dwelling clusters were privately owned developments; later nonprofit cooperatives and cooperatives with index-linked mortgages (similar to U.S. variable-rate mortgages), as well as rental units, were introduced, but the most frequent tenure type is still based on private ownership.

A typical communal dwelling cluster is formed by twelve to thirty independent homes, each with its own kitchen and private outdoor space. The building types used for homes are predominantly detached or attached single-family houses, one or two stories in height, often with an open-plan interior layout and a split-level arrangement, and grouped closely together reflecting their communality. The common house, or *Faelleshus*, is usually centrally located and its floor area is a function of the size of the community; each household has access to it as well as to shared open space.

Communal child care and the provision of an appropriate social environment for the upbringing of children is another attraction of these communities. Nuclear families with one or two children, not to mention single parents, are rarely in a position to provide an optimum environment for their children with adequate social contacts, not only with their peers, but with adults as well. By joining a communal housing development, families naturally extend the social network of their children as well as their own. They become part of a large family, whose individual members have various kinds of expertise and are willing to share the responsibility for looking after each other's children. A safe and healthy outdoor environment, the presence of different age groups of children, and social contacts with adults, with whom they are at ease, create good conditions for the growth and development of children. Usually, a wide range of social and recreational activities is available to adults and children alike, such as singing, dancing, gardening, and sports, in addition to hobbies like photography and sewing.

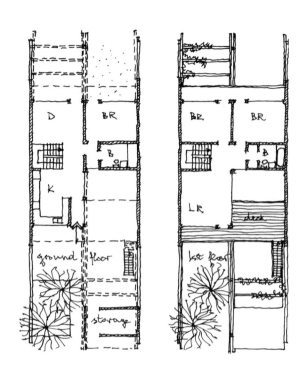

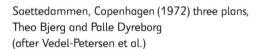

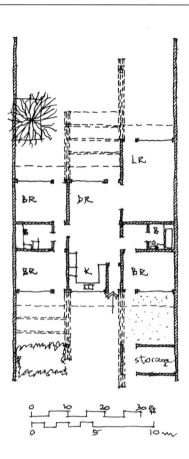

Saettedammen, Copenhagen (1972) three plans,
Theo Bjerg and Palle Dyreborg
(after Vedel-Petersen et al.)

Of course, members have to accept some responsibilities upon joining a residential community administered by a residents' association. Since all decisions are made through a democratic process, membership entails attendance at an annual general meeting, monthly meetings, and special committee meetings. Although some flexibility exists about how many working obligations are assumed voluntarily, some work and participation in the administration of the community is unavoidable.

One of the first communal housing projects based on privately owned homes was built near Copenhagen, in Hillerod, and completed in 1972. Designed by architects Theo Berg and Palle Dyreborg, this community, called Saettedammen, consists of twenty-seven private dwelling units and a common house. At the outset, there were two types of attached town houses to choose from: single-story or two-story. Subsequently, a few dwellings, whose original occupants left the community, were expanded and others converted into smaller rental units. The common house consists of a well-equipped kitchen, a dining hall, TV room, playroom, laundry, and a sauna with dressing rooms and showers.

Every afternoon at three, tea is served in the common house to all residents. Communal dining is organized for the participating group, numbering about forty persons, from Sunday to Friday, and every member of this group over 18 years of age must take turns in buying food and preparing meals. A music group rehearses weekly and another group meets regularly to do physical exercise. A teenager is hired to look after the children, but is supervised by adult residents on a rotating basis. Considerable attention is paid to the maintenance of common grounds, which include play areas for children, ball courts, a small pond used in winter for skating, kitchen gardens, and an orchard. Vehicular movement on the site is restricted to the garage court near the entrance. The land-use efficiency of this development is almost twice as high as Levittown's.

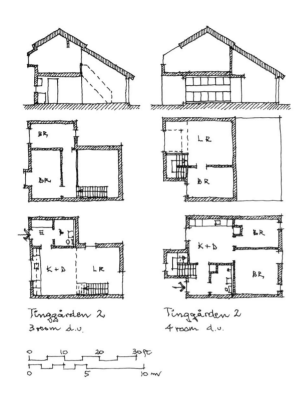

Tinggården 2 (1984), Vandkunsten and Karsten Vibild
(after M. Kjeldsen)

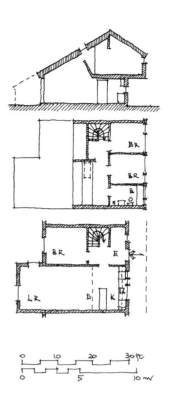

Attached dwellings, Fuglsangpark (1983), Vandkunsten
(after M. Kjeldsen)

A large nonprofit communal housing project, with 155 attached dwellings, is Tinggården 1 and Tinggården 2 (1979–84) at Herfolge, near the provincial town of Koge. While Tinggården 1 has a garden ambiance, Tinggården 2 is more urban in character with a focus on pedestrian streets. Designed by Atelier Vandkunsten and Karsten Vibild, this development has seven different types of dwellings, mostly two-story, with sloping ceilings and mezzanines, giving the homes a spatial quality rarely seen in subsidized housing.

Danish communal housing developments can be compared to the small PUDs (Planned Unit Developments) of North America. However, in Danish Bofaellesskaber cooperation among residents extends beyond security concerns and embraces several well-structured social services, from day-nurseries and teenage clubs to communal dining. Several communal housing developments modeled on Danish examples were established not only in neighboring Sweden and Norway, but also in other European countries and, more recently, in North America.

After studying several Danish examples, Kathryn McCamant and Charles Durrett, in their book *Cohousing: A Contemporary Approach to Housing Ourselves*, outlined the advantages of living in dwelling clusters in communal housing. A couple of years after the publication of *Cohousing* (a term coined by the authors and protected by trademark), a communal residential development with thirty dwelling units was founded in Winslow, Washington, a town on Bainbridge Island in Puget Sound. Designed by Seattle architect Ed Weinstein, the gabled dwellings with wood siding are similar in appearance to the traditional farmhouses of the island. The Winslow communal housing group, consisting of forty-five adults—mostly professional people—and twenty-five children, lives on a beautiful five-acre wooded site in the countryside, yet they can reach downtown Seattle by ferry in thirty minutes.

Communal housing groups seem to function best, and with less friction, if their members share similar values and have similar backgrounds. This is one of the reasons they are so successful in Denmark, a country with a culturally homogeneous population. It is tempting to compare the members of communal housing to a large extended family or a clan, but there are two basic distinctions: (1) membership is voluntary, and (2) as there is no patriarch or chief, all important decisions are made democratically.

There are several significant attractions about Bofaellesskaber. First, individuals have the option at all times either to enjoy the privacy of their own homes or to engage in social activities in the community's common areas. Second, these residential communities foster voluntary social interaction as well as social and environmental responsibility; most communities practice composting and recycling. Last, but not least, they foster first-hand experience in harmonious communal living; not unlike members of band-type food-gathering societies, they learn to compromise after realizing that what is good for the individual may not always be in the best interest of the community.

RESIDENTIAL CONVERSIONS

The conversion of factories and warehouses into loft apartment buildings is a phenomenon of the second half of the twentieth century. After World War II, the vacancy rate in loft buildings was high because of the gradual departure of manufacturing industries and warehouses from inner-city locations. The economic base in North American cities shifted from manufacturing to service industries, and the dispersal of factories was aided by the new interstate highways. The first loft conversion was probably made clandestinely by an artist in search of a studio and, although it was illegal, a place to live for a reasonable rent.

A well-documented loft conversion area in New York City is SoHo (named for its location south of

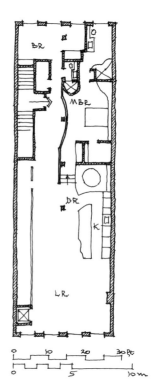

Loft dwelling, New York City, Alan Buchsbaum and Stephen Tilly
(after Mildred F. Schmertz)

Houston Street). Before the mid-nineteenth century, SoHo was a fashionable residential neighborhood, but when residents moved to uptown Manhattan, garment industries and wholesalers moved into newly erected five- to six-story loft buildings, many with cast-iron façades, in SoHo. Just before World War I, garment factories and wholesalers moved to the upper Thirties along Seventh Avenue (the present garment district) and left their vacated loft buildings for low-profile commercial enterprises.

In the early fifties artists began to move into SoHo loft buildings. They were drawn not only by cheap rent, but also because they required space for their artwork, which had a tendency to be on a large scale. For sculptors, industrial buildings were ideal for studios since they were designed for heavy live loads and were serviced by freight elevators. Apart from painters and sculptors, other artists, for example, dancers, graphic designers, architects, and musicians, also found the typical deep lofts exciting spaces to live and work in.

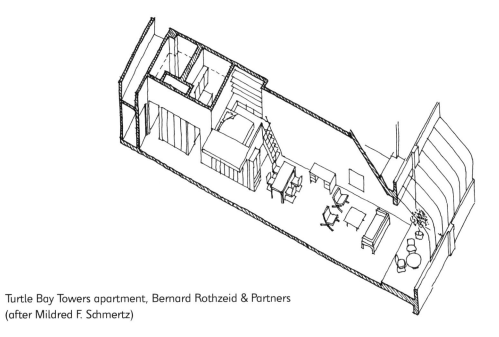

Turtle Bay Towers apartment, Bernard Rothzeid & Partners
(after Mildred F. Schmertz)

By the early sixties, SoHo was an important residential neighborhood for artists and soon thereafter, when smart shops and restaurants moved in, the area also became attractive to the modish middle-class. "Loft spaces were sought after not only because they were part of a new chic scene in New York, but also because they were reasonably priced living spaces—in fact, comparative bargains—in the expensive and tight housing market of New York" (Hudson 1987, 95).

In Lowell, Massachusetts, textile mills built next to sources of water power and later abandoned were converted into subsidized housing for the elderly and low-income residents. But it was not only New England textile mills that were converted into housing, but also heavy industrial buildings, as exemplified by the industrial structures (decommissioned in 1974) of Boston's Charlestown Navy Yard. The spine of the foundry and the machine-shop building were converted into six-story-high atriums, the main circulation space of the 367 apartment units of this project, called Constitution Quarters; ground-floor apartment units are entered from the spine, like town houses from a small stoop. Although the interiors of the dwelling units are up-to-date, the historic integrity of the buildings' exteriors from the 1850s remained essentially intact.

In Boston Harbor's Lewis Wharf is the 400-ft (122-m) long and 80-ft (24-m) wide Granite Building, which was built during the 1830s but after World War I gradually lapsed into disuse. In 1972, Carl Koch and Associates converted this old six-story warehouse into a mixed-use building. The ground floor was transformed into shops and restaurants, the floor above into offices, and the top four floors into dwellings. Built for the well-to-do, the dwellings are generally roomy with high ceilings. In contrast to the crowded housing built in the inner city, the Lewis Wharf rehabilitation project offers the advantage of a distant view over the harbor, and the luxury not only of mooring a yacht and parking a car close to home, but also of living within walking distance of downtown.

New York City high-rise office buildings, too, have been transformed into apartment buildings. Turtle Bay Towers, a twenty-four-story typical stepped-back office building with 12-ft (3.6-m) ceilings and 8-ft (2.4-m) high windows, erected in 1929 on Manhattan's East Side, was converted by Bernard Rothzeid & Partners into a luxurious residential building with 341 apartment units. The addition of greenhouses, the full width of several apartments, located adjacent to set-back ledges, as well as the provision of bedroom lofts to the linear dwelling units, created an interesting spatial zoning. This project was carried out under a New York City tax abatement program to encourage the conversion of commercial properties into residential use to give a boost to inner-city housing.

Abandoned schools in old residential neighborhoods have also been successfully converted into housing, often the only adaptive reuse acceptable to a neighboring community. Churches, too, have been converted into dwellings, but their transformation into private homes is much more difficult in comparison to an institutional conversion, for example, a library. Most nonresidential building types, however, do lend themselves to conversion into dwellings, and the limits of the existing physical envelope seldom hampers the ingenuity of architects, as many projects illustrate.

NEOTRADITIONAL DWELLING DESIGN AND NEW URBANISM

As at the turn of the previous century, when young British architects sought inspiration in the simplicity and homeyness of indigenous architects after having rejected the formalism of classicism in domestic design, so today, a new generation of architects seeks design inspiration from the traditional houses of small towns and cities, for a more humane living environment than that created during the second half of the twentieth century.

Homes, as mere "machines to live in," as the modernists proclaimed, are unacceptable to most people today. Similarly, the soulless neighborhoods of suburbia also foster discontent. In a sense, it is natural that at the very same time when technological inventions (TVs, VCRs, computers, cellular phones, etc.) enable people to live in voluntary isolation at home, the desire to live in a comprehensible neighborhood that conjures up images of stability and security of a bygone age, is becoming important.

The New Urbanism movement represents a planning and urban design approach based on tra-ditional development patterns predating the so-called rational residential neighborhoods of the Modern movement, when communities were built for people, not cars. Then, communities had narrower streets and were more compact; walking, bicycling, and using public transit were more common than driving alone in a car, and face-to-face interaction among neighbors was natural. At the time, traditional communities were also heterogeneous, comprising all levels of income. In contrast, access to both neotraditional domestic design and communities planned in accordance with principles of New Urbanism are so far limited to well-to-do families, which distinguishes them from the "real" communities they attempt to emulate.

PORT GRIMAUD

One of the first architects who adopted a neotraditional approach to both dwelling and urban design was François Spoerry, builder of Port Grimaud (1966), a lagoon town in the Bay of St. Tropez. An ardent sailor enamored of the sea, Spoerry set about to establish a community consisting of a series of islands where every home faced a private quay in the front and a street in the back. With the creation of a lagoon city, he increased the sea frontage by about 9 miles, or 14 kilometers, and thereby relieved the pressure for high-density residential development. Although modern on the inside, the exterior of Port Grimaud's homes reflect the feeling of permanence innate to the region's vernacular architecture, where no home is identical to another one, yet all have a sense of unity, because similar building materials and technology were used in their contruction. Port Grimaud replicates the charm of old villages of the area, and, at first sight, it is hard to distinguish its shaded narrow streets from those of neighboring villages, such as Ramatuelle, Cogolin or "old" Grimaud.

Port Grimaud is also one of the first communities that was built, perhaps instinctively, in conformity with the guidelines of New Urbanism. Emphasis is on pedestrian traffic, with vehicular access limited to the occasional unloading at a

'Canal du Nord' Port Grimaud, Bay of St. Tropez (1966), François Spoerry
(after F. Spoerry)

Port Liberté, New Jersey, François Spoerry
(after F. Spoerry)

homeowner's dwelling, or to vans making deliveries to shops. A large supervised parking lot on the mainland, in proximity to the entrance, is used for temporary parking and general car storage. The community is served by a post office, banks, shops, restaurants, cafés, and a communal hall seating three hundred. Twice a week an outdoor farmers' market is held in Port Grimaud. Situated on a little central island, this lagoon city's largest building is an ecumenical church with beautiful stained glass windows by the artist Victor de Vasarely.

PORT LIBERTÉ

A more recent Spoerry-designed neotraditional community is Port Liberté, a North American example of a medium-rise housing development. Built on an abandoned railway- and dockyard in

Jersey City, New Jersey, only a stone's throw from the tip of Manhattan Island, this picturesque community, with 2,000 dwellings, recalls the East Coast's traditional urban dwellings. Ranging in height from three to eight stories, the wood, brick, and pastel-colored stucco buildings have an old look, in spite of the fact that the site, as recently as 1984, was a desolate area with rusting old locomotives, railway cars, and the rotting hulks of Liberty ships. Port Liberté has its own town square, shopping, entertainment, and recreational facilities. With yachts moored to the quays of excavated canals, this new lagoon city, like its predecessor, Port Grimaud, was designed for the well-to-do, who are amused by the mélange of neotraditional domestic vernacular and Disneyesque urban design.

SEASIDE

One of the earliest North American examples of a neotraditional community is Seaside, a resort community for well-to-do residents that evokes nostalgia for the comfortable middle-class life of the turn-of-the-century. Designed by Andres Duany and Elizabeth Plater-Zyberk, and built in the 1980s by developer Robert Davis, Seaside is a picturesque community located on the seashore of the Florida Panhandle. Most Seaside homes are traditional two-story detached houses, with painted wood siding, double-hung windows, large porches, widow's walks on top of sloped roofs, and picket fences. Although Seaside's homes reflect nineteenth-century American domestic architecture externally, their interiors are contemporary, not only in appointments and fixtures, but also in their layout. The "open plan" of the servantless house is paramount. Essentially, Seaside attempts to replicate life in a small southern American town more than half a century ago.

A critic observed that Seaside "was a completely artificial place inhabited only by yuppies, with none of the nitty-gritty problems of a real town with a diverse population, real economic concerns, and a history"(Kunstler 1993, 257). This may be so, but the fact is that people prefer to live in a

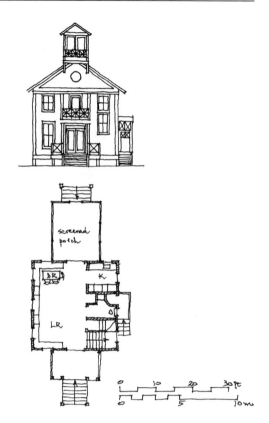

Cooper House I, Seaside, Cooper Johnson Smith (after D. Mohney and K. Easterling)

Cooper House II, Seaside, Cooper Johnson Smith (after D. Mohney and K. Easterling)

coherent Traditional Neighborhood Development (TND). Duany and Plater-Zyberk were swamped with requests to design neotraditional communities in many other parts of North America.

The Beach Cottage, Windsor, Florida, Craig Roberts (after Duany and Plater-Zyberk)

WINDSOR

One neotraditional community designed by Duany and Plater-Zyberk is built on the site of a former grapefruit grove in Florida. Windsor (1989) is yet another attempt by the designers to restore living conditions to the "earlier model of villages, towns and neighbourhoods" (Duany 1989, 31). A strict discipline is applied to buildings, controlling their siting and height as well as their appearance. Two-story homes are built right on the property line to liberate much land normally wasted on front lawns. The exterior appearance of Windsor's residences attempts to emulate the Anglo-Caribbean vernacular homes of former British colonists in the West Indies.

CELEBRATION

One of the latest examples of neotraditionalism and New Urbanism is a community near Orlando, Florida, on the outskirts of Disney World. Michael Eisner, Disney's CEO, commissioned a design team including Robert A. M. Stern, Andres Duany, and Elizabeth Plater-Zyberk, as well as Jaquelin Taylor Robertson, among others, to design a self-contained town for about 20,000, where residents could live in security, shop in an attractive town center with stores, restaurants, and movie houses, and enjoy a public park.

Celebration is planned as a community where children as well as the elderly can feel at home, with well-funded schools and modern health center. Celebration is not envisaged as a gated community with security guards manning its entryways. Instead, it is hoped that the distance from Orlando and a very wide green belt around the new town will give sufficient protection (though at least one family has experienced a break-in).

In his article on Celebration, Russ Rymer muses that, instead of being a neotraditional community, it is really a protocorporate contemporary "town off the shelf, meant not to be built but to be consumed by its residents" and what "Celebration celebrates, oddly, is an American community that existed precisely in that time before corporations made it their business to build communities" (Rymer 1996, 76–77).

Without the presence of moderate- and low-income families, Celebration's idealized small-town life is make-believe, and is scarcely more realistic than Disney World's illusory "Main Street U.S.A"—a street designed for leisure where there are neither vacancies nor "for rent" signs. Scores of charwomen, gardeners, city workers, as well as sales clerks and clerical workers, who cannot afford to live in Celebration, have to come in on weekdays to sustain this new community. Yet there is no doubt that neotraditional dwellings in New Urbanism residential settings are popular. These new communities emulate the scale of towns predating the proliferation of private cars and they emphasize pedestrian movement within their boundaries.

CONCLUSION

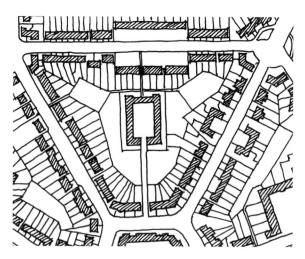

Next to alimentation and procreation, shelter, in most climates, is the most basic requirement for human survival. The various means by which food is procured by people is reflected in the nature of their dwellings. Food gatherers and hunters who live a nomadic existence live in ephemeral or episodic shelters, while nomadic tribes with a pastoral economy live in portable tentlike dwellings, with their frame and cover carried by beasts of burden from campsite to campsite. In contrast to the nomadic existence intrinsic to food-gathering and pastoralism, the domestication of plants implied a more sedentary life. The state of agricultural technology employed in cultivation determines the length of time cultivators may inhabit their dwelling, a range that can vary from a few years, in the case of rudimentary slash-and-burn farming, to several generations, when an advanced agricultural economy was reached with the aid of compound tools and fertilization. It was at this stage of surplus food production that conditions were conducive to the evolution of urban civilization.

Rural dwellings of agricultural societies were emulated by ancient urban societies that eventually evolved into the typical introverted oriental urban houses, which open upon an enclosed courtyard, a private "well of heaven," with an emphasis on a short-range view of private space. Unfortunately, several nations where the oriental courtyard house was indigenous for several millennia began to abandon this house form during the twentieth century and adopt occidental house forms. The few voices that advocate the improvement rather than the abandoning of domestic architectural heritage are not heeded. Paradoxically, during the twentieth century, several architects discovered the advantages of the inward-oriented house and successfully used them in several residential developments in western Europe.

The inward orientation of oriental urban houses is in marked contrast to the outward orientation of their occidental counterparts, which are extroverted dwellings with views from their principal rooms of public streets and squares. This difference in orientation accounts in part for the great disparity between the narrow alleyways of the oriental city and the wide streets, avenues, and squares of the occidental city.

The externalization of the occidental urban house dates from the Middle Ages, when each gabled house asserted its individuality toward the street. For a period this individuality was abandoned in favor of a collective unity expressed in a palatial façade, but the outward orientation of the dwelling remained unaltered. The emphasis upon individuality returned during the nineteenth century with the detached villas and the tasteful cottages of the well-to-do middle class; attention to the external appearance of the house became a challenge with Andrew Jackson Downing's claim, that much of the character of a homeowner may be read in his house.

That the outward orientation of the occidental dwelling contributed to the segregation of social classes in neighborhoods of various income levels is a plausible supposition, since rich and poor live as neighbors in cultures where the inward-looking courtyard house prevails. At a time when homogeneous precincts of tanners or other craftsmen of the medieval city were small, every citizen, rich and poor, was served by the same community facilities; they went to the same place of worship, the same school, the same marketplace. However, in the wake of the Industrial Revolution, when workers' districts became large urban entities and their residents were so numerous that they acquired their own church, school, and market street, people of lower- and upper-income groups seldom met.

The phenomenal urban growth initiated by the Industrial Revolution resulted in a deterioration of city life, which no longer symbolized freedom as it did during the Middle Ages, but a yoke of misery for far too many. Thus, fertile ground was created for the acceptance of Ebenezer Howard's Garden City concept, which, essentially, was a mere confirmation of an anti-urban trend that already had manifested itself decades before when the well-to-do left the city and built their homes in the countryside, within commuting distance of the city. The nineteenth century also set the scene for the socioeconomic polarization of dwellings—the low-density single-family house at one extreme, and the high-density apartment or tenement on the other.

Le Corbusier eloquently presented this choice between extremes. In his opinion, the low-rise choice meant living in individual houses with a questionable charm that entailed a great waste of urban land resources, while the second choice implied living in high-rise apartment buildings in a parklike setting, a more attractive solution and also more efficient in its land use. It is questionable, however, whether choices between housing forms were truly as limited as Le Corbusier thought.

During the interwar period, improvements in domestic architecture, including workers' housing,

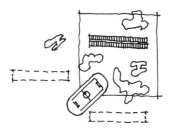

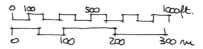

Le Corbusier: comparison of high- and low-density housing
(after Le Corbusier and de Pierrefeu, 1948)

led to spatial and safety standards unknown before World War I. Two housing forms—the single-family and the multifamily dwelling—were compared and debated. While single-family homes, freestanding or attached, gave greater independence to their residents, distances to the workplace, schools, shopping streets, etc. increased due to an inefficient land use; multifamily dwellings, on the other hand, were more economical in the utilization of land and enhanced the communal spirit, but diminished the independence of their residents. The former was preferred and attainable in North America, while the second was favored in European countries. There was a consensus that dwellings in residential neighborhoods should have easy access to collective institutions for their residents to lead a healthy life.

After World War II, the realization of the American Dream initiated an exodus of city dwellers to the suburbs. In consequence, cities, in contrast to thriving suburbs with a young and dynamic population, began showing signs of decline. They inherited an unfair social burden, looking after citizens in need and, at the same time, maintaining an expensive urban infrastructure for people who worked in the city but lived and paid taxes in the suburbs. With commerce following the flight to the suburbs, the tax base of parent cities was further eroded, while social liabilities increased even more.

Most large North American cities became obsessed in the fifties and sixties with "urban renewal" as a tool for razing slums, building housing, improving existing traffic arteries, and providing new limited-access autoroutes. In the process dilapidated, overcrowded, and substandard homes were demolished and uprooted residents rehoused in new housing "projects." The greatest attraction of urban renewal was generous funding—if approved by the governments. The insensitive and drastic measures with which urban renewal was implemented often meant that entire residential neighborhoods were erased, resulting not only in the uprooting of families, but also the severance of many social and business ties.

The choice between the two extreme dwelling types still haunts the urban dweller of the twenty-first century. We have inherited a housing stock of bungalows and high-rise apartments more than adequate to meet the demand for these extreme types of dwellings for the foreseeable future. Dwellings that occupy the range between these two extremes must now be explored. Similarly, the contemporary urban land-use inefficiency created by single-use zoning patterns must be alleviated through mixed zoning to ensure the twenty-four-hour use of the expensive infrastructure that the modern city depends upon. Apart from economic benefits derived from mixed zoning, the real impact would be the vitality that such measures would produce in cities.

While cities decay, suburbs thrive today as never before. It is ironic that for centuries, during the Middle Ages people living in suburbs, so-called *faubourgs*, waited patiently for the privilege of being admitted to live in the city, because at the time, cities rather than suburbs symbolized freedom, safety, and security. Today, regretfully, the reverse is true. The potential revival of cities, the urbane places that older people remember and most young people have never experienced, is only possible by bridging the social and economic gulf that allowed suburbs to separate from their parent cities. It may be hoped that suburbs will learn to keep the parent city alive and well.

An even greater challenge of self-preservation is for all people to become friendly towards nature. The occidental world's accustomed standard of living is unsustainable in the long run. We have to learn to do with less. Nature is not a foe to conquer, but rather an ally if we live in harmony with its rules. To do otherwise is foolish and leads to calamity. In fact, until fairly recently, the majority of people did live in harmony with nature. Paradoxically, only since ecology became a household word has both the magnitude and frequency of mismanagement of our natural habitat become alarming.

For 6,000 years, dwellings in their incredibly rich diversity were built to traditional social norms and physical standards that evolved over a very long period and withstood the test of time. This fact alone carries with it the assurance of both viability and sustainability.

BIBLIOGRAPHY

Adams, Annmarie. "Eden Smith and the Canadian Revival." *Urban History Review* XXI 2 (March 1993): 104–15.

———. "The Eichler Home: Intention and Experience in Postwar Suburbia." In *Gender, Class, and Shelter: Perspectives in Vernacular Architecture V*, ed. Elizabeth Collins, 164–78. Knoxville: University of Tennessee Press, n.d.

Agus, Irving A. *Urban Civilization in Pre-Crusade Europe*. Vols. I and II. New York: Yeshiva University Press, 1965.

Allen, Edward. *Stone Shelters*. Cambridge: MIT Press, 1969.

Allingham, Helen, and Stewart Dick. *The Cottage Homes of England*. London: Bracken, 1984.

Alpern, Andrew. *Apartments for the Affluent: A Historical Survey of Buildings in New York*. New York: McGraw-Hill, 1975.

Andersen, Kaj Blegvad. *African Traditional Architecture*. Nairobi: Oxford University Press, 1977.

Anderson, Cardwell Ross. "Primitive Shelters." *AIA Journal*, (October 1961): 33–39.

Anderson, Stanford, Ed. *On Streets*. Cambridge: MIT, 1978.

Anheisser, Roland. *Das mittelalterliche Wohnhaus in deutschstämmigen Landen*. Stuttgart: Strecker and Schroeder, 1934.

"Apartments with Inner Street: The Oaklands, Toronto. Architects: DuBois & Associates." *The Canadian Architect*, 27 (January 1982): 16–18.

Arquitectonica, "The Atlantis" and "The Palace." In *GA Document 7*. Tokyo: A.D.A. Editor, 1983.

Ashihara, Yoshinobu, Ed. *World Collective Houses: 200 in the 20th Century*. Tokyo: Daikyo, 1990.

Ashworth, William. *The Genesis of Modern British Town Planning: A Study in Economic and Social History of the Nineteenth and Twentieth Centuries*. London: Routledge & Kegan Paul, 1954.

Aslet, Clive, and Alan Powers. *The National Trust Book of the English House*. Harmondsworth: Viking in association with the National Trust, 1985.

Aston, Michael, and James Bond. *The Landscape of Towns*. London: J. M. Dent, 1976.

Atkinson, Adrian. "Bernese Middle Land Farmhouses." In *Shelter and Society*. New York: Frederick Praeger, 1969.

Babelon, Jean-Pierre. *Demeures Parisiennes sous Henry IV et Louis XIII*. Paris: Le Temps 1965.

Bach, Ira J. *Chicago on Foot*. Chicago: Rand McNally, 1979.

Bacon, Edmund N. *Design of Cities*. New York: Penguin, 1976.

Badawy, Alexander. *A History of Egyptian Architecture*. Berkeley: University of California Press, 1968.

Bannister, Turpin C. "Oglethorpe's Sources for the Savannah Plan." *Journal of the Society of Architectural Historians*, 20(1) (March 1961): 47–62.

Bardi, P. M. "America Before Columbus." In *History of the House*, ed. Ettore Camasasca. New York: G. P. Putnam, 1971.

Barley, M. W. *The House and Home*. London: Vista, 1963.

Basista, Andrzej. "Kadhemiya—Zespol Tradycyjnej Zabudowy W Bagdadzie." *Kwartalnik Architektury i Urbanistyki*, 21(3) (1976a): 217–37.

———. "Plany Przeksztalcenia Kadhemiyi, Zabytkowej Dzielnicy Bagdadu." *Kwartalnik Architektury i Urbanistyki*, 21(4) (1976b): 337–58.

Bates, Marston. *Man in Nature*. Englewood Cliffs, NJ: Prentice Hall, 1961.

Beijing Architectural Research Institute. *Blueprints of Working Drawings*. Montreal: McGill University School of Architecture, 1991.

Bekaert, Geert. *Cogels-Osylei: Anvers-Antwerpen-Antwerp. Architecturae Liber XI*. Liege: Pierre Mardaga,1984.

Bemis, Albert Farwell, and John Burchard III. *The Evolving House*. Vol. 1. Cambridge, MA: Technology Press, 1933.

Benevolo, Leonardo. *History of Modern Architecture*. Vol. 2. Cambridge: MIT, 1977.

Beritic, Luksa. *Utvrdenja Grada Dubrovnika*. Zagreb: Jugoslavenska Akademija Znanosti i Umjetnosti, 1955.

Berning, Maria, Michael Braum, and Engelbert Lütke-Daldrup. *Berliner Wohnquartiere: Ein Führer durch 40 Siedlungen*. Berlin: Dietrich Reimer, 1990.

Beyer, Glenn H. *Housing and Society*. New York: Macmillan, 1965.

Beyer Blinder & Belle Architects and Planners. "Alwyn Court Restoration." *Building Stone Magazine 3*(4) (1984): 37–38.

Bhatt, Vikram. "Architecture for a Developing India." *Harvard Design Magazine* (Summer 1999): 28–32.

Bhatt, Vikram and Peter Scriver. *Contemporary Indian Architecture: After the Masters*. Ahmedabad: Mapin, 1990.

Bjørkto, Roar. *Atriumhus i norsk klima*. Oslo: Norges Byggforskningsinstitutt, 1965.

Bloc, André. "Reconstruction en Tunesie." *L'architecture d'aujourd'hui, 20* (October 1948): 1–110.

Boas, Franz. *The Central Eskimo*. Lincoln: University of Nebraska Press, 1964.

Boegner, Toni. *Rothenburg*. Munich: Piper, 1912.

Boesiger, W. *Le Corbusier: Oeuvre complete 1938–1946*. Erlenbach-Zurich: Les Editions d'Architecture, 1946.

Boesiger, W. and Girsberger, H. *Le Corbusier 1910–60*. Zurich: Girsberger, 1960.

Bott, Gerhard. *Von Morris zum Bauhaus: Eine Kunst gegründed auf Einfachheit*. Hanau, Germany: Dr. Hans Peters, 1977.

Boyd, Andrew. *Chinese Architecture and Town Planning: 1500 B.C.–A.D. 1911*. London: Alec Tiranti, 1962.

Boyd, Robin. *New Directions in Japanese Architecture*. New York: George Braziller, 1968.

Boyer, Christine. *Manhattan Manners: Architecture and Style, 1850–1900*. New York: Rizzoli, 1985.

Briggs, Martin S. *Muhammadan Architecture in Egypt and Palestine*. New York: Da Capo, 1974.

Brochmann, Odd. *By og Bolig*. Oslo: Cappelens, 1958.

Bruemmer, Fred. *The Arctic*. New York: New York Times Book Company, 1974.

Burke, Gerald. *Towns in the Making*. London: Arnold, 1971.

Cahnman, Werner J. *How Cities Grew*. Madison, NJ: Florham Park, 1959.

Camesasca, Ettore, Ed. *History of the House*. New York: Putnam, 1971.

Cantacuzino, Sherban. *European Domestic Architecture*. London: Studio Vista, 1969.

Cardwell, Kenneth H. *Bernard Maybeck: Artisan, Architect, Artist*. Santa Barbara: Peregrine Smith, 1977.

Carskadon, Thomas R. *Houses for Tomorrow*. New York: Twentieth Century Fund, 1944.

Carter, Francis W. *Dubrovnik (Ragusa): A Classical City-State*. London: Seminar Press, 1972.

Castro, Ricardo L. *Rogelio Salmona*. Bogota: Villegas Editores, 1998.

Çelik, Zeynep. "Cultural Intersections: Re-visioning Architecture and the City in the Twentieth Century." In *At the End of the Century: One Hundred Years of Architecture*, ed. R. Ferguson, 191–228. Los Angeles: Museum of Contemporary Art and Harry N. Abrams, 1998.

Chagnon, Napoleon A. *Yanomamö*. New York: Holt, Rinehart & Winston, 1968.

Chalklin, C. W. *The Provincial Towns of Georgian England*. London: Arnold, 1974.

Chambers, James. *The English House*. London: Thames Methuen, 1985.

Chan, Katherine. "Traditional Housing in China." Unpublished student essay. Montreal: McGill University School of Architecture, 1973.

Chbib, Adnan M. *Casablanca Bidonvilles Study*. Montreal: Unpublished thesis, Faculty of Graduate Studies and Research. McGill University, 1975.

Cheng, James K. M. and Coal Harbour Architectural Group. "Architectural Seclusion: Willow Arbor Townhouses, Vancouver." *The Canadian Architect*, 27(10) (1982):38–41.

Choay, Françoise. *The Modern City: Planning in the 19th Century*. New York: George Braziller, 1969.

Cockburn, Charles. "Fra-Fra House: Damongo, Ghana." *Architectural Design* 32 (June 1962): 299–300.

Cohen, Jean-Louis. "Urban Architecture and the Crisis of the Modern Metropolis." In *At the End of the Century: One Hundred Years of Architecture*, ed. R. Ferguson, 229–274). Los Angeles: The Museum of Contemporary Art and Harry N. Abrams, 1998.

Coon, Carleton S. *The Hunting Peoples*. Boston: Little Brown, 1971.

Cornforth, John. "Birthplace of Urban Conservation: The Royal Mile, Edinburgh." *Country Life*, August 3, 1981.

Crawford, David. *A Decade of British Housing: 1963–1973*. London: Architectural Press, 1975.

Creese, Walter L. *The Search for Environment. The Garden City: Before and After*. New Haven: Yale University Press, 1966.

Creswell, K.A.C. *Early Muslim Architecture*. Oxford: Clarendon Press, 1940.

——. *The Muslim Architecture of Egypt*. Vol. 1. Oxford: Clarendon Press, 1952.

Culot, Maurice. "Belgium: Red Steel and Blue Aesthetic." In *Art Nouveau Architecture*, ed. Frank Russell. London: Academy Editions, 1983.

Curinschi, Gheorghe, et al. "Centrul Istoric al Orasului Medias." In *Studii si Proiecte*. Bucharest: Institutul de Architectura Ion Mircu, 1964.

Davey, Peter. *Arts and Crafts Architecture*. London: Phaidon, 1980.

Davis, Sam. "The House Versus Housing." In *The Form of Housing*, ed. Sam Davis. New York: Van Nostrand Reinhold, 1977.

de Carlo, Giancarlo, and Bruno Zevi. "Marriage Italian Style." *The Architectural Forum*, 124(4) (1966): 62–67.

de la Croix, Horst. *Military Considerations in City Planning: Fortifications*. New York: George Braziller, 1972.

d'Espouy, H. *Monuments Antiques*. Paris: Librairie Générale de l'Architecture et des Arts Décoratifs, 1910.

Development Workshop. *Indigenous Building and the Third World*. Tehran: Building and Housing Research Center, 1976.

Doxiadis, Constantinos A. *Architecture in Transition*. New York: Oxford University Press, 1963.

Duany, Andres, and Elizabeth Plater-Zyberk. "The New Town of Windsor, Florida: 1989." *Architectural Design Profile No.15* (1993): 31–49.

Duchscherer, Paul, and Douglas Keister. *The Bungalow: America's Arts & Crafts Home*. New York: Penguin Studio, 1995.

Durant, Will. *The Life of Greece*. New York: Simon and Schuster, 1939.

——. *Caesar and Christ*. New York: Simon and Schuster, 1944.

——. *The Age of Faith*. New York: Simon and Schuster, 1950.

——. *Our Oriental Heritage*. New York: Simon and Schuster, 1954.

Ecochard, Michel. "Habitat Musulman au Maroc." *L'Architecture d'Aujourd'hui* (June 1955): 36–41.

"Enter the Wonderful World of Eichler." Advertising brochure, n.d.

Epstein, David G. *Brasília, Plan and Reality: A Study of Planned and Spontaneous Urban Development*. Berkeley: University of California Press, 1973.

Eschebach, Hans. *Die Städtebauliche Entwicklung des Aniken Pompeji*. Heidelberg: F. H. Kerle, 1970.

Evans, Joan. *Life in Medieval France*. London: Phaidon, 1969.

Evans-Pritchard, E. E. *The Nuer*. Oxford: Clarendon Press, 1940.

Evenson, Norma, *Paris: A Century of Change, 1878–1978*. New Haven: Yale University Press, 1979.

Faegre, Torvald. *Tents, Architecture of the Nomads*. Garden City, NY: Anchor, 1979.

Fagan, Brian M. *People of the Earth*. Boston: Little Brown, 1977.

Feilberg, C. G. *La Tente Noire*. Copenhagen: Nationalmuseets Skrifter, Etnografisk Raekke, II, Nordisk Forlag, 1944.

Fils, Normand. *Paris Moderne, ou Choix de Maisons*. Paris: Carilian-Goeury, Librairie, 1837.

Fisher, Thomas. "Housing Lessons in Hong Kong." *Progressive Architecture*, 67(3) (1986): 39–41.

Fitch, James Marston, and Daniel P. Branch. "Primitive Architecture and Climate." *Scientific American* (December 1960): 134–44.

Foltyn, Ladislav. *Volksbaukunst in der Slowakei*. Prague: Artia, 1960.

Fonseca, Rory. "The Walled City of Old Delhi." In *Shelter and Society*. New York: Praeger, 1969.

Ford, James. *Slums and Housing*. Cambridge: Harvard University Press, 1936.

Frampton, Kenneth. *Modern Architecture: A Critical History*. New York: Oxford University Press, 1980.

Franck, Klaus. *The Works of Affonso Eduardo Reidy*. New York: Praeger, 1960.

Franz-Pascha. "Die Baukunst des Islam." In *Handbuch der Architektur*. Darmstadt: Arnold Bergstrasser, 1987.

Fraser, Douglas. *Village Planning in the Primitive World*. New York: George Braziller, 1968.

Futagawa, Yukio. "Adriatic Sea." In *Villages and Towns*. No. 2. Tokyo: A.D.A. Edita, 1974.

Gallet, Michel. *Stately Mansions: Eighteenth-Century Paris Architecture*. New York: Praeger, 1972.

Galotti, Jean. *Moorish Houses and Gardens of Morocco*. New York: William Helburn, 1925.

Gardi, René. *Indigenous African Architecture*. New York: Van Nostrand Reinhold, 1973.

Gerle, János, Kovács Attila, and Makovecz Inre. *A Századfordulo Magyar Épitészete*. Budapest: Szépirodalmi Könykiadó - Bonex, 1990.

Giedion, Sigfried. *Space, Time and Architecture*. Cambridge: Harvard University Press, 1954a.

——. *Walter Gropius: Work and Teamwork*. London: Architectural Press, 1954b.

Goldberg, Bertrand, illustrations. "Marina City, Chicago, Etats-Unis." *L'architecture d'aujourd'hui*, 34(117), (November 1964): 32–37.

Goldman, Irving. *The Cubeo*. Urbana: University of Illinois Press, 1963.

Goodwin, Philip L., photographs by G. E. Kidder Smith. *Brazil Builds: Architecture New and Old 1652–1942*. New York: Museum of Modern Art, 1943.

Greceanu, Eugenia. *Monumente Medievale din Medias*. Bucharest: Meridiane, 1968.

Green, A. Mowbray. *The Eighteenth-Century Architecture of Bath*. Bath: Gregory, 1904.

Grinberg, Donald I. *Housing in the Netherlands, 1900–1940*. Rotterdam: Delft University Press, 1977.

Grossman, Irving. *Le Corbusier, Architects of Modern Thought*. Toronto: CBC, 1962.

Grote, Ludwig, Ed. *Die Deutsche Stadt im 19. Jahrhundert*. Munich: Prestel, 1974.

Gruber, Karl. *Die Gestalt der Deutschen Stadt*. Munich: Callwey, 1952.

Guicestre, G. "Appartement." In *Encyclopédie de l'Architecture*. Vol.1, ed. Paul Amédée Planat. Paris: Dujardin, 1839–1911.

Guidoni, Enrico. *La Citta Europea*. Milan: Electa, 1978.

Gutkind, E. A. *Revolution of Environment*. London: Kegan Paul, Trench, Trubner, 1946.

——. *Urban Development in Central Europe*. London: Collier-Macmillan, 1964.

——. *Urban Development in Southern Europe: Spain and Portugal*. New York: Free Press, 1967.

Hackney, Rod. *The Good, the Bad and the Ugly: Cities in Crisis*. London: Frederick Muller, 1990.

Hajnoczi, Gyula. *Irak Epitészete*. Budapest: Corvina Kiado, 1974.

Hall, Charles Francis. *Arctic Research and Life Among the Esquimaux*. New York: Harper, 1866.

Hamblin, Dora Jane. *The First Cities*. Alexandria, VA: Time-Life Books, 1973.

Handlin, David P. *The American Home: Architecture and Society, 1885–1915*. Boston: Little, Brown, 1979.

Hassenpflug, Gustav, and Paulhans Peters. *Scheibe, Punkt und Hügel: Neue Wohnhochhäuser*. Munich: Callwey, 1966.

Hassan, Riaz. "Islam and Urbanization in the Medieval Middle-East." *Ekistics* (February 1972): 108–12.

Hauser, Philip M. "World and Asian Urbanization in Relation to Economic Development and Social Change." In *Urbanization in Asia and the Far East*. Calcutta: UNESCO Research Center, 1957.

Hautecoeur, Louis. *Histoire de L'Architecture Classique en France*. Paris: Picard, 1955.

Hilberseimer, Ludwig. *Mies van der Rohe*. Chicago: Paul Theobald, 1956.

Hiorns, Frederick R. *Town-Building in History*. London: Harrap, 1956.

Hiort, Esbjørn. *Housing in Denmark: Since 1930*. London: Architectural Press, 1952.

Hitchcock, Henry-Russell. *Architecture: Nineteenth and Twentieth Centuries*. Harmondsworth: Penguin, 1958.

Hoag, John D. *Islamic Architecture*. New York: Abrams, 1977.

Holly, Henry Hudson. *Modern Dwellings in Town and Country: Adapted to American Wants and Climate*. New York: Harper, 1878.

Home Planning. 2 x 4 Home Plan: 200 Examples. Tokyo: Asahi Newspaper Publishing, 1976.

Home Sweet Home: Housing Designed By the London County Council and Greater London Council Architects, 1888–1975. London: Academy Editions, 1976.

"Housing at Flemingdon Park, Ont." *The Canadian Architect*, 6 (May 1961): 44–51.

Howard, Ebenezer. *Garden Cities of To-Morrow*. London: Faber and Faber, 1946.

Huber, Rudolt, and Renate Rieth. *Glossarium Artis: Burgen und feste Plätze—Chateaux-forts et places fortes*. Tübingen: Niemeyer, 1971.

Hubert, Pirsson & Hoddick. "New York Flats and French Flats." *The Architectural Record*, 2 (July-September 1892).

Hubka, T.C. *Big House, Little House, Back House, Barn: The Connected Farm Buildings of New England*. Hanover, NH: University Press of New England, 1984.

Hudson, James R. *The Unanticipated City: Loft Conversions in Lower Manhattan.* Amherst, MA: University of Massachusetts Press, 1987.

Hunter, Christine. *Ranches, Rowhouses, and Railroad Flats.* New York: Norton, 1999.

Improvements and Town Planning Committee of the Corporation of London. *The City of London.* London: Architectural Press, 1951.

Ionescu, Grigore. *Architectura Populara Romineasca.* Bucharest: Editura Tehnica, 1957.

Isham, Norman M., and Albert F. Brown. *Early Connecticut Houses: An Historical and Architectural Study.* New York: Dover, 1965.

Ismail, Adel A. "Origin, Ideology, and Physical Patterns of Arab Urbanization." *Ekistics* (February 1972): 113–23.

Ison, Walter. *The Georgian Buildings of Bath.* London: Faber and Faber, 1948.

Israels, Charles Henry. "New York Apartment Houses." *The Architectural Record,* 11 (July, 1911).

Ivekovic, Cirillo M. *Dubrovnik-Ragusa, Bau- und Kunstdenkmale in Dalmatien.* Vol. V. Vienna: Anton Schroll, 1927a.

———. *Split-Spalato, Bau- und Kunstdenkmale in Dalmatien.* Vol. IV. Vienna: Anton Schroll, 1927b.

Jackson, Frank. *Sir Raymond Unwin: Architect, Planner and Visionary.* London: A. Zwemmer, 1985.

Jacobs, Jane. *The Death and Life of Great American Cities.* New York: Random House, 1961.

Jain, Kulbhushan. "Jaisalmer, India: Morphology of a Desert Settlement." *Architecture and Urbanism* (February 1977): 13–24.

———. "Morphostructure of a Planned City, Jaipur, India." *Architecture and Urbanism* (August 1978): 107–20.

Jékely, Zsolt, and Alajos Sódor. *Budapest épitészete a XX. században.* Budapest: Müszaki Könyvkiadó, 1980.

Joedicke, Jürgen, and Christian Plath. *die weissenhofsiedlung / the Weissenhof colony / la cité de weissenhof.* Stuttgart: Karl Krämer, 1984.

Kalman, Harold. *A History of Canadian Architecture.* Vol. 2. Toronto: Oxford University Press, 1994.

Kastner, Joseph. "Alexander Jackson Davis." In *Three Centuries of Notable American Architects,* ed. Joseph J. Thorndike. New York: American Heritage, 1981.

Kaufman, Michael T. "Tough Times for Levittown." *New York Times Magazine,* September 24, 1989.

Kelly, Barbara M. *Expanding the American Dream: Building and Rebuilding Levittown.* Albany: State University of New York Press, 1993.

Kerr, Robert. "Observations on the Plan of Dwelling-Houses in Towns." *Journal of the Royal Institute of British Architects* (1893/94): 201–228.

Kertész, K. Robert, and Gyula Sváb. *The Peasant Dwellings in Hungary.* Budapest: The Hungarian Engineers and Architects Association, n. d.

Khattab, Omar. "A Report on the International Study Visit to Beijing, China, May 30–June 4, 1994." *Open House International,* 19(4) (1994): 42–43.

Kjeldsen, Marius. *Industrialized Housing in Denmark: 1965–76.* Copenhagen: Danish Building Centre, 1976 and 1988.

Klima, George J. *The Barabaig, East African Cattle-Herders.* New York: Holt, Rinehart and Winston, 1970.

Klöckner, Karl. *Alte Fachwerkbauten.* Munich: Callwey, 1991.

Knapp, Ronald G. *The Chinese House.* Hong Kong: Oxford University, 1990.

Koestler, Frank. *Modern City Planning and Maintenance.* London: McBride, Nast, 1915.

"Kollektivhuset Høje Søborg." *Arkitekten* 12 (1952): 4–12.

Kopp, Anatole. *Town and Revolution: Soviet Architecture and City Planning 1917–1935,* trans. by T. E. Burton. New York: George Braziller, 1970.

Korn, Arthur. *History Builds the Town.* London: Lund Humphries, 1961.

Kretzschmar, Frank, and Ulrike Wirtler. *Das Bürgerhaus in Konstanz, Meersburg und Überlingen.* Tübingen: Wasmuth, 1977.

Kriesis, Anthony. "Ancient Greek Town Building." In *Architects' Yearbook 10.* London: Elek, 1962.

Kroll, atelier Lucien. *BIO, PSYCHO, SOCIO/ ECO 1: Ecologies Urbaines.* Paris: Editions L'Harmattan, 1997.

Kubach, Hans Erich. *Romanesque Architecture.* New York: Abrams, 1975.

Kultermann, Udo. *New Japanese Architecture.* London: The Architectural Press, 1960.

———. "The Architects of Egypt." *MIMAR: Architecture in Development* #4 (1982): 56–61.

Kunstler, James Howard. *The Geography of Nowhere: The Rise and Decline of America's Man-Made Landscape.* New York: Simon and Schuster, 1993.

Lampl, Paul. *Cities and Planning in the Ancient Near East.* New York: George Braziller, 1968.

"Landia." *Architectural Forum,* 94(2) (February 1951): 140–46.

Langdon, Philip. *American Houses.* New York: Stewart, Tabori & Chang, 1987.

Latham, Ian. *Joseph Maria Olbrich*. London: Academy Editions, 1980.

Laubin, Reginald, and Gladys Laubin. *The Indian Tipi: Its History, Construction, and Use.* New York: Ballantine, 1971.

Lavas, G. P. "Settlements in Ancient Greece." *Ekistics* (November 1974): 330–5.

Leavitt, Jacqueline. "Two Prototypical Designs for Single Parents: The Congregate House and the New American House." In *New Households, New Housing*, eds. Karen A. Frank and Sherry Ahrentzen, 161–186. New York: Van Nostrand Reinhold, 1989.

Le Corbusier. *Creation is a Patient Search.* New York: Frederick Praeger, 1960.

Le Corbusier, and François de Pierrefeu. *The Home of Man.* London: Architectural Press, 1948.

Leonard, Jonathan Norton. *The First Farmers.* Alexandria, VA: Time-Life, 1973.

Lewis, Harold MacLean. *Planning the Modern City, Vol. 2.* New York: John Wiley, 1949.

Liermur, Jorge Francisco. "Latin America: The Places of the 'Other.' In *At the End of the Century: One Hundred Years of Architecture*, ed. R. Ferguson, 277–320. Los Angeles: The Museum of Contemporary Art and Harry N. Abrams, 1998.

Lindsay, Ian G. "The Scottish Burgh." *The Stones of Scotland*, ed. George Scott-Moncrieff. London: B.T. Batsford, 1938.

Lissitzky, El. *Russia: An Architecture for World Revolution*, trans. Eric Dluhosch. London: Lund Humphries, 1970.

Longfellow, William P. P. *A Cyclopedia of Works of Architecture in Italy, Greece, and the Levant.* New York: Scribner, 1895.

Lorenzen, Vilh. *Vore Byer: Studier i Bybygning.* Vol. 1. Copenhagen: G.E.C. Gad, 1947.

Lubove, Roy. "I. N. Phelps Stokes: Tenement Architect, Economist, Planner." *Journal of the Society of Architectural Historians*, 23(2) (May 1964): 75–87.

Luz, Oskar. "Proud Primitives, the Nuba People." *National Geographic* (November 1966): 673–699.

Lynes, Russell. *The Tastemakers.* New York: Grosset & Dunlap, 1954.

McCamant, Kathryn, and Charles Durrett with Ellen Hertzman. *Cohousing: A Contemporary Approach to Housing Ourselves.* Berkeley: Ten Speed Press, 1994.

McCoy, Esther. *Five California Architects.* New York: Reinhold, 1960.

McDonough, Yona Zeldis. *Frank Lloyd Wright.* New York: Chelsea House, 1992.

Macintosh, Duncan. *The Modern Courtyard House: A History.* London: Lund Humphries, 1973.

McKay, A. G. *Villas and Palaces in the Roman World.* London: Thames and Hudson, 1977.

Mackay David. *Modern Architecture in Barcelona: 1854–1939.* New York: Rizzoli, 1989.

McKenna, H. Dickson. *A House in the City.* New York: Van Nostrand Reinhold, 1971 .

MacLeish, Kenneth. "Stone Age Cavemen of Mindanao." *National Geographic* (August 1972): 218–49.

MacLeod, Robert. *Charles Rennie Mackintosh.* Middlesex, England: Country Life Books, 1968.

Marshall, John. *A Guide to Taxila.* Cambridge: Cambridge University Press, 1960.

———. *Mohenjo-Daro and the Indus Civilization.* Vols. I and II. Delhi Varanasi: Indological Book House, 1973.

Master Mason, A. "The Building of a Parisian House." *The Architectural Record, 14* (September 1903).

Marsan, Jean-Claude. *Montréal in Evolution.* Montreal: McGill-Queen's University Press, 1981.

Mathiassen, Therkel. *Eskimoerne in Nutid og Fortid.* Copenhagen: P. Haase, 1929.

Mayer, Eugen. *Das Bürgerhaus zwischen Ostalb und oberer Tauber.* Tübingen: Wasmuth, 1978.

Mazade, Fernand. "Living in Paris on an Income of $3,000 a Year, Parts 1, 2, and 3." *The Architectural Record, 13* (April–June 1903).

Melchers, von Bernd. *China, Vol. II.* Hagen, Germany: Folkwang, 1921.

Mellaart, James. *Earliest Civilizations of the Near East.* New York: McGraw-Hill, 1965.

"Mies van der Rohe." *Architectural Forum, 97*(5) (1952): 93–111.

Mimura, Hiroshi. Notes and drawings sent to the author.

Mindeleff, Cosmos. "Localization of Tusayan Clans." In *Nineteenth Annual Report of the U. S. Bureau of American Ethnology (1886–1887)*, 635–653. Washington, DC: Government Printing Office, 1891.

Mohney, David, and Keller Easterling. *Seaside: Making a Town in America.* New York: Princeton Architectural Press, 1991.

Moholy-Nagy, Sibyl. *Carlos Raul Villanueva and the Architecture of Venezuela.* New York: Praeger, 1964.

Mohr, Christoph. "Die Villenkolonie Buchschlag bei Darmstadt." In *Von Morris zum Bauhaus: Eine Kunst gegründed auf Einfachheit.* Hanau, Germany: Dr. Hans Peters, 1977.

Morgan, Lewis H. *Houses and House-Life of the American Aborigines.* Chicago: University of Chicago Press, 1965.

Morris, A. E. J. *History of Urban Form.* London: Godwin, 1972.

Morris, Eleanor Smith. "Tepozlan: Native Genius in Town Planning." In *Architects' Yearbook 11.* London: Elek, 1965.

Morse, Edward S. *Japanese Homes and Their Surroundings.* New York: Dover, 1961.

Moulton, Robert H. "A $40,000 Bungalow on the Roof of a Chicago Apartment House: William E. Walker, Architect." *Architectural Record,* 42 (1917): 149–152.

Mumford, Lewis. *The City in History: Its Origins, Its Transformations, and Its Prospects.* New York: Harcourt Brace Jovanovich, 1961.

Münz, Ludwig, and Gustav Künstler. *Adolf Loos: Pioneer of Modern Architecture.* London: Thames and Hudson, 1966.

Murdock, George P. "The Current Status of the World's Hunting and Gathering Peoples." In *Man the Hunter.* Chicago: Aldine, 1968.

Muthesius, Hermann. *Das englische Haus.* Vols.1, 2, and 3. Berlin: Wasmuth, 1904.

Naylor, Gillian. *Hector Guimard.* New York: Rizzoli, 1978.

Nettlefold, J. S. *Practical Housing.* Letchworth, England: Garden City Press, 1908.

Newman, Oscar. *Defensible Space: Crime Prevention through Urban Design.* New York: Macmillan, 1972.

Nicolaisen, Johannes. *Ecology and Culture of the Pastoral Tuareg. National Museets Skrifter, Etnografisk Raekke, ix.* Copenhagen: National Museum, 1963.

Nishi, Kazuo, and Kazuo Hozumi. *What is Japanese Architecture? A Survey of Traditional Japanese Architecture.* Tokyo: Kodansha International, 1983.

Notman, William. *Photographic Archives.* Montreal: McCord Museum of Canadian History, n.d.

Ojeda, Oscar Riera, and Lucas H. Guerra. *Moore Ruble Yudell: Houses and Housing.* Washington, D.C.: American Institute of Architects Press, 1994.

Olbrich, Joseph Maria. Postkarte "Haus Olbrich." Darmstadt: Museum Künstlerkolonie, 1901.

———. *Ideen von Olbrich* (Reprint of second edition, 1904). Stuttgart: Arnold'sche Verlagsanstalt, 1992.

O'Neill, Daniel. *Sir Edwin Lutyens: Country Houses.* New York: Whitney Library of Design, 1980.

Oppenheim, A. Leo. *Ancient Mesopotamia.* Chicago: University of Chicago Press, 1977.

Orthmann, Winfried. *Der alte Orient.* Berlin: Propylaen, 1975.

Pantin, W. A. "Medieval English Town-House Plans." In *Medieval Archaeology, Vols. 6 and 7* (202-239). London: The Society for Medieval Archaeology, 1964.

"Paris." In *Meyers Konversations-Lexicon, Fourth Edition.* Vol. 12. Leipzig: Bibliographisches Institut, 1890.

Parker, John Henry. *Some Account of Domestic Architecture in England, from Edward I to Richard II.* Oxford and London: Parker, 1882.

Parry, Sir William Edward. *Three Voyages for the Discovery of a North-west Passage from the Atlantic to the Pacific and an Attempt to Reach the North Pole.* London: J. Murray, 1835.

Paulsson, Thomas. *Scandinavian Architecture: Buildings and Society in Denmark, Finland, Norway, and Sweden from the Iron Age until Today.* London: Leonard Hill, 1958.

Pawley, Martin. *Architecture versus Housing.* New York: Frederick Praeger, 1971.

Pedersen, Johan. *Arkitekten Arne Jacobsen.* Copenhagen: Arkitektens Forlag, 1954.

Pelli, Cesar & Associates. "Four-Leaf Towers and Four Oaks." In *GA Document 12* (104–108). Tokyo: A.D.A. Editor, 1985.

Perks, Sydney. *Residential Flats.* London: Batsford, 1905.

Peters, Paulhans. *Wohnhochäuser: Punkthäuser, Point Blocks, Immeubles Tours.* Munich: Callwey, 1958.

———. *Atriunhäuser: Städtische Wohnhäuser mit Gartenhöfen.* Munich: Callwey, 1961.

Petrie, W. M. Flinders. *Kahun, Gurab, and Hawara.* London: Kegan Paul, Trench, Trubner, 1980.

———. *Illahun, Kahun, and Gurab.* London: Nutt, 1981.

Pevsner, Nikolaus. *Studies in Art, Architecture and Design: Victorian and After, Vol.2.* New York: Walker, 1968.

"Philadelphia Town Houses." *Architectural Forum, 118,* (April 1963): 90.

Pirenne, Henri. *Medieval Cities.* Garden City, NY: Doubleday, 1925.

Place, Charles A. *Charles Bulfinch: Architect and Citizen.* New York: Da Capo, 1968.

Platt, Colin. *The English Medieval Town.* London: Phaidon, 1969.

Plunz, Richard. *A History of Housing in New York*

City: Dwelling Type and Social Change in the American Metropolis. New York: Columbia University Press, 1990.

Posener, Julius. *Anfänge des Funktionalismus: Von Arts and Crafts zum Deutschen Werkbund.* Berlin: Ullstein, 1964.

Pott, Janet, "Old Bungalows in Bangalore, South India." *Architectural Association Quarterly,* 8(2) (1974): 36–47.

Preusser, C. *Die Wohnhäuser in Assur.* Berlin: Wissenschaftliche Veröffentlichungen der Deutschen Orient-Gesellschaft, 1954.

Price, Charles Matlack. "A Pioneer in Apartment House Architecture." *The Architectural Record,* 36 (July 1914): 74–76.

Procos, Dimitri. "Mixed Land Use." *The Canadian Architect, 16* (July 1971), 23–41.

Purdom, C. B. *The Building of Satellite Towns.* London: J. M. Dent, 1949.

Quennell, C. H. B. "English Domestic Architecture." *The Studio: Yearbook of Decorative Art,* 1910.

Quincy, Anthony. *The Traditional Buildings of England.* London: Thames and Hudson, 1990.

Rasmussen, Steen Eiler. *London: The Unique City.* Harmondsworth: Penguin, 1934.

———. *Towns and Buildings.* Liverpool: University Press of Liverpool, 1951.

———. *Rejse i Kina.* Copenhagen: Carit Andersens Forlag, 1958.

Raulin, Henri, and Georges Ravis-Giordani. *Corse.* Paris: Musée National des Arts et Traditions Populaires, 1978.

Rayside, Ron. "Heaven Round, Earth Square, The Peking House." Unpublished student essay. Montreal: McGill University School of Architecture, 1971.

Reed, William V., and Elizabeth Ogg. *New Homes for Old, Public Housing in Europe and America.* New York: The Foreign Policy Association, 1940.

Reinhold-Postina, Eva. *Jugendstil, Traditionalismus, und Heimatliche Bauweise (Darmstädter Architekturgeschichte 3: Die Jugendstiljahre).* Darmstadt: Eduart Roether, 1991.

Reps, John W. *The Making of Urban America, A History of City Planning in the United States.* Princeton: Princeton University Press, 1965.

Reuther, Oscar. *Die Innenstadt von Babylon* (Merkes). Leipzig: Wissenschaftliche Veröffenlichungen der Deutschen Orient-Gesellschaft, 1926.

Revault, Jacques. *Palais et Demeures de Tunis.* Paris: Edition du Centre National de la Recherche Scientifique, 1971.

Richardson, C. J. *The Englishman's House.* London: Chatto and Windus, 1874.

Riefenstahl, Leni. *The Last of the Nuba.* New York: Harper & Row, 1973.

Riis, Jacob A. *How the Other Half Lives.* New York: Dover, 1971.

Robinson, Peter. "The Scottish Tennement: a lasting contribution to a city streetscape." *RIBA Journal* (November 1982).

Roe, Derek. *Prehistory.* London: Paladin, 1970.

Roper, Laura Wood. *A Biography of Frederick Law Olmsted.* Baltimore: John Hopkins University Press, 1973.

Rowe, Peter G. *Making a Middle Landscape.* Cambridge: MIT, 1991.

———. "Housing Density, Type, and Urban Life in Contemporary China." *Harvard Design Magazine* (Summer 1999): 40–44.

Royal Commission on the Ancient Monuments of Scotland. *The City of Edinburgh.* Edinburgh: His Majesty's Stationary Office, 1951.

Rudofsky, Bernard. *The Prodigious Builders.* London: Secker and Warburg, 1977.

———. *Architecture Without Architects.* New York: Museum of Modern Art, 1964.

Rumler, E. "Hôtels privés." In *Encyclopédie de l'Architecture,* Vol. 5, ed. Paul Amédée Planat. Paris: Dujardin, 1839–1911.

Rusk, David. *Cities without Suburbs.* Baltimore, MD: The Woodrow Wilson Center Press/ Johns Hopkins University Press, 1993.

Ruttenbaum, Steven. *Mansions in the Clouds.* New York: Balsam Press, 1986.

Rybczynski, Witold, Dr. Avi Friedman, and Susan Ross. *The Grow Home, Project Paper No. 3.* Montreal: Affordable Homes Program, McGill University School of Architecture, 1990.

Rymer, Russ. "Back to the Future: Disney Reinvents the Company Town." *Harper's Magazine* (October 1996): 65–78.

Saalman, Howard. *Medieval Cities.* New York: Braziller, 1968.

Safdie, Moshe. *For Everyone a Garden,* ed. J. Wolin. Cambridge: MIT, 1974.

Saint, Andrew. *Richard Norman Shaw.* New Haven: Paul Mellon Centre for Studies in British Art (London) Ltd., Yale University Press, 1976.

Salokorpi, Asko. *Modern Architecture in Finland.* New York: Frederick Praeger, 1970.

Sanders, Isabel, and Cindy Schoenberger. *The Historic Garden District: An Illustrated Guide and Walking Tour.* New Orleans: Voulez-Vous, 1988.

Sauvaget, J. *Alep.* Paris: Librairie Orientaliste Paul

Geuthner, 1941.

Schäfer, Dietrich. *Das Bauernhaus im Deutschen Reiche und seinen Grenzgebieten.* Hanover: Curt R. Vincentz, 1906.

Schmertz, Mildred F., Ed. *New Life for Old Buildings.* New York: Architectural Record Book/McGraw Hill, 1982.

Schmitt, Karl Wilhelm. *Multistory Housing.* New York: Praeger, 1966.

Schoenauer, Norbert. *Cities, Suburbs, Dwellings: In the Postwar Era.* Montreal: McGill University School of Architecture, 1994.

——. *Arts and Crafts/Art Nouveau Dwellings.* Montreal: McGill University School of Architecture, 1996.

Schoenauer, Norbert, and Seeman, Stanley. *The Court-Garden House.* Montreal: McGill University Press, 1962.

Scott, M. H. Baillie. "An Ideal Suburban House." *The Studio 4* (1894): 127–32.

Scully Jr., Vincent J. *The Shingle Style and the Stick Style: Architectural Theory and Design from Richardson to the Origins of Wright.* New Haven: Yale University Press, 1971.

Sembach, Klaus-Jürgen. *Art Nouveau, Utopia: Reconciling the Irreconcilable.* Cologne: Benedikt Taschen, 1991.

Sergeant, John. *Frank Lloyd Wright's Usonian House.* New York: Whitney Library of Design, 1975.

Service, Alastair. *Edwardian Architecture: A Handbook to Building Design in Britain 1890–1914.* New York: Oxford University Press, 1977.

Seton-Watson, R. W. *A History of the Roumanians.* N. P.: Archon Books, 1963.

Severin, Timothy. *Vanishing Primitive Man.* New York: American Heritage, 1973.

Shabad, Theodore. "Peking." *Encyclopedia Britannica, 17.* Chicago: Benton, 1961.

Shah, Mahendra. "Udaipur." Unpublished student essay. Montreal: McGill University School of Architecture, 1973.

Shah, Mahendra, and Vikram Bhatt. "Morphology of Urban Housing: Ahmadabad Housing Case Study." Unpublished student essay. Montreal: McGill University School of Architecture, 1974.

Sharma, G. N. *Social Life in Medieval Rajasthan (A.D. 1500–1800).* Agra: Lakshmi Narain Agarwal, 1968.

Sharp, Thomas. *Newer Sarum: A Plan for Salisbury.* London: Architectural Press, 1949.

Shaw, Thomas. *Travels, or Observations Relating to Several Parts of Barbary and the Levant.* Oxford, England: printed at the Theatre, 1738.

Short, John R. *Housing in Britain: The Post-War Experience.* London: Methuen, 1982.

Sinclair, Fiona. *Scotstyle: 150 Years of Scottish Architecture.* Edinburgh: Royal Incorporation of Architects in Scotland and the Scottish Academic Press, 1984.

Sirén, Osvald. *The Walls and Gates of Peking.* London: John Lane the Bodley Head, 1924.

Sitte, Camillo. *The Art of Building Cities,* trans. Charles T. Stewart. New York: Reinhold, 1945.

Skaarup, Hans Hartvig. "Dubrovnik." *Arkitekten,* 63(9): 166–173.

Small House Designs. Ottawa: Central Mortgage and Housing Corporation, October 1958.

Smith, J. T., P. A. Faulkner, and Anthony Emery. *Studies in Medieval Domestic Architecture.* London: Royal Archaeological Institute, 1975.

Spoerry, François. *Gentle Architecture: from Port-Grimaud to Port-Liberté.* Chichester: Pheon Books in association with John Wiley & Sons Limited, 1991.

Stamp, Gavin, and André Goulancourt. *The English House 1860–1914: The Flowering of English Domestic Architecture.* Chicago: University of Chicago Press, 1986.

Steele, James. *An Architecture for People: The Complete Works of Hassan Fathy.* New York: Whitney Library of Design, 1997.

Stein, Clarence S., *Toward New Towns for America.* New York: Reinhold, 1957.

Stein, Rudolf. *Das Bürgerhaus in Schlesien.* Tübingen, Germany: Wasmuth, 1966.

Stern, Robert A. M. "Planned Communities." In *Housing: Symbol, Structure, Site,* 68–69. New York: Rizzoli, 1982.

Stickley, Gustav. *More Craftsman Houses.* New York: Dover, 1982.

Stiehl, Otto. *Der Wohnbau des Mittelalters, Handbuch der Architektur.* Leipzig: Kröner, 1908.

Stirling, James. "Town Centre housing Runcorn New Town." *LOTUS international* 10 (1975): 105–123.

Storgård, J.P., Jørn Ørum-Nielsen, Hanne Marcussen, and Anne Ørum-Nielsen. "Boligbebyggelsen Galgebakken, Herstederne." *Arkitektur,* 18(3) (1974): 81–91.

Stübben, J. *Der Städtebau, Handbuch der Architektur.* Stuttgart: Kröner, 1907.

Summerson, John. *Georgian London.* London: Pleiades Books, 1945.

——. "The London Suburban Villa." *The Architectural Review* (August 1948).

——. *Architecture in Britain, 1530–1830.* Harmondsworth: Penguin, 1953.

Survey of London. *The Parish of St. Gilles-in-the-*

Fields, part II. London: London County Council, Spring Gardens, 1914.

———. *St. George's Fields*. London: London County Council. 1955.

———. *The Parish of St. Paul, Covent Garden*. London: Athlone Press, 1970.

Sutcliffe, Anthony. *Multi-Story Living: The British Working-Class Experience*. London: Croom Helm, 1974.

Svensson, Ole. *Planning for Low-Rise Urban Housing Areas*, SBI-Byplanlaegning 56. Copenhagen: Danish Building Research Institute, 1988.

Székely, András. *Kós Károly*. Budapest: Corvina Kiadó, 1979.

"The Tall One." *The Architectural Forum*, *133*(1) (1970): 36–42.

Tarn, J. N. *Working-Class Housing in 19th-Century Britain*. London: Lund Humphries, 1971.

———. "French Flats for the English in Nineteenth-century London." In *Multi-Story Living*, ed. Anthony Sutcliffe. London: Croom Helm, 1974.

Tauranac, John. *Elegant New York: The Builders and the Buildings 1885–1915*. New York: Abbeville Press, 1985.

Taylor, Lisa, ed. *Housing: Symbol, Structure, Site*. New York: Cooper-Hewitt Museum/Rizzoli, 1982.

Thomas, Elizabeth Marshall. "Bushmen of the Kalahari." *National Geographic* (June 1963): 866–88.

Toth, János. *Az Orségek Népi Epitészete*. Budapest: Müsaki Könyvkiado, 1975.

Traquair, Ramsay. *The Old Architecture of Quebec: A Study of the Buildings Erected in New France From the Earliest Explorers to the Middle of the Nineteenth Century*. Toronto: MacMillan, 1947.

Trippett, Frank. *The First Horsemen*. Alexandria, VA: Time-Life, 1974.

Turnbull, Colin. *The Forest People*. New York: Simon and Schuster, 1961.

Turnbull, William Jr. *Global Architecture: MLTW/Moore, Lyndon, Turnbull and Whitaker. The Sea Ranch, California*. Tokyo: A.D.A. Edita, 1970.

Unger, Eckhard Axel Otto. *Babylon: Die Heilige Stadt Nach der Beschreibung der Babylonier*. Berlin and Leipzig: W. de Gruyter, 1931.

United Nations Development Program (UNDP). *Human Development Report 1999*. New York: Oxford University Press, 1999.

van der Bent, T. J. *The Planning of Apartment Houses, Tenements and Country Homes*. New York: Brentano, n.d.

Van Eyck, Aldo. "Architecture of the Dogon." *Architectural Forum* (September 1961): 116–21, 186.

Vedel-Petersen, Finn, Eric B. Jantzen, and Karen Ranten. *Bofaellesskaber: En Eksempelsamling*, SBI-Rapport 187. Copenhagen: Statens Byggeforskningsinstitut, 1988.

Vitruvius. *The Ten Books on Architecture*. New York: Dover, 1960.

Völckers, Otto. *Das Grundrisswerk*. Stuttgart: Julius Hoffmann, 1949.

———. *Dorf und Stadt*. Bamberg, Germany: Staackmann, 1956.

von Erffa, Wolfram. *Das Bürgerhaus im Westlichen Oberfranken*. Tübingen: Wasmuth, 1977.

Waagensen, Bent, and Jenny Rubin. *Kollektivhuset og dets Forudsaetninger*. Copenhagen: Nyt Nordisk-Forlag/Arnold Busk, 1949.

Wagg, Susan. *Percy Erskin Nobbs: Architect, Artiste, Artisan-Architect, Artist, Craftsman*. Kingston, Montreal: McGill-Queen's University Press, 1982.

Walters, Sir Roger, ed. *Home Sweet Home: Housing designed by the London County Council and Greater London Council Architects, 1888–1975*. London: Academy Editions, 1976.

Watson, Richard A. and Patty Jo Watson. *Man and Nature: An Anthropological Essay in Human Ecology*. New York: Harcourt Brace Jovanovich, 1969.

White, William H. "Paris Houses." In *The Builder*, 33 (December 1875).

Whitlock, Ralph. *Salisbury Plain*. London: Robert Hale, 1955.

Whittick, Arnold, Ed. *Encyclopedia of Urban Planning*. New York: McGraw-Hill, 1974a.

———. *European Architecture in the 20th Century*. New York: Abelard-Schuman, 1974b.

Wood, Margaret. *The English Mediaeval House*. London: Phoenix House, 1965.

Woodbridge, Sally B. *Bernard Maybeck: Visionary Architect*. New York: Abbeville Press, 1992.

Wong, Sie-Khiang. "Chinese Court House." Unpublished student essay. McGill University School of Architecture, 1973.

Woolley, C. Leonard. *Ur of the Chaldees*. London: Benn, 1929.

The World Population Situation in 1977: New Beginnings and Uncertain Ends. Population Studies 63. New York: United Nations, 1979.

Worsdall, Frank. *The Tenement: A Way of Life*. Edinburgh: Chambers, 1979.

Wright, Frank Lloyd. *The Disappearing City*. New York: William Farquhar Payson, 1932.

———. *The Story of the Tower: The Tree that Escaped*

the Crowded Forest. New York: Horizon, 1956.

———. *The Natural House.* New York: The American Library, 1963.

Wright, Olgivamura Lloyd. *Frank Lloyd Wright: His Life, His Work, His Words.* New York: Horizon, 1966.

Yorke, F. R. S., and Frederick Gibberd. *Modern Flats.* London: Architectural Press, 1958.

Zehrfuss, B. H. and J. Kyriakopoulos. "La Maison Minima Tunisienne." *L'architecture d'aujourd'hui* 20 (October 1948): 70–76.

Zillich, Heinrich. *Siebenbürgen: Ein Abendländisches Schicksal.* Königstein im Taunus, Germany: Langewiesche, 1957

Acknowledgments

I began writing this book during the early sixties when a graduate program in housing was launched at the School of Architecture of McGill University, and students in the program needed a textbook on the history of dwellings. Then, the absence of a proper textbook reflected the view of many architectural historians that common dwellings were not true architecture. This was ironic because the megaron, an ancient Hellenic dwelling form, served as the basic building block of classical Greek temples, and other prototypes of indigenous dwellings provided the bases for other building types.

For help and support in assembling the first edition of *6,000 Years of Housing* in 1981, I am indebted to William G. Salo, Jr., senior editor of Garland STPM Press; Professors John Bland and Arthur Acheson; librarians Eva Doelle and Salwa Ferahian; and McGill graduates Athena Kovatsi, Katherine Cienciala, and John Lindley. Dr. Julius Gorynski invited me to travel with him to Baghdad, as a Pol-Service consultant on housing and urban planning issues, which rekindled my fascination with the court-garden house.

Many colleagues helped with the revision of the 2000 edition of *6,000 Years of Housing*. Heartfelt thanks go to all of them: Nancy Green, senior editor of W. W. Norton, discovered the previous edition of *6,000 Years of Housing* on a library shelf and proposed to republish an updated version of it.

Annmarie Adams supplied information on Eichler Homes and Eden Smith; Bruce Anderson provided information on Montreal architects; Vikram Bhatt reviewed my essay on twentieth-century housing in India. David Covo helped to find source material on New Orleans shotgun and camelback houses and Carl Koch's conversion work in Boston's harbor, reviewed the Chinese chapter, and assisted in the transliteration of Chinese words. Avi Friedman supplied information on the Grow Home. Adrian Sheppard located illustrations on turn-of-the-century Parisian urban life as well as information on Belgian Art Nouveau. Ricardo Castro reviewed my essay on Latin America. Pieter Sijpkes helped to unravel the contributions to domestic design by Dutch and Belgian architects, and gave constant moral support. Marilyn Berger found invaluable reference material. Helen Dyer edited additions to Parts II and III of this book, and helped with my e-mail woes. I relied on Kathleen Innes-Prevost for secretarial work and for printing and saving files of my manuscript; Dr. Donald Chan set up my computer workstations and was always there to help me when I ran into computer problems; David Morin transferred my Word Perfect text to Word 5 and scanned illustrations from my previous books to facilitate their reuse. Mahmoud Essam Hallak helped me with the transliteration of Arabic nouns related to dwellings; Tatsuyuki Setta helped me to translate Japanese text; Liang Gao, Ming-Yi Wong, and Louis Huang assisted with the translation of some Chinese text. Christine Habermaas did the meticulous work of copyediting this edition.

Words cannot convey the gratitude I feel to Maureen Anderson for her selfless devotion to the task of editing, and for her insightful criticism of my manuscripts over three decades.

After my initial studies of architecture in Budapest, and before emigrating to Canada, I spent six years working and studying in Denmark, where I learned to speak Danish and acquired a Danish outlook on domestic architecture. This experience had a profound influence upon my life; during this period I met my wife, Astrid, who for years has endured my absentmindedness.

Finally, I must express gratitude to McGill University, for providing me with an academic home in which to study and teach for nearly forty years.

INDEX

Page numbers in *italics* refer to illustrations.

Aborigines, 11, 15, 19–20
Acoma Indians, 68
acropolis, 125
actus, 127
Afghanistan, *46*, 47
Africa, 11, 15, 16–19, 42, 45, 47, 49, 51, 52, 54, 55, 58, 60, 62, 63, 64, 151
agora, 125
agricultural societies
    advanced, 73–74. *see also* permanent rural
        dwellings
    China, 119
    development of Industrial Revolution, 289, 290,
        291
    High Middle Ages, 234
    hoe peasant, 57–58, 60, 66, 68
    origins of urban societies, 96, 100, 101–2, 108–9,
        113, 119, 120, 123, 215–16, 473
    pastoral nomads, 41
    pre-urban dwelling types, 12, 93, 473
    root crop cultivation, 32–33
    seminomadic peoples, 48, 49
    slash-and-burn cultivation, 32–34
    social characteristics, 57
Ahmadabad, 179, 189–92
air-shaft buildings, 299–300
Äir-Tuareg people, 44–45
alae, 136–37
alagados, 412
Alakaluk Indians, 15
Alcazabah, 218–19
al-Fustat house, 151–53
Algeria, *46*
aling aling, 99
al-Kazimiyah, 172–74, 175

allotment gardens, 399
almshouses, 293
al-Qahira, 161
amphithalamos, 130
amphitheaters, Roman, 219–20
Amsterdam School, 377–79
Anatolia, 71–72
ànbar, 171
andron, 131
andronitis, 130
animal husbandry
    among seminomadic people, 48, 49, 51–52, 54–55
    among semipermanent societies, 62, 68
    ancient Indus civilization, 113
    in pastoral nomadism, 41
apa, 19
apartment hotels, 341–43
apartment houses
    garden apartments, 383
    nineteenth century
        Great Britain, 323–32
        mid-rise, 452
        New York, 332–43
        Paris, 311–23
    studio apartments, 339–41
    twentieth century, 387–88, 394–96, 399–405, 412
        high-rise tenements, 437–42
        luxury high-rise, 432–37
        mid-rise, 452–60
arcaded urban houses, medieval European, 262–65
arch construction, 113
argol, 42
arsala, 44
Art Deco, 432
Art Nouveau, 369–72

Arts and Crafts movement, 304, 311, 344, 355
    in North America, 356–67
Arunta Aborigines, 19–20
Ashley, Lord, 292, 296
Asia, 42, 45, 47
assabiyyats, 148
Assur, 105–7
Athens, 123, 124, 132–33
atriolum, 142
atrium, 127
atrium house, 136–44
audlitiving, 25
aul, 44
Australia, 11, 15, 19–20
Austria, 89, 398–400, 457–59
automobile, 386
    benefits of mixed-use building design, 448
    suburban sprawl and, 415, 418
    town house design and, 426–27
Awuna people, 62–63

bab, 171
babanu, 105
bab assir, 153
Babylon, 105, 107
back-to-back housing, 293–95
Baghdad, 168–72, 178
bahu, 154
Bali, 99
Baltimore, Md., 439, 440
Baluchi, 47
BaMbuti people, 18–19, 96
bands. *see* nomadic bands
bangala, 362
Barabaig, 54–55
barbican, *235*
Barrett, Samuel Augustus, 292
barriada, 412
barrios, 412
bastides, 267
battlements, *235*
Bauernburgen, 236
bawab, 172
bays, 258
bayts, 153
beaux-quartiers, 312
Bedouin, 45–47, 96
beehive-type huts, 11, 15, 16–17, 18–19, 20
bel étage, 313
Berbers, 44, 47
Berlage, Henrik Petrus, 377
Bernese farmhouse, 85–87

bibliothèque, 316
bidonvilles, 159
bitanu, 105
Blackfoot Indians, 29, 30
Bloomsbury, England, 275–77
boarium, 128
bode, 258
Bofaellesskaber, 212, 462, 466
bohio, 38
Bok, Edward William, 358
boma, 52–54
Boston, 286–87, 467
box-machicoulis, 233
Brazil, 38
brise-soleil, 410
British Guiana, 34
brownstones, 288
building codes and regulations
    early urban worker housing, 298
    mixed-use zoning, 445
bungalow courts, 382
bungalows, 362–63
    twentieth-century North American, 418–19
Bürgerhöfe, 251
burghs, 224–25
Bushmen, 11, 15, 16–17
bylaw houses, 298

cabinet de toilette, 318
cabinet de travail, 316
Cairo, 161–68
calefactorium, 225
camelback house, 420
campsite layout, 96
    pastoral nomads, 44
    primitive hunting and gathering societies, 17, 19, 20
    see also settlement organization
Canada, 89, 450–51, 459
Cape Cod house, 87–89
Caraya Indians, 38
Casablanca, 160–61
castrum, 127
catering flats, 327–29
cave dwellings, 15–16, 91
    China, 75–77
Cayuga Indians, 39–40
cella ostiaria, 140
cenacula, 128
chajjas, 184
chatris, 185
chatta, 180
chatuhsala, 119

chaupala, 182
chaupars, 187
chemin-du-ronde, 235
cheng, 120
Cheyenne Indians, 29, 96
Chicago, 388, 432–34, 446–48
Chile, 15
China, 56, 75, 95
    Beijing, 120, 121
        historical evolution, 193–96
        modern architecture, 201–3
        traditional dwelling, 196–201
    high-rise public housing, 441–42
    urban dwellings, 119–22, 193–203
chowk, 180
chowkidar, 180
chowkris, 185
cieng, 52
circular dwellings, 12, 15, 91–92
circus, 127
cité-jardin, 355–56, 390–91
citta nuova, 220
citta vecchia, 220
city-states, 123
civitates, 127
classical architecture, 99
classification of pre-urban dwelling types, 11–12
class relations, 57
    in advanced agricultural societies, 73
    Chinese building design and, 199
    courtyard housing and social segregation, 424
    effects of Industrial Revolution, 290, 291, 473
    in Greek urban housing of classical period, 130
    in medieval Europe, 242
    trends in twentieth-century urban living, 414
claustrum, 225
cloister, 214
close, 276, 349
cob cottages, 74, 75
codes and regulations. *see* building codes and regulations
collective habitation, 403–4, 406, 407–8, 454, 460–62
Colombia, 457
colonia patricia, 218
colosseum, 127
Comanche Indians, 29
communal structures
    episodic dwellings, 32–38
    igloos, 27
    in modern era, 462–66
    in Soviet Russia, 406–8

storehouses of seminomadic people, 49
    see also collective habitation
compluvium, 137
conflict between peoples
    ancient China, 120
    ancient Egypt, 109
    ancient Greece, 123
    ancient Mesopotamian civilization, 100, 101
    European Dark Ages, 217–18, 219, 223, 224
    evolution of medieval European fortress cities, 234–36, 237, 243, 267
    occidental urban design and, 215
    pastoral nomadic societies, 41, 42
Constantinople, 129, 218
cooperatives and condominiums, 334–35, 339, 402–4
    ownership concepts, 323
Cordova, 218–19
corps-de-logis, 315
Corsica, 231–33
cour d'honneur, 315
courette, 321
courtinae, 137
courtyards, 35, 473
    ancient Chinese, 121, 122
    ancient Egyptian, 111, 112
    ancient Greek, 125
    ancient Indus civilization, 115, 116
    ancient Mesopotamian, 102, 105
    Awuna cluster dwelling, 62, 63
    Chinese dwellings, 198
    Dogon cluster dwelling, 64, 65
    evolution of urban housing, 96–99, 209, 210–12, 216
    Greek peristyle house, 129–30
    Indian urban house, 179, 182, 187–88, 189
    medieval Europe, 251, 256–57
    medieval Islamic, 147–48, 159, 175
    Mesakin Quisar cluster dwelling, 60, 61
    nineteenth-century apartment buildings, 315
    North African Islamic urban, 154–55
    occidental urban house, 216
    Renaissance European, 277–79
    Roman house, 136
    tenement buildings, 296
    twentieth-century court-garden house, 422–26
Cree Indians, 29
Crow Indians, 29
Cubeo Indians, 37
cubicula, 137
cuescomatl, 67
culina, 137
Cyprus, 70
Czechoslovakia, 39, 79

Danubian people, *39*, 40
danyuanlo, 201
dar, 154–59
daraj, 172
Dark Ages, 129
    origins of, 217–18
    sociocultural effects, 213
decoration and ornamentation
    ancient Egyptian urban dwellings, 111
    Art Nouveau movement, 369–72
    Bernese farmhouse, 87
    Chinese dwellings, 197
    Kazakh yurt, 47
    medieval Islamic urban houses, 158, 162
    Mesakin Quisar dwelling, 61–62
    modern apartment housing, 432
    Roman house, 136
Deir el Medina, 111
Delos, 133–35
Denmark, 404–5, 422–23, 427–28, 454, 460–62,
    464–65, 466
Detroit, Michigan, 414
development of housing forms, 12–13, 16, 66, 91–93
    ancient urban housing, 95–99, 108–9, 113–14,
        119–22
    future challenges, 474
    historical course, 472–73
    medieval Islamic cities, 145–78
    nineteenth-century cities, 293–302
        apartment buildings, 311–43
    occidental urban, 213–16
        Industrial Revolution, 289, 290–93, 473
        medieval era, 228, 229–33, 247, 249–53,
            256–66
        modern era, 288
    portable dwellings, 47
    Renaissance
        residential squares and crescents, 270–82
        town houses, 282–88
    seasonal dwellings, 56
    semipermanent dwellings, 70–72
    suburban housing, 302–11
    twentieth century
        apartment houses, 432–37
        attached town-house dwellings, 422–26
        avant-garde movements, 369–81
        court-garden house, 422–26
        Europe, 344–55, 388–406
        high-rise public housing, 437–42
        Latin America, 410–12
        loft conversions, 466–68

mid-rise housing, 452–60
New Urbanism, 468–71
North America, 344–55, 356–69, 382–88
point block projects, 442–45
post–World War II detached houses, 418–22,
    474
Russia, 406–10
between World Wars, 382–412, 473
diele, 83, 264
dirka, 162
dododa muhog, 55
Dogon people, 64–66
dolan, 171
domkommunas, 406–8
domus, 99, 136
Donse, 85
dormitoria, 225
douar, 96
Downing, Andrew Jackson, 305
dozoh, 206
du, 120
Duboy, Paul Émile, 342–43
Dubrovnik, 222–23, 240–48
dukkan, 162
dumbbell tenements, 302
duplex apartment, 335, 387
durqā'ah, 162
durra, 60
dwelling towers, 215, 229, 230–33, 249–50

Egypt, 95, 100
    ancient, 108–12
    medieval urban house, 151–54, 161–68
energy-efficient design, 418, 432
entre cour et jardin, 315
entresol, 313
environmental determinism, 11
    ancient Chinese urban design, 121
    episodic/temporary dwellings, 23
    occidental urban housing, 214
    origins of urban society, 95, 100
    periodic dwellings, 42
    seasonal dwellings, 48, 49
    semipermanent dwellings, 58
    tropical climates, 34
environmental impact
    of advanced agricultural societies, 74
    future challenges, 474
    of hunting and gathering societies, 22
    of mid-rise developments, 459–60
    of sedentary societies, 57

ephemeral/transient dwellings, 12
    characteristics, 14, 15
    examples, 16–20
    prehistoric and historic development, 15, 16, 20–21
    social organization associated with, 14
episodic temporary dwellings, 12
    characteristics, 22, 23
    communal, 32–38
    examples, 23–32, 34–38
    geographic distribution, 23
    prehistoric and historic development, 38–40
    social organization associated with, 22–23
    see also periodic temporary dwellings
ergastuae, 136
Erigbaagtsa Indians, 36–37
Eskimo. see Inuit people
Etruscan house, 98, 136
Europe, 211–12
    court-garden house developments, 422–24
    Dark Ages, 129
    Lapps, 31–32
    point blocks, 442–45
    prehistoric episodic dwellings, 38–39, 40
    Renaissance, 267–87
    see also medieval Europe; specific country
exedra, 142
Eyre, William, 358–59

Faelleshus, 463
faskije, 171
faubourgs, 474
fauces, 136
favela, 412
Federal style, 288
festsaal, 84
Finland, 380–81, 405–6
fisqiyyah, 162
flats, 323
flett, 84
folk community, 57
Forest Hills Gardens, New York, 367–69
forms of buildings
    determinants of, 11, 91
    developmental patterns, 12, 91–93
    global distribution, 12
    pre-urban, 12, 91–93
forum, 127
France, 89, 219–20, 262, 269–70, 311–23, 390–93, 423–24, 434–35, 441, 442, 452
French Guiana, 38
fundus regius, 236

fusuma, 206
futon, 205

gabled house, 215, 216, 229–30
gali, 180
gallery house, 90
garden apartments, 383
garden cities/Garden City movement, 292, 344, 350, 356, 375–76, 473
Garden City, New York, 309, 367
Garden of Sind, 112–13, 117
Gaudí y Cornet, Antonio, 372
ged, 55
gemütlich, 376
geographical distribution
    black tent, 46–47
    ephemeral dwellings, 15
    episodic dwellings, 23
    historical hunting and gathering societies, 21
    pastoral nomadic societies, 42
    pre-urban building forms, 12
Germany, 83–85, 229–30, 231, 248, 372, 374, 376, 393–98, 442, 445, 454–57
Ghana, 62
gheid, 54–55
Giedion, Sigfried, 322
gol, 52
granaries, 49
grand escalier, 313
Great Britain, 71, 74, 75, 261, 270–71, 440–41, 444–45, 452–54
    Bath, England, 271–75
    Bedford Park, London, 309–11
    Industrial Revolution, 289–93
    nineteenth century
        apartment buildings, 323–32
        worker housing, 292–99
    twentieth-century housing, 344–55, 388–90, 423
    villa houses, 303–5
Greece
    classical period of urban development, 123
    foreign conquest by, in ancient world, 109, 117, 118, 126, 146
    peristyle house, 129–36
    Roman architectural styles and, 126–27
Greene, Charles Sumner, 360–62
Greene, Henry Mather, 360–62
Guimard, Hector, 370, 371
Gurunsi, 63–64
gynaeconitis, 130

hacienda, 211
Haida Indians, 40
Hakka people, 77
hall-type housing, 261–62
hammam, 145, 146
Hampstead Garden Suburb, 354–56
haramlik, 150
Hardenbergh, Henry Janeway, 334, 335–37
harem, 151
havelis, 185
health and quality of life
    building codes and regulations, 298
    early Industrial Revolution, 291, 292
    nineteenth-century urban housing, 293, 294, 330
    pre–World War II housing, 382, 390
herkos, 130
Herrentrinkstube, 251
Herrgottswinkel, 87
Hill, Octavia, 292
Hippodamus of Miletus, 124
hisbah, 146
hoe peasant societies
    agricultural practice, 57–58, 60, 66, 68
    pre-urban dwelling types, 12
    social organization and behavior, 57
höfe, 399
hofje, 377
hogan, 49–51, 56
Hohe Haus, 249
holitarium, 128
Hopi Indians, 68
horrea, 128
Horta, Victor, 370
hortulus, 136
hosh, 162
hosh murraba', 170
hospitia, 136
hôtel particulier, 312
Howard, Ebenezer, 349, 350, 352
Hsiung-nu, 47
Hubert, Philip G., 334–35, 341–42
huland, 55
Hungary, 81, 89, 379–80
Hunt, Richard Morris, 333–34, 339
hunting and gathering societies, 93, 472
    advanced forms, 22–23
    Arunta Aborigines, 19–20
    BaMbuti Pygmies, 18–19
    characteristics, 14–15
    dwelling types, 12
    episodic/temporary dwellings, 22–23

    historical evolution, 21
    Kung Bushmen, 16–17
    primitive forms, 14–16
    in slash-and-burn societies, 33
Hus, 258

igdluarn, 25
igdluling, 25
igloo, 23–28
impluvium, 137
India, 15, 95
    Ahmadabad dwellings, 189–92
    Jaipur dwellings, 184–89
    Jaisalmer dwellings, 181–84
    modern architecture, 190–92
    occidental influences in, 180, 190, 192
    Udaipur dwellings, 188
    urban design characteristics, 179–80
Indic civilization, 112–19
Industrial Revolution, 216
    demographic changes in, 291
    energy supply for, 289–90
    evolution of urban worker housing, 290, 291–302
    health and quality of life, 291, 293, 295
    origins of, 289
    significance of, 289
    urban development and, 290–91, 473
infrastructure costs, 421
    advantages of mixed-use buildings, 451–52
    mid-rise developments, 459–60
insulae, 128
interior decoration, 359
Inuit people, 23–28
Iraq, 168, 175–77
Iroquois Indians, 39–40
Islamic city
    Baghdad architecture, 168–72, 178
    Cairo architecture, 161–68
    characteristics, 145–51
    historical development, 145
    in medieval Europe, 218–19
    North African houses, 151–61
Israel, 70
Italy, 77, 92, 450
itiner, 127
iwanat, 151
iwentshes, 172

jacal, 67
Jacobsen, Arne, 405
Jaipur, 184–89

Jaisalmer, 181–84
jami' mosque, 145–46
Japan, 56
    urban housing, 204–8
Jeanneret, Charles Edouard (Le Corbusier), 391–93,
    410–11, 434–35
jian, 199
Jordan, 70–71
Jugendstil movement, 372

kachelofen, 87
kædehus, 428
Kahun (Egypt), 109–11
Kalmuck people, 42
Kammerfach, 85
kang, 75–76, 200
Karankawa Indians, 21
Kazakh tent, 47
kebishkans, 172
keeping room, 88
Kenya, 52, 55, 58
khadaki, 189
khana, 42, 145
khanchos, 180
khans, 147
khazneh, 164
khizaneh, 166
kiosk, 164
Kirchenburg, 236
Kirgiz people, 42, *43*
kiva, 70
Købmandsgaard, 258
kota, 31
kraal, 51
Krier, Robert, 454–56
kucha, 180
Kung Bushmen. *see* Bushmen
Kurds, 47
Kwakiutl Indians, 40
Kyoto, 204–8

Lacan, L. C., 319
ladang, 32
Lapps, 31–32
lararium, 142
Latin America, 410–12
Le Corbusier. *see* Jeanneret, Charles Edouard
Letchworth, England, 350–52
Levittown, New York, 415–16
lit clos, 324
Llewellyn Park, New Jersey, 307

loess, 75
loft conversions, 466–68
loge, 313
London, England, 292, 295–99, 309–11, 327–32
longhouses, 39–40
Loos, Adolf, 399
Low German farmstead, 83–85
Luo people, 58, 59
Lutyens, Edwin, 344, 347–48, 354, 355
Luyia people, 58–59

machicolations, 235–36
machiya, 205
Mackintosh, Charles Rennie, 344, 346–47
Maclure, Samuel, 363
madrasah, 146
mahalahs, 148
mashrabiyyahs, 150
Maidu Indians, 56
maisons-à-loyer, 312
majaz, 171
Makiritare community, *33*, 38
Mali, 64
maloca, 36–38
malqafs, 151
Mandan Indians, 56
mandarh, 111
maq'ad, 159
maristans, 147
Masai tribes, 52–54, 96
maskan, 149
matbakh, 171
Mauretania, *46*
Mayan people, 66–67
Maybeck, Bernard Ralph, 363
maydan, 146, 147
Mazade, Fernand, 320–22
Medias, 237, *238*
medieval Europe
    emergence of cities, 223–28
    fortress cities, 234–58, 267
    late period urban dwellings, 258–66
megaron, 129
Menes, 108
merlons, *235*
Mesakin Quisar, 60–61, 96
mesauloe, 130
Mesopotamia, 95
    emergence of city-states, 100–102
    urban house, 102–7, 150
Mexico, 66, 67

mid-rise housing, 452–60
Mies van der Rohe, Ludwig, 432–34
Miletus, 124
milpa, 32
mirhad, 172
mise, 205
moda, 182
Modern movement, 391, 411, 432, 468
modh, 188
Mogollon Indians, 56
mohallas, 179
Mohawk Indians, 39–40
Mohenjo-Daro, 113–17
monasteries, 225–26
Mongol people, 42, 47
Moors, 218–19
Moor tent, 46
moran, 52
Morris, William, 304, 311
mortgage financing, 388, 391
    suburban sprawl and, 415
Motilone Indians, 38
muhaled, 55
multiplex houses, 364–65
mundahs, 42
municipium, 127

nakonoma, 205
National Romantic style, 380–81
Navaho Indians, 49–51
neem, 171
neotraditional design, 468–71
Netherlands, 377–79, 400–402
New Gourna, 167–68
Newman, Oscar, 438–39
New Objectivity, 402
New Realism, 394
New Urbanism, 468–71
New York City, 287–88, 298–99, 387–88, 448–50
    nineteenth-century apartment buildings, 332–43
    public housing, 438–39, 440
    residential conversions, 466–68
Nîmes, 220
nineteenth-century occidental housing
    apartment buildings
        Great Britain, 323–32
        mid-rise, 452
        New York, 332–43
        Paris, 311–23
    building codes and regulations, 298
    effects of Industrial Revolution, 289–93

evolution of suburbs, 302–11
    urban worker housing, 293–302
Nobbs, Percy, 364
nomadic bands
    Arunta Aborigines, 19–20
    dwelling types, 12, 472
    ephemeral dwellings of, 14
    episodic/temporary dwellings, 22–23
    Inuit, 23–28
    Kung Bushmen, 16
    Lapps, 31–32
    Plains Indians, 28–30
    seminomadic peoples, 48–49
    social relations within, 22
    Tungus people, 30–31
    see also pastoral nomads
nomes, 108
Nördlingen, 239, 240
North America, 21, 24–30, 39–40, 50, 56, 68, 87,
        279, 286–88, 305, 356–69
    see also Canada; United States; *specific city*
Norway, 258–61
Nuba people, 112
Nuer people, 51–52

Oak Park, Illinois, 308–9
occidental urban housing
    after fall of Roman Empire, 217–23
    decline of American cities, 413–15, 474
    environmental influences on design, 214–16
    future challenges, 474
    historical evolution, 472–73
    Industrial Revolution effects, 290–93
    influence in India of, 180, 190, 192
    influence of Japanese design on, 206–7
    influence on Asian design by, 201–3, 207–8
    medieval era
        fortress cities, 234–58, 267
        late period, 258–66
        origins of, 223–28
    nineteenth century, 293–302, 473
        apartment buildings, 311–43
    oriental urban housing and, 210–12, 213–14, 228,
        472
    Renaissance
        residential squares and crescents, 270–82
        town houses, 282–88
    residential precincts, 210–11
    rural heritage, 215–16
    twentieth century. *see* twentieth-century housing
oda, 169

oecus, 132, 137
Olbrich, Joseph Maria, 373–75
Olmsted, Frederick Law, 308
Olynthos, 130–32
Ona Indians, 21
Oneida Indians, 39–40
Onondoga Indians, 39–40
open spaces, 292, 306–7, 391, 392
oriental urban housing
    ancient Egyptian, 108–12
    characteristics, 209–10, 212, 472
    Chinese cities, 119–22, 193–203
    historic origins, 95, 209
    India, 179–92
    Indus civilization, 112–19
    Japan, 204–8
    medieval Islamic cities, 145–51
    Mesopotamian societies, 100–107
    occidental urban housing and, 210–12, 213–14, 228
    residential precincts, 210
    Roman urban housing and, 144
otta, 190
Ottomans, 161–62, 245
Oud, Jacobus Johannes Pieter, 400–402
Ouled tent, *46*
ovra, 182
ownership and property rights concepts
    in advanced agricultural societies, 73
    among seminomadic peoples, 48
    among semipermanent societies, 57, 64, 68
    cooperatives and condominiums, 323
    Islamic law, 174–75
    medieval urban Europe, 258
    in primitive hunting and gathering societies, 14, 16

Palestine, 100
parcelhuse, 405
Paressi Indians, 38
pargetted cottages, *74, 75*
Paris, 311–23
Parker, Richard Barry, 348–49, 351–52
parsal, 189
pastas, 130
pastoral nomads
    periodic temporary dwellings of, 41, 42
    pre-urban dwelling types, 12
patio houses, 211, 424–26
pattasala, 182
Pelche Indians, 21
periodic temporary dwellings, 12
    characteristics of, 41–42

examples, 42–47
    prehistoric and historic, 47
    social organization associated with, 41
peristyle house, 97–98, 129–36
permanent rural dwellings, 12
    characteristics, 74–75
    examples, 75–90
    social organization associated with, 73–74
Persia, 109, 124
petit salon, 316
Philadelphia, 279, 286, 426
Philippines, 15
piano nobile, 247, 283
Piaroa Indians, 38
piau, 115
piazza, 271
piscarium, 128
piscina, 142
pistrinum, 140
pitvar, 82
plague, 217, 243–44, 267
Plains Indians, 28–30, 56, 96
planned communities, 307
point blocks, 442–45
Pokot people, 55–56
pol, 189
Poland, *39*
polis, 123
Pollard, George, 340–41
pomoerium, 242
Pompeii, 126, 127, 137–44
population density
    advanced agricultural societies, 74
    ancient Rome, 128
    ancient Sumeria, 102
    cities of India, 190
    Cordova, 219
    decline of Roman Empire, 217, 218
    evolution of suburban housing, 306
    feudal Kyoto, 204
    historical trends, 96
    Industrial Revolution, 291
    medieval European cities, 239, 267
    nineteenth-century Paris, 312
    pastoral nomadic societies, 41
    primitive hunting and gathering societies, 15
    slash-and-burn societies, 33
    urban living, 96
        post–World War II United States, 413, 414
        Wright's Broadacre City, 386
portcullis, *235*

porte cochere, 258, 313, 316
portiers, 313
portón, 211
post-and-beam construction, 87, 88
posticum, 140
prehistoric dwellings, 15–16, 20–21, 91
    episodic, 38–40
    portable dwellings, 47
    seasonal dwellings, 56
    semipermanent, 70–72
pre-urban dwellings
    classification, 11–12. *see also specific category*
    determinants of form, 11, 91
    patterns of development, 12–13, 91–93
Priene, 135–36
privacy
    evolution of court-garden house, 99, 209
    exclusive residential communities, 307
    medieval Islamic urban life, 150
    occidental urban house, 210–11
    oriental urban house, 209, 210
property rights. *see* ownership and property rights
    concepts
prostas, 130
prostasis, 220
prothyron, 130
public housing, 437–42
public places, 58, 66, 409
    ancient Greek cities, 125
    ancient Indus civilization, 115
    ancient Mesopotamian civilization, 101
    medieval Islamic cities, 147–48
    oriental *vs.* occidental urban design, 210–11
    urban India, 180, 189
pueblo, 68–70
Pueblo Indians, 68
Punjab, 112, 117
punkthus, 442
puras, 179
purdah, 187
Pushtun tent, 46
Pygmies, 15, 18–19

qāʾah, 164
qata, 45
qaysariyyah, 147
Queen Anne style, 304
Querandi Indians, 21

Radburn-type communities, 386–87
Radiant City, 392–93
Ragusa (Dubrovnik), 222–23, 240–48

railroad flats, 299
ramada, 49, 51
ranchos, 412
ranch-type house, 418
ravelin, 243
rear house, 299
recreational space, 391, 409
religious and spiritual space, 98–99
    ancient Egyptian urban dwellings, 111
    cloister, 214
    European monasteries, 225–26
    Greek peristyle house, 130
    historical development, 58
    India, 182
    medieval Islamic city, 145–46
    occidental, 210
    Pueblo Indians, 69–70
    Roman house, 136, 140
Renaissance Europe
    building construction, 268
    origins of, 267
    residential squares and crescents, 270–82
    social relations, 269–70
Riverside, Illinois, 307–9
Roman empire
    architectural style, 126–27, 144
    atrium house, 136–44
    decline and fall, 213, 217–23
    extent, 127
rond-points, 312
Roth, Emery, 387–88
Rothenburg ob der Tauber, 248–53
row houses, 293–95
Rowland, Henrietta Octavia, 292, 354
ruag, 45
Rumania, 81
Russia, 39, 406–10

Safdie, Moshe, 458, 459
sakan, 149
salamlik, 150, 151
Salisbury, 254–58
Salish Indians, 40
salle à manger, 316
salon, 316
salsabils, 151
saltbox, 88
Samelat, 31
samod, 55
san du, 199
sath, 169
Savannah, Georgia, 279–82

Saxons, 236–38

Scandinavia, 402–6

Scotland, 323–27

Scythians, 47

seasonal dwellings, 12
- characteristics, 48–49
- examples, 49–56
- prehistoric and historic development, 56

security concerns
- advantages of mixed-use urban building design, 445
- high-rise housing projects, 438–40
- twentieth-century urban living, 414

semipermanent dwellings, 12
- characteristics, 58
- examples, 58–70
- prehistoric and historic development, 70–72
- social organization associated with, 57–58

Seneca Indians, 39–40

senzai, 206

serdab, 171

Sert, José Luis, 424

settlement houses, 292

settlement organization
- Dogon people, 64, 65–66
- European farmsteads, 89
- evolution of court-garden house, 96
- Mayan villages, 66
- seminomadic people, 48–49, 50, 51, 52, 55
- semipermanent societies, 58
- *see also* campsite layout; urban design and layout

shabono, 35

shah-neshin, 170

Shaw, Norman, 304, 309–10, 331

shenashil, 169

Shingle style, 356

shoji, 206

shopping centers and malls, 413

Shoshone Indians, 29

shotgun houses, 420

Siberia, 30

sidillahs, 163

siheyuan, 198

similarities in building form, 11

simple and complex social organization, 11, 12

Sioux Indians, 29

sirdloang, 25

Sirkap, 118–19

Sirsukh, 119

Sitte, Camillo, 354–55

sizes of buildings, 12
- determinants of, 93
- episodic/temporary dwellings, 23

social status and, 258

urban dwellings of India, 183

skerm, 16

slash-and-burn cultivation, 12, 32–34

slate cottages, 74, 75

Slovakian farm houses, 79–81

Smith, Eden, 363–64

social organization and behavior
- advanced agricultural societies, 73–74
- ancient China, 120
- ancient Egypt, 108–9
- ancient Indus civilization, 113–14
- ancient Mesopotamian civilization, 100–101
- ancient Rome, 128, 129
- Arunta Aborigines, 19, 20
- BaMbuti, 18, 19
- Chinese cities, 196, 197, 198, 199
- classification of pre-urban forms, 11–12
- collective habitation, 406, 407–8, 460
- communal dwellings, 462–66
- complexity, 11, 12
- court-garden housing and, 424
- crime in high-rise housing, 438–40
- Cubeo Indians, 37, 38
- Dark Ages, 213
- decline of Roman Empire, 217
- decline of U.S. cities, 413, 414, 474
- determinants of building form, 11
- developmental patterns, 12, 21
- effects of building design, 438
- Erigbaagtsa Indians, 36–37
- European Dark Ages, 224–25
- evolution of court-garden house, 98–99
- evolution of suburban housing, 305–6
- feudal Japan, 204–5
- Greek cities of classical period, 123–24, 126
- High Middle Ages, 234–35
- hoe peasant societies, 57–58, 60, 62
- hunting and gathering economy
  - advanced, 22–23
  - primitive, 14–16
- Industrial Revolution, 291, 292, 474
- Kung Bushmen, 16, 17
- Masai tribes, 52, 54
- Mayan village, 66
- medieval Europe, 236, 241–42
  - family life, 258–61
  - mercantilism in, 226–27
- medieval Islamic urban life, 145–47, 148, 169, 174–75
- modern apartment housing, 432
- Navaho Indians, 50, 51

need for, 14

nineteenth-century apartment residents, 315, 318, 322

nomadic bands, 12, 14, 22, 23

Nuer, 52

oriental *vs.* occidental architecture, 228

pastoral nomads, 41, 42

Pueblo Indians, 68, 69–70

Renaissance Europe, 269–70, 284

seminomadic people, 48–49

semipermanent societies, 63

size of buildings and, 93

slash-and-burn cultivators, 32, 33–34

tribal societies, 41

Tungus people, 31

twentieth-century American suburbs, 417

urban life in india, 179–80, 182, 183

Wai-Wai people, 34–35

South America, 21, 33, 34, 36, 37, 410–12

Spain, 211, 218–19

Spalato, 220–22

speicher, 87

spirit wall, 99, 115, 121, 198, 209

split-level house, 418–20

sprawl, suburban, 415–18

squares, town, 271–82

squatter settlements, 412

St. Louis, Missouri, 439–40

Stickley, Gustav, 357–58

stöckli, 87

Stokes, I. N. Phelps, 302

Stone Age cultures, 91

storehouses

advanced agricultural societies, 78, 84

ancient Roman, 128

medieval urban Europe, 260

seminomadic people, 49

semipermanent societies, 58, 59, 61, 62–63, 65, 67

Strokenbouw, 402

studio apartments, 339–41

stupa, 118

suarium, 128

suburbs

court-garden house developments, 422–26

design and layout, 415–18

future challenges, 474

landscaping, 416, 417–18

origins and development, 302–11

post–World War II, 413–14

pre–World War II, 382, 386–87, 388–91, 393, 394–98, 399, 400

relationship with parent city, 414–15

Sudan, 51, 60, 112

Sumer, 100–102, 123, 155–56

urban dwellings, 102–7

suq, 145, 146

surplus economy, 12

suweqah, 149

Sweden, 402–4, 442–44, 460

Switzerland, 85, 263

Syria, 100

tabernae, 128

tablinum, 136

tabulum, 136

Takshasila. *see* Taxila

taktabosh, 171

Tanzania, 52, 54

tarmah, 170

Tasaday, 15–16, 91

tatami, 206

Taxila, 117–18

technology

advanced agricultural societies, 73

advanced hunting and gathering societies, 22

development of building forms, 92–93

high-rise construction, 435–36

hoe peasant society, 57

slash-and-burn cultivation, 32

Tehuelche Indians, 21

Tell-'Amarna, 111–12

Tell-Asmar, 105

temporary dwellings

see episodic temporary dwellings; periodic temporary dwellings

tenement buildings, 292, 293, 296–97, 299–302

high-rise, 437–42

tents

Äir-Tuareg, 44–45

Bedouin, 45–47

Inuit, 28

of Lapps, 31–32

of pastoral nomads, 41–42

Plains Indians, 28–30

Tungus people, 30–31

yurts, 42–44

tepees, 28–30

thalamos, 130

thermae, 127

thermopolium, 140

Thunström, Olof, 442–43

thyron, 130

tianjing, 121

Tibet, 47

Tigris-Euphrates valleys, 95, 100
timber-framed structures, *74*, 75, 85, 229–30
    medieval Europe, 257–58
tlār, 170
toguna, 66
tokonoma, 206
Toledo, 218
tooriniwa, 206
tower-houses, 442
towers, dwelling. *see* dwelling towers
town houses, 282–88, 288, 302–3, 418, 426–32
Transylvania, 89, 236–38, 379–80
travois, 22
tribal societies
    characteristics, 41
    seminomadic peoples, 48
triclinium, 137
Troglodyte dwellings, 76–77
tropical regions
    dwelling design, 34
    slash-and-burn cultivators, 32
trullo, 77–78
tsuboniwa, 206
Tungus people, 30–31
Tunisia, 76, *157*, 158–60
tupiq, 28
Turkic people, 42
turnpike stair apartment, 324
twentieth-century housing
    apartment houses, 387–88, 394–96, 399–405
    avant-garde movements, 369–81
    decline of American cities, 413–15, 474
    Europe, 344–55, 388–406
    North America, 355–69, 382–88
    post–World War II
        apartment houses, 432–37
        attached town-house dwellings, 422–26
        court-garden house, 422–26
        current trends, 468–71
        detached housing, 418–22
        high-rise public housing, 437–42
        loft conversions, 466–68
        mid-rise housing, 452–60
        mixed-use urban buildings, 445–52
        point-block projects, 442–45
    between World Wars, 382–412

uadling, 25
Udaipur, 188
'*ummah*, 148
undercroft, 261
underground dwellings, China, 75–77

United States, 87, 382–88, 445–50, 465, 469–71
    evolution of suburban housing, 305–9, 415–18
    post–World War II
        apartment houses, 432–37
        attached town-house dwellings, 422–26
        court-garden house, 422–26
        decline of cities, 413–15, 474
        detached house design, 418–22, 474
        high-rise public housing, 437–42
        mixed-use buildings, 445–50
        residential conversions, 466–68
    town houses, 288
universitas, 236
Unwin, Raymond, 348–49, 351–52
Upper-Volta, 62, 63, 64
Ur, 102–7
urban design and layout
    ancient Egyptian cities, 109–10, 111–12
    ancient Greek cities, 118, 123–26, 130, 133
    ancient Indic cities, 113–15, 118–19
    ancient Mesopotamia, 102–4, 105–6
    Chinese cities
        ancient, 120–22, 193–96
        modern, 201–3
    effects of high-rise structures, 436
    fortress cities of medieval Europe, 234–36, 242–43,
        245, 247–49, 254–56, 267
    future challenges, 474
    garden cities, 350–52, 474
    historical development, 95–96
    impact of automobiles, 386
    Indian cities, 179, 180, 181, 184–87, 189
    Industrial Revolution, 290–91, 292–93
    Islamic city, 146, 147–50, 161, 173–74, 177–78
    Kyoto, Japan, 204
    medieval European cities
        early dwelling design, 229–33
        emergence of, 223–26, 228
        fortress cities, 237–40
        late period dwellings, 258–66
    mid-rise developments, 452–60
    mixed-use zoning, 445, 451–52
    nineteenth-century Paris, 312, 322
    oriental *vs.* occidental, 210, 213–14, 228
    population trends, 96
    Renaissance Europe, 268
        residential squares and crescents, 270–82
        town houses, 282
    Roman, 127–29, 137–38
    Soviet Russia, 408–10
    twentieth-century concepts and plans, 386, 390,
        391–93, 394, 408–10, 411–12, 445

urban renewal, 414, 474
ursi, 169
Ute Indians, 21
Utzen, Jørn, 422

vadies, 189
van de Velde, Henry Clemens, 369–70
Venezuela, *33*, 35, 38
Venice, Italy, 222
vestibulium, 136
via, 127
vici, 129
Viennese Secession, 372–74
villa houses, 303–5, 327
    twentieth-century designs, 393
Ville Radieuse, 392–93
vinarium, 128
viridarium, 140
Vitruvius, 130
Voysey, F. A., 344–46

Wai-Wai people, 34–35
wast-eddar, 154
wattle and daub, 52, 85, 88
Waura Indians, 38
wec, 52
werf, 17

wheelhouses, 71, 72
Wohnstube, 85
worker housing, 326, 376, 377–78
    evolution of suburban housing, 306
    Industrial Revolution effects, 290, 291–93
    Soviet Russian, 406–8, 409
    twentieth-century urban, 392
    urban nineteenth-century, 293–302
Wright, Frank Lloyd, 308–9, 358, 359–60, 384–86, 445–46

xian, 120
xystus, 142

Yaguan Indians, 21
Yanomamö Indians, 35–36, 97
Yecuana Indians, 38
yi, 120
Young Ones, 379–80
yurt, 42–44

zaguan, 211
zarookhas, 184
zashiki, 205
zufa, 163
Zuni Indians, 68